YOUR TEXAS BUSINESS

SECOND EDITION

What you should know to start and run a business in Texas today

Richard Alderman
Tom Oldham

Gulf Publishing Company
Houston, London, Paris, Zurich, Tokyo

This edition has been updated by the authors and reprinted December 1995.

to Janie and Chaille

YOUR TEXAS BUSINESS

SECOND EDITION

Gulf Publishing Company
Book Division
P.O. Box 2608 □ Houston, Texas 77252-2608

10 9 8 7 6 5 4 3 2

Library of Congress Cataloging-in-Publication Data

Alderman, Richard M.
Your Texas business: what you should know to start and run a business in Texas today/Richard Alderman, Tom Oldham.—2nd ed.
p. cm.
Includes index.
ISBN 0-88415-024-0
1. Business enterprises—Texas. 2. Business law—Texas. I. Oldham, Tom. II. Title.
KFT1405.Z9A38 1992
346.764′065—dc20
[347.640665] 92-22080
CIP

Contents

Chapter 4

The Limited Partnership, 23

Chapter 5

The Corporation, 31

Chapter 6

Hiring and Firing, 44

Chapter 7

Miscellaneous State and Federal Taxes, Fees, and Statutes, 51

Chapter 8

The Texas Deceptive Trade Practices Act, 57

Chapter 9

Warranties, 63

Chapter 10

Cash or Credit, 71

Chapter 11

Getting Paid, 77

Chapter 12

You and Your Lawyer, 85

Appendix A

Statutory Supplement, 89

Appendix B

Sample Documents and Agreements, 137

Appendix C

State Publications and Forms to Be Filed with the State of Texas, 175

Appendix D

Federal Publications, 245

Federal Tax Material, 246

OSHA, 337

Appendix E

Immigration Law Supplement, 341

Index, 362

Acknowledgments

We would like to thank Juanita Alt for her tireless and careful secretarial help. She made this project much easier to complete. We are also indebted to Betsy Smith and other students at the University of Houston Law Center who provided research assistance, as well as employees of the City of Houston One Stop Business Center, and other governmental offices, who were quite helpful.

Introduction

A Texas business person must answer vital legal questions every day. Knowing the law is essential if you are going to start or operate a business. It is not smart business to make decisions without considering the legal implications.

This book will help you understand these implications by explaining important legal issues, helping you recognize potential legal problems, and showing you how to avoid or solve them. In many cases a slight change in how you say or do things can save you thousands of dollars in liability. For example, if you tell a customer "the bolts will be delivered on Tuesday," and fail to deliver, you could be responsible for three times your customer's damages. But if you say, "I will do my best to see that the bolts get there on Tuesday," no liability will exist.

To help you understand the law and deal with legal problems, we discuss the most common legal questions that arise when you start or operate a business. We have also provided forms and models to help you prepare certain documents yourself. One of the most common questions business people ask is, "can I do it myself, or do I need a lawyer?" In very lawyerly fashion we have adopted a compromise position. Whenever possible we have provided you with the forms and information necessary to complete basic legal tasks, such as forming a partnership or incorporating. But we do this with a **big warning:** Doing it yourself can be dangerous, it is easy to make mistakes, and every situation is just a little different. So the compromise approach we suggest is that you use this book to help you prepare your own documents and tentatively make important legal decisions, and then let an attorney review what you have done. This way you get the best of both worlds. You save substantial sums of legal fees by preparing documents yourself, and you have the protection of an attorney's review before an important decision is made. Of course, if you are comfortable with the documents you have prepared, you may consider using them without an attorney's review. But remember that it can be difficult, even with the help of this book, for a non-lawyer to make legal decisions without the help of a lawyer. You might not realize that something about your particular situation makes some general statement inapplicable to you. If you are making a significant decision regarding your business, or completing an important transaction, we encourage you to discuss it with a lawyer.

We should also point out that although we have done everything we could to make sure that all the important information you need is in this book, law is not unchanging. The information in this book is accurate as of June 1992.

Texas law or federal law could change after that date. The Texas legislature and Congress have the power to change the laws we discuss, and courts could make rulings that affect their application. While such changes are unlikely, this is another reason why an attorney or appropriate government office should be consulted before an important decision is made.

Finally, a quick review of the Table of Contents indicates that some of the chapters apply to everyone, while some apply to only those persons starting a business. We suggest that anyone who is thinking about starting a business, or who has just started one, should review the entire book, paying particular attention to Chapters 1 through 5. If you are already operating an established business, and are comfortable with the form of the business you have chosen, you may want to skip Chapters 1 through 4. You should still read Chapter 5, however, to make sure that you do not wish to consider another form of operation. We also encourage you to read Chapter 12 at your leisure. While there may not be an immediate need for an attorney, it is helpful to be prepared if the need arises.

Richard Alderman
Tom Oldham

1

Starting a Business: Preliminary Considerations

If you are reading this book, you either are running a business or thinking about starting one. For those of you who have not yet taken the plunge we strongly recommend that you seriously consider your decision to start a business, and talk to some people who have done it. It is a terrific amount of work, and many new businesses fail. Do not underestimate the commitment you will be making if you start a business.

We do not mean to scare you away from starting a new business. Many people find it one of the most satisfying things they have ever done. Still, you should choose to do it "with your eyes open." Starting a business is a major financial and personal commitment, and you must consider all of the ramifications. For example, do you have the financial resources you will need, the expertise, the time, and the necessary drive? Have you considered the effect the time commitment will have on your family and your social life? These are just some of the things you should consider, and talk over with friends, family, and experts.

If you do decide to open a business, some of your first decisions will be among the most important. In this chapter, we discuss some of the things we believe you should consider when making these decisions. These are not just legal points, but practical economic factors as well. And by the way, if you have already started a business you may still want to read this chapter. But if you are concerned only with the legal aspects of a going concern, you might want to skip to Chapter 2.

Choosing Partners vs. "Going It Alone"

One of the most important decisions you will make when starting a business is your choice of who, if anyone, will be involved in the business with you. Many new businesses are sad stories of people with good intentions, who did not get along. Before you decide to involve someone in the venture, have a long talk with him or her. Do you have the same goals? How much time and money do each of you want to devote to the venture? Do you enjoy working together, or is it at least tolerable? Can you trust each other? How will decisions be made, particularly if you disagree? Remember, just because you are friends doesn't mean you can be business associates.

You may decide to "go it alone." This has certain obvious advantages. You get to make all the decisions, and the business will "make it or break it" based upon them. Also, you will receive all the profits. But starting a business by yourself can cause other problems. There is no other owner who could provide funds, and no other owner is available to supervise the business if you need to do something else. Sometimes you may want to share the responsibilities a new business imposes.

As you can see, there is no right or wrong decision regarding whether you should include one or more additional partners in your venture. If you do decide to include other owners, however, be very careful about the people you choose.

Obtaining Seed Money

When you decide to start a business, the first problem to solve is obtaining enough seed money for the business. This really presents three different problems. First, how much money is needed? Second, when will it be needed? Third, who will pay it?

How Much Money Is Needed?

When a business is started, "seed money" is needed. All businesses require some outlay of cash before the business opens its doors. For example, inventory might have to be purchased, rent might have to be prepaid, telephones and other equipment generally is needed, some salary probably must be paid, accountant's and lawyer's fees may be necessary, and some advertising normally is necessary. Some or all of these expenditures may require cash; it is quite difficult for a new business to obtain a significant amount of credit.

Also, after the business is started, it probably initially will be unprofitable. Normally a business is not profitable until a significant number of people realize that the business exists, and a substantial group of repeat customers has been established. Remember how long it takes *you* to discover that a new business has been opened in your area. Anyone starting a new business must make a financial plan so the business can weather this initial period of financial losses.

For example, assume you start a flower shop with some friends. Each person contributes $5,000 seed money. Much of this is used to buy plants and decorate the store that has been rented. No plan is made for obtaining additional money. If the business is not successful immediately, how will you pay the rent or the salaries of your employees? What if only one of you has additional capital? Can you force each person to contribute more, or do you just close up shop? If you need credit in a hurry, it will probably be hard to get, and the terms will probably be terrible.

Few businesses have sufficient capital when they are started, in large part because people don't plan ahead and prepare. And not having enough money puts a great deal of strain on the business. People starting a business have a tendency to make financial plans based upon a very rosy picture of the initial success of the business. Be realistic when you estimate your budget. Be prepared if the business is not an immediate cash machine. Few new businesses are. Talk to others who are familiar with the type of business you are planning to start. Find out how long it takes for this type of business to become profitable. What initial capital expenditures are required? Can some expenditures be postponed? Can some things be rented, rather than purchased? How much inventory will be needed initially? Can some things be obtained on credit?

One way to help protect against early financial problems is to estimate a proposed budget for the business. Prepare a "worst case" budget. Could the business lose money? If so, for how long? How will these losses be financed? You may want to speak with an accountant to get some professional help in estimating your expenses. Remember, underestimating the costs of your new business could mean a business failure.

When Will the Money Be Needed?

Not only is it necessary to determine how much money you will need, you also need to determine when certain funds will be needed. This frequently will be the period immediately after the business starts, but in some instances a significant payment may be necessary at some later point. You must consider if such funds may be necessary and how they will be raised if they are.

For example, assume Juanita and Elvia start a restaurant. Initially they rent a small restaurant, but they had always planned to move to a larger space. The restaurant is successful, and they decide to move but now suddenly find they don't have the money to pay for the move, or any plans for raising it. Early planning might have eliminated this dilemma. An agreed upon line of credit with a bank, for example, would have given them the flexibility to expand when they wanted.

Who Will Contribute the Seed Money?

Once you determine how much money you need, and when you will need it, you must decide how to obtain the money. Basically there are three choices: you; a bank; or other investors. Obviously the simplest solution is for you to contribute the money. This is not, however, always the most desirable, or feasible, solution. Many entrepreneurs do not have a significant amount of cash to contribute to a new business. And even if you have the cash, you may not want to risk it in the venture. For these reasons, many entrepreneurs attempt to obtain seed money from other sources. Ideally this money will be provided in a manner such that the other party, not you, assumes the risk of failure.

When most people think of money they think of banks, and a bank is a second possible source of funds. This funding approach has advantages and disadvantages. On one hand, the bank probably will not want to be involved in the operation of the business, nor would it want a percentage of the profits of the business. A bank will usually let you, the entrepreneur, retain all rights to the profits of the business if it is successful, and it won't interfere in the day to day operation of the business. But the bank isn't going to just "give" a new business money. It will probably want collateral or a "personal guarantee" from the business owner, you. This way if the loan isn't paid the bank can then either take the collateral or sue the business owner and attach his personal assets, in addition to the assets of the business, to collect the loan amount unpaid. Some owners do not want to take such a risk with their personal assets. As a practical matter, however, it is very difficult to borrow money on any other terms for a new business. Be prepared to run a personal financial risk if you start a business.

But banks sometimes do give unsecured loans to a corporate business without obtaining a personal guarantee from the owner. If this kind of loan is obtained, and the business is unsuccessful, the owner's personal assets are not at risk. However, banks generally would only do this for a good customer who had started successful companies in the past. Banks frequently are unwilling to give unsecured loans to new businesses without a personal guarantee from the owner.

You also should shop around for the best financial package. New businesses frequently fail. Because of this risk, a bank might try to charge a high interest rate. Still, the banking business is very competitive, and you may find different rates. Additionally, if you agree to do all your banking with a lender, allow the bank to do your payroll, or factor your accounts, the bank might be willing to make cost concessions. Further, the more money you have in non-interest-bearing, or low-interest-bearing accounts, the more likely a bank is to make concessions in loan transactions.

Private investors are another source of money, especially seed money. Investors normally do not make loans to the business. Instead, they contribute funds to the new business in exchange for a percentage of the profits of the business. So, if the business is unsuccessful, they receive nothing; if the business is successful, they receive a portion of the profits of the business. This funding source, therefore, can reduce the owner's share of the profits of the business. Carefully weigh whether this form of funding is worth the financial risk it eliminates.

Not all investors are strangers. Some new business owners ask their friends to become involved in a new venture. This should be done only after much reflection. Friends and business partners relate quite differently. After a friend invests in your business, you may find that the friendship has been ruined. This is particularly likely if the business is not successful.

The Bottom Line

Almost all new businesses need "seed money." This money is needed to establish the business and cover any initial losses of the business. If you are starting a new business, you must realistically determine how much seed money is necessary. If, after deciding how much seed money will be needed, you do not have that amount of money or for some other reason do not want to contribute your money, another source of the seed money must be found. Banks sometimes will loan money to new companies, but usually want a personal guarantee and charge high rates. Alternatively, investors might be sought. Personal liability can be avoided by doing this, but you will lose some of the profits, and possibly control, of the business.

Liability Concerns

When you start a new business you are frequently concerned, and should be concerned, about what will happen if the business is unsuccessful or is the subject of a large lawsuit. Many people have accumulated assets that they do not want to risk losing as a result of the new business. Even if you do not now have assets, *future* accumulations can be jeopardized due to a business failure now. This can happen, because a creditor may get a judgment against you, and this judgment can be used to attach assets acquired in the future. Some business risks can, and should, be insured against, but others may not be covered by insurance. For these reasons, you understandably want to organize your business in such a way that your personal assets will be safe, no matter what happens to the business. There are a number of ways these concerns can be met.

The Structure of the Business

A new business can be structured as one of a number of common types of business organization forms that are used for businesses. Almost all new businesses can be established either as a proprietorship, partnership, or corporation. The particular form chosen depends upon the needs and tax concerns of the owner, rather than any characteristic of the business. For example, think of the businesses you frequent. Do you have any idea whether the business is a proprietorship, partnership, or corporation? Generally this is not very clear to the public, and the public normally does not care. The particular business form chosen depends solely upon the concerns of the owner. It usually doesn't affect the day to day operations of the business.

You should remember to try to keep you and your business separate once you have begun operations. When a business is started, typically many documents must be signed. And what they say, and how they are signed, will affect your liability. Remember that **there is no such thing as a "form" anything!** Do not sign anything until you have reviewed it carefully, thought about it, and determined that it is fair and consistent with your understanding. Anything you sign can make you personally liable, sometimes for a significant amount of money. Take your time. Every time you put your signature on a piece of paper, it is important.

What follows is a very brief discussion of the various business forms. A more detailed discussion of each business form can be found in later chapters.

The Proprietorship

The simplest form of doing business is the proprietorship. No filing with any governmental body is required to form a proprietorship. The business is owned by one person, and that person makes all the decisions regarding the business. No rules specify how those decisions are to be made. This is the simplest business organization form.

But proprietorships are not the best form for all businesses. For example, there may be more than one owner. If so, it cannot be a proprietorship, since a proprietorship only has one owner. Also, a proprietorship does not exist separate from its owner. This means that a creditor of a proprietorship can attach the personal assets of the owner if the proprietorship does not pay the claim. You may not want to jeopardize personal assets when you start a business. Tax concerns will also affect your decision. Proprietorship income is taxed at the marginal tax rate of the owner. If you have significant other income, you may want to see if the corporate tax rate would be lower. (Proprietorships are discussed further in Chapter 2.)

Partnership

A partnership is similar to a proprietorship in many ways. It is quite informal. No formal agreement or filing is required to form one. For example, you may even have established one and not know it. Consider this:

> Frank and Tom buy a four-plex apartment building, taking title jointly. Both collect rents, show apartments to prospective tenants, and sign leases. Frank and Tom have agreed to share all profits or losses generated by the building. They are partners, regardless of whether or not they think they are.

There are certain disadvantages to partnerships. For example, all partners can manage the business of the partnership. But this can complicate things if the partners do not agree. Also, each partner's personal assets can be attached, for the total amount due by the partnership, if the partnership does not pay a partnership debt. Finally, the income of the partnership is taxed according to the marginal personal tax rate of each individual partner.

Some of the problems of a partnership can be solved by forming a limited partnership. In order to form a limited partnership, a filing must be made with the Texas secretary of state. Only "general" partners can manage a limited partnership; "limited" partners are passive investors. The personal assets of limited partners cannot be attached to collect partnership debts; however, the personal assets of any general partners can be attached. For this reason, it is quite common for corporations to be the general partner. (Partnerships and limited partnerships are discussed in Chapters 3 and 4.)

Corporations

Many times the best way to do business is to form a corporation. A corporation is formed by filing a certificate of incorporation with the secretary of state. Corporations have certain advantages, the most important of which is limited liability. Only the assets of the corporation can be attached to collect claims against the business. Even if these assets are not sufficient to pay all creditors of the business, creditors cannot attach personal assets of the owners. Also, even if there are a number of owners, a corporation is managed by the president and the board of directors of the business. Lines of authority are clear.

Tax consequences are also different for a corporation. Normal "C" corporations pay tax at corporate tax rates, regardless of the incomes of the shareholder-owners. This can be good or bad, depending upon the marginal tax rates of the owners. If the company decides to distribute money to the owners as a dividend, the owners must pay income tax on that distribution.

Sometimes owners want their corporation to be treated for tax purposes as if it were a partnership. If this is desired, an "S" corporation election is possible. Such a corporation is treated for liability purposes like a corporation, and for tax purposes like a partnership. There are also other types of corporations, such as non-profit corporations and professional corporations, all with special attributes. (Corporations are discussed in Chapter 5.)

Summary

There are many factors that will affect your decision whether to operate your business as a proprietorship, general partnership, limited partnership, or corporation. No one can give you an absolute rule regarding when one form is better than the others. We encourage you to read Chapters 2 through 5, where we discuss in detail the different characteristics of each business form. But here is a summary of the types of businesses that would want to use each type of business form.

A **sole proprietorship** is a good choice when:

1. The business has one owner.
2. The type of business has little risk of liability.
3. The owner is not concerned about any tax savings that might result from forming a corporation (or no tax savings would result).

A **general partnership** is a good choice when:

1. The business has more than one owner.
2. All wish to manage the business.
3. All partners know one another and have some degree of trust in one another.
4. Any tax savings that could result from a corporation are not desired (or no tax savings would result).
5. The business has little risk of liability.

A **limited partnership** is desirable when:

1. The business has more than one investor and some want to manage the business while others do not.
2. Some investors want limited liability.
3. Tax savings that could result from a corporation are not desired (or no tax savings would result).

A business should **incorporate** when:

1. There is a significant risk of liability.
2. Clear delegation of management authority is desired.
3. Corporate tax benefits are desired.
4. The business is expected to continue even if the principals should withdraw or die.

The Bottom Line

Your choice of a business form is very important and must be based on an analysis of your particular needs and the law. You should carefully read the following chapters before making a decision of how you will do business.

Signing a Lease

Many new business owners almost immediately sign a lease. The terms of the lease can constitute crucial legal and business decisions. It is vital that you read and understand the terms of the lease before you sign. Remember, as we will say many times in this book, there is no such thing as a form *anything*. Everything can be negotiated.

The Identity of the Lessee

Your first concern when signing a lease is the identity of the "lessee," the person or entity who is agreeing to pay the rent. As discussed, if the lessee is a corporation, you generally will not be personally liable for the rent if the business is unsuccessful and the corporation can't pay the rent. However, if you personally are the lessee, if the lessee is a general partnership and you are a partner, or if the lessee is limited partnership and you are the general partner, you will be personally responsible for the lease payments if the business is unsuccessful. Also, you will be personally liable for the lease payments if you personally "guarantee" the lease, even if the lessee is a corporation.

The identity of the lessee is obviously a major concern. The landlord is likely to be reluctant to have the lessee be a corporation, particularly if the corporation is new and does not have many assets. The landlord may well want you to personally guarantee the corporation's lease payments. If you do this, you will be personally responsible for the lease payments if the business is unsuccessful and the corporation can't pay the rent.

If you are personally liable for the lease, this may affect your thoughts about other terms of the lease. For example, maybe you then would want a very short lease term (such as a month-to-month, or, at most, a fixed six-month term), while retaining some option on your part to extend the lease term if your business is successful. If the lease term is short, this means your personal liability will be relatively low even if the business is not successful. Of course, it also means the landlord may raise the rent or change the lease terms after a very short term.

Other Important Lease Terms

It is difficult to set forth all possible important terms that could be included in a lease. However, we will try to list a few here:

- **How long is the lease term?** On one hand, you might want a long term, because this makes it definite you will have a right to the space for a significant period, and you will not have to move. However, if the business is unsuccessful and you are personally liable, a long-term lease could be quite expensive. One option that is favorable to tenants is to agree to a relatively short term, but retain an option to extend the lease for an additional term once you determine how successful the business is. If you want such an option to extend, you should include in the lease when you must notify the landlord that you wish to extend, and what the rent will be for the additional term. If the landlord is not very interested in a short lease term, it may be to your advantage to offer a pay a little higher rent for the initial period in order to induce the landlord to accept a short lease term.
- **What is the rent?** Will the landlord offer any concessions? During the recent business downturn, landlords were willing to make many concessions to induce tenants to sign a lease. For example, will the landlord improve or modify the property to make it more desirable? Will the landlord accept a lower rent for an initial period while the business is beginning?
- **Determine whether any additional amounts will be added to the agreed-upon rent.** For example, if the landlord's real-estate taxes or repair costs increase, can the landlord pass these increased costs to you? If so, do you agree to this? Are the included "costs" clearly set forth? Also, wil the rent be adjusted each year for inflation? If so, do you understand how this adjustment will be done, and do you think it is fair?
- **Who will be responsible for utilities and repairs?** In Texas, the expense of utilities can be significant. What happens if something breaks, the toilet backs up, the roof leaks, or the plumbing leaks? If the damage requires you to close your business for a period, who will bear the loss?
- **Are the premises clearly appropriate for your uses?** For example, can the premises adequately deal with any needs you have for electricity for computers or other equipment? Is the parking adequate for your employees and any visitors you expect? What are the rules regarding signs? Verify that the landlord will not object to any signs you plan to use, and that these signs comply with all local laws.
- **Is the area appropriate for your business?** Are you familiar with the crime rate and the accessibility to the area?
- **Can you sublease or assign the lease?** This may be useful. If rental rates go up after you sign the lease and you have this right you could sublease the premises and make a profit.
- **If your business is successful, how will that affect your space needs?** Think about the future. You may want to include, in your lease, your right to lease certain additional space. You may want to describe the additional space, specify when you would have to exercise the option to rent the additional space, and what the rental terms would be.

Retaining a Lawyer and an Accountant

Finally, if you are considering starting a business, it may be very helpful to retain a lawyer and an accountant. The accountant can, among other things, help ensure that the seed money estimates and budgets are reasonable, help you set up decent records, and assist with tax preparation. The lawyer can talk to you about the best form for the business, and can tell you what actions should be taken before the business is begun. A lawyer can also review important documents before you sign them, and keep you up to date with various changes in the law. It does not cost much money to consult a lawyer and an accountant before starting a business, and significant later problems can be avoided. (Hiring a lawyer is discussed in Chapter 12.)

Getting Other Assistance

Various government and university offices and programs offer help to people starting a new business. For example, the Texas Employment Commission publishes a free monthly publication entitled "Texas Business Today." You can subscribe by writing them at 101 E. 15th St., Austin, Texas 78778. You also may want to contact one of these small business development centers convenient to where you live:

Angelo State University
2601 West Ave. N.
San Angelo, TX 76909
915-942-2119

City of Houston
One Stop Business Center
P.O. Box 1562
City Hall
901 Bagby St.
Houston, TX 77251
713-663-7867

Corpus Christi Chamber of Commerce
1201 North Shoreline
P.O. Box 640
Corpus Christi, TX 78403
512-882-6161

Dallas County Community College
1402 Corinth St.
Dallas, TX 75202
214-565-5832

El Paso Community College
103 Montana Ave. #202
El Paso, TX 79904
915-534-3410

Galveston College
Galveston Chamber of Commerce
621 Moody #300
Galveston, TX 77550
409-763-4426

Lamar University
855 Florida Ave.
Beaumont, TX 77705
409-880-2254

Laredo State University
Division of Business Administration
West End Washington St.
Laredo, TX 78040
512-722-8001

McLennan Community College
4601 North 19th St., A-15
Waco, TX 76708
817-750-3600

Tarrant County Junior College
1500 Houston
Fort Worth, TX 76102
817-877-9254

Texas Tech University
College of Business Administration
1313 Broadway #1
Lubbock, TX 79401
806-744-5343

University of Houston
601 Jefferson #2330
Houston, TX 77002
713-752-8444

University of Texas @ San Antonio
College of Business
San Antonio, TX 78285
512-224-0791

University of Texas, Permian Basin
4901 E. University #298
Odessa, TX 79762
915-367-2190

West Texas University
T. Boone Pickens College of Business
1800 S. Washington #110
Amarillo, TX 79102
806-372-5151

2

The Sole Proprietorship

The simplest business structure to select, if there is only one owner, is the sole proprietorship. No documents must be filed with any governmental office and no other agreement of any kind is needed to form one or keep the business in good standing. This minimizes organizational costs of starting the business.

A proprietorship is created every time one person starts a business. Any name can be chosen as the name of the business, and the name does not have to include the word *proprietorship*. But you should be sure that no one else has previously started a business by the same name. If they have, you may not have the right to use that name. While you probably won't get into any trouble if you innocently use someone else's name, you can be forced to stop using it and this can cost you money when you have to start all over again with printing and advertising costs. At a minimum, you ought to contact the secretary of state's office, in Austin, and the county clerk's office, where you are doing business, to see if someone else has registered the name. You may also want to consider hiring a name search company to protect you if you are going to make a big investment in advertising or promotional materials. Name search companies exist who will check for you whether anyone else is using your proposed business name.

One of the best things about doing business as a proprietorship is that decisions can be informally made. No board of directors meetings or other formal authorizations or record-keeping is needed. You simply act as the business. This reduces the expense and increases the ease of operating a business.

But sole proprietorships do have certain disadvantages. Certain tax advantages available to a corporation, such as deductible medical insurance plans, disability insurance plans, and life insurance plans, are not available to an owner of a sole proprietorship. These tax advantages of a corporation are discussed in Chapter 5.

In a proprietorship, there is only one owner. This can create a problem if you get sick, want to take a vacation, or need to be out of town. There may be no other responsible person you would trust to run the business when you cannot.

And even more importantly, a creditor of a sole proprietorship can attach the personal assets of the owner, if the proprietorship does not pay the claim. This "unlimited liability" feature of the sole proprietorship can be quite scary to a person starting a new business. Consider what happened to poor Mary:

> Mary recently started a small dry cleaning business by the name of Mary's Cleaners. She signed a 2-year lease when she started the business. Things went fine, until business dropped off after six months and Mary could no longer make a profit. She closed up, but now the landlord demands the remaining 18 months rent. Because she operated the business as a sole proprietorship, Mary is individually liable for the remainder of the lease term.

Here are some of the things you should consider before starting a sole proprietorship.

Tax Concerns

Before deciding to operate a business as a sole proprietor, you need to understand the income tax effects of this choice. The sole proprietorship is not considered a separate entity for tax purposes. The income (or loss) is treated as personal income of the owner. So, if in 1991 the owner and his spouse have other income of $50,000, and net income from the proprietorship business of $30,000, the couple would pay income tax, based upon individual tax rates, on both the $50,000 other income and the $30,000 business income. Unless they had any deductions, the total income for the year would be $80,000. In a proprietorship business, the marginal tax rate for this couple on the business income would be 31%; the tax due on the $30,000 income would be $9,300.

But if the couple in the example above operated the business as a corporation, the tax effect would be very different. The tax rate on the $30,000 business income would be 15%, or $4,500. This is much better than the $9,300 proprietorship tax due. But there are disadvantages to this corporate savings as well.

In a proprietorship, income is only taxed once. The income is taxed when the proprietorship makes it. The money can then be taken out by the owner, and no tax is due on such a withdrawal. In a corporation, however, the business pays tax on its income according to corporate tax rates. (As we have shown, these rates might be lower than the owner's personal marginal tax rates.) If you wish to take money out of the corporation, however, this withdrawal is called a "dividend" and is considered income to you, and you must pay taxes *again*, at personal tax rates. This is commonly referred to as the corporate "double tax." Of course, the double tax does not have to be paid if you plan to keep profits in the business for some reason, such as for capital improvements or to buy inventory. In most cases, however, owners do want profits paid out, so the double tax is a problem.

If your business makes money, a proprietorship can also be desirable, from a tax standpoint, for reasons other than the double tax. Personal tax rates are graduated. In 1990 the lowest rate was 15% and the highest rate was 31%. The profits of a proprietorship business are taxed based upon these rates (plus all other income you earn). All other income of the owner (and the owner's spouse) for the tax year is added to compute the owner's total taxable income for the year. If the owner will not have significant other income, and the business is not going to make much money, it might be desirable to pay taxes based upon the personal tax rates.

Therefore, tax treatment of a proprietorship may be advantageous for some successful businesses and not for others. If your business will lose money initially, the proprietorship is normally a better business form than a corporation, from a tax standpoint. Losses from the proprietorship business can offset other personal income. If you plan to lose money initially (and many new businesses do), this characteristic of the proprietorship can be helpful. In contrast, in Chapter 5 you will discover that if a corporation loses money during any one year this loss generally cannot be used by a shareholder to offset other income. The loss can only be carried over to offset future business income. While this shouldn't be your only concern, the ability to write off losses may be a big plus for a sole proprietorship.

Running the Business

A proprietorship can sign agreements just like any business organization. For example, the proprietorship can sign a lease, purchase inventory, or borrow money. You simply sign the name of the business.

More complicated arrangements are also possible. If you want to motivate employees or a manager, you might want to compensate the employee at least partially in terms of the profitability of the business. This can be set forth in an employment agreement between the employee and the proprietorship. Some sample employment agreements are set forth in Appendix B, Forms 9 and 10.

But you should remember that agreements involving a proprietorship business really are agreements obligating you as the owner, since proprietorships do not have limited liability. Any agreements involving the business should clarify this. For example:

> Assume Janie Alt is running a florist shop by the name of "The Green Thumb" as a proprietorship. If she signs a lease for space, the lease should be between the landlord and Janie Alt, d/b/a (doing business as) The Green Thumb.

In this example, the signature line on the lease could look like this:

____
Janie Alt, d/b/a The Green Thumb

But the bottom line is that it is not important how you sign agreements for a proprietorship, because in a proprietorship business *you* are personally liable for the obligations set forth in the contract.

Liability and Bankruptcy

We have said that an owner of a proprietorship business is personally liable for all claims against a business. This means that a creditor of the business can attach any property owned by you that is not exempt under Texas law, regardless whether the property was used in the business. (Exemptions are discussed in Chapter 11.) Also, if you don't have any property the creditor can attach, or if you don't have enough property to fully satisfy the creditor's claim, the creditor can get a court judgment against you for the claim. If this happens, the creditor can attach any non-exempt property you acquire in the future.

For these reasons, the unlimited liability of a proprietorship can have terrible consequences. If you start a proprietorship business, try to minimize the likelihood you will lose your personal assets. For example, consider obtaining insurance regarding foreseeable possible claims. For instance, will anyone operate a car or truck on behalf of the business? If so, be sure there is adequate auto liability insurance. Similarly, are you selling or making a product that could hurt someone if it malfunctions or is defective? If so, consider product liability insurance.

Unfortunately, there is no way to obtain insurance that your business will be successful. If a business is unsuccessful, there can be a significant number of unpaid creditors. And in many cases, bankruptcy is the only way to deal with all of the money the business owes.

Under federal bankruptcy law, any legal entity may file a petition and generally be released, or discharged, from most debts it owes. For example, a corporation can go out of business, file bankruptcy, and basically leave its shareholders suffering only the loss of their investment. But as we have pointed out, a sole proprietorship is not a separate legal entity. The law treats it as one and the same as its owner. Even if it is the business that has run up debts the owner must file personal bankruptcy. For example:

> Sam recently started a small fix-it shop in his back yard workshop. Business got better and soon he had a store in a local mall. Within a few years he was making a nice profit and gave up his other job. Then things started getting worse. Business went down, he owed thousands of dollars in bills, and he was sued by a customer after a stove he fixed exploded. Unfortunately he didn't have insurance, and when the customer won a lawsuit for $150,000 Sam couldn't pay it. The only choice was to go out of business, and file bankruptcy. But because Sam was operating the business as a sole proprietorship, he will have to file personal bankruptcy, and in all likelihood his wife will have to file as well. Sam won't owe any money anymore, and he probably will get to keep his house, and most of his property, but he will lose his savings, his IRA, and the stocks and bonds he has saved for his kids' education.

We are not trying to scare you, but a business failure can mean personal financial ruin. The best way to avoid this is to have proper insurance coverage, and if you want to fully protect your personal assets, consider incorporating.

Assumed Name Certificate

Most proprietorship businesses have a name that is different from the owner's name. For example, Harold might start a tailoring business under the name of Harold's Tailoring, or The Alteration Shop. In either case Harold should file an assumed name certificate, since he would be doing business under a name different from his own name. The manner in which an assumed name certificate is filed is set forth in Chapter 7.

Miscellaneous Taxes and Fees

Although forming and operating a proprietorship is relatively simple, proprietorship businesses must comply with tax withholding rules and other regulations applicable to all businesses, such as workmen's compensation and social security. These state and federal requirements are discussed in Chapter 7.

The Bottom Line

Sole proprietorships are easy to form and easy to run, but remember, you and the business are one and the same.

SUMMARY

A proprietorship is very simple to form and operate. You as owner can make all the decisions and you can do it informally. Also, you can keep all the profits of the business. But there may be a high price for this independence. You as the owner are personally liable for all claims against the business. In addition, there may be no one else you would trust to help run the business if you get sick or need to be away.

3

The General Partnership

In Chapter 2 we discussed the sole proprietorship, the simplest business form. As we told you, a sole proprietorship is run and owned by one person. This form may not be appropriate for many businesses, however, because often a business is started by more than one person. If there is to be more than one owner of the business, another business form is necessary. A general partnership, limited partnership, or a corporation might be the best choice in this situation.

A general partnership is a business form where all the owners are *general partners*. In other words, all the partners run the business and have full responsibility. This may sound like a good idea and it may be what you want, but before you make the decision to form a general partnership you should consider the benefits and drawbacks to this form. Here are some of the key aspects of the general partnership:

No Limited Liability

In Chapters 4 and 5 we will discuss the idea of *limited liability* for an owner. If a business form has limited liability, the investor is assured that, at worst, the investor will lose only the capital invested. Many people starting a business are not particularly concerned about the extent of their potential liability. The euphoria of the moment blinds them to the possibility that the business might be unsuccessful. Business founders, however, must remain aware that many new businesses are not successful; the risk relating to each possible business form should be carefully considered before the business form is selected. For example:

> Assume Frank and Bob start a discotheque. They need to borrow a significant amount of money to decorate the club. A bank loans money to the business for these expenses. If the business is unsuccessful, Frank and Bob would not be personally liable for the bank loan if the business was a corporation or they were limited partners.

But in a general partnership, the partners *do not have* limited liability. This means that a creditor of the partnership can attach the assets of any partner to collect a debt of the partnership. It doesn't even matter whether a partner is a "silent" partner. Compare this example with the one you just considered:

> Steve and Lynn recently formed a general partnership. Steve runs the day-to-day operations and Lynn put up most of the cash. An employee of the partnership ran over a woman with a car while doing something for the partnership, and the injured person sued the partnership and Steve and Lynn. If the injured person won, she could attach the individual assets of the partners if the partnership does not have adequate assets. Additionally, either Steve or Lynn could owe the full amount if the other couldn't pay.

The result would be the same if the debt stemmed from a business failure, instead of an accident. For example:

> The business is unsuccessful and is closed six months after it was opened. If the business signed a lease for two years on the property used for the business, the lessor could sue the partners individually for all amounts due under the partnership's lease.

The importance of the unlimited liability that arises from a general partnership depends upon the circumstances of the individual partners. For example, if one or more partners have significant personal assets, this aspect of partnership law could scare them a great deal. Also, even if the partners do not have assets now, they may accumulate assets later that could be made liable for claims against the partnership. Before the general partnership form is chosen the problem of unlimited liability must be considered.

If you are considering forming a general partnership, think about the type of business you plan to open and what types of claims could be made against that type of business. For example, will any employees of the business have to drive a car to make sales or deliver items? If so, you need to consider possible personal injury claims that could stem from the driver's negligence. Some types of specific liability, such as an accident, can be insured against. Also, "umbrella" liability coverage to protect you against excessive loss is available. But although adequate insurance is one way of minimizing some of the risks involved in a general partnership, many risks, such as a business failure, cannot be insured against and you will be personally responsible.

The Bottom Line

Each partner has unlimited liability for the debts of the partnership. If you do form a partnership you must consider this and at a minimum make sure you have sufficient insurance.

The Registered Limited Liability Partnership

In 1991, the Texas legislature created a "registered limited liability partnership." This business form, not accepted in any other state, apparently permits a general partner not to be personally liable for claims arising from the negligence of another partner. Any type of business can obtain this status. Under the new statute, partners wishing to have limited liability must file an application with the Texas secretary of state. The partnership's name must include the phrase "registered limited liability partnership" or the abbreviation "L.L.P." Also, the fee for obtaining this status is $100 per partner per year. The registration must be renewed each year, presumably by filing another document with the secretary of state. The business must also carry insurance of at least $100,000 for damage caused by negligence of employees of the business.

In other chapters, we discuss the other business forms (the limited partnership and the S corporation) that have limited liability. These forms have been used for a long time, and we would advise, if limited liability is important, to continue to use these other forms, rather than the limited liability partnership, until it is more clear how Texas courts will construe the limited liability recently created for this new type of partnership. In any event, be sure to consult with your attorney if you decide to set up a limited liability partnership to ensure all the legal prerequisites are fulfilled.

Decision Making

In a general partnership, all partners normally participate in the management of the business. This management arrangement may or may not be what the owners desire. If you do not want to share all management decisions, you should have an agreement saying so. For example, the partners might agree that one partner should be the "managing partner," and that others should only be consulted for big decisions. If the partnership manages a shopping center, here's an example of how such an agreement might look:

> Managing Partner's Authority. The Managing Partner shall have the full, exclusive and complete authority of management and control of the affairs of the Partnership consistent with the provisions hereof; he shall make all decisions affecting the Partnership affairs and shall have full power and authority to negotiate the terms of and to execute such documents and instruments relating to the Partnership affairs as may in his opinion be appropriate, necessary or advisable in the conduct of the Partnership business, including, without limitation, leases, tenancy agreement, and subordination agreements, provided such document or instrument covers or relates to the Property and business of the Partnership; provided, however, the Managing Partner shall not be authorized to sell or encumber any portion of the Property, to borrow any funds on behalf of the Partnership, or enter into any contracts with any related person or entity of the Managing Partner without the written consent of the Investing Partner.
>
> Investing Partner's Authority. Except as otherwise provided in this Agreement, the Investing Partner shall not take an active part in the management of the Partnership business or transact any business for the Partnership, and shall have no power to sign for or to bind the Partnership.
>
> Managing Partner's Obligations. Upon the decision of the Partnership to proceed with any development, the Managing Partner shall do all things as may be necessary or appropriate to complete such development substantially in accordance with the plans and specifications. To such end, the Managing Partner shall obtain all

necessary architectural, engineering, surveying and other assistance necessary to develop such shopping center, shall engage a contractor or contractors to construct such shopping center, and shall oversee and manage the entire development process. The Managing Partner shall manage the Partnership and its affairs in a prudent, businesslike manner in accordance with good practices in the industry. The Managing Partner shall prepare an annual rental budget (pursuant to paragraph 8.05(k) below) and shall use its best efforts to consummate leases with tenants for occupancy of any development. The Partnership may engage ________ to develop the Property, but any such engagement shall be invalid unless contained in a written contract executed by the Investing Partner on behalf of the Partnership.

Financing. The Managing Partner shall use its best efforts to obtain interim construction financing and permanent financing for any development of the Partnership, but all costs and expenses involved in obtaining such financing shall be borne by the Partnership.

Prohibited Transactions. Notwithstanding any language contained herein to the contrary, the Managing Partner shall not, without the written consent or ratification of the specific act by the Investing Partner, have the power or authority to do any of the following:

(a) Do any act in contravention of this Agreement.
(b) Do any act which would make it impossible to carry on the ordinary business of the Partnership.
(c) Confess a judgment against the Partnership.
(d) Possess Partnership property, or assign such Partner's rights in the Partnership property for other than Partnership purposes.
(e) Admit a person as a partner.
(f) Execute or deliver any assignment for the benefit of the creditors of the Partnership.
(g) Lend to any persons any of the funds of the Partnership.
(h) Mortgage, encumber, pledge or otherwise hypothecate any of the assets of the Partnership or extend, renew, replace, or substantially modify such financing.
(i) Sell any portion of the Property or improvements thereon.
(j) Develop or lease any portion of the Property not used for construction of a shopping center.
(k) Lease on behalf of the Partnership (as lessor) any portion of the shopping center at a rate (taking into account all free rent) less than that approved by the Investing Partner based on a budget prepared by the Managing Partner. Such budget shall include (i) a minimum rent below which no leases shall be made without Investing Partner's consent, (ii) a budgeted average rent, and (iii) a percentage of the total rentable square feet which shall be the maximum number of square feet which may be leased at a rent below the budgeted average rent (but not below the minimum rent) without Investing Partner's consent.

The Bottom Line

Unless partners agree otherwise, all partners can manage the business. If some other arrangement is desired, an agreement is necessary.

Liability for Partner's Acts

A general partnership is liable for all wrongs done by *any* partner in connection with its business. For this reason it is very important that you know and trust all partners. For example:

> Smith and Jones form a law partnership. In connection with a real estate transaction for a client, Jones is given some funds from the client to hold in escrow until the sale closes. If Jones steals the money, Smith probably would be liable to the client for the money stolen, if Jones disappeared or spent the stolen money.

Of course, partners are not liable for everything done by another partner. A partner is not liable for an act of another partner if the act is unrelated to the business. For example, if Barb and Sue run a shoe store in Dallas, and Sue has a car accident in Austin while doing something unrelated to the shoe store's business, Barb is not liable for this.

The Bottom Line

Partners are personally liable for negligent acts of a partner done in connection with the partnership's business. If you are thinking about becoming a partner in a general partnership, be sure that you trust your partners and believe they are all responsible.

Taxes

General partners pay individual income taxes (or get individual deductions) based upon the results of the business of the partnership. There is no separate "partnership tax." For example:

> Smith and Jones, a general partnership, makes a profit of $50,000 for the calendar year. Smith and Jones are equal partners. Both Smith and Jones must report personal income of $25,000 for that year. The partnership pays no tax (although an "information return" must be filed with the IRS).

or:

> Smith and Jones, a general partnership, loses $50,000 for the calendar year. Smith and Jones are equal part-

ners. Smith and Jones can each deduct $25,000 on their personal tax returns for that year, as long as they both actively manage the business.

The examples above assume that the partners are 50–50 partners. Of course, partners can share profits and losses differently, such as 40–60, or 30–70. Also, there can be more than two partners. And remember, unless you provide otherwise in your agreement the law presumes you are equal partners.

The taxable income or loss of each partner is determined by the income or loss of the partnership. It does not matter whether money was actually transferred from the partnership to the partner, or from the partner to the partnership.

The Bottom Line

There is no separate partnership tax. Partners pay personal income tax on their respective share of the partnership's profits.

Forming A Partnership

No formal action need be taken to form a general partnership. No written agreement is normally required, and nothing normally must be filed with any state or local office, unless the partnership owns realty. Also, nothing must be done or filed with any state office to keep the partnership in good standing, other than the miscellaneous taxes and fees discussed in Chapter 7. For example, partnerships still must withhold federal income tax and social security for employees, and workmen's compensation payments must be made. **We do strongly recommend, however, that partners sign a written partnership agreement.** What follows are some suggested important subjects that should be addressed in your agreement.

But first we should emphasize that partners need not consider themselves "partners" to establish a partnership. Under Texas law, a partnership is defined as "an association of two or more persons to carry on as co-owners a business for profit." If owners agree to share profits, and both owners participate in the management of the venture, they probably will be considered partners, unless it can be established that some other arrangement was agreed upon. This can sometimes come as quite a surprise. For example:

> Smith and Jones agree that Smith will contribute $10,000 to purchase timber, and Jones will supervise the milling of the timber. They agree to split the profits. If the enterprise is unprofitable, it is likely that they would be considered partners, and would share any losses. Also, each would be personally liable for the losses.

If Smith and Jones had signed a written agreement that clarified that Jones was an employee of the business, not a partner, and that his compensation was one-half of the profits of the business, Jones would not be a partner, and would not be liable for the losses. Smith would be liable for all losses. Written agreements can clarify the relationship between people who are doing business, as well as their respective rights and duties. This is one of the many reasons why we recommend written agreements.

The Bottom Line

No formal action is needed to form a partnership. If you are sharing profits with someone and both of you exercise management power in the business, you will probably be considered partners. If this is not desired, clarify this in a written agreement.

THE PARTNERSHIP AGREEMENT

Introduction

As we have pointed out, a general partnership can be established without an agreement. Texas has enacted a statute, the Uniform Partnership Act (the "UPA"), that creates an agreement for the partners if the partners do not negotiate one between themselves. This statute, reproduced in Appendix A, contains some controversial provisions that many business owners would not accept if they considered them. Some of these provisions will be discussed below. If partners want to change these provisions, an agreement is necessary. Also, a written agreement is always a good idea, so parties can remember the terms of the deal.

Here are some examples of points you may want to consider in your partnership agreement, to change that result.

The Partnership Name

The name of a partnership is obviously important to identify the business. It also normally is a partnership asset. If this is not the intention of the parties, the understanding should be clarified. For example, after the business is no longer operated by the partners, who will have the rights to use the name? Consider this:

> Jim and Bob start a night club named "Fast and Cool." This club becomes quite popular. People in other towns

want to buy the rights to use the name. Who should receive this money, Bob, Jim or the Partnership? A provision in the partnership agreement could clarify that the name "Fast and Cool" is a partnership asset.

For example, one clause could be:

Partnership Name. All rights in and to the partnership name, "Fast and Cool," shall belong to the partnership, and not to any individual partner.

Authority of Partners

A partnership can only do business through the partners or their agents, and you should be concerned with the right of each partner to bind the partnership. For example, suppose your partner goes out and buys some new lavish furniture for the business for $20,000, when all you told him to spend was $2,500. The partnership, and in turn you as a partner, probably would be responsible for this debt even though it was not what you expected. Unless you say otherwise, every partner has the right to bind the partnership for matters "in the ordinary course of business." If you wish to limit this right, for example by giving only one partner the right to make decisions for the partnership, you must do so by agreement.

If your agreement provided that only you had the right to make purchasing decisions, and your partner, without your authority, bought expensive furniture, the partnership might not be responsible for the bill. We say "might" because even though you had an agreement giving you the sole right to make purchasing decisions, your partner could still be viewed as the partnership's agent, and would by law have authority to bind the partnership.

Let's say that in the past your partner has always purchased furniture for the business, and the partnership had always paid the bills for expenses he incurred in the name of the partnership. Under the law, he now has what is called *apparent authority* to bind the partnerships. Even though your agreement provides otherwise, the law gives him the right to make decisions binding the partnership, if the person dealing with him does not know of any restriction upon his authority. This is designed to protect people who in good faith rely on the appearance of authority that you have allowed to exist.

Remember, the partnership agreement may limit a partner's authority to bind the partnership, but the law may still impose liability when innocent people deal with the unauthorized partner. The best way to protect yourself from this happening is to closely supervise all transactions between the partnership and others.

The Bottom Line

Unless your agreement says otherwise, each partner has the right to enter into contracts and bind the partnership. If you are not happy with that result, make sure you have a partnership agreement. And remember, even with an agreement, repeatedly allowing anyone to act on behalf of the business may result in liability to you, even for unauthorized acts.

Making Decisions

Under the law, unless you say otherwise, a majority of partners must approve important decisions. This can cause strange results if some partners have a large interest in the venture, and some partners have a small interest. For example:

Smith, Jones, and Hernandez form a general partnership. Hernandez has a right to 60% of the profits, and Smith and Jones each have a right to 20% of the profits. Unless the parties had agreed to another arrangement, Smith and Jones could make important decisions over the objections of Hernandez.

To many people, this does not seem fair. Hernandez should have more control than Smith and Jones. For this reason many partners agree that voting should be based upon a majority *in interest*, not a majority *of the partners*. For example, here is a clause Hernandez may want included in the agreement:

Management Decisions. Management decisions shall be decided by a majority vote. In such a vote, partners shall have different voting power, based upon their respective interests in the partnership. So, for example, if the interests of the three partners are 25 percent, 20 percent, and 55 percent, respectively, the voting power of each partner shall be based upon these relative interests.

The Bottom Line

Unless you have another agreement, important decisions will be made by a majority of the *partners*, regardless of their ownership percentages. If you want another arrangement, this needs to be included in an agreement.

Compensation for Services

General partners are *not* entitled to any salary from the partnership, unless there is an express agreement approving it. Consider the problem of Smith and Jones:

> Smith and Jones form a general partnership. Smith and Jones both contribute seed money, and Jones manages the business. They agree to share profits. Jones will not be entitled to any salary, unless there is an agreement providing for compensation. Both would simply split the profits equally.

Many times one partner will render more services than another partner. In this situation, it may seem fair to compensate the partner for these services. But unless there is an agreement about being paid, the partner will not have a claim against the partnership. For this reason, if one partner will be rendering services and others will not, the compensation issue should be considered and provided for in the agreement. Here is how such a clause might look:

> Compensation of Manager. __________ will manage the business of the partnership. He will devote a reasonable amount of time to the partnership's business. In consideration of these management services, he will be paid a monthly management fee of $______.

Also, if a partner is going to do anything else on behalf of the partnership and wants to receive payment for any of these other services rendered on behalf of the partnership, such as a real estate commission, or a legal or accounting fee, this should be specified and approved by all the partners in the agreement.

The Bottom Line

If you think you, or your partner, should be paid for the services contributed to the partnership you had better say so in the agreement. If you don't, you will simply share the profits *equally*, regardless of any services performed.

Dividing Profits and Losses

Under Texas law, profits and losses are divided equally after each partner's capital contribution has been returned. The results can be surprising if partners have contributed varying amounts to the partnership.

> Smith and Jones form a general partnership. Smith contributed $5,000, and Jones contributed $15,000. Assume the business makes a profit of $120,000 during the first year. Unless there is some agreement, Smith will receive his $5,000 contribution and Jones will receive his $15,000. Then the remaining $100,000 of the profits will be divided equally. In other words, Smith will receive $55,000 and Jones $65,000. This may not be what they intended.

Smith and Jones could have agreed to share profits according to their respective contributions. If the partnership agreement contained a provision such as this, the profits would have been split differently:

> Profit Share. After capital contributions of all partners have been returned to the partners from the partnership, any additional profits shall be divided among the partners based upon the relative amounts of their respective capital contributions.

The Bottom Line

Profits of a partnership are split equally, unless there is an agreement to the contrary. If you want a different arrangement, you need an agreement.

Capital Contributions

New businesses almost always need seed money. Owners must decide the relative initial capital contributions to be made. Some owners might want to make their initial contribution in installments, rather than in a lump sum. If so, the owners should decide whether the company's budget can accommodate such an installment arrangement.

Owners also may want to contribute property instead of cash. If property that has appreciated in value is to be contributed, the contributing partner might have to pay tax on the increased value. For example, assume one partner had purchased a building for $10,000 in 1970. If the building is now worth $50,000, and the partner wants to contribute the building to the partnership, there could be a tax due. A tax counselor should be consulted if this is a concern.

Once the partners have decided the capital contributions to be made, each partner's share of profits should be clarified. Are profits to be divided based upon capital contributions, or on some other basis?

Some partners might want to contribute services rather than cash or property. If this is to be done, the amount and type of services should be clarified, as well as the profit percentage the "service" partner will obtain and whether the partner will receive any compensation other than the profit percentage. For example, what type of service is contemplated, and approximately how many hours per week will be needed? What happens if the partner ends up working much more or less than initially predicted? Also, will there be any limit upon the "service" partner's right to receive profits (for example, such as a maximum annual payment), or will the service partner be treated like all other partners? For example:

Assume one partner will manage the partnership's restaurant, and one contributes capital. The basic arrangement is that the partners will split the profits. If the restaurant is *very* successful, would some other profit split be fairer?

Texas law provides that partners do not receive any interest from the partnership on capital contributions, unless the partners agree otherwise. This question should be discussed by the partners. Here is how a clause would look that gives a partner interest on capital contributions:

Interest on Capital Contributions. In addition to the profit share of each partner, each partner shall be entitled to an annual interest payment from the partnership, each year on December 1, until the partner has had his initial capital contribution repaid in full by the partnership. The interest payment shall be _____% of the amount of capital contribution not repaid as of December 1 of that year.

Additional Capital

When a business is started, owners normally try to estimate the amount of seed capital that business will need. This, of course, is only an estimate and can be very wrong. Many new businesses find that they need more money after the business has been started. There can be many reasons for this need for additional capital. For example, the business might be less profitable initially than planned, or more money might be needed for expansion, advertising, or inventory.

This need for additional capital can cause problems. For example, assume that Tom and Becky have started a video store, and that each contributed $10,000. They have agreed to share profits equally. What if they discover three months after the business has opened that the business needs more money? Assume Becky has some money and Tom doesn't. If Becky contributes more money, will this change her profit percentage? If so, how will it change it?

The agreement should address what happens if this occurs. First, who decides whether the business needs more capital? After it is decided that more money is needed, who must contribute, and how much? Should each partner have to contribute the portion of the additional capital based upon the partner's percentage of profits? What if one partner does not have any more funds, or does not want to contribute any more funds?

The Bottom Line

Owners of a new business need to consider what will happen if the initial "seed money" is inadequate and additional capital is needed. If you don't do this, it will be unclear to the partners what each partner's obligations are, if the business needs more money.

Partnership Draws

Simply saying partners share profits doesn't mean much. More importantly, when do you get whatever money you are entitled to? Partners need to decide when payments will be made to partners, in addition to any salary payments agreed to. New businesses need seed capital, and most are initially unprofitable. It frequently is unwise to drain the business of its capital via payments to partners. Many agreements provide the procedure for approving partnership draws. For example, the agreement could provide that two-thirds of the partners must approve a payment arrangement before the partners could receive a payment from the partnership. Alternatively, the agreement could state that, except for partners receiving a salary from the partnership, no payment would be made until the business is profitable for a three-month period.

The Bottom Line

The amount and timing of partnership draws can be quite controversial in a partnership. Partners should discuss how the partnership will determine when draws are appropriate.

Bank Accounts and Signing Checks

Businesses need bank accounts. An important management decision for the partnership is who should be able to make withdrawals from the account. This may be determined by the mechanics of the business. For example, if one partner is running the business, he probably will be the one authorized to make withdrawals.

The decision regarding banking for the business highlights an issue of trust among the owners. If one person has the right to make withdrawals, that person could steal money from the business. This does sometimes occur. As a safeguard, many businesses require two people to authorize withdrawals from a business account.

After you and your partners have decided upon the best arrangement for withdrawals, this can be worked out with your bank for the business. When the account for the business is opened, one important provision of the account agreement is who is authorized to make withdrawals. Partners should go to the bank and clarify with the bank officer the arrangement desired, and this arrangement should be set forth in the new account agreement.

The Bottom Line

Control of the bank account means control of the funds of the partnership. Be sure to work with your bank to ensure that funds are not misappropriated.

Partnership Property

A partnership is considered a separate entity that can own property. Partners can also let the partnership use property owned by a partner. If the agreement does not clarify the status of property, it can be unclear whether a partner has given the partnership certain property, thereby making property partnership property, or whether the partner has merely let the partnership use property. To the extent possible, it is always a good idea to clarify what property is being given to the partnership, and what property is merely being used by the partnership. For example:

> Richard and Janie start an athletic equipment store. Richard owns some typewriters and computers and lets the store use them. When the business ends and the assets of the partnership are being divided, this equipment may be divided up as a partnership asset.

If a partner is contributing property to the partnership, he should receive credit for contributing the full value of the property, less any liens on the property. If the partner is letting the partnership use property, he should be given credit for the rental value of the property. This clarifies that the property is not partnership property.

The Bottom Line

Make sure it is always clear whether property belongs to the partnership or an individual partner.

The Partnership Business

Partners obviously should clarify the type of business the partnership will carry on. For example, it could be quite a shock if a partner contributed money to a partnership he thought would be operating a restaurant, and then the other partners decided that they would sell flowers instead. To solve this problem, the agreement should set forth the type of business of the partnership, and all the approval of all partners should be necessary to make any change in that provision. For example, a clause could look like this:

> Partnership Business. The purpose of the Partnership shall be to develop, lease, or sell approximately 100 acres of real property located at 400 Wildcrest, Tomville, Texas, which real property is more fully described on Exhibit "A" attached hereto. Such real property and any improvement thereon shall be hereinafter referred to as the "Property." The purposes of the Partnership shall include the acquisition, ownership, holding for investment purposes, development, encumbering, leasing (as lessor), maintaining, operating, and disposing of all or part of such Property.

The Bottom Line

Silly as it may sound, be sure to decide what type of business your partnership will be in before you agree to it. Remember, you may be personally liable for the losses of the business.

Opening a Competing Business

Fortunately most partners can get along well. However, some find that they cannot work together, and one or more decide to leave. Before this happens to you, you must consider whether any departing partner should have the right to open a business that competes with the partnership. If you decide that this shouldn't be allowed, you must consider what a reasonable noncompetition period and area would be. Then a noncompetition provision must be added to the partnership agreement.

Also, even without an express agreement, partners cannot operate a business that competes with the partnership, or is similar to the partnership business, as long as the partner is still a partner, unless the partnership agreement permits this. This surprises many partners. For example, assume Bob and Ray agree to be partners in an oil and gas venture regarding one location. If Bob found another promising oil and gas location, he would have to offer Ray an opportunity to participate in this other venture. This may not be what Bob expected. Bob and Ray might want to be partners as to the one parcel, but don't want to have to offer each other any other parcels discovered. If so, this should be set forth in the agreement. A sample provision might look like this:

> Partner's Activities. The Managing Partner shall devote to the Partnership business such time as, in his sole discretion, he deems reasonably necessary. Any Partner or person with any interest in such Partner may engage in or possess an interest in other business ventures of any nature or description, independently or with others, even if such ventures are in direct competition with the Partnership, which ventures may include, but are not limited to, the real estate business in all its phases which

shall include, without limitation, ownership, operation, management, syndication and development of real property, and neither the Partnership nor any partner shall have any rights in or to such independent ventures or income or profits derived therefrom; provided, however, neither the Managing Partner, nor any of his affiliates shall, without the written consent of the Investing Partner, directly or indirectly participate in any way in the development, ownership, leasing or operation of any type of shopping center within _____ miles of the Property at any time while the Partnership, the Investing Partner or the shareholders of the Investing Partner have any ownership interest in the Property.

Some partners also might have ownership interests in businesses that are similar to that contemplated by the partnership. If so, this should be disclosed to the partners. The agreement should set forth the approval by the other partners of the competing business, and what activities the partner will be permitted to do without violating any of his rights to the partnership. If such a provision is not added, the partner with the competing business interest could be considered in violation of his duties to the partnership.

The Bottom Line

Under the law a partnership is a serious commitment and it prohibits you from going out on your own in similar ventures. If this isn't what you want, say so in your agreement.

Adding New Partners

No matter how carefully you plan at first, you may find that you want to add a new partner after the business is started. For example, additional money might be needed, or the new partner might have expertise that would be useful for the business. Similarly, you might want to add new partners in connection with an expansion of the business, or to give an employee more of a stake in the business. This is a topic that should be covered in your partnership agreement. For example, partners should consider whether a partner should be admitted by a majority vote, or whether all partners must approve a new member.

Also, if a new partner is to be added, how much will he have to contribute, and what will he get for the contribution? Sometimes the specifics of the arrangement are left to be decided by the partners when the new partner is to be admitted.

When a new partner is added, the partnership should clarify the interest the new partner holds. For example, for what period does the partner's profit percentage apply? Similarly, what debts and liabilities is the new partner responsible for? The UPA provides that the new partner is personally liable for debts that arise after the new partner becomes a partner, but is not personally liable for prior debts. If another arrangement is desired, this should be clarified.

The Term of the Partnership

When you start a business, it is important to consider the term of your commitment. Is the business to be operated indefinitely, or should some end point be set forth? For example:

Harold and Carolyn invest in an apartment, and will manage it. When should the apartment be sold? What if one partner wants to sell, or leaves Texas, and the other doesn't want to sell?

A possible answer to the problem of Harold and Carolyn would be a clause like this:

Sale of Partnership Property. The Partnership property shall be sold, and the proceeds divided, when any partner desires to sell the property and wind up the business of the partnership.

Ending a Partnership

A partnership is perceived as a special relationship, and according to the law, it only continues to exist as long as all the initial partners remain. If one dies, desires to sell his interest, or is thrown out, the relationship is disturbed. This "break" in the relationship is called *dissolution*.

You might say, so what? Well, the effects of a dissolution can be significant. Unless partners agree otherwise, at dissolution any partner normally can force the partnership business to be broken up and sold. Once a business has developed significant goodwill, this can be a terrible result. For example:

Bill, Bob and Tom start a restaurant in Houston called "George's" which becomes quite successful. Bill wants to withdraw from the partnership and start a restaurant in Los Angeles. If the partners had no agreement, Bill could force the partnership to liquidate, even though the business is successful.

When one partner quits or dies, the remaining partners normally want to carry on the business of the partnership. If the agreement deals with this and sets forth that the remaining partners can continue the business, this is effective. Most agreements therefore contain fairly long provisions about these problems. For example, a portion of such a clause might look like this:

> In the event of the withdrawal of a partner, for whatever reason, the partnership shall not be dissolved, but the partnership business may be continued uninterrupted by the remaining partners.

The Bottom Line

Unless you say otherwise, a partnership lasts only so long as all the partners are alive and want it to continue. Any partner can end it at any time. If you don't want this result you'd better have a clause in your agreement.

Buyout Arrangements

Any business needs to plan for what happens if one owner dies, or for some other reason needs to withdraw. As we have just told you, if a partner wants out he can force the sale of the partnership. Two basic questions are presented when planning for this problem. First, how is the interest to be valued? Second, once a value is determined, who will buy the interest?

There are a number of formulas that can be used to value businesses. For example, the net value of the assets of the business could be used. This is what the law will do if you don't say otherwise. This might not be a bad way to value the worth of a very new business. However, this does not incorporate a factor for the "goodwill" of the business, the value of the business as an ongoing concern. For example, common sense tells us that a successful business is worth more than the value of its assets; a successful business is also an income stream, and this has value.

The goodwill component can be satisfied in a few ways. For example, a formula could be set forth to quantify the value. One formula commonly used is a specified multiple of the earnings of the business. Alternatively, the partners could agree to set a value each year for the business; if any partner needed to sell that year, the value of the interest would be a pro rata percentage of the agreed value. Another common method used is to obtain an appraisal (or three) of the value of the business from specified appraisers.

A partnership does not have to have one valuation method for all purposes. For example, one valuation method, such as the book value method, could be used if the partner has only been a partner for a short period, while another method could be used if the person has been a partner for a long period. Similarly, one method could be used to value the interest if the partner dies, but another method could be used if the partner merely wants to leave the business.

As you can see, it is important that the agreement establish the value of a buyout. But in addition to value you should consider the terms of the sale. For example, does the buyout have to be in cash, or can some or all of the payment be made over time? If it can be made over time, what amount of interest should be paid? Sometimes the interest rate is tied in some way to the prime rate, as it changes. For example, the former partner could receive interest payments for each year based upon that year's average prime rate plus 2% on all monies until paid.

Once the value of the interest is established, the identity of the payor must be set forth. All of the partners might wish to buy out the partner. On the other hand, only some might want to, or none might want to. Some buyout agreements give the business the right to buy the interest first; this does not change the relative ownership interests of the other partners. If the business does not buy it, some mechanism must be established for determining which partner (or partners) can buy the share.

An important issue is whether the partners *must* buy the interest, or whether they only have the option to buy the interest. Many partners do not want to make it possible for the interest to be sold to a third party, since they do not want to have a new partner whom they might not trust or enjoy working with.

The Bottom Line

Many complications can arise if a partner dies, wants to withdraw, or wants to sell his interest and the partnership agreement does not address this. If this is not planned for, it is unclear how the partnership would value and purchase the interest of a departing partner. It is a good idea to include a detailed provision in your partnership agreement, regarding the manner in which a withdrawing partner's share will be valued and paid.

Selling an Interest

Your partnership agreement should deal with what happens if a partner wants to sell his interest. Does the partner have the right to sell to a third party? Any third party? Must the interest be offered to the partnership or the other partners first? What valuation method will be used to value the interest? To solve these questions you need a specific clause in your agreement. For example, a clause could look like this:

> 10.03 Right of First Refusal. If any Partner desires to sell its interest in the Partnership (the "Selling Partner"), it must first give notice of same to all of the non-selling Partners (the "Remaining Partners") including

> the name of the proposed purchaser and the net price and terms of the proposed sale. In such event, the Remaining Partners shall be entitled, during a period of ninety (90) days from the date of receipt of such notice, to participate in the purchase of the Selling Partner's interest at the same net price and terms. In the event more than one Remaining Partner desires to purchase a portion of the Selling Partner's interest at such price and terms, such interest shall be divided among them as they may agree, or if they fail to agree within such ninety (90) day period, in proportion to their respective Capital Interests in the Partnership. The purchase price of such Selling Partner's interest shall be allocated among the purchasing Partners in proportion to the respective portion of the interest purchased by each of them.
>
> 10.04 Sale to Third Parties. If the Remaining Partners do not exercise their right of first refusal as provided in paragraph 10.03 above within the ninety (90) day period provided therein, the Selling Partner may sell his interest to a third party provided such sale is (a) to the purchaser specified and at the price and terms specified in the notice to the Remaining Partners, and (b) such sale is consummated within sixty (60) days of the termination of the right of first refusal provided for in paragraph 10.03 above. Notwithstanding any provision of this Agreement to the contrary, except for transfers due to death or incapacity, the Managing Partner shall not, without the written consent of the Investing Partner, (i) sell or transfer a portion of his Capital Interest to more than one person or entity other than his immediate family, or (ii) sell or transfer during any Development Stage any portion of the Partnership Interest which would result in its remaining Capital Interest being less than twenty-five percent (25%).

You also should know that the law permits a partner to sell his right to profits from the partnership, and this does not dissolve the partnership. The person buying the rights to profits does not become a "partner" and cannot exercise management power or participate in decisions. Is this arrangement desired? If not, the agreed upon terms should be set forth.

The sale of an interest in a partnership can create tax liabilities. A tax counselor should be consulted before such a sale is effected to be sure that there is no excess tax liability incurred in connection with the transaction.

Expelling a Partner

Sometimes a partnership might want to expel a partner. This obviously is a drastic step, and should be undertaken only rarely when no other solution seems workable. The grounds and procedure for expulsion should be set forth in the agreement.

If a provision regarding expulsion is included, other terms need to be addressed, such as how the expelled partner's interest is to be valued and paid. Presumably the partner's interest in the partnership's profits would stop when he is expelled, but this should also be clarified.

Bankruptcy of a Partner

Under the UPA the bankruptcy of a partner dissolves the partnership. Many partners do not want this arrangement. If so, the agreement should provide that the bankruptcy of one partner does not dissolve the partnership. One common approach is to expel a partner if he becomes bankrupt; the remaining partners would buy out the bankrupt partner and continue the business of the partnership, if the agreement states that the remaining partners have this power.

Death of a Partner

If a partner dies, this presents both dissolution and buyout issues. Under the UPA, the death of a partner dissolves the partnership. If this is not desired, this should be set forth.

The buyout procedure should be set forth. For example, how is the interest to be valued? Who purchases the interest? What are the terms of the sale?

Other Partnership Agreement Issues

Some common partnership agreement subjects are mentioned above. Still, every new business is unique. Think about your business. Imagine various scenarios for the business. Consider what the business will be like if it becomes successful; does the agreement deal with the significant matters that would arise? Similarly, imagine what would happen if the business is not successful. Does the agreement cover all significant matters that would arise? If you are planning to prepare the partnership agreement yourself, we do encourage you to have a lawyer review the agreement. The lawyer can then tell you whether anything needs to be changed or added.

Miscellaneous Partnership Information

Partners do not have to be individuals. In Texas a corporation, trust, estate, a general partnership, or limited partnership can be a partner of a general partnership. A general partnership can have any number of partners, as long as there are at least two. All partners of a general partnership are general partners.

A *joint venture* is a partnership for a specific limited purpose, and in many ways is treated as a general partnership.

SUMMARY OF ADVANTAGES AND DISADVANTAGES

There are a number of desirable features of a general partnership. It is quite simple to form and operate, no special filing with any state office normally is required, and no minutes of meetings of any kind must be maintained. This simplicity can save owners time and legal fees. Also, there is no partnership tax; owners of a general partnership only pay taxes individually.

Other features of a general partnership can cause problems. General partners have no limited liability; their personal assets can be attached to collect claims against the partnership. Also, management of a general partnership is not centralized; the law presumes that all general partners have the right to make normal management decisions and obligate the partnership. If owners want to centralize management of the business in one owner, the general partnership format does not work well.

4

The Limited Partnership

In Chapter 3 the characteristics of a general partnership were discussed. The general partnership has certain advantages, but for many new businesses it has significant drawbacks. The general partnership presumes that all partners want to manage the business, and that they are all willing to assume unlimited liability for the debts of the business. However, in many instances, one partner is the manager, and all others wish only to be passive investors. Also, many investors want some limit to their liability; they do not want to be personally liable for all claims against the business. In such situations a "limited" partnership has significant advantages over a general partnership.

There are some significant differences between a general partnership and a limited partnership. For example, a limited partnership has two types of partners: general partners and limited partners. General partners manage the business and have the unlimited liability normally associated with general partners. Limited partners are essentially investors who do not manage the business and who have limited liability. They can lose, at most, the amount they invest in the business; creditors of the business cannot attach the other assets of a limited partner. This new class of "limited partner" is the significant difference between a limited partnership and a general partnership. The liability of a limited partner resembles that of a shareholder in a corporation.

The limited partnership can be useful if some owners are concerned about the unlimited liability that results from a general partnership, and these owners do not want to manage the business of the partnership. These owners can be limited partners, and their liability is limited to the investment in the partnership. Those partners who manage the business would be the general partners, and they would not have limited liability.

There must be at least one general partner and at least one limited partner to create a limited partnership. Of course, there can be many partners of both types, if this is desired. One person or entity can be both a general and a limited partner. In Texas a corporation, a general partnership, a limited partnership, a trust, or an estate can be a general or limited partner, if this is desired.

People forming a limited partnership frequently designate a corporation as the sole general partner of a limited partnership; all individuals are designated limited partners. When this is done, no person is forced to incur unlimited individual liability for debts of the business. The corporate general partner has limited liability due to its corporate form, and the limited partners have limited liability from their designation as limited partners.

Limited partnerships and general partnerships are similar in many ways. For example, they are taxed in the same way. There is no limited partnership tax, so partners pay only individual tax, according to their respective profit percentage. Also, many issues that should be resolved in a general partnership agreement need to be included in a limited partnership agreement. These issues will be discussed below.

Forming a Limited Partnership

Unlike a general partnership, something must be filed with the Texas secretary of state to form a limited partnership. If this limited partnership "certificate" is not filed, the business normally will be considered a general partnership, and all partners can be considered general partners, even those who believed they were limited partners. This can create quite a problem, since limited partners generally do not want unlimited liability. To avoid this problem, if you want to form a limited partnership, be sure to file a certificate that satisfies all the requirements of Texas law. Specifically, you must meet the requirements of the Revised Limited Partnership Act enacted in 1987.

The information that must be included in a limited partnership certificate is set forth in Section 2.01 of the Revised Limited Partnership Act (see Appendix A).

The certificate must include the name of the partnership, the location of the principal place of business, the name, mailing address, and street address of the business or residence of each general partner, the address of the registered office, and the name and address of the agent for service of process.

A filing fee must be paid to the secretary of state when the certificate is filed. The fee is $750.00. The certificate should be sent to the Texas Secretary of State, P.O. Box 13697, Austin, TX 78711. For information about this filing process, call the secretary of state at 512-463-5782. The certificate should be amended if the identity of the partners change, or some other term in the agreement is changed.

The Bottom Line

To form a limited partnership, a certificate must be filed with the Texas secretary of state. If you decide to form a limited partnership, be sure you file a certificate that satisfies Texas law.

Partnership Name

The certificate should set forth the name of the partnership business. The partnership agreement should also clarify whether the rights to this name will be a partnership asset.

Before a name is selected, it is important to determine whether anyone else has used the name before. If someone has, you may not have the right to use the name.

The name of a limited partnership must include "limited partnership," "limited," "L.P.," or "Ltd." The surname of a limited partner should not be included in the name of a limited partnership. If this is done, the limited partner can be treated as a general partner. There is a fear that if the surname of a limited partner is included in the name of the business, creditors could rely upon the credit of such a limited partner when extending credit to a limited partnership. In order to clarify the limited liability status of limited partners, no surname of a limited partner should be included in the name of the business.

Powers of Limited Partners

Limited partners cannot take an active role in the management of the limited partnership. If they do, they can be considered general partners, and they lose their limited liability as a limited partner. It is vital for limited partners to be aware of this when a limited partnership business is doing poorly. In this situation, a limited partner can be tempted to become more involved in the business to try to salvage his investment. The partner must be aware that too active a role can lead to his being considered a general partner. If this occurs, the limited partner might not lose just his initial investment, but his other personal assets.

Limited partners can participate in important decisions, however, without losing limited liability. The statute sets forth certain things a limited partner can do. For example, a limited partner can advise the general partner about the operation of the business, guarantee partnership debts and provide collateral for partnership loans, be employed by the partnership, and act as an officer, director, or shareholder of a corporate general partner. In addition, the limited partners can be given the right to approve certain important things, such as a plan to dissolve the partnership, an amendment to the limited partnership certificate, and a sale of all the assets of the partnership. If the limited partners want any of these powers, the agreement should specify this.

The Bottom Line

Limited partners cannot exercise normal management powers. They can be given the power to approve important decisions, if the agreement provides for this.

Tax Treatment of Limited Partners

A limited partnership normally is taxed as a partnership, not a corporation. So, the partnership profits are allocated among the partners, and these partners pay individual income tax on the profits. However, if a limited partnership looks too much like a corporation to the Internal Revenue Service, the IRS can take the position that the limited partnership really is a corporation and should be taxed as one. This can be quite a costly result, since corporations have to pay a corporate income tax on the profits of the business, and then shareholders have to pay a tax on money distributed to them. (This is discussed in detail in Chapter 5.) Technical rules have evolved to determine whether a limited partnership will be taxed as a partnership or a corporation. If you want to form a limited partnership, and it is important to you whether the business will be treated as a corporation or a partnership for tax purposes, consult a tax advisor to verify that the business will be taxed as a partnership.

Securities Regulation

Limited partnership interests are considered "securities." Because of this, rules regarding the sale of securities should be followed when forming a limited partnership. If these rules are not followed, a limited partner has the right to have his investment refunded to him by the general partner. In an extreme case, the general partner could also be fined and possibly even jailed if the securities laws are not followed. Securities laws will be discussed in Chapter 5.

Interstate Business

If the partnership wants to do business in other states, it's likely that the business will have to "qualify" to do business there. In order to "qualify" to do business in another state, some filing must be made with the appropriate state office. This filing normally requires a filing fee, and the partnership must agree to appear in court in that state if there is a dispute involving business transacted in that state. The partnership must also designate an agent for service of process in connection with any such dispute. This filing in each state should be made before the partnership transacts any business in that state.

Assumed Name Certificate

If the business plans to do business under a name other than the name of the partnership, an assumed name certificate must be filed. This is discussed in Chapter 7.

The Limited Partnership Agreement

The limited partnership agreement should set forth the terms of the understanding between the parties. If the partners have no express agreement, Texas law provides an agreement for the partners. This is the Texas Revised Limited Partnership Act (RLPA). However, partners frequently want to change the RLPA terms in some ways. Some important issues that frequently are dealt with in a limited partnership agreement will be mentioned below.

Contributions by the Partners

The agreement should specify how much each partner must contribute, as well as when the amount should be contributed. Such a provision could look like this:

> General Partner's Initial Capital Contribution. The General Partner has previously contributed to the Partnership as his Initial Capital Contribution (i) the sum of Fifty and No/100 Dollars ($50.00) upon the formation of the Partnership, and (ii) his entire interest in the Tract and all contracts therefor, plans and specifications, construction contracts, financing commitments, and other items involved in the purchase of the Tract and construction of Improvements.

> Limited Partners' Capital Contributions. By the execution and delivery of this Agreement, each Limited Partner agrees to contribute to the Partnership the sum of money set forth opposite such Limited Partner's name on the signature pages hereof. The total of the Limited Partner's Capital Contributions shall be Two Million Three Hundred Thousand and No/100 Dollars ($2,300,000.00), comprised of Ninety-Two (92) Units of Twenty-Five Thousand and No/100 Dollars ($25,000.00) each. Each Limited Partner's Initial Capital Contribution shall be the sum of Four Thousand and No/100 Dollars ($4,000.00) for each Unit purchased by such Limited Partner. Each Limited Partner's Additional Capital Contribution shall be the sum of Twenty-One Thousand and No/100 Dollars ($21,000.00) for each Unit purchased by such Limited Partner, to be paid to the Partnership over a five year period plus interest at a per annum interest rate equal to One Percent (1%) over the prime commercial lending rate charged from time to time by _____ Bank, N.A., Houston, Texas to its most creditworthy customers, in accordance with the following schedule: $7,500.00 per Unit plus accrued interest on or before February 15, 1992; $6,500.00 per Unit plus accrued interest on or before February 15, 1993; $4,000.00 per Unit plus accrued interest on or before February 15, 1994; and $3,000.00 per Unit plus accrued interest on or before February 15, 1995. Each such Additional Capital Contribution shall be evidenced by a Promissory Note to be executed and delivered upon the admission to the Partnership of such Limited Partner. The proceeds of such Capital Contributions, including the Promissory Notes evidencing a portion of same, may be used by the General Partner for any proper Partnership purpose, including securing any Partnership borrowings. Each Promissory Note is to be secured by the delivery by the respective Limited Partner of a certificate of deposit, letter of credit or other security accept-

able to the General Partner in the amount of Twenty-one Thousand and No/100 Dollars ($21,000.00) per Unit represented by such Limited Partner's Promissory Note, such Security Instrument to continue in force until the Promissory Note is paid in full.

General Partner's Additional Capital contributions. In the event the Partnership requires additional operating funds, the General Partner shall be obligated to contribute such funds to the Partnership as an Additional Capital Contribution.

Permissible Partnership Contributions

A limited partner cannot acquire an interest in a limited partnership in exchange for future services. A partner can contribute cash, other property, the value of past services rendered, or a promissory note in exchange for a partnership interest.

Additional Contributions

If any additional contributions are to be required, the respective amounts and dates of these contributions should be specified. For example, should each partner have to contribute a pro rata amount, based upon each partner's interest in the partnership? If so, many agreements set forth what will occur if a partner defaults on his obligation to make an additional contribution. This is one such provision:

Advances by Other Partners. In the event a Partner fails to make a Capital Contribution to the Partnership at any time when required to do so, and such default continues for a period of ten (10) days from receipt of written notice of such default from the General Partner (or any other Partner if the General Partner is in default), the General Partner (provided he is not the Partner in default) shall be entitled to elect to advance to the Partnership any such amount which the defaulting Partner has failed to contribute. In the event the General Partner does not elect to advance or cause to be advanced any amount which a Partner failed to contribute within thirty (30) days of the original notice to the defaulting Partner, then the General Partner (or any other Partner if the General Partner is in default) shall send written notice of such default to all other Partners, and all non-defaulting Partners shall be entitled, during the period that such defaulting Partner continues to be in default, to elect to participate in the making of any such advance. The advances by the non-defaulting Partners electing to so advance funds shall be apportioned among them as they may agree, or if they fail to agree, such advances shall be made in proportion to the respective Capital Interests of the non-defaulting Partners electing to make such advances. Any advances pursuant to this Paragraph 15.01 shall be deemed to be a loan by each Partner making such an advance to the defaulting Partner, and any such Advancing Partner shall earn interest on such advance at the maximum rate of interest allowed by law, but if no such maximum rate then exists, at Twenty-Four Percent (24%) per annum. Any and all distributions which otherwise would be distributed to the defaulting Partner in accordance with the terms hereof shall instead be distributed to the Advancing Partners in partial repayment of any interest accrued on such advances, and then in repayment of any advances made in accordance with this Paragraph 15.01, until such advances plus accrued interest have been fully repaid, such repayments to be allocated among the Advancing Partners in proportion to their respective advances on behalf of such defaulting Partner or in addition to there being an Advancing Partner the defaulting Partner additionally owes funds to the Partnership.

The Bottom Line

Partners need to plan for what will occur if the business needs more capital. The agreement should deal with who will have the obligation to provide this additional capital, and what benefits will result from making such an additional contribution.

Profit Percentage

The respective profit percentages of each partner obviously should be set forth. The Texas Revised Limited Partnership Act provides that, unless the partners make another arrangement, all partners share profits in proportion to their respective capital contributions. For example:

Assume three limited partners contribute $5,000, $10,000, and $20,000 to a venture, respectively, and the general partner contributes $15,000. Assume the business makes a profit of $150,000. Unless the partners made another agreement, after the capital contributions are returned to the partners the remaining $100,000 of profit would be divided in a proportion to the amount contributed.

Profit division provisions can be simple or quite complicated. For example, limited partners might be given a fixed profit percentage regardless of the extent of the profits of the business. On the other hand, the general partners might want the profit percentage of the limited partners to be limited after the partners receive a certain return on their investment.

The Bottom Line

Profits are normally shared based upon each partner's capital contribution. If a different arrangement is desired, an agreement is necessary.

Dividing Losses

Losses normally are shared in the same manner as profits. A different arrangement can be made, if the partners all agree.

Compensation of General Partner

The general partner normally manages the business of the limited partnership. Unless there is another agreement, a partner is not compensated for services rendered in the partnership business. The agreement should set forth the compensation, if any, to be received by the general partner for any work. For example, the partner might receive a salary; most would agree that a partner should at least receive reimbursement for expenses. This is an example of one such provision:

> Compensation of General Partner. The General Partner shall receive no compensation for his services as General Partner. If the General Partner, however, renders services to the Partnership other than as required hereunder, the General Partner shall be entitled to reasonable compensation for such services. The General Partner shall be entitled to be reimbursed by the Partnership out of Partnership funds for any and all direct costs and expenses incurred by it in relation to the formation of the Partnership and the operation of the Partnership affairs.

The Bottom Line

Partners are not entitled to be compensated for services rendered to the partnership, unless the agreement so provides.

Obligation to Repay Contributions of Limited Partners

If a limited partnership is unsuccessful, the limited partners normally lose their investment. In some instances the general partner will guarantee the return of the contributions made by the limited partners. If this is the partners' understanding, the agreement should include this guarantee.

Partnership Business

The agreement should set forth the types of business to be conducted by the partnership. This gives the limited partners some protection. If this is done, the general partner cannot change the character of the business without obtaining the consent of the limited partners. This is an example of one such provision:

> The purposes of the Partnership are to (i) acquire, own and hold the Tract containing approximately 10.7522 acres out of the _____ Survey, Houston, Harris County, Texas, (ii) construct the Improvements on the Tract, (iii) manage, operate and lease (as lessor) apartments in the Project, (iv) encumber and obtain financing for the Project, and (v) sell, transfer, convey, and exchange the Project. The Partnership shall have the power to do everything necessary, advisable, proper or convenient for the accomplishment of the purposes specified above; provided, however, nothing contained in this Article 3 or elsewhere in this Partnership Agreement shall obligate the General Partner to take any action on behalf of the Partnership if he deems such action inappropriate or not necessary to accomplish the Partnership purposes.

Partnership Property

If partners plan to let the partnership use property owned by a partner, the agreement should clarify what property will be owned by the partnership, and what property will be considered still owned by a partner. Alternatively, partners can contribute property to the partnership instead of cash. If this is done, the agreement should clarify that such property will be owned by the partnership.

Term of the Partnership

If the partners plan to do business only for a known period of time, this should be set forth in the agreement. In contrast, if partners do not know when the business will end, some provision should be made for how this decision will be made. This is one such provision:

> Partnership Term. The term of the Partnership commenced November 22, 1991 and shall continue until December 31, 2021 unless sooner terminated in accordance with the provisions of this Partnership Agreement.

Competing Businesses

Limited and general partners have a fiduciary duty to each other regarding the business. Because of these duties, unless the agreement provides otherwise partners must refer to the partnership all business related to the partnership's business. This can be a significant problem, since many business people have more than one investment in the same type of business. For example:

> Texas Properties, Ltd., is a limited partnership. Smith is the general partner. The business of the partnership is real estate development. Unless the agreement provides

> otherwise, Smith must do all his real estate development transactions through Texas Properties, Ltd.

Many general partners do not want this arrangement, since they may be the general partner of a number of real estate developments, or may want to develop some property in their individual capacity. If this is desired, the scope of the partnership business should be carefully described, and the agreement should outline the types of activities the general partner can be involved in as an individual. This is an example of one such provision:

> General Partner's Activities. The General Partner shall devote to the Partnership business such time as he reasonably shall deem necessary to manage the business and affairs of the Partnership. The General Partner may engage in or possess an interest in other business ventures of any nature or description, independently or with others, even if such ventures are in direct competition with the Partnership, which ventures may include, but are not limited to, the real estate business in all its phases including ownership, operation, management, syndication and development of apartment complexes and other real property, and neither the Partnership nor any Partner shall have any rights in or to such independent ventures or income or profits derived therefrom.

The Bottom Line

A partner cannot carry on any other business that is at all competitive with the partnership. If a partner wants to do this, all partners must approve.

Adding New Partners

The limited partnership agreement should deal with how new partners will be added. It normally is not very important how limited partners are added. Since they are passive investors in many respects, the only the new partner.

The addition or replacement of a general partner is much more significant. The agreement should address this process in much more detail.

Buyout Arrangement

Limited partnership interests normally are not very marketable. For this reason, some arrangement must be provided for the sale of shares. These provisions can apply if a limited partner dies, becomes bankrupt, or for some other reason wants to sell. If a partner dies or becomes bankrupt, some means for establishing the value of the partnership interest should be established. Various means of doing this were discussed in Chapter 3. Also, the identity of the purchaser (that is, the partnership or the limited partners) should be clarified, as well as the terms of the purchase (that is, all cash, or in installments).

Different issues are presented if a limited partner wants to sell his interest. Sometimes partners want a "right of first refusal" if this occurs. This is an example of one such provision:

> 12.02 Right of First Refusal. If any Partner desires to sell his Partnership Interest (the "Selling Partner"), he must first give written notice of same to the General Partner, including the name of the proposed purchaser and the net price and terms of the proposed sale. In such event, the General Partner shall be entitled, during a period of ten (10) days from the date of receipt of such notice, to elect to purchase the Selling Partner's Partnership Interest at the same net price and terms. In the event the General Partner does not elect to purchase the Selling Partner's Partnership Interest as provided above, the General Partner shall distribute the Selling Partner's notice to all other Partners, and the Partners other than the Selling Partner shall be entitled, during a period of twenty (20) days from the date of the Selling Partner's original notice, to elect to participate in the purchase of the Selling Partner's Partnership Interest at the same net price and terms as contained in such notice. In the event more than one Partner elects to purchase a portion of the Selling Partner's Partnership Interest, such Partnership Interest shall be divided among them as they may agree, or if they fail to agree within such twenty (20) day period, in proportion to their respective Capital Interests. The purchase price of a Selling Partner's Partnership Interest under this Paragraph 12.02 shall be allocated among the purchasing Partners in proportion to the respective portion of the Partnership Interest purchased by each of them. Any purchase under this Paragraph 12.02 shall be closed within thirty (30) days of the above-referenced election to purchase.
>
> 12.03 Sale to Third Parties. If the General Partner and the Remaining Partners do not exercise their right of first refusal as provided in paragraph 12.02 above within the twenty (20) day period provided therein, or any such purchase is not closed within the thirty (30) day period provided therein, the Selling Partner may sell his interest to a third party provided such sale is (i) to the purchaser specified and at the price and terms specified in the notice to the General Partner, and (ii) such sale is consummated within forty-five (45) days of the termination of the right of first refusal provided for in paragraph 12.02.

The Bottom Line

Texas law does not provide clear rules regarding how a partner's interest should be valued and paid for if he dies or withdraws. Partners should specify how a partnership interest will be valued in that event. Also, the partners should consider what should occur if a partner wants to sell his interest to a third party.

Firing the General Partner

Limited partners sometimes grow disenchanted with the general partner. Unless the agreement addresses this subject, the limited partners have no right to "fire" the general partner. Some limited partners want to have this right, if at least 50% or 67% of the limited partners want to remove the general partner. Such a provision should set forth the grounds for which the general partner can be removed; if no reason is needed, this should be set forth. The effect of such a removal upon the profit percentage of the removed general partner also should be specified.

Distributions to the Limited Partners

Someone must decide when the limited partner will receive distributions from the partnership. Normally this decision is made by the general partner. If the limited partners want to limit the discretion of the general partner, this should be set forth. This is an example of one provision regarding distributions:

> 6.02 Current Distributions. The General Partner shall distribute to the Partners, not less often than quarterly, the Distributable Funds of the Partnership (if any), being all cash generated from the operation of the Project, after the retention of adequate working capital and the establishment of a reasonable reserve for current, future and contingent liabilities, as reasonably determined by the General Partner. All such distributions shall be made to the Partners in the proportion of their respective Capital Interests.

Reports to the Limited Partners

Limited partners desire financial information about the partnership. The agreement should state how often reports will be sent to the partners, and what kind of reports will be prepared. This is an example of one kind of provision:

> 7.05 Monthly Statements. The General Partner shall prepare or cause to be prepared monthly statements showing the income and expenses of the Partnership and the assets and liabilities thereof as of the end of each calendar month. Such monthly statements shall be distributed to the Partners within thirty (30) days after the end of each calendar month.

Making Important Decisions

Under Texas law, a general partner has general management power. Limited partners frequently want to participate in important management decisions affecting the business of the partnership, as long as the powers do not subject them to personal liability for exercising control, as mentioned above. Decisions requiring the approval of the limited partners should be clarified. This is an example of one such provision:

> 9.02 Approval Rights. Anything to the contrary contained in this Partnership Agreement notwithstanding, without the written consent of Limited Partners owning three-quarters (3/4) of the Capital Interests owned by Limited Partners, the General Partner shall not:
>
> (a) Do any act in contravention of this Partnership Agreement.
> (b) Except for a permitted dissolution of the Partnership or sale of the Project, do any act which would make it impossible to carry on the ordinary business of the Partnership.
> (c) Confess a judgment against the Partnership.
> (d) Possess Partnership property or assign their rights in specific Partnership property, for other than a Partnership purpose.
> (e) Admit a person as a general partner.
> (f) Except to the extent otherwise permitted in this Partnership Agreement, admit a person as a limited partner.
> (g) Refinance and replace any Permanent Loan with another loan secured by a lien against the Project, but nothing contained herein shall require the consent of any Limited Partners to the initial Permanent Loan or other proper Partnership borrowings which are not secured by an interest in the Project.
> (h) Sell or exchange any real property interest in the Project.

Death or Bankruptcy of a Partner

The agreement should set forth whether the business of the partnership can be carried on after the death or bankruptcy of a limited or general partner. Also, as mentioned above, a means for valuing the partner's interest should be set forth.

The agreement should specify whether the business can be continued if a limited or general partner dies, retires, is declared bankrupt, or sells his interest. Most businesses want to have such a right. If the business is to be continued after the general partner dies or retires, a means for selecting a substitute general partner should be set forth.

Other Limited Partnership Agreement Issues

This chapter has discussed some common partnership agreement subjects. Still, every new business is unique. Imagine various scenarios for your business. Consider what will happen if it becomes successful; does the agreement deal with the significant matters that would arise? Similarly, imagine what would happen if the business is not successful. Does the agreement cover all significant matters that would arise? If you are planning to prepare the partnership agreement yourself, we do encourage you to have a lawyer review the agreement. The lawyer can tell you whether anything needs to be changed or added.

Advantages and Disadvantages of a Limited Partnership

The limited partnership form has a number of advantages. Limited partners have limited liability. This enables the partnership to attract investors who are willing to invest a certain amount of money in the venture, but only if their liability is limited. Also, management of the business is centralized in the general partner. This can be desirable, since in many instances not all investors want to manage the business. Limited partnerships do not pay a partnership tax, so frequently there is a tax advantage to the limited partnership form. Also, if the business loses money it may be possible for the limited partners to use these losses to shelter personal income from other sources.

There are a few disadvantages. To form a limited partnership, a filing must be made with the Texas secretary of state. Also, securities law requirements must be obeyed. Limited partners cannot control the general partner or manage the business. This can be a problem if the general partner is doing a poor job. Certain tax benefits available to a corporation, such as preferred treatment of life insurance, health insurance, and disability insurance, cannot be obtained in a limited partnership.

5

The Corporation

Whenever they think of "doing business," many people immediately think "corporation." To a beginning entrepreneur, forming a corporation is the American dream. But although many people think that an essential requirement of starting a business is to incorporate, that just isn't true. As we have shown you in Chapters 2, 3, and 4, there are several other forms of doing business, and in many cases one of them may be the best way. The corporation, however, does have one attribute different from all the other forms of businesses: it is a legal entity separate from its individual investors. Perhaps that is why in fiscal year 1990 there were 2,763 limited partnerships formed in Texas, as compared to 35,304 corporations. As you will see, the reason that so many corporations are formed and exist is in large part due to this distinction.

The Separate Entity

As we have pointed out, one aspect of a corporation makes it very different from the types of business forms discussed in the earlier chapters. A corporation is considered an entity separate from the individual owners. This *separate entity* concept has a number of effects.

For example, the corporation normally pays a corporate tax on its profits, and then the individual owners also pay a tax when money is distributed to them from the corporation. (This is not true of an S corporation, which will be discussed shortly.)

The separate entity idea also affects the liability of the owners of the business. A corporation has *limited liability*. Limited liability means that creditors of the corporation can only reach assets of the corporation; the assets of the owners cannot be reached.

In these respects the corporation is quite different from the sole proprietor, the newly created limited liability partnership, and the general partnership, as described in Chapters 2 and 3. Neither the sole proprietor nor the general partnership pays an additional tax on the profits of the business, and neither the proprietor, nor the limited liability partnership, nor any general partner has limited liability. The limited partnership also does not pay a separate tax on its profits. Limited partners do have limited liability, while a general partner in a limited partnership does not. But remember, a limited partner pays a high price for this protection: he cannot manage the partnership's business.

Continuity and Marketability

A second major difference between a corporation and the other forms of business is that the corporation, as a separate legal entity, exists independently of its owners or managers and ownership interests can be transferred simply through the sale of its stock. For example, a partnership generally is automatically dissolved when one of its partners dies. A corporation, on the other hand, usually continues to exist even if its major shareholder or its president dies. Unless a corporation is organized in a manner that provides for its dissolution upon the happening of a certain event, the business will continue to exist, and have the legal authority to do business, regardless of what happens to the individuals who control it.

And because the corporation is independent of its owners and managers, the sale of a corporation usually may be effectuated much easier than the sale of a partnership or sole proprietorship. Ownership of a corporation is based on the amount of stock in the corporation that a person owns, and this stock may often be sold and transferred with ease. Of course we don't expect that shares in your beginning corporation will be as easy to sell as shares in General Motors, but they will most likely be easier to sell than a partial interest in a partnership or sole proprietorship.

If you are thinking about establishing a business that will endure beyond your lifetime, or one that you can easily sell or transfer to another, you should consider incorporating.

Identity of the Manager

In a corporation, it is clear who will manage the business. A corporation is managed by its "officers." The chief officer is the "president." Regardless of how many different owners there are, the president operates the business. Corporations also must have an officer called a "secretary," who is responsible for maintaining corporate records. In a small business, it is common for the same person to be both the president and the secretary. A corporation can also choose to have other officers, such as vice presidents, executive vice presidents, a treasurer, and assistant treasurers and assistant secretaries. An officer can be a shareholder or a member of the board of directors, but does not have to be.

Corporate officers are selected by the "board of directors." The board of directors approves significant business decisions. The board may be comprised of only one person, or the owners may choose to have a much larger board. The size of the board of directors is set forth in the articles of incorporation, which will be discussed below.

The members of the board are normally selected by the owners of the business, who are called the *shareholders*. Board members are elected by a majority vote of the shareholders, whose relative voting power stems from the number of shares owned. The initial members of the board are set forth in the articles of incorporation. A member of the board can also be a shareholder, but does not have to be.

Issuing Shares

The shareholders are issued shares in proportion to their percentage interest in the business. So, for example, if there are two owners, and owner A has a 40% interest and owner B has a 60% interest, if there are 100 shares total, owner A would receive 40 shares and owner B would receive 60 shares.

Authority of Shareholders

The shareholders do not participate in most management decisions; these are made by the board of directors and the officers. However, the shareholders do select the board of directors, and can remove the board of directors at any time, if the internal rules of the business provide for it. In such situations the shareholders do effectively control decisions of the board.

In small businesses it is quite common for a shareholder to be an officer and a member of the board of directors. There can be one shareholder or many shareholders.

Do not be overwhelmed by all these technicalities. It's not normally that complicated. For example, in many small businesses the same person is the president and secretary, the sole director, and the only shareholder. In this situation, the owner for all practical purposes operates the business himself, even though there is a corporation.

FORMATION OF A CORPORATION

Where to Incorporate

You may have noticed that many large corporations are "incorporated" in unlikely places, such as Delaware and Nevada. This is possible because a corporation can be "formed" anywhere; it does not matter where the corporation will actually do business. A corporation is "formed" by filing articles of incorporation with the appropriate governmental office in the chosen state.

A large corporation might choose Delaware due to certain complex transactions the company plans to complete. The law of Delaware might facilitate these transactions more than the law of other states. Also, the law of Delaware makes it more difficult for shareholders to sue the officers for bad decisions, so corporate management might prefer it.

It is possible for Texas residents to form a corporation in a state other than Texas, even if the business of the corporation will be conducted only in Texas. However, for the normal small business it is cheaper and simpler to form a Texas corporation. Even if the corporation is formed in another state, if the corporation does business in Texas the business will have to "qualify" to do business in Texas. In order to qualify to do business, a filing must be made with the Texas secretary of state, and the filing fees and franchise tax due are $1,100. This qualification fee is more expensive than the fee for forming a Texas corporation. For this reason, there is an initial financial incentive to incorporate in Texas.

During the past few years, Texas courts have established exceptions to the general rule of limited liability for corporations. These exceptions appear to be broader than the rules of some other states. At this time, it is not clear whether these Texas "piercing-the-corporate-veil" rules will be applied to corporations formed in other states whose principal place of business is Texas.

If you are considering forming a corporation, talk to your lawyer before you do so to determine whether or not it would be advisable to form the corporation in another state to minimize the risk that you could have personal liability for claims against your corporation. All states, however, accept some exceptions to the general rule that owners of corporations will not be personally liable for claims against the corporation. For this reason, regardless of where you form your corporation, we urge you to:

1. Keep corporate money separate from personal money;
2. Pay corporate debts with corporate money (and personal debts with personal money);
3. Properly document corporate actions with corporate minutes (which should then be placed in the corporation's minute book);
4. Make a reasonable attempt to ensure, in light of the corporation's capital and insurance, that the corporation is adequately capitalized for foreseeable claims.

The discussion below summarizes the procedure for forming a corporation in Texas.

Creating a Corporation

To form a corporation, articles of incorporation must be filed with the Texas secretary of state. In order to be sure that the corporation is properly formed, it is important that you obey the rules regarding the contents of the articles, and the proper procedure for filing them.

Choosing a Name

The secretary of state frequently does not accept articles of incorporation because the name of the proposed corporation is identical or too similar to the name of an existing Texas corporation. In order to avoid this result, you can "reserve" the name you want. Before the secretary of state will let you reserve the name, the availability of the name will be checked. The best way to check the availability of a corporate name is by attempting to reserve the name with the secretary of state. A sample letter to reserve a name is set forth here.

Application for Reservation of Corporate Name

Secretary of State
Corporations Section
P.O. Box 13697
Austin, TX 78711

Dear Secretary of State:

Pursuant to Article 2.06 of the Texas Business Corporation Act, I would like to reserve the name "Texas Software, Inc." for 120 days. Enclosed is my check payable to your office in the amount of $40.

Dated: December 1, 1991

Signed by:

____

Albert Einstein
5000 Montrose Blvd.
Ste. 200
Houston, TX 77006
(713-523-1000)

This name reservation letter should be sent by someone who plans to sign the articles of incorporation.

If the secretary of state discovers that the name requested is not available, he will tell you this, and your $40 check will be returned. If the secretary of state determines that the name is available, you will be permitted to reserve the name. This "reservation" is good for 120 days, and the cost is $40.

As we said above, if you have enough time to go through this process with the secretary of state, the written name reservation request is the best way to clarify whether the name you desire is available. If you do not have time to reserve the name before the articles are filed, telephone the secretary of state at 512-463-5555 to determine if the name is available. An employee of the secretary of state will tell you whether the name is available. This is only an unofficial check of name availability, and the secretary of state may later determine that the name is not available. Still, it is better than nothing.

The name of a corporation must include the word *corporation, company*, or *incorporated*, or some abbreviation of any of these words (*corp., co.*, or *inc.*). The name can include arabic numerals, as well as other symbols commonly found on a typewriter, such as "!, ″, $, %, ′, ( ), *, ?, =, @, [ ], /, +, &, and -."

Even if the secretary of state accepts the articles of incorporation, or allows you to reserve the name, this does not mean you have the right to use the chosen name in the state of Texas. The secretary of state only searches names of corporations in Texas. Another corporation could have established an interest in the name by using the name in another state before you started your business, or a sole proprietorship or partnership could have used the name in Texas. A more thorough name search must be made if you want to be sure that you have the sole right to use the name in Texas.

Where to Send the Articles

Articles of incorporation must be signed by at least one person, and all signatures must be notarized. People who sign articles of incorporation are called *incorporators*. Articles of incorporation signed by all incorporators, plus one copy, should be sent to the Texas Secretary of State, Corporate Section, P.O. Box 13697, Austin, TX 78711. The filing fee for the articles is $300. The check should be made out to the Texas Secretary of State.

Contents of the Articles

The Texas Business Corporation Act, art. 3.02, lists the information that must be included in the articles of incorporation. This law is included in Appendix A. For example, the articles must include the name of the business, the period of time the corporation will do business, the type of business to be carried on, the total number of shares of stock, and the different classes of shares, that the corporation is authorized to issue, whether the corporation is authorized to issue preferred shares, the statement that the business will not be started until the owners have paid at least a total of $1,000 for the shares of the business, the street address of its office and the registered agent for the business, the number of directors that the corporation will have, the names and addresses of the persons who will be members of the board, and the name and address of each person who signs the articles of incorporation. A basic form for articles of incorporation is included in Appendix B, Form 5a.

The description of the articles of incorporation above sounds complicated. However, in many instances a standard form articles of incorporation is finc. For example, Figure 5-1 (page 35) is a sample articles of incorporation for Texas Software, Inc. Assume that Albert Einstein has already reserved the name, and that he intends to be the sole shareholder and director of the company.

Although articles of incorporation can be quite simple, depending upon your situation it may be a good idea to make some changes in the basic sample set forth above. For example, the corporation might want to eliminate "preemptive rights" of the shareholders, create different classes of stock, or elect to be a "close corporation." In order to do any of these things, the simple form of article shown in Figure 5-1 cannot be used. For this reason it is a good idea to have a lawyer review your articles of incorporation to be sure that the articles best suit your needs.

Corporations normally are formed by mail. This process can take a few weeks. It normally is a good idea to tell the secretary of state to form the business as of the date the secretary of state received the articles of incorporation. They will do this, if you ask. Otherwise, the articles can sit on someone's desk for weeks, and the corporation's existence would begin weeks later. This could be a problem if the corporation is doing business or signing contracts in the interim.

An alternative way of incorporating is available for a small extra fee ($10) if you need to incorporate immediately. This is the "expedited special handling" service provided by the secretary of state. If this service is requested, the secretary of state tries to complete the incorporation procedure by mail in two days. If you go to the office of the secretary of state, incorporation can be completed while you wait. This expedited service can be a good idea if you plan to do business right away. This facilitated incorporation service verifies that the articles were accepted, the name is available, and the corporation is in existence when the business is begun. If business is conducted before the corporation is formed, this can create personal liability for the owners. We strongly encourage you not to do this. **Wait until the corporation is formed before you conduct business or sign agreements.**

If the articles in the form filed satisfy Texas law, the name is available, and the appropriate filing fee is enclosed, the secretary of state will file the articles of incorporation. The incorporator will be notified of this when the secretary sends the incorporator a "certificate of incorporation." After this certificate is issued by the secretary of state, the corporation exists,

ARTICLES OF INCORPORATION OF TEXAS SOFTWARE, INC.

Article One:
The name of the corporation is Texas Software, Inc.

Article Two:
The period of its duration is perpetual.

Article Three:
The purpose for which the corporation is organized is the transaction of any lawful business for which corporations may be incorporated under the Texas Business Corporation Act.

Article Four:
The aggregate number of shares that the corporation shall have authority to issue is one hundred (100) shares, without par value.

Article Five:
The corporation will not commence business until it has received for the issuance of its shares consideration of the value of not less than one thousand dollars ($1000), consisting of money, labor done, or property actually received.

Article Six:
The street address of its initial office is 5000 Montrose Blvd., Ste. 200, Houston, TX 77006, and the name of its initial registered agent at this address is Albert Einstein.

Article Seven:
The number of directors constituting the initial board of directors is one, and the name and address of the person who will serve as director until the first meeting of the shareholders, or until his successor is elected and qualifies is Albert Einstein, 5000 Montrose, Ste. 200, Houston, TX 77006.

Article Eight:
The name and address of the incorporator is Albert Einstein, 5000 Montrose, Ste. 200, Houston, TX 77006.

____

Albert Einstein, incorporator

State of Texas
County of Harris

Before me, a notary public, on this day personally appeared Albert Einstein, known to me to be the person whose name is subscribed to the foregoing document and, being by me first duly sworn, declared that the statements therein contained are true and correct.

Given under my hand and seal of office December 1, 1991.

(Notary Seal) ______________________________

My commission expires:
________________, 19____

Figure 5-1. An example of articles of incorporation.

and no owner normally is personally liable for claims against the business that arise after this date.

After the corporation is formed, you should order a book of stock certificates, a corporate seal, and a minute book. These three items are normally sold as a corporate kit. A number of companies sell these corporate kits. The kits generally cost less than $50. The stock certificates are used as the stock in the corporation. Each shareholder receives a certificate; the certificate states how many shares the certificate represents. The corporate seal is sometimes needed to authorize action on behalf of the corporation. The minute book is used to hold records of corporate actions.

Incorporating an Ongoing Business

It is possible to incorporate an ongoing business. Some or all of the assets of the business can be transferred to the corporation (after the corporation is formed) in exchange for stock in the corporation. The tax consequences of the transaction are important, so talk to an accountant or lawyer about this before you do it.

The incorporation of an ongoing business may also need to comply with the "Bulk Transfer Act." Consult your lawyer regarding whether this is required in your case. Usually, such an incorporation is "exempt."

When you are incorporating an ongoing business, be sure to notify your creditors in writing that you are doing this. Also, if you are not going to change the name of the business, art. 1302-2.02 of the Miscellaneous Corporation Laws of Texas requires you to publish once a week for at least four consecutive weeks in a newspaper in the county where the company does business a notice of your intention to incorporate. If you don't do this, you can be personally liable for the corporation's debts.

Issuing the Shares of Stock

After the articles of incorporation are filed, and the secretary of state issues a certificate of incorporation, the corporation is in existence, and the corporation has a board of directors, as named in the articles. The board then needs to authorize the issuance of shares to the investor-owners. There can be only one shareholder or many shareholders, depending upon what is desired. The board needs to decide both the price of each share to be issued, as well as the identity of the shareholders. The price of each share should be determined after it is decided how much capital the corporation needs, and each investor decides how much money he wants to invest. The price of the shares obviously depends upon how many shares are to be issued. For example, if it is decided that capitalization of $1,000 is adequate for the business, if there are going to be two equal owners, each will contribute $500. If only one share is to be issued to each shareholder, the stock will cost $500 per share. If 500 shares are to be issued to each shareholder, each share would cost $1. Stock should be sold for at least the "par value" of the shares, if the shares have a par value.

In many small businesses, the identities of the shareholders normally are known before the articles are filed. The investors normally know one another, decide to form the business, and choose the corporate form. The investors frequently are also directors. After the issuance of the shares is authorized by the board, shares can be issued to each shareholder, when the shareholder presents a check to the corporation for the agreed value of the shares to be purchased. In most instances stock is issued in exchange for a check, but stock can also be issued in exchange for property or past services. Stock cannot be issued for a promissory note or a promise of future services. Shares are "issued" by a corporate officer filling out a share certificate for each shareholder, signing the certificate, affixing the corporate seal, and noting on the certificate how many shares of the company the shareholder purchased. After this is done, the corporation will then have some initial capital, and shareholders will exist.

Texas law requires shareholders to contribute a total amount of at least $1,000. In some instances, it is a good idea to contribute a higher amount. Under Texas law, in some circumstances shareholders can lose their limited liability if it is determined that the corporation was grossly undercapitalized by the founders, in light of the probable needs of the business. So, before the amount to be contributed is determined, the owners must prepare a projected budget and estimate how much initial capital the business will need, and how much insurance the company will maintain. When deciding upon the initial capitalization of the company, it is a good idea to discuss this with an accountant. A corporation should have adequate capital and insurance to satisfy foreseeable claims.

Shares of a corporation are "securities." The sale of securities in a corporation therefore must satisfy state and federal rules governing the issuance of securities. These rules are discussed on pages 38–39.

The First Board Meeting

After the corporation is formed, it is a good idea to have the board of directors adopt resolutions so that the corporation will be ready to function. For example, it was mentioned above that the board should authorize the issuance of shares, so the company will then have stockholders. A number of other things should be done by the board as soon as possible after the corporation is formed.

These resolutions can be adopted by the board at a meeting of the board of directors, or the board can adopt these resolutions by written consent, if all directors approve. Many small businesses find board meetings a stupid legal formality, and adopt simple resolutions by written consent. This is particularly useful if there is only one director.

At the first meeting of the directors the board should elect the officers of the corporation. Each Texas corporation must have a president and a secretary; additional offices are possible, if desired, such as treasurer, vice president, assistant secretary, and assistant treasurer. One person can hold more than one of these offices; for that matter, one person can hold all the offices. It is a good idea to have more than one officer, though, so that if one person is out of town there is someone who can act for the corporation.

The board of directors normally does a number of things in its first meeting, in addition to authorizing the issuance of shares and the election of officers. Significant agreements to be signed by the corporation should be approved at this first meeting of the board. For example, if the business is signing a lease, the board should approve the terms of the lease, and authorize an officer to signing the lease on behalf of the corporation. Any other significant agreements, such as employment agreements, shareholder agreements, or purchase contracts should be approved at this time, if the corporation is to be a party. The board also normally authorizes an officer to open a bank account at a certain bank, and the authorized signatories are specified. The form of the corporate stock certificate and the corporate seal are approved. An example of resolutions adopted by directors at a first meeting is included in Appendix B, Form 7.

At the first meeting of the board, the board approves the *bylaws* for the company. The bylaws essentially are the rules that will govern the operation of the business. For example, the different officers of the corporation are specified, such as the president, vice president, secretary and treasurer, and the functions and authority of the various officers are set forth. Also, the procedure for the election of directors is established. The frequency of shareholder and board meetings is also established, as is the manner in which notice of additional meetings is to be sent. An example of corporate bylaws is included in Appendix B, Form 6.

A number of other matters might be considered at the first meeting of the board. For example, the business sometimes selects a fiscal year. Also, it is a good idea to select the registered agent for service of process on the corporation, as well as the address of the principal executive office or location of the business. The S corporation election and Section 1244 stock will be discussed later. If either of these elections are desired, the board must approve the necessary filings. Also, if the corporation is going to conduct business under a name other than its corporate name, an assumed name certificate must be filed with the secretary of state, and the board must approve this.

After the articles are filed, shares are issued, and the first meeting of the board of directors has occurred, the corporation is prepared to begin doing business. The corporate entity exists, and the corporation has shareholders, officers, and a board of directors. Before the corporation commences business, however, the corporation should also comply with all federal, state, and local rules regarding tax withholding, social security, workmen's compensation, and other matters. These matters are discussed in Chapter 7.

The Shareholders' Agreement

Owners of a new corporate business should consider whether they need a shareholders' agreement. When people agree to start a business together, they normally do it because of a special relationship between the owners. If the business is successful and continues for a significant period, it is likely that one owner will die or for some other reason want to sell his shares. This can create a number of problems, if a procedure for transferring shares has not been arranged. First, the other owners may not want a stranger to be an owner. The stranger might not have the particular talent that attracted them to the person who is selling the shares. Also, there probably will not be much of a market for the shares of a small business. It would violate the securities law to advertise that the shares were available, so not many people will know the shares are for sale. In addition, few people might want to get involved in the small business.

So, most people try to work out an arrangement so that the other shareholders, or the company, will buy back the shares from a shareholder if a shareholder dies or for some other reason wants to sell. If this arrangement is chosen, some procedure must be set forth for valuing the shares. These various valuation methods were discussed in Chapter 3 in connection with general partnerships. The agreement should address whether the shares will be purchased pursuant to some specific valuation procedure, or whether the company (or the shareholders) need only to match any offer to buy the shares made by a third party. The agreement should also specify whether each shareholder must buy his pro rata share of the seller's shares, or whether each other shareholder merely has the right to buy them, but doesn't have to.

If shareholders choose to have an agreement regarding these matters, the shareholders need to consider what situations will create the buyout right for the other shareholders. For example, what if one shareholder divorces, and the divorce court grants the spouse some shares? What happens if a shareholder goes bankrupt?

If there are two equal shareholders, it is a good idea to try to plan for what would happen if the shareholders disagree regarding fundamental business matters. If there is a "deadlock" in such a situation, the business can become paralyzed.

A copy of one shareholders' agreement is in Appendix B, Form 8.

The Bottom Line

Formation of a corporation is not very difficult. For many small businesses simple forms can be used, and it normally is not complicated. Still, some businesses might have special needs not addressed by the simple forms. If you do plan to incorporate, it is a good idea at least to have a lawyer review your incorporation papers.

SELLING SECURITIES

If you are receiving an interest in a limited partnership or a corporation, you are receiving a "security." Sales of securities are regulated by both federal and Texas law. Many people have been defrauded in connection with sales of securities, and laws have been enacted to try to prevent this.

As a general rule, securities can only be sold, in Texas, after a "registration statement" has been filed with the U.S. Securities & Exchange Commission (the SEC), and after the sale has been "qualified" by the Texas Securities Commission. This process is very expensive, however. Detailed disclosure documents must be prepared about the company, and many hours must be spent dealing with the state and federal securities offices. Most small businesses want to be able to issue securities without spending this much time and money. Federal law and Texas law do permit this, but only if the exemptions set forth below are satisfied.

Federal Law

Under federal law, securities can be sold without a registration statement if the sale is one "not involving any public offering." Unfortunately, it is not clear what constitutes such an exempt private offering. If one person or a husband and wife are forming a corporation, and there will be no other stockholders, this clearly would be an exempt offering. Such an offering requires no filing with any government office. If shares will be sold to more than one person, whether the sale would constitute an exempt private offering would depend upon a number of things, such as the wealth and business experience of the investors, and whether the investors had a prior business or social relationship before the securities were sold. If you are planning to sell shares in your corporation to others, it is not clear whether the sale would be an exempt private offering; it therefore would be best to rely upon a more definite exemption to be sure that the sale complies with the law. One useful exemption for small businesses is "Rule 504," promulgated by "Regulation D." Under this Rule 504, a small business can raise up to $500,000 over twelve months, if certain rules are satisfied. No advertising or public solicitation can be made regarding the stock, resale of the shares must be restricted (this will be discussed), and a form must be filed with the SEC.

If Rule 504 is complied with, the company does not have to file a registration statement with the SEC.

Texas Law

Texas has created exemptions from its qualification requirement for certain nonpublic sales of stock by a small business. For example, if one person or a husband and wife form a corporation and buy shares, this would be an exempt offering under Texas law, and no filing of any kind would be required. However, if you want to sell stock to others, Texas exemption rules are more complicated. Texas has not adopted the federal "Rule 504" exemption mentioned above.

Under Texas law, a sale is exempt if, after sale, the company will have thirty-five or fewer shareholders. There are very technical rules regarding how the number of shareholders will be determined. (For example, holders of corporate debt are considered shareholders.)

Even if it is determined that there will be thirty-five or fewer shareholders after the issuance, the issuance is only exempt if there is no "public solicitation." The Texas Securities Board has established regulations that clarify that this means more than merely no advertising. To satisfy this test, the seller, after reasonable inquiry, must reasonably believe one of these two things:

1. That all buyers are "sophisticated" and "well informed."
2. That all buyers are "well-informed" and have a trusting relationship with the company or its executive officers or directors.

A person is "well-informed" if, before the decision to purchase is made, he receives material from the issuer of the securities that fairly describes the history of the business, its business plans, all risks facing the business, and the proposed use of the proceeds to be received. Available financial information also should be provided.

To determine whether a person is "sophisticated," these factors are relevant:

- The financial capacity of the buyer—that is, the total amount invested, should not constitute a "material" portion of the buyer's total net worth. If the investment is less than 10% of the investor's total net worth, it is not "material."
- The buyer's, or the buyer's advisor's, general knowledge about investments; and the experience and skill of the buyer, or the buyer's advisor, regarding investments.

Only private sales of stock can be exempt in Texas. No advertising is permitted, and offering material should be given to a prospective investor *only* after the company reasonably believes the buyer will satisfy one of the exemption standards set forth above. Call the Texas Securities Commission at 512-474-2233, or write them at P.O. Box 13167, Capitol Station, Austin, TX, 78711, for more information about the Texas securities laws.

If the sale is an exempt transaction under Texas law, the sale does not have to be qualified with the Texas Securities Board. A filing normally should be made with the Texas Securities Commission, however. The necessary form depends upon the exemption statute relied upon.

Resales of Shares

Shares sold pursuant to a private offering exemption are "restricted" shares. The shares cannot be resold to another, unless that sale complies with the securities laws.

OPERATING THE CORPORATION

In many respects a corporate business is operated just like any other business. If you are the sole owner and the president of the corporation, you will make all the decisions regarding the business. If there are other owners, they will want to be consulted regarding important decisions, as would any owner. However, if you operate your business as a corporation you need to satisfy a few additional requirements.

Corporate Funds

You should keep corporate funds separate from your individual funds. This is very important. If you mix your funds with the funds of the business, it is quite likely that a court later would hold all your assets liable to creditors of the business.

Signing Contracts

Similarly, contracts and promissory notes regarding the business should be signed in the name of the corporation, not in your name alone. This is vital if you want limited liability.

Example 1. John Smith is making a contract for himself as an individual. The contract says that he is a party to the contract, and the signature line looks like this:

____
John Smith

John Smith is a party to this contract, and is personally responsible for performing it.

Example 2. John Smith is president of Texas Software, Inc. John is making a contract for the company. The contract says that Texas Software is the party responsible for satisfying the terms of the contract, and the signature line on the contract looks like this:

Texas Software, Inc.

BY ______________________________
John Smith, as its president

Texas Software is a party to this contract; John Smith is not. If there is a breach of this contract, the other party can sue Texas Software and attach its assets, but not John Smith's assets.

If the procedure set forth above is not followed, it is quite possible that John Smith could find himself personally liable for the debts of the corporation.

Example 3. John Smith is president of Texas Software, Inc. and is making a contract for the company. Assume the signature line of the contract looks like this:

Texas Software, Inc.

____
John Smith

John Smith is probably personally liable if he signs this contract. **When signing a contract or a promissory note on behalf of a business, it is very important to make it clear in what capacity you are signing.**

If you are signing something on behalf of a corporation, make sure the signature line states that you are signing for that entity, states your relationship to the entity (e.g., its president), and be sure the entity is correctly referred to. If you don't do this, there is a good chance you will be personally liable for the contract or note you have signed. Since most business people do not want this result, they should read contracts very carefully before they sign.

For example, a recent case involved a situation where a corporation (E.D. Jones Co.) was doing business under another name (Industrial Telephone Systems). The president of the company signed a contract under its trade name, Industrial Telephone Systems. The contract did not state that Industrial Telephone Systems was the fictitious business name of E.D. Jones Co. The other party to the contract was able to sue the president of the company *individually* because the correct identity of the corporation was not disclosed when the contract was made.

People signing things on behalf of a business should have the authority to do what they are doing. It is common for the board of directors to approve important transactions involving the business. The board then authorizes a certain officer to do what was approved, such as sign an agreement or a promissory note. This clarifies that the person has the authority to bind the business.

Corporate Formalities

Even in a small business, it is a good idea each year for the shareholders to elect directors, and for the directors to elect officers. This makes sure that there are people authorized to act on behalf of the corporation. Also, the directors should approve important transactions involving the corporation. Copies of documents reflecting these actions should be placed in the corporation's minute book.

These corporate formalities clarify whether the company has properly approved a certain transaction, and keeps a current list of officers able to act on behalf of the company.

These "corporate formalities" also serve another purpose. If the limited liability of the shareholders is ever an issue, many courts consider it important whether the corporation complied with these procedures. In small businesses, particularly when the same person is the president and the sole director and sole shareholder, it does seem silly to have to go through with the formality of director approval of important decisions. Still, it can be important.

Texas Taxes

When operating your corporate business, you should comply with the various licensing requirements and pay all taxes and fees due for the business and the employees. Some of these are discussed in Chapter 7. It is particularly important that all Texas franchise taxes are paid. If you do not do this, the secretary of state can suspend the corporation, and the officers and directors of the corporation can be personally liable for debts created after that happens.

The Bottom Line

You can operate a corporate business much like any other business. Still, there are a few things to remember. Keep your personal funds separate from corporate funds. Try to keep good records of directors' meetings and shareholder meetings. Also, when signing contracts on behalf of the business, be sure that it is clear that you are signing these contracts on behalf of a corporation, and that the name of the corporation is correctly set forth.

Corporations and Federal Taxes

In the 1970s, a business operated as a corporation enjoyed a number of tax advantages, as compared to the tax treatment of partnerships and sole proprietorships. One large advantage was that a corporation could deduct from its income much larger pension contributions for employees than could sole proprietors or partnerships. A number of these advantages have been eliminated by recent amendments to the Internal Revenue Code. For example, rules regarding pension contributions are now essentially the same for all business forms.

Corporations do still offer some tax advantages. The main advantages are fringe benefits that a corporation can provide for employees. The benefits are valuable, but are not taxed as income to the employee. Even though the benefits are not taxed as income to the employee, the corporation is able to deduct the expense of the benefit from its income.

For example, an individual can only deduct medical expenses to the extent that the expenses exceed 7.5% of the individual's adjusted gross income. Most people do not deduct any medical expenses, since their medical expenses never reach that portion of their income. In contrast, a corporation is permitted to adopt a medical and dental expense reimbursement plan for its employees and their dependents. All amounts paid to the employees under the plan as expense reimbursements are deductible by the corporation (if the corporation chooses to purchase health insurance, then the price of the premiums is deductible), and the employee does not have to pay tax on the amount received.

Similar benefits are available for disability insurance and life insurance. The corporation can purchase up to $50,000 worth of life insurance for an employee, and the expense is deductible by the corporation but is not income to the employee. Also, disability insurance can be purchased for an employee, and the cost of this insurance is deductible by the corporation and is not income to the employee.

In many small businesses there is only one employee of the business: the owner. In this instance, if the owner establishes insurance protection for himself through the company, there will be significant tax savings.

The discussion above mentions that various expenditures are "deductible" by the corporation. This is a significant concern for corporations, since normal "C" corporations pay a tax on income. This is the *corporate tax*. Shareholders pay additional personal income tax when funds are distributed to them as a dividend, and dividends are not deductible by the corporation. Because of this system, it is said that corporations are subject to a "double tax." First corporate income tax is paid by the corporation, and then personal income tax is paid by the shareholders on dividends.

In light of this double tax, why would anyone ever choose to do business as a corporation? The tax penalty, or advantage, depends upon the particular business. For example, for tax years beginning after July 1, 1987, the tax rate for the first $50,000 of corporate income is 15%; this is significantly lower than the marginal personal tax rate of most Americans. If the business plans to retain its profits (for example, to buy inventory or equipment) and not pay them to shareholders, it might be a good idea for tax purposes to incorporate. If the business does plan to pay its profits to its shareholders, however, there may be a tax penalty due to the corporate status.

Many small businesses pay their owners salaries for working for the business. "Salaries" are deductible; "dividends" are not. The IRS frequently wages war with small business owners over whether certain payments really were salary payments or dividends. In any event, after the payment of salaries, many small businesses have little taxable income, so the corporate double tax is not too important.

If you want to operate your business as a corporation, but are concerned about the double tax, there is an alternative that many find useful. An "S" corporation is a corporation that is taxed like a partnership. In order to be an S corporation, the corporation must have 35 or fewer shareholders. Also, there must be only one class of stock, all shareholders must be individuals, and no shareholder may be a non-resident alien. In order to be an S corporation, the corporation and all shareholders must sign an election form and file it with the IRS. This election is then valid until the corporation revokes it.

S corporations are taxed like a partnership, so there is no double tax. Shareholders merely report as income their share of the income of the company. S corporations do have limited liability.

S corporations lose many of the tax benefits of a corporation that were discussed above. For example, an S corporation cannot deduct the cost of insurance for employees, if the employees are shareholders.

The tax effects of incorporating and the S corporation election can be quite significant. It is a good idea to discuss these tax consequences with your accountant or your lawyer before you incorporate or make an S corporation election.

If a regular "C" corporation has a loss for any tax year, the company can carry this loss over to the next year to offset it against any future income, but the shareholders cannot offset the loss against personal income they have from other sources. Before the 1986 tax reform law, shareholders of an S corporation could offset losses of the business against income from most other sources. After the 1986 law, if the loss is a "passive" loss under the new rules, the shareholder can only use the loss to offset other "passive" income.

The Bottom Line

Corporations still offer certain tax advantages. An owner of a small business can have the business provide him with various fringe benefits, such as family medical and dental insurance, disability insurance, and life insurance. The cost of this insurance is not taxable to the employee-owner, and the business can deduct the cost.

Also, due to the separate tax rate for corporate income, a business might pay less tax as a corporation than the personal tax the owner would have to pay if the business was a partnership or proprietorship. If the corporation plans to accumulate profits in the business, and the owner's marginal tax rate is high, a corporation can offer tax savings. In contrast, if the corporation plans to distribute its profits to its owners, there may be a tax disadvantage to the normal "C" corporation.

Miscellaneous Issues

If a corporation is unsuccessful, and the business goes bankrupt, under normal circumstances the investment loss by the shareholders is considered a *capital loss*. There is a limit upon the amount of capital losses that can be used to shelter income from other sources; only $3,000 per year can be used. If the corporation issues shares under Internal Revenue Code Sec. 1244, a shareholder can deduct all losses up to $50,000 ($100,000 for a husband and wife filing jointly) if the business is unsuccessful. In order to qualify for 1244 treatment, the capitalization for the corporation must be less than $1 million, and the corporation must earn less than 50% of its revenue from passive sources like royalties, dividends, interest, and rents. When issuing corporate shares, discuss with your lawyer or accountant whether the 1244 election would be desirable.

If you want a Texas corporation to do business in another state, the corporation should "qualify" to do business there before any business is conducted in the state. Each state's qualification procedure is different, but all generally want the corporation to agree to be sued in the state regarding disputes arising from business transacted in the state, and a certain filing fee will be due. Contact the secretary of state or department of corporations of each state in which you want to do business, and see what needs to be done to qualify.

SUMMARY OF ADVANTAGES AND DISADVANTAGES

The corporation offers some advantages for the owner of a small business. The owners enjoy limited liability; they are not personally liable for claims against the business. Also, management power is easily centralized in the president. This is desirable if one owner wants to run the business, and the others do not. Ownership interests are relatively easy to transfer, and the business clearly continues even if one owner retires or dies.

The "C" corporation can provide tax savings. Owner-employees can receive tax-advantaged fringe benefits. Also, money can be accumulated in the corporation at lower corporate tax rates, compared to the personal marginal tax rate of most Americans.

The corporation has some disadvantages, however. It is somewhat expensive to form, since expenditures for both lawyer's fees and filing fees will be required. Also, it is cumbersome to operate, since shareholders' meetings and board meetings are necessary.

The Limited Liability Company

In 1991, the Texas legislature established a new type of entity under Texas law. This entity is known as a "limited liability company." Many of the characteristics of the limited liability company are similar to those of a corporation. For example, a limited liability company has limited liability, as long as the required filing is made with the Texas secretary of state. The only major difference between a "C" corporation and the limited liability company is that it appears that, in most instances, the limited liability company does not have to pay a federal corporate tax on its income. ("C" corporations and limited liability companies both must pay Texas franchise tax. See Chapter 7.) Of course, owners of a limited liability company have to pay federal taxes as individuals on their pro rata share of the company's income, just like a partner in a partnership; however, no separate tax is due. This lack of a double tax makes it much like the "S" corporation. The potential advantage is that the limited liability company could be available in situations where the "S" corporation is not, such as where the company has more than 35 investors, or when an investor is a nonresident alien. If avoidance of this double tax is important to you, you must be sure that you draft your organizational documents in a way so that the company qualifies as an entity not subject to the double tax. At a minimum, when you form this type of organization, be sure you have your accountant or lawyer look at the organizational documents to be sure that you receive the tax consequences you desire. If there is only one owner of a limited liability company, it appears that the entity will be taxed like a corporation and a corporate federal tax on income will be due, regardless of how you draft the organizational documents. So, if there will be only one owner, and you desire a business form with limited liability and no double tax, consider an "S" corporation.

The limited liability company is a new type of business form in Texas. It is as yet somewhat unclear how this type of entity will be taxed by the federal government and how this type of entity will be treated by courts in Texas and in other states. In contrast, rules for "S" corporations are well-developed and clear. Also, the "S" corporation is available in most instances, unless there are more than 35 owners or there is a nonresident alien owner. For this reason, we suggest that if you want an entity with limited liability and no double tax, use the "S" corporation, as long as that is available.

CORPORATION FORMATION CHECKLIST

These are the basic documents you need to prepare to form a Texas corporation:*

- Name reservation letter
- Articles of incorporation
- Minutes of board of directors meeting
- Bylaws
- Stock certificates
- Bank account card for company account

You should also consider whether these documents would be advisable:

- Shareholders' agreement
- S Corporation election
- Section 1244 plan election for stock issuance
- Securities filings with the SEC and the Texas Securities Board

* There are several companies that sell what are called "corporate kits," which contain most of the documents necessary to complete the formation of your corporation once the articles of incorporation have been filed. These relatively inexpensive kits, costing less than $50, may be ordered from: Lawyer's Aid Service, Inc., P.O. Box 848, Austin, TX 78767-0848, (512) 474-2002.

6

Hiring and Firing

When you start a business, one of the first things you have to do is hire employees. When hiring people, you need to comply with the various rules applicable to withholding for taxes, social security, workmen's compensation, and so on, as we discuss in Chapter 7. But you also need to be aware of other kinds of legal problems that relate to hiring employees. In particular you should know that your personal beliefs about people of a different age, sex, race, or religion are not a legal basis upon which to decide whom you will employ.

Federal law says that if you have 15 or more employees you may not discriminate based on color, sex, religion, national origin, age, or physical or mental disability, with respect to:

- Job advertisements
- Recruitment
- Testing
- Hiring and firing
- Compensation, assignment, or classification
- Transfer, promotion, layoff, or recall
- Use of company facilities
- Training and apprenticeship programs
- Fringe benefits such as life and health insurance
- Pay, retirement plans, and disability leave
- Causing or attempting to cause a union to discriminate
- Other terms and conditions of employment

Age Discrimination

Consider this:

> Susan and Cindy have formed a catering business. Wilma, a woman 57 years old, interviewed for a job with the company. Susan and Cindy decided that they wanted to hire a younger person who would tire less easily, and they did hire a younger person for the job. Wilma probably can sue the business for age discrimination in hiring. In addition to the wages Wilma lost by not getting the job, Wilma could also possibly recover damages for pain and suffering.

Under Federal law it is illegal to discriminate in employment on the basis of age against anyone over the age of 39, unless the employer can establish that, for the particular task involved, age is a "bona fide occupational qualification." This exception is very hard to establish.

So, as a practical matter, what does this mean you should do when interviewing prospective employees? First, *never* advertise that you are looking for a "young" person for a job. Every qualified applicant should be considered for a job. But even if you follow this policy, you can still be sued for unlawful discrimination. The best way to protect yourself from such suits is to keep a record of all interviews. Note on the interview record the reason the interviewee was not hired. For example, was the interviewee late, poorly dressed, or did the references provided state something negative? If the employment decision is ever challenged, it is quite useful to have a record of the thoughts of the interviewer. A good idea is to have printed interview forms to ensure that you question, and evaluate, each applicant the same way.

Racial Discrimination

Race discrimination in hiring is illegal, even if it seems "logical" to you. Consider the following:

> Bob and Jim start a business selling golf equipment to golf pro shops. They need to hire sales people to contact golf pro shops and talk to the golf professional at various golf courses. Bob and Jim perceive that a white person could relate better to the golf pros than a black person could, so Bob and Jim do not hire an otherwise qualified black applicant. The applicant could sue the business for racial discrimination.

The federal civil rights laws prohibit racial discrimination in hiring. It does not matter whether in fact you, as an employer, are correct in your belief that a person of one race might incur more problems trying to deal with the customers of the business in question. Hiring must be done on the basis of ability to perform the job. Your perception that a white, black, or brown may do better, or worse, is not a sufficient basis upon which to discriminate. Make a decision based on race and you invite a lawsuit. Again, keeping good records of each interview, and asking the same questions of each applicant, can help prevent lawsuits.

Sex Discrimination

Like age and race discrimination, sex discrimination in employment is prohibited.

> Diego and Juan have formed a business to sell tires to gas stations. Diego and Juan believe that a man would be better able to do this job than a woman. If Diego and Juan did not hire a qualified woman based on this belief, the woman could sue the business for sex discrimination.

It is illegal to discriminate on the basis of sex in hiring decisions, unless sex is a "bona fide occupational qualification." This exception is construed quite narrowly by the courts. Your personal belief that a man could do the job better is probably not sufficient justification for discriminating against a woman.

Sexual Harrassment

Sexual harassment in the workplace is nothing new, but it is against the law. Victims of sexual harassment must no longer choose between putting up with a bad situation or leaving their jobs. Now they can sue their employers for allowing offensive conduct in the workplace.

The most important thing for employers to understand about sexual harassment is that they will likely be held responsible for it even if they do not know that it is happening. Therefore, an employer must not only know what kind of behavior could be construed as sexual harassment, but must also do everything possible to prevent such behavior in the workplace by employees.

Sexual harassment involves basing hiring, firing, promoting, and salary decisions on an employee's submission to sexual demands. Sexual harassment also includes conduct that creates an intimidating, hostile, or offensive working environment. For example:

> Jane is a clerk in a small store. She acquiesces to her supervisor's sexual demands out of fear of losing her job. Jane may sue the owner of the store for sexual harassment even if the owner did not have knowledge of the supervisor's conduct.

The Bottom Line

The employer's best line of defense against suits for sexual harassment is to provide a grievance or complaint mechanism for employees who feel they are being sexually harassed. This mechanism should not be limited to contacting their immediate supervisor. Complaints of sexual harassment should be taken seriously.

The EEOC (Equal Employment Opportunity Commission) has established guidelines concerning sexual harassment in the workplace. If you need more information, call 1-800-USA-EEOC.

Hiring the Disabled

Approximately 43 million Americans have one or more physical or mental disabilities, and these individuals are often discriminated against in employment. With the passage of the American With Disabilities Act in 1990, such discrimination is no longer legal. Business owners should immediately take steps to familiarize themselves with this law and ensure that it is not violated. As with most laws, it is not a defense to say "I didn't know that was the law."

To give businesses time to comply with the law, it doesn't go into effect for employers with more than 25 employees until July 1992. For those with 15–24 employees, the effective date is extended until July 1994. Employers with less than 15 employees are exempt from the equal-employment provisions of the Act.

The purpose of the American With Disabilities Act, commonly referred to as the ADA, is to ensure equal opportunity and full participation in our society. The law applies to anyone with a disability. A disability is defined as "a physical or mental impairment that substantially limits one or more of the major life activities of such individual." A person may establish that they are disabled if they either have a record of such impairment, or are regarded as having such an impairment. Major life activities include the daily functions, such as caring for one's self, walking, eating, talking, breathing, learning, working, or performing manual tasks. Contagious diseases, including AIDS, are covered under the Act.

Under the ADA, an employer is expected to treat the disabled the way it treats anyone else. This means equality in all aspects of employment, recruiting, hiring, firing, and training. It is important to note that the law does not require preferential treatment for the disabled, just equal treatment. A disabled worker who does not properly perform can be fired just as any other worker. Similarly, an employer can continue to give exams or tests to its prospective employees, provided that the test does not screen out the disabled.

The law also requires that employers take reasonable steps to accommodate the disabled. What is reasonable will depend on the facts, but clearly all employers must take simple inexpensive steps. For example, employers could increase or decrease the height of chairs or tables, and add wooden ramps where it could be done without great cost. Similarly, work schedules must be adjusted when doing so would not disrupt the business. If an employee can only work four days a week because of a disability, he or she must be given the opportunity to do so unless it would cause an undue hardship on the business. Other accommodations, such as increasing the size of doors and entry ways, adding special equipment for the deaf or blind, or modifying restrooms, will be evaluated on a case by case basis. In all likelihood, small businesses will not be required to make accommodations that cost thousands of dollars.

The Bottom Line

The ADA will affect the way you do business. To avoid problems you should immediately get job descriptions in order, so that you can establish that you are filling a job based on essential duties and not discriminating against the disabled. Where accommodations can be made without undue expense or hardship, make them. Doors should be widened and ramps should be built wherever reasonable. Finally, treat disabled workers as you would any other. Don't keep them if they are not performing their job, and hire them if they are qualified. If you have questions about this law you can call the Department of Justice ADA Hotline, 202-514-0301.

Other Prohibited Discrimination

In addition to the rules outlined above, federal law prohibits discriminating in hiring on the basis of religion, national origin, or handicap. Remember that "handicap" can be broadly construed. For example, there is now a dispute over whether AIDS victims are "handicapped," and it appears that the courts will say they are. This doesn't mean you have to hire someone with AIDS, but it does mean that if that is your only reason for not hiring a qualified applicant, you may be illegally discriminating.

The Bottom Line

When you interview applicants for a job, be sure you interview all qualified people who apply. When you decide not to hire someone, keep a record of the reason or reasons you didn't hire that person. Be particularly careful about keeping such a record when the person rejected is a racial minority, a woman, a person over the age of 39, or a handicapped person. You do not *have to hire* such a person; however, the employment decision must be based upon some rational factor. If you need more information about employment discrimination, call 1-800-USA-EEOC.

Immigration Law*

As most of you already know, Congress recently enacted new immigration laws making it illegal to hire an alien knowing that the alien is not a lawful permanent resident of this country or does not have legal permission to be employed. It is a criminal offense to do this. The Act does not require, however, that you verify employees who were working for you prior to the effective date of the Act. In other words, the new law basically says that **if you hire someone you must verify that they are working here legally.**

To comply with the Act you should examine certain documents to determine if the person is working here legally and is who they say they are. You are not required to establish the validity of the document, but you must see if it reasonably appears to be valid. Here is a list of documents that you can use:

1. The individual's United States passport.
2. The individual's Certificate of United States Citizenship.

* The U.S. Department of Justice, Immigration and Naturalization Service, publishes the employment Eligibility Verification Form and Handbook for Employers.

3. The individual's Certificate of Naturalization.
4. The individual's unexpired foreign passport if such passport has a notation of an unexpired endorsement from the INS authorizing the individual's employment in the United States.
5. The individual's resident alien card or "green card" or any other form of alien registration card if it contains a photograph of the individual or any other personal identifying information relating to that individual and is evidence of authorization of employment in the United States.

Any of these documents will be sufficient to establish the person's identity and employment authorization, as required by the law. You may also use separate documents to establish each of these prerequisites. For example, you may verify identity with either of the following:

1. The individual's driver's license or similar document issued for purposes of identification by a state provided that it contains a photograph of the individual or such other personal identifying information relating to that individual as required by regulations.
2. When the individual is under 16 years of age or is in a state which does not provide an identification card or document other than a driver's license, production of documentation of personal identity as deemed acceptable for identification purposes under INS regulations.

Authorization to work may be proven by:

1. The individual's social security account number card, provided such card does not state on its face that it does not authorize employment in the United States or contain similar language.
2. The individual's certificate of birth in the United States or an authorized certificate establishing U.S. nationality at birth.
3. Any other documentation evidencing employment authorization in the United States granted by the INS.

Immigration laws can be very tough on employers. Before you hire someone, take steps to ensure that they are who they say they are and that they have the legal right to work here. You also should contact your attorney, the Department of Labor, or the Department of Immigration to find out exactly what the law requires. Remember, this is a new law that will be constantly changing as new rules and regulations are enacted.

The Bottom Line

The immigration law places a burden on employers to make sure that their workers are here legally. If you violate this law you may suffer stiff criminal penalties. Make sure that you understand this law before you hire anyone. For more information about this law, contact the local office of the Immigration and Naturalization Service.

Employment Contracts

In most instances, employees are "hired" by the boss simply telling the applicant he or she has a job. No written contract is signed, and no definite term of employment is specified. This creates what a lawyer would call "at will" employment. So, the employer or the employee can terminate the relationship at any time. As long as the employee works, however, the employer is bound by this oral contract to pay the employee at the agreed upon salary rate.

And even though you do not have any sort of a formal contract, you and your employee are bound to perform in a certain manner. Suppose you hire a new employee to work at your store. Nothing much is said except that the salary will be $5.00 per hour, and she should start next Monday. Do you have a contract? Yes, you do. The terms of your contract are everything said, basically just $5.00 an hour, start on Monday, and everything that one would normally imply in such an agreement. For example, your employee would be expected to work an eight hour day, with a reasonable time for lunch and a break similar to everyone else. If you have given your employees vacation pay in the past your agreement with the new employee would probably incorporate similar items. In other words, the law implies an agreement based on what a reasonable employee and employer would expect in similar circumstance. If you acted differently, for example, by refusing to give the new employee vacation time as you did the others, you could be found to have breached your employment contract. Of course, because this is still an employment-at-will contract you have the right to fire the employee at any time. (Turn to page 49 for more on this point.)

But at-will employment with no formal contract is not always a good idea for an employer. For example, you may be training the employee at significant expense. Do you care whether the employee quits immediately after training, and takes the knowledge to a competitor? If you do, you need to have an employment agreement that states what happens if the employee does this. We have included some model agreements in Appendix B, Forms 9a and 9b, but you probably should have your lawyer help you with this contract because each one is slightly different.

You also should know that if you want to hire an employee for a term of more than one year, the contract with the employee must be in writing. Other kinds of contracts don't have to be in writing. However, a written agreement is always a good idea, so at a later date parties can refer back to what was agreed to. For example, it might be a good idea to set forth what kind of fringe benefits or expense account will be provided the employee. Also, when will the employee be considered for a raise or promotion? Will the employer pay any moving expenses? What will be the employee's duties and responsibilities?

If you decide to enter into a written contract with your employees you probably should try to cover the major terms of your agreement. It isn't necessary that every little detail be covered but you can avoid problems by setting out each party's duties and responsibilities. For example, here are some of the things you may want to include:

- Amount and method of payment
- Length of employment period, if it is known
- Description of job to be performed
- Vacation terms
- Termination terms
- Dispute resolution terms
- Liability and indemnification terms
- Any other terms special to your situation.

For an example of such an agreement, see Appendix B, Form 10.

Additionally, you may want to consider protecting your investment by limiting the rights of your employees to compete with you. For example:

> Melanie and Joyce start a company that sells tires to gas stations. They hire Shirley as a sales person to call on the stations. Shirley gradually builds up a relationship with the customers. If Melanie and Joyce have no agreement with Shirley, she at any time can quit and start a new company that would sell tires to her old customers.

People like Melanie and Joyce frequently do not want Shirley to be able to do this. To stop Shirley from doing this, Melanie and Joyce should have Shirley sign a "covenant not to compete" with their business.

Historically, Texas courts have been reluctant to enforce covenants not to compete. In 1989, a law was passed that makes covenants not to compete enforceable if these two factors are present:

1. The covenant not to compete is made in conjunction with an employment contract or some other enforceable contract and in exchange for valuable consideration, and
2. The covenant not to compete is reasonable as to the geographic area covered by the agreement, the time limitations, and the activities addressed by the covenant.

Despite this statute, Texas courts still look with disfavor upon covenants not to compete. If you decide to ask an employee to sign a covenant not to compete, at a minimum ask the employee to sign the covenant at the time he is hired, and include only reasonable limits regarding the geographic area covered, the time limitations, and the activities addressed by the covenant. If a covenant not to compete is important to you, as an employer, we suggest that you offer an employee additional money if he agrees to the covenant. For example, offer an annual salary of $20,000 without the covenant, and $25,000 with the covenant. This will increase the likelihood a Texas court will enforce the covenant.

You also may want to protect the ideas that your employees come up with.

> Jim and Bob start a medical research business. Part of their business is a research laboratory where employees of the business do experiments regarding new medical equipment and drugs. Deborah is a research chemist for the company. Assume Deborah gets a great idea and wants to quit her job and start a new company to sell her new product.

Employers normally own research created by employees while on the job. Still, it is a good idea in such situations to clarify in the employment agreement that any patents will be in the name of the employer and the employee will not be compensated for assigning the patent rights to the employer. Also, the agreement should clarify that the employee cannot divulge to anyone any confidential information regarding any company projects, even after the employee quits or is fired. For an example of such an agreement, see Appendix B, Forms 10 and 11.

The agreement regarding not divulging trade secrets could also have another advantage. The Texas Supreme Court has stated that, if the employer allows the employee access to confidential information in exchange for the employee's promise not to disclose the information and not to compete with the employer for a certain reasonable period, the covenant not to compete would be enforced.

Independent Contractors

As we said before, if you hire anyone as an employee you are responsible for complying with state and federal laws regarding employees, and probably are responsible for the acts of your employees while on the job. If you use an independent contractor, however, you may avoid some of the legal hassle and liability.

> Ace Construction builds small homes. They employ about twenty people and do almost all the work themselves. They do not, however, have a person who can build brick chimneys. Instead of hiring a new employee, the president decides to hire an outside contractor to do the occasional jobs they need done. The contractor would not be considered an employee, withholding would not have to be taken out, social security would not have to be paid, and he would not be covered under workers compensation.

If you hire an independent contractor, your obligations toward that person are much less than if he or she is an employee. To be an independent contractor you usually must show that the person you hire meets these criteria:

1. Has his or her own place of business at a definite location.
2. Doesn't perform all of his services at your place of business.
3. Holds himself out as being independent.
4. Uses his or her own tools.
5. Is responsible for the final result.
6. Is not controlled by you.

These are not absolute tests but usually they must be met to qualify the person as an independent contractor.

Remember that the law doesn't allow you to hire an employee and call him an independent contractor just to avoid compliance with employer-employee laws. As an employer, you need to be careful about whether someone is treated by you as an independent contractor and not an employee. For example, if you do treat someone as an independent contractor and do not withhold taxes from compensation, if the IRS later establishes that the person was an employee, significant penalties can be imposed.

The Bottom Line

Employment contracts may be as formal or informal as you wish. But to protect yourself, and make sure that there are no misunderstandings, a written contract is usually helpful.

Terminating Employment

As of this writing, the law regarding your right to fire someone in Texas is simple: If you don't have a contract the agreement is "at-will" and you can fire without cause, without notice.* If you have a contract, or union agreement, you can only fire in accordance with that agreement. The only major exceptions to this are the discrimination laws. For example, you may not fire a person based on race, religion, sex, or because they are handicapped. The Texas Supreme Court has also ruled that you may not fire an employee because he has refused to perform an illegal act.

But consider the following:

> Juanita recently hired a new employee to work in her secretarial pool. She had twenty other employees and for the past few years she had followed a policy of giving each employee one week vacation, and two weeks severance pay to anyone who was fired. The new employee started and then business got slow so Juanita fired her. Juanita didn't pay any severance pay, and didn't give the employee any notice. Juanita believed that under the employment-at-will doctrine she could fire at any time without notice. She didn't have a written contract with the employee that said anything different.

Juanita may be wrong. The employment-at-will doctrine says you can fire without cause, without notice, but if there is a contract, the terms of the contract control. Even though Juanita didn't have a written contract, Juanita has an implied agreement with the employee, basically saying that she will treat her the way she treats other employees. In this case, Juanita had established a policy of giving two weeks severance pay and that policy probably became part of her agreement with the new employee. **Just because nothing is said doesn't mean you don't have an agreement. Past action can establish a policy that becomes part of your contractual agreement with your employees.**

One final point on firing employees. If your employees are unionized you must follow the terms of your agreement with the Union. Firing is one of the terms that is subject to bargaining and will be covered in the collective bargaining agreement. Make sure you don't violate it.

* This is a rapidly changing area of law with much litigation. Before relying on the information in this section, you may want to make sure that the "employment-at-will doctrine" has not been changed.

The Bottom Line

Texas law gives employers great latitude in dealing with employees. Under the employment-at-will doctrine you can usually fire anyone, whenever you want. But be careful not to violate discrimination laws, or any contracts you have with your employees.

Drug Testing and Polygraph

As of the writing of this book, a private employer in Texas has the right to require his or her employees to submit to drug testing and can fire them if they refuse. This is in line with the employment-at-will doctrine, which allows you to fire without cause. Similarly, if you have a union agreement or employment contract, that will determine your rights to test your employees. The law prohibits lie detector tests, however, except in very limited situations. An employee may be asked to submit to a lie detector test if it is part of an ongoing investigation and the employer has a reasonable suspicion that an employee was involved. **This is a fast-changing area of law. Before requiring testing check with your lawyer to make sure that the law has not changed.**

7

Miscellaneous State and Federal Taxes, Fees, and Statutes

TAXES

Taxes are a fact of life for your business. As was discussed in Chapter 1, federal income tax normally will be imposed on the profits of your business, regardless of whether you operate your business as a sole proprietorship, a partnership, or a corporation. Texas has no corporate income or personal income tax. A business in Texas is also subject to municipal taxes, state taxes, and other federal taxes. These will be discussed below.

To help you keep track of your business income and make it easier for you to compute your taxes, it is a good idea to hire an accountant who can help you get started on a bookkeeping system that is suitable for your business. He or she can tell you what taxes you will have to pay, when you will have to pay them, and what filings need to be made. An accountant can also make you aware of all the deductions that you can take, and how to properly document them. But even more importantly, the accountant can help you establish an effective recordkeeping system, vital to the success of your business. A good recordkeeping system will not only help you manage your business more efficiently, it will help you comply with the tax laws. Your records should clearly indicate the source of your receipts, keep track of your deductible expenses, allow you to figure your depreciation deductions, and maintain a record of all amounts withheld from employees' wages.

Federal Taxes

The federal tax laws and regulations are very complicated. For example, employers have the obligation to withhold from employees' wages amounts for social security (FICA) and personal income tax, and employers must make contributions for social security and unemployment compensation. The IRS has published a helpful guide entitled "Employer's Tax Guide" (Circular E). We encourage all business owners to read this.

Tax Identification Number

When you file your individual federal tax return you can use your social security number as your taxpayer identification number. It may be necessary, however, for you to have an employer identification number (EIN) as well, once you are in business. Every partnership and corporation (including S Corporations) must have an EIN to use as a taxpayer identification number. A sole proprietor must also have an EIN if either of the following is true:

1. It pays wages to one or more employees.
2. It is required to file any excise tax returns, including those for alcohol, tobacco, or firearms.

To apply for an EIN, use Form SS-4, Application for Employer Identification Number. This form is available from the Internal Revenue Service, and if you have any questions they will be glad to help you—at no cost.

Withholding

As an employer, you have certain tax responsibilities for your employees. In general, you must withhold income tax from an employee's taxable wages based on the employee's wage level, marital status, and number of withholding allowances claimed. Each employee is required to file with you a Form W-4 which will provide the employee's social security number and all information you need regarding the employee's withholding allowances. The IRS "Employer's Tax Guide" contains tables from which you can determine how much to withhold.

You will also be required to withhold amounts from employee's wages for contributions to FICA (social security). Currently 7.65% of the employee's wages must be paid by the employee; however, in 1990 if an employee earned more than $53,400 annually any such additional wages were not subject to FICA. This number changes each year, so be sure to check what the current social security ceiling is. An employer must match the FICA contribution made by its employees. So, if $50 is withheld from an employee's wages for FICA during a pay period, the employer must pay an equal amount.

Amounts withheld from employee's pay must be deposited within a reasonable time with the Federal Reserve Bank in your area, or with a financial institution authorized to accept these deposits. Check with the Federal Reserve Bank in your area to learn what institutions can accept these deposits.

IRS employees have informed us that the frequency of the deposits depends upon the amount of the taxes owed. For example, if you owe less than $500 at the end of any quarter, you don't have to deposit the money. You can merely send it to the IRS, with a Form 941. If you owe more than $500 for the quarter, a deposit will have to be made. The deposits should be made with a Form 8109 federal deposit coupon. Copies of these coupons will be sent to you by the IRS after you apply for a federal employer identification number. Instructions for using this coupon are included in the coupon book. Until you have received your coupon book, you can use the blank Form 8109-B, available from the IRS. If you owe less than $500 in taxes for any one month, you do not have to make a deposit; you can wait until the next month. If you owe more than $500, but less than $3,000, at the end of any month, the amount owed must be deposited within 15 days after the end of the month. If your monthly tax bill significantly exceeds $3,000, it may be necessary to make more than one deposit per month. Additional copies of the Form 8109 can be obtained from the IRS by using the reorder form included in the coupon book. Be sure to check with your accountant and the IRS about when and where you should make these deposits. There is a 10% penalty for late payments.

Remember that the IRS considers an employer, as well as other "responsible individuals," as trustees for amounts withheld from employees' wages. If amounts withheld are not paid to the IRS, the employer and all responsible persons will be liable for all such taxes, plus a 100% penalty. Criminal sanctions are also possible.

A Form 941 must be filed quarterly with the IRS regarding withheld income tax and social security tax. These quarterly returns must be filed within 30 days after the end of each calendar quarter. For Texas businesses, the return should be sent to the Social Security Administration, Albuquerque Data Operations Center, Albuquerque, NM 87180.

You must fill out a Form W-2 wage and tax statement for each employee, and the employee must receive it by January 31 for the prior calendar year. The W-2 should include all wages the employee received, as well as "other compensation." This includes certain payments considered taxable income that are not subject to withholding, such as reimbursement of moving expenses. Copy A of all W-2 Forms prepared for each employee should be filed annually with the Social Security Administration with the Form W-3.

A Form W-3, Transmittal of Income and Tax Statements, must be filed by the end of February with the Social Security Administration, Albuquerque Data Operations Center, Albuquerque, NM 87180.

If you are self-employed, you have to pay a self-employment tax. This is essentially a social security payment. Schedule SE (form 1040) is used to compute the amount owed.

Federal Unemployment Tax Act (FUTA)

The federal unemployment tax system, together with the state systems, provides for payments of unemployment compensation to workers who have lost their jobs. If you pay wages of at least $1,500, or if you employ at least one person for some period during 20 different weeks during a calendar year, you are subject to this tax. This tax is 6.2% of the first $7,000 earned by each employee for each calendar year. However, if you are an employer subject to the Texas Unemployment Insurance Tax, which is discussed below under Texas Taxes, a credit will be given for contributions to the Texas fund. This credit can be as much as 5.4% of the first $7,000 of wages, which may very significantly reduce the amount you will pay under this federal tax. Form 940 is used to report and pay the aggregate federal unemployment compensation tax due. FUTA payments should be made with Form 8109 deposit coupons relating to other federal taxes due. If additional FUTA payments are due at the end of the year, this payment should accompany the Form 940. This Form 940 must be filed by January 31, to the IRS at Austin, TX 73301. This is not a tax that you withhold from your employees' wages; the employer pays this tax.

To order any forms or information booklets relevant to federal taxes, write to: Internal Revenue Service, P.O. Box 9903, Bloomington, IL 61799. The forms may also be obtained by calling 800-829-3676. Some of the publications that might be of particular interest to you are:

- Publication 583—Information for Business Taxpayers
- Publication 334—Tax Guide for Small Business
- Publication 589—Tax Information on S Corporations
- Publication 541—Tax Information on Partnerships
- Publication 542—Tax Information on Corporations
- Publication 552—Recordkeeping for Individuals and a List of Tax Publications
- Publication 539—Employment Taxes
- Publication 937—Business Reporting
- Publication 535—Business Expenses
- Publication 15—Circular E—Employer's Tax Guide
- Form W-2—Wage and Tax Statement
- Form W-3—Transmittal of Income and Tax Statements
- Form W-4—Employee's Withholding Allowing Certificate
- Form 940—Employer's Quarterly
- Form 941—Employer's Quarterly Federal Tax Return
- Form 1120—U.S. Corporation Income Tax Return
- Form 1120S—U.S. Income Tax Return for an S Corporation
- Form 1120-W—Corporation Estimated Tax
- Form 1040—Schedule SE—Social Security Self-Employment Tax
- Form 2553—Election by a Small Business Corporation.
- Form SS-4—Application for Employer Identification Number

Many of the forms and publications may be found in the Appendix.

Texas Taxes

Franchise Tax on Corporations

As of January 1, 1992, the Texas franchise tax was significantly changed. Prior to that time, the tax was solely based upon a company's capital. As of January 1, 1992, the tax is based upon either the company's capital or its earnings, depending upon which would yield the highest tax payment.

The tax on "net taxable capital" is now .25%. For corporations, the net taxable capital is essentially the sum of its stated capital and its capital surplus. For limited liability companies, the net taxable capital is the sum of the contributions of all members.

The tax on "taxable earned surplus" is 4.5%. The definition of this term is quite complex, but it basically is the reportable taxable income of the corporation for federal tax purposes. For S corporations, the reportable taxable income is the income reported as taxable to the corporation's shareholders.

The franchise tax due is the higher of the tax computed based upon the net taxable capital or that based upon the taxable earned surplus. The computation of the tax is explained in more detail in Appendix C. The tax applies to corporations (including S corporations) and limited liability companies; proprietorships, general partnerships, and limited partnerships do not have to pay this tax. The first report under the new system is due on May 15, 1992, and will be based upon 1991 earnings and capital. It is not necessary to apply for a franchise tax account or permit.

If a corporation does business in more than one state, the tax due is prorated, based upon the percentage of the company's business that is conducted in Texas. For more information, call the comptroller's office at 1-800-252-5555.

Sales Taxes

A sales tax is a tax on the sale, lease, or rental of property or services. To determine if your business must pay a sales tax, you should call the Comptroller's office. The tax is added to the price of the good or service and collected from the customer. Every business selling, renting, or leasing taxable items or providing taxable services in Texas must apply to the Comptroller of Public Accounts for a sales tax permit. A sales tax permit should be obtained for each Texas place of business. For more information and the application for the permit, write to: The Tax Administration Division, Comptroller of Public Accounts, Austin, Texas 78774.

There is no charge for a sales tax permit. You may be required to furnish the comptroller a bond or security to ensure payment of the taxes you collect. The amount of the bond necessary will vary in accordance with the amount of taxes you expect to collect. The bond or security will be returned if all sales tax due is paid on time for two consecutive years. However, this bond requirement may be waived if you are entering business for the first time and your bond is calculated to be $3,000 or less.

If you are buying an existing business, you should request that the comptroller notify you if the business has an outstanding sales tax liability. If you purchase the business, it is strongly advised that you withhold from the purchase price an amount sufficient to pay any sales taxes that the firm may still owe the state. By purchasing the firm, you may become liable for any sales tax owed by the firm, up to the amount of the purchase price.

You are required by law to collect sales tax and to file tax returns and pay the tax to the comptroller. If you collect less than $1,500 per quarter in state sales tax, you may file a quarterly report with the comptroller. If your business collects more than $1,500 per quarter in state sales tax, you will be required to file and pay monthly. Your return is filed on preprinted forms which will be sent to you by the comptroller at the appropriate intervals.

The current state sales tax is 6.25% on all retail sales, leases, and rentals of taxable items. Cities in Texas have the option of imposing an additional 1% sales tax. Heavily populated areas can also create Metropolitan Transit Authority taxing districts that fund improved mass transit systems. These taxes can add another 1%. For example, in Houston in 1990 the sales tax rate was 8.25% (6.25% + 1% + 1%).

Sales taxes are not imposed if an item is purchased for resale. However, you do need a sales tax permit even if you only purchase goods for resale. If your business is buying goods for resale, give the seller a resale certificate. A copy of it should be given to the supplier. It should *not* be sent to the comptroller of public accounts. Use the resale certificate each time tangible personal property is purchased for resale. This will exempt you from the state and local sales and use taxes. An item is purchased for resale if you intend to sell, lease, or rent the item within the United States in the regular course of your business. If your business only purchases items for resale, you can give your supplier a "blanket" resale certificate. For a "blanket" resale certificate, use the Texas Sales Resale Certificate and describe the property in general terms. Your supplier can rely on this blanket certificate until it is revoked in writing. Forms of the resale certificates are available from the comptroller.

For more information about Texas taxes, call the comptroller's one-stop tax information hotline (512) 463-4600, or 1-800-252-5555 toll free from anywhere in Texas. The address is: Comptroller of Public Accounts, 111 East 17th Street, Austin, Texas 78774.

Unemployment Insurance Tax

If you are an employer who has paid $1,500 or more in wages in a calendar quarter, or you have employed one or more workers on any day in 20 different weeks in a calendar year, you are subject to the Texas Unemployment Compensation Act.

Under this law, the initial tax rate is 2.7% of the first $9,000 earned by each worker during the calendar year. All employers are taxed at this rate for six to eight consecutive quarters. After that, the employer will become eligible for an experience rating. Experience ratings are determined by the employer's taxable payroll and the unemployment benefits charged to the employer during this period. The experience tax rates can range from 0.0% to a maximum of 6.0%.

As a Texas employer, you are required to file a form C-1, Status Report, and a C-3a(186), Employer's Quarterly Report, with the Texas Employment Commission. The address is: Controller—TEC, P.O. Box 2908, Austin, TX 78769. Copies of these forms are in Appendix B, Form 9.

For more information about the Texas Unemployment Compensation Tax, contact the Texas Employment Commission, 101 East 15th Street, Austin, Texas 78778, (512) 463-2222.

Workers' Compensation

Workers' Compensation Insurance protects an employer from lawsuits arising out of the death or personal injury sustained by his employees in the course of their employment. Although obtaining workers' compensation insurance is optional in Texas, it can save you a lot of money and prevent large lawsuits against you by your employees. If you are unsure about workers' compensation you should talk with your attorney. If you decide to purchase workers' compensation you can do so through the Texas Employment Insurance Association or through any insurance company authorized to sell liability or accident insurance in Texas.

To get further information about workers' compensation insurance, contact: Workers' Compensation Section of the State Board of Insurance, 1110 San Jacinto, Austin, Texas 78701-1998, (512) 463-6311. To order the "List of Authorized Insurance Companies," contact: Publications Dept., 1110 San Jacinto, Austin, Texas 78701-6153. There is a small charge for this booklet.

FEDERAL REGULATION OF SAFETY AND HEALTH

Occupational Safety and Health Act (OSHA)

Under a federal law called the Occupational Safety and Health Act of 1970, every employer has the "general duty" to provide a workplace that is safe and healthful, free from recognized hazards. The Occupational Safety and Health Administration, which is part of the U.S. Department of Labor, has put into effect specific standards and regulations that employers must follow which are relevant to occupational safety and health. These standards vary in accordance with the kind of workplace you have. An employer is "any person engaged in a business affecting commerce who has employees." Self-employed persons and farms at which only the immediate members of the farm employer's family are employed are not covered under this Act.

OSHA standards fall into four major categories: General Industry, Maritime, Construction, and Agriculture. As an employer, it is your responsibility to become familiar with the standards applicable to your particular establishment and to be sure that your employees have, and use, personal protective gear and equipment when required for safety. As it is not possible to include the specific standards that may apply to your establishment in the scope of this chapter, please refer to the fact sheet in Appendix D to learn how to obtain some publications containing the applicable standards.

The law also requires that you must display the official "OSHA poster," which describes rights and responsibilities under OSHA's law, in a prominent place so that your employees can readily see it. In general, your employees have a right to know which OSHA standards apply to your workplace. To get the poster, contact your regional OSHA office.

If you employ 11 or more employees, you must maintain records of occupational injuries and illnesses as they occur. OSHA recordkeeping is not required for employers with no more than 10 full- or part-time employees at any one time in the previous calendar year. Also exempt from the recordkeeping requirements are all employers in retail trade, finance, insurance, and real estate. Service industries are exempt, except for building materials and garden supplies, general merchandise and food stores, hotels and other lodging places, repair services, amusement and recreational services, and health services.

If you are not exempt from the recordkeeping obligation, record each injury on OSHA Form No. 200, which is called the Log and Summary. Not every injury or illness occurring in the workplace is recordable. Definitions on the back of OSHA Form No. 200 explain which cases must be recorded. Then, prepare a supplementary record of occupational injuries and illnesses for recordable cases either on OSHA Form No. 101 or on a worker's compensation report giving the same information. Every year, prepare the annual summary, which is also OSHA Form No. 200, and post it no later than February 1. It should be kept posted until March 1. The form itself will explain in detail how and when to post it. A good place to post it would be near the official OSHA poster. You need to retain these records for at least five years. To obtain this form, contact your regional OSHA office (see Appendix D for a list of addresses and phone numbers). OSHA also publishes a *Handbook for Small Businesses*. This free booklet sumarizes OSHA requirements and is intended to help small businesses comply with the law.

Reporting of Fatalities or Multiple Hospitalization Accidents

You must report every accident which results in one or more deaths or in hospitalization of five or more employees. This is necessary even if you are exempt from the routine recordkeeping described above. The report must be made within 48 hours after the occurrence of the accident. You can report either in writing or orally to the OSHA area director. (Please see Appendix D for the addresses of the district and area offices.)

Licenses and Permits

One of your start-up business requirements will be to secure the licenses and permits that may be required by the county or city in which you plan to operate. The kinds of permits and licenses necessary will vary in accordance with the type of business you plan to operate. For instance, the permits necessary for the operation of a restaurant may differ from those required for an automobile repair shop.

If you are picking a new site for your business, it is advisable to visit the county clerk's office to obtain any information about deed restrictions that may apply. Deed restrictions may impose additional restrictions and requirements, such as: setbacks, height and size, architectural specifications, signs, maintenance, parking, refuse storage and collection, noise, odors, smoke, and others. Any applicable zoning rules should also be complied with.

Your city or county may require that you get some of the following permits or approvals for your business. Check with your city or county offices about:

- Certificate of occupancy
- Building permit approval
- Development plat approval
- Wastewater capacity reservation
- Sign administration
- Fire marshall
- Finance and administration
- Health department; consumer health services
- Public works department; industrial waste
- Texas Alcoholic Beverage Commission (if alcoholic beverages are to be served)
- Bureau of Alcohol, Tobacco, and Firearms
- Additional permits—occupational permits

Some cities have Business Assistance Centers that will supply you with the information you need about license, permits, and fees in a central location. For the office nearest you, refer to list on page 7.

Assumed Name Certificate

If your firm will be doing business under an assumed name, any name other than that of the owners, you need to file an "assumed name certificate" with the county clerk's office in the county where your business will operate. The assumed name certificate is a relatively simple form. A small filing fee normally is due; in Harris County, for example, the fee is $5. Contact the office in your county to determine the exact form needed and the filing fee.

If you are doing business as a corporation, and you plan to use a name other than the exact corporate name given in your Articles of Incorporation, you must file an assumed name certificate with the secretary of state of Texas as well as with the county clerk of the county where the principal office of your corporation is located. If your registered office is not located in the same county as your principal office, a certificate must also be filed in that county. If you plan to use more than one assumed name, you will have to file a certificate for each one. The assumed name certificate is valid for ten years and may be renewed. A sample of the Assumed Name Certificate for an Incorporated Business is in Appendix B, Form 18. The fee for filing with the secretary of state is $10.

8

The Texas Deceptive Trade Practices Act

Dealing with Customers

The typical business person believes that legal questions concerning the business arise, and are answered, before the business is opened. When a business person thinks of "legal questions," he may think of decisions regarding the form of the venture, the arranging of financing, and the satisfaction of state and federal employment and tax requirements. These issues are resolved when a business starts. From that point on, the business usually operates under the old maxim *caveat emptor*, let the buyer beware. So long as you do not intentionally defraud or mislead your customers and business contacts, you assume that you have no liability.

Unfortunately, a number of legal problems can arise after the business is started. Consider the following:

> Joe recently opened a car dealership. He took in trade a late model car and was told by the customer "I have had no problems. It is good as new." An independent mechanic verifies that there is nothing wrong. Joe sells the car and tells the customer "The car is good as new." Due to a hidden defect the car breaks down the day after the sale. **Joe may be liable for up to three times the buyer's damages and attorney's fees.**

Or what about this:

> Sally's travel agency recently received a beautiful brochure from the Sea Isle Hotel. The picture shows a beautiful hotel with a large pool. Sally tells the customer "The Sea Isle has a beautiful pool." The customer takes the trip and the hotel has filled in the pool to make room for more tennis courts. **Sally may be liable to the customer for up to three times the traveler's damages and attorney's fees.**

And finally:

> Melanie owns and operates a computer store. She recently received a notice from a large manufacturer that their latest computer was to be replaced with a new model, selling for substantially less. A customer comes in and wants to buy the old model, and Melanie says nothing about the new model and the discount price. **Melanie may be liable to the buyer for up to three times the difference in price, plus attorney's fees.**

These are just a few examples of an important Texas law that changes the way business should operate in this state. The law is called the Texas Deceptive Trade Practices Act, and it is one of the most powerful consumer protection laws in the nation. Under this law the maxim *caveat emptor* has been replaced with a new credo, *caveat vendor*. This law doesn't require intent, doesn't require knowledge, and doesn't allow you to escape liability by claiming that it was only a good faith mistake. You generally can't contractually avoid the law and if you violate it you are responsible for up to three times the person's damages plus all court costs and attorney's fees.

And don't think that this law doesn't apply to you because you don't deal with "consumers." Under the law, a consumer is anyone, except a business entity with over $25 million dollars in assets. As you will see, it is mandatory that you know who this law applies to, what it covers, how you can avoid liability, and what to do when you are threatened with action under the Deceptive Trade Practices Act.

Who Is Covered by the Law?

The Deceptive Trade Practices Act applies to any person or entity that is a *consumer*. A consumer is a person, partnership, corporation, or government entity who acquires or seeks to acquire, goods or services by purchase or lease—in other words, any person or entity that buys goods or services from you, or that tries to. This law applies even if you do not finalize the transaction. Consider this example:

> You recently opened a health club and ran an ad in your local paper advertising your trained staff. In response to your ad, Janie came to your club and received a free demonstration.While using one of the machines, her expensive watch was damaged because the staff member helping her was untrained and forgot to tell her to take it off.

Even though Janie did not pay you anything, she has a claim under the Deceptive Trade Practices Act based on your ad. The statement in your ad that you had trained personnel was untrue with respect to the assistance she received, and Janie was a consumer because she was seeking to purchase services. The only exception in the law is for businesses with more than $25 million in assets. Everyone else is a "consumer" under Texas Law.

The Bottom Line

Assume whenever you deal with anyone that the Deceptive Trade Practices Act applies. Probabilities are that it does.

When Can I Be Sued Under This Law?

The Deceptive Trade Practices Act allows a consumer to sue whenever they have been harmed by any one of the following:

1. A violation of the provisions of the Act.
2. Any breach of warranty.
3. Any unconscionable action.

First, the Act itself has a list of 25 things that are expressly prohibited by law. This list, generally called the "laundry list" of violations, covers nearly every aspect of a business. This is what the law prohibits, in the actual language of the Act:

1. Passing of goods or services as those of another;
2. Causing confusion or misunderstanding as to the source, sponsorship, approval, or certification of goods or services;
3. Causing confusion or misunderstanding as to affiliation, connection or association with, or certification by, another;
4. Using deceptive representations or designations of geographic origin in connection with goods or services;
5. Representing that goods or services have sponsorship, approval, characteristics, ingredients, uses, benefits, or quantities which they do not have, or that a person has a sponsorship, approval, status, affiliation, or connection which he does not;
6. Representing that goods are original or new if they are deteriorated, reconditioned, reclaimed, used, or second-hand;
7. Representing that goods or services are of a particular standard, quality, or grade, or that goods are of a particular style or model, if they are of another;
8. Disparaging the goods, services, or business of another by false or misleading representation of facts;
9. Advertising goods or services with intent not to sell them as advertised;
10. Advertising goods or services with intent not to supply a reasonable, expectable public demand, unless the advertisements disclosed a limitation of quantity;
11. Making false or misleading statements of fact concerning the reasons for, existence of, or amount of price reductions;
12. Representing that an agreement confers or involves rights, remedies, or obligations which it does not have or involve, or which are prohibited by law;
13. Knowingly making false or misleading statements of fact concerning the need for parts, replacement, or repair service;
14. Misrepresenting the authority of a salesman, representative or agent to negotiate the final terms of a consumer transaction;
15. Basing a charge for the repair of any item, in whole or in part, on a guaranty or warranty instead of on the value of the actual repairs made, or work to be performed on the item, without stating, separately, the charges for the work and the charge for the warranty or guaranty, if any;
16. Disconnecting, turning back, or resetting the odometer of any motor vehicle so as to reduce the number of miles indicated on the odometer gauge;
17. Advertising of any sale by fraudulently representing that a person is going out of business;
18. Using or employing a chain-referral sales plan in connection with the sale or offer to sell of goods, merchandise, or anything of value which uses the sale's technique, plan, arrangement, or agreement in which the buyer or prospective buyer is offered the opportunity to purchase merchandise or goods and, in connection with the purchase, receives the seller's promise or representation that the buyer shall have the right to receive compensation or consideration, in any form, for furnishing to the seller the names of other prospective buyers, if re-

ceipt of the compensation or consideration is contingent upon the occurrence of an event subsequent to the time the buyer purchases the merchandise or goods;

19. Representing that a guaranty or warranty confers or involves rights or remedies, which it does not have or involve, provided, however, that nothing in this subchapter shall be construed to expand the implied warranty of merchantability, as defined in Section 2.314 through 2.318 of the Business & Commerce Code to involve obligations in excess of those which are appropriate to the goods;

20. Selling or offering-to-sell, either directly or associated with the sale of goods or services, a right of participation in a multilevel distributorship. As used herein, "multilevel distributorship" means a sales plan for the distribution of goods or services in which promises of rebate or payment are made to individuals, conditioned upon those individuals recommending or securing additional individuals to assume positions in the sales operation, and where the rebate or payment is not exclusively conditioned on, or in relation to proceeds from the retail sales of goods;

21. Representing that work or services have been performed on, or parts replaced in, goods when the work or services were not performed or the parts not replaced;

22. Filing suit, founded upon a written contractual obligation of and signed by the defendant, to pay money arising out of or based on a consumer transaction for goods, services, loans, or extensions of credit intended primarily for personal, family, household, or agricultural use in any county other than in the county in which the defendant resides at the time of the commencement of the action or in the county in which the defendant in fact signed the contract; provided, however, that a violation of this subsection shall not occur where it is shown by the person filing such suit he neither knew nor had reason to know that the county in which such suit was filed was neither the county in which the defendant resides at the commencement of the suit, nor the county in which the defendant in fact signed the contract; or

23. The failure to disclose information concerning goods or services which was known at the time of the transaction if such failure to disclose such information was intended to induce the consumer into a transaction into which the consumer would not have entered had the information been disclosed.

24. Using the term "corporation," "incorporated," or an abbreviation of either of these terms in the name of a business entity that is not incorporated under the laws of this state or another jurisdiction.

25. Taking advantage of a disaster declared by the governor under Chapter 418, Government Code, by (a) selling or leasing fuel, food, medicine, or another necessity at an exorbitant or excessive price; or (b) demanding an exorbitant or excessive price in connection with the sale or lease of fuel, food, medicine, or another necessity.

It is essential that every business person read this list carefully to understand what the law prohibits. Remember, if you do one of the specified acts listed above, you are automatically liable. It is not a defense to say you acted in good faith, or it was a mistake, or that you didn't intend to deceive the person. For example, the law prohibits misrepresenting the geographic origin of a product. If you honestly believe that a rug is from Pakistan, and this is what the wholesaler told you, you violate the law if you sell the rug as such and it turns out to be from India. Simply put, this law makes you an absolute guarantor of what you say. **If you say something it had better be true.** If it is not, you may pay three times the damages.

Finally, although most, if not all of this list is self-explanatory, some provisions should be pointed out. For example, subsection 12, misrepresenting that an agreement confers rights when it does not, can apply if you demand payment that the contract really doesn't authorize. Even if you acted in good faith and believed that you were owed the money, it is unlawful to misrepresent a contractual obligation. And subsection 23 may come as a shock to anyone schooled under the rules of caveat emptor. Under this law it is no longer lawful to just sit back and say nothing. If you know the product has a defect, or is going to be discontinued, or is going on sale, and you know that the buyer wouldn't buy the product at the price you asked if he or she knew these facts, the law imposes an obligation to disclose this information. If you don't you could find yourself on the wrong side of a substantial law suit.

But the "laundry list" is not the only way you may find yourself involved with the Deceptive Trade Practices Act. As we stated in the beginning of this section the law also applies to any "breach of warranty" and to any "unconscionable" action. As you will see, this is a broad area of liability. Here are two examples of warranties that you may not be aware of:

Rid-a-bug exterminator agrees to exterminate a house. The employee is careless, and improperly applies the chemicals, damaging the property and not getting rid of the bugs. Under the law, the company impliedly warranted that they would perform in a workmanlike manner, and the failure to do so could result in treble liability under the Deceptive Trade Practices Act.

Store sells a new toaster which we discover causes fire damage to the customer's house. The company that manufactured the toaster has filed bankruptcy. The store, which has warranted the toaster to be merchantable, may be liable for treble damages under the Deceptive Trade Practices Act.

It is very important that you read and understand Chapter 9 on warranties because any warranty can give rise to liability under the Deceptive Trade Practices Act. As you will see in Chapter 9, there are ways to eliminate and limit liability under warranty law, and this will help to protect you under the Deceptive Trade Practices Act. The bottom line, however, is that, in Texas, any breach of warranty action is automatically a Deceptive Trade Practices Act claim. If the consumer is successful, the claim may be trebled and attorney's fees will be awarded.

Last, but surely not least, the Deceptive Trade Practices Act makes it unlawful for you to engage in any *unconscionable* act. This term is defined in the law as follows:

> (5) Unconscionable action or course of action means an act or practice which, to a person's detriment, takes advantage of the lack of knowledge, ability, experience, or capacity of a person to a grossly unfair degree.

In other words, under Texas law it is unlawful to take advantage of a person's lack of bargaining capacity. If you are in a position where you have superior abilities, knowledge, experience, or capacity, you cannot use this advantage to drive a grossly unfair bargain. On the other hand, if the parties have equal abilities, the law will not disrupt what otherwise might appear to be an unfair bargain. For example:

> Abe is an experienced car salesperson. Sandy, who is about to buy her first car, approaches Abe and lets him know that she has never bought a car and wants to spend no more than $2,500. Abe shows her a car on the lot that he had just recently offered to someone else for $1,000. He tells Sandy it is a great buy and a steal at $2,500. Abe's conduct could be considered unconscionable because he took advantage of Sandy's lack of knowledge and experience.

> George is an independent businessperson who runs a small oil company. He has been in the business for over 20 years. Casey owns a company that sells used drilling equipment. George contacted Casey about purchasing some used equipment. Casey had recently tried to sell the equipment to another buyer for $35,000. George asked Casey how much she wanted and she replied, "I couldn't take less than $50,000." George offered $45,000 and Casey accepted. Even if the price is grossly excessive, the bargain is probably not unconscionable because both parties have equal abilities, capacities, and knowledge.

It should be obvious that the Deceptive Trade Practices Act has altered what were the generally accepted norms of doing business. No longer can you drive the best bargain at any cost to the consumer; no longer can you take advantage of your superior knowledge about the product or service you sell; and no longer can you make representations concerning the goods or services without standing behind them. Penalties for violation of the Deceptive Trade Practices Act can be extreme, and remember if you lose you will also have to pay the consumer's attorney's fees, an amount often in excess of the consumer's damages.

The Bottom Line

The Deceptive Trade Practices Act affects everything you, as a business person, do. Carefully read the next section and find out how some minor changes in the way you do business can help you avoid problems with the Deceptive Trade Practices Act.

Avoiding Deceptive Trade Practices Act Liability

The first thing that has to be pointed out is that basically the only way to avoid liability under the Deceptive Trade Practices Act is to not act in a way that violates the law. Once a violation has occurred there is little in the way of a legal defense. As stated earlier, your good faith or honest mistake will not get you off. And don't think that you can put up a sign, or have the customer sign a release, to avoid liability. Under the law, the Deceptive Trade Practices Act may not be waived or disclaimed. In other words, once you have violated its provisions you had better consider settling the matter with the consumer.

But there are some things you can do to prevent a violation of the Act. First, and foremost, don't say anything about your goods or services unless you are willing to stand behind the statement 100%. For example, if you tell a client that the computer program you designed will serve his needs for one year, and it doesn't, you are responsible under this law. You are responsible even if the reason that the program doesn't work is because business increased tenfold, a totally unexpected condition. To avoid liability you must state precisely what you are willing to guarantee. Tell the consumer, "As far *as I can tell*, this will last you for the next year." Now you will have no liability if the product doesn't last because it was just an opinion, an opinion based on the present facts. Here are some other helpful hints to help prevent problems:

1. Never make absolute representations of facts. Whenever possible qualify your statements to present conditions. Say, "Based on your present conditions, it should last a year," *not* "It will last a year."

2. Whenever you rely on another source, say so. "This resort has a beautiful pool," may result in liability if it doesn't. "According to their brochure they have a beautiful pool," is the proper way to say it.
3. Always state your opinions as such. "As far as I am concerned it is good as new," *not* "It is good as new."
4. Be honest. Don't try to hide anything. Remember, under the law you can be liable if you try to induce a person into something by not disclosing everything you know.

Finally, there is one very important part of the Deceptive Trade Practices Act that can save you a lot of money. **Under the law you must get notice of the consumer's complaint 60 days before any legal action is taken.** After you receive this notice you can offer a written settlement of the matter. If you offer to settle in full, the consumer may not collect treble damages or attorney's fees. In fact, if you offer to settle in full and the consumer still goes to court, you may be entitled to your attorney's fees. Even if you do not offer to settle in full, a partial settlement can still help you. If the amount you offer to settle for is the same or substantially the same as what a court finally awards the consumer, the consumer does not get the amount trebled and may not get attorney's fees. Most consumers will, therefore, accept a reasonable offer of settlement. **Remember, if you do not offer to settle and you are found liable, you may owe three times the amount plus attorney's fees.**

> Customer is told by your mechanic that his car is repaired and the brakes are "as good as new." Due to a mix-up with repair orders, however, the mechanic didn't really make the repairs. Shortly after leaving the station, the car crashes. Customer is not hurt but his car is damaged. Customer sends you a notice that he is going to sue for $5,000 under the Deceptive Trade Practices Act. You receive the letter and recognize that you may be responsible. You believe, however, that the damage to the car will cost no more than $2,000 to repair.

If you do nothing, the consumer will proceed to court, and if the jury agrees with you that his actual damages were only $2,000 it will award that amount. The $2,000, however, may be multiplied by three, to $6,000, and you will owe attorney's fees, possibly as much as $10,000. Of course, you have also paid your own attorney's fees, let's say another $10,000. Thus, you are now out about $26,000 for a claim you originally estimated at $2,000. But, suppose that you took advantage of the law and proposed a settlement of $2,000. The consumer may simply accept this amount, and that is the end of the matter. You save as much as $24,000. But what if the consumer does not and still goes to court? The consumer will still collect the $2,000, but it will not be increased and the consumer's attorney may not recover his or her fees. Thus you will still have saved a substantial amount of money.

The Bottom Line

Whenever you feel that you may ultimately bear some responsibility, propose a settlement within the sixty day limit. As a practical matter many settlement offers are accepted, and even if it is not accepted it may save you a lot of money if the matter proceeds to a trial.

Your Worst Enemy, Your Best Friend

The Deceptive Trade Practices Act could be considered the business person's worst enemy. This is the law that your customers will use when you make an error or sell a defective product. But this same law protects you when you are the consumer. Remember, under this law anyone, including a business, can be a consumer, as long as you do not have assets in excess of $25 million. For example:

> Laura and Mark recently opened a new shoe store in the most fashionable part of town. Business is booming and the new fall season is near. To make sure that they have all the best new shoes, Mark and Laura placed an order with the shoe supply company for 500 new pairs. Because they are concerned with when the shoes will arrive they ask the company when they should expect delivery. The salesperson responds "The shoes will be at your store by September 1." Relying on this statement they plan a big sale for the first week of September. Unfortunately, the shoes never arrive and they lose hundreds of sales, as well as the good will they had developed with their customers.

If Mark and Laura sue they could sue under the Deceptive Trade Practices Act and recover up to three times their damages. They are consumers under the act even though they were buying inventory, and the salesman misrepresented the goods by saying they would arrive by September 1 when they did not.

You should reread all of the material in this chapter and understand that the obligations it imposes on you are also imposed on the people you deal with as a buyer. Your suppliers, accountants, and lawyers are all subject to this law if they deceive you, mislead you, act unconscionably, or breach a warranty.

The Bottom Line

The Deceptive Trade Practices Act places an obligation on sellers of goods or services to live up to their customers' obligations. This law is your best friend when you are the purchaser, but beware when you are the seller.

9

Warranties

Most people think of a warranty as something that comes on a product attached to a little tag, which tells you what the manufacturer might do if a product doesn't work. If you are a businessperson you don't pay much attention to warranties because they are the manufacturer's, not yours.

Well, we have some news for you. This is not what warranty law is all about. In fact, every time you sell something or perform a service you probably give a warranty to your customer. And if you breach that warranty, by not doing what you said, or selling goods that are defective, you are in big trouble. **In Texas, any breach of warranty is automatically a violation of the Deceptive Trade Practices Act, and you may be responsible for three times the customer's damages plus attorney's fees** (see Chapter 8). Here's an example of how warranty law can affect you:

> Fred and Sara recently opened a small appliance store. They sell stoves, refrigerators, toasters and microwaves. The other day a customer came in the store and asked if a certain microwave would work in her apartment complex. The customer explained that the complex had special wiring and that there was less power than usual coming through the lines. Fred had just read that the Expo model 980 worked on lower power and told the customer "The Expo 890 is just what you need, it will work in your apartment." Unfortunately for Fred he was wrong. The microwave did not work; in fact, it exploded and set off a small fire causing $500 in damage. The Expo, which cost $300, was also destroyed. When the customer came back and told Fred the story Fred said he would check with Expo to see what they would do. As you might expect with a product like this, Expo had gone out of business. Fred told the customer he was sorry, there was nothing he could do.

If the customer sued Fred she could recover $2,400 in damages plus the attorney's fees which could amount to several thousand dollars more. By saying the Expo would work Fred had made an express warranty to the customer, and by selling a product to do a specific job he made an implied warranty that the product was fit. Both of these warranties were breached, and the Deceptive Trade Practices Act violated, when the microwave did not work. The customer is therefore entitled to her damages ($500 for the fire, $300 for the microwave) times three. **If you are going into business in this state you had better know warranty law.**

What Is a Warranty?

Basically a warranty is a promise that a product or a service will do a certain thing in a certain way. Warranties may be made in two ways: expressly, by your words or conduct; or impliedly, arising as a matter of law simply by virtue of the fact that a sale occurred. These two types of warranties are generally called *express warranties* and *implied warranties*.

WARRANTIES IN THE SALE OF GOODS

Express Warranties

An express warranty is any promise about a good. One may arise out of the contract between you and your customer, from the statement made by you or your salesperson to the customer, from your conduct, or even from the statements of the customer to you. For example, if the customer describes the goods she wants to buy, and then you supply them, the customer's description becomes your express warranty.

The most common examples of express warranties are those made by manufacturers, in writing, whenever a product is sold. Whenever the product sold is a consumer good, and this includes most things you will sell, the warranty is subject to a federal law called the Magnuson-Moss Warranty Act. This law imposes certain obligations on the warrantor.

If You Write Your Own Warranties

The Magnuson-Moss warranty law was passed by congress in response to the many problems that existed in state warranty law. Basically this law requires that any written warranty be in simple and readily understandable language. It also requires that all written warranties must be labeled *full* or *limited*. Under the law any warranty that is not a full warranty must be clearly labeled *limited* and the only warranties that can be labeled *full* are those that meet the following requirements:

1. The warrantor (the person making the warranty) must repair or replace the product, or give the consumer a refund within a reasonable time and at no charge if the product does not conform with the warranty.
2. The warrantor may not impose any limitation on the duration of any implied warranty (those warranties that arise by operation of law and are discussed on pages 66–68).
3. The warrantor may not exclude or limit consequential damages (those caused by the defective product) unless the exclusion is conspicuously written on the face of the warranty.
4. If the product can't be repaired after a reasonable number of attempts, the consumer must be permitted to elect to receive a refund or a replacement.
5. The warranty is good for anyone who owns the product during the warranty period.

As we said, under the law, a warranty can be labeled *full* only if it meets *all* of these requirements.

Magnuson-Moss also places restrictions on the content of written warranties. By law, your written warranty must include certain basic information about:

1. What parts of the product or what types of problems the warranty covers (and, if necessary for clarity, what parts or problems it does not cover).
2. What the period of coverage is.
3. What you will do to correct problems (and, if necessary for clarity, what you will not do).
4. How the customer can get warranty service.
5. How state law may affect certain provisions of the warranty.

In addition, if there are limitations or conditions on the warranty coverage you provide, you must include a statement of them in your warranty. You may want to consider what conditions and limitations you really need and eliminate those that are unnecessary.

If your warranty contains certain particular conditions or restrictions, you must include additional information. Check the FTC's Rule on Disclosure of Written Consumer Product Warranty Terms and Conditions to determine what you must disclose in your warranty.

Finally, the law requires that your warranty include a title that indicates whether it is *full* or *limited*. What these terms mean and how to use them in titling your warranty are explained in detail in this manual.

Of course, you should consult your lawyer to ensure that your warranty meets all the requirements of both federal and state warranty law.

There are also some things you want to make sure are not included in your warranty. For example, promotional statements, instructions to service agents, and other extraneous material in a warranty may confuse customers about the purpose of the document. Include only necessary information in your warranty. A concise, straightforward warranty will promote your product better than a crowded document full of praise for your product.

If you feel that it is necessary to include promotional material about your product with your written warranty, keep it separate from the warranty. If possible, put it in a separate brochure. If you put promotional statements on the same page as your warranty, clearly set apart your warranty, for example, by placing a border around it. The customer should be able to separate at a glance the warranty from the promotional material.

One way to make sure that your warranty covers all the necessary material, and does so in a clear concise manner, is to use the basic elements required by law as headings for your warranty. The Federal Trade Commission, which enforces federal warranty law, recommends that you use the following headings:

- What the Warranty Covers (and, if necessary for clarity, What it Does *not* Cover)
- What the Period of Coverage Is
- What We (the Company) Will Do to Correct Problems (and, if necessary for clarity, What the Company Will *Not* Do)
- How You (the Customer) Can Get Service
- How State Law Relates to the Warranty

You may need to use additional headings in your warranty if all of the conditions and limitations cannot be dealt with adequately using only the recommended headings.

Regardless of which headings you use to organize your warranty, be sure the headings are specific and informative. You may, for example, want to use questions as headings because they reflect what consumers ask about warranty coverage. We do not recommend headings that consist of a single noun or a string of nouns. These are usually vague and general and do not give readers enough information to let them know what follows in the text. For example, the following headings, all of which come from one warranty, are not very useful or informative:

Parts Warranty
Extended Porcelain Finish Warranty
Warranty Service
Extended Warranty Service Labor Allowance
Ownership
Warranty Conditions
Federal Regulatory Provisions
Purchaser's Responsibility
Purchase Registration
Model and Serial Numbers
Factory Assistance

A warranty does not have to be just "full" or "limited." Different parts may be covered by different warranties, or the warranty may change after a period of time. For example, Figure 9-1 shows (page 66) a "full" and "limited" warranty.

Figure 9-2 (page 67) gives an example of a limited warranty, with pro-rata coverage.

Warranties are a very important part of any sale. For this reason they are regulated by federal law and the Texas Deceptive Trade Practices Act. If you are going to give your customers a written warranty you should be careful to comply with the law. If you would like more, free, information about written warranties, you can write the Federal Trade Commission, 6th & Pennsylvania Ave. N.W., Washington, D.C. 20580, or call the Office of Consumer and Business Education, 202-326-3650, and ask for their booklet "Writing Readable Warranties."

The Bottom Line

Written express warranties are strictly regulated by Federal law. If you give your customers a written warranty be sure that it complies with Magnuson-Moss and is labeled *Full* or *Limited*.

Oral Express Warranties

Express warranties do not have to be written. In fact, few small businesses make written express warranties, relying instead on the warranties made by the manufacturer. But oral representations about the quality of the goods can also turn out to be legally binding as a warranty.

Under the law, any representation about the goods, or a promise relating to them, constitutes a warranty. For example, if you tell a customer that the product is finished with "100% oil base enamel" it better be, because you just warranted it. And don't say that the table is "stain resistant" unless you know for a fact it is because the buyer could sue for breach of warranty and recover treble damages. Be careful about what you or your salespeople say about a product. Any affirmation of fact about a product, or a description of its qualities or benefits can become an express warranty. The only major exceptions to this are statements of your opinion. A mere statement of opinion, salesperson "puffing" does not constitute a warranty. So if you say that the spark plug is the "best made" it may not constitute a warranty. But be careful, most courts to have considered whether a statement is "puffing" or a warranty generally favor the consumer and find that it is a warranty. To protect yourself be sure to say "in my opinion," or "as far as I am concerned." This will let the buyer know that it is just your opinion and not a warranty.

The Bottom Line

Representations about a product, whether oral or written, can easily become warranties if they enter into the bargain. Be careful about what you and your employees say. To fully protect yourself you may also want to consider limiting your warranty liability contractually. This alternative is discussed on pages 61–62.

Full Two Year Warranty On The Black Star 2001 Clothes Washer

What is Covered:	For How Long:	What Black Star Will Do:
Any defect in your 2001 Clothes Washer.	Two years after the date you bought your 2001 Clothes Washer.	Repair, or if repair is not possible, either replace your 2001 Clothes Washer, or refund the purchase price, whichever you prefer.

Limited Warranty on Parts for the Third Through Fifth Years

What is Covered:	For How Long:	What Black Star Will Do:
Any defect in your 2001 Clothes Washer.	From the start of the third year after you bought your 2001 Clothes Washer until the end of the fifth year after you bought it.	Provide free new or rebuilt replacement parts, but not labor to install the parts. Any servicer you choose can do service during this period.

How to Get Service: Contact any Black Star Dealer or any Authorized Black Star Service Center. See the Yellow Pages under "Appliance Repair" for the name of a Black Star Servicer near you, or call 800-111-1111.

Your Rights Under State Law: This warranty gives you specific legal rights, and you may also have other rights which vary from state to state.

Figure 9-1. A "full" and "limited" warranty.

Implied Warranties

Many people think that a warranty is something that arises only if a seller makes a promise, or guarantee, to a buyer about a product. Many sellers think that as long as they don't make any promises they don't have to worry about warranty law. Well think again. **Under the law any time you sell something the law implies certain warranties.** These implied warranties arise simply by virtue of the sale; you do not have to do or say anything special. For example, consider this:

> Janie and her friend Bess recently opened a small shop to sell wool and knitting supplies. Both had a lot of experience with knitting but little with business. They were doing pretty well, however, and even made a small profit. Generally, they made their money from the sale of wool, and offered their advice as part of their customer service

Polarity Corporation Limited Warranty

What is Covered?

This warranty covers all defects in workmanship or materials in your Polarity Automobile Battery.

How Long is the Coverage Period?

The warranty coverage runs for 36 months from the date you buy your Polarity Automobile Battery.

What Will Polarity Corporation Do?

If your Polarity Auto Battery fails during:	Polarity will provide you with a credit of:
The 1st through the 9th month	100%
The 10th through the 18th month	75%
The 19th through the 27th month	50%
The 28th through the 36th month	25%

The credit will be a percentage of the original price you paid for the battery. The credit will be good only toward purchase of a new Polarity Auto Battery of the same or equivalent model.

How Can You Get Service?

Bring the battery and proof of date and amount of purchase to any retailer that carries Polarity products. Check the Yellow Pages under "Auto Parts" for the name and address of a Polarity dealer near you.

How Does State Law Apply?

This warranty gives you specific legal rights, and you may also have other rights which vary from state to state.

Figure 9-2. A limited warranty with pro-rata coverage.

program. All of the wool they sold was provided by a local wholesaler. The wool was marked with a written guarantee by the manufacturer against defects in workmanship.

About four weeks ago a customer came in and bought $75 worth of wool for a sweater. The customer didn't know much about wool and told Janie she needed a heavy-duty wool that would be good for a ski sweater. Janie gave her the wool she would use. Needless to say, the wool was defective and after the sweater was finished, while she was on a ski vacation, the sweater came apart, and the customer got frostbitten as a result.

Even though Janie never "guaranteed" the wool, or said anything about its quality, she has violated the implied warranty of merchantability and the implied warranty of fitness for a particular purpose. If the customer were to sue, she would be entitled to the cost of the wool and her damages from the frostbite, times five, under the Texas Deceptive Trade Practices Act. Of course Janie could sue the wool company, but if they have gone out of business, Janie still owes her customer.

Basically, the law imposes a warranty upon a seller guaranteeing that the goods sold are what they are supposed to be. This is called the "implied warranty of merchantability," and the law reads like this:

> (1) Unless excluded or modified, a warranty that the goods shall be merchantable is implied in a contract for their sale if the seller is a merchant with respect to goods of that kind. Under this section the serving for value of food or drink to be consumed either on the premises or elsewhere is a sale.
> (2) Goods to be merchantable must be at least such as:
>
> (a) pass without objection in the trade under the contract description; and
> (b) in the case of fungible goods, are of fair average quality within the description; and
> (c) are fit for the ordinary purposes for which such goods are used; and
> (d) run, within the variations permitted by the agreement, of even kind, quality and quantity within each unit and among all units involved; and
> (e) are adequately contained, packaged, and labeled as the agreement may require; and
> (f) conform to the promises or affirmation of fact made on the container or label if any.

Without boring you with all the details, this law basically means that whenever a merchant sells something he guarantees the buyer that the buyer is getting a product that will do what it is supposed to do, in the way in which it is supposed to, for the amount of time it usually does.

And there is one other implied warranty that arises when you sell goods, called *the implied warranty of "Fitness for a Particular Purpose."* This law reads as follows:

> "Where the seller at the time of contracting has reason to know any particular purpose for which the goods are required and that the buyer is relying on the seller's skill or judgment to select or furnish suitable goods, there is unless excluded or modified under the next section an implied warranty that the goods shall be fit for such purpose."

In our example above, Janie made this warranty because her customer needed wool for a "particular purpose," a ski sweater, and the buyer relied on Janie's judgment. Because the wool was not fit for any purpose, Janie would have breached both the warranty of merchantability and the warranty of fitness for a particular purpose. **If you are in a business where your customers rely on your skill and judgment to choose products for them, remember that you are probably warranting that what you sell will do what the customer asked for.**

Implied warranties, however, are not absolute. They can be disclaimed and may not arise in the sale of used goods. Implied warranties are considered part of the contract, and as such they can be disclaimed by a seller. For example, if you sell something "as is" there are no implied warranties. Also, many Texas courts have held that there are no implied warranties when you sell used goods. But there is one big exception to your right to get out of liability under this warranty. Under the Magnuson-Moss Warranty Act, a seller who makes any written express warranties may not disclaim implied warranties. For example, if you give your customer a 30-day written guarantee on parts, you may not disclaim the implied warranties that go along with the sale. **You may, however, limit the period of time of the implied warranties to the same period as your express warranty.** To find out more about disclaiming warranties, read the next section.

The Bottom Line

Remember, anytime you sell something an implied warranty probably arises. Be sure to either take steps to disclaim this warranty, or make sure that you have sufficient insurance to protect yourself.

Limiting Warranty Liability

Warranty is a creature of contract, and because it is you may contractually limit, or disclaim, your warranty liability. **But contractually limiting warranty liability may have no effect on your liability under the Texas Deceptive Trade Practices Act.** Consider this:

> Bob, a car dealer, recently sold a used car to Mr. and Mrs. Jones. Before they signed the contract Bob said "This car is a real gem. It has been completely overhauled." Unfortunately for the Jones' that was not true. But the contract the parties signed said "Seller has made no representations about the quality of the car. There are no warranties except those contained in this written contract. Seller disclaims all other warranties express and implied including the warranty of merchantability. Buyer accepts the car 'as is.'" Even though the contract is probably sufficient to limit Bob's liability for breach of warranty, he would still be liable under the Deceptive Trade Practices Act.

Liability under the Deceptive Trade Practices Act may not be contractually limited or disclaimed. Even though you may be able to insulate yourself from warranty liability for oral promises, you can't do so under the Deceptive Trade Practices Act. **In Texas if you say it you had better be willing to stand behind it 100%.**

Keeping in mind the limited effect of disclaiming warranty liability, there are ways that you can do so. First, oral promises, even if they are sufficient to give rise to a warranty, are not enforceable if the written contract states that it is your complete agreement and that there are no other promises. For example, language such as this would probably be sufficient to eliminate warranty liability based on an oral statement:

> This contract is the full and complete expression of the parties' warranty liability. The entire agreement of the parties regarding warranties is contained herein and no evidence of any prior or contemporaneous agreement, whether agreement, representation, understanding, or the like, may be used to add to, subtract from, or modify the content of the warranties here set forth. **There are no warranties that extend beyond the description of the goods contained in this contract and only such warranties are given as we expressly set out herein.**

If the contract your customer signed contained this statement you probably would not be responsible for any express warranties that arose out of your conversations, or those of your salesperson, with the customer before the contract was signed.

A second way to limit your express warranty liability is to limit the buyer's remedy. For example, the following clause could be used in a written contract to limit the buyer to repair of the goods or a refund of the purchase price, and limit damages.

> Buyer's exclusive remedy. In the event of a breach of this contract by seller, the Buyer's exclusive remedy shall be to return the goods or any part thereof which may be defective or nonconforming and receive repayment by the Seller of all, or in the case of a partial breach, a prorata share of the purchase price that has been paid by the buyer at the time of the breach. Repayment of the purchase price shall discharge the Seller from all obligations under this contract. Buyer shall in no event recover consequential damages.

Here is an example of how these two clauses would work:

> Frank recently opened a small auto parts store. Recently he sold a fuel pump to Texas Super Truckers, a long distance hauling company. His salesperson told the buyer the pump "would last at least a year." The fuel pump cost $189.00 and the trucking company and its mechanic installed it.

As it turns out the pump only lasted six months, an otherwise reasonable length of time. It broke down during a long haul of refrigerated vegetables and caused the loss of the entire load. Texas Trucker had insurance to cover the loss, but not the income they would have made. They now want to sue Frank for $189.00 plus the $750 profit they would have made on the hauling. Of course, this amount would be tripled under the Deceptive Trade Practices Act.

If Frank did not have a written agreement with the trucker he probably will have to settle because if he goes to court he is going to lose. The salesperson's statement probably constituted an express warranty about the pump.

On the other hand, if Frank's invoice or contract of sale contained the two above clauses he would have only limited contract liability for breach of warranty. The first clause would prevent the buyer from using the oral statement as a warranty and the second clause would probably be sufficient, even if liability arose, to limit his damages to return of the purchase price. **Remember, unless you act to limit damages you will be responsible for all foreseeable damages that result from your breach of warranty.** For example, if the buyer didn't have insurance Frank might have been liable for the cost of the damaged vegetables as well.

Finally, there is one more way to eliminate most of your warranty problems: sell the good "as is." If the contract is clearly indicated to be on an "as is" basis you probably have no warranty liability, unless the buyer can establish that you made an express warranty. To eliminate even this problem use a contract that contains the clause excluding oral warranties with your "as is" clause. But again remember that even a contract "as is" does not affect Deceptive Trade Practices Act liability. For example, if your salesperson tells the buyer the car is in great condition, and then you sell it "as is," you would be responsible if what the salesman said wasn't true. You wouldn't have any warranty liability because of the "as is" but you would have Deceptive Trade Practices liability because of the misrepresentation about the goods.

The Bottom Line

It is possible to contractually limit or eliminate warranty liability and you should consider doing so. But remember, Texas law favors buyers and the Deceptive Trade Practices Act may not be waived. Best advice . . . don't say it unless you will stand behind it.

WARRANTIES IN SERVICE TRANSACTIONS

Most of the rules discussed with respect to warranties in the sale of goods apply to warranties arising out of a service transaction. For example, express warranties are created by a service provider's representations regarding the service. As creatures of contract these warranties may also be disclaimed or limited in your contract.

There is one major distinction, however, between warranties in the sale of goods and service warranties. In service contracts, the implied warranty may not be disclaimed.

Recently, the Texas Supreme Court held that in any service contract involving the repair or modification of tangible property, there is an implied warranty that the service was performed "in a good and workmanlike manner." This means that there is a guarantee that the service was done the way a competent person would do it. It is not a guarantee of results. For example, assume:

> Frank recently hired Ralph to repair his truck. Frank picked up the truck and paid for it on Tuesday. On Wednesday morning the truck broke down with the same problem, injuring Frank.

Under the implied warranty of good and workmanlike performance, Frank has a claim against Ralph if the repairs were not done the way a competent mechanic would have done them. On the other hand, if the mechanic did everything properly, but the truck still broke down, there would be no breach of the warranty.

The implied warranty of good and workmanlike performance requires that service providers perform at a reasonable leel of competency. As noted above, this warranty may not be waived or limited by contract. In fact, trying to do so may even violate the Texas Deceptive Trade Practices Act, discussed in Chapter 8.

One final note. So far the Texas Supreme Court has applied this warranty only to service providers who repair or modify tangible property. It has not said it applies to professionals, such as accountants, lawyers, or doctors. This is not to say, however, that it will not be so extended, and it is a good idea to keep up with developments in this area of law.

10

Cash or Credit

CASH

It goes without saying that the best way to do business is to have your customers pay you in cash, at or before delivery. But unfortunately most people don't pay in cash; a check or some form of credit is the more usual method of payment. And even though you probably consider a check and cash to be one and the same, because no extension of credit is involved, there are some subtle differences you should be aware of.

First, remember that a check is nothing more than a person's order to his or her bank to pay you money. If the money isn't there the bank has no liability to pay you. In other words, taking a check means relying on the honesty of the person that gave it to you. But there are some ways you can decrease the risks inherent in taking a check. First, make sure that you have proper identification from the person writing the check. If it is a forgery you will be out of luck. A drivers license or other picture ID card, at a minimum, should be required. Second, there are several check verification services you can subscribe to that you can call and have the check guaranteed. These services charge a small fee for each check but it will be worth it if one of the checks bounces. Finally, you should know that if a customer gives you a check without having money in the bank to cover it, this is a criminal offense and you can have the person arrested. To find out more about this law, read page 83 dealing with collection.

As you can see, there are risks involved in accepting a check, but if you require proper identification the risks may be minimal, and the threat of criminal prosecution is a big help in collecting on a bad check. Whenever in doubt about an individual's honesty or ability to pay, however, demand cash, or a cashier's or certified check. You have the legal right to do so.

CREDIT

Credit has become an essential part of any business. If you purchase goods or supplies you may want to buy them on credit, and if you sell goods or services your customers may want to pay on credit. Even though we all know that the easiest way to do business is to do it on a cash-only basis, a commercial reality is that to exist and compete in today's marketplace you will probably have to give your customers an alternative way to pay. No one wants to lose a sale because the customer went somewhere else where he could pay it off on time.

So what are your alternatives to selling things only for cash? Well first, as we just pointed out, taking a check is not really an alternative. The law treats checks as cash, and you and your customers should also. Payment by a check obligates the person who wrote the check to have money on hand in the bank to cover it, and may allow you to use the criminal courts to collect if the check bounces. In other words, it is not an extension of credit. The only real alternative to cash is some form of credit, and here you have two choices: you may extend the credit yourself; or you can rely on third-party credit grantors.

Third Party Credit

Credit, by definition, involves a risk; the risk that the debtor will not pay and the creditor will suffer a loss. The best way to ensure that you will not suffer this loss is to arrange for someone else to extend the credit. This is what we are talking about when we use the term *third party credit*. Perhaps the most common example of this arrangement is the credit card. For example, suppose you sell $900 worth of goods to a customer who needs several months to pay off the bill. The customer gives you a credit card to pay the $900. You then collect from the credit card company, and the credit card company extends credit to your customer. If the customer doesn't pay, the credit card company, not you, bears the loss. Additionally, all of the terms of the credit agreement, the problems of compliance with federal disclosure laws and state usury laws, and the process of collection are handled by the credit card company. **Accepting credit cards is the simplest, safest way of extending credit.** But as you might expect, this simplicity and safety does not come free.

Credit card companies make their money two ways. First, they charge the customer a fee for the card and interest on any money borrowed. Second, they charge a fee to you when you accept the card. How much you pay the credit card company will depend on how many credit card transactions you process and the amount each transaction is for. Generally you can expect to pay the credit card company anywhere from 1–5% of the transaction amount as a commission for their services. For example, in the case above, the customer would sign a credit card draft in the amount of $900. You would deposit this in your bank and be credited with $900 minus the credit card commission. If it was 5% you would receive $855. As you can tell, credit card commissions can add up—but remember, you have taken no risk if the customer doesn't pay, and you have your money relatively quickly. **Each credit card company, and many of the banks that issue credit cards, have their own commission and payment terms. Shop around for the best buy. You can decide how many, if any, credit cards you will accept.** Be sure to find out:

- How much do I have to pay for the use of the card?
- Will this amount increase or decrease depending upon the number or dollar amount of my transactions?
- How soon will I receive the funds for the charge?

Once you do enter into an agreement with a credit card company or bank, be sure to read the agreement carefully and make sure you comply with its terms. For example, in many cases the credit card company will hold you responsible if you forget to get a transaction approved, and the customer doesn't pay.

Another way of using third party credit, which is feasible only if you deal in large transaction amounts, is to refer the customer to a lending institution to get the cash to pay you. For example, if your business is home repair, you can have your customers go to their bank and arrange for a home improvement loan to pay you cash at the time you do the work. Before you do this very often, however, there are several things to keep in mind.

First, if the customer is going to borrow money against their home to pay you for your work, make sure the loan is approved by the bank and the bank has arranged for payment *before* you do any work. Ask to see a written commitment from the bank for the loan, and have the checks issued in either your name, your name *and* the customer's name, or a third party, such as a general contractor, whom you trust. **Texas law is very strict when it comes to loans secured by a homestead.** Reread the material on liens, pages 83–84, and talk with the bank before you do anything.

A second problem you may face if you use this type of third party credit is compliance with federal disclosure laws. Under federal law you can be treated as a creditor and subject to various penalties, if you are what the law calls an "arranger of credit." An arranger of credit is someone who regularly arranges for the extension of credit more than 25 times a year. For example, if you sold cars, and each of your customers was referred by you to a finance company for his or her loan, you would, under this law, be treated as a creditor if you did this more than 25 times in a calendar year period. Without going into a lot of detail about just what this means, suffice it to say that if the bank or creditor messed up, you could be responsible. Only use this type of third party credit occasionally. If you are going to regularly refer your customers to another for financing, you must take steps to ensure that the creditor has complied with all the federal disclosure laws. You or your attorney should examine the creditor's forms, and ask to see a copy of the completed contract before delivering the goods or performing the services.

The Bottom Line

Third party credit is simple. Letting someone else be the creditor avoids all of the risk and most of the hassle of extending credit yourself. But, this protection does cost money, and if you regularly refer your customers to another for credit, you may end up being treated as a creditor yourself.

Special Credit Card Rules

If you accept credit cards you should know about the special federal laws that protect consumers who use them. Although these laws actually deal with the consumers' rights against the credit card company, and not you, as you will see, whenever the credit card company has to give back these consumers' money, the company in turn will debit your account.

Let's start with an example:

> Your business has been booming and you discover a new, untapped, market—mail order. After you place several ads in local papers you begin to receive orders, which you promptly fill and send back to the customers. Because your product is not very large or heavy you use the U.S. mail to send it. You also allow your customers to pay by credit card and most have chosen to do so. Each of your devices sells for $69.95, and you include an extra $4.00 for postage and handling. Everything is fine until you suddenly receive a memo from your bank that the credit card company has debited your account for over $700. It turns out that ten customers have written the credit card company to dispute their bill because they did not receive your product. Your records show that they were shipped, but you have no other proof.

Under federal laws you are probably out of luck. The law states that a consumer may dispute his bill, and refuse to pay, whenever there is a "billing error." Most billing errors are between the credit card company and the consumer; however, a charge for goods which were not received is considered a billing error. If your product never arrived, and you will have to prove it did, the consumer doesn't have to pay the credit card company. The credit card company, in turn, has the right to debit your account.

If you ship goods and accept credit cards as payment, be sure to use a method of shipment that allows you to prove that the goods have been received and accepted. For example, although goods mailed through the U.S. mails do not have a receipt, goods shipped by United Parcel Service must be signed for and you would have proof of receipt. But even if the goods are shipped and accepted you may still not get your money. Consider this:

> Your business is still flourishing. You have resolved your problem of undelivered goods by using UPS and profits are rolling in. One day you receive a large order over the phone. You get all the information and call the order in to be approved, which it is. You then ship the 10 items. A few days later you get a call from the consumer that all of the items were broken when they arrived. You don't believe you have any responsibility for the shipping company so you tell the consumer to take it up with them. A few weeks later you find out that the credit card company has debited your account because the consumer refused to pay his bill, saying that the goods were defective and that he doesn't owe you the money.

Under the same federal law that protects buyers when goods do not arrive, a consumer doesn't have to pay his credit card bill if he has a dispute with the merchant. In most cases when the customer disputes the bill the credit card company will debit your account and ask for your side of the story. Only if you can show that the customer's dispute is invalid will they give you back your money. In most other cases the credit card company will tell you to resolve the problem yourself with the customer. **Don't think that when you take a credit card your rights against the customer are secured.** Under federal law the customer may raise his claims against you, against the credit card company any time the following three requirements are met:

1. The cardholder has made a good faith attempt to settle the matter with the merchant.
2. The goods or services cost over $50.
3. The transaction took place within the cardholder's home state, or within 100 miles of his home.

Whenever you take a credit card, and a dispute arises with a customer, be sure to try and resolve it. Don't take the attitude that you have the money and the customer has to try and get it back. Under federal law it is very easy for the customer to turn the tables on you by simply disputing the charge.

The Bottom Line

Taking credit cards is convenient, but federal law offers the customer special protection against the credit card company if the goods don't arrive, or are defective. These laws are important to you because if the credit card company has to pay the cardholder, they will simply debit your account to get their money back.

Extending Credit

Let's begin with a warning: **Extending credit is very risky, both financially and legally.** You are aware of the financial risks when you extend credit; you may not get paid back. You may not, however, be aware of the legal risks. Credit laws are very specific and failure to comply with any of the many federal and state laws could be very costly. Consider this:

> Susan recently opened a new catering service. After just a few weeks in business she was contacted by one of the city's best known and wealthiest families. They wanted her to cater a large party for over 500 people. The total cost of the affair would be nearly $10,000. Susan was elated. This would be bigger than all her previous jobs combined, and it also would establish her as one of the "in" caterers in the city. Everything was perfect until they discussed payment. When the client asked for 60 days to pay, the "usual" in the catering business, Susan didn't know what to do. She had often given people the right to pay off their bill in four or five installments with a small interest charge but she had never dealt with this much money. When she told the client she would have to charge him interest, he said, "O.K., just pick a fair amount." Susan suggested 10% and he approved. She then drew up a quick agreement on a piece of paper, saying that the client agreed to pay 10% interest, or $1,000, for the right to pay the bill in 60 days. Susan then told him that as far as she was concerned, their handwritten agreement was all they needed and it was a legally valid contract.

Even though Susan has acted in complete innocence she could be in real trouble. Susan has probably violated Texas usury laws and may owe the client twice the interest, or $2,000. She has probably violated federal credit laws and owes him another $1,000, and she may well have violated the Texas Deceptive Trade Practices Act, for which she could owe another $3,000. In other words, Susan's little mistake, of charging too much interest and telling the client that everything was legal, could cost her $6,000 plus whatever court cost and attorney's fees were involved. **If you ever decide to extend credit, be careful! Credit laws have high penalties for those who fail to follow them.**

So what are the credit laws you should be aware of? First, Texas, like every other state, has usury statutes that regulate how much interest you can charge. **Usury laws are very complicated.** There is no one amount that you can always use as a ceiling to be safe. The amount of legally permissible interest depends upon the nature of the transaction, the nature of the parties, and the prevailing treasury bill rate. The best advice we can give you is before you agree on a rate of interest, check with your attorney or accountant to find out the maximum legal rate you can charge. **If you charge an amount in excess of the legal rate, you may be responsible for a penalty in the amount of twice the interest you charged.** You also may find yourself subject to additional penalties under the Texas Deceptive Trade Practices Act, if you represent to your customer that the law allows you to charge the amount you have, when in fact usury law prohibited it. Under this law you are liable for up to three times the customer's damages. (To find out more about the Deceptive Trade Practices Act turn to Chapter 8.) Again, check with someone before you decide how much to charge for interest.

And once you have determined the proper amount of interest, you must be very careful how you disclose it and what your loan agreement looks like. If you begin to regularly extend credit, that is, 25 times or more a year, you are subject to Truth-in-Lending, a federal law that regulates how the terms of a credit transaction are disclosed.* For example, Figure 10-1 (page 75) shows a credit sale model form a creditor subject to Truth-in-Lending should use.

Here is an example of how the Federal Reserve Board recommends you complete this form. Suppose that you sold a car for a cash price of $7,500 with a down payment of $1,500. You charge interest at an 8% add on rate (under the law interest must be disclosed an Annual Percentage Rate) and the term is three years, with 36 equal payments. The credit life insurance premium and filing fees are also financed by you. There is a $25 credit report fee paid by the buyer before the sale. The form when complete should look like the example in Figure 10-2 (page 76).

As you can tell, some of the terms used in this form appear to have special meaning under the law. Federal law requires the use of certain terms in every credit contract. For example, the finance charge is defined as follows:

> (a) *Definition.* The finance charge is the cost of consumer credit as a dollar amount. It includes any charge payable directly or indirectly by the consumer and imposed directly or indirectly by the creditor as an incident to or a condition of the extension of credit. It does not include any charge of a type payable in a comparable cash transaction.

You may have assumed that the interest you charged was part of the finance charge, but did you know that all of the following are also included in the legal definition of that term:

> (1) Interest, time price differential, and any amount payable under an add-on or discount system of additional charges.

* This law also prohibits discrimination. See Appendix A-4 for a copy of the Federal Rules regarding credit discrimination.

ANNUAL PERCENTAGE RATE The cost of your credit as a yearly rate.	FINANCE CHARGE The dollar amount the credit will cost you.	Amount Financed The amount of credit provided to you or on your behalf.	Total of Payments The amount you will have paid after you have made all payments as scheduled.	Total Sale Price The total cost of your purchase on credit, including your downpayment of $ ________.
%	$	$	$	$

You have the right to receive at this time an itemization of the Amount Financed.
☐ I want an itemization. ☐ I do not want an itemization.

Your payment schedule will be:

Number of Payments	Amount of Payments	When Payments Are Due

Insurance
Credit life insurance and credit disability insurance are not required to obtain credit, and will not be provided unless you sign and agree to pay the additional cost.

Type	Premium	Signature
Credit Life		I want credit life insurance. ________ Signature
Credit Disability		I want credit disability insurance. ________ Signature
Credit Life and Disability		I want credit life and disability insurance. ________ Signature

You may obtain property insurance from anyone you want that is acceptable to (creditor). If you get the insurance from (creditor), you will pay $ ________.

Security: You are giving a security interest in:
☐ the goods or property being purchased.
☐ (brief description of other property).

Filing fees $ ________ **Non-filing insurance** $ ________

Late Charge: If a payment is late, you will be charged $ ________ / ________ % of the payment.

Prepayment: If you pay off early, you
☐ may ☐ will not have to pay a penalty.
☐ may ☐ will not be entitled to a refund of part of the finance charge.

See your contract documents for any additional information about nonpayment, default, any required repayment in full before the scheduled date, and prepayment refunds and penalties.

____
e means an estimate

Figure 10-1. Credit sale model form.

(2) Service, transaction, activity, and carrying charges, including any charge imposed on a checking or other transaction account to the extent that the charge exceeds the charge for a similar account without a credit feature.
(3) Points, loan fees, assumption fees, finder's fees, and similar charges.
(4) Appraisal, investigation, and credit report fees.
(5) Premiums or other charges for any guarantee or insurance protecting the creditor against the consumer's default or other credit loss.
(6) Charges imposed on a creditor by another person for purchasing or accepting a consumer's obligation, if the consumer is required to pay the charges in cash, as an addition to the obligation, or as a deduction from the proceeds of the obligation.
(7) Premiums or other charges for credit life, accident, health, or loss-of-income insurance, written in connection with a credit transaction.
(8) Premiums or other charges for insurance against loss of or damage to property, or against liability arising out of the ownership or use of property, written in connection with a credit transaction.
(9) Discounts for the purpose of inducing payment by a means other than the use of credit.

This may appear to be a lot of legal gobbledygook, but it is the law! Don't think that you can just say to someone "that will be 10% a year interest." Under the

Big Wheel Auto Alice Green

ANNUAL PERCENTAGE RATE The cost of your credit as a yearly rate.	FINANCE CHARGE The dollar amount the credit will cost you.	Amount Financed The amount of credit provided to you or on your behalf.	Total of Payments The amount you will have paid after you have made all payments as scheduled.	Total Sale Price The total cost of your purchase on credit, including your downpayment of $ 1500 –
14.84 %	$1496.80	$6107.50	$7604.30	$9129.30

You have the right to receive at this time an itemization of the Amount Financed.
☐ I want an itemization. ☒ I do not want an itemization.

Your payment schedule will be:

Number of Payments	Amount of Payments	When Payments Are Due
36	$211.23	Monthly beginning 6-1-91

Insurance
Credit life insurance and credit disability insurance are not required to obtain credit, and will not be provided unless you sign and agree to pay the additional cost.

Type	Premium	Signature	
Credit Life	$120 –	I want credit life insurance.	Alice Green Signature
Credit Disability		I want credit disability insurance.	Signature
Credit Life and Disability		I want credit life and disability insurance.	Signature

Security: You are giving a security interest in:
☒ the goods being purchased.
☐ ____________________.

Filing fees $ 12.50 **Non-filing insurance** $ ________

Late Charge: If a payment is late, you will be charged $10.

Prepayment: If you pay off early, you
☐ may ☐ will not have to pay a penalty.
☒ may ☐ will not be entitled to a refund of part of the finance charge.

See your contract documents for any additional information about nonpayment, default, any required repayment in full before the scheduled date, and prepayment refunds and penalties.

I have received a copy of this statement.

Alice Green 5-1-91
Signature Date

e means an estimate

Figure 10-2. Example of completed credit sale form.

Truth-in-Lending law, there is no such thing as interest, there is a "finance charge." And this finance charge must be disclosed as an "annual percentage rate," another defined term that involves a very complicated formula. **The easiest way to determine the annual percentage rate is to use charts prepared by the Federal Reserve Board.** If you don't want to bother with these charts, ask your accountant. There are also special provisions dealing with disclosure of pay, net amounts and dates, insurance, late fees, prepayment penalties, and the taking of any security for the loan.

The Bottom Line

Compliance with federal credit laws is very complicated and a mistake can be very costly. Before you begin regularly extending credit yourself, ask your attorney to approve all of your forms and advise you on how they should be filled out. For the occasional loan, however, the promissory notes in Appendix B, Forms 12a and 12b, should be sufficient.

* If you find yourself extending credit very often, you should write the Federal Reserve Board, Washington D.C., and ask for a free copy of Regulation Z—Truth-in-Lending.

11

Getting Paid

Whether you are selling goods or providing a service the bottom line is always the same: if you are not paid for what you do, you will soon be out of business. And as you will see, in Texas getting your money from a recalcitrant debtor can be difficult. So the best advice is: **Whenever possible, make sure you are paid either before or at the same time you perform.** In other words, try not to deliver goods on credit and try to get paid in advance for the services you perform. Here is an example of what can happen if you don't:

> Joe is a plumber who recently went into business on his own. He thought he was lucky when a large apartment complex hired him to do all its repairs. For several months things went well, then he wasn't paid for the past month's work. When he asked about it he was told, "don't worry, we will get you a check next week." After working for six weeks Joe was finally given a check. Relieved, he put the check in the bank and paid his bills. Unfortunately the check bounced, the company filed bankruptcy, and all of Joe's checks to his creditors bounced.

This story points out two things about getting paid. First, you must always remember a check isn't exactly the same as cash. Until the bank pays the check you have only the promise of the person who gave you the check to rely on. **Don't assume that once you have a check you have been paid . . . wait until it clears the bank.** Second, if someone who owes you money files bankruptcy, you will probably never be paid. Even though you are allowed to file a claim in bankruptcy court to get your share of what the person owed, there usually is very little money left to pay the average creditor.

So what can you do to prevent this from happening to you? First, don't wait long periods of time between payments from an unknown creditor. Arrange a payment plan whereby you will be paid every week, instead of every month. Next, if you are going to take a check, ask for a cashier's check, a bank draft, or a certified check. Without going into all the legal reasons why, these checks almost assure that you will get your money because the bank stands behind them. Finally, if possible get partial payment in advance, something like the security deposit landlords have tenants pay. And if you extend credit, which you often must, get a credit report to make sure you are not dealing with a person with a bad credit history.

But no matter how diligent you are, there will be times that you have to extend credit, and then try to collect. When this happens you should know that there are laws that regulate what you do in your role as debt collector, and violating them can be costly.

Debt Collection

Whenever you try to collect money you are owed, you are subject to the Texas Debt Collection Laws. Under the law, wrongful and abusive debt collection may result in civil liability. Additionally, if the debt involves a consumer you are subject to the Debt Collection Practices Act. This Act prohibits most harassing and deceptive practices, and a violation could result in civil and criminal penalties. Here is what the law says you may not do:

Threats or Coercion

No debt collector may collect or attempt to collect any debt alleged to be due and owing by any threats, coercion, or attempts to coerce which employ any of the following practices:

(a) using or threatening to use violence or other criminal means to cause harm to the person or property of any person;
(b) accusing falsely or threatening to accuse falsely any person of fraud or any other crime;
(c) representing or threatening to represent to a third party or any other person, that a consumer is willfully refusing to pay a non-disputed debt when the debt is in dispute for any reason and the consumer has notified such debt collector in writing of the dispute;
(d) threatening to sell or assign to another the obligation of the consumer with an attending false representation that the result of such sale or assignment would be that the consumer would lose any defense to the alleged debt or would be subject to illegal collection attempts;
(e) threatening that the debtor will be arrested for nonpayment of an alleged debt without proper court proceedings; however, nothing herein shall prevent a debt collector from informing the debtor that the debtor may be arrested after proper court proceedings in cases where the debtor has violated the criminal laws of this state;
(f) threatening to file charges, complaints, or criminal action against a debtor when in fact the debtor has not violated any criminal laws; provided, however, nothing herein shall prevent a debt collector from threatening to institute civil lawsuits or other judicial proceedings to collect a debt;
(g) threatening that nonpayment of an alleged debt will result in the seizure, repossession, or sale of any property of that person without proper court proceedings; however, nothing herein shall prevent a debt collector from exercising or threatening to exercise a statutory or contractual right of seizure, repossession, or sale which does not require court proceedings; or
(h) threatening to take any action prohibited by law.

Harassment; Abuse

In connection with the collection of or attempt to collect any debt alleged to be due and owing by a consumer, no debt collector may oppress, harass, or abuse any person by methods which employ the following practices:

(a) using profane or obscene language or language that is intended to unreasonably abuse the hearer or reader;
(b) placing telephone calls without disclosure of the name of the individual making the call, and with the willful intent to annoy or harass or threaten any person at the called number;
(c) causing expense to any person in the form of long distance telephone tolls, telegram fees, or other charges incurred by a medium of communication, without first disclosing the name of the person making the telephone call or transmitting the communication; or
(d) causing a telephone to ring repeatedly or continuously or making repeated and continuous telephone calls, with the willful intent to harass any person at the called number.

Unfair or Unconscionable Means

No debt collector may collect or attempt to collect any debt by unfair or unconscionable means employing the following practices:
(a) seeking or obtaining any written statement or acknowledgment of life where the obligation was not in fact incurred for such necessaries; or
(b) collecting or attempting to collect any interest or other charge, fee, or expense incidental to the obligation unless such interest or incidental fee, charge, or expense is expressly authorized by the agreement creating the obligation or legally chargeable to the consumer. However, creditors may charge reasonable reinstatement fees as consideration for renewal of a real estate loan or contract of sale, after default, if the additional fees are included in a written contract executed at the time of renewal.

Fraudulent, Deceptive, or Misleading Representations

No debt collector may collect or attempt to collect debts or obtain information concerning a consumer by any fraudulent, deceptive, or misleading representations which employ the following practices:
(a) using any name while engaged in the collection of debts other than the true business or professional name or the true personal or legal name of the debt collector; or failing to maintain a list of all business or professional names known to be used or formerly used by individual persons collecting debts or attempting to collect debts for the debt collector;
(b) falsely representing that the debt collector has information in his possession or something of value for the consumer in order to solicit or discover information about the consumer;
(c) failing to clearly disclose, in any communication with the debtor, the name of the person to whom the debt has been assigned or is owed at the time of making any demand for money (provided, however, this subsection shall not apply to persons servicing or collecting real estate first lien mortgage loans);
(d) failing to clearly disclose, in any communication with the debtor, that the debt collector is attempting to collect a debt, unless such communication is for the purpose of discovering the whereabouts of the debtor;
(e) using any written communication which fails to clearly indicate the name of the debt collector and the debt collector's street address, when the written notice

refers to an alleged delinquent debt; (the foregoing shall not require disclosure of names and addresses of employees of debt collectors);
(f) using any written communication which demands a response to a place other than the debt collector's or creditor's street address or post office box; (the foregoing shall not require response to the address of an employee of a debt collector);
(g) misrepresenting the character, extent, or amount of a debt against a consumer, or misrepresenting its status in any judicial or governmental proceedings;
(h) falsely representing that any debt collector is vouched for, bonded by, affiliated with, or an instrumentality, agent, or official of this state or any agency of federal, state, or local government;
(i) using, distributing, or selling any written communication which simulates or falsely represents to be a document authorized, issued, or approved by a court, an official, a governmental agency, or any other legally constituted or authorized governmental authority, or which creates a false impression about its source, authorization, or approval; or using any seal or insignia or design which simulates that of any governmental agency;
(j) representing that a debt may be increased by the addition of attorney's fees, investigation fees, service fees, or other charges when there is no written contract or statute authorizing such additional fees or charges;
(k) representing that a debt will definitely be increased by the addition of attorney's fees, investigation fees, service fees, or other charges when the award of such fee or charge is discretionary by a court of law;
(l) falsely representing the status or true nature of the services rendered by the debt collector or his business;
(m) using any written communication which violates or fails to conform to the United States postal laws and regulations;
(n) using any communication which purports to be from any attorney or law firm, when in fact it is not;
(o) representing that a debt is being collected by an attorney when it is not; or
(p) representing that a debt is being collected by an independent, bona fide organization engaged in the business of collecting past due accounts when the debt is being collected by a subterfuge organization under the control and direction of the person to whom the debt is owed; however, nothing herein shall prohibit a creditor from owning or operating its own bona fide debt collection agency.

Deceptive Use of Credit Bureau Name

No person shall use the term "credit bureau," "retail merchants," or "retail merchants association" in his business or trade name unless such person is in fact engaged in gathering, recording, and disseminating favorable as well as unfavorable information relative to the credit worthiness, financial responsibility, paying habits, and other similar information regarding individuals, firms, corporations, and any other legal entity being considered for credit extension so that a prospective creditor may be able to make a sound decision in the extension of credit. This paragraph shall not apply to any nonprofit retail trade association consisting of individual members and qualifying as a bona fide business league as defined by the United States Internal Revenue Service, and which nonprofit retail trade association does not engage in the business of debt collection or credit reporting.

And don't think because this law uses "their debt collector" it doesn't apply to you. Anyone who collects debts, including their own, is a debt collector under this law.

So how should you go about collecting a debt? First, after you have read the law very carefully, make reasonable phone calls and send a reasonable letter letting the person who owes you money know that you expect to be paid and if you are not, you will take all available steps to try and collect through the courts. Sometimes the threat of a lawsuit, which usually increases the amount owed through the addition of court costs and attorney's fees, is enough to get your money. You also should consider trying to work out a payment plan with the debtor, or even taking less than 100 cents on a dollar. Remember, a bird in the hand is worth two in the bush. As I told you before, it is very difficult, and sometimes impossible, to make someone pay who just refuses to do so.

If after sending your letters and making your phone calls you still don't have your money, you now have three options:

1. Give up, and take a loss (learning a lesson and knowing never to deal with that person again).
2. Give the account to a collection agency. (The collection agency may charge you a small amount up front but usually takes its money from the amount it ultimately collects).
3. Sue (either in small claims court or with an attorney).

The decision of what to do at this point depends on what you think the likelihood of getting your money through continued efforts is. Remember, everything you do from this point on will cost you in terms of time and money. If the amount is small, or recovery unlikely (read pages 82–83 to determine if you will be able to collect) you may be better off to just chalk this one up as a lesson of doing business. On the other hand, if there is a good chance you will get your money, you may want to sue; and contrary to what you may think, you can do this without a lawyer if the amount is under $5,000.

When You Have to Sue

Now that you have made the decision that you are owed enough money that it is worth your time and effort to sue, you must next decide whether to do it yourself or with an attorney. **If the amount you are owed is less than $5,000 you can sue in small claims court without the assistance of an attorney.** Small claims court is easy and efficient and usually gets you the money you are owed, but there are some reasons why you might want to consider hiring an attorney to file your suit in District Court:

1. Small claims court is limited to $5,000. If your claim is for more than that you *must* file in District or County Court. Also, remember that if your claim was brought under the Deceptive Trade Practices Act (see Chapter 8) you are entitled to up to three times your damages (five times in special circumstances).
2. Your claim is legally or factually complicated. An attorney may be better able to successfully resolve the problem.
3. The person you are suing is going to fight the claim. If you win in small claims court the person you sue has an absolute right to file an appeal and start the whole thing all over again. While this is not the usual case, if the person you are suing makes it clear that he is going to fight you all the way, it may be better to get an attorney and start in District or County Court. Appeal from this court is not absolute and only issues of law can be appealed.
4. You are uncomfortable representing yourself. Don't be embarrassed to admit that going to court to represent yourself scares you. You are not alone. There is an old saying that the man who represents himself has a fool for a client. Sometimes this applies to us all.
5. Finally, the use of an attorney may let the other party know you are serious and result in an early settlement. Even though you have written letters telling the other person you are going to sue, they may still not take you seriously until they receive a letter from a real attorney.

Remember, in most cases when you sue for money owed you for payment you will be entitled to attorney's fees from the other side if you win. Therefore, hiring an attorney may not really cost too much if you do recover a judgment. Once you decide to hire an attorney, read Chapter 12, and by all means make sure you find out how much he is going to charge, and how and when he is going to collect his fee, before you hire an attorney.

Going To Small Claims Court

Suing in small claims court is easy. You can sue anyone who is actually in Texas, or who has a permanent home in Texas, or who is doing business in Texas. To sue a sole proprietorship, the proprietor must be in Texas; to sue a partnership, the partners must be in Texas; and, to sue a corporation it must do business in the state. For more information on each of these forms of business re-read Chapters 1–5.

There are many small claims courts, so after you decide to go to court you must find the proper location for your complaint. Generally you must sue in the court that covers the area where the person you are suing lives or where your business operates or where the transaction took place. For example, suppose you repair a garage in a rental unit for a man who lives in another part of town. You could sue either where the rental property is located or where the man responsible lives. If you sue anywhere else he has the right to have it moved back to one of those courts.

Small claims courts are part of the Justice Courts, so look in the phone book under Justice of the Peace. If you are not sure which precinct covers the location where your claim arises, call any of the clerks and ask for their help. Small claims clerks are generally very helpful.

After you find the right court go down to the clerk's office and fill in what is called a *petition*. This is the document that starts the lawsuit. Make sure that you have the correct name and address of the person you are suing. If you do not, the court will be unable to serve them with your papers and the suit will never be brought to court. If you are suing a corporation call the secretary of state in Austin (512) 463-5555, and ask for the name of the "agent for service." This is the person who is designated to accept legal papers for the corporation.

Figure 11-1 (page 81) shows a typical petition. **Read it over, fill it in, and give it to the clerk. Remember, if you have any questions, ask.**

You, the person suing, are called the *plaintiff*. After you file the petition and pay your fees (about $50), the court will have the constable or sheriff serve the *defendant*, the person or business being sued, with the papers. The defendant will then have a short period of time to answer your complaint; that is, state his side of the story and say why you should not win. If the de-

In the Small Claims Court of __________ County, Texas

Plaintiff
vs.
Defendant
State of Texas
County of __________

(Plaintiff), whose post office address is

____

Street and Number

______________________, ______________________,

City County,

Texas, being duly sworn, on his oath deposes and says that (defendant), whose post office address is

____, __________

County, Texas, is justly indebted to him in the sum of __________ Dollars and __________ Cents ($_____), for ____

____

(here the nature of the claim should be stated in concise form and without technicality, including all pertinent dates), and that there are no counter claims existing against the plaintiff, except ______

____

____

Plaintiff

Subscribed and sworn to before me this _____ day of __________, 19__.

____

Judge

Figure 11-1. Typical small claims court petition.

fendant thinks *you owe him money*, he can counterclaim and ask the court to award him a judgment against you. If the defendant does nothing, he is considered to be in default, and you will win so long as you can convince the judge that you are entitled to the money. Make sure that you ask for the cost of your lawsuit in your petition so the judgment will cover your damages plus the costs incurred.

If the defendant answers, a date will be set for trial. Either party has the right to ask for a jury trial. If you do not, the judge will hear the case alone. Most small court hearings are very informal. Both sides have a chance to tell their story to a judge and then the judge may ask some questions. Be sure to be prepared. If you have any evidence such as invoices, receipts, pictures, etc., bring them with you. The better prepared party usually wins. Also, if you have any witnesses, for example, the worker who completed the work, bring them along.

Usually the other side will not have an attorney in small claims court, but if he does don't be intimidated. The judge will make sure that you are treated fairly and have a fair chance to tell your side of the story. This isn't television, the judge won't allow the lawyer to jump up and object to everything you say.

After both sides have had their chance to talk the judge will make a ruling. Usually the judge acts as soon as you are through but he may wait a brief period of time to think about it. In most cases once a ruling is made that is the end. If you win you are usually paid promptly, and if you lose you know that you had a fair day in court. But two problems can arise. First, as we said before, either side can appeal this judgment and start the whole thing over again. You will have to wait to see if the defendant is going to appeal. If you lose and want to appeal you will probably need an attorney to help you and you will have to post a bond. Remember, you have 30 days to appeal so act promptly. The more serious problem that can arise, however, is getting your money once you win if the defendant does not voluntarily pay. As you will see, Texas is a debtor's paradise.

The Bottom Line

Small claims court really is a "people's court"; don't be afraid to use it. It is fast, simple, and very often just filing suit gets you the money you are owed.

Collecting a Judgment

After you go to court and win, whether it is small claims court or district court, the judge will award you a judgment. Basically this is an official pronouncement that you are right and the defendant owes you the money you said he did. The problem is that simply getting a judgment does not put any money in your pocket. As we said before, most people will voluntarily pay a judgment once they lose, but you should know what your legal rights are if they don't; and as you will see, in Texas it can be very difficult to get your money after you win in court.

Once you have a judgment, the next step is to use the available legal proceedings to enforce that judgment, and force the debtor to pay. For example, let's say that you recently sold a $350 washing machine to someone who never paid you. You went to small claims court and won. Now what do you do with this judgment? Well, basically you go back to the court to have the court *execute* on your judgment. In other words, you ask the court to have the constable or sheriff go out and take some of the debtor's property, sell it, and give you the money you are owed. And there are two ways the court can do this. First, they can issue what is called an *abstract of judgment*. This is a piece of paper that you file in the county courthouse to get a lien on the debtor's real estate. If the person you sue owns non-exempt real estate, you have the right to force its sale to get your money. As a more practical matter the abstract will tie up any purchase or sale of real estate by the debtor and will appear on his credit report. This usually is enough to get you your money.

The second method of forcing payment is called a *writ of execution*. This is a court order to the constable telling him to take the debtor's non-exempt personal property such as a boat, or a valuable painting, and sell it to pay you the money you are owed. Similar to this device is a *writ of garnishment* which allows you to get money or property of the debtor that another person is holding. For example, if you know the debtor has money in the bank, or an IRA, or stocks and bonds, you can get a writ of garnishment to have these funds seized and sold to pay you off. If you have any questions about getting your money after you have won in court, don't be afraid to ask the clerk for help.

Exempt Property

Now that you have just finished reading how to sue someone, and what devices there are to get your money, it is time to fill you in on the truth about Texas law. **Texas is a debtor's state. If the person you sue doesn't want to pay you it is very hard to force them to do so.** This is because of the Texas exemption laws. You probably noted that whenever we told you what property you could get to satisfy your judgment we referred to it as *non-exempt*. You are only allowed to take the debtor's non-exempt property, and in Texas that is not very much. In Texas much of an average debtor's property is exempt from execution. That means that you cannot force the sale of this property to pay your debt. Here is a list of the property that most creditors cannot touch:

1. All current wages.
2. The homestead. (That includes, in a city, one acre of land with all improvements regardless of value.)
3. Personal property valued at $30,000 for an individual and $60,000 for a family, if the personal property is any of the types listed below:
   - Furnishings of a home, including family heirlooms, and provisions for consumption.
   - All of the following: implements of farming or ranching; tools, equipment, apparatus (including a car or a boat), and books used in any trade or profession; wearing apparel; two firearms; athletic and sporting equipment; and jewelry (up to 25% of limit).
   - A two-, three-, or four-wheel vehicle for each member of the family with a driver's license.
   - Various animals.
   - The present value of any life insurance policy to the extent that a member or members of the family of the insured person or a dependent or dependents of a single, adult person is a beneficiary thereof.

As you can see, for most debtors there is very little non-exempt property left for you to collect against. In most cases the only property you can get is money in the bank, stocks and bonds, rental property, or personal property in excess of that exempted by law. If you are thinking of suing someone, you should find out whether they have any non-exempt property. If they do not, and you do not think an adverse credit report will be enough to compel payment, you may be better off just writing off the debt. A lawsuit could be throwing good money after bad.

The Bottom Line

Small claims court is easy to use, and you are ensured your day in court. But winning a judgment in Texas doesn't guarantee you will be paid. Try to find out if your debtor has any non-exempt assets before you throw good money after bad.

Ways to Protect Against Nonpayment

As you have seen from reading this chapter, collecting money that people owe you can often be difficult, or impossible. To protect yourself from this happening there are basically two things you can do. You can demand payment in cash, cashier's check, or certified check; in advance; or you can take steps to ensure that if you are not paid you have some of the debtor's property to go after. Taking a personal check is also fairly safe. Even though a check may bounce you are still substantially protected. **Giving someone a check that bounces, in exchange for goods or services, is criminal.** In Texas you can criminally prosecute someone who gives you a bad check. Here is what this law says:

Issuance of Bad Check

(a) A person commits an offense if he issues or passes a check or similar sight order for the payment of money knowing that the issuer does not have sufficient funds in or on deposit with the bank or other drawee for the payment in full of the check or order as well as all other checks or orders outstanding at the time of issuance.
(b) This section does not prevent the prosecution from establishing the required knowledge by direct evidence; however, for purposes of this section, the issuer's knowledge of insufficient funds is presumed (except in the case of a postdated check or order) if:

(1) he had no account with the bank or other drawee at the time he issued the check or order; or
(2) payment was refused by the bank or other drawee for lack of funds or insufficient funds on presentation within 30 days after issue and the issuer failed to pay the holder in full within 10 days after receiving notice of that refusal.

(c) Notice for purposes of Subsection (b)(2) of this section may be notice in writing, sent by registered or certified mail with return receipt requested or by telegram with report of delivery requested, and addressed to the issuer at this address shown on:

(1) the check or order;
(2) the records of the bank or other drawee; or
(3) the records of the person to whom the check or order has been issued or passed.

(d) If notice is given in accordance with Subsection (c) of this section, it is presumed that the notice was received no later than five days after it was sent.

So, if you take cash or a check you are usually protected, but many customers will not want to pay in advance, or will need time to pay off a large sum. In these cases you should protect yourself by taking a *lien* on some of their property. Even though you may not have thought about it, you are probably already familiar with how this works. For example, when you bought your car you probably gave the bank a lien on the car to ensure that you would pay the note. **A lien gives the creditor the right to take a specific piece of property, and sell it, in the event he is not paid.** In the case of your car, if you don't pay the bank or finance company, they have the right to take your car, sell it, and apply the proceeds to your debt. Basically there are two types of liens you should know about, the security interest and the mechanic's or materialman's lien.

A security interest is a voluntary agreement, between you and your customer, where your customer agrees to let you have the property back if he doesn't pay you. Your interest in the property is called a "security interest" and you file a form, called a financing statement, with either the county clerk or the secretary of state to make your interest superior to everyone else's. (A copy of a security agreement may be found in Appendix B, Form 16.) Once you have a security interest the law lets you take the property back yourself, sell it, and apply the proceeds to the amount you are owed. The only major restriction on your rights is that you must take the property back peacefully; that is, without any action that results in, or is likely to result in, violence. Here is an example of how you might take advantage of this legal device:

Marvin sells appliances. Most of his sales are on credit and the average price for an appliance is $500. Recently he sold a washing machine to Mary. Mary paid $100 down and agreed to pay the rest in monthly installments of $25. Marvin had Mary sign a promissory note, gave all the proper disclosures **(Read Chapter 10 carefully)** and took a security interest in the machine. After a few months Mary came upon hard times and stopped paying.

If Marvin didn't take a security interest, his only right would be to try and collect the $350 Mary still owes by sending letters and by taking her to court if necessary. And as we just explained, even if he wins in court he may not get anything. On the other hand, because he has a security interest he has the right to go to her home and ask for the return of the machine. If he gets it he can sell it and keep the money he gets. If she refuses he can go to court and in a relatively simple proceeding have the court order her to give him the machine. Of course he would be entitled to collect whatever costs he incurred.

It should be obvious that a security interest gives you a much greater chance of getting paid in full. But it does take additional time and cost a few extra dollars to create one. If you think this device is what your business needs, speak with your attorney. For a small fee he or she should be able to provide you with all the forms you need and tell you just what to do to protect yourself. **You should not have to pay much for this information. Be sure to shop around for an attorney you can afford.**

A second way to achieve a result similar to a security interest is by taking what is generally called a mechanic's or materialman's lien. This lien is similar to the security interest in that it gives you rights against a debtor's property without the need to sue and get a judgment and in spite of exemption laws. The basic difference is that this lien can arise automatically; that is, there is not always the need for the debtor to sign an agreement before the work is done. For example:

> Sylvia is a mechanic who specializes in expensive German cars. Recently she repaired a car for a customer, who didn't have the money to pay and asked for credit. Sylvia learned long ago not to extend credit, so she said no, when you pay you can have the car. The customer told her it was his car and he wanted it back.

Under the law Sylvia has a mechanic's lien on the car for the value of the repairs she has done. This means that she can keep the car until she is paid, and if she is not paid she can sell the car, take the money she is owed, and give the rest, if any, back to her customer. We also should point out that if the customer were to give Sylvia a bad check to get the car back, Sylvia would have the right to re-take the car when the check bounced. Similar rules help the person who repairs or supplies materials for the repair of a home.

> L and L Construction recently agreed to remodel Fred's house. The contract price was $15,000 with periodic payments as the work progressed. The final payment of 20% was to be made after completion. Everything went fine until the work was complete and Fred refused to pay. L and L knew that filing a lawsuit was expensive and often useless, but fortunately they had taken the proper steps to create a mechanic's lien on Fred's homestead. They now have the right to file their lien and if he still doesn't pay they can sell his home to get their money.

Whenever a person repairs or improves the property of another they are entitled to a mechanic's lien on the property. Also, when you supply the materials for such work you can get a lien for the value of the materials. **But there are certain legal prerequisites that must be met before such a lien is valid.** If you do not follow these rules, you may not have a lien, and trying to assert a lien when you don't have one can get you in lots of trouble. For example, to get a lien on a homestead, you must:

1. Have a written contract before any work is done.
2. If the owner is married both spouses must sign.
3. The lien must be filed with the county clerk.

For example, if you began work before the contract was signed you would not have a lien. **These liens are not very complicated, but you should talk to your attorney to find out exactly what you should do and how and when you should do it.** Once your attorney gives you the basic instructions you can do it yourself from then on.

One last point for those of you who do home repair. Under the law an owner is required to withhold 10% of the contract price owed a contractor for 30 days after the work is completed. An owner who does this is usually relieved of any obligations to unpaid sub-contractors or suppliers. This means that if you have a claim against the owner based on the fact that you were not paid by a general contractor, you had better assert it within 30 days after completion. If you don't, you may lose your lien.

The Bottom Line

There are ways to protect yourself when it comes to being paid. First, try and insist on cash or a cashier's or certified check. Second, when you must extend credit have your attorney help you prepare the papers necessary for you to get a lien on your customer's property.

12

You and Your Lawyer

Let's face facts. No matter how many self-help books you buy, no matter how much you learn about the law, and no matter how hard you try to avoid legal hassles, nearly every business-person finds that, sooner or later, he or she needs a lawyer. And unfortunately, some who use a lawyer discover that they sometimes have problems dealing with lawyers. Studies have shown that many people avoid lawyers because they do not trust them. We can't emphasize enough that this approach is wrong. If you feel that the advice of a lawyer is necessary by all means get it! But protect yourself by taking steps to ensure that you choose a lawyer who is right for you, and that you know your rights if a problem arises.

Finding a Lawyer Who's Right for You

We would like to be able to tell you that now that you own this book you will never need the assistance of a lawyer, but unfortunately that isn't so. No matter how much law you learn from reading this book there will still be times when the advice and assistance of a professional is necessary; either because the problem is too complex to resolve yourself, or because the amount involved is so large and the risk so great, that you want to make sure things are done properly. When this happens you should know how to locate lawyers, what questions to ask to make sure that the one you choose is the best one for you, and how to deal with a lawyer once he or she has been hired. One thing you should always keep in mind: **The lawyer you hire works for you, and with you. It is essential that you find someone you trust, whom you can communicate with, and who will treat you fairly.**

Shop Around and Compare

The first thing to remember when you are looking for a lawyer is that there are probably many lawyers in your area who can competently help you, and you should shop around before you make the decision of who to hire. For example, one of the authors did a television report recently and called more than twenty lawyers asking what they would charge for a basic will. They were all given the same information and asked for a price. Their prices ranged from $45 to over $600. A reporter went and got the $45 will and showed it to an expert who stated that it was a perfectly fine will and did everything that was requested. Perhaps the lawyer who charged $600 would have done more, but that is not the point. All that was asked for was a simple will, and paying for things you don't need is a waste of money. As this points out, a few simple phone calls can save you a lot of money, especially on standard legal services such as incorporation, partnership agreements, bills of sale, leases, promissory notes, and security agreements.

So how do you decide who to call? Well, do the same thing you would do if you needed a doctor or mechanic or a plumber. (Lawyers love to be compared to plumbers and mechanics.) Ask your friends. See if they have dealt with a lawyer lately and what they thought of him or her. Next, try the yellow pages and other advertising. Lawyer advertising is still relatively new, and more and more lawyers are starting to use it. Granted, some lawyer advertising is sleazy, but that doesn't mean you should not consider calling the lawyer who has a tasteful ad in the yellow pages. Review lawyer advertising the same way you would any other ads. The advertising is a good reflection of the lawyer's character. If you still haven't come up with enough names, the legal community itself has organizations to help you. Local and state bar associations maintain lawyer referral services that list attorneys who specialize in certain areas, and who have agreed to talk with you for a very small fee. Call these organizations and tell them what type of a lawyer you need. They will give you several names of people in your area for you to call.

Once you get several names you should arrange to speak with several before choosing one. It may even be a good idea to get a lawyer before you have problems. Once you think about starting your business, find yourself an attorney who will represent you if you have any problems or have to make big decisions. View the attorney as the family doctor, someone you call in an emergency. The probabilities are that some time in the future you will need an attorney. Find one before a crisis arises.

The Bottom Line

Find a lawyer you trust whose judgment you respect. Contact the lawyer before you sign an agreement or complete a significant transaction. At this point the lawyer can help you structure the transaction to protect you and your business.

Talking With Your Lawyer

So what should you ask the lawyer when you first meet with him or her? Well first, talk about what you are interested in and get a feel for what kind of person the lawyer is. For example, if you think you will need someone that you can call every couple of days and ask questions, let the attorney know. Ask how he or she would feel about that. Are they in their office a lot or do they do mostly trial work? How many other clients do they have with problems like you will have? How long have they been in practice? Where did they get their college degrees? And finally, but most importantly, how are they going to charge you and how much are they going to charge you? Remember, many lawyers charge differently, and things that sound similar can be quite different.

Some lawyers charge an hourly fee, so your fee will depend upon how many hours the lawyer spends on the matter. Other lawyers will agree to a set fee, regardless of how much time is spent. If you are asking a lawyer to sue someone, some lawyers will accept as their fee a percentage of whatever they recover for you. With this type of fee arrangement, you only pay a fee if the lawyer recovers something. However, most lawyers would want you to pay the costs of the lawsuit, such as court filing fees, no matter what happens in the case.

Make sure you understand how any given situation will be billed. Let's say that you want a lawyer to incorporate you. One tells you that it will cost $250 and another says $500. The first one is cheaper, right? Not necessarily. If the filing fees charged by the State of Texas are included in the second one, and they are not included in the first, then the second attorney would actually be charging you less. **Always ask what the total fee will be and how it will be computed.**

Also, be sure to ask if the attorney uses paralegals, nonlawyer personnel who help and are billed at a different rate, and how phone calls are billed. Most lawyers have minimum billing units. You may be surprised to find that you were charged for a quarter of an hour every time you called to see how your case was going. This could happen if the lawyer's minimum billing unit was a quarter of an hour.

Ask if the lawyer will handle your case personally or if it will be given to another person in the firm to handle. It doesn't do you any good to be impressed with one person only to find that you have hired another.

And finally, one piece of advice on how to deal with the lawyer who doesn't want to be bothered with all these questions and tells you, "I don't have to answer all these questions. I have been practicing law for a long time and if you don't trust me find another lawyer." Take his advice—find another lawyer.

The Bottom Line

Talk with the attorney before you hire him or her. If you are uncomfortable talk some more, or talk to someone else. Until you find a lawyer you trust and are comfortable with, keep looking.

Problems With Your Attorney

It is unfortunate, but many people have disputes with their lawyer. In most cases these disputes could have been avoided through better communication and more complete understanding of exactly what the attorney was going to do, how long it would take, and what it would cost. As we have emphasized, it is extremely important to talk with prospective lawyers and feel comfortable before you choose one. By doing this, it is much less likely that a dispute will arise. But it is still no guarantee, and if you have a problem with your attorney you should know what rights you have if it can't be resolved.

But before you even consider pursuing your rights against your lawyer, talk with him/her. Many disputes are simply misunderstandings and can be resolved through better communication. If after talking with your lawyer you are still dissatisfied, there are two alternatives: you can sue your lawyer; or you can file a complaint with the State Bar Grievance Committee. Unlike most professions, lawyers depend upon a license issued by the state to practice their trade. And the organization that issues that license, the Texas State Bar, also regulates the profession and maintains a grievance committee to hear complaints about lawyers and to discipline them, if that is warranted. Although many argue that self-regulation is too easy on lawyers, each year hundreds are either suspended from the practice of law for a period of time, or disbarred and prohibited from practicing in this state.

Filing a Grievance

So what types of problems should you consider filing a grievance about? Lawyers are governed by what is called a "Code of Ethics," and if they violate that Code they are subject to discipline. Without going into all of the details, there are certain things that lawyers may not do, and if they do any of them they will be considered to be acting unethically, and subject to being suspended, or removed, from the practice of law. For example, lawyers may not:

- Take a client's property.
- Abandon a client's case.
- Lie to a client.
- Refuse to talk with a client.
- Represent a client if there is a conflict of interest that has not been disclosed.
- Fail to perform for a client.
- Act incompetently.

As you read this list you probably have noted one thing that is missing: disputes about fees. In most cases disputes about fees are not reviewable by the grievance committees. If the fee is grossly excessive, however, it could constitute unethical conduct on the part of the lawyer and could therefore be reviewed by the grievance committee.

If your lawyer engages in any of the above acts, it would be appropriate to file a grievance with the State Bar. The Bar will then investigate, and if it feels it is appropriate the Bar will hold a hearing. To get more information about filing a complaint against a lawyer you should contact: Office of the General Counsel, State Bar of Texas, P.O. Box 12487, Capital Station, Austin, Texas 78711, (800) 932-1900.

Remember, filing a complaint against a lawyer is a very serious matter. The lawyer may lose the right to practice if you are successful. If you are not sure about your complaint, talk with your lawyer and ask him or her to explain what is going on. You may be surprised to find out that there was a reasonable explanation for what you believed was unethical conduct. On the other hand, if you truly believe your lawyer has acted in an unethical manner, you should not hesitate to file a grievance with the Bar.

Suing Your Attorney

It shouldn't come as a surprise that lawyers, like anyone else, can be sued when they mess up. Just like doctors, a lawyer who acts negligently, or who lies, can be sued for malpractice. And if you can prove that your lawyer deceived you or didn't live up to the standards of other lawyers in your area, you may be able to recover damages. We say maybe because you must show more than just the fact that your lawyer messed up; you probably must also show that if he or she hadn't, you would have won your suit.

So what should you do if you believe your lawyer has acted negligently? Simple, see another lawyer. Although some lawyers have been reluctant to take cases against other lawyers, many now will, and will tell you if you have a case. You also should know that lawyers are subject to the law just like anyone else. This means that the Texas Deceptive Trade Practices Act, discussed in Chapter 8, applies to lawyers. If you can show that your lawyer violated this law, by either charging a grossly excessive fee or deceiving you, you can recover up to three times your damages plus your court costs. To use this law it is not necessary that you show your lawyer acted negligently, only that he or she misrepresented what they were going to do for you, or took advantage of you, or charged you a grossly excessive price. Make sure that you discuss the possibility of suing under the Texas Deceptive Trade Practices Act when you talk about suing your lawyer.

The Bottom Line

Lawyers are not above the law, and in fact are one of the most regulated professions. If you believe your lawyer has misled, deceived, or not properly represented you, consider filing a grievance with the State Bar or suing for malpractice.

Appendix A

Statutory Supplement

Appendix A

Statutory Supplement

1. Texas Uniform Partnership Act

TEXAS UNIFORM PARTNERSHIP ACT
[Revised Civil Statutes]

PART I.
PRELIMINARY PROVISIONS

Art. 6132b-1. **Name of Act**

This Act shall be known and may be cited as the Texas Uniform Partnership Act.

Art. 6132b-2. Definition of Terms

In this Act, "court" includes every court and judge having jurisdiction in the case.

"Business" includes every trade, occupation, or profession.

"Person" includes individuals, partnership, corporations, and other associations.

"Bankrupt" includes bankrupt under the Federal Bankruptcy Act or insolvent under any State Insolvent Act.

"Conveyance" includes every assignment, lease, mortgage, or encumbrance.

"Real property" includes land and any interest or estate in land.

"Registered limited liability partnership" means a partnership registered under Section 45-A and complying with Sections 45-b and 45-C.

Art. 6132b-3. Interpretation of Knowledge and Notice

(1) A person has "knowledge" of a fact within the meaning of this Act not only when he has actual knowledge thereof, but also when he has knowledge of such other facts as in the circumstances shows shows bad faith.

(2) A person has "notice" of a fact within the meaning of this Act when the person who claims the benefit of the notice:

(a) States the fact to such person, or

(b) Delivers through the mail, or by other means of communication, a written statement of the fact to such person or to a proper person at his place of business or residence.

Art. 6132b-4. Rules of Construction

(1) The rule that statutes in derogation of the common law are to be strictly construed shall have no application to this Act.

(2) The law of estoppel shall apply under this Act.

(3) The law of agency shall apply under this Act.

(4) This Act shall be so interpreted and construed as to effect its general purpose to make uniform the law of those states which enact it.

(5) This Act shall not be construed so as to impair the obligations of any contract existing when the Act goes into effect, nor to affect any action or proceedings begun or right accrued before this Act takes effect.

Art. 6132b-5. Rules for Cases Not Provided for in This Act

In any case not provided for in this Act the rules of law and equity, including the law merchant, shall govern.

PART II.
NATURE OF A PARTNERSHIP

Art. 6132b-6. Partnership Defined

(1) A partnership is an association of two or more persons to carry on as co-owners a business for profit.

(2) But any association formed under any other statute of this state, or any statute adopted by authority, other than the authority of this state, is not a partnership

under this Act, unless such association would have been a partnership in this state prior to the adoption of this Act; but this Act shall apply to limited partnerships except in so far as the statutes relating to such partnerships are inconsistent herewith.

(3) An association is not a partnership under this Act if:

(a) The word "association" or "associates" is part of and always used in the name under which it transacts business, and

(b) Its assumed name certificates, filed in accordance with law, contain a statement substantially as follows: "This association intends not to be governed by the Texas Uniform Partnership Act," and

(c) The business it transacts is wholly or partly engaging in an activity in which corporations cannot lawfully engage.

This Subsection shall not be construed to change in any way the law applicable to associations which are not partnerships under this Act.

Art. 6132b-6-A. Persons Who May be Partners

(1) In this section, "person" includes without limitation:

(a) A corporation;
(b) A general or limited partnership;
(c) A trustee or trust;
(d) An executor, administrator, or estate; and
(e) A natural person.

Art. 6132b-7. Rules for Determining the Existence of a Partnership

In determining whether a partnership exists, these rules shall apply:

(1) Except as provided by Section 16 persons who are not partners as to each other are not partners as to third persons.

(2) Joint tenancy, tenancy in common, tenancy by the entireties, joint property, common property, or part ownership does not of itself establish a partnership, whether such co-owners do or do not share any profits made by the use of the property.

(3) The sharing of gross returns does not of itself establish a partnership, whether or not the persons sharing them have a joint or common right or interest in any property from which the returns are derived.

(4) The receipt by a person of a share of the profits of a business is prima facie evidence that he is a partner in the business, but no such inference shall be drawn if such profits were received in payment:

(a) As a debt by installments or otherwise,

(b) As wages of an employee or rent to a landlord,

(c) As an annuity to a widow or representative of a deceased partner,

(d) As interest on a loan, though the amount of payment vary with the profits of the business,

(e) As the consideration for the sale of a good will of a business or other property by installments or otherwise.

(5) Operation of a mineral property under a joint operating agreement does not of itself establish a partnership.

Art. 6132b-8. Partnership Property

(1) All property originally brought into the partnership stock or subsequently acquired by purchase or otherwise, on account of the partnership, is partnership property.

(2) Unless the contrary intention appears, property acquired with partnership funds is partnership property.

(3) Any estate in real property may be acquired in the partnership name. Title so acquired can be conveyed only in the partnership name.

(4) A conveyance to a partnership in the partnership name, though without words of inheritance, passes the entire estate of the grantor unless a contrary intent appears.

PART III.
RELATIONS OF PARTNERS
TO PERSONS DEALING
WITH THE PARTNERSHIP

Art. 6132b-9. Partner Agent of Partnership as to Partnership Business

(1) Every partner is an agent of the partnership for the purpose of its business, and the act of every partner, including the execution in the partnership name of any instrument, for apparently carrying on in the usual way the business of the partnership of which he is a member binds the partnership, unless the partner so acting has in fact no authority to act for the partnership in the particular matter, and the person with whom he is dealing has knowledge of the fact that he has no such authority.

(2) An act of a partner which is not apparently for the carrying on of the business of the partnership in the usual way does not bind the partnership unless authorized by the other partners.

(3) Unless authorized by the other partners or unless they have abandoned the business, one or more but less than all the partners have no authority to:

(a) Assign the partnership property in trust for creditors or on the assignee's promise to pay the debts of the partnership.

(b) Dispose of the good-will of the business,

(c) Do any other act which would make it impossible to carry on the ordinary business of a partnership,

(d) Confess a judgment,

(e) Submit a partnership claim or liability to arbitration or reference.

(4) No act of a partner in contravention of a restriction on authority shall bind the partnership to persons having knowledge of the restriction.

Art. 6132b-10. Conveyance of Real Property of the Partnership

(1) Where title to real property is in the partnership name, any partner may convey title to such property by a conveyance executed in the partnership name; but the partnership may recover such property unless the partner's act binds the partnership under the provisions of paragraph (1) of Section 9, or unless such property has been conveyed by the grantee or a person claiming through such grantee to a holder for value without knowledge that the partner, in making the conveyance, has exceeded his authority.

(2) Where title to real property is in the name of the partnership, a conveyance executed by a partner, in his own name, passes the equitable interest of the partnership, provided the act is one within the authority of the partner under the provisions of paragraph (1) of Section 9.

(3) Where title to real property is in the name of one or more but not all the partners, and the record does not disclose the right of the partnership, the partners in whose name the title stands may convey title to such property, but the partnership may recover such property if the partners' act does not bind the partnership under the provisions of paragraph (1) of Section 9, unless the purchaser or his assignee, is a holder for value, without knowledge.

(4) Where the title to real property is in the name of one or more or all the partners, or in a third person in trust for the partnership, a conveyance executed by a partner in the partnership name, or in his own name, passes the equitable interest of the partnership, provided the act is one within the authority of the partner under the provisions of paragraph (1) of Section 9.

(5) Where the title to real property is in the names of all the partners a conveyance executed by all the partners passes all their rights in such property.

(6) Nothing in this Section shall be deemed to modify the statutes of limitations of actions for lands.

Art. 6132b-11. Partnership Bound by Admission of Partner

An admission or representation made by any partner concerning partnership affairs within the scope of his authority as defined by this Act is evidence against the partnership.

Art. 6132b-12. Partnership Charged with Knowledge of or Notice to Partner

Notice to any partner of any matter relating to partnership affairs, and the knowledge of the partner acting in the particular matter, acquired while a partner or then present to his mind, and the knowledge of any other partner who reasonably could and should have communicated it to the acting partner, operate as notice to or knowledge to the partnership, except in the case of a fraud on the partnership committed by or with the consent of that partner.

Art. 6132b-13. Partnership Bound by Partner's Wrongful Act

Where, by any wrongful act or omission of any partner acting in the ordinary course of the business of the partnership or with the authority of his co-partners, loss or injury is cause to any person, not being a partner in the partnership, or any penalty is incurred, the partnership is liable therefor to the same extent as the partner so acting or omitting to act.

Art. 6132b-14. Partnership Bound by Partner's Breach of Trust

The partnership is bound to make good the loss:

(a) Where one partner acting within the scope of his apparent authority receives money or property of a third person and misapplies it; and

(b) Where the partnership in the course of its business receives money or property of a third person and the money or property so received is misapplied by any partner while it is in the custody of the partnership.

Art. 6132b-15. NATURE OF PARTNER'S LIABILITY IN ORDINARY PARTNERSHIP AND IN REGISTERED LIMITED LIABILITY PARTNERSHIP.

(1) Except as provided by paragraph (2) of this Section, all partners are liable jointly and severally for all debts and obligations of the partnership including those under Sections 13 and 14.

(2) A partner in a registered limited liability partnership is not individually liable for debts and obligations of the partnership arising from errors, omissions, negligence, incompetence, or malfeasance committed in the course of the partnership business by another partner or a representative of the partnership not working under the supervision or direction of the first partner at the time the errors, omissions, negligence, incompetence, or malfeasance occurred, unless the first partner:

(a) was directly involved in the specific activity in which the errors, omissions, negligence, incompetence, or malfeasance were committed by the other partner or representative; or

(b) had notice or knowledge of the errors, omissions, negligence, incompetence, or malfeasance by the other partner or representative at the time of occurrence.

(3) Paragraph (2) does not affect the joint and several liability of a partner for debts and obligations of the partnership arising from any cause other than those specified in paragraph (2).

(4) Paragraph (2) does not affect the liability of partnership assets for partnership debts and obligations.

Art. 6132b-16. Partner by Estoppel

(1) When a person, by words spoken or written or by conduct, represents himself, or consents to another representing him to any one, as a partner in an existing partnership or with one or more persons not actual partners, he is liable to any such person to whom such representation has been made, who has, on the faith of such representation, given credit to the actual or apparent partnership, and if he has made such representation or consented to its being made in a public manner he is liable to such person, whether the representation has or has not been made or communicated to such person so giving credit by or with the knowledge of the apparent partner making the representation or consenting to its being made:

(a) When a partnership liability results, he is liable as though he were an actual member of the partnership;

(b) When no partnership liability results, he is liable jointly with the other persons, if any, so consenting to the contract or representation as to incur liability, otherwise separately.

(2) When a person has been thus represented to be a partner in an existing partnership, or with one or more persons not actual partners, he is an agent of the persons consenting to such representation to bind them to the same extent and in the same manner as though he were a partner in fact, with respect to persons who rely upon the representation. When all the members of the existing partnership consent to the representation, a partnership act or obligation results; but in all other cases it is the joint act or obligation of the persons acting and the persons consenting to the representation.

(3) A represention that a person is an "associate" or a "non-partner member" of a partnership is not a representation that he is a partner in the partnership.

Art. 6132b-17. Liability of Incoming Partner

A person admitted as a partner into an existing partnership is liable for all the obligations of the partnership arising before his admission as though he had been a partner when such obligations were incurred, except that this liability shall be satisfied only out of partnership property.

PART IV.
RELATIONS OF PARTNERS
TO ONE ANOTHER

Art. 6132b-18. Rules Determining Rights and Duties of Partners and Employees

(1) The rights and duties of the partners in relation to the partnership shall be determined, subject to any agreement between them, by the following rules:

(a) Each partner shall be repaid his contributions, whether by way of capital or advances to the partnership property, and share equally in the profits and surplus remaining after all liabilities, including those to partners, are satisfied; and must contribute toward the losses, whether of capital or otherwise, sustained by the partnership according to his share in the profits.

(b) The partnership must indemnify every partner in respect of payment made and personal liabilities, reasonably incurred by him in the ordinary and proper conduct of its business, or for the preservation of its business or property.

(c) A partner, who in aid of the partnership makes any payment or advance beyond the amount of capital which he agreed to contribute, shall paid interest from the date of the payment or advance.

(d) A partner shall receive interest on the capital contributed by him only from the date when repayment should be made.

(e) All partners have equal rights in the management and conduct of the partnership business.

(f) No partner is entitled to remuneration for acting in the partnership business, except that a surviving partner is entitled to reasonable compensation for his services in winding up the partnership affairs.

(g) No person can become a member of a partnership without the consent of all the partners.

(h) Any difference arising as to ordinary matters connected with the partnership business may be decided by a majority of the partners; but no act in contravention of any agreement between the partners may be done rightfully without the consent of all the parties.

(2) By written agreement, the partners may establish various classes of partners (such as "senior partners," "junior partners," "managing partners" and others) and may provide for their varying rights and duties in relation to the partnership.

(3) By written agreement, the partners may establish various classes of non-partner employees (such as "associates," "non-partner members" and others) and may provide for their varying rights and duties in relation to the partnership.

Art. 6132b-19. Partnership Books

The partnership books shall be kept, subject to any agreement between the partners, at the principal place of business of the partnership, and every partner shall at all times have access to and may inspect and copy any of them.

Art. 6132b-20. Duty of Partners to Render Information

Partners shall render on demand true and full information of all things affecting the partnership to any partner or the legal representative of any deceased partner or partner under legal disability.

Art. 6132b-21. Partner Accountable as a Fiduciary

(1) Every partner must account to the partnership for any benefit, and hold as trustee for it any profits derived by him without the consent of the other partners from any transaction connected with the formation, conduct, or liquidation of the partnership or from any use by him of its property.

(2) This Section applies also the representative of a deceased partner engaged in the liquidation of the affairs of the partnership as the personal representatives of the last surviving partner.

Art. 6132b-22. Right to an Account

Any partner shall have the right to a formal account as to partnership affairs:

(a) If he is wrongfully excluded from the partnership business or possession of its property by his co-partners,

(b) If the right exists under the terms of any agreement,

(c) As provided by Section 21,

(d) Whenever other circumstances render it just and reasonable.

Art. 6132b-23. Continuation of Partnership beyond Fixed Term

(1) When a partnership for a fixed term or particular undertaking is continued after the termination of such term or particular undertaking without any express agreement, the rights and duties of the partners remain the same as they were at such termination, so far as is consistent with a partnership at will.

(2) A continuation of the business by the partners or such of them as habitually acted therein during the term, without any settlement or liquidation of the partnership affairs is prima facie evidence of a continuation of the partnership.

PART V.
PROPERTY RIGHTS IN
PARTNERSHIP

Art. 6132b-24. Extent of Property Rights of a Partner

The property rights of a partner are (1) his rights in specific partnership property, (2) his interest in the partnership, and (3) his right to participate in the management. The community property rights of a partner's spouse are stated in Section 28-A.

Art. 6132b-25. Nature of a Partner's Right in Specific Partnership Property

(1) A partner is co-owner with his partners of specific partnership property holding as a tenant in partnership.

(2) The incidents of this tenancy are such that:

(a) A partner, subject to the provisions of this Act and to any agreement between the partners, has an equal right with his partners to possess specific partnership property for partnership purposes; but he has no right to possess such property for any other purpose without the consent of his partners.

(b) A partner's right in specific partnership property is no assignable except in connection with the assignment of rights of all the partners in the same property.

(c) A partner's right in specific partnership property is not subject to attachment or execution, except on a claim against the partnership. When partnership property is attached for a partnership debt the partners, or any of them, or the representatives of a deceased partner, cannot claim any right under the homestead or exemption laws.

(d) On the death of a partner his right in specific partnership property vests in the surviving partner or partners, except where the deceased was the last surviving partner, when his right in such property vests in his legal representative. Such surviving partner or partners, or the legal representative of the last surviving partner, has no right to possess the partnership property for any but a partnership purpose.

(e) A partner's right in specific partnership property is not subject to dower, curtesy, or allowances to widows, heirs, or next of kin.

Art. 6132b-26. Nature of Partner's Interest in the Partnership

A partner's interest in the partnership is his share of the profits and surplus, and the same is personal property for all purposes.

Art. 6132b-27. Assignment of Partner's Interest

(1) A conveyance by a partner of his interest in the partnership does not of itself dissolve the partnership, nor, as against the other partners in the absence of agreement, entitle the assignee, during the continuance of the partnership, to interfere in the management or administration of the partnership business or affairs; it merely entitles the assignee to receive in accordance with this contract the profits to which the assigning partner would otherwise be entitled and, for any proper purpose, to require reasonable information or account of partnership transactions and to make reasonable inspection of the partnership books.

(2) In case of a dissolution of the partnership, the assignee is entitled to receive his assignor's interest.

Art. 6132b-28. Interest in Partnership Subject to Charging Order

(1) On due application to a competent court by any judgment creditor of a partner (or of any other owner of an interest in the partnership), the court which entered the judgment, order, or decree, or any other court, may charge the interest of the debtor partner (or such other owner) with payment of the unsatisfied amount to such judgment debt with interest thereon; and may then or later appoint a receiver of his share of the profits, and of any other money due or to fall due to him in respect of the partnership, and make all other orders, directions, accounts and inquiries which the debtor partner (or such other owner) might have made, or which the circumstances of the case may require.

(2) The interest charged may be redeemed at any time before foreclosure, or in case of a sale being directed by the court may be purchased without thereby causing a dissolution:

(a) With separate property, by any one or more of the partners, or

(b) With partnership property, by any one or more of the partners with the consent of all the partners whose interests are not so charged or sold.

(3) Nothing in this Act shall be held to deprive a partner (or other owners) of his right, if any, under the exemption laws, as regards his interest in the partnership.

Art. 6132b-28-A. Extent of Community Property Rights of a Partner's Spouse

(1) A partner's rights in specific partnership property are not community property.

(2) A partner's interest in the partnership may be community property.

(3) A partner's right to participate in the management is not community property.

Art. 6132b-28-B. Effect of Death or Divorce on Interest in the Partnership

(1)(A) On the divorce of a partner, the partner's spouse shall, to the extent of such spouse's interest in the partnership, be regarded for purposes of this Act as an assignee and purchaser of such interest from such partner.

(B) On the death of a partner, such partner's surviving spouse (if any) and such partner's heirs, legatees or personal representative, shall to the extent of their respective interests in the partnership, be regarded for purposes of this Act as assignees and purchasers of such interests from such partner.

(C) On the death of a partner's spouse, such spouse's heirs, legatees or personal representative shall, to the extent of their respective interests in the partnership, be regarded for purposes of this Act as assignees and purchases of such interests from such partner.

(2) A partnership is not dissolved by the death of a partner's spouse unless the agreement between the partners provides otherwise.

(3) Nothing in this Act shall impair any agreement for the purchase or sale of an interest in a partnership at the death of the owner thereof or at any other time.

PART VI.
DISSOLUTION AND WINDING UP

Art. 6132b-29. Dissolution Defined

The dissolution of a partnership is the change in the relation of the partners caused by any partner ceasing to be associated in the carrying on as distinguished from the winding up of the business.

Art. 6132b-30. Partnership Not Terminated by Dissolution

On dissolution the partnership is not terminated, but continues until the winding up of partnership affairs is completed.

Art. 6132b-31. Causes of Dissolution

Dissolution is caused:

(1) Without violation of the agreement between the partners,

(a) By the termination of the definite term or particular undertaking specified in the agreement,

(b) By the express will of any partner when no definite term or particular undertaking is specified,

(c) By the express will of all the partners who have not assigned their interests or suffered them to be charged for their separate debts, either before or after the termination of any specified term or particular undertaking,

(d) By the expulsion of any partner from the business bona fide in accordance with such a power conferred by the agreement between the partners;

(2) In contravention of the agreement between the partners, here the circumstances do not permit a dissolution under any other provision of this Section, by the express will of any partner at any time;

(3) By any event which makes it unlawful for the business of the partnership to be carried on or for the members to carry it on in partnership;

(4) By the death of any partner unless the agreement between the partners provides otherwise;

(5) By the bankruptcy of any partner or the partnership;

(6) By decree of court under Section 32.

Art. 6132b-32. Dissolution by Decree of Court

(1) On application by or for a partner the court shall decree a dissolution whenever:

(a) a partner has been declared mentally disabled in any judicial proceeding or is shown to be of unsound mind;

(b) a partner becomes in any other way incapable of performing his part of the partnership contract;

(c) a partner has been guilty of such conduct as tends to affect prejudicially the carrying on of the business;

(d) a partner wilfully or persistenly commits a breach of the partnership agreement, or otherwise so conducts himself in matters relating to the partnership business that it is not reasonably practicable to carry on the business in partnership with him;

(e) the business of the partnership can only be carried on at a loss; or

(f) other circumstances render a dissolution equitable.

(2) On the application of the purchaser of a partner's interest under Section 27 and 28:

(a) After the termination of the specified term or particular undertaking,

(b) At any time if the partnership was a partnership at will when the interest was assigned or when the charging order was issued.

Art. 6132b-33. General Effect of Dissolution on Authority of Partner

Except so far as may be necessary to wind up partnership affairs or to complete transactions begun but not then finished, dissolution terminates all authority of any partner to act for the partnership:

(1) With respect to the partners,

(a) When the dissolution is not by the act, bankruptcy or death of a partner; or

(b) When the dissolution is by such act, bankruptcy or death of a partner, in cases where Section 34 so requires.

(2) With respect to persons not partners, as declared in Section 35.

Art. 6132b-34. Right to Partner to Contribution from Co-partners after Dissolution

Where the dissolution is caused by the act, death or bankruptcy of a partner, each partner is liable to his co-partners for his share of any liability created by any partner acting for the partnership as if the partnership had not been dissolved unless:

(a) The dissolution being by act of any partner, the partner acting for the partnership had knowledge of the dissolution, or

(b) The dissolution being by the death or bankruptcy of a partner, the partner acting for the partnership had knowledge or notice of the death or bankruptcy.

Art. 6132b-35. Power of Partner to Bind Partnership to Third Persons after Dissolution

(1) After dissolution a partner can bind the partnership except as provided in paragraph (3):

(a) By any act appropriate for winding up partnership affairs or completing transactions unfinished at dissolution;

(b) By any transaction which would bind the partner if dissolution had not taken place provided the other party to the transaction:

(I) Was a creditor of the partnership at the time of dissolution or had extended credit to the partnership within two years prior to dissolution and, in either case, had no knowledge or notice of his want of authority; or

(II) Though he was not such a creditor or had not so extended credit, had nevertheless known of the partnership prior to dissolution, and, having no knowledge or notice of dissolution, the fact of dissolution had not been advertised in a newspaper of general circulation in the place (or in each place if more than one) at which the partnership business was regularly carried on.

(2) The liability of a partner under Paragraph (1b) shall be satisfied out of partnership assets alone when such partner had been prior to dissolution:

(a) Unknown as a partner to the person with whom the contract is made; and

(b) So far unknown and inactive in partnership affairs that the business reputation of the partnership could not be said to have been in any degree due to his connection with it.

(3) The partnership is in no case bound by any act of a partner after dissolution:

(a) Where the partnership is dissolved because it is unlawful to carry on the business, unless the act is appropriate for winding up partnership affairs; or

(b) Where the partner has become bankrupt; or

(c) Where the partner has no authority to wind up partnership affairs; except by a transaction with one who:

(I) Was a creditor of the partnership at the time of dissolution or had extended credit to the partnership within two years prior to dissolution and, in either case, had no knowledge or notice of his want of authority; or

(II) Though he was not such a creditor or had not so extended credit to the partnership prior to dissolution; and, having no knowledge or notice of his want of authority, the fact of his want of authority has not been advertised in the manner provided for advertising the fact of dissolution in Paragraph (1bII).

(4) Nothing in this Section shall affect the liability under Section 16 or any person who after dissolution represents himself or consents to another representing him as a partner in a partnership engaged in carrying on business.

Art. 6132b-36. Effect of Dissolution on Partner's Existing Liability

(1) The dissolution of the partnership does not of itself discharge the existing liability of any partner.

(2) A partner is discharged from any existing liability upon dissolution of the partnership by an agreement to that effect between himself, the partnership creditor and the person or partnership continuing the business; and such agreement may be inferred from the course of dealing between the creditor having knowledge of the dissolution and the person or partnership continuing the business.

(3) Where a person agrees to assume the existing obligations of a dissolved partnership, the partners whose obligations have been assumed shall be discharged from any liability to any creditor of the partnership who, knowing of the agreement, consents to a material alteration in the nature or time of payment of such obligations.

(4) The individual property of a deceased partner shall be liable for all obligations of the partnership incurred while he was a partner but subject to the prior payment of his separate debts.

Art. 6132b-37. Right to Wind Up

Unless otherwise agreed the partners who have not wrongfully dissolved the partnership or the legal representative of the last surviving partner, not bankrupt, has the right to wind up the partnership affairs; provided, however, that any partner, his legal representative or his assignee, upon cause shown, may obtain winding up by the court.

Art. 6132b-38. Rights of Partners to Application of Partnership Property

(1) When dissolution is caused in any way, except in contravention of the partnership agreement, each partner, as against his co-partners and all persons claiming through them in respect of their interests in the partnership, unless otherwise agreed, may have the partnership property applied to discharge its liabilities, and the surplus applied to pay in cash the net amount owing to the respective partners. But if dissolution is caused by expulsion of a partner, bona fide under the partnership agreement and if the expelled partner is discharged from all partnership liabilities, either by payment or agreement under Section 36(2), he shall receive in cash only the net amount due him from the partnership.

(2) When dissolution is caused in contravention of the partnership agreement the rights of the partners shall be as follows:

(a) Each partner who has not caused dissolution wrongfully shall have,

(I) All the rights specified in Paragraph (1) of this Section, and

(II) The right, as against each partner who has caused the dissolution wrongfully, to damages for breach of the agreement.

(b) The partners who have not caused the dissolution wrongfully, if they all desire to continue the business in the same name, either by themselves or jointly with others, may do so, during the agreed term for the partnership and for that purpose may possess the partnership property, provided they secure the payment by bond approved by the court, or pay to any partner who has caused the dissolution wrongfully, the value of his interest in the partnership at the dissolution, less any damages recoverable, under clause (2aII) of this Section, and in like manner indemnify him against all present or future partnership liabilities.

(c) A partner who has caused the dissolution wrongfully shall have:

(I) If the business is not continued under the provision of paragraph (2b) all the rights of a partner under paragraph (1), subject to clause (2aII), of this Section,

(II) If the business is continued under paragraph (2b) of this Section the right as against his co-partners and all claiming through them in respect of their interests in the partnership, to have the value of his interest in the partnership, less any damages caused to his co-partners by the dissolution, ascertained and paid to him in cash, or the payment secured by bond approved by the court, and to be indemnified against all existing liabilities of the partnership; but in ascertaining the value of the partner's interest the value of the goodwill of the business shall not be considered.

Art. 6132b-39. Rights Where Partnership is Dissolved for Fraud or Misrepresentation

Where a partnership contract is rescinded on the ground of the fraud or misrepresentation of one of the parties thereto, the party entitled to rescind is, without prejudice to any other right, entitled:

(a) To a lien on, or right of retention of, the surplus of the partnership property after satisfying the partnership liabilities to third persons for any sum of money paid by him for the purchase of an interest in the partnership and for any capital or advances contributed by him; and

(b) To stand, after all liabilities to third persons have been satisfied, in the place of the creditors of the partnership for any payments made by him in respect to the partnership liabilities; and

(c) To be indemnified by the person guilty of the fraud or making the representation against all debts and liabilities of the partnership.

Art. 6132b-40. Rules for Distribution

In settling accounts between the partners after dissolution, the following rules shall be observed, subject to any agreement to the contrary:

(a) The assets of the partnership are:

(I) The partnership property,

(II) The contributions of the partners necessary for the payment of all the liabilities specified in clause (b) of this paragraph.

(b) The liabilities of the partnership shall rank in order of payment, as follows:

(I) Those owing to creditors other than partners,

(II) Those owing to partners other than for capital and profits,

(III) Those owing to partners in respect of capital,

(IV) Those owing to partners in respect of profits.

(c) The assets shall be applied in the order of their declaration in clause (a) of this paragraph to the satisfaction of the liabilities.

(d) The partners shall contribute, as provided by Section 18(a) the amount necessary to satisfy the liabilities; but if any, but not all, of the partners are insolvent, or, not being subject to process, refuse to contribute, the other partners shall contribute their share of the liabilities, and, in the relative proportions in which they share the profits, the additional amount necessary to pay the liabilities.

(e) An assignee for the benefit of creditors or any person appointed by the court shall have the right to enforce the contributions specified in clause (d) of this paragraph.

(f) Any partner or his legal representative shall have the right to enforce the contributions specified in clause (d) of this paragraph, to the extent of the amount which he has paid in excess of his share of the liability.

(g) The individual property of a deceased partner shall be liable for the contributions specified in clause (d) of this paragraph.

(h) When partnership property and the individual properties of the partners are in possession of a court for distribution, partnership creditors shall have priority on partnership property and separate creditors on individual property, saving the rights of lien or secured creditors as heretofore.

(i) Where a partner has became bankrupt of his estate is insolvent the claims against his separate property shall rank in the following order:

(I) Those owing to separate creditors,

(II) Those owing to partnership creditors,

(III) Those owing to partners by way of contribution.

Art. 6132b-41. Liability of Persons Continuing the Business in Certain Cases

(1) When any new partner is admitted into an existing partnership, or when any partner retires and assigns (or the representatives of the deceased partners assigns) his rights in partnership property to two or more of the partners, or to one or more of the partners, and one or more third persons, if the business is continued without liquidation of the partnership affairs, creditors of the first or dissolved partnership are also creditors of the partnership so continuing the business.

(2) When all but one partner retire and assign (or the representative of a deceased partner assigns) their rights in partnership property to the remaining partner, who continues the business without liquidation of partnership affairs, either alone or with others, creditors of the dissolved partnership are also creditors of the person or partnership so continuing the business.

(3) When any partner retires or dies and the business of the dissolved partnership is continued as set forth in paragraphs (1) and (2) of this Section, with the consent of the retired partners or the representative of the deceased partner, but without any assignment of his right in partnership property, rights of creditors of the dissolved partnership and of the creditors of the person or partnership continuing the business shall be as if such assignment had been made.

(4) When all the partners of their representatives assign their rights in partnership property to one or more third persons who promise to pay the debts and who continue the business of the dissolved partnership, creditors of the dissolved partnership are also creditors of the person or partnership continuing the business.

(5) When any partner wrongfully causes a dissolution and the remaining partners continue the business under the provisions of section 38(2b), either alone or with others, and without liquidation of the partnership affairs, creditors of the dissolved partnership are also creditors of the person or partnership continuing the business.

(6) When a partner is expelled and the remaining partners continue the business either alone or with others, without liquidation of the partnership affairs, creditors of the dissolved partnership are also creditors of the person or partnership continuing the business.

(7) The liability of a third person becoming a partner in the partnership continuing the business, under this Section, to the creditors of the dissolved partnership shall be satisfied out of partnership property only.

(8) When the business of a partnership after dissolution is continued under any conditions set forth in this Section the creditors of the dissolved partnership, as against the separate creditors of the reitring or deceased partner or the representative of the deceased partner, have a prior right to any claim of the retired partner or the representative of the deceased partner against the person or partnership continuing the business, on account of the retired or deceased partner's interest in the dissolved partnership or on account of any consideration promised for such interest for his right in partnership property.

(9) Nothing in this Section shall be held to modify any right of creditors to set aside any assignment on the ground of fraud.

(10) The use by the person or partnership continuing the business of the partnership name, or the name of a deceased partner as part thereof, shall not of itself make the individual property of the deceased partner liable for any debts contracted by such person or partnership.

Art. 6132b-42. Rights of Retiring or Estate of Deceased Partner When the Business is Continued

When any partner retires or dies, and the business is continued under any of the conditions set forth in Section 41(1, 2, 3, 5, 6) or Section 38(2b), without any settlement of accounts as between him or his estate and the person or partnership continuing the business, unless otherwise agreed, he or his legal representative as against such persons or partnership may have the value of his interest at the date of dissolution ascertained, and shall receive as an ordinary creditor an amount equal to the value of his interest in the dissolved partnership with interest, or, at his option or at the option of his legal representative, in lieu of interest, the profits attributable to the use of his right in the property of the dissolved partnership; provided that the creditors, or the representative of the retired or deceased partner, shall have priorty on any claim arising under this Section as provided by Section 41(8) of this Act.

Art. 6132b-43. Accrual of Actions

The right to an account of his interest shall accrue to any partner, or his legal representative, as against the winding up partners or the surviving partners or the person or partnership continuing the business, at the date of dissolution, in the absence of any agreement to the contrary.

Art. 61326-45-A. REGISTERED LIMITED LIABILITY PARTNERSHIPS.

(1) To become a registered limited liability partnership, a partnership must file with the secretary of state an application stating the name of the partnership, the address of its principal office, the number of partners, and a brief statement of the business in which the partnership engages.

(2) The application must be executed by a majority in interest of the partners or by one or more partners authorized by a majority in interest of the partners.

(3) The application must be accompanied by a fee of $100 for each partner.

(4) The secretary of state shall register or renew any partnership that submits a completed application with the required fee.

(5) Registration if effective for one year after the date the registration is filed, unless voluntarily withdrawn by filing with the secretary of state a written withdrawal notice executed by a majority in interest of the partners or by one or more partners authorized by a majority in interest of the partners.

(6) The secretary of state may provide forms for application for or renewal of registration.

Sec. 45-B. NAME OF REGISTERED LIMITED LIABILITY PARTNERSHIPS. A registered limited liability partnership's name must contain the words "registered limited liability partnership" or the abbreviation "L.L.P." as the last words or letters of its name.

Sec. 45-C INSURANCE OF REGISTERED LIMITED LIABILITY PARTNERSHIPS. A registered limited liability partnership must carry, if reasonably available, at least $100,000 of liability insurance of a kind that is designed to cover the kinds of errors, omissions, negligence, incompetence, or malfeasance for which liability is limited by Section 15(2).

2. Texas Revised Limited Partnership Act

[Portions of the new Texas Revised Limited Partnership Act are set forth below.]

Senate Bill 563

BE IT ENACTED BY THE LEGISLATURE OF THE STATE OF TEXAS:

SECTION 1. The Texas Revised Limited Partnership Act is enacted to read as follows:

Sec. 1.01. SHORT TITLE. This Act may be cited as the Texas Revised Limited Partnership Act.

Sec. 1.03 PARTNERSHIP NAME. The name of a limited partnership as stated in its certificate of limited partnership, a reserved or registered name, or the name under which a foreign limited partnership is permitted to register to do business in Texas as contained in its application for registration as a foreign limited partnership must contain the words "Limited Partnership," Limited," or the abbreviation "L.P." or "Ltd." as the last words or letters of its name and may not:

(1) contain the name of a limited partner unless:

(A) that name is also the name of a general partner; or

(B) the business of the limited partnership or foreign limited partnership had been carried on under that name before the admission of that limited partner;

(2) contain a word or phrase indicating or implying that it is organized other than for a purpose stated in its partnership agreement;

(3) be the same as or deceptively similar to the name of a corporation or limited partnership that exists under the laws of Texas, that has a certificate of authority to transact business as a foreign corporation in Texas, or that is registered as a foreign limited partnership in Texas, or a name that has been reserved or registered for a corporation, limited partnership, or foreign limited partnership under the laws of Texas, except that a limited partnership or foreign limited partnership may adopt, reserve, or register, as appropriate, a name that is similar if written consent is obtained from the corporation, limited partnership, or foreign limited partnership having the name considered similar or from the person for whom the name considered similar is reserved or registered in the office of the secretary of state; or

(4) contain a word or phrase indicating or implying that it is a corporation.

Sec. 1.04. RESERVATION OF NAME. (a) The exclusive right to the use of a name may be reserved by:

(1) a person intending to organize a limited partnership under this Act and adopt that name;

(2) a domestic limited partnership or a foreign limited partnership registered in Texas that proposes to change its name to that name;

(3) a foreign limited partnership intending to register in Texas and adopt that name; or

(4) a person intending to organize a foreign limited partnership and intending to have it registered in this state and adopt that name.

(b) A specified name may be reserved by filing with the secretary of state an application executed by the applicant or an attorney or agent of the applicant, together with a duplicate copy of the application, which need not be an executed original or a photocopy of an executed original, and paying the applicable filing fee. If the secretary of state finds that the name is available for use by a domestic or foreign limited partnership, the secretary of state shall reserve the name for the exclusive use of the applicant for a period of 120 days. An applicant may reserve the same name for one or more successive 120-day periods by filing a new application and paying the applicable filing fee before the effective 120-day reservation period expires. The right to the exclusive use of a reserved name may be transferred to another person by filing with the secretary of state a notice of the transfer executed by the applicant for whom the name was reserved that specifies the name and address of the transferee and paying the applicable filing fee.

Sec. 1.07. RECORDS TO BE KEPT; ACCESS TO INFORMATION. (a) A domestic limited partnership shall keep and maintain the following records in its principal office in the United States or make them available in that office within five days after the date of receipt of a written request under Subsection (d) of this section:

(1) a current list that states:

(A) the name and mailing address of each partner, separately identifying in alphabetical order the general partners and the limited partners;

(B) the last known street address of the business or residence of each general partner;

(C) the percentage or other interest in the partnership owned by each partner; and

(D) if one or more classes or groups are established in or under the partnership agreement, the names of the partners who are members of each specified class or group;

(2) copies of the limited partnership's federal, state, and local information or income tax returns for each of the partnership's six most recent tax years;

(3) a copy of the partnership agreement and certificate of limited partnership, all amendments or restatements, executed copies of any powers of attorney under which the partnership agreement, certificate of limited partnership, and all amendments or restatements to the agreement and certificates have been executed, and copies of any document that creates, in the manner provided by the partnership agreement, classes or groups of partners;

(4) unless contained in the written partnership agreement, a written statement of:

(A) the amount of the cash contribution and a description and statement of the agreed value of any other contribution made by each partner, and the amount of the cash contribution and a description and statement of the agreed value of any other contribution that the partner has agreed to make in the future as an additional contribution;

(B) the times at which additional contributions are to be made or events requiring additional contributions to be made;

(C) events requiring the limited partnership to be dissolved and its affairs wound upl and

(D) the date on which each partner in the limited partnership became a partner; and

(5) correct and complete books and records of account of the limited partnership.

(b) A limited partnership shall maintain its records in written form or in another form capable of conversion into written form within a reasonable time.

(c) A limited partnership shall keep in its registered office in Texas and make available to partners on reasonable request the street address of its principal United States office in which the records required by this section are maintained or will be available.

(d) A partner or an assignee of a partnership interest, on written request stating the purpose, may examine and copy, in person or by the partner's or assignee's representative, at any reasonable time, for any proper purpose, and at the partner's information regarding the business, affairs, and financial condition of the limited partnership as is just and reasonable for the person to examine and copy.

(e) On the written request by any partner or an assignee of a partnership interest made to the person and address designated in the partnership agreement or, if there is no designation, to a general partner at the partnership's principal United States office, the partnership shall provide to the requesting partner or assignee without charge true copies of:

(1) the partnership agreement and certificate of limited partnership and all amendments or restatements; and

(2) any of the tax returns described in Subdivision (2) of Subsection (a) of this section.

Sec. 1.09. NATURE OF BUSINESS PERMITTED. (a) A limited partnership formed under this Act may engage in any lawful business unless a more limited purpose is stated in its partnership agreement.

(b) A limited partnership engaging in a business that is subject to regulation by another Texas statute may be formed under this Act only if it is not prohibited by the other statute. The limited partnership is subject to all limitations of the other statute.

Sec. 1.10. BUSINESS TRANSACTIONS OF PARTNER WITH PARTNERSHIP. Except as otherwise provided by the partnership agreement, a partner may lend money to and transact other business with the limited partnership and, subject to other applicable law, has the same rights and obligations with respect to those matters as a person who is not a partner.

Sec. 2.01. CERTIFICATE OF LIMITED PARTNERSHIP. (a) To form a limited partnership, the partners must enter into a partnership agreement and one or more partners, including all of the general partners, must execute a certificate of limited partnership. The filing fee and the certificate shall be filed with the secretary of state. The certificate must contain:

(1) the name of the limited partnership;

(2) the address of the registered office and the name and address of the registered agent for service of process required to be maintained by Section 1.06 of this Act;

(3) the address of the principal office in the United States where records are to be kept or made available under Section 1.07 of this Act;

(4) the name, the mailing address, and the street address of the business or residence of each general partner; and

(5) other matters that the general partners determine to include.

(b) A limited partnership is formed at the time of the filing of the initial certificate of limited partnership with the secretary of state or at a later date or time specified in the certificate if there has been substantial compliance with the requirements of this section.

Sec. 2.02. AMENDMENT TO CERTIFICATE. (a) A certificate of limited partnership may be amended by paying the filing fee and filing a certificate of amendment with the secretary of state. The certificate of amendment must set forth:

(1) the name of the limited partnership; and

(2) the amendment to the certificate.

(b) A general partner shall file a certificate of amendment reflecting the occurrence of one or more of the following events not later than the 30th day after the date of the occurrence of the event:

(1) the admission of a new general partner;

(2) the withdrawal of a general partner;

(3) a change in the name of the limited partnership; or

(4) except as provided by Subsection (b) or (h) of Section 1.06 of this Act, a change in the address of the registered office or a change in the name or address of the registered agent of the limited partnership.

(c) A general partner who becomes aware that a statement in a certificate of limited partnership was false when made or that a matter described in the certificate has changed, making the certificate false in any material respect, shall promptly amend the certificate to make it accurate.

(d) A certificate of limited partnership may be amended at any time for any other proper purpose determined by the general partners.

(e) Unless otherwise provided by this Act, a certificate of amendment is effective when filed with the secretary of state or at a later date or time specified in the certificate if there has been substantial compliance with the requirements of this section.

Sec. 2.03. CERTIFICATE OF CANCELLATION. (a) A certificate of limited partnership shall be cancelled by paying the filing fee and filing a certificate of cancellation with the secretary of state:

(1) on the completion of the winding up of the partnership;

(2) when there are no limited partners; or

(3) subject to Subsection (c) of this section, on a merger or consolidation as provided by Subsection (b) of Section 2.11 of this Act.

(b) A certificate of cancellation must contain:

(1) the name of the limited partnership;

(2) the date of the filing of its certificate of limited partnership;

(3) the reason for filing the certificate of cancellation;

(4) the future effective date or time, which shall be a date or time certain, of cancellation if it is not to be effective on the filing of the certificate; and

(5) any other information determined proper by the person filing the certificate of cancellation.

(c) If, the case of merger or consolidation, one or more limited partnerships formed or registered under this Act are not the surviving partnership or partnerships, the certificate of merger filed under Subsection (b) of Section 2.11 of this Act is sufficient, without a filing under this section, to cancel the certificate of limited partnership of those nonsurviving partnerships.

Sec. 2.04. EXECUTION. (a) Each certificate required by this article to be filed with the secretary of state shall be executed in the following manner:

(1) an initial certificate of limited partnership must be signed by all general partners, unless signed and filed by a person under Subdivision (1) of Subsection (a) of Section 3.04 of this Act;

(2) a certificate of amendment or restated certificate must be signed by at least one general partner and by each other general partner designated in the certificate of amendment as a withdrawing or a new general partner, unless signed and filed by a person under Subdivision (1) of Subsection (a) of Section 3.04 of this Act;

(3) a certificate of cancellation must be signed by all general partners or, if there is no general partner, by a majority in interest of the limited partners;

(4) a certificate of merger must be signed by all general partners of each limited partnership affected by the merger or consolidation; and

(5) a certificate filed under Section 2.06 of this Act must be signed by the person designated by the court.

(b) Any person may sign a certificate or partnership agreement or amendment or restated certificate by an attorney in fact. A power of attorney relating to the signing of a certificate or partnership agreement or amendment or restated certificate by an attorney in fact need not be sworn to, verified, or acknowledged, and need not be filed with the secretary of state, but shall be retained with the partnership records under Section 1.07 of this Act.

(c) The execution of a certificate by a general partner or the execution of a written statement by a person under Subdivision (2) of Subsection (a) of Section 3.04 of this Act constitutes an oath or affirmation, under the penalties for perjury, that, to the best of the executing party's knowledge and belief, the facts stated in the certificate or statement are true.

Sec. 2.07. FILING. (a) The original signed copy and one duplicate copy, which need not be an executed original or a photocopy of an executed original, of a certificate of limited partnership, a certificate of amendment or cancellation, a judicial decree of amendment or cancellation, a certificate of merger, or a restated certificate shall be delivered to the secretary of state. A person who executed a certificate as an agent or fiduciary need not exhibit evidence of that person's authority as a prerequisite to filing. Unless the secretary of state finds that a certificate does not conform to law, on receipt of all applicable filing fees required by law the secretary of state shall certify that the certificate or decree has been filed in the secretary of state's office by endorsing on the original the word "Filed" and the date of the filing, file and index the endorsed certificate or decree, and return the duplicate copy, similarly endorsed, to the person who filed it or to the person's designated representative. The secretary of state's endorsement is conclusive of the date of the filing in the absence of actual fraud.

(b) On the filing of a certificate of amendment, judicial decree of amendment, or certificate restated with the secretary of state, or on the future effective date or time of the certificate or decree provided in the certificate or decree, the certificate of limited partnership is amended or restated. The certificate of limited partnership is canceled on:

(1) the filing of a certificate of cancellation or a judicial decree of cancellation;

(2) the future effective date or time of the certificate or decree provided in the certificate or decree; or

(3) as specified by Subsection (d) of Section 1.06 of this Act. A merger takes effect on the filing of a certificate of merger.

Sec. 3.03 LIABILITY TO THIRD PARTIES. (a) Except as provided by Subsection (d) of this section, a limited partner is not liable for the obligations of a limited partnership unless the limited partner is also a general partner or, in addition to the exercise of the limited partner's rights and powers as a limited partner, the limited partner participates in the control of the business. However, if the limited partner does participate in the control of the business, the limited partner is liable only to persons who transact business with the limited partnership reasonably believing, based on the limited partner's conduct, that the limited partner is a general partner.

(b) For the purposes of this section, a limited partner does not participate in the control of the business by virtue of the limited partner's having or acting in one or more of the following capacities or possessing or exercising one or more of the following powers:

(1) acting as a contractor for or an agent or employee of the limited partnership or of a general partner, an officer, director, or stockholder of a corporate general partner, or a partner of a partnership that is a general partner of the limited partnership;

(2) consulting with or advising a general partner on any matter, including the business of the limited partnership;

(3) acting as surety, guarantor, or endorser for the limited partnership, to guarantee or assume one or more specific obligations of the limited partnership, or to provide collateral for borrowing of the limited partnership;

(4) calling, requesting, attending, or participating in a meeting of the partners or the limited partners;

(5) winding up a limited partnership under Section 8.04 of this Act;

(6) taking any action required or permitted by law to bring or peruse a derivative action in the right of the limited partnership;

(7) serving on a committee of the limited partnership or the limited partners; or

(8) proposing, approving, or disapproving, by vote or otherwise, one or more of the following matters:

(A) the dissolution and winding up of the limited partnership;

(B) the sale, exchange, lease, mortgage, assignment, pledge, or other transfer of, or granting of a security interest in, an asset or assets of the limited partnership;

(C) the incurring, renewal, refinancing, or payment or other discharge of indebtedness by the limited partnership;

(D) a change in the nature of the business of the limited partnership;

(E) the admission, removal, or retention of a general partner;

(F) the admission, removal, or retention of a limited partner;

(G) a transaction or other matter involving an actual or potential conflict of interest;

(H) an amendment to the partnership agreement or certificate of limited partnership;

(I) if the limited partnership is qualified as an investment company under the federal Investment Company Act of 1940 (15 U.S.C. Section 80a-1 et seq.):

(i) electing directors or trustees of the investment company;

(ii) approving or terminating investment advisory or underwriting contracts;

(iii) approving auditors; and

(iv) acting on any other matters that the Investment Company Act of 1940 (15 U.S.C. Section 80a-1 et seq.) requires to be approved by the holders of beneficial interests in the investment company;

(J) indemnification of a general partner under Article 11 of this Act;

(K) any other matter stated in the partnership agreement; or limited partners under this Act and not specifically enumerated in this subsection.

(c) The enumeration in Subsection (b) of this section does not mean that having or acting in other capacities or possessing or exercising other powers by a limited partner constitutes participation by that limited partner in the control of the business of the limited partnership.

(d) A limited partner who knowingly permits that limited partner's name to be used in the name of the limited partnership, except under circumstances permitted by Subdivision (1) of Section 1.03 of this Act is liable to creditors who extend credit to the limited partnership without actual knowledge that the limited partner is not a general partner.

(e) This section does not create rights of limited partners. Those rights may be created only by the certificate, partnership agreement, or other sections of this Act.

Sec. 5.01. FORM OF CONTRIBUTION. The contribution of a limited partner may be in cash, property, or services rendered, or a promissory note or other obligation to pay cash or transfer property to the limited partnership.

Sec. 5.03. ALLOCATION OF PROFITS AND LOSSES. The profits and losses of a limited partnership shall be allocated among the partners in the manner provided by a written partnership agreement. If a written partnership agreement does not otherwise provide, the profits and losses shall be allocated in accordance with the then current percentage or other interest in the partnership stated in partnership records of the kind described in Subsection (a) of Section 1.07 of this Act. If the allocation of profits and losses is not provided by a written partnership agreement or in partnership records of the kind described in Subsection (a) of Section 1.07, profits and losses shall be allocated in proportion to capital accounts.

Sec. 5.04. SHARING OF DISTRIBUTIONS. Distributions of cash or other assets of a limited partnership shall be made to the partners in the manner provided by a written partnership agreement. If a written partnership agreement does not otherwise provide, distributions that are a return of capital shall be made on the basis of the agreed value, as stated in the partnership records required to be kept under Subsection (a) of Section 1.07 of this Act, of the contributions made by each partner to the extent that the contributions have not been returned, and distributions that are not a return of capital shall be made in proportion to the allocation of profits as determined under Section 5.03 of this Act.

Sec. 7.02. ASSIGNMENT OF PARTNERSHIP INTEREST. (a) Unless otherwise provided by the partnership agreement:

(1) a partnership interest is assignable in whole of in part;

(2) an assignment of a partnership interest does not dissolve a limited partnership or entitle the assignee to become, or to exercise rights or powers of, a partner;

(3) an assignment entitles the assignee to be allocated income, gain, loss, deduction, credit, or similar items, and to receive distributions, to which the assignor was entitled, to the extent those items are assigned; and

(4) until the assignee becomes a partner, the assignor partner continues to be a partner and to have the power to exercise any rights or powers of a partner, except to the extent those rights or powers are assigned; however, on the assignment by a general partner of all of the general partner's rights as a general partner, the general partner's status as a general partner may be terminated by the affirmative vote of a majority in interest of the limited partners.

(b) Until an assignee of the partnership interest in a limited partnership becomes a partner, the assignee has no liability as a partner solely as a result of the assignment.

(c) A written partnership agreement may provide that a partner's partnership interest may be evidenced by a certificate of partnership interest issued by the limited partnership, may provide for the assignment or transfer of partnership interest represented by a certificate, and may make other provisions with respect to the certificate.

Sec. 7.03. RIGHTS OF JUDGMENT CREDITOR. (a) On application to a court of competent jurisdiction by a judgment creditor of a partner or of any other owner of a partnership interest, the court may charge the partnership interest of the partner or other owner with payment of the unsatisfied amount of the judgment, with interest, may then or later appoint a receiver of the debtor partner's share of the partnership's profits and of any other money payable or that becomes payable to the debtor partner with respect to the partnership, and may make all other orders, directions, and inquiries that the circumstances of the case require. To the extent that the partnership interest is charged in this manner, the judgment creditor has only the rights of an assignee of the partnership interest.

(b) The partnership interest charged may be redeemed at any time before foreclosure or, in case of a sale directed by the court, may be purchased without a dissolution being caused:

(1) with separate property of any general partner, by any one or more of the general partners; or

(2) with respect to partnership property, by any one or more of the general partners whose interests are not charged, on the consent of all general partners whose interests are not charged and a majority in interest of the limited partners, excluding limited partnership interests held by any general partner whose interest is charged.

(c) The remedies provided by Subsection (a) of this section are exclusive of others that may exist, including remedies under laws of this state applicable to partnerships without limited partners.

(d) This section does not deprive any partner of the benefit of any exemption laws applicable to that partner's partnership interest.

Sec. 7.04. RIGHT OF ASSIGNEE TO BECOME LIMITED PARTNER. (a) An assignee of a partnership interest, including an assignee of the partnership interest of a general partner, may become a limited partner if and to the extent that:

(1) the partnership agreement provides; or

(2) all partners consent.

(b) An assignee who becomes a limited partner has, to the extent assigned, the rights and powers and is subject to the restrictions and liabilities of a limited partner under a partnership agreement and this Act. Unless otherwise provided by a written partnership agreement, an assignee who becomes a limited partner also is liable for the obligations of the assignor to make contributions as provided by Section 5.02 of this Act, but is not obligated for liabilities unknown to the assignee at the time the assignee became a limited partner and which could not be ascertained from a written partnership agreement.

(c) Whether or not an assignee of a partnership interest becomes a limited partner, the assignor is not released from the assignor's liability to the limited partnership under Articles 5 and 6 of this Act.

Sec. 12.01. FEES. The secretary of state shall collect for the use of the state:

(1) for filing a certificate of limited partnership under Section 2.01 of this Act, or an application for registration as a foreign limited partnership under Section 9.02 of this Act, a fee of $750;

(2) for filing a certificate of amendment under Section 2.02 of this Act, a certificate of cancellation under Section 2.03 of this Act, a restated certificate of limited partnership under Section 2.10 of this Act, a correction certificate under Section 9.05 of this Act, or a certificate of cancellation under Section 9.06 of this Act, a fee of $200;

(3) for filing an application for reservation of name, an application for renewal of reservation, a notice of transfer of reservation under Subsection (b) of Section 1.04 of this Act, or an application for registration of name or an application for renewal of registration of name under Section 1.05 of this Act, a fee of $75;

(4) for filing a statement for change of registered office, registered agent, or both, under Subsection (b) of Section 1.06 of this Act, or a statement for change of location of registered office under Subsection (h) of Section 1.06 of this Act, a fee of $50, except that the maximum fee for simultaneous filings by a registered agent for more than one limited partnership may not exceed $2,500;

(5) for preclearance of any document for filing, a fee of $50; and

(6) for filing any instrument under this Act not expressly provided for above, a fee of $25.

Sec. 13.02. APPLICATION. (a) Before September 1, 1992, this Act applies only to:

(1) a domestic limited partnership formed on or after the effective date of this Act;

(2) a partnership foreign limited transacting business in the state that has not qualified to transact business in Texas before the effective date of this Act; and

(3) a domestic limited partnership formed before the effective date of this Act, or a foreign limited partnership that has qualified to transact business in Texas before the effective date of this Act, that elects, as provided by this section, to be governed by this Act.

(b) After August 31, 1992, this Act applies to all domestic limited partnerships and all foreign limited partnerships transacting business in Texas.

(c) Before September 1, 1992, a domestic limited partnership formed before the effective date of this Act and a foreign limited partnership qualified before the effective date of this Act to transact business in Texas may voluntarily elect, by complying with the procedures provided in its partnership agreement for amending the partnership agreement, to adopt this Act and may become subject to its provisions by filing with the secretary of state a certificate of limited partnership or an application for registration as a foreign limited partnership that complies with this Act or a certificate of amendment that would cause its certificate of limited partnership to comply with this Act and that specifically states that the partnership is electing to adopt this Act. On the filing of a document complying with this subsection, this Act applies to that partnership.

(d) If, after August 31, 1992, a domestic limited partnership formed before the effective date of this Act or a foreign limited partnership qualified to transact business in Texas before the effective date of this Act has not amended its certificate of limited partnership or application for registration as a foreign corporation in accordance with Subsection (c) of this section, the partnership is not considered to have failed to comply with this Act solely because the name of the partnership does not conform with Section 1.02 of this Act, if the name conforms with the other provisions of this Act and all other laws of Texas, or solely because its certificate of limited P or application for registration as a foreign limited partnership does not state the address of its registered office and the name and address of its registered agent for service of process, in which case service of process on that limited partnership may be made as provided by Section 9.10 of this Act. If such a partnership amends its certificate of limited partnership or application for registration as a foreign limited partnership, as the case may be, after August 31, 1992, the limited partnership must, at the time of or before filing the amendment with the secretary of state, take any action that is necessary to cause the limited partnership to conform to the provisions of this Act.

Sec. 13.03. CASES NOT PROVIDED FOR BY THIS ACT. In any case not provided for by this Act, the Texas Uniform partnership Act (Article 6132b, Vernon's Texas Civil Statutes) and the rules of law and equity, including the law merchant, govern.

SECTION 3. This Act takes effect September 1, 1987.

3. Texas Business Corporations Act—Corporate Formation Sections

Art. 3.01. Incorporators

A. Any natural person of the age of eighteen (18) years or more, or any partnership, corporation, association, trust, or estate (without regard to place of residence, domicile, or organization) may act as an incorporator of a corporation by signing and verifying the articles of incorporation for such corporation and by delivering the original and a copy of the articles of incorporation to the Secretary of State.

(1955 ch. 64, 1975 ch. 134, 1979 ch. 120 eff. May 9, 1979)

Art. 3.02. Articles of Incorporation

A. The articles of incorporation shall set forth:

(1) The name of the corporation;

(2) The period of duration, which may be perpetual;

(3) The purpose or purposes for which the corporation is organized which may be stated to be, or to include, the transaction of any or all lawful business for which corporations may be incorporated under this Act;

(4) The aggregate number of shares which the corporation shall have authority to issue; if such shares are to consist of one class only, the par value of each of such shares, or a statement that all of such shares are without par value; or, if such shares are to be divided into classes, the number of shares of each class, and a statement of the par value of the shares of each class or that such shares are to be without par value;

(5) If the shares are to be divided into classes, the designation of each class and statement of the preferences, limitations, and relative rights in respect of the shares of each class;

(6) If the corporation is to issue the shares of any preferred or special class in

series, then the designation of each series and a statement of the variations in the relative rights and preferences as between series insofar as the same are to be fixed in the articles of incorporation, and a statement of any authority to be vested in the board of directors to establish series and fix and determine the variations in the relative rights and preferences as between series;

(7) A statement that the corporation will not commence business until it has received for the issuance of shares consideration of the value of a stated sum which shall be at least One Thousand Dollars ($1,000), consisting of money, labor done, or property actually received;

(8) Any provision limiting or denying to shareholders the preemptive right to acquire additional or treasury shares of the corporation;

(9) If a corporation elects to become a close corporation in conformance with Part Twelve of this Act, any provision (a) required or permitted by this Act to be stated in the articles of incorporation of a close corporation, (b) contained in a shareholders' agreement in conformance with Part Twelve of this Act which the incorporators elect to set forth in articles of incorporation, or (c) that makes a shareholders' agreement in conformance with Part Twelve of this Act part of the articles of incorporation of a close corporation in the manner prescribed in Section F, Article 2.22 of this Act, but any such provision, other than the statement required by Section A, Article 12.11 of this Act, shall be preceded by a statement that the provision shall be subject to the corporation remaining a close corporation in conformance with Part Twelve of this Act;

(10) Any provision, not inconsistent with law, including any provision which under this Act is required or permitted to be set forth in the bylaws, which the incorporators elect to set forth in the articles of incorporation for the regulation of the internal affairs of the corporation;

(11) The street address of its initial registered office and the name of its initial registered agent at such address;

(12) The number of directors constituting the initial board of directors and the names and addresses of the person or persons who are to serve as directors until the first annual meeting of shareholders or until their successors be elected and qualify, or, in the case of a close corporation that, in conformance with Part Twelve of this Act, is to be managed in some other manner pursuant to a shareholders' agreement by the shareholders or by the persons empowered by the agreement to manage its business and affairs, the names and addresses of the person or persons who, pursuant to the shareholders' agreement, will perform the functions of the initial board of directors provided for by this Act;

(13) The name and address of each incorporator.

B. It shall not be necessary to set forth in the articles of incorporation any of the corporate powers enumerated in this Act.

Art. 3.03. Filing of Articles of Incorporation

A. The original and a copy of the articles of incorporation shall be delivered to the Secretary of State. If the Secretary of State finds that the articles of incorporation conform to law, he shall, when all fees have been paid as required by law:

(1) Endorse on the original and the copy the word "Filed," and the month, day, and year of the filing thereof.

(2) File the original in his office.

(3) Issue a certificate of incorporation to which he shall affix the copy.

B. The certificate of incorporation, together with the copy of the articles of incorporation affixed thereto by the Secretary of State, shall be delivered to the incorporators or their representatives.

Art. 3.04. Effect of Issuance of Certificate of Incorporation

A. Upon the issuance of the certificate of incorporation, the corporate existence shall begin, and such certificate of incorporation shall be conclusive evidence that all conditions precedent required to be performed by the incorporators have been complied with and that the corporation has been incorporated under this Act, except as against the State in a proceeding for involuntary dissolution.

Art. 3.05. Requirement before Commencing Business

A. A corporation shall not transact any business or incur any indebtedness, except such as shall be incidental to its organization or to obtaining subscriptions to or payment for its shares, until it has received for the issuance of shares consideration of the value of at least One Thousand Dollars ($1,000.00) consisting of money, labor done, or property actually received.

Art. 3.06. Organization Meeting of Directors

A. After the issuance of the certificate of incorporation, an organization meeting of the initial board of directors named in the articles of incorporation shall be held, either within or without this State, at the call of a majority of the directors named in the articles of incorporation, for the purpose of adopting bylaws, electing officers, and transaction such other business as may come before the meeting. The directors calling the meeting shall give at least three (3) days notice thereof by mail to each director so named, stating the time and place of the meeting.

4. Equal Credit Opportunity

PART 202—EQUAL CREDIT OPPORTUNITY

Sec.

Regulation B (Equal Credit Opportunity)

§ 202.1 Authority, scope and purpose.

(a) *Authority and scope.* This regulation is issued by the Board of Governors of the Federal Reserve System pursuant to title VII (Equal Credit Opportunity Act) of the Consumer Credit Protection Act, as amended (15 USC 1601 et seq.). Except as otherwise provided herein, the regulation applies to all persons who are creditors, as defined in § 202.2(1). Information collection requirements contained in this regulation have been approved by the Office of Management and Budget under the provisions of 44 USC 3501 et seq. and have been assigned OMB No. 7100-0201.

(b) *Purpose.* The purpose of this regulation is to promote the availability of credit to all creditworthy applicants without regard to race, color, religion, national origin, sex, marital status, or age (provided the applicant has the capacity to contract); to the fact that all or part of the applicant's income derives from a public assistance program; or to the fact that the applicant has in good faith exercised any right under the Consumer Credit Protection Act. The regulation prohibits creditor practices that discriminate on the basis of any of these factors. The regulation also requires creditors to notify applicants of action taken on their applications; to report credit history in the names of both spouses on an account; to retain records of credit applications; and to collect information about the applicant's race and other personal characteristics in applications for certain dwelling-related loans.

§ 202.2 Definitions.

For the purposes of this regulation, unless the context indicates otherwise, the following definitions apply.

(a) *Account* means an extension of credit. When employed in relation to an account, the word *use* refers only to open-end credit.

(b) *Act* means the Equal Credit Opportunity Act (title VII of the Consumer Credit Protection Act).

(c) *Adverse action.* (1) The term means:

(i) A refusal to grant credit in substantially the amount or on substantially the terms requested in an application unless the creditor makes a counteroffer (to grant credit in a different amount or on other terms) and the applicant uses or expressly accepts the credit offered;

(ii) A termination of an account or an unfavorable change in the terms of an account that does not affect all or a substantial portion of a class of the creditor's accounts; or

(iii) A refusal to increase the amount of credit available to an applicant who has made an application for an increase.

(2) The term does not include:

(i) A change in the terms of an account expressly agreed to by an applicant.

(ii) Any action or forbearance relating to an account taken in connection with inactivity, default, or delinquency as to that accounnt;

(iii) A refusal or failure to authorize an account transaction at a point of sale or loan, except when the refusal is a termination or an unfavorable change in the terms of an account that does not affect all or a substantial portion of a class of the creditor's accounts, or when the refusal is a denial of an application for an increase in the amount of credit available under the account;

(iv) A refusal to extend credit because applicable law prohibits the creditor from extending the credit requested; or

(v) A refusal to extend credit because the creditor does not offer the type of credit or credit plan requested.

(3) An action that falls within the definition of both paragraphs (c)(1) and (c)(2) of this section is governed by paragraph (c)(2).

(d) *Age* refers only to the age of natural persons and means the number of fully elapsed years from the date of an applicant's birth.

(e) *Applicant* means any person who requests or who has received an extension of credit from a creditor, and includes any person who is or may become contractually liable regarding an extension of credit. For purposes of § 202.7(d), the term includes guarantors, sureties, endorsers and similar parties.

(f) *Application* means an oral or written request for an extension of credit that is made in accordance with procedures established by a creditor for the type of credit requested. The term does not include the use of an account or line of credit to obtain an amount of credit that is within a previously established credit limit. A *completed application* means an application in connection with which a creditor has received all the information that the creditor regularly obtains and considers in evaluating applications for the amount and type of credit requested (including, but not limited to, credit reports, any additional information requested from the applicant, and any approvals or reports by governmental agencies or other persons that are necessary to guarantee, insure, or provide security for the credit or collateral). The creditor shall exercise reasonable diligence in obtaining such information.

(g) *Business credit* refers to extensions of credit primarily for business or commercial (including agricultural) purposes, but excluding extensions of credit of the types described in § 202.3 (a), (b), and (d).

(h) *Consumer credit* means credit extended to a natural person primarily for personal, family, or household purposes.

(i) *Contractually liable* means expressly obligated to repay all debts arising on an account by reason of an agreement to that effect.

(j) *Credit* means the right granted by a creditor to an applicant to defer payment of a debt, incur debt and defer its payment, or purchase property or services and defer payment therefor.

(k) *Credit card* means any card, plate, coupon book, or other single credit device that may be used from time to time to obtain money, property, or services on credit.

(l) *Creditor* means a person who, in the ordinary course of business, regularly participates in the decision of whether or not to extend credit. The term includes a creditor's assignee, transferee, or subrogee who so participates. For purposes of §§ 202.4 and 202.5(a), the term also includes a person who, in the ordinary course of business, regularly refers applicants or prospective applicants to creditors, or selects or offers to select creditors to whom requests for credit may be made. A person is not a creditor regarding any violation of the act or this regulation committed by another creditor unless the person knew or had reasonable notice of the act, policy, or practice that constituted the violation before becoming involved in the credit transaction. The term does not include a person whose only participation in a credit transaction involves honoring a credit card.

(m) *Credit transaction* means every aspect of an applicant's dealings with a creditor regarding an application for credit or an existing extension of credit (including, but not limited to, information requirements; investigation procedures; standards of creditworthiness; terms of credit; furnishing of credit information; revocation, alteration, or termination of credit; and collection procedures).

(n) *Discriminate against an applicant* means to treat an applicant less favorably than other applicants.

(o) *Elderly* means age 62 or older.

(p) *Empirically derived and other credit scoring systems*—(1) *A credit scoring system* is a system that evaluates an applicant's creditworthiness mechanically, based on key attributes of the applicant and aspects of the transaction, and that determines, alone or in conjunction with an evaluation of additional information about the applicant, whether an applicant is deemed creditworthy. To qualify as an *empirically derived, demonstrably and statistically sound, credit scoring system*, the system must be:

(i) Based on data that are derived from an empirical comparison of sample groups or the population of creditworthy and noncreditworthy applicants who applied for credit within a reasonable preceding period of time;

(ii) Developed for the purpose of evaluating the creditworthiness of applicants with respect to the legitimate business interests of the creditor utilizing the system (including, but not limited to, minimizing bad debt losses and operating expenses in accordance with the creditor's business judgment);

(iii) Developed and validated using accepted statistical principles and methodology; and

(iv) Periodically revalidated by the use of appropriate statistical principles and methodology and adjusted as necessary to maintain predictive ability.

(2) A creditor may use an empirically derived, demonstrably and statistically sound, credit scoring system obtained from another person or may obtain credit experience from which to develop such a system. Any such system must satisfy the criteria set forth in paragraph (p)(1) (i) through (iv) of this section; if the creditor is unable during the development process to validate the system based on its own credit experience in accordance with paragraph (p)(1) of this section, the system must be validated when sufficient credit experience becomes available. A system that fails this validity test is no longer an empirically derived, demonstrably and statistically sound, credit scoring system for that creditor.

(q) *Extend credit* and *extension of credit* mean the granting of credit in any form (including, but not limited to, credit granted in addition to any existing credit or credit limit; credit granted pursuant to an open-end credit plan; the refinancing or other renewal of credit, including the issuance of a new credit card in place of an expiring credit card or in substitution for an existing credit card; the consolidation of two or more obligations; or the continuance of existing credit without any special effort to collect at or after maturity).

(r) *Good faith* means honesty in fact in the conduct or transaction.

(s) *Inadvertent error* means a mechanical, electronic, or clerical error that a creditor demonstrates was not intentional and occurred notwithstanding the maintenance of procedures reasonably adapted to avoid such errors.

(t) *Judgmental system of evaluating applicants* means any system for evaluating the creditworthiness of an applicant other than an empirically derived, demonstrably and statistically sound, credit scoring system.

(u) *Marital status* means the state of being unmarried, married, or separated, as defined by applicable state law. The term "unmarried" includes persons who are single, divorced, or widowed.

(v) *Negative factor or value*, in relation to the age of elderly applicants, means utilizing a factor, value, or weight that is less favorable regarding elderly applicants than the creditor's experience warrants or is less favorable than the factor, value, or weight assigned to the class of applicants that are not classified as elderly and are most favored by a creditor on the basis of age.

(w) *Open-end credit* means credit extended under a plan under which a creditor may permit an applicant to make purchases or obtain loans from time to time directly from the creditor or indirectly by use of a credit card, check, or other device.

(x) *Person* means a natural person, corporation, government or governmental subdivision or agency, trust, estate, partnership, cooperative, or association.

(y) *Pertinent element of creditworthiness*, in relation to a judgmental system of evaluating applicants, means any information about applicants that a creditor obtains and considers and that has a demonstrable relationship to a determination of creditworthiness.

(z) *Prohibited basis* means race, color, religion, national origin, sex, marital status, or age (provided that the applicant has the capacity to enter into a binding contract); the fact that all or part of the applicant's income derives from any public assistance program; or the fact that the applicant has in good faith exercised any right under the Consumer Credit Protection Act or any state law upon which an exemption has been granted by the Board.

(aa) *State* means any State, the District of Columbia, the Commonwealth of Puerto Rico, or any territory or possession of the United States.

[Reg. B, 50 FR 48026, Nov. 20, 1985, as amended at 54 FR 50485, Dec. 7, 1989]

§ 202.3 Limited exceptions for certain classes of transactions

(a) *Public utilities credit*—(1) *Definition.* Public utilities credit refers to extensions of credit that involve public utility services provided through pipe, wire, or other connected facilities, or radio or similar transmission (including extensions of such facilities), if the charges for service, delayed payment, and any discount for prompt payment are filed with or regulated by a government unit.

(2) *Exceptions.* The following provisions of this regulation do not apply to public utilities credit:

(i) Section 202.5(d)(1) concerning information about marital status;

(ii) Section 202.10 relating to furnishing of credit information; and

(iii) Section 202.12(b) relating to record retention.

(b) *Securities credit*—(1) *Definition.* Securities credit refers to extensions of credit subject to regulation under section 7 of the Securities Exchange Act of 1934 or extensions of credit by a broker or dealer subject to regulation as a broker or dealer under the Securities Exchange Act of 1934.

(2) *Exceptions.* The following provisions of this regulation do not apply to securities credit:

(i) Section 202.5(c) concerning information about a spouse or former spouse;

(ii) Section 202.5(d)(1) concerning information about marital status;

(iii) Section 202.5(d)(3) concerning information about the sex of an applicant;

(iv) Section 202.7(b) relating to designation of name, but only to the extent necessary to prevent violation of rules regarding an account in which a broker or dealer has an interest, or rules necessitating the aggregation of accounts of spouses for the purpose of determining controlling interests, beneficial interests, beneficial ownership, or purchase limitations and restrictions;

(v) Section 202.7(c) relating to action concerning open-end accounts, but only to the extent the action taken is on the basis of a change of name or marital status;

(vi) Section 202.7(d) relating to the signature of a spouse or other person;

(vii) Section 202.10 relating to furnishing of credit information; and

(viii) Section 202.12(b) relating to record retention.

(c) *Incidental credit.* (1) *Definition.* Incidental credit refers to extensions of consumer credit other than credit of the types described in paragraphs (a) and (b) of this section:

(i) That are not made pursuant to the terms of a credit card account;

(ii) That are not subject to a finance charge (as defined in Regulation Z, 12 CFR 226.4); and

(iii) That are not payable by agreement in more than four installments.

(2) *Exceptions.* The following provisions of this regulation do not apply to incidental credit:

(i) Section 202.5(c) concerning information about a spouse or former spouse;

(ii) Section 202.5(d)(1) concerning information about marital status;

(iii) Section 202.5(d)(2) concerning information about income derived from alimony, child support, or separate maintenance payments;

(iv) Section 202.5(d)(3) concerning information about the sex of an applicant, but only to the extent necessary for medical records or similar purposes;

(v) Section 202.7(d) relating to the signature of a spouse or other person;

(vi) Section 202.9 relating to notifications;

(vii) Section 202.10 relating to furnishing of credit information; and

(viii) Section 202.12(b) relating to record retention.

(d) *Government credit*—(1) *Definition.* Government credit refers to extensions of credit made to governments or governmental subdivisions, agencies, or instrumentalities.

(2) *Applicability of regulation.* Except for section 202.4, the general rule prohibiting discrimination on a prohibited basis, the requirements of this regulation do not apply to government credit.

[Reg. B, 50 FR 48026, Nov. 20, 1985, as amended at 54 FR 50485, Dec. 7, 1989]

§ 202.4 General rule prohibiting discrimination.

A creditor shall not discriminate against an applicant on a prohibited basis regarding any aspect of a credit transaction.

§ 202.5 Rules concerning taking of applications.

(a) *Discouraging applications.* A creditor shall not make any oral or written statement, in advertising or otherwise, to applicants or prospective applicants that would discourage on a prohibited basis a reasonable person from making or pursuing an application.

(b) *General rules concerning requests for information.* (1) Except as provided in paragraphs (c) and (d) of this section, a creditor may request any information in connection with an application.[1]

(2) *Required collection of information.* Notwithstanding paragraphs (c) and (d) of this section, a creditor shall request information for monitoring purposes as required by § 202.13 for credit secured by the applicant's dwelling. In addition, a creditor may obtain information required by a regulation, order, or agreement issued by, or entered into with, a court or an enforcement agency (including the Attorney General of the United States or a similar state official) to monitor or enforce compliance with the act, this regulation, or other federal or state statute or regulation.

(3) *Special purpose credit.* A creditor may obtain information that is otherwise restricted to determine eligibility for a special purpose credit program, as provided in §§ 202.8 (c) and (d).

(c) *Information about a spouse or former spouse.* (1) Except as permitted in this paragraph, a creditor may not request any information concerning the spouse or former spouse of an applicant.

(2) *Permissible inquiries.* A creditor may request any information concerning an applicant's spouse (or former spouse under paragraph (c)(2)(v)) that may be requested about the applicant if:

(i) The spouse will be permitted to use the account;

(ii) The spouse will be contractually liable on the account;

(iii) The applicant is relying on the spouse's income as a basis for repayment of the credit requested;

(iv) The applicant resides in a community property state or property on which the applicant is relying as a basis for repayment of the credit requested is located in such a state; or

(v) The applicant is relying on alimony, child support, or separate maintenance payments from a spouse or former spouse as a basis for repayment of the credit requested.

(3) *Other accounts of the applicant.* A creditor may request an applicant to list any account upon which the applicant is liable and to provide the name and address in which the account is carried. A creditor may also ask the names in which an applicant has previously received credit.

(d) *Other limitations on information requests*—(1) *Marital status.* If an applicant applies for individual unsecured credit, a creditor shall not inquire about the applicant's marital status unless the applicant resides in a community property state or is relying on property located in such a state as a basis for repayment of the credit requested. If an application is for other than individual unsecured credit, a creditor may inquire about the applicant's marital status, but shall use only the terms "married," "unmarried," and "separated." A creditor may explain that the category "unmarried" includes single, divorced, and widowed persons.

(2) *Disclosure about income from alimony, child support, or separate maintenance.* A creditor shall not inquire whether income stated in an application is derived from alimony, child support, or separate maintenance payments unless the creditor discloses to the applicant that such income need not be revealed if the applicant does not want the creditor to consider it in determining the applicant's creditworthiness.

(3) *Sex.* A creditor shall not inquire about the sex of an applicant. An applicant may be requested to designate a title on an application form (such as Ms., Miss, Mr., or Mrs.) if the form discloses that the designation of a title is optional. An application form shall otherwise use only terms that are neutral as to sex.

(4) *Childbearing, childrearing.* A creditor shall not inquire about birth control practices, intentions concerning the bearing or rearing of children, or capability to bear children. A creditor may inquire about the number and ages of an applicant's dependents or about dependent-related financial obligations or expenditures, provided such information is requested without regard to sex, marital status, or any other prohibited basis.

(5) *Race, color, religion, national origin.* A creditor shall not inquire about the race, color, religion, or national origin of an applicant or any other person in connection with a credit transaction. A creditor may inquire about an applicant's permanent residence and immigration status.

[1] This paragraph does not limit or abrogate any federal or state law regarding privacy, privileged information, credit reporting limitations, or similar restrictions on obtainable information.

(e) *Written applications.* A creditor shall take written applications for the types of credit covered by § 202.13(a), but need not take written applications for other types of credit.

§ 202.6 Rules concerning evaluation of applications.

(a) *General rule concerning use of information.* Except as otherwise provided in the Act and this regulation, a creditor may consider any information obtained, so long as the information is not used to discriminate against an applicant on a prohibited basis.[2]

(b) *Specific rules concerning use of information.* (1) Except as provided in the act and this regulation, a creditor shall not take a prohibited basis into account in any system of evaluating the creditworthiness of applicants.

(2) *Age, receipt of public assistance.* (i) Except as permitted in this paragraph (b)(2), a creditor shall not take into account an applicant's age (provided that the applicant has the capacity to enter into a binding contract) or whether an applicant's income derives from any public assistance program.

(ii) In an empirically derived, demonstrably and statistically sound, credit scoring system, a creditor may use an applicant's age as a predictive variable, provided that the age of an elderly applicant is not assigned a negative factor or value.

(iii) In a judgmental system of evaluating creditworthiness, a creditor may consider an applicant's age or whether an applicant's income derives from any public assistance program only for the purpose of determining a pertinent element of creditworthiness.

(iv) In any system of evaluating creditworthiness, a creditor may consider the age of an elderly applicant when such age is used to favor the elderly applicant in extending credit.

(3) *Childbearing, childrearing.* In evaluating creditworthiness, a creditor shall not use assumptions or aggregate statistics relating to the likelihood that any group of persons will bear or rear children or will, for that reason, receive diminished or interrupted income in the future.

(4) *Telephone listing.* A creditor shall not take into account whether there is a telephone listing in the name of an applicant for consumer credit, but may take into account whether there is a telephone in the applicant's residence.

(5) *Income.* A creditor shall not discount or exclude from consideration the income of an applicant or the spouse of an applicant because of a prohibited basis or because the income is derived from part-time employment or is an annuity, pension, or other retirement benefit; a creditor may consider the amount and probable continuance of any income in evaluating an applicant's creditworthiness. When an applicant relies on alimony, child support, or separate maintenance payments in applying for credit, the creditor shall consider such payments as income to the extent that they are likely to be consistently made.

(6) *Credit history.* To the extent that a creditor considers credit history in evaluating the creditworthiness of similarly qualified applicants for a similar type and amount of credit, in evaluating an applicant's creditworthiness a creditor shall consider:

(i) The credit history, when available, of accounts designated as accounts that the applicant and the applicant's spouse are permitted to use or for which both are contractually liable;

(ii) On the applicant's request, any information the applicant may present that tends to indicate that the credit history being considered by the creditor does not accurately reflect the applicant's creditworthiness; and

(iii) On the applicant's request, the credit history, when available, of any account reported in the name of the applicant's spouse or former spouse that the applicant can demonstrate accurately reflects the applicant's creditworthiness.

(7) *Immigration status.* A creditor may consider whether an applicant is a permanent resident of the United States, the applicant's immigration status, and any additional information that may be necessary to ascertain the creditor's rights and remedies regarding repayment.

(c) *State property laws.* A creditor's consideration or application of state property laws directly or indirectly affecting creditworthiness does not constitute unlawful discrimination for the purposes of the Act or this regulation.

§ 202.7 Rules concerning extensions of credit.

(a) *Individual accounts.* A creditor shall not refuse to grant an individual account to a creditworthy applicant on the basis of sex, marital status, or any other prohibited basis.

(b) *Designation of name.* A creditor shall not refuse to allow an applicant to open or maintain an account in a birth-given first name and a surname that is the applicant's birth-given surname, the spouse's surname, or a combined surname.

(c) *Action concerning existing open-end accounts*—(1) *Limitations.* In the absence of evidence of the applicant's inability or unwillingness to repay, a creditor shall not take any of the following actions regarding an applicant who is contractually liable on an existing open-end account on the basis of the applicant's reaching a certain age or retiring or on the basis of a change in the applicant's name or marital status:

(i) Require a reapplication, except as provided in paragraph (c)(2) of this section;

(ii) Change the terms of the account; or

(iii) Terminate the account.

(2) *Requiring reapplication.* A creditor may require a reapplication for an open-end account on the basis of a change in the marital status of an applicant who is contractually liable if the credit granted was based in whole or in part on income of the applicant's spouse and if information available to the creditor indicates that the applicant's income may not support the amount of credit currently available.

(d) *Signature of spouse or other person*—(1) *Rule for qualified applicant.* Except as provided in this paragraph, a creditor shall not require the signature of an applicant's spouse or other person, other than a joint applicant, on any credit instrument if the applicant qualifies under the creditor's standards of creditworthiness for the amount and terms of the credit requested.

(2) *Unsecured credit.* If an applicant requests unsecured credit and relies in part upon property that the applicant owns jointly with another person to satisfy the creditor's standards of creditworthiness, the creditor may require the signature of the other person only on the instrument(s) necessary, or reasonably believed by the creditor to be necessary, under the law of the state in which the property is located, to enable the creditor to reach the property being relied upon in the event of the death or default of the applicant.

(3) *Unsecured credit—community property states.* If a married applicant requests unsecured credit and resides in a community property state, or if the property upon which the applicant is relying is located in such a state, a creditor may require the signature of the spouse on any instrument necessary, or reasonably believed by the creditor to be necessary, under applicable state law to make the community property available to satisfy the debt in the event of default if:

(i) Applicable state law denies the applicant power to manage or control sufficient community property to qualify for the amount of credit requested under the creditor's standards of creditworthiness; and

(ii) The applicant does not have sufficient separate property to qualify for the amount of credit requested without regard to community property.

(4) *Secured credit.* If an applicant requests secured credit, a creditor may require the signature of the applicant's spouse or other person on any instrument necessary, or reasonably believed by the creditor to be necessary, under applicable state law to make the property being offered as security available to satisfy the debt in the event of default, for example, an instrument to create a valid lien, pass clear title, waive inchoate rights or assign earnings.

(5) *Additional parties.* If, under a creditor's standards of creditworthiness, the personal liability of an additional party is necessary to support the extension of the credit requested, a creditor may request a cosigner, guarantor, or the like. The applicant's spouse may serve as an additional party, but the creditor shall not require that the spouse be the additional party.

(6) *Rights of additional parties.* A creditor shall not impose requirements upon an additional party that the creditor is prohibited from imposing upon an applicant under this section.

(e) *Insurance.* A creditor shall not refuse to extend credit and shall not

---

[2] The legislative history of the Act indicates that the Congress intended an "effects test" concept, as outlined in the employment field by the Supreme Court in the cases of *Griggs* v. *Duke Power Co.*, 401 U.S. 424 (1971), and *Albemarle Paper Co.* v. *Moody*, 422 U.S. 405 (1975), to be applicable to a creditor's determination of creditworthiness.

terminate an account because credit life, health, accident, disability, or other credit-related insurance is not available on the basis of the applicant's age.

§ 202.8 Special purpose credit programs.

(a) *Standards for programs.* Subject to the provisions of paragraph (b) of this section, the act and this regulation permit a creditor to extend special purpose credit to applicants who meet eligibility requirements under the following types of credit programs:

(1) Any credit assistance program expressly authorized by federal or state law for the benefit of an economically disadvantaged class of persons;

(2) Any credit assistance program offered by a not-for-profit organization, as defined under section 501(c) of the Internal Revenue Code of 1954, as amended, for the benefit of its members or for the benefit of an economically disadvantaged class of persons; or

(3) Any special purpose credit program offered by a for-profit organization or in which such an organization participates to meet special social needs, if:

(i) The program is established and administered pursuant to a written plan that identifies the class of persons that the program is designed to benefit and sets forth the procedures and standards for extending credit pursuant to the program; and

(ii) The program is established and administered to extend credit to a class of persons who, under the organization's customary standards of creditworthiness, probably would not receive such credit or would receive it on less favorable terms than are ordinarily available to other applicants applying to the organization for a similar type and amount of credit.

(b) *Rules in other sections.* (1) *General applicability.* All of the provisions of this regulation apply to each of the special purpose credit programs described in paragraph (a) of this section unless modified by this section.

(2) *Common characteristics.* A program described in paragraph (a)(2) or (a)(3) of this section qualifies as a special purpose credit program only if it was established and is administered so as not to discriminate against an applicant on any prohibited basis; however, all program participants may be required to share one or more common characteristics (for example, race, national origin, or sex) so long as the program was not established and is not administered with the purpose of evading the requirements of the act or this regulation.

(c) *Special rule concerning requests and use of information.* If participants in a special purpose credit program described in paragraph (a) of this section are required to possess one or more common characteristics (for example, race, national origin, or sex) and if the program otherwise satisfies the requirements of paragraph (a) of this section, a creditor may request and consider information regarding the common characteristic(s) in determining the applicant's eligibility for the program.

(d) *Special rule in the case of financial need.* If financial need is one of the criteria under a special purpose program described in paragraph (a) of this section, the creditor may request and consider, in determining an applicant's eligibility for the program, information regarding the applicant's martial status; alimony, child support, and separate maintenance income; and the spouse's financial resources. In addition, a creditor may obtain the signature of an applicant's spouse or other person on an application or credit instrument relating to a special purpose program if the signature is required by Federal or State law.

§ 202.9 Notifications.

(a) *Notification of action taken, ECOA notice, and statement of specific reasons* —(1) *When notification is required.* A creditor shall notify an applicant of action taken within:

(i) 30 days after receiving a completed application concerning the creditor's approval of, counteroffer to, or adverse action on the application;

(ii) 30 days after taking adverse action on an incomplete application, unless notice is provided in accordance with paragraph (c) of this section;

(iii) 30 days after taking adverse action on an existing account; or

(iv) 90 days after notifying the applicant of a counteroffer if the applicant does not expressly accept or use the credit offered.

(2) *Content of notification when adverse action is taken.* A notification given to an applicant when adverse action is taken shall be in writing and shall contain: a statement of the action taken; the name and address of the creditor; a statement of the provisions of section 701(a) of the Act; the name and address of the Federal agency that administers compliance with respect to the creditor; and either:

(i) A statement of specific reasons for the action taken; or

(ii) A disclosure of the applicant's right to a statement of specific reasons within 30 days, if the statement is requested within 60 days of the creditor's notification. The disclosure shall include the name, address, and telephone number of the person or office from which the statement of reasons can be obtained. If the creditor chooses to provide the reasons orally, the creditor shall also disclose the applicant's right to have them confirmed in writing within 30 days of receiving a written request for confirmation from the applicant.

(3) *Notification to business credit applicants.* For business credit, a creditor shall comply with the requirements of this paragraph in the following manner:

(i) With regard to a business that had gross revenues of $1,000,000 or less in its preceding fiscal year (other than an extension of trade credit, credit incident to a factoring agreement, or other similar types of business credit), a creditor shall comply with paragraphs (a) (1) and (2) of this section, except that:

(A) The statement of the action taken may be given orally or in writing, when adverse action is taken;

(B) Disclosure of an applicant's right to a statement of reasons may be given at the time of application, instead of when adverse action is taken, provided the disclosure is in a form the applicant may retain and contains the information required by paragraph (a)(2)(ii) and the ECOA notice specified in paragraph (b)(1) of this section;

(C) For an application made solely by telephone, a creditor satisfies the requirements of this paragraph by an oral statement of the action taken and of the applicant's right to a statement of reasons for adverse action.

(ii) With regard to a business that had gross revenues in excess of $1,000,000 in its preceding fiscal year or an extension of trade credit, credit incident to a factoring agreement, or other similar types of business credit, a creditor shall:

(A) Notify the applicant, orally or in writing, within a reasonable time of the action taken; and

(B) Provide a written statement of the reasons for adverse action and the ECOA notice specified in paragraph (b)(1) of this section if the applicant makes a written request for the reasons within 60 days of being notified of the adverse action.

(b) *Form of ECOA notice and statement of specific reasons.*

(1) *ECOA notice.* To satisfy the disclosure requirements of paragraph (a)(2) of this section regarding section 701(a) of the Act, the creditor shall provide a notice that is substantially similar to the following:

The Federal Equal Credit Opportunity Act prohibits creditors from discriminating against credit applicants on the basis of race, color, religion, national origin, sex, marital status, age (provided the applicant has the capacity to enter into a binding contract); because all or part of the applicant's income derives from any public assistance program; or because the applicant has in good faith exercised any right under the Consumer Credit Protection Act. The Federal agency that administers compliance with this law concerning this creditor is (name and address as specified by the appropriate agency listed in Appendix A of this regulation).

(2) *Statement of specific reasons.* The statement of reasons for adverse action required by paragraph (a)(2)(i) of this section must be specific and indicate the principal reason(s) for the adverse action. Statements that the adverse action was based on the creditor's internal standards or policies or that the applicant failed to achieve the qualifying score on the creditor's credit scoring system are insufficient.

(c) *Incomplete applications*—(1) *Notice alternatives.* Within 30 days after receiving application that is incomplete regarding matters that an applicant can complete, the creditor shall notify the applicant either:

(i) Of action taken, in accordance with paragraph (a) of this section; or

(ii) Of the incompleteness, in accordance with paragraph (c)(2) of this section.

(2) *Notice of incompleteness.* If additional information is needed from an applicant, the creditor shall send a written notice to the applicant specifying the information needed, designating a reasonable period of time for the applicant to provide the information, and informing the applicant that fail-

ure to provide the information requested will result in no further consideration being given to the application. The creditor shall have no further obligation under this section if the applicant fails to respond within the designated time period. If the applicant supplies the requested information within the designated time period, the creditor shall take action on the application and notify the applicant in accordance with paragraph (a) of this section.

(3) *Oral request for information.* At its option, a creditor may inform the applicant orally of the need for additional information; but if the application remains incomplete the creditor shall send a notice in accordance with paragraph (c)(1) of this section.

(d) *Oral notifications by small-volume creditors.* The requirements of this section (including statements of specific reasons) are satisified by oral notifications in the case of any creditor that did not receive more than 150 applications during the preceding calendar year.

(e) *Withdrawal of approved application.* When an applicant submits an application and the parties contemplate that the applicant will inquire about its status, if the creditor approves the application and the applicant has not inquired within 30 days after applying, the creditor may treat the application as withdrawn and need not comply with paragraph (a)(1) of this section.

(f) *Multiple applicants.* When an application involves more than one applicant, notification need only be given to one of them, but must be given to the primary applicant where one is readily apparent.

(g) *Applications submitted through a third party.* When an application is made on behalf of an applicant to more than one creditor and the applicant expressly accepts or uses credit offered by one of the creditors, notification of action taken by any of the other creditors is not required. If no credit is offered or if the applicant does not expressly accept or use any credit offered, each creditor taking adverse action must comply with this section, directly or through a third party. A notice given by a third party shall disclose the identify of each creditor on whose behalf the notice is given.

[Reg. B, 50 FR 48026, Nov. 20, 1985, as amended at 54 FR 50485, Dec. 7, 1989]

§ 202.10 Furnishing of credit information.

(a) *Designation of accounts.* A creditor tht furnishes credit information shall designate:

(1) Any new account to reflect the participation of both spouses if the applicant's spouse is permitted to use or is contractually liable on the account (other than as a guarantor, surety, endorser, or similar party); and

(2) Any existing account to reflect such participation, within 90 days after receiving a written request to do so from one of the spouses.

(b) *Routine reports to consumer reporting agency.* If a creditor furnishes credit information to a consumer reporting agency concerning an account designated to reflect the participation of both spouses, the creditor shall furnish the information in a manner that will enable the agency to provide access to the information in the name of each spouse.

(c) *Reporting in response to inquiry.* If a creditor furnishes credit information in response to an inquiry concerning an account designated to reflect the participation of both spouses, the creditor shall furnish the information in the name of the spouse about whom the information is requested.

§ 202.11 Relation to state law.

(a) *Inconsistent state laws.* Except as otherwise provided in this section, this regulation alters, affects, or preempts only those state laws that are inconsistent with the act and this regulation and then only to the extent of the inconsistency. A state law is not inconsistent if it is more protective of an applicant.

(b) *Preempted provisions of state law.* (1) A state law is deemed to be inconsistent with the requirements of the Act and this regulation and less protective of an applicant within the meaning of section 705(f) of the Act to the extent that the law:

(i) Requires or permits a practice or act prohibited by the Act or this regulation;

(ii) Prohibits the individual extension of consumer credit to both parties to a marriage if each spouse individually and voluntarily applies for such credit;

(iii) Prohibits inquiries or collection of data required to comply with the act or this regulation;

(iv) Prohibits asking or considering age in an empirically derived, demonstrably and statistically sound, credit scoring system to determine a pertinent element of creditworthiness, or to favor an elderly applicant; or

(v) Prohibits inquiries necessary to establish or administer as special purpose credit program as defined by § 202.8.

(2) A creditor, state, or other interested party may request the Board to determine whether a state law is inconsistent with the requirements of the Act and this regulation.

(c) *Laws on finance charges, loan ceilings.* If married applicants voluntarily apply for and obtained individual accounts with the same creditor, the accounts shall not be aggregated or otherwise combined for purposes of determining permissible finance charges or loan ceilings under any federal or state law. Permissible loan ceiling laws shall be construed to permit each spouse to become individually liable up to the amount of the loan ceilings, less the amount for which the applicant is jointly liable.

(d) *State and Federal laws not affected.* This section does not alter or annul any provision of state property laws, laws relating to the disposition of decedents' estates, or Federal or state banking regulations directed only toward insuring the solvency of financial institutions.

(e) *Exemption for state-regulated transactions.* (1) *Applications.* A state may apply to the Board for an exemption from the requirements of the Act and this regulation for any class of credit transactions within the state. The Board will grant such an exemption if the Board determines that:

(i) The class of credit transactions is subject to state law requirements substantially similar to the Act and this regulation or that applicants are afforded greater protection under state law; and

(ii) There is adequate provision for state enforcement.

(2) *Liability and enforcement.* (i) No exemption will extend to the civil liability provisions of section 706 or the administrative enforcement provisions of section 704 of the Act.

(ii) After an exemption has been granted, the requirements of the applicable state law (except for additional requirements not imposed by Federal law) will constitute the requirements of the Act and this regulation.

§ 202.12 Record retention.

(a) *Retention of prohibited information.* A creditor may retain in its files information that is prohibited by the Act or this regulation in evaluating applications, without violating the Act or this regulation, if the information was obtained:

(1) From any source prior to March 23, 1977;

(2) From consumer reporting agencies, an applicant, or others without the specific request of the creditor; or

(3) As required to monitor compliance with the Act and this regulation or other Federal or state statutes or regulaticns.

(b) *Preservation of records*—(1) *Applications.* For 25 months (12 months for business credit) after the date that a creditor notifies an applicant of action taken on an application or of incompleteness, the creditor shall retain in original form or a copy thereof:

(i) Any application that it receives, any information required to be obtained concerning characteristics of the applicant to monitor compliance with the Act and this regulation or other similar law, and any other written or recorded information used in evaluating the application and not returned to the applicant at the applicant's request;

(ii) A copy of the following documents if furnished to the applicant in written form (or, if furnished orally, any notation or memorandum made by the creditor):

(A) The notification of action taken; and

(B) The statement of specific reasons for adverse action; and

(iii) Any written statement submitted by the applicant alleging a violation of the Act or this regulation.

(2) *Existing accounts.* For 25 months (12 months for business credit) after the date that a creditor notifies an applicant of adverse action regarding an existing account, the creditor shall retain as to that account, in original form or a copy thereof:

(i) Any written or recorded information concerning the adverse action; and

(ii) Any written statement submitted by the applicant alleging a violation of the act or this regulation.

(3) *Other applications.* For 25 months (12 months for business credit) after the date that a creditor receives an application for which the creditor is not required to comply with

the notification requirements of § 202.9, the creditor shall retain all written or recorded information in its possession concerning the applicant, including any notation of action taken.

(4) *Enforcement proceedings and investigations.* A creditor shall retain the information specified in this section beyond 25 months (12 months for business credit) if it has actual notice that it is under investigation or is subject to an enforcement proceeding for an alleged violation of the act or this regulation by the Attorney General of the United States or by an enforcement agency charged with monitoring that creditor's compliance with the act and this regulation, or if it has been served with notice of an action filed pursuant to section 706 of the Act and § 202.14 of this regulation. The creditor shall retain the information until final disposition of the matter, unless an earlier time is allowed by order of the agency or court.

(5) *Special rule for certain business credit applications.* With regard to a business with gross revenues in excess of $1,000,000 in its preceding fiscal year, or an extension of trade credit, credit incident to a factoring agreement or other similar types of business credit, the creditor shall retain records for at least 60 days after notifying the applicant of the action taken. If within that time period the applicant requests in writing the reasons for adverse action or that records be retained, the creditor shall retain records for 12 months.

[Reg. B, 50 FR 48026, Nov. 20, 1985, as amended at 54 FR 50486, Dec. 7, 1989]

§ 202.13 Information for monitoring purposes.

(a) *Information to be requested.* A creditor that receives an application for credit primarily for the purchase or refinancing of a dwelling occupied or to be occupied by the applicant as a principal residence, where the extension of credit will be secured by the dwelling, shall request as part of the application the following information regarding the applicant(s):

(1) Race or national origin, using the categories American Indian or Alaskan Native; Asian or Pacific Islander; Black; White; Hispanic; Other (Specify);

(2) Sex;

(3) Marital status, using the categories married, unmarried, and separated; and

(4) Age.

"Dwelling" means a residential structure that contains one to four units, whether or not that structure is attached to real property. The term includes, but is not limited to, an individual condominium or cooperative unit, and a mobile or other manufactured home.

(b) *Obtaining of information.* Questions regarding race or national origin, sex, marital status, and age may be listed, at the creditor's option, on the application form or on a separate form that refers to the application. The applicant(s) shall be asked but not required to supply the requested information. If the applicant(s) chooses not to provide the information or any part of it, that fact shall be noted on the form. The creditor shall then also note on the form, to the extent possible, the race or national origin and sex of the applicant(s) on the basis of visual observation or surname.

(c) *Disclosure to applicant(s).* The creditor shall inform the applicant(s) that the information regarding race or national origin, sex, marital status, and age is being requested by the Federal government for the purpose of monitoring compliance with Federal statutes that prohibit creditors from discriminating against appliants on those bases. The creditor shall also inform the applicant(s) that if the applicant(s) chooses note to provide the information, the creditor is required to note the race or national origin and sex on the basis of visual observation or surname.

(d) *Substitute monitoring program.* A monitoring program required by an agency charged with administrative enforcement under section 704 of the Act may be substituted for the requirements contained in paragraphs (a), (b), and (c).

§ 202.14 Enforcement, penalties and liabilities.

(a) *Administrative enforcement.* (1) As set forth more fully in section 704 of the Act, administrative enforcement of the Act and this regulation regarding certain creditors is assigned to the Comptroller of the Currency, Board of Governors of the Federal Reserve System, Board of Directors of the Federal Deposit Insurance Corporation, Office of Thrift Supervision, National Credit Union Administration, Interstate Commerce Commission, Secretary of Agriculture, Farm Credit Administration, Securities and Exchange Commission, Small Business Administration, and Secretary of Transportation.

(2) Except to the extent that administrative enforcement is specifically assigned to other authorities, compliance with the requirements imposed under the act and this regulation is enforced by the Federal Trade Commission.

(b) *Penalties and liabilities.* (1) Sections 706 (a) and (b) and 702(g) of the Act provide that any creditor that fails to comply with a requirement imposed by the Act or this regulation is subject to civil liability for actual and punitive damages in individual or class actions. Pursuant to sections 704 (b), (c), and (d) and 702(g) of the Act, violations of the Act or regulations also constitute violations of other Federal laws. Liability for punitive damages is restricted to nongovernmental entities and is limited to $10,000 in individual actions and the lesser of $500,000 or 1 percent of the creditor's net worth in class actions. Section 706(c) provides for equitable and declaratory relief and section 706(d) authorizes the awarding of costs and reasonable attorney's fees to an aggrieved applicant in a successful action.

(2) As provided in section 706(f), a civil action under the Act or this regulation may be brought in the appropriate United States district court without regard to the amount in controversy or in any other court of competent jurisdiction within two years after the date of the occurrence of the violation, or within one year after the commencement of an administrative enforcement proceeding or of a civil action brought by the Attorney General of the United States within two years after the alleged violation.

(3) Sections 706 (g) and (h) provide that, if an agency responsible for administrative enforcement is unable to obtain compliance with the Act or this regulation, it may refer the matter to the Attorney General of the United States. On referral, or whenever the Attorney General has reason to believe that one or more creditors are engaged in a pattern or practice in violation of the Act or this regulation, the Attorney General may bring a civil action.

(c) *Failure of compliance.* A creditor's failure to comply with §§ 202.6(b)(6), 202.9, 202.10, 202.12 or 202.13 is not a violation if it results from an inadvertent error. On discovering an error under §§ 202.9 and 202.10, the creditor shall correct it as soon as possible. If a creditor inadvertently obtains the monitoring information regarding the race or national origin and sex of the applicant in a dwelling-related transaction not overed by § 202.13, the creditor may act on and retain the application without violating the regulation.

[Reg. B, 50 FR 48026, Nov. 20, 1985, as amended at 54 FR 53539, Dec. 29, 1989]

Appendix A to Part 202—Federal Enforcement Agencies

The following list indicates the Federal agencies the enforce Regulation B for particular classes of creditors. Any questions concerning a particular creditor should be directed to its enforcement agency.

National Banks

Comptroller of the Currency, Consumer Examinations Division, Washington, DC 20219.

State Member Banks

Federal Reserve Bank serving the district in which the state member bank is located.

Nonmember Insured Banks

Federal Deposit Insurance Corporation Regional Director for the region in which the nonmember insured bank is located.

Savings institutions insured under the Savings Association Insurance Fund of the FDIC and federally chartered saving banks insured under the Bank Insurance Fund of the FDIC (but not including state-chartered savings banks insured under the Bank Insurance Fund).

The District Director of the Office of Thrift Supervision in the District in which the institution is located.

5. Texas Deceptive Trade Practices Act

DECEPTIVE TRADE PRACTICES— CONSUMER PROTECTION ACT (AS AMENDED THROUGH 1991)

Sec. 17.41. Short Title

This subchapter may be cited as the Deceptive Trade Practices—Consumer Protection Act.

Sec. 17.42. Waivers: Public Policy

(a) Any waiver by a consumer of the provisions of this subchapter is contrary to public policy and is unenforceable and void; provided, however, that a waiver is valid and enforceable if a defendant in an action or claim under this subchapter pleads and proves:

(1) the consumer is not in a significantly disparate bargaining position;

(2) the consumer is represented by legal counsel in seeking or acquiring goods or services, other than the purchase or lease of a family residence occupied or to be occupied as the consumer's residence, by a purchase or a lease for a consideration paid or to be paid that exceeds $500,000; and

(3) the consumer waives all or part of this subchapter, other than Section 17.555, by an express provision in a written contract signed by both the consumer and the consumer's legal counsel; and provided, however, that a business consumer with assets of $5 million or more according to the most recent financial statement of the business consumer prepared in accordance with generally accepted accounting principles that has knowledge and experience in financial and business matters that enable it to evaluate the merits and risks of a transaction and that is not in a significantly disparate bargaining position may by written contract waive the provisions of this subchapter, other than Section 17.555.

(b) The existence or absence of a disparate bargaining position may not be established as a matter of law solely by evidence of the consumer's financial position relative to other parties to the contract or by matters contained in a written contract relating to the relative bargaining position of the parties.

Sec. 17.43. Cumulative Remedies

The provisions of this subchapter are not exclusive. The remedies provided in this subchapter are in addition to any other procedures or remedies provided for in any other law; provided, however, that no recovery shall be permitted under both this subchapter and another law of both actual damages and penalties for the same act or practice. A violation of a provision of law other than this subchapter is not in and of itself a violation of this subchapter. An act or practice that is a violation of a provision of law other than this subchapter may be made the basis of an action under this subchapter if the act or practice is proscribed by a provision of this subchapter or is declared by such other law to be actionable under this subchapter. The provisions of this subchapter do not in any way preclude other political subdivisions of this state from dealing with deceptive trade practices.

Sec. 17.44. Construction and Application

This subchapter shall be liberally construed and applied to promote its underlying purposes, which are to protect consumers against false, misleading, and deceptive business practices, unconscionable actions, and breaches of warranty and to provide efficient and economical procedures to secure such protection.

Sec. 17.45. Definitions

As used in this subchapter:

(1) "Goods" means tangible chattels or real property purchased or leased for use.

(2) "Services" means work, labor, or service purchased or leased for use, including services furnished in connection with the sale or repair of goods.

(3) "Person" means an individual, partnership, corporation, association, or other group, however organized.

(4) "Consumer" means an individual, partnership, corporation, this state, or a subdivision or agency of this state who seeks or acquires by purchase or lease, any goods or services, except that the term does not include a business consumer that has assets of $25 million or more, or that is owned or controlled by a corporation or entity with assets of $25 million or more.

(5) "Unconscionable action or course of action" means an act or practice which, to a person's detriment:

(A) takes advantage of the lack of knowledge, ability, experience, or capacity of a person to a grossly unfair degree; or

(B) results in a gross disparity between the value received and the consideration paid, in a transaction involving transfer of consideration.

(6) "Trade" and "commerce" mean the advertising, offering for sale, sale, lease, or distribution of any good or service, of any property, tangible or intangible, real, personal, or mixed, and any other article, commodity, or thing of value, wherever situated, and shall include any trade or commerce directly or indirectly affecting the people of this state.

(7) "Documentary material" includes the original or a copy of any book, record, report, memorandum, paper, communication, tabulation, map, chart, photograph, mechanical transcription, or other tangible document or recording, wherever situated.

(8) "Consumer protection division" means the antitrust and consumer protection division of the attorney general's office.

(9) "Knowingly" means actual awareness of the falsity, deception, or unfairness of the act or practice giving rise to the consumer's claim or, in an action brought under Subdivision (2) of Subsection (a) of Section 17.50, actual awareness of the act or practice constituting the breach of warranty, but actual awareness may be inferred where objective manifestations indicate that a person acted with actual awareness.

(10) "Business consumer" means an individual, partnership, or corporation who seeks or acquires by purchase or lease, any goods or services for commercial or business use. The term does not include this state or a subdivision or agency of this state.

Sec. 17.46. Deceptive Trade Practices Unlawful

(a) False, misleading, or deceptive acts or practices in the conduct of any trade or commerce are hereby declared unlawful and are subject to action by the consumer protection division under Sections 17.47, 17.58, 17.60, and 17.61 of this code.

(b) Except as provided in Subsection (d) of this section, the term "false, misleading, or deceptive acts or practices" includes, but is not limited to, the following acts:

(1) passing off goods or services as those of another;

(2) causing confusion or misunderstanding as to the source, sponsorship, approval, or certification of goods or services;

(3) causing confusion or misunderstanding as to affiliation, connection, or association with, or certification by, another;

(4) using deceptive representations or designations of geographic origin in connection with goods or services;

(5) representing that goods or services have sponsorship, approval, characteristics, ingredients, uses, benefits, or quantities which they do not have or that a person has a sponsorship, approval, status, affiliation, or connection which he does not;

(6) representing that goods are original or new if they are deteriorated, reconditioned, reclaimed, used, or secondhand;

(7) representing that goods or services are of a particular standard, quality, or grade, or that goods are of a particular style or model, if they are of another;

(8) disparaging the goods, services, or business of another by false or misleading representation of facts;

(9) advertising goods or services with intent not to sell them as advertised;

(10) advertising goods or services with intent not to supply a reasonable expectable public demand, unless the advertisements disclosed a limitation of quantity;

(11) making false or misleading statements of fact concerning the reasons for, existence of, or amount of price reductions;

(12) representing that an agreement confers or involves rights, remedies, or obligations which it does not have or involve, or which are prohibited by law;

(13) knowingly making false or misleading statements of fact concerning the need for parts, replacement, or repair service;

(14) misrepresenting the authority of a salesman, representative or agent to negotiate the final terms of a consumer transaction;

(15) basing a charge for the repair of any item in whole or in part on a guaranty or warranty instead of on the value of the actual repairs made or work to be performed on the item without stating separately the charges for the work and the charge for the warranty or guaranty, if any;

(16) disconnecting, turning back, or resetting the odometer of any motor vehicle so as to reduce the number of miles indicated on the odometer gauge;

(17) advertising of any sale by fraudulently representing that a person is going out of business;

(18) using or employing a chain referral sales plan in connection with the sale or offer to sell of goods, merchandise, or anything of value, which uses the sales technique, plan, arrangement, or agreement in which the buyer or prospective buyer is offered the opportunity to purchase merchandise or goods and in connection with the purchase receives the seller's promise or representation that the buyer shall have the right to receive compensation or consideration in any form for furnishing to the seller the names of other prospective buyers if receipt of the compensation or consideration is contingent upon the occurrence of an event subsequent to the time the buyer purchases the merchandise or goods;

(19) representing that a guarantee or warranty confers or involves rights or remedies which it does not have or involve, provided, however, that nothing in this subchapter shall be construed to expand the implied warranty of merchantability as defined in Sections 2.314 through 2.318 of the Business & Commerce Code to involve obligations in excess of those which are appropriate to the goods;

(20) selling or offering to sell, either directly or associated with the sale of goods or services, a right of participation in a multi-level distributorship. As used herein, "multi-level distributorship" means a sales plan for the distribution of goods or services in which promises of rebate or payment are made to individuals, conditioned upon those individuals recommending or securing additional individuals to assume positions in the sales operation, and where the rebate or payment is not exclusively conditioned on or in relation to proceeds from the retail sales of goods;

(21) representing that work or services have been performed on, or parts replaced in, goods when the work or services were not performed or the parts replaced;

(22) filing suit founded upon a written contractual obligation of and signed by the defendant to pay money arising out of or based on a consumer transaction for goods, services, loans, or extensions of credit intended primarily for personal, family, household, or agricultural use in any county other than in the county in which the defendant resides at the time of the commencement of the action or in the county in which the defendant in fact signed the contract; provided, however, that a violation of this subsection shall not occur where it is shown by the person filing such suit he neither knew or had reason to know that the county in which such suit was filed was neither the county in which the defendant resides at the commencement of the suit nor the county in which the defendant in fact signed the contract;

(23) the failure to disclose information concerning goods or services which was known at the time of the transaction if such failure to disclose such information was intended to induce the consumer into a transaction into which the consumer would not have entered had the information been disclosed; or

(24) using the term "corporation," "incorporated," or an abbreviation of either of those terms in the name of a business entity that is not incorporated under the laws of this state or another jurisdiction.

(c)(1) It is the intent of the legislature that in construing Subsection (a) of this section in suits brought under Section 17.47 of this subchapter the courts to the extent possible will be guided by Subsection (b) of this section and the interpretations given by the Federal Trade Commission and federal courts to Section 5(a)(1) of the Federal Trade Commission Act [15 U.S.C.A. § 45(a)(1)].

(2) In construing this subchapter the court shall not be prohibited from considering relevant and pertinent decisions of courts in other jurisdictions.

(d) For the purposes of the relief authorized in Subdivision (1) of Subsection (a) of Section 17.50 of this subchapter, the term "false, misleading, or deceptive acts or practices" is limited to the acts enumerated in specific subdivisions of Subsection (b) of this section.

Sec. 17.47. Restraining Orders

(a) Whenever the consumer protection division has reason to believe that any person is engaging in, has engaged in, or is about to engage in any act or practice declared to be unlawful by this subchapter, and that proceedings would be in the public interest, the division may bring an action in the name of the state against the person to restrain by temporary restraining order, temporary injunction, or permanent injunction the use of such method, act, or practice.

Nothing herein shall require the consumer protection division to notify such person that court action is or may be under consideration. Provided, however, the consumer protection division shall, at least seven days prior to instituting such court action, contact such person to inform him in general of the alleged unlawful conduct. Cessation of unlawful conduct after such prior contact shall not render such court action moot under any circumstances, and such injunctive relief shall lie even if such person has ceased such unlawful conduct after such prior contact. Such prior contact shall not be required if, in the opinion of the consumer protection division, there is good cause to believe that such person would evade service of process if prior contact were made or that such person would destroy relevant records if prior contact were made, or that such an emergency exists that immediate and irreparable injury, loss, or damage would occur as a result of such delay in obtaining a temporary restraining order.

(b) An action brought under Subsection (a) of this section which alleges a claim to relief under this section may be commenced in the district court of the county in which the person against whom it is brought resides, has his principal place of business, has done business, or in the district court of the county where the transaction occurred, or, on the consent of the parties, in a district court of Travis County. The court may issue temporary restraining orders, temporary or permanent injunctions to restrain and prevent violations of this subchapter and such injunctive relief shall be issued without bond.

(c) In addition to the request for a temporary restraining order, or permanent injunction in a proceeding brought under Subsection (a) of this section, the consumer protection division may request a civil penalty of not more than $2,000 per violation, not to exceed a total of $10,000, to be paid to the state.

(d) The court may make such additional orders or judgments as are necessary to compensate identifiable persons for actual damages or to restore money or property, real or personal, which may have been acquired by means of any unlawful act or practice. Damages may not include any damages incurred beyond a point two years prior to the institution of the action by the consumer protection division. Orders of the court may also include the appointment of a receiver or a sequestration of assets if a person who has been ordered by a court to make restitution under this section has failed to do so within three months after the order to make restitution has become final and nonappealable.

(e) Any person who violates the terms of an injunction under this section shall forfeit and pay to the state a civil penalty of not more than $10,000 per violation, not to exceed $50,000. In determining whether or not an injunction has been violated the court shall take into consideration the maintenance of procedures reasonably adapted to insure compliance with the injunction. For the purposes of this section, the district court issuing the injunction shall retain jurisdiction, and the cause shall be continued, and in these cases, the consumer protection division, or the district or county attorney with prior notice to the consumer protection division, acting in the name of the state, may petition for recovery of civil penalties under this section.

(f) An order of the court awarding civil penalties under Subsection (e) of this section applies only to violations of the injunction incurred prior to the awarding of the penalty order. Second or subsequent violations of an injunction issued under this section are subject to the same penalties set out in Subsection (e) of this section.

Sec. 17.48. Duty of District and County Attorney

(a) It is the duty of the district and county attorneys to lend to the consumer protection division any assistance requested in the commencement and prosecutions of action under this subchapter.

(b) A district or county attorney, with prior written notice to the consumer protection division, may institute and prosecute actions seeking injunctive relief under this subchapter, after complying with the prior contact provisions of Subsection (a) of Section 17.47 of this subchapter. On request, the consumer protection division shall assist the district or county attorney in any action taken under this subchapter. If an action is prosecuted by a district or county attorney alone, he shall make a full report to the consumer protection division including the final disposition of the matter. No district or county attorney may bring an action under this section against any licensed insurer or licensed insurance agent transacting business under the authority and jurisdiction of the State Board of Insurance unless first requested in writing to do so by the State Board of Insurance, the commissioner of insurance, or the consumer protection division pursuant to a request by the State Board of Insurance or commissioner of insurance.

Sec. 17.49. Exemptions

(a) Nothing in this subchapter shall apply to the owner or employees of a regularly published newspaper, magazine, or telephone directory, or broadcast station, or billboard, wherein any advertisement in violation of this subchapter is published or disseminated, unless it is established that the owner or employees of the advertising medium have knowledge of the false, deceptive, or misleading acts or practices declared to be unlawful by this subchapter, or had a direct or substantial financial interest in the sale or distribution of the unlawfully advertised good or service. Financial interest as used in this section relates to an expectation which would be the direct result of such advertisement.

(b) Nothing in this subchapter shall apply to acts or practices authorized under specific rules or regulations promulgated by the Federal Trade Commission under Section 5(a)(1) of the Federal Trade Commission Act [15 U.S.C.A. 45(a)(1)]. The provisions of this subchapter do apply to any act or practice prohibited or not specifically authorized by a rule or regulation of the Federal Trade Commission. An act or practice is not specifically authorized if no rule or regulation has been issued on the act or practice.

Sec. 17.50. Relief for Consumers

(a) A consumer may maintain an action where any of the following constitute a producing cause of actual damages:

(1) the use or employment by any person of a false, misleading, or deceptive act or practice that is specifically enumerated in a subdivision of Subsection (b) of Section 17.46 of this subchapter;

(2) breach of an express or implied warranty;

(3) any unconscionable action or course of action by any person; or

(4) the use or employment by any person of an act or practice in violation of Article 21.21, Texas Insurance Code, as amended, or rules or regulations issued by the State Board of Insurance under Article 21.21, Texas Insurance Code, as amended.

(b) In a suit filed under this section, each consumer who prevails may obtain:

(1) the amount of actual damages found by the trier of fact. In addition the court shall award two times that portion of the actual damages that does not exceed $1,000. If the trier of fact finds that the conduct of the defendant was committed knowingly, the trier of fact may award not more than three times the amount of actual damages in excess of $1,000, provided that:

(A) the provisions of Chapters 33 and 41, Civil Practice and Remedies Code, shall govern the determination of the consumer's right under this subchapter to recover actual and other damages, including exemplary damages, and the amount of those damages that may be recovered by the consumer under this subchapter, in an action seeking damages for (i) death; (ii) personal injury other than mental anguish or distress associated with a violation of this subchapter that does not involve death or bodily injury; or (iii) damage to property other than the goods acquired by the purchase or lease that is involved in the consumer's action or claim if that damage arises out of an occurrence that involves death or bodily injury; and

(B) only in an action under this subchapter that is subject to Paragraph (A) of this subdivision, the consumer's right to recover damages shall be subject to any defense or defensive matter that could be considered by the trier of fact in an action subject to Chapter 33, Civil Practice and Remedies Code, in determining the percentage of responsibility attributable to the consumer claimant under that chapter;

(2) an order enjoining such acts or failure to act;

(3) orders necessary to restore to any party to the suit any money or property, real or personal, which may have been acquired in violation of this subchapter; and

(4) any other relief which the court deems proper, including the appointment of a receiver or the revocation of a license or certificate authorizing a person to engage in business in this state if the judgment has not been satisfied within three months of the date of the final judgment. The court may not revoke or suspend a license to do business in this state or appoint a receiver to take over the affairs of a person who has failed to satisfy a judgment if the person is a licensee of or regulated by a state agency which has statutory authority to revoke or suspend a license or to appoint a receiver or trustee. Costs and fees of such receivership or other relief shall be assessed against the defendant.

(c) On a finding by the court that an action under this section was groundless and brought in bad faith, or brought for the purpose of harassment, the court shall award to the defendant reasonable and necessary attorneys' fees and court costs.

(d) Each consumer who prevails shall be awarded court costs and reasonable and necessary attorneys' fees.

Sec. 17.505. Notice: Offer of Settlement

(a) As a prerequisite to filing a suit seeking damages under Subdivision (1) of Subsection (b) of Section 17.50 of this subchapter against any person, a consumer shall give written notice to the person at least 60 days before filing the suit advising the person in reasonable detail of the consumer's specific complaint and the amount of actual damages and expenses, including attorneys' fees, if any, reasonably incurred by the consumer in asserting the claim against the defendant. During the 60-day period a written request to inspect, in a reasonable manner and at a reasonable time and place, the goods that are the subject of the consumer's action or claim may be presented to the consumer. If the consumer unreasonably refuses to permit the inspection, the court shall not award the two times actual damages not exceeding $1,000, as provided in Subsection (b) of Section 17.50 of this subchapter.

(b) If the giving of 60 days' written notice is rendered impracticable by reason of the necessity of filing suit in order to prevent the expiration of the statute of limitations or if the consumer's claim is asserted by way of counterclaim, the notice provided for in Subsection (a) of this section is not required, but the tender provided for by Subsection (c) of this section and by Subsection (d), Section 17.506 of this subchapter may be made within 60 days after the filing of the suit or counterclaim.

(c) Any person who receives the written notice provided by Subsection (a) of this section may, within 60 days after the receipt of the notice, tender to the consumer a written offer of settlement, including an agreement to reimburse the consumer for the attorneys' fees, if any, reasonably incurred by the consumer in asserting his claim up to the date of the written notice. A person who does not receive such a written notice due to the consumer's suit or counterclaim being filed as provided for by Subsection (b) of this section may, within 60 days after the filing of such suit or counterclaim, tender to the consumer a written offer of settlement, including an agreement to reimburse the consumer for the attorneys' fees, if any, reasonably incurred by the consumer in asserting his claim up to the date the suit or counterclaim was filed. Any offer of settlement not accepted within 30 days of receipt by the consumer shall be deemed to have been rejected by the consumer.

(d) A settlement offer made in compliance with Subsection (c) of this section, if rejected by the consumer, may be filed with the court together with an affidavit certifying its rejection. If the amount tendered in the settlement offer is the same as or more than, or if the court finds that amount to be substantially the same as the actual damages found by the trier of fact, the consumer may not recover an amount in excess of the amount tendered in the settlement offer or the amount of actual damages found by the trier of fact, whichever is less. Such settlement offer shall not be admissible as evidence before a jury.

Sec. 17.506. Damages: Defenses

(a) In an action brought under Section 17.50 of this subchapter, it is a defense to the award of any damages or attorneys' fees if the defendant proves that before consummation of the transaction he gave reasonable and timely written notice to the plaintiff of the defendant's reliance on:

(1) written information relating to the particular goods or service in question obtained from official government records if the written information was false or inaccurate and the defendant did not know and could not reasonably have known of the falsity or inaccuracy of the information;

(2) written information relating to the particular goods or service in question obtained from another source if the information was false or inaccurate and the defendant did not know and could not reasonably have known of the falsity or inaccuracy of the information; or

(3) written information concerning a test required or prescribed by a government agency if the information from the test was false or inaccurate and the defendant did not know and could not reasonably have known of the falsity or inaccuracy of the information.

(b) In asserting a defense under Subdivision (1), (2), or (3) of Subsection (a) of Section 17.506 above, the defendant shall prove the written information was a producing cause of the alleged damage. A finding of one producing cause does not bar recovery if other conduct of the defendant not the subject of a defensive finding under Subdivision (1), (2), or (3) of Subsection (a) of Section 17.506 above was a producing cause of damages of the plaintiff.

(c) In a suit where a defense is asserted under Subdivision (2) of Subsection (a) of Section 17.506 above, suit may be asserted against the third party supplying the written information without regard to privity where the third party knew or should have reasonably foreseen that the information would be provided to a consumer; provided no double recovery may result.

(d) In an action brought under Section 17.50 of this subchapter, it is a defense to a cause of action if the defendant proves that he received notice from the consumer advising the defendant of the nature of the consumer's specific complaint and of the amount of actual damages and expenses, including attorneys' fees, if any, reasonably incurred by the consumer in asserting the claim against the defendant, and that within 30 days after the day on which the defendant received the notice the defendant tendered to the consumer:

(1) the amount of actual damages claimed; and

(2) the expenses, including attorneys' fees, if any, reasonably incurred by the consumer in asserting the claim against the defendant.

Sec. 17.55. Promotional Material

If damages or civil penalties are assessed against the seller of goods or services for advertisements or promotional material in a suit filed under Section 17.47, 17.48, 17.50, or 17.51 of this subchapter, the seller of the goods or services has a cause of action against a third party for the amount of damages or civil penalties assessed against the seller plus attorneys' fees on a showing that:

(1) the seller received the advertisements or promotional material from the third party;

(2) the seller's only action with regard to the advertisements or promotional material was to disseminate the material; and

(3) the seller has ceased disseminating the material.

Sec. 17.555. Indemnity

A person against whom an action has been brought under this subchapter may seek contribution or indemnity from one who, under the statute law or at common law, may have liability for the damaging event of which the consumer complains. A person seeking indemnity as provided by this section may recover all sums that he is required to pay as a result of the action, his attorney's fees reasonable in relation to the amount of work performed in maintaining his action for indemnity, and his costs.

Sec. 17.56. Venue

An action brought which alleges a claim to relief under Section 17.50 of this subchapter may be commenced in the county in which the person against whom the suit is brought resides, has his principal place of business, or has a fixed and established place of business at the time the suit is brought or in the county in which the alleged act or practice occurred or in a county in which the defendant or an authorized agent of the defendant solicited the transaction made the subject of the action at bar.

Sec. 17.565. Limitation

All actions brought under this subchapter must be commenced within two years after the date on which the false, misleading, or deceptive act or practice occurred or within two years after the consumer discovered or in the exercise of reasonable diligence should have discovered the occurrence of the false, misleading, or deceptive act or practice. The period of limitation provided in this section may be extended for a period of 180 days if the plaintiff proves that failure timely to commence the action was caused by the defendant's knowingly engaging in conduct solely calculated to induce the plaintiff to refrain from or postpone the commencement of the action.

Sec. 17.57. Subpoenas

The clerk of a district court at the request of any party to a suit pending in his court which is brought under this subchapter shall issue a subpoena for any witness or witnesses who may be represented to reside within 100 miles of the courthouse of the county in which the suit is pending or who may be found within such distance at the time of trial. The clerk shall issue a separate subpoena and a copy thereof for each witness subpoenaed. When an action is pending in Travis County on the consent of the parties a subpoena may be issued for any witness or witnesses who may be represented to reside within 100 miles of the courthouse of a county in which the suit could otherwise have been brought or who may be found within such distance at the time of the trial.

Sec. 17.58. Voluntary Compliance

(a) In the administration of this subchapter the consumer protection division may accept assurance of voluntary compliance with respect to any act or practice which violates this subchapter from any person who is engaging in, has engaged in, or is about to engage in the act or practice. The assurance shall be in writing and shall be filed with and subject to the approval of the district court in the county in which the alleged violator resides or does business or in the district court of Travis County.

(b) The acceptance of an assurance of voluntary compliance may be conditioned on the stipulation that the person in violation of this subchapter restore to any person in interest any money or property, real or personal, which may have been acquired by means of acts or practices which violate this subchapter.

(c) An assurance of voluntary compliance shall not be considered an admission of prior violation of this subchapter. However, unless an assurance has been rescinded by agreement of the parties or voided by a court for good cause, subsequent failure to comply with the terms of an assurance is prima facie evidence of a violation of this subchapter.

(d) Matters closed by the filing of an assurance of voluntary compliance may be reopened at any time. Assurances of voluntary compliance shall in no way affect individual rights of action under this subchapter, except that the rights of individuals with regard to money or property received pursuant to a stipulation in the voluntary compliance under Subsection (b) of this section are governed by the terms of the voluntary compliance.

Sec. 17.59. Post Judgment Relief

(a) If a money judgment entered under this subchapter is unsatisfied 30 days after it becomes final and if the prevailing party has made a good faith attempt to obtain satisfaction of the judgment, the following presumptions exist with respect to the party against whom the judgment was entered:

(1) that the defendant is insolvent or in danger of becoming insolvent; and

(2) that the defendant's property is in danger of being lost, removed, or otherwise exempted from collection on the judgment; and

(3) that the prevailing party will be materially injured unless a receiver is appointed over the defendant's business; and

(4) that there is no adequate remedy other than receivership available to the prevailing party.

(b) Subject to the provisions of Subsection (a) of this section, a prevailing party may move that the defendant show cause why a receiver should not be appointed. Upon adequate notice and hearing, the court shall appoint a receiver over the defendant's business unless the defendant proves that all of the presumptions set forth in Subsection (a) of this section are not applicable.

(c) The order appointing a receiver must clearly state whether the receiver will have general power to manage and operate the defendant's business or have power to manage only a defendant's finances. The order shall limit the duration of the receivership to such time as the judgment or judgments awarded under this subchapter are paid in full. Where there are judgments against a defendant which have been awarded to more than one plaintiff, the court shall have discretion to take any action necessary to efficiently operate a receivership in order to accomplish the purpose of collecting the judgments.

Sec. 17.60. Reports and Examinations

Whenever the consumer protection division has reason to believe that a person is engaging in, has engaged in, or is about to engage in any act or practice declared to be unlawful by this subchapter, or when it reasonably believes it to be in the public interest to conduct an investigation to ascertain whether any person is engaging in, has engaged in, or is about to engage in any such act or practice, an authorized member of the division may:

(1) require the person to file on the prescribed forms a statement or report in writing, under oath or otherwise, as to all the facts and circumstances concerning the alleged violation and such other data and information as the consumer protection division deems necessary;

(2) examine under oath any person in connection with this alleged violation;

(3) examine any merchandise or sample of merchandise deemed necessary and proper; and

(4) pursuant to an order of the appropriate court, impound any sample of merchandise that is produced in accordance with this subchapter and retain it in the possession of the division until the completion of all proceedings in connection with which the merchandise is produced.

Sec. 17.61. Civil Investigative Demand

(a) Whenever the consumer protection division believes that any person may be in possession, custody, or control of the original copy of any documentary material relevant to the subject matter of an investigation of a possible violation of this subchapter, an authorized agent of the division may execute in writing and serve on the person a civil investigative demand requiring the person to produce the documentary material and permit inspection and copying.

(b) Each demand shall:

(1) state the statute and section under which the alleged violation is being investigated, and the general subject matter of the investigation;

(2) describe the class or classes of documentary material to be produced with reasonable specificity so as to fairly indicate the material demanded;

(3) prescribe a return date within which the documentary material is to be produced; and

(4) identify the members of the consumer protection division to whom the documentary material is to be made available for inspection and copying.

(c) A civil investigative demand may contain a requirement or disclosure of documentary material which would be discoverable under the Texas Rules of Civil Procedure.

(d) Service of any demand may be made by:

(1) delivering a duly executed copy of the demand to the person to be served or to a partner or to any officer or agent authorized by appointment or by law to receive service of process on behalf of that person;

(2) delivering a duly executed copy of the demand to the principal place of business in the state of the person to be served;

(3) mailing by registered mail or certified mail a duly executed copy of the demand addressed to the person to be served at the principal place of business in this state, or if the person has no place of business in this state, to his principal office or place of business.

(e) Documentary material demanded pursuant to this section shall be produced for inspection and copying during normal business hours at the principal office or place of business of the person served, or at other times and places as may be agreed on by the person served and the consumer protection division.

(f) No documentary material produced pursuant to a demand under this section, unless otherwise ordered by a court for good cause shown, shall be produced for inspection or copying by, nor shall its contents be disclosed to any person other than the authorized employee of the consumer protection division without the consent of the person who produced the material. The consumer protection division shall prescribe reasonable terms and conditions allowing the documentary material to be available for inspection and copying by the person who produced the material or any duly authorized representative of that person. The consumer protection division may use the documentary material or copies of it as it determines necessary in the enforcement of this subchapter, including presentation before any court. Any material which contains trade secrets shall not be presented except with the approval of the court in which the action is pending after adequate notice to the person furnishing the material.

(g) At any time before the return date specified in the demand, or within 20 days after the demand has been served, whichever period is shorter, a petition to extend the return date for, or to modify or set aside the demand, stating good cause, may be filed in the district court in the county where the parties reside, or a district court of Travis County.

(h) A person on whom a demand is served under this section shall comply with the terms of the demand unless otherwise provided by a court order.

(i) Personal service of a similar investigative demand under this section may be made on any person outside of this state if the person has engaged in conduct in violation of this subchapter. Such persons shall be deemed to have submitted themselves to the jurisdiction of this state within the meaning of this section.

Sec. 17.62. Penalties

(a) Any person who, with intent to avoid, evade, or prevent compliance, in whole or in part, with Section 17.60 or 17.61 of this subchapter, removes from any place, conceals, withholds, or destroys, mutilates, alters, or by any other means falsifies any documentary material or merchandise or sample of merchandise is guilty of a misdemeanor and on conviction is punishable by a fine of not more than $5,000 or by confinement in the county jail for not more than one year, or both.

(b) If a person fails to comply with a directive of the consumer protection division under Section 17.60 of this subchapter or with a civil investigative demand for documentary material served on him under Section 17.61 of this subchapter, or if satisfactory copying or reproduction of the material cannot be done and the person refuses to surrender the material, the consumer protection division may file in the district court in the county in which the person resides, is found, or transacts business, and serve on the person, a petition for an order of the court for enforcement of Sections 17.60 and 17.61 of this subchapter. If the person transacts business in more than one county, the petition shall be filed in the county in which the person maintains his principal place of business, or in another county agreed on by the parties to the petition.

(c) When a petition is filed in the district court in any county under this section, the court shall have jurisdiction to hear and determine the matter presented and to enter any order required to carry into effect the provisions of Sections 17.60 and 17.61 of this subchapter. Any final order entered is subject to appeal to the Texas Supreme Court. Failure to comply with any final order entered under this section is punishable by contempt.

Sec. 17.63. Application

The provisions of this subchapter apply only to acts or practices occurring after the effective date of this subchapter, except a right of action or power granted to the attorney general under Chapter 10, Title 79, Revised Civil Statutes of Texas, 1925, as amended, prior to the effective date of this subchapter.

6. Information Regarding the Federal Securities Laws

What are the Federal securities laws?

The securities laws were, in large part, enacted as a reaction to the chaotic securities markets of the 1920's, when stocks and bonds were often sold on the basis of glittering promises of fantastic profits, without disclosure of any meaningful information to investors. These conditions were major contributors to the disastrous Stock Market Crash of 1929. In response, the Congress passed the Securities Act of 1933 (Securities Act) and the Securities Exchange Act of 1934 (Exchange Act), and set up the Securities and Exchange Commission (SEC) to administer those laws.

The Securities Act requires a company to make "full disclosure" of all material facts before it offers its securities to the public. In enforcing this law, the SEC has no authority to evaluate the quality of securities offered nor to pass judgement on the merits of each offering. Rather, the "disclosure" approach permits a company to offer its securities for sale, regardless of the merit of the investment, so long as it has disclosed sufficient, accurate information about the business it conducts or proposes to conduct.

The Exchange Act sets up requirements for continued disclosure by most publicly held companies on a periodic basis. The company has an obligation under the Exchange Act to keep its shareholders informed of its business operations, financial condition and management.

There are, however, alternatives to registration under the Securities Act, and exemptions from the Exchange Act reporting requirements, which are discussed elsewhere in this brochure.

Is any special help available for small businesses that want to sell securities?

The SEC's primary responsibility under the securities laws is to protect investors and ensure that the capital markets operate in a fair and orderly manner. However, the Commission believes that its regulations should not have the effect of inadvertently impairing capital formation by small businesses. Therefore, the SEC has for some time been examining steps that might be taken to facilitate capital raising by small businesses and reduce undue regulatory burdens arising from the Federal securities laws.

The Office of Small Business Policy

In furtherance of this effort, the SEC, in 1979, established the Office of Small Business Policy within its Division of Corporation Finance. The mission of this Office is to:

- spearhead the SEC's small business rulemaking initiatives;
- review and comment upon the impact of various SEC rule proposals on smaller issuers; and
- serve as a liaison with Congressional committees, government agencies, and other groups concerned with small business.

Registration Alternatives and Exemptions

The SEC has adopted a number of measures which are designed to facilitate capital formation by small business. Alternatives to, or exemptions from full registration are discussed in detail elsewhere in this brochure. It is hoped that these regulations will ease the burden of regulation for those small businesses which qualify to take advantage of them, and will enable these companies to raise needed capital.

Should my company "go public"?

The first thing to be considered when a small business is seeking additional capital is whether or not "going public" is the right step to take. There are both advantages and disadvantages to making a registered public offering of your securities and these should be carefully considered. Some of the factors to be weighed are listed below.

Advantages

- Your company may become more widely known.
- Future financing may be more easily obtainable since the company can offer investors a security that is liquid--more freely tradeable--and that has an ascertainable market value.
- Controlling shareholders of the company have a ready market for their shares, which means that they can more easily sell their interests at retirement or for some other reason.
- The company may be able to attract and retain more highly qualified personnel if it can offer stock options, bonuses, or other incentives that have an ascertainable market value.

Disadvantages

- The company assumes additional responsibilities to its shareholders and the general public, the most important of which is its continuing obligations to inform its shareholders of the company's business operations, financial condition, and management. Such disclosure may be expensive and time consuming, and exposes the company and its management to certain liabilities.
- The management of a company may lose some flexibility in directing the company's affairs, particularly with regard to actions requiring shareholder approval.

How does a small business "go public"?

Section 5 of the Securities Act requires that a registration statement be filed with the SEC before securities are offered for sale to the public, and prohibits the sale of those securities until the registration statement becomes "effective". The basic registration statement consists of two principal parts:

Part I is the legal offering or "selling" document, called the prospectus, which must be furnished to all purchasers of the securities. The company--the "issuer" of the securities--is required to put the essential facts regarding its business operations, financial condition, and management in the printed prospectus. This document must be made available to everyone who buys the new issue, and also to anyone who has been made an offer to purchase the securities.

Part II contains supplemental information which is available for inspection by the public at the SEC. (Copies of all disclosure documents filed with the SEC may be obtained by mail, for a nominal copying charge.)

Basic Registration of Securities

The basic registration form, Form S-1, requires, among other things, a description of the company's business; its properties; material transactions between the company and its officers and directors; competition; identification of officers and directors and their remuneration; certain pending legal proceedings; the plan for distributing the securities and the intended use of the proceeds. It is not prepared as a fill-in-the-blank form like a tax return, but, rather, is similar to a brochure, with the information provided in a narrative format. In addition, there are detailed requirements concerning financial statements, including that such statements be audited by an independent certified public accountant. In addition to the information expressly required by the form, the company must also provide any other information that is necessary to make the statements complete and not misleading. If there are sufficient adverse or risk factors concerning the offering and the issuer--such as lack of business operating history, adverse economic conditions in a particular industry, lack of market for the securities offered, dependence upon key personnel, etc.--they must be set forth prominently in the prospectus, usually in the beginning.

Alternative Registration for Small Issues

In April 1979, the SEC adopted a simplified registration form for use by certain domestic or Canadian issuers, as an alternative to

Form S-1. Form S-18 is available for the registration of securities to be sold to the public for cash not exceeding an aggregate offering price of $5 million, provided such issuers are not subject to the SEC's continuous reporting requirements under the Exchange Act. Form S-18 provides for reduced disclosure requirements and has other attributes which are intended to result in a more timely and less expensive registration process for the smaller issuer who wishes to gain access to the public capital markets.

Although many of the requirements for an S-18 registration statement are the same as those for a full registration, Form S-18 permits the issuer:

- to provide audited financial statements for two fiscal years prepared in accordance with generally accepted accounting principals, whereas Form S-1 requires the issuer to provide audited financial statements for three fiscal years prepared in accordance with more detailed SEC regulations;

- to include less extensive narrative disclosure, particularly in the areas of the description of business, than that required by Form S-1;

- to file with either the SEC's Regional Office nearest the place where the company's principal business operations are conducted, or with the SEC's Division of Corporation Finance, in Washington, D.C., where all Form S-1 registration statements are filed and reviewed. The primary advantage of regional filing is that Regional Office personnel may be more familiar with local economic conditions, the business community, the financial environment, and, in some cases, the background and history of the company.

After a company becomes "public", what are its disclosure obligations?

The Exchange Act requires a company to file certain periodic reports once its registration statement has been declared effective. This obligation continues indefinitely unless, at the beginning of any subsequent fiscal year, the class of securities offered is held of record by less than 300 persons, or at the beginning of any subsequent fiscal year, other than the two fiscal years immediately succeeding the year the registration statement became effective, all securities offered are held of record by less than 500 persons and the issuer has had less than $3 million in total assets for each of its last three fiscal years. In these cases, the reporting obligation is suspended. This means that a company must continuously disclose certain information about its operations, its officers, directors and certain shareholders (including salary, various fringe benefits, and inside transactions between the company and management), the financial condition of the business (including audited financial statements by an independent certified public accountant), its competitive position, material terms of certain contracts or lease agreements, etc.

Even if a company has not filed a registration statement which has been declared effective, the Exchange Act requires all companies with total assets exceeding $3 million and a class of equity securities held by 500 or more persons, to register these securities, and file the same supplementary, periodic, and current reports as noted above. In addition, the Commission's rules require that if proxies are solicited from holders of securities registered under the Exchange Act, the company must furnish all shareholders proxy statements disclosing all of the material facts concerning the matters on which they are being asked to vote. If the proxy solicitation by management relates to an annual meeting at which directors are to be elected, the Commission's proxy rules require the company to furnish each shareholder an annual report that discloses certain information about the company, including audited financial statements for its latest fiscal year.

Are there ways to sell securities legally without registering with the SEC?

The Securities Act provides several exemptions from the registration requirements, and the most common of them are discussed below. It should be pointed out, however, that the purchase or sale of even an exempt security is subject to the antifraud provisions of the Federal securities laws. This means that there is a risk of exposure to private or government legal action, including criminal sanctions, for false or misleading statements, whether oral or written. It should also be noted that if all of the conditions of the exemptions discussed below are not met, each purchaser may seek to have his purchase price refunded. In addition, the fact that an offering may be exempt from certain provisions of the Federal securities laws does not necessarily mean that it is exempt from the notice and filing obligations of various state laws. Accordingly, an issuer is cautioned to check with the appropriate state authority before proceeding with an offering in reliance on any of the exemptions discussed below.

Intrastate Offering Exemption

Section 3(a)(11) of the Securities Act is generally known as the "intrastate offering exemption." It exempts from registration any security which is a part of an issue offered and sold only to persons who are residents of a single state or territory, where the issuer of such security is a person who is both a resident and is doing business within that state or territory. This exemption is intended to facilitate the local financing of local business operations. In order to qualify for the exemption, the company:

- must be incorporated in the state in which it is making the offering;
- must carry out a significant amount of its business in such state; and
- must make offers and sales only to residents of the state.

Although there is no fixed limit on the size of the offering or the number of purchasers, the company has the obligation to determine the residence of each purchaser. If any of the securities are offered or sold to one out-of-state purchaser, the exemption may be lost. In addition, if any of the securities are resold by an original resident purchaser to a person resident outside the state within nine months after the offering by the issuer is completed, the entire transaction may be in violation of the Securities Act. Therefore, there is usually no significant after-market for any securities issued in an intrastate offering during the nine month period following the initial sale and, consequently, they must normally be sold at a discount.

It is difficult for an issuer to rely on the intrastate exemption unless the company knows the purchasers and the sale is directly negotiated with them. In addition, a company that has some of its assets outside of the state or derives a substantial portion of its revenues outside of the state in which it proposes to offer its securities will, in all probability, have a difficult time in justifying the availability of the exemption.

The SEC has adopted Rule 147, a "safe-harbor" rule, which may be followed by companies that want to be certain they meet the requirements for this exemption. However, it is possible that transactions that do not meet all of the requirements of Rule 147 may still qualify for the exemption.

Private Offering Exemption

Section 4(2) of the Securities Act provides an exemption from registration for "transactions by an issuer not involving any public offering." There has been much uncertainty, however, as to the precise limits of this "private offering exemption". Generally, sales to persons directly managing the business fall within the intended scope of the exemption. However, as the number of purchasers increase, and their relationship to the company and its management becomes more remote, it becomes more difficult for an issuer to demonstrate that it does, in fact, qualify for the exemption.

Generally, in order to qualify the offering under this exemption, it is necessary that the persons to whom the security is sold:

- have sufficient knowledge and experience in financial and business matters that they are capable of evaluating the risks and merits of the investment, or are able to bear the economic risk of the investment;

- have access to the type of information that would normally be provided in a prospectus; and

- agree not to resell or distribute the securities.

In addition, the offering may not be made by means of any form of public solicitation or general advertising.

It should be noted that if the security is offered for sale to even one person who does not meet the necessary conditions, the entire offering may be in violation of the Securities Act.

The SEC has adopted Rule 506, a "safe-harbor" rule, which provides objective standards upon which businessmen may rely in order to be certain they meet the requirements of this exemption. Rule 506 is a part of Regulation D, which is described more fully below.

Regulation A

Section 3(b) of the Securities Act gives the SEC authority to exempt from registration certain offerings where the securities to be offered involve relatively small dollar amounts. Under this provision, the SEC has adopted Regulation A. Regulation A is a conditional exemption from registration for certain public offerings, not exceeding $1.5 million in any 12-month period. An offering statement, consisting of a notification, offering circular and exhibits, must be filed with the SEC's Regional Office in the region in which the company's principal business activities are conducted. Although Regulation A is technically an exemption from the registration requirements of the Securities Act, it is often referred to as a "short form" of registration, since the offering circular, which is similar in content to a prospectus, must be supplied to each purchaser, and the securities issued are freely tradeable in an aftermarket. The principal advantages of Regulation A offerings as opposed to full registration on either Form S-1 or S-18 are:

- the required financial statements are simpler and need not be audited, and

- there are no periodic SEC reporting requirements, other than sales reports following the sale of the securities, unless the issuer has more than $3 million in assets and more than 500 shareholders.

All types of companies may utilize Regulation A, with the exception of investment companies registered or required to be registered under the Investment Company Act of 1940. In addition, in most cases Regulation A may be utilized by shareholders for the resale of up to $100,000 of securities.

Regulation D

In March, 1982, the SEC adopted Regulation D under Sections 4(2) and 3(b) of the Securities Act to coordinate the various limited offering exemptions and to streamline the existing requirements applicable to private offers and sales of securities. The Regulation establishes three exemptions from registration in Rules 504, 505, and 506.

Rule 504 - Rule 504 provides an exemption for non-reporting companies for offerings up to $500,000. Under the Rule:

- The sale of up to $500,000 of securities is permitted in a 12-month period.

- No limitation is placed on the number of persons purchasing securities.

- The offering may not be made through any form of general solicitation or general advertising and the securities received in the offering are "restricted securities" unless the offering is made only in states which provide for the registration of the securities and the delivery of a disclosure document.

- Within 15 days after the first sale of securities under the Rule, a Form D notice must be filed with the headquarters office of the SEC.

Unlike Rules 505 and 506, Rule 504 does not mandate that specified disclosure must be provided to purchasers. However, the businessperson should take care that sufficient information is provided to meet the full disclosure obligations which exist under the antifraud provisions of the securities laws.

Rule 505 - Rule 505 was adopted by the SEC in order to provide small businesses more flexibility in raising capital than under Rule 504, but without the uncertainty of determining the quality of the purchasers that generally is involved in using Rule 506. The Rule provides a limited offering exemption for issuers for sales of securities totaling up to $5 million in any 12-month period. Under Rule 505:

- The total offering price of each issue of securities under Rule 505 may not exceed $5 million per issue.

- The issuer may sell the securities to an unlimited number of "accredited investors" and to 35 non-accredited persons. There are no requirements of "sophistication" or "wealth" for persons to whom the securities are sold.

- The offering may not be made by means of any form of general solicitation or general advertising.

- The term "accredited investor" is defined to include banks, insurance companies, registered investment companies, business development companies, or small business investment companies, and certain employee benefit plans for which investment decisions are made by a bank, insurance company, or registered investment adviser; any employee benefit plan within the meaning of Title I of the Employee Retirement Income Security Act with total assets in excess of $5 million; private business development companies; charitable organizations with assets in excess of $5 million; directors, executive officers and general partners of the issuer; persons purchasing at least $150,000 of securities, where the total purchase price does not exceed 20 percent of the purchaser's net worth; natural persons with a net worth of at least $1 million; and natural persons with an income of at least $200,000 per year for two years preceding the offering and for the year in which the offering is made.

- There is no specified information which the issuer must furnish to investors, if only accredited investors are involved in the offering. However, if the offering involves one or more non-accredited persons, the issuer must furnish all purchasers with the same kind of information as that specified in Part I of Form S-18. The information is normally referred to as an "offering memorandum" or "circular." Only financial statements for the most recent fiscal year need be certified by an independent public accountant. If an issuer, other than a limited partnership, cannot obtain audited financial statements without unreasonable effort or expense, then only the issuer's balance sheet, which shall be dated within 120 days of the start of the offering, must be audited. If the issuer is a limited partnership and cannot obtain the required financial statements without unreasonable effort or expense, it may furnish financial statements that have been prepared on the basis of federal income tax requirements and examined and reported on in accordance with generally accepted auditing standards by an independent public or certified accountant. The issuer must also be available to answer questions which prospective purchasers may have about the issuer or the offering.

- A company must take whatever steps are necessary to ensure that the purchasers are acquiring securities for investment only, and not with a view to resale. This means that the securities are "restricted" and investors must be informed that they may not be able to sell their investment for at least two years.

- The issuer is not required to file any offering materials with the Commission. Fifteen days after the first sale in the offering, the issuer must file a notice of sales on Form D. The notice also contains an undertaking by the issuer under Rule 505 to furnish the Commission, upon its staff's request, any information furnished to non-accredited purchasers in connection with the offering.

Rule 506 - Under Rule 506:

- There is no ceiling on the amount which may be raised.

- The issuer may sell its securities to an unlimited number of accredited investors and 35 non-accredited purchasers in reliance on the Rule. All non-accredited purchasers, either alone or with a purchaser representative, must have such knowledge and experience in financial and business matters that they are capable of evaluating the merits and risks of the prospective investment.

- No general solicitation or general advertising is permitted.

- The term "accredited investor" is defined the same as for Rule 505 (See discussion under Rule 505, above).

- There is no specified information which the issuer must furnish to investors, if only accredited investors are involved in the offering. However, if the offering involves one or more non-accredited persons, the issuer must furnish all purchasers with the same kind of information as they would receive if furnished a prospectus filed under a registration statement. In the case of an offering under $5 million, the information requirements would be the same as those for Rule 505, above. In the case of an offering over $5 million, the information would be the same kind as would be specified on the registration form the issuer would be entitled to use, except that if the issuer cannot obtain audited financial statements without unreasonable effort or expense, then the issuer may provide financial statements in accordance with the special treatment described under Rule 505, above. The issuer must also be available to answer questions which prospective purchasers may have about the issuer or the offering.

- The securities sold pursuant to Rule 506 are restricted securities, as under Rule 505.

- A company is required to file a notice of the offering on Form D at the SEC's headquarters office in Washington, D.C., within 15 days after the first sale in the offering. There is no requirement to file the offering memorandum with the Commission.

Accredited Investor Exemption: Section 4(6)

The Small Business Investment Incentive Act of 1980 created a new statutory exemption from registration under the Securities Act for transactions involving offers and sales of securities by any issuer solely to one or more "accredited investors." Under new Section 4(6):

- The total offering price of each issue of securities under the exemption may not exceed the limit on small offerings set by Section 3(b) the Securities Act, which currently is $5 million per issue.

- The offering may not be made by means of any form of advertising or public solicitation.

- The term "accredited investor" is defined to include the same individuals and entities as included for purposes of Rules 505 and 506.

- The issuer is required to file a notice of sales on Form D with the Commission 15 days after the initial sale is made in reliance on the exemption.

- The Section 4(6) exemption does not contain any specific disclosure requirements. The issuer is cautioned however, that, as in the case of the other exemptions, Section 4(6) does not exempt the issuer from the antifraud provisions of the securities laws.

Are there state law requirements in addition to those under the Federal securities laws?

The Federal government and the state governments each have separate and autonomous securities laws and regulations. Compliance with the laws and rules of one, does not constitute compliance with the laws and regulations of the other. A company selling securities must comply with the laws of each state in which it intends to offer its securities. At a minimum, it must comply with at least two sets of requirements--the Federal securities laws and the laws of the state in which the securities are to be sold (if sold in only one state). In addition, the fact that a particular offering may be exempt from certain provisions of the Federal securities laws does not necessarily mean that it is exempt from the notice and filing requirements of various state laws.

In certain states, the law permits a state official to judge the merits of an offering. In these "merit states", even though a company complies with the registration or filing procedures, the state may prohibit the offering because the state official does not consider it to be "fair, just and equitable" for purchase by citizens of his state. Consequently, an issuer of securities must be careful to make sure that there is compliance with all of the appropriate state requirements, as well as with the Federal securities laws.

Where can I go for more information?

The staff of the Office of Small Business Policy, as well as the personnel of the SEC's Regional Offices, will be glad to assist you with any questions you may have with respect to the Federal securities laws. For information regarding state securities laws, contact the appropriate state securities commissioner, whose office is usually located in the capital city.

The entire text of the Commission's rules and regulations is available through the U.S. Government Printing Office or from several private publishers of legal information. In addition, numerous books on this subject have been published, and some are available at most metropolitan public libraries. As of this writing, the following items were available from the Government Printing Office:

Title 17 of the Code of Federal Regulations *(The SEC's rules and and regulations)* April 1, 1982

Vol. I – Parts 1 to 239. SEC Organization; Conduct & Ethics; Info & Requests; Rules of Practice; Regulation S-X and Securities Act of 1933.
Stock No. 022-003-94463-0. . . . . $8.50

Vol. II – Parts 240 to End. Securities Exchange Act of 1934; Public Utility Holding Company, Trust Indenture, Investment Company, Investment Advisers, and Securities Investor Protection Corporation Acts.
Stock No.022-003-94464-8 . . . . $8.00

To order the items on this page, send a check or money order to:

Superintendent of Documents
Government Printing Office
Washington, D.C. 20402

For advice concerning matters relating particularly to small business:

Office of Small Business Policy
U.S. Securities and Exchange Commission
450 Fifth Street, N.W.
Washington, D.C. 20549
Telephone: (202) 272-2644

For copies of Commission forms, and recently-adopted rules:

Publications Section
(same address as above)
Telephone: (202) 272-7460

For information concerning alternative ways of financing small business activities:

Office of Chief Counsel for Advocacy
U.S. Small Business Administration
1441 L Street, N.W.
Washington, D.C. 20416
Telephone: (202) 653-6533

For further information with regard to any aspect of the SEC's operations, you may contact the Regional Office listed on the following two pages, that is most convenient for you.

Regional and Branch offices

New York
Region 1

NEW YORK REGIONAL OFFICE
26 Federal Plaza New York, N.Y. 10278
212-264-1636
Region: New York and New Jersey

Boston
Region 2

BOSTON REGIONAL OFFICE
150 Causeway Street
Boston, Massachusetts 02114
617-223-2721
Region: Maine, New Hampshire, Vermont, Massachusetts, Rhode Island and Connecticut

Atlanta
Region 3

ATLANTA REGIONAL OFFICE
1375 Peachtree Street, N.E.
Suite 788
Atlanta, Georgia 30367
404-881-2524
Region: Tennessee, Virgin Islands, Puerto Rico, North Carolina, South Carolina, Georgia, Alabama, Mississippi, Florida and Louisiana east of the Atchafalaya River

MIAMI BRANCH OFFICE
Dupont Plaza Center
300 Biscayne Blvd., Way, Suite 500
Miami, Florida 33131
305-350-5765

Chicago
Region 4

CHICAGO REGIONAL OFFICE
Everett McKinley Dirksen Bldg.
219 South Dearborn Street, Room 1204
Chicago, Illinois 60604
312-353-7390
Region: Michigan, Ohio, Kentucky, Wisconsin, Indiana, Iowa, Minnesota, Missouri, and Illinois

DETROIT BRANCH OFFICE
1044 Federal Bldg.
Detroit, Michigan 48226
313-226-6070

Fort Worth
Region 5

FORT WORTH REGIONAL OFFICE
411 W. Seventh St.
Fort Worth, Texas 76102
817-334-3821
Region: Oklahoma, Arkansas, Texas Louisiana west of the Atchafalaya River and Kansas

HOUSTON BRANCH OFFICE
7500 San Felipe, Suite 550
Houston, Texas 77063
713-266-3671

Denver
Region 6

DENVER REGIONAL OFFICE
410 17th Street, Suite 700
Denver, Colorado 80202
303-844-2071

Region: North Dakota, South Dakota, Wyoming, Nebraska, Colorado, New Mexico, and Utah

SALT LAKE BRANCH OFFICE
Boston Bldg. Suite 810
9 Exchange Place
Salt Lake City, Utah 84111
801-524-5796

Los Angeles
Region 7

LOS ANGELES REGIONAL OFFICE
5757 Wilshire Blvd., Suite 500 East
Los Angeles, California 90036-3648
213-468-4511

Region: Nevada, Arizona, California, Hawaii, and Guam

SAN FRANCISCO BRANCH OFFICE
450 Golden Gate Avenue, Box 36042
San Francisco, California 94102
415-556-5264

Seattle
Region 8

SEATTLE REGIONAL OFFICE
3040 Federal Building
915 Second Avenue
Seattle, Washington 98174
206-442-7990
Region: Montana, Idaho, Washington, Oregon, and Alaska

Washington
Region 9

WASHINGTON REGIONAL OFFICE
Ballston Center Tower 3
4015 Wilson Blvd.
Arlington, Virginia 22203
703-235-3701
Region: Pennsylvania, Delaware, Maryland, Virginia, West Virginia, and District of Columbia

PHILADELPHIA BRANCH OFFICE
William J. Green, Jr. Federal Bldg.
600 Arch Street, Room 2204
Philadelphia, Pennsylvania 19106
215-597-3100

U.S. Securities and Exchange Commission

450 Fifth Street,
N. W. Washington, D. C.
20549

Office Locations

SEC 1753 3-85

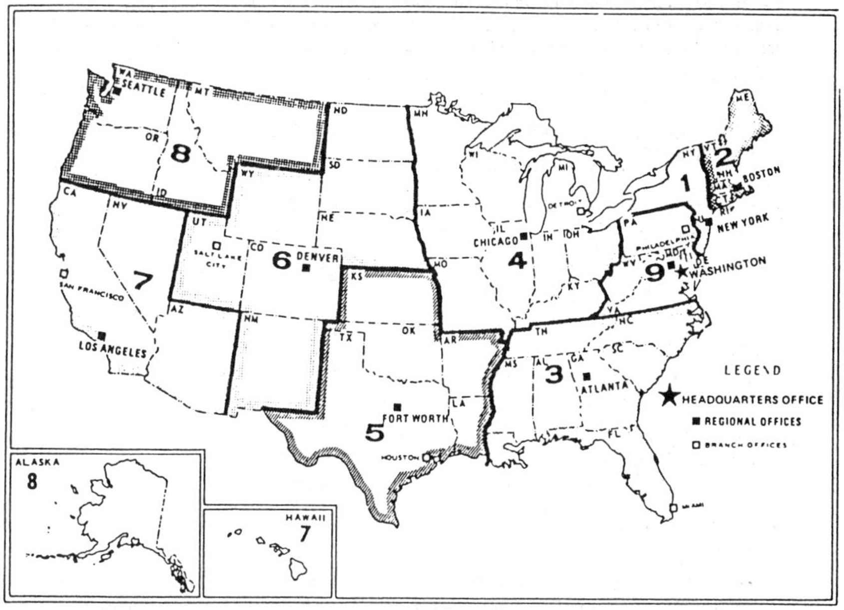

---

7. Forms to Be Filed with the Securities and Exchange Commission and the Texas Securities Commission

FORM D

OMB APPROVAL
OMB Number: 3235-0076
Expires: April 30, 1991
Estimated average burden hours per response . . . 16.00

UNITED STATES
SECURITIES AND EXCHANGE COMMISSION
Washington, D.C. 20549

FORM D

NOTICE OF SALE OF SECURITIES PURSUANT TO REGULATION D, SECTION 4(6), AND/OR UNIFORM LIMITED OFFERING EXEMPTION

SEC USE ONLY	
Prefix	Serial
DATE RECEIVED	

Name of Offering (☐ check if this is an amendment and name has changed, and indicate change.)

Filing Under (Check box(es) that apply): ☐ Rule 504 ☐ Rule 505 ☐ Rule 506 ☐ Section 4(6) ☐ ULOE

Type of Filing: ☐ New Filing ☐ Amendment

A. BASIC IDENTIFICATION DATA

1. Enter the information requested about the issuer

Name of Issuer (☐ check if this is an amendment and name has changed, and indicate change.)

Address of Executive Offices (Number and Street, City, State, Zip Code)	Telephone Number (Including Area Code)
Address of Principal Business Operations (Number and Street, City, State, Zip Code) (if different from Executive Offices)	Telephone Number (Including Area Code)

Brief Description of Business

Type of Business Organization

☐ corporation ☐ limited partnership, already formed ☐ other (please specify):

☐ business trust ☐ limited partnership, to be formed

Actual or Estimated Date of Incorporation or Organization: Month ☐☐ Year ☐☐ ☐ Actual ☐ Estimated

Jurisdiction of Incorporation or Organization: (Enter two-letter U.S. Postal Service abbreviation for State: CN for Canada; FN for other foreign jurisdiction) ☐☐

GENERAL INSTRUCTIONS

Federal:

Who Must File: All issuers making an offering of securities in reliance on an exemption under Regulation D or Section 4(6), 17 CFR 230.501 et seq. or 15 U.S.C. 77d(6).

When To File: A notice must be filed no later than 15 days after the first sale of securities in the offering. A notice is deemed filed with the U.S. Securities and Exchange Commission (SEC) on the earlier of the date it is received by the SEC at the address given below or, if received at that address after the date on which it is due, on the date it was mailed by United States registered or certified mail to that address.

Where to File: U.S. Securities and Exchange Commission, 450 Fifth Street, N.W., Washington, D.C. 20549.

Copies Required: Five (5) copies of this notice must be filed with the SEC, one of which must be manually signed. Any copies not manually signed must be photocopies of the manually signed copy or bear typed or printed signatures.

Information Required: A new filing must contain all information requested. Amendments need only report the name of the issuer and offering, any changes thereto, the information requested in Part C, and any material changes from the information previously supplied in Parts A and B. Part E and the Appendix need not be filed with the SEC.

Filing Fee: There is no federal filing fee.

State:

This notice shall be used to indicate reliance on the Uniform Limited Offering Exemption (ULOE) for sales of securities in those states that have adopted ULOE and that have adopted this form. Issuers relying on ULOE must file a separate notice with the Securities Administrator in each state where sales are to be, or have been made. If a state requires the payment of a fee as a precondition to the claim for the exemption, a fee in the proper amount shall accompany this form. This notice shall be filed in the appropriate states in accordance with state law. The Appendix to the notice constitutes a part of this notice and must be completed.

ATTENTION

Failure to file notice in the appropriate states will not result in a loss of the federal exemption. Conversely, failure to file the appropriate federal notice will not result in a loss of an available state exemption unless such exemption is predicated on the filing of a federal notice.

SEC 1972 (2-89) 1 of 8

A. BASIC IDENTIFICATION DATA

2. Enter the information requested for the following:
   - Each promoter of the issuer, if the issuer has been organized within the past five years;
   - Each beneficial owner having the power to vote or dispose, or direct the vote or disposition of, 10% or more of a class of equity securities of the issuer;
   - Each executive officer and director of corporate issuers and of corporate general and managing partners of partnership issuers; and
   - Each general and managing partner of partnership issuers.

Check Box(es) that Apply: ☐ Promoter ☐ Beneficial Owner ☐ Executive Officer ☐ Director ☐ General and/or Managing Partner

Full Name (Last name first, if individual)

Business or Residence Address (Number and Street, City, State, Zip Code)

Check Box(es) that Apply: ☐ Promoter ☐ Beneficial Owner ☐ Executive Officer ☐ Director ☐ General and/or Managing Partner

Full Name (Last name first, if individual)

Business or Residence Address (Number and Street, City, State, Zip Code)

Check Box(es) that Apply: ☐ Promoter ☐ Beneficial Owner ☐ Executive Officer ☐ Director ☐ General and/or Managing Partner

Full Name (Last name first, if individual)

Business or Residence Address (Number and Street, City, State, Zip Code)

Check Box(es) that Apply: ☐ Promoter ☐ Beneficial Owner ☐ Executive Officer ☐ Director ☐ General and/or Managing Partner

Full Name (Last name first, if individual)

Business or Residence Address (Number and Street, City, State, Zip Code)

Check Box(es) that Apply: ☐ Promoter ☐ Beneficial Owner ☐ Executive Officer ☐ Director ☐ General and/or Managing Partner

Full Name (Last name first, if individual)

Business or Residence Address (Number and Street, City, State, Zip Code)

Check Box(es) that Apply: ☐ Promoter ☐ Beneficial Owner ☐ Executive Officer ☐ Director ☐ General and/or Managing Partner

Full Name (Last name first, if individual)

Business or Residence Address (Number and Street, City, State, Zip Code)

Check Box(es) that Apply: ☐ Promoter ☐ Beneficial Owner ☐ Executive Officer ☐ Director ☐ General and/or Managing Partner

Full Name (Last name first, if individual)

Business or Residence Address (Number and Street, City, State, Zip Code)

(Use blank sheet, or copy and use additional copies of this sheet, as necessary.) 2 of 8

B. INFORMATION ABOUT OFFERING

1. Has the issuer sold, or does the issuer intend to sell, to non-accredited investors in this offering? .... Yes ☐ No ☐

   Answer also in Appendix, Column 2, if filing under ULOE.

2. What is the minimum investment that will be accepted from any individual? .... $_______

3. Does the offering permit joint ownership of a single unit? .... Yes ☐ No ☐

4. Enter the information requested for each person who has been or will be paid or given, directly or indirectly, any commission or similar remuneration for solicitation of purchasers in connection with sales of securities in the offering. If a person to be listed is an associated person or agent of a broker or dealer registered with the SEC and/or with a state or states, list the name of the broker or dealer. If more than five (5) persons to be listed are associated persons of such a broker or dealer, you may set forth the information for that broker or dealer only.

Full Name (Last name first, if individual)

Business or Residence Address (Number and Street, City, State, Zip Code)

Name of Associated Broker or Dealer

States in Which Person Listed Has Solicited or Intends to Solicit Purchasers

(Check "All States" or check individual States) .... ☐ All States

[AL]	[AK]	[AZ]	[AR]	[CA]	[CO]	[CT]	[DE]	[DC]	[FL]	[GA]	[HI]	[ID]
[IL]	[IN]	[IA]	[KS]	[KY]	[LA]	[ME]	[MD]	[MA]	[MI]	[MN]	[MS]	[MO]
[MT]	[NE]	[NV]	[NH]	[NJ]	[NM]	[NY]	[NC]	[ND]	[OH]	[OK]	[OR]	[PA]
[RI]	[SC]	[SD]	[TN]	[TX]	[UT]	[VT]	[VA]	[WA]	[WV]	[WI]	[WY]	[PR]

Full Name (Last name first, if individual)

Business or Residence Address (Number and Street, City, State, Zip Code)

Name of Associated Broker or Dealer

States in Which Person Listed Has Solicited or Intends to Solicit Purchasers

(Check "All States" or check individual States) .... ☐ All States

[AL]	[AK]	[AZ]	[AR]	[CA]	[CO]	[CT]	[DE]	[DC]	[FL]	[GA]	[HI]	[ID]
[IL]	[IN]	[IA]	[KS]	[KY]	[LA]	[ME]	[MD]	[MA]	[MI]	[MN]	[MS]	[MO]
[MT]	[NE]	[NV]	[NH]	[NJ]	[NM]	[NY]	[NC]	[ND]	[OH]	[OK]	[OR]	[PA]
[RI]	[SC]	[SD]	[TN]	[TX]	[UT]	[VT]	[VA]	[WA]	[WV]	[WI]	[WY]	[PR]

Full Name (Last name first, if individual)

Business or Residence Address (Number and Street, City, State, Zip Code)

Name of Associated Broker or Dealer

States in Which Person Listed Has Solicited or Intends to Solicit Purchasers

(Check "All States" or check individual States) .... ☐ All States

[AL]	[AK]	[AZ]	[AR]	[CA]	[CO]	[CT]	[DE]	[DC]	[FL]	[GA]	[HI]	[ID]
[IL]	[IN]	[IA]	[KS]	[KY]	[LA]	[ME]	[MD]	[MA]	[MI]	[MN]	[MS]	[MO]
[MT]	[NE]	[NV]	[NH]	[NJ]	[NM]	[NY]	[NC]	[ND]	[OH]	[OK]	[OR]	[PA]
[RI]	[SC]	[SD]	[TN]	[TX]	[UT]	[VT]	[VA]	[WA]	[WV]	[WI]	[WY]	[PR]

(Use blank sheet, or copy and use additional copies of this sheet, as necessary.) 3 of 8

C. OFFERING PRICE, NUMBER OF INVESTORS, EXPENSES AND USE OF PROCEEDS

1. Enter the aggregate offering price of securities included in this offering and the total amount already sold. Enter "0" if answer is "none" or "zero." If the transaction is an exchange offering, check this box ☐ and indicate in the columns below the amounts of the securities offered for exchange and already exchanged.

Type of Security	Aggregate Offering Price	Amount Already Sold
Debt	$________	$________
Equity	$________	$________
☐ Common ☐ Preferred		
Convertible Securities (including warrants)	$________	$________
Partnership Interests	$________	$________
Other (Specify ____________)	$________	$________
Total	$________	$________

Answer also in Appendix, Column 3, if filing under ULOE.

2. Enter the number of accredited and non-accredited investors who have purchased securities in this offering and the aggregate dollar amounts of their purchases. For offerings under Rule 504, indicate the number of persons who have purchased securities and the aggregate dollar amount of their purchases on the total lines. Enter "0" if answer is "none" or "zero."

	Number Investors	Aggregate Dollar Amount of Purchases
Accredited Investors	________	$________
Non-accredited Investors	________	$________
Total (for filings under Rule 504 only)	________	$________

Answer also in Appendix, Column 4, if filing under ULOE.

3. If this filing is for an offering under Rule 504 or 505, enter the information requested for all securities sold by the issuer, to date, in offerings of the types indicated, in the twelve (12) months prior to the first sale of securities in this offering. Classify securities by type listed in Part C - Question 1.

Type of offering	Type of Security	Dollar Amount Sold
Rule 505	________	$________
Regulation A	________	$________
Rule 504	________	$________
Total	________	$________

4. a. Furnish a statement of all expenses in connection with the issuance and distribution of the securities in this offering. Exclude amounts relating solely to organization expenses of the issuer. The information may be given as subject to future contingencies. If the amount of an expenditure is not known, furnish an estimate and check the box to the left of the estimate.

Transfer Agent's Fees	☐ $________
Printing and Engraving Costs	☐ $________
Legal Fees	☐ $________
Accounting Fees	☐ $________
Engineering Fees	☐ $________
Sales Commissions (specify finders' fees separately)	☐ $________
Other Expenses (identify) ________	☐ $________
Total	☐ $________

4 of 8

C. OFFERING PRICE, NUMBER OF INVESTORS, EXPENSES AND USE OF PROCEEDS

b. Enter the difference between the aggregate offering price given in response to Part C - Question 1 and total expenses furnished in response to Part C - Question 4.a. This difference is the "adjusted gross proceeds to the issuer." .... $________

5. Indicate below the amount of the adjusted gross proceeds to the issuer used or proposed to be used for each of the purposes shown. If the amount for any purpose is not known, furnish an estimate and check the box to the left of the estimate. The total of the payments listed must equal the adjusted gross proceeds to the issuer set forth in response to Part C - Question 4.b above.

	Payments to Officers, Directors, & Affiliates	Payments To Others
Salaries and fees	☐ $________	☐ $________
Purchase of real estate	☐ $________	☐ $________
Purchase, rental or leasing and installation of machinery and equipment	☐ $________	☐ $________
Construction or leasing of plant buildings and facilities	☐ $________	☐ $________
Acquisition of other businesses (including the value of securities involved in this offering that may be used in exchange for the assets or securities of another issuer pursuant to a merger)	☐ $________	☐ $________

Repayment of indebtedness	☐ $________	☐ $________
Working capital	☐ $________	☐ $________
Other (specify): ________________	☐ $________	☐ $________
________________		
________________	☐ $________	☐ $________
Column Totals	☐ $________	☐ $________
Total Payments Listed (column totals added)	☐ $________	

D. FEDERAL SIGNATURE

The issuer has duly caused this notice to be signed by the undersigned duly authorized person. If this notice is filed under Rule 505, the following signature constitutes an undertaking by the issuer to furnish to the U.S. Securities and Exchange Commission, upon written request of its staff, the information furnished by the issuer to any non-accredited investor pursuant to paragraph (b)(2) of Rule 502.

Issuer (Print or Type)	Signature	Date
Name of Signer (Print or Type)	Title of Signer (Print or Type)	

ATTENTION

Intentional misstatements or omissions of fact constitute federal criminal violations. (See 18 U.S.C. 1001.)

5 of 8

E. STATE SIGNATURE

1. Is any party described in 17 CFR 230.252(c), (d), (e) or (f) presently subject to any of the disqualification provisions of such rule? Yes ☐ No ☐

See Appendix, Column 5, for state response.

2. The undersigned issuer hereby undertakes to furnish to any state administrator of any state in which this notice is filed, a notice on Form D (17 CFR 239.500) at such times as required by state law.

3. The undersigned issuer hereby undertakes to furnish to the state administrators, upon written request, information furnished by the issuer to offerees.

4. The undersigned issuer represents that the issuer is familiar with the conditions that must be satisfied to be entitled to the Uniform limited Offering Exemption (ULOE) of the state in which this notice is filed and understands that the issuer claiming the availability of this exemption has the burden of establishing that these conditions have been satisfied.

The issuer has read this notification and knows the contents to be true and has duly caused this notice to be signed on its behalf by the undersigned duly authorized person.

Issuer (Print or Type)	Signature	Date
Name (Print or Type)	Title (Print or Type)	

Instruction:
Print the name and title of the signing representative under his signature for the state portion of this form. One copy of every notice on Form D must be manually signed. Any copies not manually signed must be photocopies of the manually signed copy or bear typed or printed signatures.

6 of 8

APPENDIX

1	2		3	4				5	
	Intend to sell to non-accredited investors in State (Part B-Item 1)		Type of security and aggregate offering price offered in state (Part C-Item1)	Type of investor and amount purchased in State (Part C-Item 2)				Disqualification under State ULOE (if yes, attach explanation of waiver granted) (Part E-Item1)	
State	**Yes**	**No**		**Number of Accredited Investors**	**Amount**	**Number of Non-Accredited Investors**	**Amount**	**Yes**	**No**
AL									
AK									
AZ									
AR									
CA									
CO									
CT									
DE									
DC									
FL									
GA									
HI									
ID									
IL									
IN									
IA									
KS									
KY									
LA									
ME									
MD									
MA									
MI									
MN									
MS									
MO									

APPENDIX

1	2		3	4				5	
	Intend to sell to non-accredited investors in State (Part B-Item 1)		Type of security and aggregate offering price offered in state (Part C-Item1)	Type of investor and amount purchased in State (Part C-Item 2)				Disqualification under State ULOE (if yes, attach explanation of waiver granted) (Part E-Item1)	
State	Yes	No		Number of Accredited Investors	Amount	Number of Non-Accredited Investors	Amount	Yes	No
MT									
NE									
NV									
NH									
NJ									
NM									
NY									
NC									
ND									
OH									
OK									
OR									
PA									
RI									
SC									
SD									
TN									
TX									
UT									
VT									
VA									
WA									
WV									
WI									
WY									
PR									

Form
133.29

State Securities Board
1800 San Jacinto
Austin, Texas 78701

Form 133.29
Intrastate Exemption Notice for Sales Under Regulation 109.13(1)

This form is for notification to the State Securities Board of an issuer's intent to sell securities under Regulation 109.13(1) and under Section 5.T of The Securities Act.

All answers required by this form must be completed and submitted to the Securities Board at least ten (10) business days before any sale may be consummated under Regulation 109.13(1).

Where Needed, Attach Answers on Legal Size Paper
Number Answers to Correspond to Numbers on Form

Name of Issuer ______________________

Contact persons and phone numbers ______________________

State of Organization ______________________

Address of principal place of business ______________________

____

1. Description of Plan of Business of Issuer ______________________

____

2. Information on securities to be sold:

(a) Description of securities to be sold including title and class; ______________________

____

(b) Total number of shares or units proposed to be sold; ______________________

____

(c) Offering price per unit at which the securities are to be sold; ______________________

____

(d) Aggregate dollar amount of securities to be sold. ______________________

____

Revised 11/10/87

3. Section 35 of The Securities Act requires payment of a fee that is equal to one-tenth (1/10) of one percent (1%) of the aggregate amount of securities described as being offered for sale, but in no case more than $500. Please indicate the amount of fees remitted.

____

4. List present Officers, Directors, Partners, Members, Trustees or Managers. Give names, date of birth, home addresses and business addresses.

____

____

____

____

5. List all persons who will actually engage in selling securities pursuant to Subsection (1). Give complete names, date of birth and addresses.

____

____

____

6. State whether the issuer or the registered dealer (as such terms are defined in Section 109.13(1) of the regulations):

   (a) Is currently subject to any administrative order issued by state or federal authorities within five (5) years of the expected offer and sale of securities in reliance upon this exemption, which order

      (1) Is based upon a finding that such person has engaged in fraudulent conduct; or

      (2) Has the effect of enjoining such person from activities subject to federal or state statutes designed to protect investors or consumers against unlawful or deceptive practices involving securities, insurance, commodities or commodity futures, real estate, franchises, business opportunities, consumer goods, or other goods and services: ____________________ If yes, give details including pertinent dates, style and numbers of case and disposition in an attached statement;

   (b) Has been convicted within five years prior to commencement of the offering of any felony or misdemeanor of which fraud is an essential element, or which is a violation of the securities laws or regulations of this state, or of any other state of the United States, or of the United States, or any foreign jurisdiction; or which is a crime involving moral turpitude; or which is a criminal violation of statutes designed to protect consumers against unlawful practices involving insurance, securities, commodities or commodity futures, real estate, franchises, business opportunities, consumer goods or other goods and services; ____________________ If yes, explain in detail giving location of Court, style and number of case, charge and disposition in an attached statement;

   (c) Is subject to any order, judgment or decree entered within 5 years prior to commencement of the offering by any court of competent jurisdiction which temporarily or permanently restrains or enjoins such person from engaging in or continuing any conduct or practice in connection with the purchase or sale of any security or involving any false filing with any state; or which restrains or enjoins such person from activities subject to federal or state statutes designed to protect consumers against unlawful or deceptive practices involving insurance, commodities or commodity futures, real estate, franchises, business opportunities, consumer goods, or other goods and services. ______________________ If yes, give details including location of court, style and number of case, and disposition in an attached statement;

STATE OF ______________________ §

COUNTY OF ______________________ §

The undersigned being duly sworn deposes and says that he has executed the foregoing application for and on behalf of the issuer named therein; that he is ______________________ of such issuer and is fully authorized to execute and file such application; that he is familiar with such application; and that to the best of his knowledge, information and belief the statements made in such application are true and any documents submitted therewith are true copies of the originals thereof.

____

Subscribed and sworn to before me the __________ day of ______________, 19 ______.

____

Notary Public in and for ______________________ County, State of ______________.

Form 133.30 12-15-80

STATE OF TEXAS
STATE SECURITIES BOARD
P.O. Box 13167, Capitol Station
Austin, Texas 78711

INFORMATION CONCERNING PROJECTED MARKET PRICES,
AND RELATED MARKET INFORMATION - SECTION 5.0(3)
TEXAS SECURITIES ACT

Section 5.0(3) provides that securities should be offered for sale at prices reasonably related to the current market price of such security at the time of sale. The Securities Board has interpreted the language "at prices reasonably related the current market price of such security at the time of sale" to mean that the market price of such security in the existing secondary market must have a basis supported by a substantial volume of bona fide sales transactions within or without this state. Additionally, the board policy provides that in the absence of a going market or where there have been only casual transactions, it shall be incumbent on the person filing the Section 5.0 Exemption Notice to prove to the Commissioner that the security will have a market price which has been fairly determined and justified at inception with reasonable assurance of continuity of the market into the future.

This procedure would include a consideration by the Commissioner of criteria established in the items set out below. If additional space is needed to complete any item, please submit attached sheets, identifying each item by number.

(Note: If the requested information is contained in a 10-K or 10-Q report submitted to our Agency, answers may be made by appropriate references.)

(a) Describe the nature and extent of the business operations of the issuer and its predecessor, if any, and the period of time during which the issuer and its predecessor, if any, has been continuously engaged in business. ______________________________

(b) The net asset value of the stock per share. ______________________________

(c) If there is a record of earning for the issuer, the value per share of the stock based upon a reasonable time-earnings factor (setting out the factor used) related to the industry represented by the issuer. ______________________________

(d) Any other basis for full justification of the value per share of the stock. ______________________________

(e) Attach a written undertaking by the issuer to furnish to its shareholders and dealers deemed by the issuer to be likely to trade the securities of the issuer a current balance sheet, a comparative three-year income statement and analysis of shareholder's equity [or for the period of the existence of the issuer, if such period of existence is less than three (3) years], and annual financial statements thereafter.

(f) Attach a written undertaking by a registered Texas securities dealer who is financially able, setting out:

(1) His willingness to make a market in the issue of securities;

(2) The price at which he will begin the market; and

(3) The procedures which he intends to follow for the purpose of assuring an orderly market.

(g) Supplementary data to assist in determining the character of the share distribution and the number of publicly held shares:

(1) Identification of 10 largest holders of record, including beneficial owners (if known) of holding of record by nominees;

Name of Holder	Number of Shs	Name of Holder	Number of Shs

(2) List of holding of 1,000 shares or more in the names of registered dealers and unregistered out-of-state dealers;

Name of Dealer	Number of Shs	Name of Dealer	Number of Shs

(3) Number of transfers and shares transferred of record during the last two years (or period of existence of the issuer, if shorter); ____________________

(4) Summary, by principal groups, of stock, owned or controlled by:

A. Officers or directors and their immediate families; ______
____
____

B. Other concentrated holdings of 10 percent or more; ______
____
____

(5) Estimates of number of non-officer employees owning stock and the total shares held; ____________________

(6) Company shares held in profit-sharing, savings, pension, or other similar funds or trusts established for the benefit of officers or employees; ______

(7) Number of round-lot and number of odd-lot holders of records and aggregate number of shares so held.

______

______

8. Magnuson-Moss Warranty Law—Rules

SUBCHAPTER G—RULES, REGULATIONS, STATEMENTS AND INTERPRETATIONS UNDER THE MAGNUSON-MOSS WARRANTY ACT

PART 700—INTERPRETATIONS OF MAGNUSON-MOSS WARRANTY ACT

AUTHORITY: Magnuson-Moss Warranty Act, Pub. L. 93-637, 15 U.S.C. 2301.

SOURCE: 42 FR 36114, July 13, 1977, unless otherwise noted.

§ 700.1 Products covered.

(a) The Act applies to written warranties on tangible personal property which is normally used for personal, family, or household purposes. This definition includes property which is intended to be attached to or installed in any real property without regard to whether it is so attached or installed. This means that a product is a "consumer product" if the use of that type of product is not uncommon. The percentage of sales or the use to which a product is put by any individual buyer is not determinative. For example, products such as automobiles and typewriters which are used for both personal and commercial purposes come within the definition of consumer product. Where it is unclear whether a particular product is covered under the definition of consumer product, any ambiguity will be resolved in favor of coverage.

(b) Agricultural products such as farm machinery, structures and implements used in the business or occupation of farming are not covered by the Act where their personal, family, or household use is uncommon. However, those agricultural products normally used for personal or household gardening (for example, to produce goods for personal consumption, and not for resale) are consumer products under the Act.

(c) The definition of "Consumer product" limits the applicability of the Act to personal property, "including any such property intended to be attached to or installed in any real property without regard to whether it is so attached or installed." This provision brings under the Act separate items of equipment attached to real property, such as air conditioners, furnaces, and water heaters.

(d) The coverage of separate items of equipment attached to real property includes, but is not limited to, appliances and other thermal, mechanical, and electrical equipment. (It does not extend to the wiring, plumbing, ducts, and other items which are integral component parts of the structure.) State law would classify many such products as fixtures to, and therefore a part of, realty. The statutory definition is designed to bring such products under the Act regardless of whether they may be considered fixtures under state law.

(e) The coverage of building materials which are not separate items of equipment is based on the nature of the purchase transaction. An analysis of the transaction will determine whether the goods are real or personal property. The numerous products which go into the construction of a consumer dwelling are all consumer products when sold "over the counter," as by hardware and building supply retailers. This is also true where a consumer contracts for the purchase of such materials in connection with the improvement, repair, or modification of a home (for example, paneling, dropped ceilings, siding, roofing, storm windows, remodeling). However, where such products are at the time of sale integrated into the structure of a dwelling they are not consumer products as they cannot be practically distinguished from realty. Thus, for example, the beams, wallboard, wiring, plumbing, windows, roofing, and other structural components of a dwelling are not consumer products when they are sold as part of real estate covered by a written warranty.

(f) In the case where a consumer contracts with a builder to construct a home, a substantial addition to a home, or other realty (such as a garage or an in-ground swimming pool) the building materials to be used are not consumer products. Although the materials are separately identifiable at the time the contract is made, it is the intention of the parties to contract for the construction of realty which will integrate the component materials. Of course, as noted above, any separate items of equipment to be attached to such realty are consumer products under the Act.

(g) Certain provisions of the Act apply only to products actually costing the consumer more than a specified amount. Section 103 applies to consumer products actually costing the consumer more than $10, excluding tax. The $10 minimum will be interpreted to include multiple-packaged items which may individually sell for less than $10, but which have been packaged in a manner that does not permit breaking the package to purchase an item or items at a price less than $10. Thus, a written warranty on a dozen items packaged and priced for sale at $12 must be designated, even though identical items may be offered in smaller quantities at under $10. This interpretation applies in the same manner to the minimum dollar limits in section 102 and rules promulgated under that section.

(h) Warranties on replacement parts and components used to repair consumer products are covered; warranties on services are not covered. Therefore, warranties which apply solely to a repairer's workmanship in performing repairs are not subject to the Act. Where a written agreement warrants both the parts provided to effect a repair and the workmanship in making that repair, the warranty must comply with the Act and the rules thereunder.

(i) The Act covers written warranties on consumer products "distributed in commerce" as that term is defined in section 101(3). Thus, by its terms the Act arguably applies to products exported to foreign jurisdictions. However, the public interest would not be served by the use of Commission resources to enforce the Act with respect to such products. Moreover, the legislative intent to apply the requirements of the Act to such products is not sufficiently clear to justify such an extraordinary result. The Commission does not contemplate the enforcement of the Act with respect to consumer products exported to foreign jurisdictions. Products exported for sale at military post exchanges remain subject to the same enforcement standards as products sold within the United States, its territories and possessions.

§ 700.2 Date of manufacture.

Section 112 of the Act provides that the Act shall apply only to those consumer products manufactured after July 4, 1975. When a consumer purchases repair of a consumer product the date of manufacture of any replacement parts used is the measuring date for determining coverage under the Act. The date of manufacture of the consumer product being repaired is in this instance not relevant. Where a consumer purchases or obtains on an exchange basis a rebuilt consumer product, the date that the rebuilding process is completed determines the Act's applicability.

[42 FR 36114, July 13, 1977; 42 FR 38341, July 28, 1977]

§ 700.3 Written warranty.

(a) The Act imposes specific duties and liabilities on suppliers who offer written warranties on consumer products. Certain representations, such as energy efficiency ratings for electrical appliances, care labeling of wearing apparel, and other product information disclosures may be express warranties under the Uniform Commercial Code. However, these disclosures alone are not written warranties under this Act. Section 101(6) provides that a written affirmation of fact or a written promise of a specified level of performance must relate to a specified period of time in order to be considered a "written warranty."[1] A product information disclosure without a specified time period to which the disclosure relates is therefore not a written warranty. In addition, section 111(d) exempts from the Act (except section 102(c)) any written warranty the making or content of which is required by federal law. The Commission encourages the disclosure of product information which is not deceptive and which may benefit consumers, and will not construe the Act to impede information disclosure in product advertising or labeling.

(b) Certain terms, or conditions, of sale of a consumer product may not be "written warranties" as that term is defined in section 101(6), and should not be offered or described in a manner that may deceive consumers as to their enforceability under the Act. For example, a seller of consumer products may give consumers an unconditional right to revoke acceptance of goods within a certain number of days after delivery without regard to defects or failure to meet a specified level of performance. Or a seller may permit consumers to return products for any reason for credit toward purchase of another item. Such terms of sale taken alone are not written warranties under the Act. Therefore, suppliers should avoid any characterization of such terms of sale as warranties. The use of such terms as "free trial period" and "trade-in credit policy" in this regard would be appropriate. Furthermore, such terms of sale should be stated separately from any written warranty. Of course, the offering and performance of such terms of sale remain subject to section 5 of the Federal Trade Commission Act, 15 U.S.C. 45.

(c) The Magnuson-Moss Warranty Act generally applies to written warranties covering consumer products. Many consumer products are covered by warranties which are neither intended for, nor enforceable by, consumers. A common example is a warranty given by a component supplier to a manufacturer of consumer products. (The manufacturer may, in turn, warrant these components to consumers.) The component supplier's warranty is generally given solely to the product manufacturer, and is neither intended to be conveyed to the consumer nor brought to the consumer's attention in connection with the sale. Such warranties are not subject to the Act, since a written warranty under section 101(6) of the Act must become "part of the basis of the bargain between a supplier and a buyer for purposes other than resale." However, the Act applies to a component supplier's warranty in writing which is given to the consumer. An example is a supplier's written warranty to the consumer covering a refrigerator that is sold installed in a boat or recreational vehicle. The supplier of the refrigerator relies on the boat or vehicle assembler to convey the written agreement to the consumer. In this case, the supplier's written warranty is to a consumer, and is covered by the Act.

[1] A "written warranty" is also created by a written affirmation of fact or a written promise that the product is defect free, or by a written undertaking of remedial action within the meaning of section 101(6)(B).

§ 700.4 Parties "actually making" a written warranty.

Section 110(f) of the Act provides that only the supplier "actually making" a written warranty is liable for purposes of FTC and private enforcement of the Act. A supplier who does no more than distribute or sell a consumer product covered by a written warranty offered by another person or business and which identifies that person or business as the warrantor is not liable for failure of the written warranty to comply with the Act or rules thereunder. However, other actions and written and oral representations of such a supplier in connection with the offer or sale of a warranted product may obligate that supplier under the Act. If under State law the supplier is deemed to have "adopted" the written affirmation of fact, promise, or undertaking, the supplier is also obligated under the Act. Suppliers are advised to consult State law to determine those actions and representations which may make them co-warrantors, and therefore obligated under the warranty of the other person or business.

§ 700.5 Expressions of general policy.

(a) Under section 103(b), statements or representations of general policy concerning customer satisfaction which are not subject to any specific limitation need not be designated as full or limited warranties, and are exempt from the requirements of sections 102, 103, and 104 of the Act and rules thereunder. However, such statements remain subject to the enforcement provisions of section 110 of the Act, and to section 5 of the Federal Trade Commission Act, 15 U.S.C. 45.

(b) The section 103(b) exemption applies only to general policies, not to those which are limited to specific consumer products manufactured or sold by the supplier offering such a policy. In addition, to qualify for an exemption under section 103(b) such policies may not be subject to any specific limitations. For example, policies which have an express limitation of duration or a limitation of the amount to be refunded are not exempted. This does not preclude the imposition of reasonable limitations based on the circumstances in each instance a consumer seeks to invoke such an agreement. For instance, a warrantor may refuse to honor such an expression of policy where a consumer has used a product for 10 years without previously expressing any dissatisfaction with the product. Such a refusal would not be a specific limitation under this provision.

§ 700.6 Designation of warranties.

(a) Section 103 of the Act provides that written warranties on consumer products manufactured after July 4, 1975, and actually costing the consumer more than $10, excluding tax, must be designated either "Full (statement of duration) Warranty" or "Limited Warranty". Warrantors may include a statement of duration in a limited warranty designation. The designation or designations should appear clearly and conspicuously as a caption, or prominent title, clearly separated from the text of the warranty. The full (statement of duration) warranty and limited warranty are the exclusive designations permitted under the Act, unless a specific exception is created by rule.

(b) Section 104(b)(4) states that "the duties under subsection (a) (of section 104) extend from the warrantor to each person who is a consumer with respect to the consumer product." Section 101(3) defines a consumer as "a buyer (other than for purposes of resale) of any consumer product, any person to whom such product is transferred during the duration of an implied or written warranty (or service contract) applicable to the product. * * *." Therefore, a full warranty may not expressly restrict the warranty rights of a transferee during its stated duration. However, where the duration of a full warranty is defined solely in terms of first purchaser ownership there can be no violation of section 104(b)(4), since the duration of the warranty expires, by definition, at the time of transfer. No rights of a subsequent transferee are cut off as there is no transfer of ownership "during the duration of (any) warranty." Thus, these provisions do not preclude the offering of a full warranty with its duration determined exclusively by the period during which the first purchaser owns the product, or uses it in conjunction with another product. For example, an automotive battery or muffler warranty may be designated as "full warranty for as long as you own your car." Because this type of warranty leads the consumer to believe that proof of purchase is not needed so long as he or she owns the product a duty to furnish documentary proof may not be reasonably imposed on the consumer under this type of warranty. The burden is on the warrantor to prove that a particular claimant under this type of warranty is not the original purchaser or owner of the product. Warrantors or their designated agents may, however, ask consumers to state or affirm that they are the first purchaser of the product.

§ 700.7 Use of warranty registration cards.

(a) Under section 104(b)(1) of the Act a warrantor offering a full warranty may not impose on consumers any duty other than notification of a defect as a condition of securing remedy of the defect or malfunction, unless such additional duty can be demonstrated by the warrantor to be reasonable. Warrantors have in the past stipulated the return of a "warranty registration" or similar card. By "warranty registration card" the Commission means a card which must be returned by the consumer shortly after purchase of the product and which is stipulated or implied in the warranty to be a condition precedent to warranty coverage and performance.

(b) A requirement that the consumer return a warranty registration card or a similar notice as a condition of performance under a full warranty is an unreasonable duty. Thus, a provision such as, "This warranty is void unless the warranty registration card is returned to the warrantor" is not permissible in a full warranty, nor is it permissible to imply such a condition in a full warranty.

(c) This does not prohibit the use of such registration cards where a warrantor suggests use of the card as one possible means of proof of the date the product was purchased. For example, it is permissible to provide in a full warranty that a consumer may fill out and return a card to place on file proof of the date the product was purchased. Any such suggestion to the consumer must include notice that failure to return the card will not affect rights under the warranty, so long as the consumer can show in a reasonable manner the date the product was purchased. Nor does this interpretation prohibit a seller from obtaining from purchasers at the time of sale information requested by the warrantor.

§ 700.8 Warrantor's decision as final.

A warrantor shall not indicate in any written warranty or service contract either directly or indirectly that the decision of the warrantor, service contractor, or any designated third party is final or binding in any dispute concerning the warranty or service contract. Nor shall a warrantor or service contractor state that it alone shall determine what is a defect under the agreement. Such statements are deceptive since section 110(d) of the Act gives state and federal courts jurisdiction over suits for breach of warranty and service contract.

§ 700.9 Duty to install under a full warranty.

Under section 104(a)(1) of the Act, the remedy under a full warranty must be provided to the consumer without charge. If the warranted product has utility only when installed, a full warranty must provide such installation without charge regardless of whether or not the consumer originally paid for installation by the warrantor or his agent. However, this does not preclude the warrantor from imposing on the consumer a duty to remove, return, or reinstall where such duty can be demonstrated by the warrantor to meet the standard of reasonableness under section 104(b)(1).

§ 700.10 Section 102(c).

(a) Section 102(c) prohibits tying arrangements that condition coverage under a written warranty on the consumer's use of an article or service identified by brand, trade, or corporate name unless that article or service is provided without charge to the consumer.

(b) Under a limited warranty that provides only for replacement of defective parts and no portion of labor charges, section 102(c) prohibits a condition that the consumer use only service (labor) identified by the warrantor to install the replacement parts. A warrantor or his designated representative may not provide parts under the warranty in a manner which impedes or precludes the choice by the consumer of the person or business to perform necessary labor to install such parts.

(c) No warrantor may condition the continued validity of a warranty on the use of only authorized repair service and/or authorized replacement parts for non-warranty service and maintenance. For example, provisions such as, "This warranty is void if service is performed by anyone other than an authorized 'ABC' dealer and all replacement parts must be genuine 'ABC' parts," and the like, are prohibited where the service or parts are not covered by the warranty. These provisions violate the Act in two ways. First, they violate the section 102 (c) ban against tying arrangements. Second, such provisions are deceptive under section 110 of the Act, because a warrantor cannot, as a matter of law, avoid liability under a written warranty where a defect is unrelated to the use by a consumer of "unauthorized" articles or service. This does not preclude a warrantor from expressly excluding liability for defects or damage caused by such "unauthorized" articles or service; nor does it preclude the warrantor from denying liability where the warrantor can demonstrate that the defect or damage was so caused.

§ 700.11 Written warranty, service contract, and insurance distinguished for purposes of compliance under the Act.

(a) The Act recognizes two types of agreements which may provide similar coverage of consumer products, the written warranty, and the service contract. In addition, other agreements may meet the statutory definitions of either "written warranty" or "service contract," but are sold and regulated under state law as contracts of insurance. One example is the automobile breakdown insurance policies sold in many jurisdictions and regulated by the state as a form of casualty insurance. The McCarran-Ferguson Act, 15 U.S.C. 1011 et seq., precludes jurisdiction under federal law over "the business of insurance" to the extent an agreement is regulated by state law as insurance. Thus, such agreements are subject to the Magnuson-Moss Warranty Act only to the extent they are not regulated in a particular state as the business of insurance.

(b) "Written warranty" and "service contract" are defined in sections 101(6) and 101(8) of the Act, respectively. A written warranty must be "part of the basis of the bargain." This means that it must be conveyed at the time of sale of the consumer product and the consumer must not give any consideration beyond the purchase price of the consumer product in order to benefit from the agreement. It is not a requirement of the Act that an agreement obligate a supplier of the consumer product to a written warranty, but merely that it be part of the basis of the bargain between a supplier and a consumer. This contemplates written warranties by third-party non-suppliers.

(c) A service contract under the Act must meet the definitions of section 101(8). An agreement which would meet the definition of written warranty in section 101(6) (A) or (B) but for its failure to satisfy the basis of the bargain test is a service contract. For example, an agreement which calls for some consideration in addition to the purchase price of the consumer product, or which is entered into at some date after the purchase of the consumer product to which it applies, is a service contract. An agreement which relates only to the performance of maintenance and/or inspection services and which is not an undertaking, promise, or affirmation with respect to a specified level of performance, or that the product is free of defects in materials or workmanship, is a service contract. An agreement to perform periodic cleaning and inspection of a product over a specified period of time, even when offered at the time of sale and without charge to the consumer, is an example of such a service contract.

§ 700.12 Effective date of 16 CFR Parts 701 and 702.

The Statement of Basis and Purpose of the final rules promulgated on December 31, 1975, provides that Parts 701 and 702 of this chapter will become effective one year after the date of promulgation, December 31,

1976. The Commission intends this to mean that these rules apply only to written warranties on products manufactured after December 31, 1976.

PART 701—DISCLOSURE OF WRITTEN CONSUMER PRODUCT WARRANTY TERMS AND CONDITIONS

AUTHORITY: 15 U.S.C. 2302 and 2309.

SOURCE: 40 FR 60188, Dec. 31, 1975, unless otherwise noted.

§ 701.1 Definitions.

(a) "The Act" means the Magnuson-Moss Warranty Federal Trade Commission Improvement Act, 15 U.S.C. 2301, et seq.

(b) "Consumer product" means any tangible personal property which is distributed in commerce and which is normally used for personal, family, or household purposes (including any such property intended to be attached to or installed in any real property without regard to whether it is so attached or installed. Products which are purchased solely for commercial or industrial use are excluded solely for purposes of this part.

(c) "Written warranty" means:

(1) Any written affirmation of fact or written promise made in connection with the sale of a consumer product by a supplier to a buyer which relates to the nature of the material or workmanship and affirms or promises that such material or workmanship is defect free or will meet a specified level of performance over a specified period of time, or

(2) Any undertaking in writing in connection with the sale by a supplier of a consumer product to refund, repair, replace, or take other remedial action with respect to such product in the event that such product fails to meet the specifications set forth in the undertaking, which written affirmation, promise or undertaking becomes part of the basis of the bargain between a supplier and a buyer for purposes other than resale of such product.

(d) "Implied warranty" means an implied warranty arising under State law (as modified by sections 104(a) and 108 of the Act) in connection with the sale by a supplier of a consumer product.

(e) "Remedy" means whichever of the following actions the warrantor elects:

(1) Repair,

(2) Replacement, or

(3) Refund; except that the warrantor may not elect refund unless: (i) The warrantor is unable to provide replacement and repair is not commercially practicable or cannot be timely made, or

(ii) The consumer is willing to accept such refund.

(f) "Supplier" means any person engaged in the business of making a consumer product directly or indirectly available to consumers.

(g) "Warrantor" means any supplier or other person who gives or offers to give a written warranty.

(h) "Consumer" means a buyer (other than for purposes of resale or use in the ordinary course of the buyer's business) of any consumer product, any person to whom such product is transferred during the duration of an implied or written warranty applicable to the product, and any other such person who is entitled by the terms of such warranty or under applicable State law to enforce against the warrantor the obligations of the warranty.

(i) "On the face of the warranty" means:

(1) Where the warranty is a single sheet with printing on both sides of the sheet or where the warranty is comprised of more than one sheet, the page on which the warranty text begins;

(2) Where the warranty is included as part of a larger document, such as a use and care manual, the page in such document on which the warranty text begins.

§ 701.2 Scope.

The regulations in this part establish requirements for warrantors for disclosing the terms and conditions of written warranties on consumer products actually costing the consumer more than $15.00.

§ 701.3 Written warranty terms.

(a) Any warrantor warranting to a consumer by means of a written warranty a consumer product actually costing the consumer more than $15.00 shall clearly and conspicuously disclose in a single document in simple and readily understood language, the following items of information:

(1) The identity of the party or parties to whom the written warranty is extended, if the enforceability of the written warranty is limited to the original consumer purchaser or is otherwise limited to persons other than every consumer owner during the term of the warranty;

(2) A clear description and identification of products, or parts, or characteristics, or components or properties covered by and where necessary for clarification, excluded from the warranty;

(3) A statement of what the warrantor will do in the event of a defect, malfunction or failure to conform with the written warranty, including the items or services the warrantor will pay for or provide, and, where necessary for clarification, those which the warrantor will not pay for or provide;

(4) The point in time or event on which the warranty term commences, if different from the purchase date, and the time period or other measurement of warranty duration;

(5) A step-by-step explanation of the procedure which the consumer should follow in order to obtain performance of any warranty obligation, including the persons or class of persons authorized to perform warranty obligations. This includes the name(s) of the warrantor(s), together with: The mailing address(es) of the warrantor(s), and/or the name or title and the address of any employee or department of the warrantor responsible for the performance of warranty obligations, and/or a telephone number which consumers may use without charge to obtain information on warranty performance;

(6) Information respecting the availability of any informal dispute settlement mechanism elected by the warrantor in compliance with Part 703 of this subchapter;

(7) Any limitations on the duration of implied warranties, disclosed on the face of the warranty as provided in section 108 of the Act, accompanied by the following statement:

Some States do not allow limitations on how long an implied warranty lasts, so the above limitation may not apply to you.

(8) Any exclusions of or limitations on relief such as incidental or consequential damages, accompanied by the following statement, which may be combined with the statement required in paragraph (a)(7) of this section:

Some States do not allow the exclusion or limitation of incidental or consequential damages, so the above limitation or exclusion may not apply to you.

(9) A statement in the following language:

This warranty gives you specific legal rights, and you may also have other rights which vary from State to State.

(b) Paragraphs (a)(1) through (9) of this section shall not be applicable with respect to statements of general policy on emblems, seals or insignias issued by third parties promising replacement or refund if a consumer product is defective, which statements contain no representation or assurance of the quality or performance characteristics of the product: *Provided* That: (1) The disclosures required by paragraphs (a)(1) through (9) of this section are published by such third parties in each issue of a publication with a general circulation, and (2) such disclosures are provided free of charge to any consumer upon written request.

§ 701.4 Owner registration cards.

When a warrantor employs any card such as an owner's registration card, a warranty registration card, or the like, and the return of such card is a condition precedent to warranty coverage and performance, the warrantor shall disclose this fact in the warranty. If the return of such card reasonably appears to be a condition precedent to warranty coverage and performance, but is not such a condition, that fact shall be disclosed in the warranty.

PART 702—PRE-SALE AVAILABILITY OF WRITTEN WARRANTY TERMS

AUTHORITY: 15 U.S.C. 2302 and 2309.

SOURCE: 40 FR 60189, Dec. 31, 1975, unless otherwise noted.

§ 702.1 Definitions.

(a) "The Act" means the Magnuson-Moss Warranty Federal Trade Commission Improvement Act, 15 U.S.C. 2301, *et seq.*

(b) "Consumer product" means any tangible personal property which is distributed in commerce and which is normally used for personal, family, or household purposes (including any such property intended to be attached to or installed in any real property without regard to whether it is so attached or installed). Products which are purchased solely for commercial or industrial use are excluded solely for purposes of this part.

(c) "Written warranty" means—

(1) Any written affirmation of fact or written promise made in connection with the sale of a consumer product by a supplier to a buyer which relates to the nature of the material or workmanship and affirms or promises that such material or workmanship is defect free or will meet a specified level of performance over a specified period of time, or

(2) Any undertaking in writing in connection with the sale by a supplier of a consumer product to refund, repair, replace or take other remedial action with respect to such product in the event that such product fails to meet the specifications set forth in the undertaking,

which written affirmation, promise, or undertaking becomes part of the basis of the bargain between a supplier and a buyer for purposes other than resale of such product.

(d) "Warrantor" means any supplier or other person who gives or offers to give a written warranty.

(e) "Seller" means any person who sells or offers for sale for purposes other than resale or use in the ordinary course of the buyer's business any consumer product.

(f) "Supplier" means any person engaged in the business of making a consumer product directly or indirectly available to consumers.

[40 FR 60189, Dec. 31, 1975, as amended at 52 FR 7574, Mar. 12, 1987]

§ 702.2 Scope.

The regulations in this part establish requirements for sellers and warrantors for making the terms of any written warranty on a consumer product available to the consumer prior to sale.

§ 702.3 Pre-sale availability of written warranty terms.

The following requirements apply to consumer products actually costing the consumer more than $15.00:

(a) *Duties of seller.* Except as provided in paragraphs (c) through (d) of this section, the seller of a consumer product with a written warranty shall make a text of the warranty readily available for examination by the prospective buyer by:

(1) Displaying it in close proximity to the warranted product, or

(2) Furnishing it upon request prior to sale and placing signs reasonably calculated to elicit the prospective buyer's attention in prominent locations in the store or department advising such prospective buyers of the availability of warranties upon request.

(b) *Duties of the warrantor.* (1) A warrantor who gives a written warranty warranting to a consumer a consumer product actually costing the consumer more than $15.00 shall:

(i) Provide sellers with warranty materials necessary for such sellers to comply with the requirements set forth in paragraph (a) of this section, by the use of one or more by the following means:

(A) Providing a copy of the written warranty with every warranted consumer product; and/or

(B) Providing a tag, sign, sticker, label, decal or other attachment to the product, which contains the full text of the written warranty; and/or

(C) Printing on or otherwise attaching the text of the written warranty to the package, carton, or other container if that package, carton or other container is normally used for display purposes. If the warrantor elects this option a copy of the written warranty must also accompany the warranted product; and/or

(D) Providing a notice, sign, or poster disclosing the text of a consumer product warranty. If the warrantor elects this option, a copy of the written warranty must also accompany each warranted product.

(ii) Provide catalog, mail order, and door-to-door sellers with copies of written warranties necessary for such sellers to comply with the requirements set forth in paragraphs (c) and (d) of this section.

(2) Paragraph (a)(1) of this section shall not be applicable with respect to statements of general policy on emblems, seals or insignias issued by third parties promising replacement or refund if a consumer product is defective, which statements contain no representation or assurance of the quality or performance characteristics of the product; provided that

(i) The disclosures required by § 701.3(a) (1) through (9) of this part are published by such third parties in each issue of a publication with a general circulation, and

(ii) Such disclosures are provided free of charge to any consumer upon written request.

(c) *Catalog and mail order sales.* (1) For purposes of this paragraph:

(i) "Catalog or mail order sales", means any offer for sale, or any solicitation for an order for a consumer product with a written warranty, which includes instructions for ordering the product which do not require a personal visit to the seller's establishment.

(ii) "Close conjunction" means on the page containing the description of the warranted product, or on the page facing that page.

(2) Any seller who offers for sale to consumers consumer products with written warranties by means of a catalog or mail order solicitation shall:

(i) Clearly and conspicuously disclose in such catalog or solicitation in close conjunction to the description of warranted product, or in an information section of the catalog or solicitation clearly referenced, including a page number, in close conjunction to the description of the warranted product, *either:*

(A) The full text of the written warranty; or

(B) That the written warranty can be obtained free upon specific written request, and the address where such warranty can be obtained. If this option is elected, such seller shall promptly provide a copy of any written warranty requested by the consumer.

(d) *Door-to-door sales.* (1) For purposes of this paragraph:

(i) "Door-to-door sale" means a sale of consumer products in which the seller or his representative personally solicits the sale, including those in response to or following an invitation by a buyer, and the buyer's agreement to offer to purchase is made at a place other than the place of business of the seller.

(ii) "Prospective buyer" means an individual solicited by a door-to-door seller to buy a consumer product who indicates sufficient interest in that consumer product or maintains sufficient contact with the seller for the seller reasonably to conclude that the person solicited is considering purchasing the product.

(2) Any seller who offers for sale to consumers consumer products with written warranties by means of door-to-door sales shall, prior to the consummation of the sale, disclose the fact that the sales representative has copies of the warranties for the warranted products being offered for sale, which may be inspected by the prospective buyer at any time during the sales presentation. Such disclosure shall be made orally and shall be included in any written materials shown to prospective buyers.

[40 FR 60189, Dec. 31, 1975, as amended at 52 FR 7574, Mar. 12, 1987]

PART 703—INFORMAL DISPUTE SETTLEMENT PROCEDURES

AUTHORITY: 15 U.S.C. 2309 and 2310.

SOURCE: 40 FR 60215, Dec. 31, 1975, unless otherwise noted.

§ 703.1 Definitions.

(a) "The Act" means the Magnuson-Moss Warranty—Federal Trade Commission Improvement Act, 15 U.S.C. 2301, *et seq.*

(b) "Consumer product" means any tangible personal property which is distributed in commerce and which is normally used for personal, family, or household purposes (including any such property intended to be attached to or installed in any real property without regard to whether it is so attached or installed).

(c) "Written warranty" means:

(1) Any written affirmation of fact or written promise made in connection

with the sale of a consumer product by a supplier to a buyer which relates to the nature of the material or workmanship and affirms or promises that such material or workmanship is defect free or will meet a specified level of performance over a specified period of time, or

(2) Any undertaking in writing in connection with the sale by a supplier of a consumer product to refund, repair, replace, or take other remedial action with respect to such product in the event that such product fails to meet the specifications set forth in the undertaking, which written affirmation, promise or undertaking becomes part of the basis of the bargain between a supplier and a buyer for purposes other than resale of such product.

(d) "Warrantor" means any person who gives or offers to give a written warranty which incorporates an informal dispute settlement mechanism.

(e) "Mechanism" means an informal dispute settlement procedure which is incorporated into the terms of a written warranty to which any provision of Title I of the Act applies, as provided in section 110 of the Act.

(f) "Members" means the person or persons within a Mechanism actually deciding disputes.

(g) "Consumer" means a buyer (other than for purposes of resale) of any consumer product, any person to whom such product is transferred during the duration of a written warranty applicable to the product, and any other person who is entitled by the terms of such warranty or under applicable state law to enforce against the warrantor the obligations of the warranty.

(h) "On the face of the warranty" means:

(1) If the warranty is a single sheet with printing on both sides of the sheet, or if the warranty is comprised of more than one sheet, the page on which the warranty text begins;

(2) If the warranty is included as part of a longer document, such as a use and care manual, the page in such document on which the warranty text begins.

§ 703.2 Duties of warrantor.

(a) The warrantor shall not incorporate into the terms of a written warranty a Mechanism that fails to comply with the requirements contained in §§ 703.3 through 703.8 of this part. This paragraph shall not prohibit a warrantor from incorporating into the terms of a written warranty the step-by-step procedure which the consumer should take in order to obtain performance of any obligation under the warranty as described in section 102(a) (7) of the Act and required by Part 701 of this subchapter.

(b) The warrantor shall disclose clearly and conspicuously at least the following information on the face of the written warranty:

(1) A statement of the availability of the informal dispute settlement mechanism;

(2) The name and address of the Mechanism, or the name and a telephone number of the Mechanism which consumers may use without charge;

(3) A statement of any requirement that the consumer resort to the Mechanism before exercising rights or seeking remedies created by Title I of the Act; together with the disclosure that if a consumer chooses to seek redress by pursuing rights and remedies not created by Title I of the Act, resort to the Mechanism would not be required by any provision of the Act; and

(4) A statement, if applicable, indicating where further information on the Mechanism can be found in materials accompanying the product, as provided in § 703.2(c) of this section.

(c) The warrantor shall include in the written warranty or in a separate section of materials accompanying the product, the following information:

(1) Either (i) a form addressed to the Mechanism containing spaces requesting the information which the Mechanism may require for prompt resolution of warranty disputes; or (ii) a telephone number of the Mechanism which consumers may use without charge;

(2) The name and address of the Mechanism;

(3) A brief description of Mechanism procedures;

(4) The time limits adhered to by the Mechanism; and

(5) The types of information which the Mechanism may require for prompt resolution of warranty disputes.

(d) The warrantor shall take steps reasonably calculated to make consumers aware of the Mechanism's existence at the time consumers experience warranty disputes. Nothing contained in paragraphs (b), (c), or (d) of this section shall limit the warrantor's option to encourage consumers to seek redress directly from the warrantor as long as the warrantor does not expressly require consumers to seek redress directly from the warrantor. The warrantor shall proceed fairly and expeditiously to attempt to resolve all disputes submitted directly to the warrantor.

(e) Whenever a dispute is submitted directly to the warrantor, the warrantor shall, within a reasonable time, decide whether, and to what extent, it will satisfy the consumer, and inform the consumer of its decision. In its notification to the consumer of its decision, the warrantor shall include the information required in § 703.2 (b) and (c) of this section.

(f) The warrantor shall: (1) Respond fully and promptly to reasonable requests by the Mechanism for information relating to disputes;

(2) Upon notification of any decision of the Mechanism that would require action on the part of the warrantor, immediately notify the Mechanism whether, and to what extent, warrantor will abide by the decision; and

(3) Perform any obligations it has agreed to.

(g) The warrantor shall act in good faith in determining whether, and to what extent, it will abide by a Mechanism decision.

(h) The warrantor shall comply with any reasonable requirements imposed by the Mechanism to fairly and expeditiously resolve warranty disputes.

Minimum Requirements of the Mechanism

§ 703.3 Mechanism organization.

(a) The Mechanism shall be funded and competently staffed at a level sufficient to ensure fair and expeditious resolution of all disputes, and shall not charge consumers any fee for use of the Mechanism.

(b) The warrantor and the sponsor of the Mechanism (if other than the warrantor) shall take all steps necessary to ensure that the Mechanism, and its members and staff, are sufficiently insulated from the warrantor and the sponsor, so that the decisions of the members and the performance of the staff are not influenced by either the warrantor or the sponsor. Necessary steps shall include, at a minimum, committing funds in advance, basing personnel decisions solely on merit, and not assigning conflicting warrantor or sponsor duties to Mechanism staff persons.

(c) The Mechanism shall impose any other reasonable requirements necessary to ensure that the members and staff act fairly and expeditiously in each dispute.

§ 703.4 Qualification of members.

(a) No member deciding a dispute shall be: (1) A party to the dispute, or an employee or agent of a party other than for purposes of deciding disputes; or

(2) A person who is or may become a party in any legal action, including but not limited to class actions, relating to the product or complaint in dispute, or an employee or agent of such person other than for purposes of deciding disputes. For purposes of this paragraph (a) a person shall not be considered a "party" solely because he or she acquires or owns an interest in a party solely for investment, and the acquisition or ownership of an interest which is offered to the general public shall be prima facie evidence of its acquisition or ownership solely for investment.

(b) When one or two members are deciding a dispute, all shall be persons having no direct involvement in the manufacture, distribution, sale or service of any product. When three or more members are deciding a dispute, at least two-thirds shall be persons having no direct involvement in the manufacture, distribution, sale or service of any product. "Direct involvement" shall not include acquiring or owning an interest solely for investment, and the acquisition or ownership of an interest which is offered to the general public shall be prima facie evidence of its acquisition or ownership solely for investment. Nothing contained in this section shall prevent the members from consulting with any persons knowledgeable in the technical, commercial or other areas relating to the product which is the subject of the dispute.

(c) Members shall be persons interested in the fair and expeditious settlement of consumer disputes.

§ 703.5 Operation of the Mechanism.

(a) The Mechanism shall establish written operating procedures which shall include at least those items specified in paragraphs (b) through (j) of this section. Copies of the written procedures shall be made available to any person upon request.

(b) Upon notification of a dispute, the Mechanism shall immediately inform both the warrantor and the consumer of receipt of the dispute.

(c) The Mechanism shall investigate, gather and organize all information necessary for a fair and expeditious decision in each dispute. When any evidence gathered by or submitted to the Mechanism raises issues relating to the number of repair attempts, the length of repair periods, the possibility of unreasonable use of the product, or any other issues relevant in light of Title I of the Act (or rules thereunder), including issues relating to consequential damages, or any other remedy under the Act (or rules thereunder), the Mechanism shall investigate these issues. When information which will or may be used in the decision, submitted by one party, or a consultant under § 703.4(b) of this part, or any other source tends to contradict facts submitted by the other party, the Mechanism shall clearly, accurately, and completely disclose to both parties the contradictory information (and its source) and shall provide both parties an opportunity to explain or rebut the information and to submit additional materials. The Mechanism shall not require any information not reasonably necessary to decide the dispute.

(d) If the dispute has not been settled, the Mechanism shall, as expeditiously as possible but at least within 40 days of notification of the dispute, except as provided in paragraph (e) of this section:

(1) Render a fair decision based on the information gathered as described in paragraph (c) of this section, and on any information submitted at an oral presentation which conforms to the requirements of paragraph (f) of this section (A decision shall include any remedies appropriate under the circumstances, including repair, replacement, refund, reimbursement for expenses, compensation for damages, and any other remedies available under the written warranty or the Act (or rules thereunder); and a decision shall state a specified reasonable time for performance);

(2) Disclose to the warrantor its decision and the reasons therefor;

(3) If the decision would require action on the part of the warrantor, determine whether, and to what extent, warrantor will abide by its decision; and

(4) Disclose to the consumer its decision, the reasons therefor, warrantor's intended actions (if the decision would require action on the part of the warrantor), and the information described in paragraph (g) of this section. For purposes of paragraph (d) of this section a dispute shall be deemed settled when the Mechanism has ascertained from the consumer that:

(i) The dispute has been settled to the consumer's satisfaction; and (ii) the settlement contains a specified reasonable time for performance.

(e) The Mechanism may delay the performance of its duties under paragraph (d) of this section beyond the 40 day time limit:

(1) Where the period of delay is due solely to failure of a consumer to provide promptly his or her name and address, brand name and model number of the product involved, and a statement as to the nature of the defect or other complaint; or

(2) For a 7 day period in those cases where the consumer has made no attempt to seek redress directly from the warrantor.

(f) The Mechanism may allow an oral presentation by a party to a dispute (or a party's representative) only if: (1) Both warrantor and consumer expressly agree to the presentation;

(2) Prior to agreement the Mechanism fully discloses to the consumer the following information:

(i) That the presentation by either party will take place only if both parties so agree, but that if they agree, and one party fails to appear at the agreed upon time and place, the presentation by the other party may still be allowed;

(ii) That the members will decide the dispute whether or not an oral presentation is made;

(iii) The proposed date, time and place for the presentation; and

(iv) A brief description of what will occur at the presentation including, if applicable, parties' rights to bring witnesses and/or counsel; and

(3) Each party has the right to be present during the other party's oral presentation. Nothing contained in this paragraph (b) of this section shall preclude the Mechanism from allowing an oral presentation by one party, if the other party fails to appear at the agreed upon time and place, as long as all of the requirements of this paragraph have been satisfied.

(g) The Mechanism shall inform the consumer, at the time of disclosure required in paragraph (d) of this section that:

(1) If he or she is dissatisfied with its decision or warrantor's intended actions, or eventual performance, legal remedies, including use of small claims court, may be pursued;

(2) The Mechanism's decision is admissible in evidence as provided in section 110(a) (3) of the Act; and

(3) The consumer may obtain, at reasonable cost, copies of all Mechanism records relating to the consumer's dispute.

(h) If the warrantor has agreed to perform any obligations, either as part of a settlement agreed to after notification to the Mechanism of the dispute or as a result of a decision under paragraph (d) of this section, the Mechanism shall ascertain from the consumer within 10 working days of the date for performance whether performance has occurred.

(i) A requirement that a consumer resort to the Mechanism prior to commencement of an action under section 110(d) of the Act shall be satisfied 40 days after notification to the Mechanism of the dispute or when the Mechanism completes all of its duties under paragraph (d) of this section, whichever occurs sooner. Except that, if the Mechanism delays performance of its paragraph (d) of this section duties as allowed by paragraph (e) of this section, the requirement that the consumer initially resort to the Mechanism shall not be satisfied until the period of delay allowed by paragraph (e) of this section has ended.

(j) Decisions of the Mechanism shall not be legally binding on any person. However, the warrantor shall act in good faith, as provided in § 703.2(g) of this part. In any civil action arising out of a warranty obligation and relating to a matter considered by the Mechanism, any decision of the Mechanism shall be admissible in evidence, as provided in section 110(a) (3) of the Act.

§ 703.6 Recordkeeping.

(a) The Mechanism shall maintain records on each dispute referred to it which shall include:

(1) Name, address and telephone number of the consumer;

(2) Name, address, telephone number and contact person of the warrantor;

(3) Brand name and model number of the product involved;

(4) The date of receipt of the dispute and the date of disclosure to the consumer of the decision;

(5) All letters or other written documents submitted by either party;

(6) All other evidence collected by the Mechanism relating to the dispute, including summaries of relevant and material portions of telephone calls and meetings between the Mechanism and any other person (including consultants described in § 703.4(b) of this part);

(7) A summary of any relevant and material information presented by either party at an oral presentation;

(8) The decision of the members including information as to date, time and place of meeting, and the identity of members voting; or information on any other resolution;

(9) A copy of the disclosure to the parties of the decision;

(10) A statement of the warrantor's intended action(s);

(11) Copies of follow-up letters (or summaries of relevant and material portions of follow-up telephone calls) to the consumer, and responses thereto; and

(12) Any other documents and communications (or summaries of relevant and material portions of oral communications) relating to the dispute.

(b) The Mechanism shall maintain an index of each warrantor's disputes grouped under brand name and subgrouped under product model.

(c) The Mechanism shall maintain an index for each warrantor as will show:

(1) All disputes in which the warrantor has promised some performance (either by settlement or in response to a Mechanism decision) and has failed to comply; and

(2) All disputes in which the warrantor has refused to abide by a Mechanism decision.

(d) The Mechanism shall maintain an index as will show all disputes delayed beyond 40 days.

(e) The Mechanism shall compile semi-annually and maintain statistics which show the number and percent of disputes in each of the following categories:

(1) Resolved by staff of the Mechanism and warrantor has complied;

(2) Resolved by staff of the Mechanism, time for compliance has occurred, and warrantor has not complied;

(3) Resolved by staff of the Mechanism and time for compliance has not yet occurred;

(4) Decided by members and warrantor has complied;

(5) Decided by members, time for compliance has occurred, and warrantor has not complied;

(6) Decided by members and time for compliance has not yet occurred;

(7) Decided by members adverse to the consumer;

(8) No jurisdiction;

(9) Decision delayed beyond 40 days under § 703.5(e)(1) of this part;

(10) Decision delayed beyond 40 days under § 703.5(e)(2) of this part;

(11) Decision delayed beyond 40 days for any other reason; and

(12) Pending decision.

(f) The Mechanism shall retain all records specified in paragraphs (a) through (e) of this section for at least 4 years after final disposition of the dispute.

§ 703.7 Audits.

(a) The Mechanism shall have an audit conducted at least annually, to determine whether the Mechanism and its implementation are in compliance with this part. All records of the Mechanism required to be kept under § 703.6 of this part shall be available for audit.

(b) Each audit provided for in paragraph (a) of this section shall include at a minimum the following:

(1) Evaluation of warrantors' efforts to make consumers aware of the Mechanism's existence as required in § 703.2(d) of this part;

(2) Review of the indexes maintained pursuant to § 703.6 (b), (c), and (d) of this part; and

(3) Analysis of a random sample of disputes handled by the Mechanism to determine the following:

(i) Adequacy of the Mechanism's complaint and other forms, investigation, mediation and follow-up efforts, and other aspects of complaint handling; and

(ii) Accuracy of the Mechanism's statistical compilations under § 703.6(e) of this part. (For purposes of this subparagraph "analysis" shall include oral or written contact with the consumers involved in each of the disputes in the random sample.)

(c) A report of each audit under this section shall be submitted to the Federal Trade Commission, and shall be made available to any person at reasonable cost. The Mechanism may direct its auditor to delete names of parties to disputes, and identity of products involved, from the audit report.

(d) Auditors shall be selected by the Mechanism. No auditor may be involved with the Mechanism as a warrantor, sponsor or member, or employee or agent thereof, other than for purposes of the audit.

§ 703.8 Openness of records and proceedings.

(a) The statistical summaries specified in § 703.6(e) of this part shall be available to any person for inspection and copying.

(b) Except as provided under paragraphs (a) and (e) of this section, and paragraph (c) of § 703.7 of this part, all records of the Mechanism may be kept confidential, or made available only on such terms and conditions, or in such form, as the Mechanism shall permit.

(c) The policy of the Mechanism with respect to records made available at the Mechanism's option shall be set out in the procedures under § 703.5(a) of this part; the policy shall be applied uniformly to all requests for access to or copies of such records.

(d) Meetings of the members to hear and decide disputes shall be open to observers on reasonable and nondiscriminatory terms. The identity of the parties and products involved in disputes need not be disclosed at meetings.

(e) Upon request the Mechanism shall provide to either party to a dispute:

(1) Access to all records relating to the dispute; and

(2) Copies of any records relating to the dispute, at reasonable cost.

(f) The Mechanism shall make available to any person upon request, information relating to the qualifications of Mechanism staff and members.

Appendix B

Sample Documents and Agreements

Appendix B

Sample Documents and Agreements

Form 1. General Partnership Agreement

GENERAL PARTNERSHIP AGREEMENT

This General Partnership Agreement is made and entered into as of the ______ day of ________, 1991, by and between

(hereinafter sometimes referred to individually as

respectively, or collectively as the "Partners").

W I T N E S S E T H

WHEREAS, the Partners own the real property more particularly described in Exhibit "A" hereto (the "Real Estate"); and

WHEREAS, each of the Partners desires to enter into a general partnership agreement upon the terms and conditions hereinafter set forth;

NOW, THEREFORE, in consideration of the mutual promises and covenants herein contained, the parties hereto agree as follows:

1. Nature of Business. The Partners hereby create and establish a general partnership (the "Partnership") for the primary purpose of holding the Real Property for investment and doing all things related to or in furtherance of that business.

2. Name and Principal Place of Business. The name of this Partnership shall be ssociates, and initially its principal place of business shall be at

provided that the business of the Partnership may be conducted at such other place or places as a majority in interest of the Partners may hereafter determine. After the execution of this agreement or a subsequent change in the membership of the Partnership, a Certificate of Fictitious Business Name, setting forth the name and residence of each Partner, shall be executed, filed and published as required by the provisions of the Business and Professions Code of California.

3. Term. The term of this Partnership shall commence as of the date hereof, and shall continue until dissolved or terminated as hereinafter provided or in accordance with applicable law.

4. Capital Contributions. The original capital of the Partnership shall consist of the entire interest of each of the Partners in the Real Estate. The Partners acknowledge that they have heretofore each expended money and contributed assets to the Partnership in addition to their interest in the Real Estate. The Partners hereby agree that the amount of such funds expended and the value of such property contributed by each shall be deemed to be pro-proportionate to their respective interests in the Real Estate, which constitute the original capital of the Partnership, and shall not result in any change in the capital account of any Partner nor shall the same be deemed to be a loan by the Partner to the Partnership. From and after the date hereof, the Partners shall from time to time contribute any additional capital in cash or property that may be necessary or desirable for the operation of the Partnership, in proportion to their respective interests in profits and losses.

5. Advances. If any Partner shall advance any moneys to the Partnership in excess of the capital agreed to be contributed by the Partners as provided in Paragraph 4 hereof, the amount of money so advanced shall be considered a loan to the Partnership and shall not be considered an increase in the Partner's capital account nor increase his share of the profits, unless a majority in interest of the Partners agree otherwise in writing. Such advance shall bear interest at the rate of 9% per annum. Repayment of each such advance shall be made within sixty (60) days following the date of the advance unless a majority in interest of the Partners agree otherwise.

6. Division of Profits and Losses. All profits and losses of the Partnership shall be allocated 50% to

7. Distributions. Within sixty (60) days after the end of each fiscal year of the Partnership there shall be distributed in cash to the Partners, in proportion to their respective shares in the Partnership's profits, an amount equal to the sum of the Partnership's net profit for that fiscal year as computed under this agreement, increased by the amounts deducted as depreciation, depletion, or amortization on the Partnership's federal income tax return, and increased by any payments received and reduced by any payments made by the Partnership during that fiscal year on account of the principal of all debt obligations (other than obligations for which provision was made in computing net profit), less a reasonable reserve for current operating requirements, emergencies, and forseeable capital improvements. Upon agreement by a majority in interest of the Partners, distributions may be made more or less frequently than as provided above.

8. Management. Each Partner shall have equal rights in the management and conduct of the business of the Partnership. No Partner shall, without the written consent of all Partners, knowingly suffer or cause anything to be done whereby Partnership property may be seized or attached or taken in execution, or its ownership or possession otherwise endangered. No Partner shall, without the written consent of a majority in interest of the Partners:

(a) Borrow money in the Partnership's name, other than in the ordinary course of the Partnership's business;

(b) Transfer, hypothecate, compromise, or release any Partnership claim except on payment in full;

(c) Subject to the provisions of Paragraph 12, sell or hypothecate the Real Estate or any interest therein, or enter into a lease of the Real Estate for a term of more than one year, or enter into any contract for any such purpose;

(d) Sell, lease or hypothecate any other Partnership property or enter into any contract for any such purpose, other than in the ordinary course of the Partnership's business.

9. Other Business Ventures. Each of the Partners may engage in other business ventures or make investments exclusively for his own account, whether or not involving real estate, and whether or not in competition with the business of the Partnership, and no Partner shall have any interest in the business ventures or investments of any other Partner. No Partner shall be obligated to offer any business opportunity to the Partnership or any other Partner, with the sole exception of opportunities to lease, sell, or otherwise dispose of the Real Estate.

10. Transfer of Partnership Interest.

(a) In the event of a proposed transfer by a Partner (the "Offering Partner") of all or any portion of his interest in the Partnership or any rights or interests therein, the other Partners shall have the option of purchasing the interest proposed to be transferred in accordance with the terms and provisions of this Paragraph 10. In the event the Offering Partner is a 50% Partner (as defined in Paragraph 19) each of the remaining Partners shall have the option to purchase the interest proposed to be transferred (the "First Option"). In the event more than one remaining Partner exercises the First Option, each remaining Partner who has done so shall be deemed to have elected to purchase a pro rata portion of the offered interest. In the event the Offering Partner is a Minority Partner (as defined in Paragraph 19), the other Minority Partner shall have the option to purchase the interest proposed to be transferred (the "First Option"), and in the event such other Minority Partner does not exercise said option, the 50% Partner shall have the option to purchase the interest (the "Second Option").

(b) At least sixty (60) days prior to a proposed transfer by the Offering Partner, the Offering Partner shall give written notice of such proposed transfer to the other Partners, which notice shall set forth the name of the proposed transferee and all terms and conditions of the proposed transfer. (The latest of the dates on which such notice is given is hereinafter referred to in this Paragraph 10(b) as the "Notice Receipt Date".) The option price hereunder and terms and conditions of purchase shall be the same as the purchase price and terms and conditions set forth in the notice from the Offering Partner. The remaining

Partner or Partners having the First Option may exercise that option only giving notice of the exercise of said option to the Offering Partner within thirty (30) days after the Notice Receipt Date. In the event said option is not so exercised, the Offering Partner shall give notice of such fact to the remaining Partner having the Second Option (if any) within 35 days after the Notice Receipt Date, and said remaining Partners may exercise the Second Option only by giving notice thereof to the Offering Partner within 50 days after the Notice Receipt Date. In the event the options granted herein are not exercised within the times above-specified, the Offering Partner may transfer his Partnership interest, but only within one hundred twenty (120) days after the Notice Receipt Date and only to the person, at the price and on the terms specified in the notice of the intended transfer. Such transfer shall not constitute the transferee a partner or entitle him to any of the rights of a partner, other than the right to receive the Offering Partner's share of distributions from the Partnership. If such purchase is not consummated within said one hundred twenty (120) day period, the Partnership interest which was proposed to be transferred shall again become subject to all of the provisions of this agreement and may not thereafter be transferred except in the manner and on the terms herein provided.

11. Death of a Partner.

(a) The death of a Partner shall not cause the dissolution of the Partnership, provided the option granted herein is exercised.

(b) Upon the death of a Partner, the surviving Partners shall have the option to purchase the entire Partnership interest of the deceased Partner in accordance with the terms of this Paragraph 11, at the option price hereinafter provided. In the event the deceased Partner is a 50% Partner, each of the surviving Partners shall have the option to purchase the entire Partnership interest of the deceased Partner (the "First Option"). In the event more than one surviving Partner exercises the First Option, each surviving Partner who had done so shall be deemed to have elected to purchase a pro rata portion of the interest of the deceased Partner. In the event the deceased Partner is a Minority Partner, the surviving Minority Partner shall have the option to purchase the entire Partnership interest of the deceased Partner (the "First Option"), and in the event such Partner does not exercise said option, the surviving 50% Partner shall have the option to purchase the interest (the "Second Option").

(c) In the event of the death of a Partner, the executor or administrator of his estate (the "Executor") shall promptly give written notice thereof to the surviving Partners in the manner prescribed in Paragraph 18 hereof. (The date such notice is given is hereinafter referred to in this Paragraph 11 as the "Notice Receipt Date".) The First Option granted herein may be exercised only by delivering written notice of the exercise thereof to the Executor within 180 days after the Notice Receipt Date. In the event said option is not so exercised, the Executor shall give notice of such fact to the surviving Partner having the Second Option (if any) within 185 days after the Notice Receipt Date, and said Partner may exercise the Second Option only by giving notice thereof to the Executor within 200 days after the Notice Receipt Date.

(d) In the event a surviving Partner elects to purchase the Partnership interest of the deceased Partner, said surviving Partner and the Executor shall consummate the purchase and sale of the Partnership interest within 230 days after the Notice Receipt Date and shall execute and deliver all deeds, instruments and documents as are necessary in connection therewith. The option price may be paid by the surviving Partner, at his option, either in cash or fifty percent (50%) in cash and fifty percent (50%) by delivery of a promissory note in the amount of fifty percent (50%) of the option price, all principal of which shall be due and payable five (5) years after the date thereof with interest payable annually at the higher of nine percent (9%) per annum or the interest rate then being charged for eighty percent (80%), thirty (30) year home loans on homes in Beverly Hills, California by American Savings and Loan Association; provided, however, that in no event shall the interest rate provided exceed the maximum interest rate permitted by law; and provided further that said note may be prepaid at any time without penalty.

(e) The option price at which the surviving Partner shall have the option of purchasing the Partnership interest of the deceased Partner hereunder shall be an amount equal to the deceased Partner's percentage interest in profits and losses multiplied by the amount by which the Partnership's total assets exceeded its total liabilities at the end of first partial or full fiscal quarter ending after the date of death of the deceased Partner, as stated on the Partnership's balance sheet prepared in the regular course of business as of said date, whether or not audited; provided, however that for purposes of computing the option price the value at which the Real Estate shall be carried on said balance sheet shall be determined as follows: Within sixty (60) days after the Notice Receipt Date, the surviving Partners shall each appoint a qualified real estate appraiser by delivering notice thereof to the

Executor. (If they choose, each surviving Partner may appoint the same real estate appraiser.) Appointment of a real estate appraiser hereunder shall not be deemed to be an election to exercise the option granted herein, but if a surviving Partner fails to make such appointment within such time, he shall be deemed to have elected not to exercise the option granted herein. Within seventy-five (75) days after the Notice Receipt Date, the Executor shall appoint a qualified real estate appraiser by delivering written notice thereof to the surviving Partners. In the event the Executor fails to do so, the surviving Partners shall name a second qualified real estate appraiser by delivering written notice thereof to the Executor within 90 days after the Notice Receipt Date. Each appraiser shall thereupon appraise the fair market value of the Real Estate in accordance with such generally recognized method or methods of appraisal as he shall select. Within one hundred twenty (120) days after the Notice Receipt Date each appraiser shall submit his written appraisal to the surviving Partner and the Executor. For purposes of computing the option price, the value at which the Real Estate shall be carried on the aforementioned balance sheet shall be the average of the appraisals submitted by the appraisers. The costs of the appraisals shall be divided equally between the surviving Partners and the estate of the deceased Partner (in the case of a deceased Partner who was a 50% Partner) or between the surviving Minority Partner and the estate of the deceased Partner (in the case of a deceased Partner who was a Minority Partner), regardless of whether or not the surviving Partner exercises the option granted herein.

12. <u>The Real Estate</u>. In the event a bona fide written offer to purchase the Real Estate at a purchase price equal to $255,000 plus fifteen percent (15%) per annum from July 1, 19 is received and a Partner or Partners having a 50% or more interest in the profits and losses of the Partnership desire to sell and the other Partner or Partners do not deliver their written acceptance of such offer to the Partners desiring to accept within 30 days after their receipt of such offer together with the written acceptance thereof by the Partner or Partners desiring to accept, the Partner or Partners refusing to sell shall be obligated to purchase the entire Partnership interest of the Partner or Partners desiring to sell at a purchase price equal to the percentage interest of the Partners desiring to sell multiplied by the amount by which the total assets of the Partnership exceeds its total liabilities at the end of the last fiscal quarter ending prior to the date the offer to purchase is received; provided, however, that for this purpose the value at which the Real Estate shall be carried on said balance sheet shall be the amount of the offer. In the event the Partner or Partners fail, within fifty (50) days after receipt of the aforementioned offer, so to purchase the Partnership interest of the Partner or Partners desiring to sell, the Partner or Partners desiring to sell shall in addition to any rights against the Partner or Partners refusing to sell, have the right to sell the Real Estate on behalf of the Partnership in accordance with such offer, and all Partners shall execute and deliver such deeds and other documents and instruments as may be necessary in connection therewith.

13. <u>Services of</u>
shall be responsible for the day-to-day contacts with tenants of the Real Estate and for arranging for the maintenance of and repairs to the Real Estate; provided, however, that any single expenditure exceeding $______________ and expenditures in any calendar month exceeding $______________ in the aggregate shall require the approval of a majority in interest of the Partners. The above services shall be provided by Mr: :y free of charge to the Partnership.

14. <u>Dissolution and Termination</u>. The Partnership shall be dissolved upon the first to occur of any of the following events:

(a) The written consent of a majority in interest of the Partners;

(b) The adjudicated bankruptcy of any Partner or the Partnership;

(c) Any event which makes it unlawful for the Partnership's business to be carried on, or for the Partners to carry it on in partnership; or

(d) A decree of a court of competent jurisdiction.

15. <u>Distribution on Dissolution and Termination of Partnership</u>. In the event the Partnership is dissolved and terminated for any cause, the Partners agree to make a true, just and final account of all matters relating to the business of the Partnership which shall thereupon be wound up and liquidated. Distribution of the Partnership assets shall then be made in the following order or priority:

(a) The payment of all debts and liabilities of the Partnership in the order of priority as provided by law;

(b) The payment of any debts of the Partnership to the Partners;

(c) The payment to the Partners of sums owing on account of their respective capital contributions;

(d) The payment to the Partners of undistributed profits and of any other surplus proceeds in the ratio of profits and losses as hereinabove set forth.

16. Salaries and Interest on Capital Accounts. No salaries shall be payable for any services rendered to the Partnership by the Partners, unless such salaries shall be agreed upon by a majority in interest of the Partners. The Partnership shall pay the reasonable expenses of each of the Partners incurred in connection with the business of the Partnership, including those expenses paid by any Partner himself, and as to the latter, a Partner shall be entitled to immediate reimbursement to the extent he paid such expenses. No interest shall be paid on the capital account of either Partner.

17. Records and Bank Accounts.

(a) The Partnership shall keep accurate books and records setting forth a true and correct copy of all transactions arising out of or connected with the conduct of the Partnership. All Partners shall have the right at all reasonable times to have access to and inspect and copy the Partnership's books and records.

(b) There shall be delivered to each Partner, within sixty (60) days after the end of each annual accounting period of the Partnership, a statement of profit and loss pertaining to said year, and a balance sheet prepared as of the close of said year, together with a copy of the Partnership information tax return (prior to filing thereof with the federal and state tax authorities), showing the profits and losses of the Partnership and distributions to each Partner for the preceding annual accounting period. All of the foregoing shall be prepared by the accountant designated by a majority in interest of the Partners and shall be prepared in accordance with generally accepted accounting principles.

(c) The Partnership shall maintain checking and savings accounts at such banks and other institutions as a majority in interest of the Partners shall agree. All funds shall be deposited in the name of the Partnership and may be withdrawn upon the signature of any Partner; provided, however, that checks exceeding $_________ shall require the signatures of a majority in interest of the Partners.

18. Notices. All notices, statements or other documents which any person shall be required or shall desire to give to another hereunder must be in writing and shall be given only in one of the following ways: (1) by personal delivery, or (2) by addressing the same as indicated below, and depositing it, registered or certified mail, postage prepaid, in the United States mail, or (3) by delivering it toll prepaid to a telegraph or cable company addressed as indicated below. If so delivered, mailed, telegraphed or cabled, each such notice, statement or other document shall be conclusively deemed to have been given when personally delivered or forty-eight (48) hours after the date of mailing, or on the date of delivery to the telegraph or cable company, as the case may be. The addresses of the Partners shall be as follows provided that either Partner may change the address to which notices to him are to be sent by giving notice thereof to the other in accordance herewith:

If to

If to Mr.

19. Definitions. As used herein the term "Minority Partner" means a Partner having less than a 50% interest in the profits and losses of the Partnership, and the term "50% Partner" means a Partner having a 50% or greater interest in the profits and losses of the Partnership, and the term "majority in interest of the Partners" means a Partner or Partners having in the aggregate more than a 50% interest in the profits and losses of the Partnership.

20. Amendment. This Partnership Agreement may be amended only by a writing executed by all of the Partners.

21. Paragraph Headings. Paragraph headings are inserted herein solely for convenience and the same shall not be used to interpret or construe any provision hereof, nor shall the same be deemed a part hereof.

22. Integration. This agreement sets forth the entire agreement of the parties hereto with respect to the subject matter hereof.

23. Governing Law. This Agreement shall be governed by the Uniform Partnership Act

IN WITNESS WHEREOF, the parties hereto have executed this Partnership Agreement as of the ______day of ________,

Form 2. Limited Partnership Agreement

LIMITED PARTNERSHIP AGREEMENT

This Limited Partnership Agreement is executed this ____ day of __________, by and between (hereinafter referred to as the "general partner"), and ______________ (hereinafter individually and collectively referred to as the "limited partners"), to form a limited partnership (the "partnership")

for the purposes and upon the terms, covenants, and conditions set forth herein.

1. Introductory Statement.

The objective of the partnership is to raise, from a total of no more than twenty (20) limited partner investors, the sum of Five Hundred Fifty Thousand Dollars ($550,000.00) (such amount, as it may be reduced by the general partner pursuant to this paragraph 1, is hereinafter referred to as the "Construction Fund") for the development, construction, and operation of a skateboard park (as hereinafter described) and incidental activities pursuant to paragraph 4 upon one of the four (4) prospective real estate properties listed on Exhibit "A" attached hereto. In addition, the general partner is authorized, but not required, in its discretion to raise an additional amount of up to, but not exceeding, Three Hundred Fifty Thousand Dollars ($350,000.00) (such amount is hereinafter referred to as the "Acquisition Fund") to be used exclusively for or toward the purchase of the real property upon which the park shall be situated. There need be no segregation of the Construction and Acquisition Funds, it being the intention of the parties that any funds in excess of the Construction Fund be applied, in the discretion of the general partner, exclusively for or toward the acquisition of the real property upon which the skateboard park shall be situated and for no other purpose whatsoever. Notwithstanding the foregoing, in the event that Four Hundred Fifty Thousand Dollars ($450,000.00) is raised, then, at the option of the general partner, the Construction Fund may thereupon be reduced, a skateboard park may be constructed, and the partnership may pursue the business purposes for which it is formed. With respect to both the Construction Fund and the Acquisition Fund, it is anticipated that one-third (1/3) of the monies raised will be in the form of capital contributions from the limited partners, and that two-thirds (2/3) of the monies raised will be in the form of loans from the limited partners to the partnership pursuant to the terms and conditions set forth in paragraph 7. This Agreement shall become binding and effective upon execution, but the partnership shall not engage in the actual construction of any skateboard park pursuant to paragraph 4 unless and until the Construction Fund is raised. Any contribution received from a limited partner shall be placed by the general partner in an interest-bearing trust account until the Construction Fund is raised. In the event that the Construction Fund is not raised by the partnership within one (1) month after the date of the execution of this Agreement, the limited partners shall receive a refund of their respective contributions, including any accrued interest at the rate of five percent (5%) per annum, and this Agreement shall be of no further force or effect. In addition, in the event that the Construction Fund is raised but the general partner, in its discretion, decides not to apply the Acquisition Fund to purchase the real property upon which the park shall be situated, the limited partners shall receive a refund of their contributions to the Acquisition Fund with accrued interest at the rate of five percent (5%) per annum. In the event that the funds raised by the partnership are more than are needed by the partnership, then the limited partners shall receive a refund of such excess pari passu with interest at the rate of five percent (5%) per annum. In all other instances, the interest rate and the terms set forth in paragraph 7(b) shall apply with respect to loans from the limited partners to the partnership.

2. Name.

The name of the partnership is Upon the execution of this Agreement, and upon any subsequent change in the partnership's membership, the partners shall sign, and shall cause to be filed and published in the county in which the principal place of business of the partnership is situated, a Fictitious Business Name Statement setting forth the name and residence of each partner and any other information as required by State law.

3. Place of Business.

The principal place of business of the partnership shall be located at until changed by designation of the general partner.

4. Purpose.

The principal purpose of this limited partnership is to develop and operate a skateboard park, and to engage in any and all general business activities related to or incidental to that purpose. The partnership shall obtain, by lease, by lease with option to purchase, or by outright purchase, real property upon which the skateboard park and any incidental activities shall be constructed, the site to be chosen from those properties listed on Exhibit "A" attached hereto, all of which are located in

5. Certificate of Limited Partnership.

The partners shall, concurrently with the execution of this Agreement, sign and acknowledge a Certificate of Limited Partnership . They shall thereafter cause the certificate to be recorded in the office of the recorder for the county in which the principal place of business of the partnership is situated. A certified copy of that certificate shall be recorded in the office of the recorder for any other county in which the partnership shall have a place of business or in which real property it owns shall be situated

6. General Partner.

(a) Authority. The general partner shall have sole and complete charge of the affairs of the partnership, and shall operate the partnership business for the benefit of all of the partners. The general partner shall have the authority to act on behalf of the partnership in all matters respecting the partnership, its business, and its property. Without limiting the generality of the foregoing, the general partner shall have the authority: (1) to employ, at the partnership's expense, such agents, employees, independent contractors, management personnel, attorneys, and accountants as it considers reasonably necessary; (2) to acquire, by lease, by lease with option to purchase, or by purchase, such real or personal property as it considers appropriate to the purposes of the partnership; (3) to alter, improve, repair, raze, replace, and rebuild the partnership property; (4) to let or lease property for any period and for any purpose; (5) to obtain necessary insurance for the proper protection of the partnership and of either (a) the general and limited partners, or (b) the general partner or the limited partners; (6) to pay, collect, compromise, arbitrate, or otherwise adjust any and all claims or demands of or against the partnership; (7) to obtain loans for the partnership or in the partnership's name; (8) to enter the partnership into partnerships, joint ventures, or other business relationships; and (9) to act for the partnership in all other transactions concerning the partnership's real or personal property or business affairs, including the execution of contracts, deeds, options, loan obligations, deeds of trust, notes, and other documents.

(b) Duties and Compensation. The general partner shall not be required to devote its full time to the affairs of the partnership, but shall devote whatever time, effort, and skill may be necessary for the efficient and successful conduct and completion of the partnership's business. The general partner may manage the partnership business and property or may engage others to assist it or to work under its direction and control in the management of the partnership business and property. The general partner shall not be compensated for management services performed by it, except to the extent of its profit participation as set forth in paragraph 8, but shall be reimbursed, on demand, for its actual costs and expenses incurred on behalf of the partnership. If the general partner is not reimbursed within fourteen (14) days after demand, it shall be entitled to receive interest at the rate of eight percent (8%) per annum from the date the cost or expense was demanded. No person, firm, or company owned or controlled by the general partner may be compensated for the performance of management services except with the prior written consent of a majority of the limited partners.

(c) Finder's Fees. The general partner is hereby authorized to pay finder's fees out of the Construction Fund in an amount not to exceed Fifty Thousand Dollars ($50,000.00) to persons who are not principals, officers, or employees of the partnership or of the general partner and who substantially assist in procuring investors for the partnership.

7. Limited Partners.

(a) Capital Contributions. The capital of the partnership shall consist of contributions made by the limited partners. Any contribution made to the partnership by a limited partner shall be allocated one-third (1/3) as a capital contribution to the partnership, and two-thirds (2/3) as a loan to the partnership repayable in accordance with the provisions of paragraph 7(b). The minimum amount to be contributed and loaned by a limited partner pursuant to this paragraph 7(a) and pursuant to paragraph 7(b) shall be Twenty-Five Thousand Dollars ($25,000.00), payable upon or, pursuant to paragraph 1, within one (1) month after the execution of this Agreement; provided, however, that there shall be no more than twenty limited partners.

(b) Loans. In addition to a capital contribution, each limited partner shall make a loan to the partnership. The aggregate amount of all such loans shall be two-thirds (2/3) of the Construction Fund and two-thirds (2/3) of the Acquisition Fund, if any. Such loans shall be repaid only out of the Net Cash Flow of the partnership pursuant to the provisions of paragraph 8(c), or upon dissolution of the partnership in accordance with the provisions set forth in paragraphs 8(d) and 9(c), with interest at the rate of eight percent (8%) per annum, accruing from and after the date upon which the full amount of the Construction Fund or Acquisition Fund is raised, respectively, with respect to loans allocated to the Construction Fund or Acquisition Fund, respectively.

The general partner shall have no liability in connection with such loans.

(c) No Additional Contributions. No limited partner shall be required to make any additional capital contribution or loan to the partnership. With the exception of the payments set forth in paragraph 6(c) all monies received by the partnership shall be devoted to the business of the partnership, including, without limitation, the construction and operation of a skateboard park and incidental activities. The general partner warrants and represents that the cost of the park currently existing at 4445 Emerald Street, Torrance, California, was approximately Five Hundred Thousand Dollars ($500,000.00) (as set forth on Exhibit "B" attached hereto), of which approximately Twenty-Three Thousand Dollars ($23,000.00) represents security deposits which are ultimately refundable. The general partner further warrants and represents that, unless the partnership is cancelled for insufficient funding pursuant to paragraph 1, the general partner shall use its best efforts to build a park from the Construction Fund in accordance with a design approved by a majority of the limited partners. In the event that any monies in excess of those in the Construction Fund are needed to complete the construction and to commence operation of a park approved by the limited partners, the general partner shall obtain the approval of a majority of the limited partners prior to obtaining and spending any such excess monies. If the approval of a majority of the limited partners is obtained, the general partner shall have the right to borrow on behalf of the partnership and any such debt shall be repaid pursuant to paragraph 8 prior to the distribution of any Net Cash Flow (as hereinafter defined) to the partners. The general partner warrants and represents that, if the consent of the limited partners is not obtained to expend more monies than are in the Construction Fund, the general partner shall nevertheless construct and open for operation a skateboard park of a reasonable design and capacity.

(d) Powers of Limited Partners. The limited partners shall take no part in the conduct or control of the partnership business and shall have no right or authority to act for or bind the partnership; provided, however, that the approval of the general partner and of the limited partners owning seventy-five percent (75%) of the contributed capital shall be necessary to effectuate: (1) the termination of the partnership, except as provided herein elsewhere; (2) amendment of the partnership agreement; or (3) sale of all or substantially all of the partnership assets.

8. Distributions and Allocations.

(a) Gross Receipts. The term "Gross Receipts" as used herein means all receipts from the conduct of the business of the partnership, except: (i) any net proceeds realized by the partnership from the sale, exchange, condemnation, or other disposition of its properties, or any portion thereof; (ii) any net proceeds from insurance payments (property or title) based upon damage, destruction, or loss of the partnership property or any portion thereof; (iii) all proceeds received from any borrowings or refinancings by the partnership; and (iv) contributions and advances made by the partners.

(b) Net Cash Flow. The term "Net Cash Flow" as used herein means the Gross Receipts of the partnership from all sources less the following: (i) all expenditures of any kind made by the partnership, including, without limitation, taxes, insurance, escrow payments, repair and maintenance expenses, expenditures made for capital improvements and replacements, accountants' and attorneys' fees, real estate commissions, lease payments, amortization payments of principal and interest and all other fees and charges paid with respect to indebtedness of the partnership (except with respect to the loans from the limited partners set forth in paragraph 7(b), and any staff salary or expense reimbursement payable pursuant to paragraph 6(b) hereof; (ii) reserves to pay anticipated expenses, including taxes, insurance, and other expenses or costs incident to the ownership of the skateboard park; and (iii) an amount equal to two percent (2%) of the Gross Receipts per month as a reserve (the "Reserve") for future expenditures for capital replacements and additions to the park. At any time the Reserve equals or exceeds the sum of Ten Thousand Dollars ($10,000.00), no further deduction from Gross Receipts shall be made until the Reserve has been depleted below such sum, in which event the general partner shall continue to reserve two percent (2%) of the Gross Receipts per month until the Reserve once again equals or exceeds the sum of Ten Thousand Dollars ($10,000.00).

(c) Distribution of Net Cash Flow and Allocation of Profit and Loss. The Net Cash Flow and the profit and loss of the partnership shall be determined on a quarterly basis in accordance with the accounting provisions set forth in paragraph 10. The Net Cash Flow, and all profit and loss (including all federal and state income and other tax deductions and credits) shall be distributed and allocated, respectively, as follows:

(i) All of the Net Cash Flow shall first be distributed, and all profit and loss (including all federal and state income and other tax deductions and credits) shall be allocated, entirely to the limited partners until the limited partners have been repaid in Net Cash Flow the amount of their respective loans to the partnership plus accrued interest at the rate of eight percent (8%) per annum, accruing pursuant to the provisions set forth in paragraph 7(b).

(ii) When all of the foregoing loans are repaid, all of the Net Cash Flow shall be distributed, and all profit and loss (including all federal and state income and other tax deductions and credits) allocated, entirely to the limited partners until the limited partners have received in Net Cash Flow an amount equal to their respective capital contributions to the partnership without interest.

(iii) When the amounts set forth in paragraphs 8(c)(i) and 6(c)(ii) have been paid in full, the Net Cash Flow shall be distributed, and the profit and loss (including all federal and state income and other tax deductions and credits) allocated, fifty percent (50%) to the general partner, and fifty percent (50%) to the limited partners collectively. The amount distributed or allocated under the immediately preceding sentence to the limited partners shall be distributed or allocated among the limited partners in a proportion corresponding to their respective capital contributions.

(d) Distributions on Sale of Partnership Assets. The sale, condemnation, or destruction of all or substantially all of the partnership property shall be an event causing the dissolution of the partnership. Upon such event there shall be first deducted from the proceeds received by the partnership such sums as are needed to pay the obligations of the partnership, other than those obligations set forth in paragraphs 8(d)(i), (ii), and (iii), and other than loans assumed by a purchaser of the partnership assets in the event of a sale, and there shall be further deducted from the proceeds such reserves as the general partner may deem reasonably necessary for the expenses of liquidation. The balance of such proceeds shall be distributed in the manner provided below:

(i) First, each limited partner shall receive a sum equal to the loan made by each such limited partner not theretofore repaid, plus interest of eight percent (8%) per annum thereon, accruing pursuant to the provisions set forth in paragraph 7(b). If the net proceeds are insufficient to allocate to each limited partner the portion thereof to which he is entitled hereunder, then the limited partners shall share the net proceeds prorata in the ratio which each such limited partner's loan bears to the total of all loans made by the limited partners.

(ii) After repayment of the loans under paragraph 8(d)(i), each limited partner shall receive a sum equal to the capital contribution made by each such limited partner not theretofore returned, less prior Net Cash Flow distributions paid to each such limited partner. If the net proceeds are insufficient to allocate to each limited partner the portion thereof to which he is entitled hereunder, then the limited partners shall share the net proceeds prorata in the ratio which each such limited partner's capital contribution bears to the total of all capital contributions of the limited partners.

(iii) After repayment of the amounts set forth in paragraphs 8(d)(i) and 8(d)(ii), any remaining net sales proceeds shall be distributed fifty percent (50%) to the general partner, and fifty percent (50%) to the limited partners prorata in the ratio which each such limited partner's capital contribution bears to the total of all capital contributions of the limited partners.

(e) Losses. No limited partner shall be required under any circumstances to contribute further sums to the capital or creditors of the partnership beyond the amount of his capital contribution as provided in paragraph 7(a) and the amount of loans as provided in paragraph 7(b).

9. Term, Dissolution, and Continuation.

(a) Term. The partnership shall dissolve on the 30th anniversary of the date of the first filing for record in Los Angeles County of the Certificate of Limited Partnership.

(b) Dissolution. The partnership shall dissolve upon the bankruptcy, dissolution, or withdrawal of the general partner; provided, however, that the partnership business shall be continued thereafter upon the written consent, made within sixty (60) days after such event, of the limited partners owning in the aggregate two-thirds (2/3) of the total contributed capital, and the election within that time of a new general partner by the same percentage of limited partners. If the partnership business is continued upon the happening of the event described in the preceding sentence, then the general partner or its legal representative shall become a limited partner of the partnership with the same interest in Net Cash Flow and distributions pursuant to paragraphs 8(d) and 9(c) which such general partner would have had had it remained the general partner, except that it shall not bear any losses in excess of its capital account as it exists from time to time.

(c) Winding Up. On dissolution of the partnership, unless it continues as provided in paragraph 9(b) above, the general partner shall wind up the partnership's affairs, liquidate the assets of the partnership, and apply its funds in the manner provided for in paragraph 8(d).

10. Books of Account.

(a) Maintenance of Records. The partnership shall maintain, at the office of the partnership or of its accountant, books, records, and accounts showing separately, in accordance with generally accepted accounting principles applied on a consistent basis, all items which in any way affect the financial and tax computations called for by this Agreement, and shall make the books, records, and accounts available for inspection by any partner, general or limited, at any reasonable time.

(b) Profit and Loss. The net profit or net loss of the partnership for each year shall be determined for accounting purposes on a quarterly basis in accordance with generally accepted accounting practices consistently applied as soon as possible after the end of each calendar quarter.

(c) Periodic Report or Audit. Within thirty (30) days after the close of each accounting period as set forth in paragraph 10(b), the general partner shall, at the expense of the partnership, cause to be prepared a report by an independent certified public accountant qualified to act as such and shall, within sixty (60) days after the close of the accounting period, cause a copy of the report to be furnished to each member of the partnership.

The report shall include a balance sheet as of the last day of the accounting period and a statement of income or profit and loss for the period. The balance sheet or accompanying comments shall set forth all of the following:

(i) The basis used in stating the valuation of assets and any changes in basis during the accounting period.

(ii) The amount, sources, and any changes in capital during the period.

(iii) The names of the partners and their prorata share of the partnership capital and losses at the beginning and at the end of the period.

(iv) Any amounts of loans or advances to or from the general partner.

(v) Any allocated but unpaid distributions to the general partner.

(vi) Total Net Cash Flow and distributions, and the amounts distributed to each partner.

The statement of income or profit and loss shall disclose the amount of and any changes in income or loss and the Net Cash Flow available for distribution compared to the immediate prior period, and shall show in particular the amounts of depreciation, depletion, amortization, interest, and extraordinary income or charges, whether or not included in operating income.

11. Bank Account. The partnership funds shall be deposited in the name of the partnership in one or more banks to be designated by the general partner and shall be withdrawn on the signature of an officer of the general partner.

12. Transfer of Interest.

(a) Assignment by Living Partners. The interest of the general partner shall not be assignable in whole or in part, except when a substitution is made pursuant to paragraph 9(b). Each limited partner may sell his interest (defined herein to include both his capital account and his loan to the partnership), subject to the provisions of this paragraph 12. Partial assignments shall not be allowed. If any limited partner (referred to in this paragraph as the "seller") desires to sell his interest in the partnership, he shall give each of the other partners thirty (30) days' written notice of the election to sell (referred to in this paragraph as the "option period"), and the other partners shall then have an option to purchase the seller's interest during the option period at the price and on the terms stated in the notice, subject to the following conditions:

(i) The interest may be purchased during the option period, with first option to each of the remaining limited partners in the proportion which the contributed capital of each bears to the total contributed capital of the partnership (less the seller's interest). If, however, any of the limited partners does not elect to purchase his share of the seller's interest, the general partner may purchase that share. If the general partner fails to exercise its option, the remaining limited partners may purchase the share, in the proportion that the contributed capital of each of those who elects to purchase the share bears to the total contributed capital of all those who so elect. The seller shall not be required to sell to the partners, however, unless his entire interest is purchased by the remaining partners. In the event the seller's interest is purchased by any of the remaining partners, then the amounts of the seller's outstanding capital contribution and loan shall be allocated prorata among the purchasers.

(ii) If the seller's entire interest is not purchased by the other partners, the seller may sell or transfer it to any person, whether or not a party to this Agreement, at not less than the price and the terms stated in the notice of election to sell. The transferee of the seller's interest shall not be a substituted limited partner and shall have only a right, upon the same terms and conditions as are applicable to the seller, to receive the distributions and allocations set forth in paragraph 8 and a share of distribution on termination of the partnership. With the consent of the general partner, however, the transferee shall become a substituted limited partner, on the same basis as the seller by an appropriate amendment of the Certificate of Limited Partnership.

(iii) If a seller is unable to sell his partnership interest to any person at not less than the price and the terms offered to the remaining partners, the seller shall, before any attempt to sell at a lower price or on more favorable terms, give the remaining partners a new notice of election to sell in accordance with the requirements stated above, and the procedure for purchase and sale shall again be followed.

(iv) Notwithstanding the foregoing, any limited partner may transfer his interest to a trust for the benefit of himself or his spouse or children, and the trust may become a substituted limited partner in the manner and on the conditions described for transferees of living partners.

(b) Transfer on Death. The heirs, devisees, and legatees of a deceased limited partner shall have the rights of a transferee of a living partner pursuant to paragraph 12(a)(ii), subject to administration of the deceased's estate, but may become substituted limited partners in lieu of the deceased partner only with the consent of the general partner pursuant to, and in the manner and on the conditions described in, paragraph 12(a)(ii).

(c) Adjustment of Basis. The partnership may elect, at the option of the general partner, pursuant to Internal Revenue Code Section 754, to adjust the basis of partnership property under the circumstances and in the manner provided in Internal Revenue Code Sections 734 and 743. The general partner shall take all necessary steps to effect the election.

13. Covenant to Sign Documents.

Each party covenants on behalf of himself and his successors and assigns to execute, with acknowledgement or affidavit if required, any and all documents and writings that may be necessary or expedient in the creation of this partnership, the achievement of the purposes of this partnership, or the consummation of any matter covered by this Agreement, specifically including, without limitation, the Certificate of Limited Partnership, any amendment to it, and any cancellation of it.

14. Power of Attorney.

Each of the limited partners irrevocably constitutes and appoints the general partner as his true and lawful attorney-in-fact, in his name, place, and stead, to make, execute, acknowledge, and file any of the following documents, this authority to be limited, however, solely to such documents as the limited partners have agreed elsewhere in this Agreement to execute and deliver:

(a) The original and any modification or amendment of the Certificate of Limited Partnership;

(b) The Fictitious Business Name Statement; and

(c) Any other instrument that may be required to be filed by the partnership under the laws of the State

This paragraph does not supersede any other paragraph of this Agreement, nor is it to be used to deprive any limited partner of his rights under this Agreement, but is intended only to provide a simplified system for the execution of documents. This power of attorney is coupled with an interest and shall survive the delivery of an assignment of a limited partnership interest.

15. Legal Fees.

It is hereby acknowledged that Esq. is a shareholder, officer, and director of each of the corporations comprising the general partner and is a partner of the law firm of It is hereby acknowledged and approved that the general partner has retained the law firm of to provide the legal services relating to the formation of the partnership, the acquisition on a lease or purchase basis of the land on which the park is to be situated, and the construction of the skateboard park, including, without limitation, the drafting of this Agreement and the architects' and contractors' agreements. A fee of Fifteen Thousand Dollars ($15,000.00) has been budgeted for such services and is hereby authorized and approved.

16. Notices.

All notices that may be required under this Agreement shall be given in writing and shall be given either personally or by prepaid certified mail directed to the parties' respective addresses as shown in the Certificate of Limited Partnership, or as later entered in the books of the partnership pursuant to written notification to the general partner. Each notice shall be signed by the party or parties giving notice. A copy of any such notice shall be sent to

17. Recovery of Attorney's Fees.

In any action between the parties to enforce any of the terms of this Agreement or of any other contract relating to the partnership, or in an action in any other way pertaining to the partnership affairs or to this Agreement, the prevailing party shall be entitled to recover expenses, including, without limitation, a reasonable attorney's fee.

18. Right to Purchase Other Property.

It is hereby expressly acknowledged that the general partner has built and operates an existing skateboard park and may build and operate, alone or with others, other skateboard parks in the future. Nothing contained in this Agreement shall preclude the general partner from building, purchasing, operating, or investing in other skateboard parks or real property of any nature whatsoever, including, without limitation, a skateboard park or real property in the locality of any skateboard park built by this partnership. Any such purchase or investment may be made without notice to the other partners, without participation by the other partners, and without liability to them or to any of them. Each limited partner waives any rights he may have against the general partner for utilizing or profiting upon information learned as a consequence of its connection with the affairs of this partnership.

19. Entire Agreement.

This Agreement contains the entire agreement between the parties and supersedes all prior writings or representations. It is binding on the parties, their executors, administrators, heirs, successors, legal representatives, and assigns.

20. Counterparts.

This partnership agreement may be executed in counterparts, and as executed shall constitute one Agreement, binding on all of the parties, even though all the parties do not sign the original or the same counterpart.

IN WITNESS WHEREOF, the parties sign this Limited Partnership Agreement.

GENERAL PARTNER

General Partnership

By ______________________

By ______________________

LIMITED PARTNERS

	AMOUNT OF CAPITAL CONTRIBUTION	AMOUNT OF LOAN
[Name]		
[Address]		
[Name]		
[Address]		

Form 3. Joint Venture Agreement

JOINT VENTURE AGREEMENT

This Joint Venture Agreement ("Agreement") is made and entered into as of the 21st day of December, by and between CORPORATION, a corporation (hereinafter "PPC", or a "Venturer"), on the one hand, and (hereinafter "Malick") and (hereinafter "TFMP"), on the other hand. Malick and TFMP shall hereinafter sometimes collectively be referred to as "Malick/TFMP", or a "Venturer".

WHEREAS, PPC and TFMP are concurrently herewith entering into an agreement (hereinafter the "Picture Agreement") for the development and possible financing, production and distribution of a theatrical motion picture (the "Picture");

WHEREAS, Malick has heretofore developed an idea for a device and/or process (hereinafter referred to as the "Process") with possible applications in motion picture technology or otherwise;

WHEREAS, the parties desire to form this venture for the purposes of further developing and exploiting the Process, all on the terms and conditions hereinbelow set forth:

NOW, THEREFORE, it is hereby agreed:

1. Formation of Joint Venture; Name.

The parties hereby form a joint venture (hereinafter the "Venture") under the firm name and style of

__________________________.

2. Business of the Venture.

The Venture is formed for the principal purpose of engaging in the development, manufacture, distribution, sale, license, or other exploitation of the Process, a description of which is set forth in Schedule "A" attached hereto.

3. Principal Office.

The principal office of the Venture shall be:

The parties may change such principal office and may establish such branch offices as they may deem necessary or appropriate for the proper conduct of the Venture's business.

4. Capital Contributions.

A. Initial Contributions.

(1) Malick/TFMP. Malick/TFMP hereby contribute to the capital of the Venture their entire right, title and interest, whether acquired before or after the date of this Agreement, in and to the concept, designs, specifications, and other information, data and proprietary rights relating to, or in, the Process and all rights related thereto, including but not limited to all rights in and to any and all derivative processes, and modifications and/or refinements of the Process, whether created before or after the date of this Agreement.

(2) PPC. PPC shall contribute cash to the capital of the Venture (whether by reimbursement or otherwise) subject to the following limitations:

a. PPC's contributions, when aggregated with expenditures and/or reimbursements to TFMP in connection with preproduction and development of the Picture pursuant to paragraph I-C of the Picture Agreement, shall not exceed $250,000.00;

b. PPC shall have the right to discontinue its contributions to the Venture at the Initial Election Point (as hereinbelow defined), notwithstanding that the aggregated expenditures or reimbursements at such point are less than $250,000; and

c. PPC shall have no obligation to furnish, or cause to be furnished, any sums in excess of the initial contributions herein specified.

B. Additional Contributions. Any additional contributions to the capital of the Venture shall be made in accordance with the terms and conditions of Paragraph 5 below.

C. Capital Accounts. For the purposes of this Agreement, the initial capital contributions of PPC, on the one hand, and Malick/TFMP, on the other hand, shall be deemed to be equal. The capital account of each party shall be equal to the value of such party's initial contribution, increased by the amount of any additional contributions made by such party and such party's share of any profits of the Venture and decreased by the amount of any distributions to such party and such party's share of any losses of the Venture.

5. Election to Proceed.

A. The Initial Election Point shall be defined as that time at which PPC approves or disapproves the budget of the Picture in accordance with the terms of paragraph II-A of the Picture Agreement. At said Initial Election Point, PPC shall elect whether or not to go forward with the development of the Process. PPC's aforesaid election shall be totally independent of PPC's election to approve or disapprove the budget of the Picture, i.e., PPC shall be entitled to go forward with the Picture and not the Process, to go forward with the Process and not the Picture, to go forward with both, or to go forward with neither.

B. If, at the Initial Election Point, PPC determines in good faith that additional monetary or other contributions are required for the further development or exploitation of the Process, PPC shall so notify Malick/TFMP in writing within ten (10) days after said Initial Election Point. Within two (2) business days after such notice is given, PPC and Malick/TFMP shall commence negotiations in good faith with regard to the manner and amount in which such contributions shall be made and the effects thereof upon the parties' respective interests in the Venture, including, without limitation, the parties' equity interests therein, it being understood that it is the intent of the parties that there shall be a reallocation of such equity interests if monies or other property, in addition to that specified in paragraph 4A above, are contributed to the Venture other than in equal amounts by both Venturers.

C. If no agreement is reached within five (5) business days after the commencement of the negotiations described in paragraph 5B above, then PPC shall have the right, at any time thereafter, to either:

(1) Refrain from making any additional contributions to the Venture; or

(2) To make, or cause to be made, additional contributions to the Venture, in which event the respective equity interests of the Venturers shall be adjusted as follows: PPC's percentage interest in the capital, profits and losses of the Venture shall be increased at the rate of one percentage point per $10,000 of additional contributions made or caused to be made by PPC and Malick/TFMP's percentage interest in the capital, profits and losses of the Venture shall be decreased in like amount; provided, however, that in no event shall Malick/TFMP's percentage interest in the capital, profits and losses of the Venture be reduced pursuant to this paragraph 5C(2) to less than ten percent (10%). Notwithstanding the foregoing, it is understood and agreed that in the event PPC elects to make additional contributions to the Venture pursuant to this paragraph 5C, it shall have no obligation to contribute any sum or sums certain and it shall at all times have the right to discontinue, or refrain from making, any further additional contributions.

6. Admission of Additional Joint Ventures.

The sole members of the Venture shall be the parties to this Agreement. No other party may be admitted to the Venture without the written consent of all members of the Venture.

7. Expenses; Compensation.

A. PPC shall reimburse Malick/TFMP for its reasonable out-of-pocket expenses incurred in connection with the business of the Venture, provided that such reimbursement and any out-of-pocket expense reasonably incurred by PPC in connection with the business of the Venture shall constitute a part of PPC's initial capital contribution and shall be subject to the provisions of paragraph 4A(2) above. After PPC shall have satisfied its obligation with respect to the initial contribution of capital, the extent to which the expenses of either party shall be reimbursed shall be determined by the management of the Venture.

B. Except as otherwise provided in this Agreement and except for its share of the profits of the Venture, no party shall be entitled to any compensation or other payment for services rendered or provided to the Venture.

8. Profit and Loss.

A. Subject to the provisions of paragraph 5 above, the profits and losses of the Venture shall be divided among and borne by the parties hereto as follows:

PPC	-	50%
MALICK/TFMP	-	50%

B. Determination of the profits and losses of the Venture, to the extent not otherwise specifically provided for in this Agreement, shall be made in the same manner as that used in preparation of the Venture's information tax return for Federal Income Tax purposes.

9. Distributions.

A. At such time or times as the Venture, in the opinion of PPC, shall have cash in excess of its foreseeable needs, the Venture shall distribute such excess cash. Such distributions shall be made wholly to PPC until such time as the aggregate of such distributions and any amounts recouped by PPC pursuant to subparagraph B. below shall equal the entire amount of PPC's contributions to the Venture, and thereafter such distributions shall be made to the Venturers in the same ratio as profits and losses are shared.

B. All sums contributed or caused to be contributed by PPC to the Venture prior to the Initial Election Point shall be included as an item of negative cost of the Picture and shall be recouped by PPC in the manner provided for the recoupment of the negative cost of the Picture pursuant to the Picture Agreement. If PPC elects to go forward with the development and/or exploitation of the Process after the Initial Election Point, such sums contributed or caused to be contributed by PPC to the Venture in connection with such development and/or exploitation as are properly chargeable to the negative cost of the Picture in accordance with generally accepted accounting principles shall be so charged. All contributions not properly chargeable to the negative cost of the Picture shall be recouped by PPC out of any amounts payable to TFMP pursuant to sections 1 and 2 of paragraph III-C of the Picture Agreement after such time as TFMP shall have received Two Hundred Fifty Thousand Dollars ($250,000.00) pursuant to said sections 1 and 2.

10. Rights/Control.

The management and control of the Venture shall be vested solely in PPC. Without limiting the generality of the foregoing, PPC shall be authorized to sell, license or otherwise dispose of any assets of the Venture, or make any other commitment on behalf of the Venture without the consent of Malick/TFMP.

11. Duties.

Malick shall be required to render services diligently and in good faith in connection with the development of the Process during the entire period of his participation in the Venture. Except for his duties in connection with the Picture, Malick shall be exclusive to the Venture until PPC's Initial Election, and in the event PPC elects to go forward with the Picture and the Process, he shall be exclusive until completion of the final answer print of the Picture. In the event PPC elects to go forward with the Process but not the Picture, Malick shall cease to be exclusive to the Venture, but he shall continue diligently to render such services as are necessary to expeditiously develop and/or exploit the Process as and when required by the Venture. Nothing herein contained shall be deemed to modify or enlarge PPC's obligation to make, or cause to be made, contributions to the Venture.

12. Books And Records; Annual Accountings, Bank Accounts.

A. The financial books and records of the Venture shall, unless otherwise agreed by each of the parties, be maintained in accordance with generally accepted accounting principles applied on a consistent basis and in a manner acceptable to the Venture's accountants. The annual accounting period of the Venture shall be the calendar year. Each party shall have full access to the books and records of the Venture.

B. Each Venturer shall receive an accounting statement from the Venture and a copy of the Venture's tax returns annually on a date to be determined by the Venturers.

C. The Venture shall maintain checking and/or savings accounts at such banks as PPC shall determine. All funds shall be deposited in the name of the Venture and may be withdrawn upon the signature of such person or persons as PPC may, in its sole discretion, designate.

13. Liability; Other Interests.

A. Liability.

Neither party shall be liable to the other party or to the Venture for any act or omission performed, or omitted to be performed by such party in good faith and on behalf of the Venture and in a manner reasonably believed by such party to be within the scope of the authority granted to such party hereunder, unless such party was guilty of gross negligence, willful misconduct or breach of this Agreement; provided, however, that Malick/TFMP shall have full responsibility and liability for, and shall indemnify the Venture and PPC in respect of, any loss, cost, damage, demand, expense, liability, claim or suit (including all attorneys' fees incurred in any such suit), or judgment incurred or suffered as a result of, or based on, the claim that the design or operation of the Process constitutes an actual or alleged infringement of a patent or other property right of a third party.

B. Other Interests.

(1) Except as otherwise provided herein, either party hereto may engage in or possess an interest in other business ventures of every nature and description, independently or with others, and neither the

Venture, nor the other party hereto shall have any right by virtue of this Agreement in and to such ventures or to the income and profits derived therefrom.

(2) No party shall be obligated to offer any business opportunity to the others or to the Venture, except opportunities which relate to the Process.

(3) Malick acknowledges that, in the event PPC goes forward with the Picture and with the Process, it is anticipated that the Process will be used in connection with the filming and/or exhibition of the Picture. Malick/TFMP hereby agrees that the Process may be used in connection with the Picture without payment of any kind to the Venture.

(4) In the event PPC abandons the Picture but goes forward with the development of the Process and Malick/TFMP sets up the Picture elsewhere pursuant to Paragraph IIB of the Picture Agreement, PPC hereby agrees that the Venture shall license the Process for use in connection with the Picture for an amount to be determined in good faith between the Venturers on the one hand, and the producer of the Picture, on the other hand. In the event of a dispute as to the value of the licensing of the Process for use in connection with the Picture after good faith negotiations, the dispute shall be submitted to and determined by arbitration in accordance with the rules of the American Arbitration Association.

14. Option To Purchase Interest.

A. The death, bankruptcy, or appointment of a guardian or conservator for the person or estate of Malick or the bankruptcy or assignment for the benefit of creditors of TFMP, or the bankruptcy or assignment for the benefit of creditors of PPC (the party suffering such event being referred to as the "Selling Venturer"), shall give rise to the right of exercise by the other party of the option hereinbelow set forth. For purposes hereof, consistent with the definition of the term "party" hereinabove contained, Malick and TFMP are considered a single party and the occurrence of the above with respect to either Malick or TFMP shall entitle PPC to exercise the option hereinbelow set forth.

B. Upon the occurrence of an event specified in subparagraph A hereof, the other party ("Buying Venturer") shall have the option (the "Option") to purchase the entire Venture interest of the Selling Venturer, including the right to return of capital, share of profit and loss and distributions in accordance with the terms of this Paragraph 14, at the price hereinafter provided.

C. Upon the occurrence of any event giving rise to the option set forth in subparagraph B hereof, the Selling Venturer, or a representative thereof, (hereinafter referred to as the "Representative"), shall promptly give written notice thereof to the Buying Venturer in the manner prescribed elsewhere in this Agreement, provided that the failure to give such notice by the Representative shall not entitle the Buying Venturer to any damages, nor prevent the Buying Venturer from exercising the Option nor have any other effect other than to extend the time to exercise the Option. (The date such notice is given is hereinafter referred to in this Paragraph 14 as the "Notice Receipt Date"). The Option may be exercised only by delivering written notice of the exercise thereof to the Representative within the period commencing upon the date of the occurrence of the event giving rise to the Option and ending, if at all, one hundred twenty (120) days after the Notice Receipt Date. In the event the Buying Venturer exercises the Option, said Buying Venturer and the Representative shall consummate the purchase and sale of the Venture interest within ninety (90) days after exercise of the Option and shall execute and deliver all instruments and documents as are necessary in connection therewith. The option price shall be payable by the Buying Venturer in cash and shall be determined in accordance with paragraph D below.

D. The option price at which the Buying Venturer shall purchase the Venture interest of the Selling Venturer hereunder shall be an amount equal to the appropriate percentage interest of the Selling Venturer in the Venture multiplied by the amount by which the Venture's total assets exceeded its total liabilities at the end of the calendar month during which the event occurred making the option first exercisable, as stated on the Venture's balance sheet prepared in the regular course of business as of said date, whether or not audited, less the amount of any distributions to the Selling Venturer made after the date of the said balance sheet.

15. Dissolution And Termination.

The Venture shall be dissolved upon the first to occur of any of the following events:

A. The written consent of all parties;

B. Any event which makes it unlawful for the Venture's business to be carried on, or for the parties to carry it on as a joint venture;

C. A decree of a court of competent jurisdiction; or

D. Thirty (30) days after receipt of all proceeds from the sale of all or substantially all of the assets of the Venture.

16. Distribution On Dissolution And Termination Of Venture.

In the event the Venture is dissolved and terminated for any cause, the parties agree to make a true, just and final account of all matters relating to the business of the Venture which shall thereupon be wound up and liquidated. All assets of the Venture (other than any patents on the Process, and the proprietary rights in the Process) shall be converted to cash as quickly as is commercially prudent and reasonable. Distribution of the Venture's assets shall then be made in the following order of priority:

A. The payment of all debts and liabilities of the Venture in the order of priority as provided by law;

B. The payment of any debts of the Venture to the parties hereto (other than for capital or profits);

C. To the parties hereto in payment of the balances in their respective capital accounts; and

D. To the extent of any excess, to the parties hereto in the same proporation as the parties share profit and loss.

17. Representations And Warranties Of Parties.

A. PPC and TFMP each represents and warrants that it is a duly organized and validly existing California corporation, with full corporate power and authority to enter into this Agreement and perform its obligations hereunder, and that this Agreement has been duly authorized, executed and delivered and constitutes PPC's and TFMP's binding agreement and obligation.

B. Malick represents and warrants that he has full capacity and right to enter into this Agreement and perform his obligations hereunder and that this Agreement constitutes his binding agreement and obligation.

C. Malick/TFMP represents and warrants that it owns all rights being contributed by it, or to be contributed by it, to the Venture free and clear of any and all liens, claims, encumbrances, rights or interest of third persons, that neither the execution, delivery or performance of this Agreement by it will be prohibited by, cause a default under, or require the consent of any person to, any agreement, instrument, court order, decree or injunction binding upon Malick or TFMP or upon the assets of either, nor has it done any act or suffered any event or condition to exist as a consequence of which any of the assets of the Venture, or its interest in the Venture, will be, or is, subject to any lien, claim, charge, encumbrance or interest of a third person.

D. Each party indemnifies and agrees to hold each other party and the Venture harmless from any loss, cost, damage, expense, claim, demand, suit, liability, or cause of action (and any and all legal fees and expenses incurred in connection therewith) which an indemnified party may suffer, or which may be asserted against an indemnified party, as a result or consequence of any breach of any warranty hereunder, and will defend the indemnified parties against any claim, suit, action or proceeding commenced, which, if successful, would require the indemnifying party to indemnify the indemnified parties.

18. Notices.

All notices, statements or other documents which any party shall be required or shall desire to give to another hereunder must be in writing and shall be given only in one of the following ways: (1) by personal delivery, or (2) by addressing the same as indicated below, and depositing it, registered or certified mail, postage prepaid, in the United States mail, or (3) by delivering it toll prepaid to a telegraph or cable company addressed as indicated below. If so delivered, mailed, telegraphed or cabled, each such notice, statement or other document shall be conclusively deemed to have been given when personally delivered or forty-eight (48) hours after the date of mailing, or on the date of delivery to the telegraph or cable company, as the case may be. The addresses of the parties shall be as follows provided that any party may change the address to which notices to him are to be sent by giving notice thereof to the others in accordance herewith:

If to PPC:

With A Copy To:

If to Malick/TFMP:

19. Amendment.

This Agreement may be amended, modified, supplemented or terminated only by a writing executed by all of the parties.

20. No Violation of Law.

Nothing herein contained shall be construed so as to require the commission of any act contrary to law, and wherever there is any conflict between any provision of this Agreement and any statute, law or ordinance contrary to which the parties have no legal right to contract, the latter shall prevail, but in such event the provision of this Agreement so affected shall be curtailed and limited only to the extent necessary to bring it within the legal requirements.

21. Further Assurances.

Malick and TFMP hereby individually and collectively agree to duly execute, acknowledge and deliver to the Venture, or procure the due execution, acknowledgment and delivery to the Venture of, any and all agreements, assignments and/or other instruments, in a form approved by counsel for PPC, necessary or expedient to carry out and effectuate the purposes and intent of the parties as expressed in this Agreement, and to convey to the Venture all rights herein granted and agreed to be granted to the Venture. Malick and TFMP, individually and collectively, further agree to procure for the Venture properly executed documents and other proof, if such is required, to establish a clear chain of title in themselves to the rights herein granted. Without limiting in any way the generality of the foregoing, in the event the Venture elects to attempt to obtain patent protection with respect to the Process, or any derivative process, application or refinement relating thereto, Malick and TFMP shall, upon request, execute all assignments and other instruments as may be required to evidence the Venture's ownership and Malick/TFMP shall use its best efforts to have the inventor execute such patent applications or other instruments as may be required in order to obtain such patent protection, vesting ownership of any and all rights in the patent application and any resulting patent in the Venture. If Malick or TFMP or both shall fail, refuse, or neglect to so execute and deliver, or cause to be so executed and delivered any such agreement, assignment or other instrument herein provided for, PPC shall be deemed, and Malick and TFMP hereby each appoint PPC, the true-and-lawful attorney-in-fact of Malick and TFMP, respectively, with full right of substitution and delegation to execute and deliver any and all documents, and to do or perform any and all acts and things, reasonably required in the premises in the name of Malick and TFMP or both or otherwise, Malick and TFMP, individually and collectively, hereby acknowledging that the power hereby granted is coupled with an interest and is irrevocable.

22. Confidentiality.

The Venturers shall use their best efforts to maintain in secrecy the Process and all derivative Processes, applications, and refinements thereof. The Venturers each recognize that the other would be seriously damaged if the Process or any information relating thereto should come into the possession of any unauthorized person, and each of them accordingly agrees to use its best efforts to prevent this from happening. In this connection, each Venturer agrees to use its best efforts to prevent any information regarding the Process from coming into the possession of any of its officers or employees except only those who are necessarily called upon to render services in connection with the development and/or exploitation of the Process and each of the Venturers shall exercise care in the selection of its employees who may be authorized to handle, use or otherwise deal with the Process. Each of the Venturers shall maintain close control over all documents, devices, or other information or equipment relating to the Process in its possession.

23. Paragraph Headings.

Paragraph headings are inserted herein solely for convenience and the same shall not be used to interpret or construe any provision hereof, nor shall the same be deemed a part hereof.

24. Integration.

This Agreement and the Picture Agreement set forth the entire agreement of the parties hereto with respect to the subject matter hereof and supersede in full all discussions, agreements or understandings of the parties respecting the subject matter hereof.

25. Governing Law.

This Agreement shall be governed by the Uniform Partnership Act

26. Successors And Assigns.

A. This Agreement shall be binding upon, and inure to the benefit of, the parties hereto and their respective heirs, successors and assigns. No person other than the parties hereto, and their respective successors and assigns, shall have any rights against any of the members of the Venture, or the Venture, by virtue of this Agreement.

B. Notwithstanding the terms of the preceding Paragraph A, Malick/TFMP shall not be entitled to assign any of its rights or obligations under this Agreement without PPC's prior written consent in each instance. Furthermore, as an essential consideration to the execution of this Agreement, without which Malick/TFMP acknowledges PPC would not enter into this Agreement, Malick/TFMP agrees that if it shall propose to enter into any transaction with a third party whereby any of Malick/TFMP's interest in the Venture or distributions from the Venture shall or may be assigned, transferred, hypothecated or encumbered, Malick/TFMP shall give PPC notice in writing of all material details and terms of such proposed transaction, including without limitation the names of the third parties, and such notice shall constitute an offer to enter into an identical transaction with PPC. PPC shall have ten (10) business days thereafter to give written notice of its acceptance or rejection of such offer, and failure to give such written notice shall be deemed rejection. If PPC shall reject such offer, Malick/TFMP shall be free for a period of thirty (30) calendar days after such rejection, but not thereafter, to consummate the proposed transaction on the terms described in said notice, but not on any other or different terms, with the third parties named in such notice, but not with anyone else.

C. PPC shall be entitled to assign this Agreement or any of its rights or obligations hereunder to any subsidiary, parent or affiliate corporation or to any person, firm or corporation which shall succeed to all or to substantially all of PPC's assets, or to all or substantially all of PPC's theatrical distribution facilities, or possessing substantially equivalent theatrical distribution facilities regardless of whether it succeeds to the remainder of PPC's assets, provided that such assignees shall, in any event, assume in writing and agree to perform all of the terms and conditions to be performed by PPC hereunder. Notwithstanding the foregoing, nothing herein contained shall be deemed or construed to limit or prevent PPC from assigning or hypothecating all or a portion of its interests in the Venture.

27. References.

All references to the singular shall, if appropriate, refer to the plural as well, and any references to the masculine shall, if appropriate, refer to the feminine and neuter, and in each case vice versa.

28. Nature of Obligations.

Each and every agreement, covenant, obligation, liability, representation, warranty and responsibility expressed herein as that of "Malick/TFMP" shall be that of Malick and TFMP jointly and severally.

29. Security Interest.

For the purpose of securing the performance of Malick/TFMP's obligations hereunder, Malick/TFMP hereby grant PPC a security interest in all of Malick/TFMP's rights, title and interest in and to, or arising under, this Agreement.

IN WITNESS WHEREOF, the parties hereto have executed this Agreement as of the 21st day of December,

By______________________

By______________________

Form 4. Stock Certificate

SAMPLE STOCK CERTIFICATE

Certificate number ________ (1) ________
For ________ (Number of) ________ Shares
Issued To:
________ (Name of shareholder) ________
________ (Address of shareholder) ________
Dated ________ (Date of issuance) ________ 19 __

From whom transferred
(4) ______________________
Dated ______________________ 19 __

No. Original Shares	No. Original Certificate	No. of Shares Transferred

Received certificate number ________
For ________ (Number of) ________ Shares
(Date of issuance)
This ________ day of ________ 19 __
________ (Shareholder's signature) ________

INCORPORATED UNDER THE LAWS OF THE STATE OF TEXAS

NO. ________

________ (name of corporation as given in articles) ________

Shares ________ (number of shares represented by certificate)

The Corporation Is Authorized To Issue ________ Common Shares — Par Value $______ Each

THE SHARES REPRESENTED BY THIS CERTIFICATE HAVE NOT BEEN REGISTERED UNDER ANY FEDERAL OR STATE SECURITIES LAW. THEY HAVE BEEN ACQUIRED FOR INVESTMENT AND MAY NOT BE TRANSFERRED WITHOUT AN EFFECTIVE REGISTRATION STATEMENT PURSUANT TO SUCH LAWS OR AN OPINION OF LEGAL COUNSEL SATISFACTORY TO THE CORPORATION THAT REGISTRATION IS NOT REQUIRED.

THIS CERTIFIES THAT ________ (name of shareholder) ________
is the owner of ________ (number of shares represented by certificate) ________
fully paid and non-assessable Shares of the above Corporation transferable only on the books of the Corporation by the holder hereof in person or by duly authorized Attorney upon surrender of this Certificate properly endorsed.

IN WITNESS WHEREOF, the said Corporation has caused this Certificate to be signed by its duly authorized officers and to be sealed with the Seal of the Corporation.

DATED ______________________

______________________ **President**

______________________ **Secretary**

Form 5a. Articles of Incorporation (Short Form)

ARTICLES OF INCORPORATION
OF
____

ARTICLE ONE

The name of the corporation is ______________________________.

ARTICLE TWO

The period of its duration is ______________________.

ARTICLE THREE

The purpose for which the corporation is organized is the transaction of any or all lawful business for which corporations may be incorporated under the Texas Business Corporation Act.

ARTICLE FOUR

The aggregate number of shares which the corporation shall have authority to issue ______________________ (__________) shares, ______________________ par value.

ARTICLE FIVE

The corporation will not commence business until it has received for the issuance of its shares consideration of the value of not less than One Thousand Dollars ($1,000) consisting of money, labor done, or property actually received.

ARTICLE SIX

The street address of its initial registered office is:

and the name of its initial registered agent at such address is:

ARTICLE SEVEN

The number of directors constituting the initial board of directors is ______________, and the names and addresses of the person or persons who are to serve as directors until the first annual meeting of the shareholders or until their successors are elected and qualified are:

ARTICLE EIGHT

The name and address of the incorporator is:

Signed (signature)______________
(typed name), Incorporator

STATE OF TEXAS

COUNTY OF ______________

Before me, a notary public, on this day personally appeared (name of incorporator)______________, known to me to be the person whose name is subscribed to the foregoing document and, being by me first duly sworn, declared that the statements therein contained are true and correct.

Given under my hand and seal of office this __________ day of ______________, A.D. ______________________.

(printed or stamped name)
Notary Public, State of Texas

(Notary Seal) My commission expires: __________, 19___

Form 5b. Articles of Incorporation (Long Form)

ARTICLES OF INCORPORATION
OF
____

The undersigned natural person of the age of eighteen (18) years or more, without regard to place of residence, domicile, or organization, acting as incorporator of a corporation (hereinafter referred to as the "Corporation"), under the Texas Business Corporation Act (hereinafter referred to as the "Act"), does hereby adopt the following Articles of Incorporation for such corporation.

ARTICLE ONE

NAME

The name of the Corporation is ______________

ARTICLE TWO

DURATION

The period of existence of the Corporation is perpetual.

ARTICLE THREE

PURPOSES AND POWERS

Section 3.01. Purposes and Powers in Addition to Statutory Powers. The purposes for which the Corporation is organized, and the powers, in addition to the general powers conferred by the Act, which the Corporation shall be entitled to exercise, all subject to the limiting provisions set forth in Section 3.03 of this Article are:

> To manage, operate or administer the business or property of any corporation, firm, or person carrying on any authorized business, and to sell or dispose of, receive and make disbursements for, or arrange for the management or administration of the whole or any part of the business or property of any corporation, firm, or person and to act as agent or manager for the development and extension of the business interests of any corporation, firm or person.
>
> To acquire, own, hold, improve, develop, operate, exploit, sell, convey, assign, lease, exchange, transfer, dispose of, pledge, mortgage, create security interests in, deal in, and loan or borrow money upon, alone or in conjunction with others, real and personal property, tangible and intangible, of every kind, character and description or any interest therein, and all kinds and forms of securities, shares of capital stock, script, bonds, debentures, coupons, mortgages, notes, bills of exchange, acceptances, assignments, accounts, fees, evidences of indebtedness, obligations, trust certificates, interim receipts, warranties and certificates issued or created by or being claimed against any corporation, association, partnership, syndicate, entity, or person, or governmental, municipal, or public subdivision, district, or authority.
>
> To further have the power to carry on any of the business and do any other acts in connection with the foregoing, and to have and exercise all the powers conferred by the laws of the State of Texas upon corporations formed under the Texas Business

Corporation Act, and to do any or all things hereinabove set forth to the same extent as a natural person might or could do.

Section 3.02. Direction of Purposes and Exercise of Powers of Directors. Subject to any limitations or restrictions imposed by the Act, by other law, or by these Articles of Incorporation, the Board of Directors hereby is authorized to direct the purposes set forth in this Article and to exercise all the powers of the Corporation without previous authorization or subsequent approval by the Shareholders.

Section 3.03. Limiting Provisions. Nothing in these Articles of Incorporation is to be construed as authorizing or attempting to authorize the Corporation:

(a) To transact any business in the State of Texas expressly prohibited by any law of the State of Texas;

(b) To engage in any activity in the State of Texas which cannot lawfully be engaged in without first obtaining a license under the laws of the State of Texas, and which license cannot be granted to a corporation; or

(c) To take any action in violation of the Anti-Trust Laws of the State of Texas.

ARTICLE FOUR

AUTHORIZED SHARES

Section 4.01. The aggregate number of shares which the Corporation shall have authority to issue is ________ of the par value of $__________ each, all of which shares shall be known as "Common Stock."

ARTICLE FIVE

INITIAL CONSIDERATION FOR ISSUANCE OF SHARES

The Corporation will not commence or transact any business or incur any indebtedness except such as shall be incidental to its organization or to obtaining subscriptions to or payment for its shares, until it has received for the issuance of its shares consideration of the value of at least One Thousand and No/100 Dollars ($1,000.00), consisting of money, labor done or property actually received.

ARTICLE SIX

RIGHTS OF DIRECTORS AND OFFICERS TO DEAL WITH CORPORATION

No Director and no Officer of the Corporation shall be disqualified by reason of his office from dealing with or contracting with the Corporation, either as vendor, seller, purchaser, vendee, buyer, mortgagee, mortgagor, or otherwise; and no transaction of this Corporation shall be void or voidable by reason of the fact that the Director or Officer of any firm in which a Director or Officer of this Corporation is a member, or any corporation of which a Director or Officer of this Corporation is a shareholder or a director or officer, is in any way interested in such transaction.

ARTICLE SEVEN

DENIAL OF PREEMPTIVE RIGHTS

Provisions limiting or denying shareholders the preemptive right to acquire additional or treasury shares of the Corporation are:

No shareholder shall be entitled, as a matter of right, to subscribe for, purchase or receive any shares of stock or any rights or options of the Corporation which it may issue or sell, whether out of the number of shares authorized by these Articles of Incorporation or by amendment thereof, or out of the shares of the stock of the Corporation acquired by it after the issuance thereof, nor shall any shareholder be entitled, as a matter of right, to subscribe for, purchase or receive any bonds, debentures or other securities which the Corporation may issue or sell that shall be convertible into, exchangeable for, stock or to which shall be attached or appertain any warrant or warrants or other instrument or instruments that shall confer upon the holder or owner of such obligations the right to subscribe for, purchase or receive from the Corporation any shares of its authorized capital stock; but all such additional issues of stock, rights and options or of bonds, debentures or other securities convertible into, or exchangeable for, stock or to which warrants shall be attached or appertain or which shall confer upon the holder the right to subscribe for, purchase or receive any shares of stock, may be issued, optioned for, and sold or disposed of by the Corporation pursuant to resolution of its Board of Directors to such persons, firms or corporations and upon such terms as may be lawful and may to such Board of Directors seem proper and advisable, without first offering such stock or securities or any part thereof to the shareholder. The acceptance of stock in the Corporation shall be a waiver of any preemptive rights or preferential rights which, in the absence of this provision might otherwise be asserted by shareholders of the Corporation of any of them.

ARTICLE EIGHT

PROHIBITION OF CUMULATIVE VOTING

At each election for Directors, every shareholder entitled to vote at such election shall have the right to vote, in person or by proxy, the number of shares owned by him for as many persons as there are Directors to be elected and for whose election he has the right to vote, but it is prohibited for any shareholder to cumulate his votes by giving one candidate as many votes as the number of such Directors multiplied by his shares shall equal, or by distributing such votes on such principle among any number of such candidates.

ARTICLE NINE

PROVISIONS FOR REGULATION OF THE CORPORATION AND ITS INTERNAL AFFAIRS

The following provisions are set forth for the regulation of the Corporation and its internal affairs to the extent that such provisions are not inconsistent with the law.

Section 9.01. Bylaws. The power to alter, amend or repeal the Bylaws and to adopt new Bylaws shall be vested in the Board of Directors and in the shareholders entitled to vote for the election of Directors; provided, however, that any Bylaw or amendment thereto as adopted by the Board of Directors may be altered, amended or repealed, or a new Bylaw in lieu thereof may be adopted, by vote of such shareholders; but no Bylaw which has been altered, amended or adopted by vote of such shareholders may be altered, amended or repealed by the Board of Directors, nor may the substance of any Bylaw repealed by vote of such shareholders be again adopted by the Board of Directors, until one year shall have expired since such action by vote of such shareholders.

Section 9.02. Other Provisions. Other provisions for the regulation of the Corporation and its internal affairs not inconsistent with law or these Articles of Incorporation may be set forth in the Bylaws, including, but not limited to, provisions regulating and providing for compensation of directors, interest of directors in contracts, provisions for working capital, liability and indemnification of directors, officers and employees, removal and discharge of directors, officers, agents and employees, and voting of shares by proxy. All rights of the shareholders, directors, officers, agents and employees of the Corporation shall be deemed subject to all provisions of the Bylaws to the fullest extent permitted by law.

ARTICLE TEN

INITIAL REGISTERED OFFICE AND AGENT

The post office address of the initial registered office of the Corporation and the name of the initial registered agent of the Corporation at such address are:

Registered Agent   Registered Office

ARTICLE ELEVEN

DIRECTORS

Section 11.01. Number. The Board of Directors of the Corporation shall consist of one or more members. The number of Directors shall be fixed by resolution of the Board of Directors and may be increased or decreased by resolution of the Board of Directors; but no decrease shall have the effect of shortening the term of any incumbent Director.

Section 11.02. Qualifications. The Directors need not be residents of the State of Texas or shareholders of the Corporation.

Section 11.03. Initial Directors. The number, names and addresses of the persons who are to serve as Directors until the first annual meeting of the shareholders or until their successors are elected and have qualified, are:

Number:

Name   Address

ARTICLE TWELVE

INCORPORATOR

The name and address of the Incorporator of the Corporation is:

Name   Address

IN WITNESS WHEREOF, I have hereunto set my hand this the _____ day of _______________, 19__.

____

THE STATE OF TEXAS §
§
COUNTY OF HARRIS §

BEFORE ME, the undersigned authority, on this day personally appeared ____________________, who being by me first duly sworn, declared that [he][she] is the person who signed the foregoing document as Incorporator, and the statements therein contained are true.

GIVEN UNDER MY HAND AND SEAL OF OFFICE on this the ____ day of __________________, 19___.

____
Notary Public in and for
the State of T E X A S

My Commission Expires:

____

Form 6. Corporate Bylaws

ARTICLE ONE

OFFICES

Registered Office

1.01 The registered office of the corporation is located at ____
____.

Registered Agent

1.02 The name of the registered agent of the corporation at such address is ____.

Principal Office

1.03 The principal office for the transaction of the business of this corporation is located at ________________________________
____.

Other Offices

1.04 The corporation may also have offices at such other places, within or without the State of Texas, where the corporation is qualified to do business, as the Board of Directors may from time to time designate, or as the business of the corporation may require.

ARTICLE TWO

SHAREHOLDERS' MEETINGS

Place of Meetings

2.01 Meetings of shareholders shall be held at any place within or without the State of Texas designated by the Board of Directors pursuant to authority hereinafter granted to the Board, or by the written consent of all persons entitled to vote thereat. In the absence of any such designation, shareholders' meetings shall be held at the principal office of the corporation. Any meeting is valid wherever held if held by the written consent of all the persons entitled to vote thereat, which consent may be given either before or after the meeting and filed with the Secretary of the corporation.

Time of Annual Meeting - Business Transacted

2.02 The annual meeting of shareholders shall be held on the first Tuesday of February of each year, at the hour of 10:00 a.m.; however, should said day fall upon a legal holiday, then at the same time on the next business day thereafter. At such meetings Directors shall be elected, reports of the affairs of the corporation shall be considered, and any other business may be transacted which is within the powers of the shareholders.

Notice of Meetings

2.03 (1) Notice of all meetings of shareholders shall be given in writing to shareholders entitled to vote by the President or Secretary or by the officer or person calling the meeting, or, in case of his neglect or refusal, or if there is no person charged with the duty of giving notice, by any Director or shareholder. The notice shall be given to each shareholder, either personally or by prepaid mail, addressed to the shareholder at his address appearing on the transfer books of the corporation.

Time of Notice

(2) Notice of any meeting of shareholders shall be sent to each shareholder entitled thereto not less than ten (10) nor more than fifty (50) days before the meeting, except in the case of a meeting for the purpose of approving a merger or consolidation agreement, in which case the notice must be given not less than twenty (20) days prior to the date of the meeting.

Contents of Notice

(3) Notice of any meeting of shareholders shall specify the place, date, and hour of the meeting. The notice shall also specify the purpose of the meeting if it is a special meeting, or

if its purpose, or one of its purposes, will be to consider a proposed amendment of the articles of incorporation, to consider a proposed reduction of stated capital without amendment, to consider a proposed merger or consolidation, to consider a voluntary dissolution or the revocation of a voluntary dissolution by act of the corporation, or to consider a proposed disposition of all, or substantially all, of the assets of the corporation outside of the ordinary course of business.

Notice of Adjourned Meeting

(4) When a shareholders' meeting is adjourned for thirty (30) days or more, notice of the adjourned meeting shall be given as in the case of an original meeting. When a meeting is adjourned for less than thirty (30) days, it is not necessary to give any notice of the time and place of the adjourned meeting or of the business to be transacted thereat other than by announcement at the meeting at which the adjournment is taken.

Calling of Special Meeting

2.04 (1) On request in writing to the President, Vice-President, or Secretary, sent by registered mail or delivered to the officer in person, by any persons entitled to call a meeting of shareholders, the officer forthwith shall cause notice to be given to the shareholders entitled to vote that a meeting will be held at a time, fixed by the officer, not less than ten (10) days after the receipt of the request. If the notice is not given within seven (7) days after the date of delivery, or the date of mailing of the request, the persons calling the meeting may fix the time of meeting and give the notice in the manner provided in these bylaws. Nothing contained in this section shall be construed as limiting, fixing, or affecting the time or date when a meeting of shareholders called by action of the Board of Directors may be held.

Persons Entitled to Call Special Meetings

(2) Special meetings of the shareholders, for any purpose whatsoever, may be called at any time by any of the following: (1) the President; (2) the Board of Directors; (3) one or more shareholders holding not less than one-tenth of all the shares entitled to vote at the meetings; (4) the Executive Committee.

Quorum of Shareholders

2.05 (1) The presence in person or by proxy of the persons entitled to vote a majority of the voting shares at any meeting constitutes a quorum for the transaction of business.

Adjournment for Lack or Loss of Quorum

(2) In the absence of a quorum or the withdrawal of enough shareholders to leave less than a quorum, any meeting of shareholders may be adjourned from time to time by the vote of a majority of the shares, the holders of which are either present in person or represented by proxy thereat, but no other business may be transacted.

Closing Transfer Books

2.06 (1) For the purpose of determining shareholders entitled to notice of or to vote at any meeting of shareholders or any adjournment thereof, or entitled to receive payment of any dividend, or in order to make a determination of shareholders for any other proper purpose, the Board of Directors may provide that the share transfer books shall be closed for a stated period not to exceed, in any case, fifty (50) days. If the transfer books shall be closed for the purpose of determining shareholders entitled to notice of or to vote at a meeting of shareholders, such books shall be closed for at least ten (10) days immediately preceding such meeting.

Record Date for Determination of Shareholders

(2) In lieu of closing the share transfer books, the Board of Directors may fix in advance a date as the record date for any such determination of shareholders, such date in any case to be not more than fifty (50) days and, in case of a meeting of shareholders, not less than ten (10) days prior to the date on which the particular action, requring such determination of shareholders, is to be taken.

Date of Notice or Resolution for Determination of Shareholders

(3) If the share transfer books are not closed and no record date is fixed for determination of shareholders entitled to notice of or to vote at a meeting of shareholders, or shareholders entitled to receive payment of a dividend, the date on which notice of the meeting is mailed or the date on which the resolution of the Board of Directors declaring such dividend is adopted, as the case may be, is the record date for such determination of shareholders.

(4) When any determination of shareholders entitled to vote at any meeting of shareholders has been made as provided in this Paragraph, such determination shall apply to any adjournment thereof except where the determination has been made through closing of the transfer books and the state period of closing has expired, in which case the Board of Directors shall make a new determination as hereinbefore provided.

Voting List

2.07 At least ten (10) days before each meeting of shareholders, the officer or agent having charge of the stock transfer books for shares of the corporation shall make a complete list of the shareholders entitled to vote at such meeting or any adjournment thereof, arranged in alphabetical order, with the address of and the number of shares held by each, which list, for a period of ten (10) days prior to such meeting, shall be kept on file at the office of the corporation and shall be subject to inspection by any shareheolder at any time during usual business hours. Such list shall also be produced and kept open at the time and place of the meeting. The original share transfer books shall be prima facie evidence as to who are the shareholders entitled to examine such list or transfer books or to vote at any meeting of shareholders. However, failure to prepare such a list shall not affect the validity of any action taken at the meeting.

Votes Per Share

2.08 Each outstanding share, regardless of class, shall be entitled to one vote on each matter submitted to a vote at a meeting of shareholders, except to the extent that the voting rights of shares of any class or classes are limited by the articles of incorporation.

Cumulative Voting

2.09 Unless prohibited by the articles of incorporation every shareholder entitled to vote at any election for Directors may cumulate his votes and give one candidate a number of votes equal to the number of Directors to be elected multiplied by the number of votes to which his shares are entitled, or distribute his votes on the same principle among any number of candidates. The candidates receiving the highest number of votes up to the number of Directors to be elected are elected. No shareholder may cumulate his votes unless he shall have given written notice of his intention so to do to the Secretary of the corporation on or before the day preceding the election at which such votes will be cumulated. If any shareholder gives written notice as provided above, all shareholders may cumulate their votes.

Voting by Voice and Ballot

2.10 Elections for Directors need not be by ballot unless a shareholder demands election by ballot at the election and before the voting begins.

Proxies

2.11 A shareholder may vote either in person or by proxy executed in writing by the shareholder or by his duly authorized attorney in fact. No proxy shall be valid after eleven (11) months from the date of its execution unless otherwise provided in the proxy. Each proxy shall be revocable unless expresaly provided therein to be irrevocable, and in no event shall it remain irrevocable for a period of more than eleven (11) months.

Waiver of Notice

2.12 Any notice required by law or these bylaws may be waived by the execution by the person entitled to the notice of a written waiver of such notice, which may be signed before or after the time stated in the notice.

Action Without Meeting

2.13 Any action which, under any provision of the Texas Business Corporation Act may be taken at a meeting of the shareholders, may be taken without a meeting if authorized by a writing signed by all of the persons who would be entitled to vote on such action a meeting, and filed with the Secretary of the corporation. Any such signed consent, or a signed copy thereof, shall be placed on the minute book of the corporation.

Appointment of Inspectors of Election

2.14 (1) In advance of any meeting of shareholders, the Board of Directors may appoint any persons, other than nominees for office, as inspectors of election to act at such meeting or any adjournment thereof. If inspectors of election are not so appointed, the chairman of any such meeting may, and on the request of any shareholder or his proxy shall, appoint inspectors of election at the meeting. The number of inspectors shall be either one or three. If appointed at a meeting on the request of one or more shareholders or proxies, the majority of shares present shall determine whether one or three inspectors are to be appointed. In case any person appointed as inspector fails to appear or fails or refuses to act, the vacancy may be filled by appointment by the Board of Directors in advance of the meeting, or at the meeting by the person acting as chairman.

Duties of Inspectors

(2) The inspectors of election shall determine the number of shares outstanding and the voting power of each, the shares represented at the meeting, the existence of a quorum, the authenticity, validity, and effect of proxies, receive votes, ballots, or consents, hear and determine all challenges and questions in any way arising in connection with the right to vote, count and tabulate all votes or consents, determine the result, and do such acts as may be proper to conduct the election or vote with fairness to all shareholders. The inspectors of election shall perform their duties impartially, in good faith, to the best of their ability and as expeditiously as is practical.

Vote of Inspectors

(3) If there are three inspectors of election, the decision, act or certificate of a majority is effective in all respects as the decision, act, or certificate of all.

Report of Inspectors

(4) On request of the chairman of the meeting or of any shareholder or his proxy the inspectors shall make a report in

writing of any challenge or question or matter determined by them and execute a certificate of any fact found by them. Any report or certificate made by them is prima facie evidence of the facts stated therein.

Conduct of Meetings

2.15 At every meeting of the shareholders, the President, or in his absence, the Vice-President designated by the President, or, in the absence of such designation, a chairman (who shall be one of the Vice Presidents, if any is present) chosen by a majority in interest of the shareholders of the corporation present in person or by proxy and entitled to vote, shall act as chairman. The Secretary of the corporation, or in his absence, an Assistant Secretary, shall act as secretary of all meetings of the shareholders. If no Secretary or Assistant Secretary is present, the chairman may appoint another person to act as secretary of the meeting.

ARTICLE THREE

DIRECTORS

Directors Defined

3.01 "Directors" or "Board", when used in relation to any power or duty requiring collective action, means "Board of Directors".

Powers

3.02 The business and affairs of the corporation and all corporate powers shall be exercised by or under authority of the Board of Directors, subject to limitations imposed by the Texas Business Corporation Act, the articles of incorporation, or these bylaws as to action which requires authorization or approval by the shareholders.

Number of Directors

3.03 The number of Directors of this corporation shall be _________, none of whom need be shareholders or residents of the State of Texas. The number of Directors may be increased or decreased from time to time by amendment to these bylaws, but no decrease shall have the effect of shortening the term of any incumbent Director.

Term of Office

3.04 The Directors named in the articles shall hold office until their successors are elected by the shareholders and the successors are qualified. Directors other than those named in the articles shall hold office until the next annual meeting and until their successors are elected and qualified.

Vacancies

3.05 (1) Vacancies in the Board of Directors shall exist in the case of the happening of any of the following events: (a) the death, resignation, or removal of any Director; (b) the authorized number of Directors is increased; or (c) at any annual, regular, or special meeting of shareholders at which any Director is elected, the shareholders fail to elect the full authorized number of Directors to be voted for at that meeting.

Declaration of Vacancy

(2) The Board of Directors may declare vacant the office of a Director in either of the following cases: (a) if he is adjudged incompetent by an order of court, or finally convicted of a felony; or (b) if within sixty (60) days after notice of his election, he does not accept the office either in writing or by attending a meeting of the Board of Directors.

Filling Vacancies by Directors

(3) Vacancies may be filled by a majority of the remaining Directors, though less than a quorum, or by a sole remaining Director. Each Director so elected shall hold office until his successor is elected at an annual, regular, or special meeting of the shareholders.

Filling Vacancies by Shareholders - Reduction of Authorized Number of Directors

(4) The shareholders may elect a Director at any time to fill any vacancy not filled by the Directors. If the Board of Directors accepts the resignation of a Director tendered to take effect at a future time, the Board or the shareholders may elect a successor to take office when the resignation becomes effective. A reduction of the authorized number of Directors does not remove any Director prior to the expiration of his term of office.

Removal of Directors

3.06 The entire Board of Directors or any individual Director may be removed from office by a vote of shareholders holding a majority of the outstanding shares entitled to vote at an election of Directors. However, unless cumulative voting has been denied by statute or by the Articles of Incorporation, and if less than the entire Board is to be removed, no one of the Directors may be removed if the votes cast against his removal would be sufficient to elect him if cumulatively voted at an election of the entire Board of Directors, or if there be classes of Directors, at an election of the class of Directors of which he is a part. If any or all Directors are so removed, new Directors may be elected at the same meeting. Whenever a class or series of shares is entitled to elect one or more Directors under authority granted by the articles, the provisions of this paragraph apply to the vote of that class or series and not to the vote of the outstanding shares as a whole.

Place of Meetings

3.07 Regular meetings of the Board of Directors shall be held at any place within or without the State of Texas which has been designated from time to time by resolution of the Board or by written consent of all members of the Board. In the absence of such designation, regular meetings shall be held at the principal office of the corporation. Special meetings of the Board may be held either at a place so designated or at the principal office. Any regular or special meeting is valid, wherever held, if held on written consent of all members of the Board given either before or after the meeting and filed with the Secretary of the corporation.

Regular Meetings

3.08 (1) Regular meetings of the Board of Directors shall be held at such time and place as shall from time to time be determined by the Board.

Call of Regular Meetings

(2) All regular meetings of the Board of Directors of this corporation shall be called by the President or, if he is absent or is unable or refuses to act, by any Vice President or by any two Directors.

Notice of Regular Meetings

(3) Written notice of the time and place of the regular meetings of the Board of Directors shall be delivered personally to each Director, or sent to each Director by mail or by other form of written communication at least seven (7) days before the meeting. If the address of a Director is not shown on the records and is not readily ascertainable, notice shall be addressed to him at the corporation's office located in the city or place in which the meetings of the Directors are regularly held. Notice of the time and place of holding an adjourned meeting of a meeting need not be given to absent Directors if the time and place are fixed at the meeting adjourned.

Validation of Meeting Defectively Called or Noticed

(4) The transactions of any meeting of the Board of Directors, however called and noticed or wherever held, are as valid as though effected at a meeting duly held after regular call and notice, if a quorum is present and if, either before or after the meeting, each of the Directors not present signs a waiver of notice, a consent to holding the meeting, or an approval of the minutes thereof. All such waivers, consents, or approvals shall be filed with the corporate records or made a part of the minutes of the meeting. Attendance by a Director at a meeting shall constitute a waiver of notice of the meeting, unless the express purpose for such attendance is to present the objection that the meeting is not lawfully called or convened.

Call of Special Meeting

3.09 (1) Special meetings of the Board of Directors of this corporation shall be called by the President or, if he is absent or is unable or refuses to act, by any Vice President or by any two Directors.

(2) Written notice of the time, place, and purpose of special meetings of the Board of Directors shall be delivered personally to each Director, or sent to each Director by mail or by other form of written communication, at least seven (7) days before the meeting. If the address of a Director is not shown on the records and is not readily ascertainable, notice shall be addressed to him at the city or place in which the meetings of the Directors are regularly held. Notice of the time and place of holding an adjourned meeting of a meeting need not be given to absent Directors if the time and place are fixed at the meeting adjourned.

Quorum

3.10 A majority of the authorized number of Directors constitutes a quorum of the Board for the transaction of business.

Majority Action

3.11 Every act or decision done or made by a majority of the Directors present at any meeting duly held at which a quorum is present is the act of the Board of Directors, unless an act of a greater number is required by the articles of incorporation or these bylaws. Each Director who is present at a meeting will be deemed to have assented to any action taken at such meeting unless his dissent to the action is entered in the minutes of the meeting, or unless he shall file his written dissent thereto with the Secretary of the meeting or shall forward such dissent by registered mail to the Secretary of the corporation immediately after such meeting.

Action by Consent of Board Without Meeting

3.12 Any action required or permitted to be taken by the Board of Directors under any provision of the Texas Business Corporation Act may be taken without a meeting, if all members of the Board shall individually or collectively consent in writing to such action. Such written consent or consents shall be filed with the minutes of the proceedings of the Board. Such action by written consent shall have the same force and effect as a unanimous vote of such Directors. Any certificate or other document filed under any provision of the Texas Business Corporation Act which relates to action so taken shall state that the action was taken by unanimous written consent of the Board of Directors without a meeting and that these bylaws authorize the Directors to so act, and such statement shall be prima facie evidence of such authority.

Adjournment

3.13 (1) In the absence of a quorum a majority of the Directors present may adjourn from time to time until the time fixed for the next regular meeting of the Board.

Notice of Adjourned Meeting

(2) Notice of the time and place of holding an adjourned meeting of a meeting need not be given to absent Directors if the time and place are fixed at the meeting adjourned.

Conduct of Meetings

3.14 At every meeting of the Board of Directors, the Chairman of the Board of Directors, if there shall be such an officer, and if not, the President, or in his absence, the Vice President designated by him, or in the absence of such designation, a chairman chosen by a majority of the Directors present, shall preside. The Secretary of the corporation shall act as Secretary of the Board of Directors. In case the Secretary shall be absent from any meeting, the chairman may appoint any person to act as Secretary of the meeting.

Compensation

3.15 Directors shall receive such compensation for their services as Directors as shall be determined from time to time by resolution of the Board. Any Directors may serve the corporation in any other capacity as an officer, agent, employee or otherwise and receive compensation therefor.

Indemnification of Directors and Officers

3.16 The Board of Directors shall authorize the corporation to pay or reimburse any present or former Director or officer of the corporation any costs or expenses actually and necessarily incurred by him in any action, suit, or proceeding to which he is made a party by reason of his holding such position; provided, however, that he shall not receive such indemnification if he be finally adjudicated therein to be liable for negligence or misconduct in office, or if such indemnification would violate Texas law. The indemnification herein provided shall also extend to good faith expenditures incurred in anticipation of, or preparation for, threatened or proposed litigation. The Board of Directors may, in proper cases, extend the indemnification to cover the good faith settlement of any such action, suit, or proceeding, whether formally instituted or not.

Interested Directors

3.17 Any contract or other transaction between the corporation and any of its Directors (or any corporation or firm in which any of its Directors is directly or indirectly interested) shall be valid for all purposes notwithstanding the presence of such Director at the meeting authorizing such contract or transaction, or his participation in such meeting. The foregoing shall, however, apply only if the interest of each such Director is known or disclosed to the Board of Directors and it shall nevertheless authorize or ratify such contract or transaction by a majority of the Directors present, each such interested Director to be counted in determining whether a quorum is present but not in calculating the majority necessary to carry such vote. This section shall not be construed to invalidate any contract or transaction which would be valid in the absence of this paragraph.

Executive Committee

3.18 The Board of Directors may at any time appoint from among its members an executive committee and one or more other committees, each of which so appointed shall have such power and authority to conduct the business and affairs of the corporation as is vested by law, the articles of incorporation, and these bylaws in the Board of Directors as a whole, except that it may not take any action that is specifically required by statute to be taken by the entire Board of Directors. Each Director shall be deemed to have assented to any action of the executive committee unless he shall, within seven (7) days after receiving actual or constructive notice of such action, deliver his written dissent thereto to the Secretary of the corporation. Members of the executive committee shall serve at the pleasure of the Board of Directors.

Other Committees

3.19 The Board of Directors, by an affirmative vote of a majority of the members constituting the Board of Directors, may appoint other committees which shall have and may exercise such powers as shall be conferred or authorized by resolution of the Board. A majority of any such committee may determine its action and fix the time and place of its meetings unless the Board of Directors shall otherwise provide. The Board of Directors, by affirmative vote, shall have the power at any time to change the powers and members of any committee of the Board, to fill vacancies, to determine the compensation of such committee members, and to dissolve any such committee.

ARTICLE FOUR

OFFICERS

Number and Titles

4.01 The officers of the corporation shall be a President, a Vice President, a Secretary, and a Treasurer. The corporation may also have, at the discretion of the Board of Directors, a Chairman of the Board, one or more additional Vice Presidents, one or more Assistant Secretaries, one or more Assistant Treasurers, and such other officers as may be appointed in accordance with the provisions of Paragraph 4.03 of this Article. One person may hold two or more offices.

Election

4.02 The officers of the corporation, except such officers as may be appointed in accordance with the provisions of Paragraph 4.03 or Paragraph 4.05 of this Article, shall be chosen annually by the Board of Directors, and each shall hold his office until he shall resign or shall be removed or otherwise disqualified to serve, or his successor shall be elected and qualified.

Subordinate Officers

4.03 The Board of Directors may appoint such other officers or agents as the business of the corporation may require, each of whom shall hold office for such period, have such authority, and perform such duties as are provided in these bylaws or as the Board of Directors may from time to time determine. The Board of Directors may delegate to any officer or committee the power to appoint any such subordinate officers, committees or agents, to specify their duties and to determine their compensation.

Removal and Resignation

4.04 Any officer may be removed, either with or without cause, by a majority of the Directors at the time in office, at any regular or special meeting of the Board, or, except in case of an officer chosen by the Board of Directors, by any committee or officer upon whom such power of removal may be conferred by the Board of Directors; provided, however, that such removal shall not be without prejudice to the contract rights, if any, of the person removed. Any officer may resign at any time by giving written notice to the Board of Directors or the President, or to the Secretary of the corporation. Any such resignation shall take effect at the date of the receipt of such notice or at any later time specified therein; and, unless otherwise specified therein, the acceptance of such resignation shall not be necessary to make it effective.

Vacancies

4.05 If the office of the President, Vice President, Secretary, Treasurer, Assistant Secretary (if any), or Assistant Treasurer (if any) becomes vacant by reason of death, resignation, removal, or otherwise, the Board of Directors shall elect a successor who shall hold office for the unexpired term, and until his successor is elected.

Chairman of the Board

4.06 The Chairman of the Board, if there shall be such an officer, shall, if present, preside at all meetings of the Board of Directors and exercise and perform such other powers and duties as may be from time to time assigned to him by the Board of Directors or prescribed by the bylaws.

President

4.07 Subject to such supervisory powers, if any, as may be given by the Board of Directors to the Chairman of the Board, if there be such an officer, the President shall be the chief executive officer of the corporation and shall, subject to the control of the Board of Directors, have general supervision, direction, and control of the business and officers of the corporation, and shall have the general powers and duties of management usually vested in the office of the President of a corporation, and shall have such other powers and duties as may be prescribed by the Board of Directors or the bylaws. Within this authority and in the course of his duties he shall:

Conduct Meetings

(1) Preside at all meetings of the shareholders, and in the absence of the Chairman of the Board, or, if there be none, at all meetings of the Board of Directors, and shall be ex officio a member of all the standing committees, including the executive committee, if any.

Sign Share Certificates

(2) Sign all certificates of stock of the corporation, in conjunction with the Secretary or Assistant Secretary, unless otherwise ordered by the Board of Directors.

(3) When authorized by the Board of Directors or required by law, execute, in the name of the corporation, deeds, conveyances, notices, leases, checks, drafts, bills of exchange, warrants, promissory notes, bonds, debentures, contracts, and other papers and instruments in writing, and unless the Board of Directors shall order otherwise by resolution, make such contracts as the ordinary conduct of the corporation's business may require.

Hire and Fire Employees

(4) Appoint and remove, employ and discharge, and prescribe the duties and fix the compensation of all agents, employees, and

clerks of the corporation other than the duly appointed officers, subject to the approval of the Board of Directors, and control, subject to the direction of the Board of Directors, all of the officers, agents, and employees of the corporation.

Meetings of Other Corporations

(5) Unless otherwise directed by the Board of Directors, attend, or designate a substitute representative to attend all meetings of the shareholders of any corporation in which this corporation holds stock.

Vice President

4.08 In the absence or disability of the President, the Vice Presidents, in order of their rank as fixed by the Board of Directors or, if not ranked, the Vice President designated by the Board of Directors, shall perform all the duties of the President, and when so acting shall have all the powers of, and be subject to all the restrictions on, the President. The Vice Presidents shall have such other powers and perform such other duties as from time to time may be prescribed for them respectively by the Board of Directors or the bylaws.

Secretary

4.09 The Secretary shall:

Sign Share Cerfificates

(1) Sign, with the President or a Vice President, certificates for shares of the corporation.

Attest Bylaws

(2) Attest and keep at the principal office of the corporation the original or a copy of its bylaws, as amended.

Minutes of Meetings

(3) Keep at the principal office of the corporation, or such other place as the Board of Directors may order, a book of minutes of all meetings of its Directors and shareholders, executive committee, and other committees, with the time and place of holding, whether regular or special, and, if special, how authorized, the notice thereof given, the names of those present at directors' meetings, the number of shares or members present or represented at shareholders' meetings, and the proceedings thereof.

Sign or Attest Documents and Affix Seal

(4) Sign or attest such documents as may be required by law or the business of the corporation, and to keep the corporate seal and affix it to such instruments as may be necessary or proper.

Notices

(5) See that all notices are duly given in accordance with the provisions of these bylaws or as required by law. In case of the absence or disability of the Secretary, or his refusal or neglect to act, notice may be given and served by an Assistant Secretary or by the President or Vice President or by the Board of Directors.

Custodian of Records and Seal

(6) Be custodian of the records and of the seal of the corporation and see that it is engraved, lithographed, printed, stamped, impressed upon or affixed to all certificates for shares prior to their issuance and to all documents, the execution of which on behalf of the corporation under its seal is duly authorized in accordance with the provisions of these bylaws.

Share Register

(7) Keep at the principal office of the corporation a share register or duplicate share register showing the names of the shareholders and their addreses; the number, date of issue, and class of shares represented by each outstanding share certificate; and the number and date of cancellation of each certificate surrendered for cancellation.

Reports and Statements

(8) See that the books, reports, statements, certificates and all other documents and records required by law are properly kept and filed.

Exhibit Records

(9) Exhibit at all reasonable times to any Director on application, or on written demand stating the purpose thereof of any person who has been a shareholder of record for at least six (6) months immediately preceding his demand or who is the holder of record of at least five (5) percent of all of the outstanding shares of the corporation, upon application, the bylaws, the share register, and minutes of proceedings of the shareholders and Directors of the corporation.

Other Duties

(10) In general, perform all duties incident to the office of Secretary, and such other duties as from time to time may be assigned to him by the Board of Directors.

Absence of Secretary

(11) In case of the absence or disability of the Secretary or his refusal or neglect to act, the Assistant Secretary, or if there be none, the Treasurer, acting as Assistant Secretary, may perform all of the functions of the Secretary. In case of the absence or disability of, or the refusal or neglect to act of both the Secretary, the Assistant Secretary and Treasurer, any person thereunto authorized by the President or Vice President or by the Board of Directors may perform the functions of the Secretary.

Assistant Secretary

4.10 At the request of the Secretary, or in his absence or disability, the Assistant Secretary, designated as set forth in preceding Subparagraph 4.10(11) of these bylaws, shall perform all the duties of the Secretary, and when so acting, he shall have all the powers of, and be subject to all the restrictions on, the Secretary. The Assistant Secretary shall perform such other duties as from time to time may be assigned to him by the Board of Directors or the Secretary.

Treasurer

4.11 The Treasurer shall:

Funds--Custody and Deposit

(1) Have charge and custody of, and be responsible for, all funds and securities of the corporation, and deposit all such funds in the name of the corporation in such banks, trust companies, or other depositaries as shall be selected by the Board of Directors.

Funds--Receipt

(2) Receive, and give receipt for, moneys due and payable to the corporation from any source whatever.

Funds--Disbursements

(3) Disburse, or cause to be disbursed, the funds of the corporation as may be directed by the Board of Directors, taking proper vouchers for such disbursements.

Maintain Accounts

(4) Keep and maintain adequate and correct accounts of the corporation's properties and business transactions including account of its assets, liabilities, receipts, disbursements, gains, losses, capital, surplus, and shares. Any surplus, including earned surplus, paid-in surplus, and surplus arising from a reduction of stated capital, shall be classified according to source and shown in a separate account.

Exhibit Records

(5) Exhibit at all reasonable times the books of account and records to any director on application, or to any person who has been a shareholder of record for a least six (6) months immediately preceding his demand or who is the holder of record of at least five (5) percent of all the outstanding shares of the corporation, on written demand stating the purpose thereof, during business hours at the office of the corporation where such books and records are kept.

Reports to President and Directors

(6) Render to the President and Directors, whenever they request it, an account of all his transactions as Treasurer and of the financial condition of the corporation.

Financial Report to Shareholders

(7) Prepare, or cause to be prepared, and certify the financial statements to be included in the annual report to shareholders and statements of the affairs of the corporation when requested by shareholders holding at least ten (10) percent of the number of outstanding shares of the corporation.

Bond

(8) Give to the corporation a bond, if required by the Board of Directors or by the President, in a sum, and with one or more sureties, or a surety company satisfactory to the Board, for the faithful performance of the duties of his office and for the restoration to the corporation, in case of his death, resignation, retirement, or removal from office, of all books, papers, vouchers, money, and other property of whatever kind in his possession or under his control belonging to the corporation.

Other Duties

(9) In general, perform all the duties incident to the office of Treasurer and such other duties as from time to time may be assigned to him by the Board of Directors.

Absence of Treasurer

(10) In case of the absence or disability of the Treasurer or his refusal or neglect to act, the Assistant Treasurer or the Secretary acting as Assistant Treasurer, may perform all of the functions of the Treasurer. In the absence or inability to act, or refusal or neglect to act, of the Treasurer, the Assistant Treasurer, and the Secretary, any person thereunto authorized by the President or Vice President or by the Board of Directors may perform the functions of the Treasurer.

Assistant Treasurer

4.12 The Assistant Treasurer, if required so to do by the Board of Directors, shall give bond for the faithful discharge of his duties, in such sum, and with such sureties as the Board of Directors shall require. At the request of the Treasurer, or his absence or disability, the Assistant Treasurer designated as set forth in preceding Subparagraph 4.11(10) of these bylaws shall perform all the duties of the Treasurer, and when so acting, he shall have all the powers of, and be subject to all the restrictions on, the Treasurer. He shall perform such other duties as from time to time may be assigned to him by the Board of Directors or the Treasurer.

Salaries

4.13 The salaries of the officers shall be fixed from time to time by the Board of Directors, and no officer shall be prevented from receiving such salary by reason of the fact that he is also a Director of the corporation.

ARTICLE FIVE

EXECUTION OF INSTRUMENTS AND DEPOSIT OF FUNDS

Authority for Execution of Instruments

5.01 The Board of Directors, except as otherwise provided in these bylaws, may authorize any officer or officers, agent or agents, to enter into any contract or execute and deliver any instrument in the name of and on behalf of the corporation, and such authority may be general or confined to specific instances; and, unless so authorized, no officer, agent, or employee shall have any power or authority to bind the corporation by any contract or engagement or to pledge its credit or to render it liable pecuniarily for any purpose or in any amount.

Execution of Instruments

5.02 Unless otherwise specifically determined by the Board of Directors or otherwise required by law, formal contracts of the corporation, promissory notes, deeds of trust, mortgages and other evidences of indebtedness of the corporation, and other corporate instruments or documents, and certificates of shares of stock owned by the corporation, shall be executed, signed or endorsed by the President or any Vice President and by the Secretary or the Treasurer, or any Assistant Secretary or Assistant Treasurer, and may have the corporate seal affixed thereto.

Bank Accounts and Deposits

5.03 (1) All funds of the corporation shall be deposited from time to time to the credit of the corporation with such banks, trust companies, or other depositaries as the Board of Directorss may select or as may be selected by any officer or officers, agent or agents of the corporation to whom such power may be delegated from time to time by the Board of Directors.

Endorsement Without Countersignature

(2) Endorsements for deposit to the credit of the corporation in any of its duly authorized depositaries may be made without countersignature by the President or any Vice President, or the Treasurer or any Assistant Treasurer, or by any other officer or agent of the corporation to whom the Board of Directors, by resolution, shall have delegated such power, or by hand stamped impression in the name of the corporation.

Signing of Checks, Drafts, Etc.

(3) All checks, drafts or other order for payment of money notes or other evidences of indebtedness, issued in the name of or payable to the corporation, shall be signed or endorsed by such person or persons and in such manner as shall be determined from time to time by resolution of the Board of Directors.

ARTICLE SIX

ISSUANCE AND TRANSFER OF SHARES

Classes and Series of Shares

6.01 The corporation may issues one or more classes or series of shares, or both, any of which classes or series may be with par value or without par value and with full limited or no voting rights, and with such other preferences, rights, privileges, and restrictions as are stated or authorized in the articles of incorporation. All shares of any one class shall have the same voting rights, conversion, redemption, and other rights, preferences, privileges, and restrictions, unless the class is divided into series. If a class is divided into series, all the shares of any one series shall have the same voting rights, conversion, redemption, and other rights, preferences, privileges, and restrictions. There shall always be a class or series of shares outstanding which has complete voting rights except as limited or restricted by voting rights conferred on some other class or series of outstanding shares.

Certificates for Fully Paid Shares

6.02 Neither shares nor certificates representing such shares may be issued by the corporation until the full amount of the consideration has been paid. When such consideration has been paid to the corporation, the shares shall be deemed to have been issued and the certificate representing such shares shall be issued to the shareholder.

Consideration for Shares

6.03 The consideration paid for the issuance of shares shall consist of money paid, labor done, or property actually received; neither promissory notes nor the promise of future services shall constitute payment or part payment for shares of the corporation.

Contents of Share Certificates

6.04 (1) Certificates for shares shall be of such form and style, printed or otherwise, as the Board of Directors may designate, and each certificate shall state of the following facts:

(a) The corporation is organized under the laws of the State of Texas.

(b) The name of the person to whom issued.

(c) The number and class of shares and the designation of the series, if any, which such certificate represents;

(d) The par value of each share represented by such certificate, or a statement that the shares are without par value.

Shares in Classes or Series

(2) If the corporation is authorized to issue shares of more than one class, the certificate shall set forth, either on the face or back of the certificate, a full summary statement of all the designation, preferences, limitations, and relative rights of the shares of each class authorized to be issued and, if the corporation is authorized to issue any preferred or special class in series, the variations in the relative rights and preferred or special class in series, the variations in the relative rights and preferences of the shares of each such series so far as the same have been fixed and determined and the authority of the Board of Directors to fix and determine the relative rights and preferences of subsequent series. In lieu of providing such a statement in full of the certificate may provide that the corporation will furnish such information to any shareholder without charge upon written request to the corporation as its principal place of business or registered office and that copies of the information are on file in the office of the Secretary of State.

Restriction on Transfer

(3) Any restrictions imposed by the corporation on the sale or other disposition of its shares and on the transfer thereof must be copied at length or in summary form on the face, or so copied on the back and referred to on the face, of each certificate representing shares to which the restriction applies. The certificate may however state on the face or back that such a restriction exists pursuant to a specified document and that the corporation will furnish a copy of the document to the holder of the certificate without charge upon written request to the corporation at its principal place of business.

Preemptive Rights

(4) Any preemptive rights of a shareholder to acquire unissued or treasury shares of the corporation which are limited or denied by the articles of incorporation must be set forth at length on the face or back of the certificate representing shares subject thereto. In lieu of providing such a statement in full on the certificate, a statement on the face or back of the certificate may provide that the corporation will furnish such information to any shareholder without charge upon written request to the corporation at its principal place of business and that a copy of such information is on file in the office of the Secretary of State.

Signing Certificates-Facsimile Signatures

6.05 All such certificates shall be signed by the President or a Vice President and the Secretary or an Assistant Secretary. The signatures of the President or Vice President, Secretary or Assistant Secretary may be facsimiles if the certificate is countersigned by a transfer agent or registered by a registrar either of which is not the corporation itself or an employee of the corporation. If the officer who has signed or whose facsimile signature has been placed on the certificate has ceased to be such officer before the certificate is issued, the certificate may be issued by the corporation with the same effect as if he were such officer at the date of its issuance.

Transfer of Lost or Destroyed Shares

6.06 (1) Where a share certificate has been lost, apparently destroyed, or wrongfully taken and the owner fails to notify the corporation of that fact within a reasonable time after he has notice of it, and the corporation registers a transfer of the share represented by the certificate before receiving such a notification, the owner is precluded from asserting against the corporation any claim for registering the transfer or any claim to a new certificate.

Replacement of Lost or Destroyed Certificates

(2) Where the holder of a share certificate claims that the certificate has been lost, destroyed, or wrongfully taken, the corporation shall issue a new certificate in place of the original certificate if: (i) the owner so requests before the corporation has notice that the share has been acquired by a bona fide purchaser; (ii) files with the corporation a sufficient indemnity bond; and (iii) satisfies any other reasonable requirements imposed by the Board of Directors.

Transfer After Replacement

(3) If, after the issue of a new security as a replacement for a lost, destroyed, or wrongfully taken certificate, a bona fide purchaser of the original certificate presents it for registration of transfer, the corporation must register the transfer unless registration would result in overissue. In addition to any rights on the indemnity bond, the corporation may recover the new security from the person to whom it was issued or any person taken under him except a bona fide purchaser.

Transfer Agents and Registrars

6.07 The Board of Directors may appoint one or more transfer agents or transfer clerks, and one or more registrars which shall be an incorporated bank or trust company, either domestic or foreign, who shall be appointed at such times and places as the requirements of the corporation may necessitate and the Board of Directors may designate.

Conditions of Transfer

6.08 A person in whose name shares of stock stand on the books of the corporation shall be deemed the owner thereof as regards the corporation: provided that whenever any transfer of shares shall be made for collateral security, and not absolutely, and written notice thereof shall be given to the Secretary of the corporation or its transfer agent, if any, such fact shall be stated in the entry of the transfer.

Reasonable Doubts as to Right to Transfer

6.09 When a transfer of shares is requested and there is reasonable doubt as to the right of the person seeking the transfer, the corporation or its transfer agent, before recording the tranfer of the shares on its books or issuing any certificate therefore, may require from the person seeking the transfer reasonable proof of his right to the transfer. If there remains a reasonable doubt of the right to the transfer, the corporation may refuse a transfer unless the person gives adequate security or a bond of indemnity executed by a corporate surety or by two individual sureties satisfactory to the corporation as to form, amount, and responsibility of sureties. The bond shall be conditioned to protect the corporation, its officers, transfer agents, and registrars, or any of them, against any loss, damage, expense, or other liability to the owner of the shares by reason of the recordation of the transfer or the issuance of a new certificate for shares.

ARTICLE SEVEN

CORPORATE RECORDS, REPORTS AND SEAL

Minutes of Corporate Meetings

7.01 The corporation shall keep at the principal office, or such other place as the Board of Directors may order, a book of minutes of all meetings of its Directors and of its shareholders or members, with the time and place of holding, whether regular or special, and, if special, how authorized, the notice thereof given, the names of those present at Directors' meetings, the number of shares or members present or represented at shareholders' or members' meetings, and the proceedings thereof.

Books of Account

7.02 The corporation shall keep and maintain adequate and correct accounts of its properties and business transactions, including accounts of its assets, liabilities, receipts, disbursements, gains, losses, capital, surplus, and shares. Any surplus, including earned surplus, paid-in surplus, and surplus arising from a reduction of stated capital, shall be classified according to source and shown in a separate account.

Share Register

7.03 The corporation shall keep at the principal office, or at the office of the transfer agent, a share register, showing the names of the shareholders and their addresses, the number and classes of shares held by each, the number and date of certificates issued for shares, and the number and date of cancellation of every certificate surrendered for cancellation. The above specified information may be kept by the corporation on punchcards, magnetic tape, or any other information storage device is capable of reproducing the information in clearly legible form for the purposes of inspection as provided in Section 7.04 of these bylaws.

Inspection of Records by Shareholders

7.04 (1) Any person who shall have been a shareholder of record for at least six (6) months immediately preceding his demand, or who is the holder of record of at least five (5) percent of all of the outstanding shares of the corporation, on written demand stating the purpose thereof, has the right to examine, in person, or by agent, accountant, or attorney, at any reasonable time or times, for any proper purpose, its books and records of account, minutes, and record of shareholders, and is entitled to make therefrom.

Inspection of Records by Directors

(2) Every Director shall have the absolute right at any reasonable time to inspect all books, records, documents of every kind, and the physical properties of the corporation, and all of its subsidiary corporations, domestic or foreign. Such inspection by a Director may be made in person or by agent or attorney, and the right of inspection includes the right to make extracts.

Annual Report to Shareholders

7.05 (1) The Board of Directors shall cause an annual report to be sent to the shareholders not later than 90 days after the close of the fiscal or calendar year.

Contents of Annual Reports

(2) The annual report shall include the following financial statements:

(a) A balance sheet as of closing date;

(b) A statement of income or profit and loss for the year ended on such closing date.

(c) Such other information as the Directors shall determine.

Preparation of Financial Statements

(3) The financial statements shall be prepared from the books and shall be in accordance therewith and shall be certified by the President, Secretary, Treasurer, or a public accountant. They shall be prepared in a form sanctioned by sound accounting practice for the particular kind of business carried on by the corporation.

Fiscal Year

7.06 The fiscal year of the corporation shall be determined by the Board of Directors.

Corporate Seal

7.07 The Board of Directors may adopt, use, and thereafter alter, the corporate seal.

ARTICLE EIGHT

AMENDMENT OF BYLAWS

Adoption, Amendment, Repeal of Bylaws by Directors

8.01 Bylaws may be altered, amended, or repealed, and new bylaws may be adopted, by the Directors, subject to repeal or change by action of the shareholders.

Certificate of Adoption of Bylaws

This is to certify:

That I am the duly elected, qualified and acting Secretary of ______________________________________, and that the above bylaws were duly adopted as the bylaws of said corporation by the Board of Directors of said corporation.

Dated:_________________________

____

___________________,Secretary

The undersigned, being all the Directors of the Corporation, hereby consent to all the foregoing this ______ day of ___________, 19___

____

____

Form 7. Corporate Minutes of First Meeting

ORGANIZATIONAL CONSENT OF DIRECTORS

OF

____

The undersigned, being all the members of the Board of Directors of ______________________________, (the "Corporation"), pursuant to Article 9.10B of the Texas Business Corporation Act, hereby consent to the adoption of the following resolutions and to the action authorized in such resolutions being taken by the Board of Directors in lieu of an Organizational Meeting thereof:

1. ADOPTION OF BYLAWS

RESOLVED, that the form of Bylaws attached to these resolutions be and the same are hereby approved and adopted as the Bylaws of the Corporation and the Secretary of the Corporation is directed to cause the originals thereof to be placed in the Minute Book of the Corporation.

2. ELECTION OF OFFICERS

RESOLVED, that the following named persons be and they are hereby elected to the office set opposite their respective names to serve until the next annual meeting of Directors or until their successors are elected and qualified:

President
Vice President
Secretary
Treasurer

3. ADOPTION OF CORPORATE SEAL

RESOLVED, that the Seal, an impression of which is shown below, be and the same is hereby adopted as the Corporate Seal of the Corporation.

4. ADOPTION OF STOCK CERTIFICATES

RESOLVED, that the attached form of stock certificate be and the same is hereby approved and adopted as the Stock Certificate of the Corporation.

5. AUTHORITY TO EXECUTE INSTRUMENTS AS MAY BE REQUIRED BY LAW

RESOLVED, that the proper officers of the Corporation be and they are hereby authorized and directed on behalf of the Corporation and under its Corporate Seal, to make and file such certificate or certificates, report or reports, or other instrument or instruments as may be required by law to be filed in the State of Texas, or any other state in which the Corporation is authorized to transact business, and the purpose for which the Corporation was incorporated.

6. QUALIFICATION IN OTHER STATES

RESOLVED, that the proper officers of the Corporation be and they are hereby authorized and directed on behalf of the Corporation and under its Corporate Seal (where a seal is required by the recipient, law or regulation under which filed) to make and file such certificates, reports, or other instruments as may be required by law to be filed in any State, Territory, Colony or Dependency of the United States, or in any foreign country, in which said officers shall find it necessary or expedient to file the same to authorize the Corporation to transact business in such State, Territory, Colony, Dependency, or foreign country.

7. PAYMENT OF ORGANIZATION FEES

RESOLVED, that the President or Treasurer is hereby authorized to pay all fees and expenses incident to and necessary for the organization of the Corporation.

8. AUTHORITY TO ISSUE SHARES OF COMMON STOCK

RESOLVED, that the proper officers of the Corporation be and they hereby are authorized to issue certificates for stock of the Corporation to the following persons for the number of shares set opposite their respective names in consideration of the cash payment by each person of $_____ per share:

____________ ________ shares
____________ ________ shares
____________ ________ shares

9. BANKING AUTHORITY

RESOLVED, that the President ~~and Treasurer~~ of the Corporation be and is hereby authorized and directed to execute and deliver such form resolutions of ______________________________, as may be required to establish such checking accounts and borrowing accounts as the President of the Corporation shall deem necessary and appropriate; and

RESOLVED FURTHER, that such form resolutions be attached to this Consent, and incorporated herein for all purposes as the official resolutions of the Corporation; and

RESOLVED FURTHER, that this resolution and the form resolutions to which it is applicable shall continue in full force and effect until official written notice of the rescission thereof by the Board of Directors of the Corporation has been given to the Bank.

10. FISCAL YEAR

RESOLVED, that the fiscal year of the Corporation shall end on ______________ of each year.

11. ADOPTION OF SHAREHOLDERS' AGREEMENT

RESOLVED, that the Corporation shall enter into a Shareholders' Agreement, containing provisions substantially similar to those contained in the sample Shareholders' Agreement attached hereto as Exhibit ____, which includes, among other provisions, restrictions on the transfer of the Corporation's shares by and between all the shareholders of the Corporation; and

FURTHER RESOLVED, that a counterpart of the Agreement shall be placed on file by the Corporation at its principal place of business and its registered office and that the same shall be subject to the same right of examination by a Shareholder of the Corporation, in person or by agent, attorney, or accountant, as are the books and records of the Corporation; and

RESOLVED, that the officers and directors of the Corporation be, and they hereby are, authorized to do any and all acts and things and to execute any and all agreements, consents and documents as in their opinion, or in the opinion of counsel to the Corporation, may be necessary or appropriate in order to carry out the purposes and intent of any of the foregoing resolutions; and

12. DATE OF ANNUAL SHAREHOLDERS' MEETING

RESOLVED, that the annual meeting of the shareholders commencing with the year 19___, shall be held each year at 10:00 A.m. on the 10th day of DECEMBER. If such day is a legal holiday, then the meeting shall be held on the next secular day following.

13. NUMBER OF DIRECTORS

RESOLVED, that the number of directors of the Corporation shall be ___ __________.

14. RESOLVED, that the directors be, and they hereby are, authorized to execute this consent in multiple counterparts.

The undersigned, being all the Directors of the Corporation, hereby consent to all the foregoing this ______ day of ___________, 19___

____

____

Form 8. Shareholders' Agreement

SHAREHOLDERS' AGREEMENT
(Redemption and Buy-Sell)
FOR
X CORPORATION

AGREEMENT, made as of this ____ day of ________, 19__, by and among X CORPORATION, a Texas corporation (hereinafter referred to as the "Corporation"), and A, B, D and D, each of ______________ County, _______ (hereinafter referred to separately and collectively as the "Shareholder" and the "Shareholders" respectively), and among the shareholders themselves.

W I T N E S S E T H:

WHEREAS, the Shareholders are the owners of all of the outstanding shares of capital sotck in the Corporation; and

WHEREAS, for good and valuable consideration, the Corporation and the Shareholders have agreed to impose certain restrictions on said capital stock; and

WHEREAS, the Shareholders mutually agree that it is to their mutual benefit and in the best interests of the capital stock Corporation to restrict the assignability of the capital stock of the Corporation, to provide for the control and disposition of the Corporation, to provide for the orderly transition of ownership in the event of death, disability or retirement of a Shareholder, or other termination of a Shareholder's interest in the Corporation, to provide for the purchase of a Shareholder's capital stock under certain specified conditions, and to provide the funds necessary to carry out such purchases.

NOW, THEREFORE, in consideration of the mutual agreements contained herein and for other valuable consideration, the sufficiency and receipt of which is hereby acknowledged, it is mutually agreed by and among the parties to this Agreement as follows:

I. DEFINITIONS

The following definitions shall control the meanings of the repective terms:

A. "Disability" or "Disabled" means with respect to Shareholders, physical or mental disability, or both, determined to be (or reasonably expected to be, based upon then available medical information) of not less than twelve (12) calendar months' duration or more. The determination (or reasonable expectancy) shall rest upon the opinion of the physician regularly attending the Shareholder who is Disabled ("Disabled Shareholder"). If the Continuing Shareholders disagree with said physician's opinion, the Continuing Shareholders may engage at their own expense a physician to examine the Disabled Shareholder, and each Shareholder a party hereto hereby consents to such examination and to waive, if applicable, any privilege between the physician and the Shareholder that may arise as a result of said examination. If, after conferring, the two physicians cannot concur on a final opinion, they shall choose a third consulting physician whose opinion shall control. The expense of the third consulting physician shall be borne equally by the Disabled Shareholder and the Continuing Shareholders. "Physician" means a medical doctor.

B. "Termination or "Terminating" means, to the extent applicable according to the provisions hereof, death, disability, severance of employment, whether voluntarily or by action of the Corporation, cessation of functioning as a Shareholder, including the loss of any rights or license necessary to continue in the employment of the Corporation, abandonment of duties or position as an officer, director, or employee of the Corporation, retirement (whether voluntary or not, or with consent of or by action of the employer), or Assignment or other transfer of an Ownership Interest (or any part thereof), and includes dissolution of marriage or permanent separation. A call to military service shall be a "termination" only to the extent allowed under the Soldiers and Sailors Relief Act.

C. "Assignment of other transfer" includes, but is not limited to, sale, exchange, hypothecation, collateral assignment, subjecting the ownership interest to a security interest. Attachment, judgment, creditor execution, bankruptcy, or other similar occurrence sanctioned by law, without the advance consent in writing of the Continuing Shareholders.

"Assignment or other transfer" shall not include a transfer or assignment by way of gift (directly or in trust) of up to but not exceeding a cumulative total of fifty percent (50%) of the Ownership Interest of a Shareholder in the Corporation to his spouse, children, or other lineal descendants, or to other employees of the Corporation or other Shareholders, however, any such assignee, transferee or donee shall be subject to the terms hereof.

D. "Continuing Shareholders" means those Shareholders who are not terminating their interest in the Corporation or who are not making an Assignment or other transfer of their Ownership Interest.

E. "Terminating Shareholder" or "Offering Shareholder" means the Shareholder who is terminating his interest in the Corporation. It includes, as required, the estate of a deceased Shareholder acting through its personal representative, which shall also be referred to as "Deceased Shareholder," or the extate of a Disabled Shareholder acting through its guardian or conservator, or, if same are not appointed, through the adult spouse of said Disabled Shareholder, or the Trustee (by trust, or in bankruptcy), receiver, or other legal representative of the Terminating Shareholder who has the power to act.

F. "Ownership Interest" means the equity interest that each Shareholder has in the Corporation which is reflected by stock ownership, regardless of class or series.

G. "Debt" means the obligation of the Corporation to repay a loan made to the Corporation by a Shareholder. Unless otherwise expressly stated herein, the debt shall be repaid according to its terms at the interest rate, interest dates, and maturity date fixed in the note, but if the note is payable on demand, is in default at the termination date, or past maturity, the debt shall be repaid upon the terms, at the interest rate, and upon the dates on which the payments in exchange for the Terminating Shareholder's Ownership Interest are made: being, for example, prorated over the installments due for the Terminating Shareholder's Ownership Interest.

H. "Receipt" or "received" refers to the date received. In the event of a dispute as to the date received, if mailed by ordinary mail, the date of receipt is three days afer the postmark date; otherwise it is the date shown on the return ship receipt. If more than two Continuing Shareholders are involved, the date received by the Shareholder who makes up the majority in mumber of the Continuing Shareholders shall be the receipt date for all the Continuing Shareholders, so that, for example, if three Continuing Shareholders are involved, A, B, and C, if A has received, but B and C have not, then the date that either B or C receives first is the date of receipt.

Unless otherwise stated specifically herein, any time period shall commence, run, and expire at 12:00 midnight, __________ time, within the stated days or months, whether the offer acceptance, or other act is to or by the Terminating Shareholder, the Corporation, or the Continuing Shareholders, acting jointly or separately, simultaneously or consecutively, and regardless of which party or parties is entitled to the first offer. All "days" shall refer to calendar days.

I. "Offerees" shall refer to the Corpoation or the Continuing Shareholders, or both, but such reference shall not alter or change any rights of the parties, and the term "Offerees" shall mean that the offer shall first be made to the Corporation and the next offers shall be made to the Continuing Shareholders, if that be required.

J. "Closing" or "Closing Date" shall mean the first business day or after the tenth day after the acceptance of an offer hereunder.

II. GENERAL TERMS

A. Delegation to Other Contractual Arrangements. Unless expressly provided herein otherwise, nothing contained in this Agreement shall discharge, release, or otherwise change, amend, or alter any sums due, or rights under any employment contract or other employment arrangement between the Corporation and any Shareholder. Further, no other contractual relationship between the Corporation and a Shareholder or among any or all of them shall be affected by this Agreement save one that attempts to define or speak to the terms of this Agreement, in which case the other contract shall be null and void unless it is in writing, it expressly indicates that it is amending this Agreement, and it is signed by the Corporation and all the Shareholders.

B. Redemption Agreement. This Agreement is intended to be a redemption agreement, and all offers required to be made hereunder shall first be made to the Corporation. If the Corporation is willing to accept the offer but does not have the financial means to accomplish the acceptance, then the Continuing Shareholders shall have the right, but not the duty, to provide to the Corporation sufficient funding, in the amounts and in the manner agreed upon between themselves, so that the Corporation may accept the offer in the first instance.

If the Corporation is for any reason unable or unwilling to accept the offer, the offer shall next be made to the Continuing Shareholders, who shall accept same, on the terms and conditions as provided herein.

C. Status of Assignees, Transferees, etc. All (i) assignees, transferees, trustees, receivers, or others who obtain an interest in the shares, whether by attachment, execution, bankruptcy law, receivership law, or otherwise by operation of law, and (ii) assignees, transferees, secured parties, creditors, and others who obtain an interest in the shares, whether or not said Assignment or other transfer occurred with the consent of the Continuing Shareholders, take subject to the terms and conditions of this Agreement. Any such act of Assignment or other transfer, whether by operation of law, voluntarily or involuntarily, or by act of a Shareholder if not consented to by the Continuing Shareholders, or, if consented to, any act, demand, or attempt to realize upon the collateral security of the shares, shall consitute the party succeeding to or attempting to succeed to the Ownership Interest of such Shareholder, a Terminating Shareholder, and the act, as described in this sentence, a termination event, so that the terms and conditions of this Agreement shall apply.

D. Rights of Continuing Shareholders. Any rights of the Continuing Shareholders shall be shared among them proportionately according to the Ownership Interest that each owns in relation to the total owned by all Continuing Shareholders. If, with the consent of the other Continuing Shareholder, one or more Continuing Shareholders decline to participate in the exercise of a right, the Continuing Shareholders so participating shall share the right proportionately according to the Ownership Interest that each owns in relation to the total owned by all of the Continuing Shareholders who exercise the right. If only one Continuing Shareholder desires to exercise the right, he may do so, and, by reason of such exercise, he shall be under no fiduciary duty to the other Continuing Shareholders wo delined to participate, and the Continuing Shareholder who elects to act may purchase control.

E. Offers, Acceptances and Communications. All offers, acceptances, communications, and the like between the Corporation, a Terminating Shareholder, and the Continuing Shareholders, or among themselves, shall be in writing. Such writing shall contain all pertinent particulars, including, as applicable, selling price, dates, terms, and conditions. A writing directed to the Corporation concerning a right that the Continuing Shareholders may exercise under this Agreement shall be sufficient as to the Continuing Shareholders, and a different or additional writing need not be directed to the Continuing Shareholders.

F. Status of Spouses. It is recognized that none of the Shareholders are married, however, in the event one of more of them shall become married, their respective spouses may have an interest in any or all shares of capital stock of the Cororation held by them to the extent such shares constitute or become community property, or are held in joint tenancy or as tenants by the entireties (included herein as "Community Property") by reason of their respective souses' rights to acquire, manage, control, or dispose of Community Property. Therefore, each of the Shareholders hereby agree and consent to the requirement that upon their marriage, they will cause their respective spouses to consent to the terms hereof, as such may affect the interest of their respective spouses and evidence such consent in writing by executing a copy of this Agreement. Furthermore, in the event of the marriage of any of the Shareholders, unless shares are issued by the Corporation to a spouse of the Shareholder, in such spouse's own name, or shares are transferred to a spouse in such spouse's own name pursuant to paragraph C of Section I hereof or otherwise, any and all references to a Shareholder or Shareholders, including the specific references incorporating such terms in Section I hereof, shall not include and shall not be interpreted to include any spouse of any of the Shareholders. In the event that circumstances cause the terms of this Agreement to be operative, whereby a Terminating Shareholder is required to offer his Ownership Interest to the Offerees, the spouse of the Terminating Shareholder shall in like manner and upon the same terms and conditions as provided herein offer any Ownership Interest and that owned by his spouse.

III CERTAIN TERMINATING EVENTS

The following terms and conditions shall control upon the occurrence of any of the following Terminating events with respect to a Shareholder:

A. Disability.

If a Shareholder is or becomes Disabled, he must offer (or be deemed to have offered automatically) to the Offerees his Ownership Interest within thirty (30) days after his Diability is finally determined; provided, however, notwithstanding any other provisions hereof, the purchase of a Disabled Shareholder's interest by the Offerees shall be optional and evidence of the Offeree's decision to accept or decline such purchase shall be communicated to the Disabled Shareholder pursuant to part iii hereof, and the following provisions shall apply:

i. The purchase price, the terms of purchase, the interest rate, the security, and the like shall be as provided in Section VII hereof.

ii. Unless the Disabled Shareholder shall consent otherwise, the Corporation, if it elects to purchase, shall purchase all (100%) of the Disabled Shareholder's Ownership Interest. If the Disabled Shareholder so consents, the Corporation and the Continuing Shareholders may purchase jointly such amounts of the Disabled Shareholder's Ownership Interst as they shall mutually agree provided that 100% of the Disabled Shareholder's Ownership Interest is so purchased.

iii. Acceptance of the offer by the Offerees shall be delivered to the Disabled Shareholder on or before the sixtieth (60th) day next succeeding the date the Offerees receive the Disabled Shareholder's offer.

B. Retirement

If a Shareholder is at the date hereof an employee of the Corporation, or thereafter becomes an employee of the Corporation and subsequently retires from such employment, the same terms and conditions as are provided in respect of the Disability of a Shareholder in subparagraphs i-iii of paragraph A of this Section III shall apply, with the term "Retired Shareholder" being substituted for the term "Disabled Shareholder". The offer period shall be measured from the date the Shareholder actually retires according to payroll records or the date mutually agreed upon by the Retired Shareholder and the Offerees.

C. Severance of employment.

If a Shareholder is at the date hereof an employee of the corporation or thereafter becomes an employee of the Corpoation and subsequently such employment is severed for eeasons other than retirement or Disability, whether or not the severance is by mutual consent or otherwise, the Terminating Shareholder shall offer (or be deemed to have offered automatically) his ownership Interest to the Offerees. The offer period shall be measured from the date of the last day of his employment, and the same terms and conditions as are provided in respect of the Disability of a Shareholder in subparagraphs i-iii of paragraph A to this Section III shall apply, with the term "Terminating Shareholder" being substituted for the term "Disabled Shareholder".

D. Divorce or Permanent Separation

In the event that a petition is filed in a court of competent jurisdiction seeking a divorce or permanent separation, by or against a Shareholder, such Terminating Shareholder shall offer (or be deemed to have offered automatically) his ownership Interest to the Offerees. The Off period shall be measured from the date of the filing of such peititon, or the date the Terminating Shareholder shall have received notice of same, whichever is later, and the same terms and conditions as are provided in respect of the Disability of a Shareholder in subparagraphs i-iii of paragraph A of this Section III shall apply with the term "Terminating Shareholder" being substituted for the term "Disabled Shareholder".

IV. ASSIGNMENT OR OTHER TRANSFER

If a Shareholder receives a bona fide offer for all or any part of his Ownership Interest from an unaffiliated third party and he desires to sell and make an Assignment or other transfer of his Ownership Interest pursuant to such offer, he shall offer to the Offerees his Ownership Interest within ten (10) calendar days after receiving the outside offer, on the following terms and conditions:

i. The purchase price, the terms of purchase, the interest rate, the security, and the like shall be as provided in Section VII hereof, except that if in the sole discretion of the Continuing Shareholders, the bona fide offer is on more favorable terms or the purchase price is less than the purchase price of the shares being offered as determined under Section VII hereof, the terms or the purchase price of the bona fide offer may be accepted by the Offerees.

ii. The Offerees shall have the period of thirty (30 days after the receipt of the Offering Shareholder's offer to elect to purchase the Offering Shareholder's Ownership Interest. The Ownership Interest offered by the Offering Shareholder to the Offerees shall be the same Ownership Interest that the Offering Shareholder proposes to sell or otherwise transfer, and the Offerees shall have the right to purchase such Ownership Interest, and no more or less, except as the Offering Shareholder shall permit.

iii. The Offering Shareholder's offer must be accepted by the Offerees in writng received by the Offering Shareholder on or before thirty (30) days after receipt of the offer. If the Offerees do not accept the offer within the thirty (30) days acceptance period, the Offering Shareholder shall be at liberty to accept the outside bona fide offer.

iv. Unless the Offering Shareholder consents otherwise, the Corporation, if it elects to purchase, shall purchase all (100%) of the Ownership Interest being offered by the Offering Shareholder. If the Offering Shareholder so consents, the Offerees may purchase jointly such amounts of the Ownership Interest being offered as they shall mutually agree provided that all (100%) of the Ownership Interest being offered by the Offering Shareholder is so purchased.

v. This first option or right in the Offerees shall be a continuing right. If the Offering Shareholder does not sell his Ownership Interest pursuant to the outside offer that is the intitial offer which initiated his offer to the Offerees, within forty-five days from the date the Offering Shareholder is first entitled to make such sale, the Offering Shareholder may not sell or otherwise transfer his ownership Interest without first offering again his Ownership Interest to the Offerees as provided above.

V. DEATH AS A TERMINATING EVENT

If a Shareholder dies, the Deceased Shareholder shall offer (or be deemd to have offered automatically) to the Offerees his Ownership Interest in the Corporation, and the following provisions shall apply:

A. Offer. The offer shall be made as soon as practical after the appointment of the decedent's personal representative, but in no event later than one hundred and twenty (120) days after the decedent's death.

B. Purchase Price. The purchase price, the terms of purchase, the interest, the security, and the like shall be as provided in Section VII hereof.

C. Purchase. Unless the Deceased Shareholder shall consent otherwise, the Corporation, if it elects to purchase, shall purchase all (100%) of the Deceased Shareholder's Ownership Interest. If the Deceased Shareholder so consents, the Corporation and the Continuing Shareholders may purchase jointly such amounts of the Deceased Shareholder's Ownership Interest as they shall mutually agree provided that 100% of the Disabled Shareholder's Ownership Interest is so purchased.

D. Acceptance. Acceptance of the offer by the Offerees shall be delivered to the Deceased Shareholder on or before the thirtieth (30th day) next succeeding the later of (a) the date Offerees received the Deceased Shareholder's offer, or (b) one hundred and twenty (120) days after the death of the Shareholder.

VI. FIRST LIEN

A. First Lien. The rights to purchase or redistribute an Ownership Interest resting in the Continuing Shareholders, as above provided, shall be a first lien or encumbrance upon the Ownership Interst of each Shareholder. This lien shall be evidence upon the books and records of the Corporation, and all indicia of an Ownership Interest shall bear a legend to that effect. Any attempted or purported transfer of an Ownership Interest in violation of this Agreement shall be deemed a termination of the Ownership Interest concerned, and the terms of this Agreement as to Disability shall apply.

B. Effect on Transfers. No transfer of an Ownership Interest pursuant to this Agreement shall be recognized by the Corporation or by the Continuing Shareholders until it is duly entered upon the books and records of the Corporation and all indicia of such Ownership Interest are changed accordingly.

C. Legend. The share certificates shall bear the following legend or a legend to the following effect:

> "The transfer of these shares is restricted. These shares may be restricted under the terms of the Securities Act of 1933, the Securities and Exchange Act of 1934, or the Securities Act of Texas (collectively called the "Securities Acts"). The restriction may involve limitations required under an exemption from said Security Acts, such as an investment representation, a residence requirement, or a holding period requirement under the Intrastate Offering exemption."
>
> "Further, the transfer of these snares is restricted under the terms of a Stock Redemption and under the terms of a Stock Redemption and Buy-Sell Agreement between the holder of this certificate and the Corporation or other shareholders, or both. Said shares may not be sold, transferred, assigned, given away, pledged, encumbered, or otherwise disposed of except in strict accordance with the terms of that agreement, and no transfer will be recognized by the Corporation until, as the case may be, counsel to the Corporation is satisfied there is no violation of the Security Acts, the other shareholders consent to the transfer, or both."
>
> "A copy of said Stock Redemption and Buy-Sell Agreement will be furnished without charge to the holder of this certificate upon receipt by the Corporation at its principal place of business or registered office of a written request from the holder hereof requesting such a copy."

VII. PURCHASE PRICE AND TERMS

A. Valuation. The value of the Corporation shall be determined as provided in Exhibit A attached hereto. Except as otherwise provided in paragraph F hereof, the purchase price payable to the Terminating Shareholder shall be the value of the Terminating Shareholder's Ownership Interest in the Corporation, without discount or adjustment. Thus, if the Terminating Shareholder's Ownership Interest is ten percent (10%) of the Corporation and the Corporation's value is one hundred dollars ($100), the purchase price shall be ten dollars ($10).

B. Payment. In the case of a Termination other than by reason of death, the purchase price shall be paid as follows: fifteen percent (15%) of the purchase price paid at Closing, with the palance paid in five (5) equal and consecutive annual installments, to commence on the first business day of the next succeeding fiscal year of the Corporation after the Closing. The unpaid principal shall bear simple annual interest payable on each principal installment date at the rate payable on the Closing Date by __________ Bank, ____________ on passbook accounts, but in no event shall the interest rate be less than ___ percent (___%). In default of either a principal installment or the interest due in respect thereof, the remaining balance of the purchase price shall become due and payable at the option of the noteholder. The entire principal balance or any part thereof, other than in the year of the Closing my be prepaid without penalty. All costs and expenses which arise in connection with collection of any amounts due shall be borne by the maker of the note, including a reasonable attorney's fee. The note to be used shall be in substantially the form attached as Exhibit B hereto.

C. Escrow. The Ownership Interest being sold to the Corporation or the Continuing Shareholders, as the case may be, and all indicia thereof, shall, at the election of the Terminating Shareholder, be retained in escrow by a disinterested third party selected by mutual agreement between the Terminating Shareholder and the Corporation or the Contintuing Shareholdes, as the case may be, with appropriate escrow instructions to the effect that the Ownership Interest shall be delivered to the Corporation or the Continuing Shareholders, as the case may be, when the purchase price, together with any accrued interest, has been paid in full, and, in the event of default thereof, the Ownership Interest shall revert to the Terminating Shareholder. However, so long as no default occurs any voting rights or oghter interests accruing to the Contintuing Shareholders by reason of their purchase of such stock shall be fully exercisable by them.

D. Secured Transaction. The terms of Article 9 of the Uniform Commercial Code, dealing with default and the taking of acollateral, then applying in the State of _______ shall govern the Terminating Shareholder' the Corpoartion's, or the Continuing Shareholders', rights and remedies in the event of default.

E. Tax Status. All proceeds payable to a Terminating Shareholder shall be regarded for income tax purposes as paid from the following sources, in the order of priority shown:

i. First, to the extent thereof, the Terminating Shareholder shall receive the balance of his salary or other employee compensation, including expense reimbursement but excluding a qualified employee plan distribution, due and owing to him for the period involved.

ii. Second, as to the balance, the Terminating Shareholder shall receive payment for his shares.

F. Death. In the case of a Termination by reason of death, all of the proceeds of any insurance owned by the Corporation or Continuing Shareholders on the life of the Deceased Shareholder shall be paid by the Corporation or Continuing Shareholders to the Deceased Shareholder in reduction or payment of the purchase price, without regard to B above. In no event shall the purchase price be less than the value of the insurance proceeds. In the event the purchase price as calculated pursuant to paragraph A hereof exceeds the value of any insurance proceeds described above, the provisions of this Section VII shall apply except that under paragraph B hereof the purchase price shall be paid at closing, with the balance paid in three equal and consecutive annual installments, to commence on the first business day of the next succeeding fiscal year of the Corporation after the Closing.

VIII. RESIGNATIONS

Effective upon the occurrence of a Terminating event, the Terminating Shareholder and his spouse will automatically be deemed to have resigned as a director or officer of the Corporation as the case may be, and such resignation shall be effective without further act of the Terminating Shareholder or his spouse. Each Shareholder confers a power of attorney upon every Continuing Shareholder and agrees that upon the occurrence of the above events, every Continuing Shareholder shall thereafter have the power to do the things and perform the acts which may be necessary to reflect the fact that neither the Terminating Shareholder nor his spouse is an officer or director of the Corporation. This power of attorney shall not be affected by the disability of the Terminating Shareholder or the lack of information as to whether he is dead or alive.

Nothing herein, however, shall act as a waiver of or release of any claim, demand, or assertion of the Terminating Shareholder against the Corporation for salary, expense reimbursement, or similar employee benefits, to the extent he is entitled to the same.

IX. NON-INTERFERENCE

A. Covenants of Terminating Shareholder. Notwithstanding that the balance of the purchase price may be due and payable to the Terminating Shareholder and the Ownership Interest is held in escrow as collateral security, the continuing interest of the Terminating Shareholer shall be solely a secured interest protecting a debt due. The Terminating Shareholder shall not have any say or right in management, and he agrees to execute whatever documents, instruments, and papers shall resonably be required by the attorney for the Corporation or the Continuing Shareholders, as the case may be, to reflect that the Terminating Shareholder has severed all relationship and connection with the Corporation save as a creditor. The Corporation or the Continuing Shareholders, as the case may be, and the Terminating Shareholder shall each have the right to send notices of the severance of the relationship.

B. Mutual Covenants. The Corporation, the Continuing Shareholders, and the Terminating Shareholder hereby mutually exchange convenants of non-interference and each agrees to refrain from any conduct, by word or act, that will reflect negatively on the character or conduct of the other.

C. Non-Competition. The terminating Shareholder, recognizing that a covenant not to compete is required to protect the business interests of the Corporation and the Continuing Shareholders, agrees that unless the Corporation or the Continuing Shareholders, as the case may be, consent in writing to the contrary, such Terminating Shareholder shall not engage in a competing business in any of the metropolitan areas surrounding cities in which the Corporation is then conducting business, for three years (1095 successive calendar days) after the Closing of the purchase transaction. A "competing business" shall mean and include a business similar or directly reltaed to the active trade or business of the Corporation or any subsidiary of the Corporation, including but not limited to, the design, manufacture and marketing of fashions, but shall not include inactive activities such as an investment not for use in the trade or business conducted by the Corporation it shall cover employment, management, and investment in any such competing business.

D Reasonableness. The Corporation and all the Shareholders expressly agree that because of the nature of the business of the Corporation, the above restrictions in paragraph C as to area and time are reasonable.

E. Preservation of Name. The Corporation now has and shall continue to have, the sole and exclusive right to use the name "X Corporation" as its corporate name and title. This right shall not be affected by the termination of asociation with the Corporation of any Shareholder, either as a shareholder, officer, director, or employee, nor by any other cause. In the event that any Shareholder ceases to be associated with or employed by the Corporation for any reason, they agree herein and hereby to not thereafter use or permit the use of the name "X Corporation" in the name or trademerk of any corporation, partnerhsip, or other business with which they are associated in any capacity, directly or indirectly, and which is engaged in a business similar in any repect to that conducted the Corporation, unless such name or trademark includes other words denoting that such business is a separate organization, business, or entity entirely distinct from and not to be confused with the Corporation, and unless such name or trademark does not contain any words stating or suggesting prior or current affiliation or connection with, or comparison in age, business, or otherwise with the Corporation.

F. Confidentiality. It is also recognized and acknowledged by the Shareholders that confidential information pertaining to the Corporation's customers and manufacturing processes which may be available to them is valuable, special and unique except as such may be in the public domain. Accordingly, each Shareholder hereby agrees that he will not at any time disclose any of such information to any person, firm, corporation, association or other entity for any reason or purpose whatsoever or make use in any other way to his advantage of such information.

IX. MISCELLANEOUS MATTERS

A. Mutual Release. The Terminating Shareholder, for his part, and the Corporation and the Continuing Shareholders, for their part, do each release and acquit the other of any and all claims that each may have against the other, save and except the obligations set forth in this Agreement. It is the intention of the parties hereto that once this Agreement becomes effective, each of the parties will look only to the rights that he or they have under this Agreement.

B. Access to Books and Records. The Corporation and each Shareholder agree that the accountant or bookkeeper, or both, regularly engaged by the Corporation to keep the Corporation's books and records and report in respect thereto, acts for the Corporation and each Shareholder, and that each Shareholder shall have free and open access to the books and records of the Corporation. As against the Corporation or any Shareholder, said accountnat may not claim an accountant-client privilege, and said accountant shall be under a duty to report all information to all Shareholders and shall be under a further affirmative duty to report any matter of concern to him, which comes to his attention in the course of his duties, to all shareholders.

C. Insurance Policies. If the Corporation is the owner and beneficiary of insurance policies on the lives of the Shareholders, the Corporation may continue to maintain such incurance in force and effect during the lifetime of each insured Shareholder. The Corporation shall have the right to obtain additional insurance on the lives of the Shareholders whenever, in the opinion of the Corporation, additional insurance may be required for the benefit of the Corporation or to enable it to carry out its obligations under this Agreement. During the term of this Agreement, the Corporation shall pay premiums on all insurance policies carried by it pursuant to this Agreeemnt as they may become due. If any premium is not paid within twenty (20) days after its due date, the Shareholder whose life is insured may pay the premium or cause it to be paid, and shall be entitled to reimbursement from the Corporation. The Corporation shall apply any dividends declared on any such policy to the payment of premiums.

D. Rights to Purchase Policies. A Terminating Shareholder shall have the right to purchase the policy or policies carried by the Corporation on his own life by paying to the Corporation an amount equal to the then net cash surrender value of such policy or policies plus the unearned portion of any premiums that may have been paid thereon. Such right of purchase shall be exercised by notice given to the Corporation, in writing, within thrty (30) days after the Closing Date of the purchase of such Terminating Shareholder's Ownership Interest and the purchase price of the issuance shall be paid in full, in cash, within such period of time. On receipt of the entire purchase price, the Corporation will deliver the policies of insurance and will execute all necessary instruments of transfer.

E. Continuation of Business. Upon the occurrence of an event of Termination for any reason whatsoever, the Continuing Shareholders shall be entitled to utilize the corporate name and to continue to conduct the business of the Corporation at the premises utilized by the Corporation at the time of the Termination event, except as provided otherwise by law.

F. Entire Agreement. This instrument contains the entire agreement of the parties hereto and supersedes all prior agreements made between the shareholders and the Corporation affecting the capital stock of the Corporation and all such prior agreements are hereby terminated. No modification, amendment, change, or discharge of any term or provision of this Agreement shall be valid or binding unless the same is in writing and signed by all the parties hereto. No waiver of any of the terms of this Agreement shall be valid unless signed by the party against whom such waiver is asserted.

G. Termination. This Agreement shall terminate on the occurrence of any of the following events:

a. Bankruptcy, receivership, or dissolution of the Corporation.

b. Death of all the Shareholders simultaneously or within a period of ninety (90) days of each other.

c. The voluntary agreement of all of the Shareholders.

H. Binding Effect. This Agreement shall be binding upon and inure to the benefit of the Shareholders and their heirs, legal representatives, successors, and assigns, and the Shareholders agree for themselves and their heirs, legal representatives, successors, and assigns, to execute any instruments in writing which may be necesary or proper in carrying out the purposes of this Agreement.

I. Applicable Law. The Shareholders mutually covenant and agree that this Agreement shall be subject to and governed by the laws of the State of __________, irrespective of the fact that one or more of the parties now is or may become a resident of a different state.

J. Damages. The parties hereby declare that it is impossible to measure in money the damages which will accrue to a party hereto or to the personal representatives of a Deceased Shareholder by reason of a failure to perform any of the obligations under this Agreement. Therefore, if any party thereto or the personal representatives of a Deceased Shareholder shall institute any action or proceeding to enforce the provisions hereof, any person (including the Corporation) against whom such action or proceeding is brought hereby waives the claim or defense therein that such party or such personal representative has or have an adequate remedy at law, and such person shall not urge in any such action or proceeding the claim or defense that such remedy at law exists.

K. Invalidity. The invalidity or unenforceability of any particular provision of this Agreement shall not affect the other provisions hereof, and the Agreement shall be construed in all respects as if such invalid or unenforceable provisions were omitted.

L. Gender. Words of any gender used in this Agreement shall be held and construed to include any other gender, and words in the singular shall be held and constured to include the plural, unless the context otherwise requires.

M. Headings. The captions or headings contained in this Agreement are inserted and included solely for convenience and shall never be considered or given any effect in construing the provisions hereof it any question of intent should arise.

N. Disability Insurance. If, during any period of Disability, the Bank or the Disabled Shareholder shall receive any proceeds of any disability insurance policy owned by the Corporation on the Disabled Shareholder, then any such payments so received by the Bank shall be paid to the Disabled Shareholder and all such payments to the Disabled Shareholder shall be applied on the purchase price as determined in accordance with the terms of this Agreement.

O. Repurchase After Divorce. In the event a Shareholder's Ownership Interest is purchased by the Offerees by reason of the Terminating Shareholder's divorce or permanent separation pursuant to the terms of this Agreement, such terminatin Shareholder shall have the exclusive right to repurchase his or her entire ownership interest in the Bank, including that of his spouse or any donees, following the entry of a final judgment and decree of divorce and the lapse of time allowed for any appeal thereof, provided no other terminating event occurs or has occurred. Such purchase shall be effected by said Terminating Shareholder giving written notice to the Offerees of his election to purchase all or any part of his Ownership Interest as provided herein within thirty (30) days of the entry of a final judgment and decree of divorce and the lapse of time allowed for any appeal thereof. If the Terminating Shareholder elects to purchase all or any part of his ownership interest as herein provided and written notice thereof is given as provided above and actually received by the Offerees within one (1) year from the date of Termination (which for purposes of this paragraph shall mean the date of the filing of any legal action regarding the Terminating Shareholder's divorce or permanent separation), the purchase price shall be the price originally paid by the Offerees to the Terminating Shareholders, otherwise the purchase price shall be determined as provided in Exhibit __ hereto, as of the date of the written notice of election.

P. Exhibits. All exhibits, attachments, annexed instruments and addenda referred to herein shall be considered a part hereof for all purposes with the same force and effect as if copied at full length herein.

Q. Dispute Resolution. Each of the Shareholders hereby agree that in the event any deadlock should arise, either among all of the holders of the Corporation's capital stock with voting rights or among all of the members of the Corporation's Board of Directors, then in the event the deadlock is among the holders of the Corporation's capital stock, the Corporation shall issue one share of a specially denominated series of Unclassified Preferred Stock, Five Dollars ($5.00) par value, which shall have full voting rights, to [Name] who shall vote such share in accordance with his best judgment. In the event the deadlock is among the Corporation's Board of Directors, the Shareholders and Common Shareholders hereby agree to increase the size of the Board of Directors by one and to elect [NAME] to the Board of Directors who shall exercise his rights as a member thereof in accordance with his best judgment. The Shareholders and the Corporation hereby agree to indemnify and hold [NAME] harmless for any action taken by him either as a holder of shares of the Corporation's capital stock or as a member of the Board of Directors.

IN WITNESS WHEREOF, the parties hereto warrant each to the other that they have read this Agreement in its entirety, understand all its terms, and execute this Agreement as of the date first above written with full knowledge of its significance.

SHAREHOLDERS:	RESPECTIVE SPOUSES:
______________________	______________________
______________________	______________________
______________________	______________________

ATTEST:	X CORPORATION
______________________ Secretary (CORPORATE SEAL)	By ______________________ President

Form 9a. Employment Agreement (Short Form)

For various considerations from ______________________ (hereinafter "Company"), I agree as follows:

1. Full Time Work for Company.

During my employment with Company:

(a) I will devote my full working time and best efforts to the service of Company and will comply with Company policies; and

(b) I will not participate in any planning, operation or management of any activity competitive with Company's interest and will not otherwise engage in any activity potentially in conflict with the interest of the Company except as authorized in writing by an officer of Company.

2. Obligation to Disclose to Company.

At Company's expense, I will both during or after my employment promptly disclose to Company all ideas, information, inventions and discoveries (whether or not patentable):

(i) which directly or indirectly relate to any of the business interests of Company in connection with which I have worked or carried responsibility or received Company confidential disclosures, and

(ii) which are conceived, made or learned by me alone or jointly with others during the term of my employment.

3. Title to Information, Ideas.

I assign unto Company all my right and title in such (see §2) ideas, information, inventions or discoveries. I will, at Company expense, cooperate both during and after my employment, in all lawful acts which may be desirable in the judgment of Company to protect for and in the name of either Company or its nominee all such ideas, information, inventions and discoveries.

4. Keep Information Proprietary and Confidential.

During my employment I may develop or be exposed to confidential or trade secret information of Company or others with whom Company does business, and maintenance of the confidential and proprietary character of such information is known to be important to Company. Accordingly, for so long either during or after my employment as any such confidential information or trade secrets may remain confidential, secret or otherwise totally or partially protectable or proprietary, I will not use or divulge such information except as permitted or required by the duties of my Company employment; and I will at all times exercise diligence to maintain any confidential, secret or proprietary character of all Company information, documents and things.

5. Restraint on Use of Company Information.

Without limitation on the obligation of section 4 above, for so long (up to two years after terminaton of my employment) as may be lawful, consistent with the place and circumstances: I will not take any employment wherein I would be aiding competition with Company and I will not undertake any owner, consultant or employment role competitive or in conflict with any interest of Company wherein the complete unhampered fulfillment of the duties of that employment would inherently or inevitably call upon me to reveal, to base judgments upon or to use any such Company confidential information or trade secrets.

6. Restraint on Diversion of Trade.

Both during and for two years after my employment I will not, within the State of Texas, directly or indirectly or by aid to others, do anything which would tend to divert from Company any trade of business (i) with any customer with whom I have any contacts or association during one year next preceding termination of my Company employment, or (ii) with any party whose identity or potential as a customer was confidential and learned by me during my employment.

7. Restraint on Soliciting Employees to Leave Company.

During my employment and for so long (up to two years after termination of my employment) as may be lawful, consistent with the time, place and circumstances, I will not either directly or indirectly induce, attempt to induce or aid others in inducing any person with whom I was acquainted while in the employ of Company, to leave the employment of Company.

8. Return of Tangible Items.

I will return to Company upon termination of my employment all documents and things, produced by me or coming into my possession by or through my employment, and which are not my personal property.

9. Other Remedies Retained by Company.

The undertakings herein shall not be construed as any limitation upon the remedies Company might have at law or equity in the absence of this Agreement.

10. Freedom to Enter into this Agreement.

I am aware of no legal obligations of mine which are inconsistent with the terms of this Agreement or with my undertaking employment with Company.

11. Severability.

If in any place or circumstance any portion of this Agreement shall be deemed wholly or partially unenforceable, I agree nevertheless to be bound by all other provisions hereof to the full lawful extent.

______________________ Date	______________________ Employee
______________________ Place of Execution	
	Company
	By: ______________________

Form 9b. Employment Agreement (Long Form)

This Employment Agreement is executed by and between ______________, a Texas corporation (hereinafter referred to as the "Company") and ______________ (hereinafter referred to as "Employee").

W I T N E S S E T H :

1. The Company hereby agrees to employ Employee, and the Employee hereby agrees to render exclusive service to the Company and perform such duties as may be assigned from time to time by the Board of Directors, or the President of the Company for a period of ______ years commencing on the date of this Agreement, subject to earlier termination as hereinafter provided.

2. Employee shall be compensated by the Company at an initial base rate of ______________ Dollars ($________) per month, payable semimonthly on the fifteenth and final days of each month during the period of Employee's employment under this greement, subject to such modifications as may be determined from ime to time by the management of the Company in its discretion. Such compensation shall be in addition to any group insurance, pension, profit sharing, and other fringe benefits which are extended from time to time to Employee in the discretion of the Board of Directors of the Company. Subject to such rules and procedures as are from time to time specified by the Company, the Company shall also reimburse Employee for all reasonable expenses incurred on behalf of the Company.

3. Employee shall devote Employee's full working time to the business of the Company; however, Employee shall be excused from performing any services for the Company hereunder during periods of temporary incapacity and during vacations conforming to the Company's standard vacation policy, without thereby in any way affecting the compensation to which Employee is entitled hereunder.

4. Without prior written consent of the Company, Employee shall not, during the period of employment herein provided, directly or indirectly invest or engage in any business which is competitive with that of the Company or accept employment with or render services to a competitor as a director, officer, agent, employee or consultant, or take any action inconsistent with the fiduciary relationship of an employee to his or her corporation.

5. In the event that the employment of Employee hereunder shall terminate for any reason, whether because of the expiration of this Agreement or otherwise, Employee agrees that during the period of _____ (____) months following the termination of his or her employment Employee will not, directly or indirectly, either through any kind of ownership (other than ownership of securities of publicly held corporations of which Employee owns less than one percent (1%) of any class of outstanding securities) or as a director, officer, agent, employee or consultant, engage in a business which is competitive with the business of the Company at the time such employment is terminated, within a radius of ______ miles from the office address where Employer was employed at the time of his termination of employment. It is expressly agreed that the remedy at law for breach of this covenant is inadequate and that injunctive relief shall be available to prevent the breach thereof.

6. All information relating to the business of the Company, including but not limited to the identity of the customers and suppliers of the Company, its arrangements with such suppliers and customers, and technical data relating to its products and services, hall be treated as confidential by Employee both during and after .e termination of Employee's employment under this Agreement. Except with the prior approval of the Company, Employee shall not disclose any of such information at any time to any person except authorized personnel of the Company or its subsidiary corporations. In the event of a breach or threatened breach by the Employee of the provisions of this paragraph, the Company shall, in addition to any other available remedies, be entitled to an injunction restraining Employee from disclosing, in whole or in part, any such information or from rendering any services to any person, firm or corporation to whom any of such information may have been disclosed or is threatened to be disclosed.

7. All data, drawings and other records and written material prepared or compiled by Employee or furnished to Employee while in the employ of the Company shall be the sole and exclusive property of the Company, and none of such data, drawings or other records, or copies thereof, shall be retained by Employee upon termination of his employment.

8. The provisions of Sections 5, 6, and 7 of this Agreement shall continue to be binding upon Employee in accordance with their terms, notwithstanding termination of Employee's employment hereunder for any reason.

9. The Board of Directors of the Company may, without cause and without advance notice, terminate Employee's employment hereunder at any time during the term of this Agreement, provided that within ten (10) days after such termination the Company shall pay to Employee all compensation earned but not previously paid prior to termination (prorated for any partial compensation period) plus the sum of ______________ Dollars ($________), as a severance payment.

10. It is agreed and understood that, except as provided in Section 9 or upon the death of Employee, the Company cannot terminate the employment of Employee under this Agreement except for good cause, and that, without prejudice to the generality of the right to terminate for good cause, each of the following contingencies shall be good cause:

(a) Should Employee by reason of injury or illness become incapable for more than thirty (30) substantially consecutive days of satisfactorily performing his or her duties as an employee under this Agreement;

(b) Should Employee for reasons other than illness or injury be absent from his or her duties without the consent of the Company for more than ten (10) consective days;

(c) Should Employee be adjudicated a bankrupt or be convicted of a crime punishable by imprisonment;

(d) Should the Employee engage in any activity that would in the opinion of the Board of Directors of the Company constitute a conflict of interest with the Company; or

(e) Should Employee be negligent or inefficient in the performance of his or her duties hereunder, or otherwise fail to comply with the terms and conditions of this Agreement.

The Company may for good cause terminate Employee's employment under this Agreement without advance notice. Termination shall not affect any of the Company's other rights and remedies.

11. Employee represents and warrants that Employee has not previously assumed any obligations inconsistent with those of this Agreement.

12. This Agreement supersedes all previous agreements, written or oral, relating to Employee's employment by the Company, and shall not be changed orally, but only by a written instrument to which the Company and the Employee are both parties.

13. This Agreement and the rights and obligations hereunder shall be binding upon and inure to the benefit of the parties hereto and their respective legal representatives, and shall also bind and inure to the benefit of any successor of the Company by merger or consolidation or any assignee of all or substantially all of its properties, but, except to any such successor or assignee of the Company, neither this Agreement nor any rights or benefits hereunder may be assigned by either party hereto.

Executed this _____ day of ______________, 19____.

____
Employee

____

By: ______________________
President

Form 10. Non-Disclosure Agreement Form

As an employee of ______________________ ("Company"), I am aware that Company is embarking on a program of rapid expansion and development of unique concepts and techniques in management, marketing and production control. I am also aware that Company contemplates allowing me to come into contact with highly confidential information concerning Company's business and that I, have a fiduciary responsibility to Company and its shareholders to not divulge this information to third parties. Accordingly, in consideration of Company allowing me access to confidential information in my continued employment with Company, I hereby agree that if I ever leave my employment with Company, I will not disclose or reveal to any other person, firm or corporation, any of the business practices, trade secrets, operating methods, techniques, or other confidential information revealed to me during my employment with Company.

Signed this _____ day of ____________, 19_____.

By: ______________________
Employee

Form 11. Invention and Patent Agreement

____________ COMPANY, INC.

INVENTION AND PATENT AGREEMENT WITH

____

In view of the fact that we are employing you in a position where you have the opportunity to become familiar with our business and to use our facilities, which may enable you to make inventions and improvements relating to this company's business, we have made the following agreement:

1. All ideas, discoveries and inventions, whether patentable or not, which you make or conceive during your employment by this company which relate to the business of this company, or the contemplated business of this company, shall be the sole and exclusive property of this company and you will fully disclose such to this company.

2. You will promptly advise your supervisor of all inventions and improvements, whether patentable or not, which you, or you and another, or others, may make during your employment by this company, which in any way relate to the business, or contemplated business this company during your employment by it.

3. You will assist in the preparation of patent applications, both domestic and foreign, upon all such inventions and improvements; sign all papers and take all oaths required in connection with such applications or applications for reissue of patents, or any divisions, continuations, continuations-in-part or substitutes of such applications; and will assist in their prosecution and in any proceedings relating to them or to patents issuing them; it being understood, however, that you will not be subjected to financial expense in connection with any of this assistance.

4. You will assign to this company your entire right, title and interest in all such inventions and improvements, and in all domestic and foreign patent applications on them , so that this company may, if it desires, obtain domestic and foreign patents on these inventions and improvements, but they shall remain the property of this company whether patented or not.

5. It is understood that you have not heretofore made any inventions or improvements which in any way relate to the business of this company and to which it is not entitled, unless those inventions and improvements are identified on the reverse side of this form.

6. You agree that you will not disclose to anyone other than authorized individuals of this company, whether during or after your employment by us, any confidential information obtained by you while in our employ, without the written consent, any technical reports, drawings, blueprints, or other reproductions, or any papers of this company, and will not employ any such papers or any such confidential information except for the benefit of this company. Nothing in this agreement will prevent you, however, from disclosing or using any information which has become public knowledge.

7. It is understood that the salary which you receive while in our employ is in full payment for your services and for acts done in performance of this agreement.

8. This agreement is binding upon you, your administrators and executors, and upon this company, its successors and assigns, and will continue during your employment and as long thereafter as may be necessary to carry out the terms of this agreement.

9. Your signature below will indicate your agreement to the provisions of this agreement.

____________ COMPANY, INC.

By: ____________________

ACCEPTED:

____
Employee

DATED this ____ day of ____________, 198___.

Form 12a. Promissory Notes

SIMPLE PROMISSORY NOTE
Form I

[Date]

[Period of time] after date [or on (date)], I promise to pay to the order of [name of payee] at [place of payment, including county] the sum of [amount].

____
[Signature of maker]

Form II

$____________ Date____________

____________after the above date I promise to pay to the order of ____________ the sum of ____________($____________), together with interest at ________percent per annum, payable at____________
____________________.

The maker and guarantor of this note further agree to waive demand, notice of nonpayment and protest, and in case suit shall be brought for the collection hereof, or the same has to be collected upon demand of an attorney, to pay reasonable attorney's fees for making such collection. Deferred interest payments to bear interest from maturity at ____________ percent per annum, payable semiannually.

(Signed) ____________________
Maker

(Signed) ____________________
Co-Maker [or Guarantor]

Due ____________

PROMISSORY NOTE
Form 3

Date:
Maker: (Debtor)
Maker's Mailing Address (including county):

Payee: (Person to be paid)
Place for Payment (including county):

Principal Amount:
Annual Interest Rate on Unpaid Principal from Date:
Annual Interest Rate on Matured, Unpaid Amounts:
Terms of Payment (principal and interst):

Maker promises to pay to the order of Payeee at the place for payment and according to the terms of payment the principal amount plus interest at the rates stated above. All unpaid amounts shall be due by the final scheduled payment date.

On default in the payment of this note, the unpaid principal balance and earned interest on this note shall become immediately due at the election of Payee. Maker and each endorser, and guarantor waive all demands for payment, presentations for payment, notices of intention to accelerate maturity, notices of acceleration of maturity, protests, and notices of protest.

If this note is given to an attorney for collection, or if suit is brought for collection, or if it is collected through probate, bankruptcy, or other judicial proceeding, then Maker shall pay Payee all costs of collection, including reasonably attorney's fees and court costs, in addition to other amounts due. Reasonable attorney's fees shall be 10% of all amounts due unless either party pleads otherwise.

Interest on the debt evidenced by this note shall not exceed the maximum amount of nonusurious interest that may be contracted for, taken, reserved, charged, or received under law; any inter- est in excess of that maximum amount shall be credited on the principal of the debtor or, if that has been paid, refunded. On any acceleration or required or permitted prepayment, any such excess shall be canceled automatically as of the acceleration or prepayment or, if already paid, credited on the principal of the debt or, if the principal of the debt has been paid, refunded. This provision overrides other provisions in this and all other instruments concerning the debt.

Each Maker is responsible for all obligations represented by this note.

____
Maker

____
Co-Maker [Guarantor]

Form 12b. Promissory Note (with Security Interest)

PROMISSORY NOTE
(to accompany Security Agreement)

Date:
Maker:
Maker's Mailing Address:

Payee:
Place for Payment:

Principal Amount:
Annual Interest Rate on Unpaid Principal from Date:
Annual Interest Rate on Matured, Unpaid Amounts:
Terms of Payment (principal and interest):

Security for Payment
A Security Interest Created and Granted in the Following Security Agreement:

Date:
Debtor:
Secured Party: Payee
County Where Collateral Located:
Collateral:

Maker promises to pay to the order of Payee at the place for payment and according to the terms of payment the principal amount plus interest at the rates stated above. All unpaid amounts shall be due by the final scheduled payment date.

On default in the payment of this note or in the performance of any obligation in any instrument securing or collateral to it, the unpaid principal balance and earned interest on this note shall become immediately due at the election of Payee. Maker and each surety, endorser, and guarantor waive all demands for payment, presentations for payment, notices of intention to accelerate maturity, notices of acceleration of maturity, protests, and notices of protest.

If this note or any instrument securing or collateral to it is given to an attorney for collection or enforcement, or if suit is brought for collection or enforcement, or if it is collected or enforced through probate, bankruptcy, or other judicial proceeding, then Maker shall pay Payee all costs of collection and enforcement, including reasonable attorney's fees and court costs, in addition to other amounts due. Reasonable attorney's fees shall be 10% of all amounts due unless either party pleads otherwise.

Interest on the debt evidenced by this note shall not exceed the maximum amount of nonusurious interest that may be contracted for, taken, reserved, charged, or received under law; any interest in excess of that maximum amount shall be credited on the principal of the debtor or, if that has been paid, refunded. On any acceleration or required or permitted prepayment, any such excess shall be canceled automatically as of the acceleration or prepayment or, if already paid, credited on the principal of the debt or, if the principal of the debt has been paid, refunded. This provision overrides other provisions in this and all other instruments concerning the debt.

Each Maker is responsible for all obligations represented by this note.

____
Maker

____
Co-Maker [or Guarantor]

Form 13. Loan Guaranty

______________, 1991

In consideration of the loan by BUDGET FINANCIAL CORPORATION, a Texas personal property broker, ("Budget") to Borrower, a Texas partnership ("Borrower"), of the sum of $500,000 on the date hereof, which loan is evidenced by a certain promissory note, of even date, executed by BORROWER and payable to BUDGET on demand (the "Note"), the undersigned jointly and severally guarantee the prompt payment in full of the Note (and all extensions, renewals or novations thereof). A copy of the Note is attached hereto as Exhibit A.

The undersigned jointly and severally further guarantee BORROWER'S prompt payment of all obligations arising under, and BORROWER'S full performance of all of the terms, conditions, and covenants contained in, any instrument of security securing the Note or arising under, or contained in, any other agreement now existing, or hereafter entered into, between BORROWER and BUDGET whereby any indebtedness is now owing, or hereafter becomes owing, by BORROWER to BUDGET.

The undersigned jointly and severally further guarantee prompt payment and performance of any and all other liabilities or obligations according to the terms thereof, which BORROWER may now or hereafter owe or incur to BUDGET, without limitation as to amount, arising in any manner whatever, whether from dealings between BORROWER and BUDGET or from other dealings by which BUDGET may be or become in any manner whatever, a creditor of BORROWER.

BORROWER and BUDGET (and any other parties thereto) may make renewals and extensions of the time of payment or performance of any liability, obligation, contract or promissory note guaranteed hereby, and may change or otherwise alter the time or manner for performance contained therein, or enter into any amendment or novation, and BORROWER and BUDGET (and all parties thereto) may freely deal with each other in all respects without in any manner whatever affecting the liability hereunder of the undersigned. BUDGET may take, surrender, or modify, vary, exchange, renew, or abstain from perfecting or taking advantage of any security, accept or make compositions or other arrangements, discharge or release any party or guarantor without in any manner whatever affecting the liability hereunder of the undersigned.

The undersigned each waives:

(a) presentment, demand, protest, notice of protest, notice of dishonor, and notice of non-payment and notices of every kind or nature, including those of any action or non-action on the part of BORROWER, or of BUDGET, or of any other person or firm;

(b) the right, if any, to the benefit of, or to direct the application of, any security hypothecated to/or for BUDGET until all indebtedness of BORROWER to BUDGET, however arising, shall have been paid;

(c) the right to require BUDGET to proceed against BORROWER, or to pursue any other remedy available to BUDGET.

(d) The right to plead any and all statutes of limitation as a defense in any action or proceeding pertaining to this Note.

Upon default by BORROWER (or by any other party required to render performance) in performance of the terms of any liability, obligation, contract or promissory note guaranteed hereby, BUDGET may proceed, without notice, directly and independently of BORROWER against the undersigned, or any of them, to collect and recover the full amount hereby guaranteed, or any portion thereof. The cessation of the liability of BORROWER for any reason other than full payment, or any extension, renewal, forbearance, change of rate of interest, amendments, novation, or acceptance, release or substitution of security, or any impairment or suspension of the remedies or rights of BUDGET against BORROWER, shall not in any manner whatever affect the liability of the undersigned, or any of them, hereunder.

The undersigned jointly and severally agree to pay reasonable attorneys' fees and all other costs and expenses which may be incurred by BUDGET in the enforcement of this Guaranty and in collection of any of said liabilities from, or the enforcement of any obligation against, BORROWER or the undersigned, or any of them.

A married woman who signs this Guaranty agrees that her separate property shall be liable for all of her obligations hereunder regardless of whether or not any such obligation is secured by a mortgage, deed of trust or other hypothecation of community property.

This Guaranty shall inure to the benefit of the assigns and successors in interest of BUDGET and each of them, and shall be binding upon the heirs, administrators, executors and assigns of the undersigned and each of them.

Any legal action or proceeding pertaining to this Guaranty shall be brought in the courts of the State of Texas. By the execution and delivery of this Guaranty, each of the undersigned irrevocably and expressly (i) submits to the jurisdiction of said courts, (ii) designates, appoints and empowers Phlip F. Marantz, Esq., whose address is Suite 530,

One Shell Plaza, Houston, Texas 77002, as the agent for service of process in any legal action or proceeding pertaining to this Guaranty, (iii) waives any right he or she may have to object to the jurisdiction or venue of said courts in which any such action or proceeding is commenced, and (iv) consents to the service of process of said courts in any such action or proceeding by the mailing thereof by air mail, postage prepaid, to the undersigned at the address set forth after the signature of the undersigned below.

This Guaranty (including, without limitation, the validity, construction and enforcement hereof) shall be governed by the internal laws of the State of Texas.

____
John Jones

Address: 5000 Montrose Blvd.
Houston, TX 77005

____
Sam Smith

Address: 4306 University Blvd
Houston, TX 77005

Form 14a. Truth-in-Lending Sale Disclosure

TRUTH-IN-LENDING (SALE) DISCLOSURE STATEMENT

(Adapted from 12 C.F.R. pt. 226 app. H (1985) for use with mechanic's lien documents prepared by the State Bar of Texas)

CREDITOR	CONSUMER

ANNUAL PERCENTAGE RATE The cost of your credit as a yearly rate.	**FINANCE CHARGE** The dollar amount the credit will cost you.	**AMOUNT FINANCED** The amount of credit provided to you or on your behalf.	**TOTAL OF PAYMENTS** The amount you will have paid after you have made all payments as scheduled.	**TOTAL SALE PRICE** The total cost of your purchase on credit, including your down payment of $________
%	$	$	$	$

You have the right to receive at this time an itemization of the Amount Financed:
☐ I want an itemization. ☐ I do not want an itemization.

Your payment schedule will be:

Number of Payments	Amount of Payments	When Payments Are Due

Security: You are giving a security interest in:
☐ the goods or property being purchased.
☐

Filing Fees $ ________ **Nonfiling Insurance $** ________

Late Charge: If a payment is late, you will be charged ________ % per annum of the late payment.

Prepayment: If you pay off early, you
(check if the loan is at simple interest) ☐ may ☐ will not have to pay a penalty.

(check if private mortgage insurance premiums are charged to the consumer) ☐ may ☐ will not be entitled to a refund of part of the finance charge.

See your contract documents for any additional information about nonpayment, default, any required repayment in full before the scheduled date, and prepayment refunds and penalties.

Additional Disclosures:

"e" means an estimate

INSURANCE DISCLOSURES

Property Insurance. You may obtain property insurance from anyone that is authorized to transact business in Texas. If you get the insurance from ________________ (creditor), you will pay $________ for ____ months.

Credit Insurance. If you want, the creditor may provide you with credit insurance for the credit term. Credit life insurance and credit disability insurance are not required to obtain credit and will not be provided unless you sign and agree to pay the additional cost. You understand that if your credit term exceeds 59 months, the premium rates for credit insurance are not fixed or approved by the Texas State Board of Insurance. If you desire insurance, you should indicate the type desired and sign below.

____ I want credit life insurance on the life of the Consumer only for a premium of $________.

____ I want credit life insurance on the lives of the Consumer and Co-Borrower for a premium of $________.

____ I want credit disability insurance (available only to Consumer) for a premium of $________.

________________ (Consumer's signature) ________________ (Co-Borrower's signature)

I have received a copy of this statement.

________ Signature ____ Date ________ Signature ____ Date

Form 14b. Truth-in-Lending Loan Disclosure

TRUTH-IN-LENDING (LOAN) DISCLOSURE STATEMENT

(Adapted from 12 C.F.R. pt. 226 app. H (1985) for use with mechanic's lien documents prepared by the State Bar of Texas)

CREDITOR	CONSUMER

ANNUAL PERCENTAGE RATE The cost of your credit as a yearly rate.	FINANCE CHARGE The dollar amount the credit will cost you.	AMOUNT FINANCED The amount of credit provided to you or on your behalf.	TOTAL OF PAYMENTS The amount you will have paid after you have made all payments as scheduled.
%	$	$	$

You have the right to receive at this time an itemization of the Amount Financed:
☐ I want an itemization. ☐ I do not want an itemization.

Your payment schedule will be:

Number of Payments	Amount of Payments	When Payments Are Due

Security: You are giving a security interest in:
☐ the goods or property being purchased.
☐

Filing Fees $__________ **Nonfiling Insurance** $__________

Late Charge: If a payment is late, you will be charged __________ % per annum of the late payment.

Prepayment: If you pay off early, you
(check if the loan is at simple interest) ☐ may ☐ will not have to pay a penalty.

(check if private mortgage insurance premiums are charged to the consumer) ☐ may ☐ will not be entitled to a refund of part of the finance charge.

See your contract documents for any additional information about nonpayment, default, any required repayment in full before the scheduled date, and prepayment refunds and penalties.

Additional Disclosures:

"e" means an estimate

INSURANCE DISCLOSURES

Property Insurance. You may obtain property insurance from anyone that is authorized to transact business in Texas. If you get the insurance from ____________________ (creditor), you will pay $__________ for _____ months.

Credit Insurance. If you want, the creditor may provide you with credit insurance for the credit term. Credit life insurance and credit disability insurance are not required to obtain credit and will not be provided unless you sign and agree to pay the additional cost. You understand that if your credit term exceeds 59 months, the premium rates for credit insurance are not fixed or approved by the Texas State Board of Insurance. If you desire insurance, you should indicate the type desired and sign below.

_____ I want credit life insurance on the life of the Consumer only for a premium of $__________.

_____ I want credit life insurance on the lives of the Consumer and Co-Borrower for a premium of $__________.

_____ I want credit disability insurance (available only to Consumer) for a premium of $__________.

____________________ (Consumer's signature)

____________________ (Co-Borrower's signature)

I have received a copy of this statement.

____________________ Signature __________ Date

____________________ Signature __________ Date

Form 14c. Truth-in-Lending Right of Rescission

TRUTH-IN-LENDING NOTICE OF RIGHT OF RESCISSION

(Notice of Right To Cancel—Refinancing)

____

(Identification of Transaction)

Your Right To Cancel

You are entering into a new transaction to increase the amount of credit provided to you. We acquired a lien on your home under the original transaction and will retain that lien in the new transaction. You have a legal right under federal law to cancel the new transaction, without cost, within three business days from whichever of the following events occurs last:

1. the date of the new transaction, which is ____________________ ; or
2. the date you received your new Truth-in-Lending disclosures; or
3. the date you received this notice of your right to cancel.

If you cancel the new transaction, your cancellation will apply only to the increase in the amount of credit. It will not affect the amount that you presently owe or the lien we already have on your home. If you cancel, the lien as it applies to the increased amount is also canceled. Within 20 calendar days after we receive your notice of cancellation of the new transaction, we must take the steps necessary to reflect the fact that our lien on your home no longer applies to the increase of credit. We must also return any money you have given to us or anyone else in connection with the new transaction.

You may keep any money we have given you in the new transaction until we have done the things mentioned above, but you must then offer to return the money at the address below. If we do not take possession of the money within 20 calendar days of your offer, you may keep it without further obligation.

How To Cancel

If you decide to cancel the new transaction, you may do so by notifying us in writing, at

(Creditor's name and business address)

You may use any written statement that is signed and dated by you and states your intention to cancel, or you may use this notice by dating and signing below. Keep one copy of this notice because it contains important information about your rights.

If you cancel by mail or telegram, you must send the notice no later than midnight of ____________________ (or midnight of the third business day following the latest of the three events listed above). If you send or deliver your written notice to cancel in some other way, it must be delivered to the above address no later than that time.

In this agreement "you" and "your" refer to the consumer, and "we" and "us" refer to the creditor.

I WISH TO CANCEL.

____________________________ ________________

Consumer's Signature Date

____

Consumer's Signature

Consumer acknowledges receipt of the Truth-in-Lending Notice of Right of Rescission with appropriate blanks completed.

____________________________ ________________

Consumer's Signature Date

____

Consumer's Signature

from 12 C.F.R. pt. 226 app. H (1985)

Form 15. Bill of Sale

Date __________________

1. ____________________, Seller, hereby sells the goods described in paragraph 2 to ____________________, Buyer.

2. The goods being sold under this bill of sale (Goods) are: ____________________

3. The purchase price for Goods is $________. In exchange for Goods, Buyer has paid Seller:

(choose one)

[] the full purchase price.
[] $________ as a down payment, balance due in ____ days.
[] $________ as a down payment and has/have executed a promissory note for the balance of the purchase price.

4. Seller(s) warrant(s) that Seller(s) is/are legal owner(s) of Goods and that Goods are free of all liens and encumbrances except ____________________

5. Seller(s) believe(s) Goods to be in good condition except for the following defects: ____________________

6. Other than the warranty of ownership in Clause 4 and the representations in Clause 5, seller makes no express warranties. THE BUYER TAKES ALL GOODS AS IS. Seller hereby disclaims the implied warranty of merchantability and all other implied warranties which may apply to the extent that such disclaimers are permitted.

7. Goods shall be delivered to Buyer in the following manner:

(choose one and fill in information if Box b or c is checked)

a. [] Buyer shall take immediate possession of Goods.
b. [] Buyer(s) assume(s) responsibility for picking up goods from ____________________ within ______ days.
c. [] In exchange for an additional delivery charge of $_____, receipt of which is hereby acknowledged, Seller will deliver Goods within ______ days to the following location: ____________________.

8. Additional terms of sale for Goods are as follows: ____________________

Signed (Seller): ____________
Address: ____________

Signed (Buyer): ____________
Address: ____________

Form 16. Security Agreement

SIMPLE SECURITY AGREEMENT

STATE OF TEXAS)
)
COUNTY OF ____________)

That I, ____,
of ____
Street Address Apt. No. City State Zip
hereinafter called "Debtor," hereby grant to_______________,
____,
Street Address Apt. No. City State Zip
hereinafter called the "Secured Party," a security interest in the following described property and all its proceeds as collateral to secure payment of the obligation described herein.

Collateral:
Obligation:

Note: Date
Amount
Maker
Payee
Terms of payment

Default in the payment of all or any part of the obligation described, or the failure to perform as agreed, is a default under this Agreement. Upon such default the Secured Party may declare all of the above-described obligation(s) immediately due and payable and shall have the remedies of a secured party under provisions of the Texas Business and Commerce Code. In the event legal action is required to enforce any provision of this Agreement, the prevailing party shall be entitled to recover reasonable attorney's fees and costs.

The Debtor hereby agrees to exercise reasonable caution and care in use of the herein-described collateral; to adequately insure or keep insured the described collateral; not to attempt to sell, assign or dispose of said collateral or his/her interest therein; not to encumber nor to permit any encumbrance against same; and not to remove said collateral from the county where the Debtor resides without written permission of the Secured Party.

EXECUTED this _________ day of _______________, 19____.

(Signed)________________________
Debtor

(Signed)________________________
Secured Party

Form 17. Assumed Name Certificate

ASSUMED NAME CERTIFICATE
OF
________ [name of corporation]

STATE OF TEXAS
COUNTY OF ______________

KNOW ALL MEN BY THESE PRESENTS:

That I, ______________ [name and title, e.g., John Doe, President] of ______________ [name of corporation], a Texas ____________ [business or nonprofit or professional or other type] corporation, for the purpose of complying with Section 36.11 of the Business and Commerce Code of the State of Texas, do hereby certify the following facts:

1. That the assumed name under which the corporation will conduct and transact business is ____________ [name] of ________ [city], ________ County, Texas.

2. That the true and full name of the corporation conducting or transacting such business is __________ [name as stated in articles of incorporation] [and the charter number or certificate of authority number is _______].

3. The state, country, or other jurisdiction under the laws of which the corporation was incorporated is ____________, and the address of its registered or similar office in that jurisdiction is ______________.

4. The corporation maintains a registered office in Texas, and the address of the registered office is ____________, Texas, and the name of its registered agent at such address is ______________.

5. The corporation will use the assumed name from ________, 19 _____, until ______________, 19 _____ [specify period not to exceed ten years].

6. The corporation ______________ [is transacting or will transact] business under its assumed name in __________ [all the counties or all the counties, except _____________ County, or ____________ County] [of] Texas.

IN TESTIMONY WHEREOF, I have hereunto set my hand this ________ day of ______________, 19____.

__________ [name of corporation]
By _______ [signature of officer]
[typed name and title of officer]

State of Texas

County of ____________

This instrument was acknowledged before me on __________, 19____, by ______________ [name], ______________ [corporate title] of _______________ [name of corporation], a __________ [Texas or other state of incorporation] corporation, on behalf of said corporation.

[Notarial seal]

____________ [signature]
Notary Public
My Commission Expires __________,
19___.

Appendix C

State Publications and Forms to be Filed with the State of Texas

Appendix C

State Publications and Forms to be Filed with the State of Texas

1. Status Report Form for Texas Unemployment Insurance

MAIL TO
CASHIER
TEXAS EMPLOYMENT COMMISSION ,
101 EAST 15TH STREET
AUSTIN, TEXAS 78778-0001

STATUS REPORT

THIS REPORT IS REQUIRED OF EVERY EMPLOYING UNIT,
AND WILL BE USED TO DETERMINE LIABILITY UNDER THE TEXAS UNEMPLOYMENT COMPENSATION ACT.
(YOU SHOULD RETAIN ONE COPY FOR YOUR FILES)

IDENTIFICATION SECTION

1. ACCOUNT NUMBER ASSIGNED BY T.E.C. (IF ANY)

2. FEDERAL EMPLOYER I.D. NUMBER

3. TYPE OF OWNERSHIP (CHECK ONE):
1 ☐ CORPORATION ☐ PROFESSIONAL ASSOCIATION ☐ STATE AGENCY
2 ☐ PARTNERSHIP ☐ LIMITED PARTNERSHIP ☐ POLITICAL SUBDIVISION
3 ☐ INDIVIDUAL (SOLE PROPRIETOR) 4 ☐ ESTATE 5 ☐ TRUST
6 ☐ OTHER (SPECIFY) ______

4. NAME

5. MAILING ADDRESS

6. CITY	7. COUNTY	8. STATE	8(a). ZIP CODE	9. PHONE NUMBER ( )

10. BUSINESS ADDRESS WHERE RECORDS OR PAYROLLS ARE KEPT: (IF DIFFERENT FROM ABOVE)	ADDRESS		PHONE NUMBER ( )
	CITY	STATE	ZIP

11. OWNERS OR OFFICERS [ATTACH ADDITIONAL SHEET IF NECESSARY]	NAME	SOCIAL SECURITY NUMBER	TITLE	RESIDENCE ADDRESS, CITY, STATE, ZIP

12. BUSINESS LOCATION IN TEXAS [ATTACH ADDITIONAL SHEET IF NECESSARY]	TRADENAME	STREET ADDRESS, CITY, COUNTY	KIND OF BUSINESS	NUMBER OF EMPLOYEES

13. IF YOUR BUSINESS IS A CORPORATION, ENTER:	CHARTER NUMBER	STATE INCORPORATED	DATE INCORPORATED	REGISTERED AGENT'S NAME
	ORIGINAL CORPORATE NAME, IF DIFFERENT THAN ABOVE			REGISTERED AGENT'S ADDRESS

EMPLOYMENT SECTION

		MONTH	DAY	YEAR
14. ENTER THE DATE ON WHICH YOUR ORGANIZATION FIRST EMPLOYED SOMEONE IN TEXAS:				
15. ENTER THE DATE ON WHICH YOUR ORGANIZATION FIRST PAID WAGES TO SOMEONE IN TEXAS:				
16. IF YOUR ACCOUNT HAS BEEN INACTIVE:	ENTER THE DATE YOUR ORGANIZATION RESUMED EMPLOYING SOMEONE IN TEXAS:			
	ENTER THE DATE YOUR ORGANIZATION RESUMED PAYING WAGES IN TEXAS:			
17. ENTER THE ENDING DATE OF THE TWENTIETH WEEK OF EMPLOYMENT IN THE CALENDAR YEAR IN WHICH THIS ORGANIZATION HAD AT LEAST ONE PERSON EMPLOYED IN TEXAS:				
18. IF YOUR ORGANIZATION HAS PAID WAGES OF $1,500 OR MORE IN A CALENDAR QUARTER, ENTER THE ENDING DATE OF THE FIRST QUARTER IN WHICH THIS OCCURRED:				
19. IF YOU HOLD AN EXEMPTION FROM FEDERAL INCOME TAXES UNDER INTERNAL REVENUE CODE SECTION 501(C)(3), ATTACH A COPY OF YOUR EXEMPTION LETTER. ALSO, ENTER THE ENDING DATE OF THE TWENTIETH WEEK OF THE CALENDAR YEAR IN WHICH 4 OR MORE PERSONS WERE EMPLOYED IN TEXAS:				

20. IF THE BUSINESS IN TEXAS WAS ACQUIRED FROM A PREVIOUS OWNER, ENTER:

PREVIOUS OWNER'S T.E.C. ACCOUNT NUMBER (IF KNOWN)	DATE OF ACQUISITION: ➡			
NAME OF PREVIOUS OWNER	ADDRESS	CITY		STATE
WHAT PORTION OF THE BUSINESS WAS ACQUIRED?	(CHECK) (ONE):	☐ ALL. ☐ PART (SPECIFY): ______		

21. ENTER THE YEAR(S) YOUR ORGANIZATION WAS LIABLE FOR TAXES UNDER THE FEDERAL UNEMPLOYMEMENT TAX ACT: (BEGIN WITH MOST RECENT YEAR) 19☐ 19☐ 19☐ 19☐

22. DOES THIS ORGANIZATION EMPLOY ANY U.S. CITIZENS OUTSIDE OF THE UNITED STATES? YES ☐ NO ☐

DOMESTIC - HOUSEHOLD EMPLOYMENT SECTION

COMPLETE 23 ONLY IF YOU HAVE DOMESTIC OR HOUSEHOLD EMPLOYEES (INCLUDES MAIDS, COOKS, CHAUFFEURS, GARDENERS, ETC.)

	MONTH	DAY	YEAR
23. ENTER THE ENDING DATE OF THE FIRST CALENDAR QUARTER IN WHICH YOU PAID GROSS WAGES OF $1000 OR MORE TO EMPLOYEES PERFORMING DOMESTIC SERVICE:			

NATURE OF ACTIVITY SECTION

24. DESCRIBE FULLY THE NATURE OF ACTIVITY IN TEXAS, AND LIST THE PRINCIPAL PRODUCTS IN ORDER OF IMPORTANCE:

25. SELECT ONE OF THE SHORT TITLES BELOW WHICH MOST CLOSELY DESCRIBES YOUR BUSINESS OPERATIONS IN TEXAS AND ENTER THE APPROPRIATE CODE IN THE SPACE PROVIDED.

INDUSTRY CODE #

CODE SHORT TITLE

01-Agricultural Production - Crops
02-Agricultural Production - Livestock
07-Agricultural Services
08-Forestry
09-Fish, Hunting, and Trapping
10-Metal Mining
12-Coal Mining
13-Oil and Gas Extraction
14-Nonmetallic Minerals, Except Fuels
15-General Building Contractors
16-Heavy Construction Contractors
17-Special Trade Contractors

Manufacturing

20-Food and Kindred Products
21-Tobacco Manufactures
22-Textile Mill Products
23-Apparel and Other Textile Products
24-Lumber and Wood Products
25-Furniture and Fixtures
26-Paper and Allied Products
27-Printing and Publishing
28-Chemicals and Allied Products
29-Petroleum and Coal Products
30-Rubber and Misc. Plastics Products
31-Leather and Leather Products
32-Stone, Clay, and Glass Products
33-Primary Metal Industries
34-Fabricated Metal Products
35-Machinery, Except Electrical

CODE SHORT TITLE

36-Electric and Electronic Equipment
37-Transportation Equipment
38-Instruments and Related Products
39-Miscellaneous Manufacturing Industries

Nonmanufacturing

40-Railroad Transportation
41-Local and Interurban Passenger Transit
42-Trucking and Warehousing
43-U.S. Postal Service
44-Water Transportation
45-Transportation by Air
46-Pipe Lines, Except Natural Gas
47-Transportation Services
48-Communication
49-Electric, Gas, and Sanitary Services
50-Wholesale Trade-Durable Goods
51-Wholesale Trade-Nondurable Goods
52-Building Material & Garden Supplies
53-General Merchandise Stores
54-Food Stores
55-Automotive Dealers & Service Stations
56-Apparel and Accessory Stores
57-Furniture and Home Furnishing Stores
58-Eating and Drinking Places
59-Miscellaneous Retail
60-Depository Institutions
61-Nondepository Credit Institutions
62-Security, Commodity Brokers & Services
63-Insurance Carriers

CODE SHORT TITLE

64-Insurance Agents, Brokers & Service
65-Real Estate
67-Holding and Other Investment Offices
70-Hotels and Other Lodging Places
72-Personal Services
73-Business Services
75-Auto Repair, Services, and Garages
76-Miscellaneous Repair Services
78-Motion Pictures
79-Amusement & Recreation Services
80-Health Services
81-Legal Services
82-Educational Services
83-Social Services
84-Museums, Botanical, Zoological Gardens
86-Membership Organizations
87-Engineering,Accounting,Research,Management
88-Private Households (Inc. Domestic Employment)
89-Miscellaneous Services
91-Executive, Legislative, and General
92-Justice, Public Order, and Safety
93-Finance, Taxation & Monetary Policy
94-Administration of Human Resources
95-Environmental Quality and Housing
96-Administration of Economic Programs
97-National Security and Intl. Affairs
99-Nonclassifiable Establishments

VOLUNTARY ELECTION SECTION

26. IF YOU ARE NOT LIABLE UNDER A COMPULSORY PROVISION OF THE TEXAS UNEMPLOYMENT COMPENSATION ACT, AND YOU WISH TO VOLUNTARILY ELECT COVERAGE FOR YOUR EMPLOYEES, SELECT ONE OF THE FOLLOWING AND ENTER THE YEAR YOU WISH LIABILITY TO BEGIN:

☐ ALL EMPLOYEES.

☐ ALL EMPLOYEES, EXCEPT THOSE PERFORMING SERVICES WHICH ARE SPECIFICALLY EXEMPT IN THE TEXAS UNEMPLOYMENT COMPENSATION ACT.

BEGINNING JAN. 1, 19: ☐ IT IS UNDERSTOOD AND AGREED THAT AT THE END OF 2 YEARS FROM THIS DATE, OR AT THE END OF ANY CALENDAR YEAR SUBSEQUENT THERETO, YOU MAY WITHDRAW THIS ELECTION BY FILING A WRITTEN REQUEST.

IF THIS ELECTION IS APPROVED, WE WILL NOTIFY YOU OF YOUR ACCOUNT NUMBER.

FARM OR RANCH EMPLOYMENT

27. DO YOU HAVE ANY EMPLOYMENT IN TEXAS ON A FARM OR RANCH? YES ☐ NO ☐
IF "YES", WE WILL SUPPLY YOU WITH A SEPARATE STATUS REPORT TO DETERMINE IF YOU ARE LIABLE FOR YOUR FARM OR RANCH EMPLOYEES.

SIGNATURE SECTION

28. I HEREBY CERTIFY THAT THE PRECEDING INFORMATION IS TRUE AND CORRECT, AND THAT I AM AUTHORIZED TO EXECUTE THIS STATUS REPORT ON BEHALF OF THE EMPLOYING UNIT NAMED HEREIN.
(THIS REPORT MUST BE SIGNED BY THE OWNER, OFFICER, PARTNER OR INDIVIDUAL FOR WHOM A VALID POWER-OF-ATTORNEY IS ON FILE WITH THE TEXAS EMPLOYMENT COMMISSION).

DRIVER'S LICENSE #

MONTH	DAY	YEAR

DATE SIGNED

SIGN HERE ⇒ ____________________ SIGNATURE ____________________ TITLE

1a. Instructions for Status Report

C-1A (987)

Instructions for Status Report (Form C-1)

Purpose of Report: The information in this report will be used to determine if liability has been incurred under the Texas Unemployment Compensation Act.

Who must File: Every individual or employing unit which operates a business or organization in Texas (including domestic and agricultural labor), or which has acquired a business or organization which has operated in Texas.

Employing Unit is defined as any individual or type of organization, including but not limited to any partnership, association, trust, estate, joint-stock company, or corporation, whether domestic or foreign, or the receiver, trustee in bankruptcy, trustee or successor thereof, or the legal representative of a deceased person, which has or, subsequent to January 1, 1936, had in its employ one (1) or more individuals performing services for it within this State.

Detail Instructions:

Item 1: Enter the account number TEC has assigned you. If you have not yet been assigned a number, leave this blank and you will be notified of your number later.

Item 2: Enter the Federal Employer Identification Number the I.R.S. has assigned you.

Item 3: Place an "X" in the appropriate box to indicate your type of business or organization.

Item 4: Enter the name(s) of the legal owner(s). For corporations, enter the corporate name. Do not enter the trade names here.

Items 5, 6, 7, 8, and 8(a): Enter the address where you want to receive your mail.

Item 9: Enter the phone number you wish us to use if we need to call you regarding TEC matters.

Item 10: Enter the address and phone number where your payroll records are kept. If it is the same as in items 5, 6, 7, and 8, leave blank.

Item 11: For each owner, officer, or responsible official, enter the name, social security number, title and residence address. If there are more than three, please enter the additional names on a separate sheet and attach it to this report.

Item 12: Enter each trade or business name under which you operate. Also enter the location, kind of business and number of employees at each location. Some examples of kinds of business are: retail store, warehouse, administrative office, factory and auto shop. If additional lines are needed, please continue the information on a separate sheet and attach it to this report.

Item 13: This section should be completed for corporations only. Enter the charter number issued by the State, the issuing State, the date issued and the original corporate name, if it is different than the name entered in item 4 above. Also enter the name and address of the corporation's registered agent.

Item 14: Enter the first date someone performed services as an employee.

Item 15: Enter the first date someone was paid for their services.

Item 16: If your account with TEC has been suspended, and you are filing this report to reactivate your account, enter the dates someone began performing services and was paid, after you resumed activity in Texas.

Item 17: Enter the ending date (Saturday) of the 20th week of the calendar year in which one or more individuals performed services in Texas. In counting weeks, include any week in which anyone performed services for any portion of a day during that week. This includes part-time and temporary, as well as permanent and full-time employees. If, when counting weeks in the first calendar year of operation, you do not reach 20 weeks, begin counting again with the first week of the second calendar year and count until you reach 20 weeks in that year.

Item 18: Enter the ending date (March 31, June 30, Sept. 30, or Dec. 31) of the first calendar quarter in which wages of $1,500.00 or more were paid.

Item 19: Same as item 17 on reverse side, except that when counting weeks, include only those weeks in which 4 or more individuals performed services. The services do not have to be performed on the same day of the week, and do not have to be performed by the same employee. Also, please be sure to attach a copy of your exemption letter from the Internal Revenue Service.

Item 20: This section should be completed if you acquired all or part of your business or organization in Texas from a previous owner. Enter the TEC account number of the previous owner if you know it. Also enter the name and address of the prior owner, the date the business or part was acquired, and check the appropriate block to indicate "all" or "part" was acquired. If you check "part", describe the part acquired. If additional space is needed, please use a separate sheet and attach it to this report.

Item 21: If you have become liable for taxes to the federal government under the Federal Unemployment Compensation Act, enter your years of liability - beginning with the most recent and working backward.

Item 22: Check the appropriate block to indicate whether you employ U.S. Citizens who perform services outside the U.S.

Item 23: Enter the ending date (March 31, June 30, Sept. 30, or Dec. 31) of the calendar quarter in which $1,000.00 or more was paid to any individual(s) who perform domestic service.

Item 24: Enter a brief description of your business activity in Texas and also list the principle product(s) you produce or the service you provide.

Item 25: Select one of the items which describes your operations in Texas and enter the appropriate code in the block.

Item 26: If your employment experience does not indicate you have become liable under a compulsory provision of the Texas Unemployment Compensation Act, you may voluntarily elect coverage for your employees. To do this, check the appropriate block to indicate whether you wish to cover all employees, or only those who are not specifically exempt by one on the sections of the law which define exempt services. If you have questions concerning exempt services, please contact a TEC Field Tax office. (See your phone book for the office nearest you.)

Item 27: Indicate if you have any employment on a farm or ranch and a separate Status Report will be provided.

Item 28: This report must be signed by an owner, corporate officer, partner, or individual for whom a valid power-of-attorney is on file with the Texas Employment Commission.

1b. Employer's Quarterly Report

TEXAS EMPLOYMENT COMMISSION
AUSTIN, TEXAS 78714-9037
(512)-463-2222

11111

EMPLOYER'S QUARTERLY REPORT

1.ACCOUNT NUMBER	2.COUNTY CODE	3.TAX AREA	4.TAX RATE	5.SIC CODE	6.FEDERAL I.D. NUMBER	7.QTR. YR.
			%			

8.EMPLOYER NAME AND ADDRESS

9.TELEPHONE NUMBER

You must FILE this return even though you had no payroll this quarter. If you had no payroll show '0' in item 13 and sign the declaration (Item 24) on this form.

ALIGNMENT

9A.QUARTER ENDING

9B.PENALTIES WILL BE ASSESSED IF REPORT IS NOT POSTMARKED BY

1st Month	2nd Month	3rd Month

10.Enter in the boxes above the number of employees employed in the pay periods that include the 12th day of the calendar month. (ENTER NUMERALS ONLY)

11.SHOW THE COUNTY CODE (see list on the back of this form) in which you had the greatest number of employees.

12.IF you have employees in more than one county in TEXAS, how many are outside the county shown in Item 11?

	DOLLARS	CENTS
13. Total Wages Paid During this Quarter to Texas Employees		
14. Taxable Wages paid this quarter to each employee up to the annual maximum amount ($7000/1987; $8000/1988; $9000/1989 and after) (If none enter "0").		
15. Tax Due (Multiply Taxable Wages By Tax Rate)		
16. Penalty 14(a), If Tax Is Past Due		
17. Penalty 14(c)(1), If Report Is Past Due		
18. Balance Due From Prior Periods (Subtract Credit Or Add Debit)		
19. Total Due - Make Remittance Payable To TEXAS EMPLOYMENT COMMISSION		

FOR TEC USE ONLY

PRINT YOUR NUMERALS LIKE THIS

0 1 2 3 4 5 6 7 8 9

	MONTH	DAY	YEAR
POSTMARK DATE C3			
POSTMARK DATE $			
EX DATE C3			
EX DATE $			

DOLLARS	CENTS	INITIALS

AMOUNT RECEIVED

	20.SOCIAL SECURITY NUMBER		1ST INIT	2ND INIT	21.EMPLOYEE NAME LAST NAME		22.TOTAL WAGES PAID THIS QUARTER
1							
2							
3							
4							
5							
6							
7							
8							
9							
10							

23. PAGE TOTAL

24. I DECLARE that the information herein is true and correct to the best of my knowledge and belief.

SIGNATURE ______________________

TITLE ______________ DATE ______________

PREPARERS NAME ______________________

PREPARERS PHONE NUMBER ______________________

MAIL REPORT AND REMITTANCE TO:

CASHIER-T.E.C.
P.O. BOX 149037
AUSTIN, TEXAS 78714-9037

DO NOT STAPLE REPORT

(Write Account No. On Check)

FORM C-3 (3/91)
SCAN3

NOTE: The County Code listed in Item 2 refers only to your mailing address. You should complete Item 11 to show the County Code in which you had the greatest number of employees.

Several Texas counties have names identical to cities located in other counties. For instance, the city of Houston is located in Harris County, Tyler in Smith County and Austin in Travis County. Please use county name and the code number which follows it.

COUNTY	CODE
Anderson	001
Andrews	003
Angelina	005
Aransas	007
Archer	009
Armstrong	011
Atascosa	013
Austin COUNTY	015
Bailey	017
Bandera	019
Bastrop	021
Baylor	023
Bee	025
Bell	027
Bexar	029
Blanco	031
Borden	033
Bosque	035
Bowie	037
Brazoria	039
Brazos	041
Brewster	043
Briscoe	045
Brooks	047
Brown	049
Burleson	051
Burnet	053
Caldwell	055
Calhoun	057
Callahan	059
Cameron	061
Camp	063
Carson	065
Cass	067
Castro	069
Chambers	071
Cherokee	073
Childress	075
Clay	077
Cochran	079
Coke	081
Coleman	083
Collin	085
Collingsworth	087
Colorado	089
Comal	091
Comanche	093
Concho	095
Cooke	097
Coryell	099
Cottle	101
Crane	103
Crockett	105
Crosby	107
Culberson	109
Dallam	111
Dallas	113
Dawson	115
Deaf Smith	117
Delta	119
Denton	121
DeWitt	123
Dickens	125
Dimmit	127
Donley	129
Duval	131
Eastland	133
Ector	135
Edwards	137
Ellis	139
El Paso	141
Erath	143
Falls	145
Fannin	147
Fayette	149
Fisher	151
Floyd	153
Foard	155
Fort Bend	157
Franklin	159
Freestone	161
Frio	163
Gaines	165
Galveston	167
Garza	169
Gillespie	171
Glasscock	173
Goliad	175
Gonzales	177
Gray	179
Grayson	181
Gregg	183
Grimes	185
Guadalupe	187
Hale	189
Hall	191
Hamilton	193
Hansford	195
Hardeman	197
Hardin	199
Harris	201
Harrison	203
Hartley	205
Haskell	207
Hays	209
Hemphill	211
Henderson	213
Hidalgo	215
Hill	217
Hockley	219
Hood	221
Hopkins	223
Houston COUNTY	225
Howard	227
Hudspeth	229
Hunt	231
Hutchinson	233
Irion	235
Jack	237
Jackson	239
Jasper	241
Jeff Davis	243
Jefferson	245
Jim Hogg	247
Jim Wells	249
Johnson	251
Jones	253
Karnes	255
Kaufman	257
Kendall	259
Kenedy	261
Kent	263
Kerr	265
Kimble	267
King	269
Kinney	271
Kleberg	273
Knox	275
Lamar	277
Lamb	279
Lampasas	281
La Salle	283
Lavaca	285
Lee	287
Leon	289
Liberty	291
Limestone	293
Lipscomb	295
Live Oak	297
Llano	299
Loving	301
Lubbock	303
Lynn	305
McCulloch	307
McLennan	309
McMullen	311
Madison	313
Marion	315
Martin	317
Mason	319
Matagorda	321
Maverick	323
Medina	325
Menard	327
Midland	329
Milam	331
Mills	333
Mitchell	335
Montague	337
Montgomery	339
Moore	341
Morris	343
Motley	345
Nacogdoches	347
Navarro	349
Newton	351
Nolan	353
Nueces	355
Ochiltree	357
Oldham	359
Orange	361
Palo Pinto	363
Panola	365
Parker	367
Parmer	369
Pecos	371
Polk	373
Potter	375
Presido	377
Rains	379
Randall	381
Reagan	383
Real	385
Red River	387
Reeves	389
Refugio	391
Roberts	393
Robertson	395
Rockwall	397
Runnels	399
Rusk	401
Sabine	403
San Augustine	405
San Jacinto	407
San Patricio	409
San Saba	411
Schleicher	413
Scurry	415
Shackelford	417
Shelby	419
Sherman	421
Smith	423
Somervell	425
Starr	427
Stephens	429
Sterling	431
Stonewall	433
Sutton	435
Swisher	437
Tarrant	439
Taylor	441
Terrell	443
Terry	445
Throckmorton	447
Titus	449
Tom Green	451
Travis	453
Trinity	455
Tyler COUNTY	457
Upshur	459
Upton	461
Uvalde	463
Val Verde	465
Van Zandt	467
Victoria	469
Walker	471
Waller	473
Ward	475
Washington	477
Webb	479
Wharton	481
Wheeler	483
Wichita	485
Wilbarger	487
Willacy	489
Williamson	491
Wilson	493
Winkler	495
Wise	497
Wood	499
Yoakum	501
Young	503
Zapata	505
Zavala	507

NOTE: Employers having 50 or more employees in Texas outside of that Texas county in which the largest number of employees is located (as reported in Item 11) are required to file Form C-97, Employer's Area Employment Report. Form C-97 should be submitted each quarter along with Form C-3, Employer's Quarterly Report. If you meet these reporting requirements and have not received Forms C-97, please request them.

22222

TEXAS EMPLOYMENT COMMISSION
AUSTIN, TEXAS 78714-9037
(512)-463-2222

EMPLOYER'S QUARTERLY REPORT CONTINUATION SHEET

1.ACCOUNT NUMBER	2.COUNTY CODE	3.TAX AREA	4.TAX RATE	5.SIC CODE	6.FEDERAL I.D. NUMBER	7.QTR. YR.
			%			

8.EMPLOYER NAME

9A.PAGE NO.	9B.UNIT NUMBER
______ OF ______	

☐☐☐ ALIGNMENT

	20.SOCIAL SECURITY NUMBER	1ST INIT	2ND INIT	21.EMPLOYEE NAME LAST NAME	22.TOTAL WAGES PAID THIS QUARTER
1					
2					
3					
4					
5					
6					
7					
8					
9					
10					
11					
12					
13					
14					
15					
16					
17					
18					
19					
20					
21					
22					
23					

RETURN THIS PAGE IF NEEDED TO COMPLETE REPORT

23. PAGE TOTAL

FORM C-4 (6/89)
SCANC4

1c. Instructions for Regular Taxed Employers

C-3 INSTRUCTIONS FOR REGULAR TAXED EMPLOYERS

IF YOU DID NOT PAY WAGES IN A CALENDAR QUARTER, YOU MUST SUBMIT A SIGNED REPORT GIVING THAT INFORMATION. IF YOU ARE NO LONGER IN BUSINESS OR IF THERE HAS BEEN A CHANGE OF ADDRESS, PHONE NUMBER, OWNERSHIP OR OTHER CHANGE, PLEASE COMPLETE THE CHANGE SHEET PRINTED ON THE BACK OF THESE INSTRUCTIONS AND RETURN IT TO THE TEXAS EMPLOYMENT COMMISSION WITH YOUR QUARTERLY REPORT.

THESE FORMS WILL BE READ BY OPTICAL SCANNING MACHINES. THEREFORE, PLEASE TYPE ENTRIES USING A TYPEWRITER OR PRINTER WITH 10 to 12 CHARACTERS PER INCH. PLEASE USE BLACK INK. Type an "X" in the alignment box to line up your typewriter or printer correctly. Do not use dollar signs, decimal points or leading zeros. If you will be preparing the wages list by computer, contact the nearest Texas Employment Commission Tax Office for a Computer Specification Sheet.

Complete the following unless the information has been preprinted:

1. Enter your Texas Employment Commission account number.
2. Enter county code from the list printed on the back of the tax report.
3. Leave this space blank.
4. Enter your tax rate. If you have not been assigned a tax rate, contact the nearest Texas Employment Commission Tax Office.
5. Leave this space blank.
6. Enter your Federal Employer Identification Number. If none has been assigned, leave blank.
7. Enter the quarter and year (1st Quarter 1989 = 1-89)
8. Enter the name of your business and your mailing address. If your business is a sole proprietorship or partnership, include the name(s) of the owner or partners.
9. If your telephone number is not printed on the form or if the printed number is incorrect, please enter the correct number in the appropriate box on the back of this form.
   A. Enter the ending date of the calendar quarter during which you paid the wages being reported (1st Quarter 1989 = 3-31-89)
   B. Enter the last day of the month after the end of the quarter.
   If you are a new employer filing for the first time, contact your nearest Texas Employment Commission Tax Office for instructions.
10. Enter the total number of Texas employees on the twelfth day of each of the three months in the calendar quarter.
11. Enter the county code of the county in which you had the greatest number of employees. (See list on the back of the quarterly report.)
12. If you had employees in more than one Texas county, enter the number of employees outside the county shown in block 11.
13. Enter the total amount of remuneration (including wages, commissions and bonuses) paid during the quarter. Include amounts paid in cash, plus the value of remuneration paid in any medium other than cash. Effective January 1, 1986, all tip income, including charged tips, reported in writing by an employee to his or her employer are wages. Payments made to corporate officers for services performed are wages and should be reported.
14. Enter the amount of taxable wages paid to each employee during this quarter. For 1987 and prior years only the first $7000 of wages paid to each employee during the calendar year are taxable. For 1988 only the first $8000 of wages paid to each employee during the calendar year are taxable and for 1989 and after only the first $9000 of wages paid to each employee during the calendar year are taxable.
15. Enter the amount of tax due. To determine the tax due for the current quarter, multiply amount entered in item 14 by item 4, tax rate.
16. Enter penalty due if payment is late (postmarked after the due date in item 9B). Multiply tax due (item 15) by 1.5% for each month past due to a maximum of 25% if due prior to 9-1-89 and 37.5% thereafter. See worksheet on back.
17. Enter penalty due if the report is late (postmarked after the due date). Use the worksheet to figure late reporting penalty or call your nearest Texas Employment Commission Tax Office.
18. Enter any past-due amounts or credits as shown on the Employer's Statement of Account (monthly billing statement). If you discover an error on a previously reported quarter, contact your nearest Texas Employment Commission Tax Office for instructions for making the adjustment. Do not attempt to make the adjustment on this form.
19. Add tax and penalty, add or subtract amounts previously due or credited. (Add items 15, 16, 17 and add or subtract item 18.)

When you need to report wages for more than ten employees, please use a continuation sheet for all wage information rather than listing part of the employees on Form C-3. You may use separate continuation sheets to report all of your employees if you wish.

20. Enter employee's nine-digit social security number.
21. Enter first initial, second initial, and employees last name.
22. Enter the total amount of remuneration (including wages, commissions, bonuses and reported tips) paid to each Texas employee. If you have more than 10 employees, contact the nearest Texas Employment Commission Tax Office for enough continuation sheets to list all of your employees.
23. Enter total of amounts listed in item 22.
24. Sign report and enter title. This report must be signed by an owner, partner or officer of the employing unit, or by a person for whom a power of attorney has been filed with the Texas Employment Commission.

Keep a copy of this report for your file.
PLEASE WRITE YOUR TEC ACCOUNT NUMBER ON YOUR CHECK
DO NOT STAPLE YOUR CHECK TO YOUR REPORT.

C-3 Instruction (990) Front

Texas Employment Commission
P.O. Box 149037
Austin, Texas 78714-9037
(512) 463-2222

IF YOUR BUSINESS OR EMPLOYMENT HAS BEEN DISCONTINUED OR IF OWNERSHIP OR NAME OR ADDRESS HAS CHANGED, OR IF YOUR ACCOUNT NUMBER, FEDERAL ID NUMBER OR TELEPHONE NUMBER HAS BEEN OMITTED OR IS INCORRECT ON YOUR PRE-PRINTED FORM, PLEASE FILL IN YOUR ACCOUNT NUMBER, ENTER YOUR CORRECTIONS AND RETURN THIS ENTIRE PAGE WITH YOUR TAX REPORT.

ACCOUNT NUMBER

Enter corrections:

Telephone Number	Federal ID Number

Enter changes below

Name: ____________________

Trade Name: ____________________

Address: ____________________

If you have discontinued employment, complete the appropriate items below:

☐ Business discontinued, no successor

☐ Business continued without employment

☐ Business acquired by a successor.

Enter the date of acquisition ____________

Date of last employment: ____________

Date Final Wages Paid: ____________

If your business was acquired by a successor, complete the following:

Successor Name: ____________

Successor Address: ____________

Successor Account Number: ____________

Was all or part of the business acquired? All________ Part ________

Which part was acquired? ____________

SIGNATURE DATE

THE FOLLOWING WORKSHEET IS INCLUDED FOR YOUR CONVENIENCE IN COMPUTING THE AMOUNT OF PENALTY DUE IF YOUR REPORT AND/OR PAYMENT IS LATE

A. COMPUTATION OF PENALTY FOR LATE PAYMENT: In accordance with Subsection 14(a) of the TUC Act, penalty for late payment of taxes is assessed at a rate of one and one-half percent (1.5%) of the amount of tax for each month or part of a month elapsed after the final due date. (Maximum penalty is 25% on taxes due prior to 9-1-89 and is 37.5% 9-1-89 forward.)

________ x .015 = ________ x ________ = ________
No. of months — Max = .375 — Amt. from Line 15 — Line 16 penalty

B. COMPUTATION OF PENALTY FOR LATE REPORT: This is in accordance with Subsection 14(c)(1) of the TUC Act. Select the period which applies to this report, compute penalty and enter in line 17.

1. Report is filed during the first 15 days after the final due date. PENALTY = *$15.00

2. Report is filed after 15 days but not later than the last day of the month after the final due date. Compute as follows:

   ________ x .0005 = ________ + *$30.00 = ________
   Amt. from Line 14 — (Line 17 penalty)

3. Report is filed during the 2nd month after the final due date

   ________ x .0015 = ________ + *$60.00 = ________
   Amt. from Line 14 — (Line 17 penalty)

4. Report is filed during or after the 3rd month after the final due date.

   ________ x .0035 = ________ + *$90.00 = ________
   Amt. from Line 14 — (Line 17 penalty)

*If report was due prior to 9-1-89, these dollar amounts are $5.00; $10.00; $20.00 and $30.00, respectively.

C-3 INSTRUCTIONS (990) Back

1d. Information Concerning Temporary Employees

The Texas Employment Commission

AT WORK

A MEMO TO TEXAS EMPLOYERS

Mary Scott Nabers
Commissioner
For Employers
1-800-TEC-MARY

TEMPORARY EMPLOYEES

Many employers continue to have the mistaken idea that a person hired for a temporary job cannot file for unemployment benefits at the end of that job.

THIS IS NOT TRUE!

The Texas Unemployment Compensation Act does not distinguish between temporary, permanent, full-time, part-time, or probationary employees. Anyone on your payroll is, under the law and for better or worse, your employee.

When a temporary job is finished, the worker who performed that job is LAID OFF FOR LACK OF WORK. This kind of job termination will NOT disqualify the worker from receiving unemployment benefits if he or she files a claim.

Whether your company will have any immediate financial liability on this kind of claim depends upon how long the person worked for you. Only BASE PERIOD EMPLOYERS have potential liability on a claim because only wages earned in the base period are used to calculate the benefit amount.

What this means, simply, is that even though the claimant draws benefits, your company will not necessarily be charged back for those benefits. How do you determine if you are or will be a base period employer when that temporary job ends? Well, first you assume a claim date and then you count backward by calendar quarters.

Let's say you hired Tom Temporary in October of 1987 for a five-month job. The job finishes, on schedule, in early March of 1988 and you assume Tom Temporary will promptly file a claim. Here is what Tom's base period looks like:

BASE PERIOD QUARTERS				LAG QUARTER	FILING QUARTER
4TH '86	1ST '87	2ND '87	3RD '87	4TH '87	1ST '88

Because Tom was not hired until the 4th quarter of 1987, your company would not fall within his base period. No liability on this claim. BUT! The scenario changes if Tom waits until April to file his claim because that moves everything up one quarter. Also, there is no guarantee that Tom will not file again next year. If that happens your company will show up in his new base period and we will notify you as a base period employer of your potential liability. Your company's account will be charged if the only reason for Tom's separation was lack of work.

In summary:

1. Temporary employees can file for unemployment benefits when the job is over.

2. Your company may or may not be immediately liable on the claim depending upon the length of time the person worked for you.

3. There is the POTENTIAL for unemployment claim liability on EVERY EMPLOYEE up to 18 months after termination.

TEC
Working for Everyone

2. Texas Application for Sales Tax Permit

TEXAS APPLICATION

• SALES TAX PERMIT • USE TAX PERMIT

JOHN SHARP • COMPTROLLER OF PUBLIC ACCOUNTS

GENERAL INFORMATION

WHO MUST SUBMIT THIS APPLICATION - You must submit this application if:
•you are a sole owner, partnership, corporation or other organization who intends to do business in Texas; AND
•you are selling tangible personal property or providing taxable services in Texas or to customers in Texas; and/or
•you acquire taxable goods or services from out-of-state suppliers that are not permitted in Texas.
NOTE: A separate application must be submitted for each business location.

DEFINITIONS - SALES TAX PERMIT: A sales tax permit is required for every individual or organization who makes sales, leases or rentals of merchandise or taxable services or repairs in Texas AND who has a business location in Texas.
SALES TAX PERMIT FEE: There is a $25 sales tax permit fee. Permits must be renewed annually for a $25 fee. *If you are moving an existing business location, an additional permit fee is not due.*
SALES TAX BOND: New taxpayers may need to post a bond or other security for this permit. To determine the amount of bond or security required, complete a "Texas Sales and UseTax Bond-Security Information" form, Form 01-707. Submit this application, your permit fee and form 01-707 to avoid delay in receiving your permit.
USE TAX PERMIT: This permit is required for every individual or organization who makes sales of merchandise or taxable services or repairs in Texas but does NOT have a business location in Texas, AND for out-of-state contractors improving realty in Texas with taxable merchandise purchased out of Texas. There is no use tax permit fee.
ENGAGED IN BUSINESS: You are engaged in business in Texas if you, or independent sales persons, make sales or take orders for merchandise or equipment rental; deliver merchandise or perform taxable services or repairs; or have lease equipment, a warehouse or other Texas location.
PLACE OF BUSINESS OR BUSINESS LOCATION: A business location is any store, office or location where you receive orders for taxable goods or services, including repairs, or make sales or rentals at least three times or more a year.
NOTE: If you have been selling without a permit, you will need to file returns and pay tax, plus applicable penalty and interest, for the period of time that you have been in business.

FOR ASSISTANCE - If you have any questions about this application, filing tax returns or any other tax-related matter, contact the Texas State Comptroller's Office at 1-800-252-5555 toll free nationwide, or call 512/463-4600.
(From a Telecommunication Device for the Deaf (TDD) ONLY call 1-800-248-4099 toll free, or call 512/463-4621.)

GENERAL INSTRUCTIONS •Please do not separate pages. •Print or type. •Write only in white areas. •Do not use dashes when entering Social Security, Federal Employer's Identification, Texas Taxpayer or Texas Vendor Identification Numbers. •If you are visually impaired and would like special assistance before you are mailed notices, check the box marked "yes" in the top section of page 1 of this application. •If you need instructions written in Spanish for completing sales tax returns, check the block marked "Si" in the top section of page 1 of this application. •Disclosure of your Social Security Number is required and authorized under law. It will be used for tax administration and identification of any individual affected by the law.
Legal cite: TEX. TAX CODE ANN. ch. 151, and 42 U.S.C.A. sec. 405 (c)(2)(C)(i)

SPECIFIC INSTRUCTIONS

Item 1 - SOLE OWNER - Enter first name, middle initial and last name.
PARTNERSHIP - Enter the legal name of the partnership.
CORPORATION - Enter the legal name exactly as it is registered with the Secretary of State.
OTHER ORGANIZATION - Enter the title of the organization.

Item 2 - Enter the complete mailing address where you want to receive mail from the Comptroller of Public Accounts.
NOTE: If you want to receive mail for other taxes at a different address, attach a letter with the other address(es).

Item 7 - If you have both a Texas Taxpayer Number and a Texas Vendor Identification Number, enter only the first eleven digits of the Vendor Identification Number.

Item 8 - If you check "Other," identify the type of organization. Example: Social club, Indep. School District, family trust.

Item 12 - PARTNERSHIP - Enter the information for ALL partners. If a partner is a corporation, enter the Federal Employer's Identification (FEI) Number instead of the Social Security Number.
CORPORATION OR OTHER ORGANIZATION - Enter the information for the principal officers (president, vice-president, secretary, treasurer).

Item 24 - If you will have an alcoholic beverage permit, your legal name in Item 1 on this application must be the same as your name on the alcoholic beverage permit.

Item 27 - You WILL be required to report interest earned on sales tax IF:
- you will make retail sales of taxable items on an installment purchase plan or deferred payment plan AND
- you charge interest on the entire balance, including sales tax, on the sale of taxable items made on installment purchase or deferred payment plans; AND
- you do your own financing on some accounts on which interest is charged; AND
- you include installment payments which were received during a reporting period in "TOTAL SALES" on your sales tax return for that period (i.e., you keep your records on a cash basis of accounting).

NOTE: If any ONE of the statements above does NOT apply to your business, then you will NOT be required to report interest earned on sales tax.

AP-100-1 (Rev. 1-91/8))

AP-100-2
(Rev. 1-91/8)

TEXAS APPLICATION

• SALES TAX PERMIT • USE TAX PERMIT

NOTE: Where space indicators are shown, please enter only one letter or number in each space and skip one space between words.

Page 1

If you are visually impaired, would you like special assistance from the Comptroller's Office before you are mailed notices? ☐ Yes ☐ No

¿Si necesita informacion sobre impuestos prefiere usted hablar con una persona que habla español? ☐ Sí ☐ No

TAXPAYER IDENTIFICATION

1. Legal name of owner *(Sole owner, first name, middle initial and last name; partnership, corporation or other name)*

2. Mailing address *(Street & no., P.O. Box or rural route and box no.)*

City — State — ZIP Code

County

3. If you are a sole owner, enter your home address *(Street & no., city, state, ZIP code)* if it is different from above.

3a. Enter the daytime phone number of the person primarily responsible for filing tax returns. (Area code and number) ▪ ( ) / —

4. Enter your Social Security Number if you are a sole owner. ▪ 2 — —

5. Enter your Federal Employer's Identification (FEI) Number, if any, assigned by the United States Internal Revenue Service. 1 —

3

6. If you are incorporating an existing business, enter the taxpayer number of the existing business.

7. Enter your taxpayer number for reporting any Texas tax OR your Texas Vendor Identification Number if you now have or have ever had one.

OWNERSHIP

8. Indicate how your business is owned. ☐ 1 - Sole owner ☐ 2 - Partnership ☐ 3 - Texas corporation ☐ 7 - Limited partnership ☐ Foreign corporation ☐ Other (explain)

9. If your business is a Texas corporation, enter the charter number and date. — Charter Number — Charter date *(Mo., day, year)*

10. If your business is a foreign corporation, enter home state, charter number, Texas Certificate of Authority Number & date. — Home state — Charter Number — Texas Cert. of Auth. No. — Cert. of Auth. date *(Mo., day, year)*

11. If your business is a limited partnership, enter the home state and identification number. — Home state — Identification number

PROPRIETORS

12. List all general partners or principal officers of your business. If you are a sole owner, skip Item 12. *(Attach additional sheets if necessary)*

Name *(First, initial, last)*

Social Security or Federal Employer's Identification (FEI) No. — Title — Phone *(Area code & no.)* / —

Home address *(Street & no., city, state, ZIP code)*

Name *(First, initial, last)*

Social Security or Federal Employer's Identification (FEI) No. — Title — Phone *(Area code & no.)* / —

Home address (Street & no., city, state, ZIP code)

Name *(First, initial, last)*

Social Security or Federal Employer's Identification (FEI) No. — Title — Phone *(Area code & no.)* / —

Home address *(Street & no., city, state, ZIP code)*

(Continue on Page 2)

For Comptroller's Use Only

JOB NAME - SALEAPP

Spanish/Visually impaired indicator

☐ PL12 ▪ 01150

☐ 0 - None
☐ 1 - Spanish
☐ 2 - Visually impaired
☐ 3 - Spanish and Visually impaired Indicator

Master name change

☐ PL10 ▪ 01170

☐ 0 - Send
☐ 1 - Do not send

Master account set up

☐ PL04 ▪ 01100

Master mailing address change

☐ PL06 ▪ 01180

County code

Master phone number add/change

☐ PL06 ▪ 01185

OF ☐ ☐ NR

State employee - A

Individual recipient - B

Ownership type

▪ 0 0 0 0

Partnership set up

☐ PL08 ▪ 01140

AP-100-3
(Rev. 1-91/8)

TEXAS APPLICATION

• SALES TAX PERMIT • USE TAX PERMIT

NOTE: Where space indicators are shown, please enter only one letter or number in each space and skip one space between words.

Page 2

13. Legal name of owner *(Same as Item 1)*

BUSINESS LOCATION

14. Trade name of your new business

15. Location of your business *(Use street & no. or directions - NOT P.O. Box or Rural Route no.)*

City State ZIP Code

County Business phone *(Area code & no.)* ( ) / —

ITEMS 16-21 REFER TO THE LOCATION AND CITY AND/OR COUNTY NAMED IN Item 15.

16. Is this location inside the city limits of the city named in Item 15? ☐ YES ☐ NO

17. Is this location engaged in business in cities that impose Texas city sales tax other than the city named in Item 15? ☐ YES ☐ NO

18. Is this location in a Metropolitan Transit Authority/City Transit Department (MTA/CTD)? ☐ YES ☐ NO

19. For this location, check all MTA(s)/CTD(s) in which you are engaged in business.
☐ Austin MTA ☐ Corpus Christi MTA ☐ Dallas MTA (DART) ☐ Ft. Worth MTA ☐ Houston MTA
☐ San Antonio MTA (VIA) ☐ El Paso CTD

20. If this location is in a MTA/CTD, will you be shipping outside the MTA/CTD? ☐ YES ☐ NO

21. Is this location engaged in business in counties that imposed Texas county or special purpose district (SPD) tax other than the tax imposed in the county in Item 15? ☐ YES ☐ NO

BUSINESS TYPE

22. Indicate your principal type of business.
☐ Retailer (52-59) ☐ Wholesaler (50-51) ☐ Manufacturer/processor (20-39) ☐ Service (70-89)
☐ Construction (15-17) ☐ Finance/Insurance (60-67) ☐ Other ________

23. Indicate your primary product or service that you sell.

24. If you will sell any type of alcoholic beverages, indicate the type of permit(s) you will hold - one or both. ☐ Mixed beverages ☐ Beer and wine

SALES/USE TAX

25. *Enter the date of the first business operation in this location that is subject to sales or use tax in Texas or the date you plan to start such business operation.* Date *(Mo., day, year)*

26. Is your business operated all year? ☐ YES ☐ NO If "NO," list months that you operate.

27. Will you be required to report interest earned on sales tax ? *(See instructions)* ☐ YES ☐ NO

28. Are you located out of state with representation in Texas? ☐ YES ☐ NO

29. List names and addresses of all representatives, agents, salesmen, canvassers or solicitors in Texas.

30. List location of all distribution points, warehouses or offices in Texas. *(Attach additional sheets if necessary.)*

31. Enter permit fee ($25.00). Permit fee must be paid with this application. (Make your payments payable to STATE TREASURER.) Permit fee *(See instructions)* $

(Continue on Page 3)

For Comptroller's Use Only

JOB NAME - SALEAPP

☐ PL15 ■ 00990

0 2 2 0

Outlet/location set up

☐ PL05 ■ 01300

Outlet number

County code

Jurisdiction codes
04 34 42

Business code

Permit set up

☐ PL14 ■ 01400

First taxable sale date

Permit type
☐ 1 - Sales
☐ 2 - Use

Seasons

Permit status

Filing type set up

☐ PL15 ■ 01590

Effective period

Filing type

☐ Payment received

AP-100-4
(Rev. 1-91/8)

TEXAS APPLICATION

• SALES TAX PERMIT • USE TAX PERMIT Page 3

32. Legal name of owner *(Sole owner, partnership, corporation or other name)(Same as item 1.)*

SUCCESSOR INFORMATION

If you purchased an existing business or business assets, complete Items 33-36. If you did not, skip to Item 37.

33. Enter the former owner's trade name. If known, enter the former owner's Texas taxpayer number.

Trade name | Taxpayer number of former owner

34. Enter the former owner's legal name. If known, enter the former owner's telephone number.

Legal name of former owner | Phone *(Area code & no.)* / –

Address of former owner *(Street & number, city, state, ZIP code)*

35. Check each of the following items you purchased. *(This includes the value of stock exchanged for assets.)*

☐ Inventory ☐ Corporate stock ☐ Equipment ☐ Real estate ☐ Other assets

36. Enter the purchase price of the business or assets purchased and the date of purchase.

Purchase price $ | Date of purchase *(Mo., day, year)*

For Comptroller's Use Only

OF ☐ NR ☐

Former owner is

☐ Active

☐ OOB

☐ TCR attached

☐ TCR previously submitted

SIGNATURES

The sole owner, all general partners, corporation president, vice-president, secretary or treasurer or an authorized representative must sign this application. Representative must submit a written power of attorney with application. *(Attach additional sheets if necessary.)*

Date of application *(Mo., day, year)*

37. I (We) declare that the information in this document and any attachments is true and correct to the best of my (our) knowledge and belief.

Type or print name and title of sole owner, partner or officer | **sign here** | Sole owner, partner or officer

Type or print name and title of partner or officer | **sign here** | Partner or officer

Type or print name and title of partner or officer | **sign here** | Partner or officer

YOUR PERMIT MUST BE PROMINENTLY DISPLAYED IN YOUR PLACE OF BUSINESS. THE INFORMATION ON YOUR PERMIT IS PUBLIC INFORMATION.

To expedite the receipt of your permit, complete this application and mail all pages to your nearest COMPTROLLER'S FIELD OFFICE

JOHN SHARP
COMPTROLLER OF PUBLIC ACCOUNTS
Austin, Texas 78774-0100

FIELD OFFICE

No. ______ Date ______
E.O. name ______ Destin. ______
Bond amount ______
Type of bond ☐ LOA ☐ LOC ☐ Surety ☐ Cash
T Code PYHOLD verified ☐
FALCON entered by ______

FOR COMPTROLLER'S USE ONLY
JURISDICTION CODES

TAXING STATUS	CITY (04)	MTA/CTD (34)	CNTY/SPD (42)
Outside jurisdiction limits, NO TAX	0	0	0
Outside jurisdiction limits, LIST	1	1	1
Inside jurisdiction limits, OUTLET	2	2	2
Inside jurisdiction limits, OUTLET LONG	3	3	3
Inside jurisdiction limits, LIST	4	4	4

** Circle the code that applies to this applicant's outlet location or sales/delivery operation and transfer the three digit number to the "Jurisdiction codes" on page 2 (04/34/42).*

3. What Is the Texas Comptroller of Public Accounts?

JOHN SHARP • TEXAS COMPTROLLER OF PUBLIC ACCOUNTS

What is the Texas Comptroller of Public Accounts?

The **Texas Comptroller of Public Accounts** is the state's chief fiscal officer, bookkeeper and economic forecaster. The Comptroller's Office has been part of our government since the 1835 provisional government of the Republic of Texas.

It is our job to collect every penny of taxes honestly due the state, but we also share your concerns about how state government spends your hard-earned money.

"I pledge to make sure you receive full value for each and every dollar you send to Austin. I guarantee that you will find the Comptroller's Office is a lean and efficient operation."

JOHN SHARP
Comptroller of Public Accounts

Tax Collections

The State Comptroller's Office collects 26 state taxes, including the sales, corporate franchise, motor fuels, motor vehicle sales, oil and natural gas production and inheritance taxes. Our field offices in major cities across the state take applications for tax permits and licenses and make sure delinquent taxpayers bring their accounts up to date. Auditors across Texas and in major cities in other states regularly check taxpayers' books to ensure compliance with the laws.

Government Accounting

The Comptroller's Office keeps track of the more than 500 separate revenue and spending funds that keep state government running. We write state payroll checks and process claims for payment from the State. We make sure state agencies stay within their budgets. We are developing uniform state accounting and payroll systems to improve the efficiency of all state financial operations.

Research

The Texas Constitution requires the Comptroller of Public Accounts to provide the Legislature with a sworn statement showing the financial condition of the State at the end of each fiscal year and an estimate of probable revenue for the coming fiscal year. We study the spending bills the Legislature writes to determine if enough money will be available to meet the budget. To accurately project state taxes, the Comptroller maintains an extensive research division that studies and reports on all sectors and geographic regions of Texas' rapidly diversifying economy.

Local Government

The Comptroller's Office works with local governments, which collect some of the State's taxes. The Local Government Division assists Texas cities and counties in their handling of state funds and in their budgeting, bookkeeping, cash management and purchasing procedures.

Economic Development

A new division of the Comptroller's Office is dedicated to helping local communities and businesses develop their economic potential. The Economic Development Division provides information about federal and state grant opportunities, distributes data about local economies and helps businesses find purchasing and training opportunities.

Tax Assistance

The Comptroller's Office maintains a toll-free hotline at **1-800-252-5555** for taxpayers with questions about taxes. Our taxpayer assistants answer an average of 625 calls an hour, every hour, every working day. The Comptroller's Office offers in-depth tax information to tax accountants on a special toll-free phone line. We help taxpayers comply with state tax laws and stay abreast of changes in the law. We routinely offer local seminars for new taxpayers and business groups.

JOHN SHARP • TEXAS COMPTROLLER OF PUBLIC ACCOUNTS

33 Comptroller offices in 25 cities provide convenient, courteous tax help near you...

Abilene
1290 South Willis, Suite 202
Commerce Plaza Office Bldg. 79605

Amarillo
6300 I-40 West, Suite 103 79106

Austin Central
111 West Sixth Street, Suite 101 78701

Austin North
3721 Executive Center Drive
Meredith Bldg., Suite 100 78731

Beaumont
6440 Concord 77708

Brownsville
1164 FM 802 78521

Bryan
1713 Broadmoor, Suite 300 77802

Corpus Christi
5155 Flynn Pkwy., Suite 106 78411

Dallas Northeast
1121 Rockingham Drive, Richardson 75080

Dallas Southeast
1331 East Highway 80, Suite 2
Mesquite 75150

Dallas Southwest
7222 S. Westmoreland Rd., Suite 100 75237

El Paso
1421 North Lee Trevino, Suite B-002 79936

Fort Worth North
4040 Fossil Creek Blvd., Suite 100 76137

Fort Worth South
4304-B Airport Freeway 76117

Houston North
211 Highland Cross, Suite 110 77073

Houston Northwest
1919 North Loop West, Suite 100 77008

Houston Southeast
650 FM 1959 77034

Houston Southwest
11150 South Wilcrest Dr., Suite 101 77099

Kerrville
125 Lehmann Drive, Suite A 78028

Laredo
602 East Calton Road, Suite 3 78041

Longview
1121 Judson Road, Suite 150
Judson Plaza 75601

Lubbock
2575 South Loop 289, Suite 103 79423

Lufkin
3213 South Medford (South Loop 287),
Suite 204 75901

McAllen
3231 North McColl Rd., Suite A 78501

Odessa
4682 East University, Suite 100 79762

San Angelo
3127 Executive Drive 76904

San Antonio Northwest
5825 Callaghan Road, Suite 100 78228

San Antonio Southwest
103 Southwest Military Drive 78221

Sherman
One Grand Centre Bldg., Suite 102
One Grand Avenue 75090

Tyler
2010 West Southwest, Loop 323 75701

Victoria
2004 Patterson Drive 77901

Waco
4315 Lake Shore Drive, Suite I 76710

Wichita Falls
3108 Fre Mar Valley (on Seymour Highway) 76301

For toll-free information, call 1-800-252-5555 and ask for the appropriate extension...

Tax Information (Ext. 34070)
- Open records requests
- Questions from the news media

Tax Publications (Ext. 34730)
- Distribute agency publications

Support Services (Ext. 34120)
- Bid applications

Claims (Ext. 34850)
- Inquiries regarding state payments
- Voucher status

Fund Accounting (Ext. 34992)
- Statewide accounting/reporting

Data Services (Ext. 34200)
- Data from major tax files (sales, franchise, motor vehicle, etc.)

Local Government (Ext. 34679)
- Local government financial management assistance

Tax Administration (Ext. 34677)
- Information for tax practitioners
- Exemptions for non-profit and other qualified organizations

Enforcement (Ext. 34600)
- Answer taxability questions
- Complaints of alleged tax law violations
- Certify Texas Alcoholic Beverage Commission (TABC) papers
- Certificates of Good Standing (walk in/same day)
- Permits and decals

Revenue Accounting (Ext. 34400)
- Copies of Lien Releases
- Refunds of bonds, overpayments
- Local tax allocations

Economic Development (Ext. 34911)
- State and regional economy
- Grant opportunities

Account Maintenance (Ext. 33601)
- Certificates of Good Standing (requested by mail)
- Certificates of Business Activity
- Filing and payment of taxes by EFT (electronic funds transfer)

Human Resources (Ext. 34800)
- Job Line Information
- Employment opportunities

Comptroller of Public Accounts, Tax Publications Division • Publication #96-128 – Revised June 1991.
For additional copies, write Comptroller of Public Accounts, Tax Correspondence/Account Maintenance, 111 E. 17th Street, Austin TX 78774-0100.

4. Texas Sales Tax Rates

July 1991

Texas Sales Tax Rates

JOHN SHARP — TEXAS COMPTROLLER OF PUBLIC ACCOUNTS

SPECIAL INFORMATION

New City Sales Tax
Effective July 1, 1991

2109144 Mount Calm
(Hill County, 76673)

Effective July 1, 1991,
the cities of

Arlington
Gilmer
Hamlin
Kemah
Marshall
Munday
New Boston
Sulphur Springs
Wills Point

will impose an additional 1/2% local sales tax for improving and promoting economic and industrial development.

New City Transit Department (CTD)
Effective July 1, 1991

The **City of Laredo** will impose a 1/4% transit tax.

Effective July 1, 1990, the state sales tax rate is $6^{1}/_{4}$%.

The cities listed in this brochure are subject to state tax plus one or more of the following:

- city tax
- additional city tax for property tax relief
- additional city tax for economic and industrial development
- transit tax (MTA/CTD)
- county/special purpose district tax (SPD)
- additional county tax for health services

If a city listed in this brochure is subject to an additional city tax, it also will be listed on page iii, "Additional City Sales Taxes."

Cities that also are subject to county/SPD or transit tax will have the county/SPD or authority listed below the city's name. Counties shown in parentheses, such as Cass shown in the example, are counties which have not adopted county sales tax.

Example:	**Local Code**	**Local Rate**	**Total Rate**
Abbott	2109064	(.01500)	.08250
Hill Co.	4109000	(.00500)	
Austin (Travis Co.)	2227016	(.01000)	.08000
Austin MTA	3227999	(.00750)	
Avinger (Cass Co.)	2034046	(.01000)	.07250

If you sell telecommunications services such as long distance phone service, pager services, or mobile phone services, different rules apply to the collection of local tax on telecommunications. For more information, call our toll-free number and ask for the publication #96-287.

If you have a question, contact the Comptroller's office toll-free at

1-800-252-5555
The local number is 512/463-4600.

County/Special Purpose District (SPD) Sales Tax

105 counties have imposed the 1/2% sales tax for property tax relief. One county, **Uvalde**, has imposed an additional 1/2% sales tax for **county health services**, increasing its total rate to 1%. Three county-wide hospital districts have imposed local sales tax. **Baylor County Hospital District** and **Ector County Hospital District** have imposed a 1% local sales tax and **Reeves County Hospital District** has imposed a 1/2% local sales tax.

Hospital districts will be referred to as **"Special Purpose Districts (SPDs)."** Tax collected for these districts will be collected, reported and paid as county sales tax.

Unincorporated areas of the following counties impose the 6 1/4% state sales tax plus the applicable county/special purpose district (SPD) sales tax.

County Name	1/2% For Property Tax Relief	1/2% For County Health Services	Special Purpose District	SPD Rate
Anderson	01-01-88			
Angelina	01-01-88			
Aransas	01-01-88			
Archer	01-01-88			
Atascosa	01-01-90			
Austin	01-01-88			
Bailey	01-01-88			
Bandera	01-01-88			
Bastrop	01-01-88			
Baylor Co. Hospital Dist.			01-01-91	1%
Bee	01-01-88			
Bell	01-01-88			
Blanco	01-01-88			
Bosque	01-01-88			
Bowie	01-01-88			
Brazoria	01-01-90			
Brazos	01-01-88			
Brewster	01-01-88			
Burleson	01-01-88			
Caldwell	01-01-88			
Calhoun	01-01-90			
Camp	01-01-88			
Castro	01-01-88			
Cherokee	01-01-88			
Childress	01-01-88			
Colorado	01-01-88			
Comal	01-01-88			
Comanche	01-01-88			
Concho	01-01-89			
Cooke	01-01-90			
Coryell	01-01-88			
Crosby	01-01-90			
Dawson	01-01-88			
Deaf Smith	01-01-88			
Dickens	01-01-88			
Dimmit	01-01-89			
Ector Co. Hospital Dist.			01-01-91	1%
El Paso	01-01-88			
Erath	01-01-88			
Falls	01-01-88			
Fannin	01-01-88			
Fayette	01-01-88			
Franklin	01-01-88			
Frio	01-01-89			

(continued)

County/Special Purpose District (SPD) Sales Tax *(continued)*

County Name	1/2% For Property Tax Relief	1/2% For County Health Services	Special Purpose District	SPD Rate
Gillespie	01-01-88			
Gonzales	01-01-88			
Gregg	01-01-88			
Grimes	01-01-89			
Guadalupe	01-01-88			
Hale	01-01-88			
Hamilton	01-01-88			
Hardeman	01-01-88			
Hays	01-01-88			
Hill	01-01-88			
Hood	01-01-88			
Hopkins	01-01-88			
Houston	10-01-90			
Hunt	01-01-88			
Jack	01-01-88			
Jefferson	01-01-88			
Karnes	01-01-88			
Kendall	01-01-88			
Kerr	01-01-88			
Lamar	01-01-90			
Lampasas	01-01-88			
Lee	01-01-88			
Leon	01-01-89			
Liberty	01-01-88			
Lubbock	01-01-88			
Marion	01-01-88			
Maverick	01-01-89			
McCulloch	10-01-90			
McLennan	01-01-88			
Medina	01-01-88			
Midland	01-01-88			
Milam	01-01-88			
Mitchell	01-01-88			
Morris	01-01-88			
Navarro	01-01-89			
Orange	01-01-90			
Palo Pinto	01-01-88			
Parker	01-01-88			
Polk	01-01-88			
Rains	01-01-88			
Red River	01-01-88			
Reeves Co. Hospital Dist.			01-01-91	1/2%
Runnels	01-01-88			
Sabine	01-01-88			
San Augustine	01-01-90			
San Jacinto	10-01-90			
San Saba	01-01-88			
Schleicher	01-01-89			
Scurry	01-01-88			
Smith	01-01-88			
Swisher	04-01-89			
Titus	01-01-88			
Tom Green	01-01-88			
Tyler	01-01-88			
Upshur	01-01-88			
Uvalde	01-01-88	01-01-91		
Victoria	10-01-90			
Walker	01-01-89			
Washington	01-01-88			
Webb	01-01-88			
Wharton	01-01-88			
Wise	10-01-90			
Wood	01-01-88			
Young	01-01-89			

Additional City Sales Taxes

Some cities have voted to increase their sales tax rate to 1 1/2% or 2%. The cities are listed below with an effective date for the applicable tax(es).

City Name	Additional 1/2% For Property Tax Relief	Additional 1/2% For Economic and Industrial Development
Abbott	01-01-88	
Abernathy	01-01-88	
Abilene	01-01-90	01-01-90
Alice	01-01-89	
Alpine	01-01-88	
Amarillo	10-01-90	04-01-90
Angus	01-01-89	
Arlington		07-01-91
Athens	10-01-90	10-01-90
Ballinger	01-01-90	
Beaumont	01-01-88	
Belton		01-01-91
Beverly Hills	01-01-90	
Big Spring	10-01-90	10-01-90
Blanco	01-01-88	
Boerne	10-01-90	
Borger	10-01-90	10-01-90
Boyd	10-01-90	
Breckenridge		10-01-90
Brownfield		07-01-90
Brownwood	10-01-90	10-01-90
Bryan	10-01-90	
Caldwell	01-01-88	
Cameron		01-01-91
Caney City	01-01-90	
Carls Corner	01-01-88	
Carrizo Springs	01-01-89	
Chandler	01-01-89	
Cleveland	01-01-90	
Coleman	10-01-90	10-01-90
College Station	10-01-90	
Colorado City	01-01-88	
Copperas Cove		10-01-90
Corrigan	01-01-89	
Corsicana	10-01-90	
Crosbyton	01-01-90	
Cuney	01-01-89	
Daingerfield	01-01-88	
Del Rio	01-01-88	
Devine	01-01-88	
Diboll	01-01-90	
Dickens	01-01-89	
Dimmitt	01-01-88	
Early	10-01-90	10-01-90
Edinburg	10-01-90	07-01-90
Edna	10-01-90	
Fairfield	01-01-88	
Farwell	01-01-88	
Flatonia	01-01-88	
Fredericksburg	01-01-89	
Galveston	01-01-89	
Gatesville	01-01-88	
George West	01-01-89	
Gilmer		07-01-91
Glen Rose	01-01-88	
Goliad	10-01-90	
Golinda	01-01-88	
Graford	10-01-90	
Granbury	01-01-88	
Hamlin		07-01-91
Harker Heights	01-01-90	
Harlingen	10-01-90	10-01-90
Hemphill	01-01-88	
Hempstead	01-01-88	
Hidalgo	01-01-90	04-01-90
Hudson Oaks	01-01-89	
Huntsville	01-01-88	
Ingleside	01-01-90	
Ingram	01-01-88	
Johnson City	01-01-89	
Kemah	01-01-89	07-01-91
Kennedale	01-01-88	
Kilgore		10-01-90
Killeen	01-01-90	
Kingsville	01-01-90	
Kyle	04-01-90	
La Feria		10-01-90
La Marque	10-01-90	10-01-90
Lampasas	01-01-88	
Livingston	01-01-88	
Llano	01-01-88	
Lometa	04-01-89	
Lufkin	01-01-88	
Lytle	01-01-89	
Madisonville	01-01-89	
Marble Falls	01-01-88	
Marion	01-01-88	
Marlin	01-01-89	
Marshall		07-01-91
Mathis	01-01-89	
McAllen	10-01-90	
Mercedes	10-01-90	10-01-90
Mexia	01-01-90	
Mineral Wells	01-01-90	
Mission	10-01-90	07-01-90
Munday		07-01-91
Mustang	01-01-88	
Nazareth	01-01-88	
New Boston		07-01-91
Nixon	01-01-88	
Northlake		04-01-90
Olney		10-01-90
Onalaska	01-01-88	
Orange Grove	01-01-88	
Overton		10-01-90
Palestine	01-01-88	
Palmview		10-01-90
Pearsall	01-01-88	
Pecos City	01-01-88	
Pharr	10-01-90	04-01-90
Pinehurst	01-01-90	
Plainview	01-01-88	
Pleasanton	10-01-90	
Port Isabel	01-01-90	
Port Lavaca	01-01-89	
Presidio	01-01-89	
Progreso Lakes	01-01-89	
Ralls	10-01-90	
Rhome	01-01-89	
Riverside	10-01-90	
Robinson	01-01-89	
Rosenberg	01-01-88	
Rotan	10-01-90	10-01-90
Round Rock	01-01-88	
San Augustine	01-01-88	
San Marcos	01-01-88	
Seadrift	10-01-90	
Seven Points	01-01-88	
Smithville	01-01-88	
Somerville	01-01-88	
Springtown	01-01-88	
Stamford		10-01-90
Stephenville	10-01-90	
Sulphur Springs		07-01-91
Sweetwater	10-01-90	10-01-90
Teague	10-01-90	10-01-90
Temple	10-01-90	
Terrell	10-01-90	10-01-90
Texarkana	10-01-90	
Trinity	01-01-88	
Tulia	01-01-88	
Valley View	01-01-89	
Vidor	01-01-90	
Village of Bee Cave	01-01-89	
Waco	01-01-88	
Weatherford	10-01-90	
Weslaco	10-01-90	10-01-90
Wharton	10-01-90	
Whitehouse	01-01-89	
Whitney	01-01-88	
Willow Park	01-01-88	
Wills Point		07-01-91
Winters	01-01-88	
Woodville	01-01-88	
Woodway	01-01-88	
Wylie		07-01-90
Zavalla	01-01-89	

5. Texas Sales and Use Tax Return

01-114
(Rev. 1-91. 15)

TEXAS SALES AND USE TAX RETURN

01

a. ■ 03200 • PLEASE PRINT YOUR NUMERALS LIKE THIS 0 1 2 3 4 5 6 7 8 9

• Do not staple or paper clip.
• Do not write in shaded areas.

Page 1 of

c. Taxpayer number	c. Filing period	e.	f. Due date
■		■	

IMPORTANT

g. Taxpayer name and mailing address (Make any necessary name or address changes below.)

• Black out this box if your mailing address has changed. Show changes by the preprinted information. 1.
• Black out this box if you are no longer in business. Write in the date you went out of business. 2.
• Black out this box if one of your locations is out of business or has changed its address. 3.

Make any necessary changes next to the incorrect information for any location.

h. ■ i. ■

(Make name or address changes below.)
8. Location (outlet) name and address
Outlet no. ■

1. TOTAL SALES (Whole dollars only) ■
2. TAXABLE SALES (Whole dollars only) ■
3. Cost of items you bought for your use (Whole dollars only) ■

9. AMOUNT OF TAX DUE FOR THIS OUTLET (Dollars and cents)
(Multiply "Amount subject to tax" by "TAX RATE" for each type of tax due)
TAX RATES

4. Amount subject to state tax (Item 2 plus Item 3) ■ X = 9a. State tax (include in Item 10a)
5. Amount subject to city tax ■ X = 9b. City tax (include in Item 10b)
6. Amount subject to MTA/CTD tax ■ X = 9c. MTA/CTD tax (include in Item 10c)
7. Amount subject to county/SPD tax ■ X = 9d. County/SPD tax (include in Item 10d)

j. ■ 03400	■ 02 STATE TAX - Column a	■ 04 CITY TAX - Column b	■ 34 MTA/CTD TAX - Column c	■ 42 COUNTY/SPD TAX - Column d
10. Total tax due (from all outlets or City, MTA/CTD and County/SPD supplements) ■				
11. Prepayment credit (See instructions)				
12. DISCOUNT (if filed and paid on time. See instructions)				
13. Net tax due (Item 10 minus Items 11 & 12)				
14. Penalty & Interest (See instructions)				
15. AMOUNT TO BE PAID (Item 13 plus Item 14)	15a. ■ 02 ■	15b. ■ 04 ■	15c. ■ 34 ■	15d. ■ 42 ■

16. TOTAL PAYMENT (Add Items 15a, 15b, 15c and 15d and enter the total → 16.

Taxpayer name

■ T Code ■ Taxpayer number ■ Period

For help call 1-800-252-5555 toll free.

01-114 (Rev. 1-91/15)

I declare that the information in this document and any attachments is true and correct to the best of my knowledge and belief.

sign here ▶ Taxpayer or duly authorized agent

Business phone (Area code & no.) | Date

x. ■

Make total for all taxes in Item 16 payable to: STATE TREASURER
Mail to JOHN SHARP
TEXAS COMPTROLLER OF PUBLIC ACCOUNTS
Austin, Texas 78774-0100

Form 01-114(Back)(Rev.1-91 15)

INSTRUCTIONS FOR COMPLETING TEXAS SALES AND USE TAX RETURN

WHO MUST FILE - Every person (sole owner, partnership, corporation or other organization) who is responsible for collection and/or payment of Texas Sales and Use Tax must file a sales tax return. (TEX. TAX CODE ANN. sec.151.403).

Returns must be filed for every period even if there is no amount subject to tax or any tax due. Complete and detailed records must be kept of all sales as well as any deductions claimed so that returns can be verified by a state auditor.

WHEN TO FILE - Returns must be filed on or before the 20th day of the month following each reporting period. If the due date falls on a Saturday, Sunday or legal state holiday, the next business day will be the due date.

BUSINESS CHANGES - It is your responsibility to notify the Comptroller's Office if your business changes or if you do not receive the correct forms to report your taxes. This will insure that you will receive the proper reporting forms.

FOR ASSISTANCE - For your convenience, call 1-800-252-5555 toll free nationwide, or call 512/463-4600, for any sales tax assistance or to request any forms. *(From a Telecommunication Device for the Deaf (TDD) ONLY call 1-800-248-4099, or call 512/463-4621.)*

SPECIFIC INSTRUCTIONS

Item c - Enter the taxpayer number shown on your Sales Tax Permit. If you have not received your Sales Tax Permit, enter your Social Security Number or your Federal Employer's Identification (FEI) Number in the space under Item c.

Item d - Enter the filing period of this report (monthly, quarterly or yearly) and the last day of the period. Examples: "Quarterly 03-31-91" "Monthly 01-31-91"

Item 1 - Enter the total amount of all sales, leases and rentals of tangible personal property and all labor and service charges made during the reporting period for each outlet. *Report only whole dollars. Enter "0" if no sales were made during the current reporting period.*

Item 2 - Enter the total amount of TAXABLE sales, leases and rentals of tangible personal property and TAXABLE labor and service charges made during the reporting period for each outlet. This amount is the total sales you made LESS any deductions.

NOTE: HOW TO HANDLE DEDUCTIONS (non-taxable sales): Deductions include all sales, leases and rentals of tangible personal property and labor and service charges on which you were NOT required to collect sales tax. Examples of deductions (non-taxable sales): - sales for resale, - sales to exempt organizations, - sales to persons using the merchandise in a manner exempted by law, - sales of non-taxable or exempt items, - sales of items which you ship to out-of-state locations, - bad debts, -repossessions, - returned goods, discounts and allowances on which tax has been paid, - non-taxable labor and service charges. All certificates, receipts and/or invoices verifying each deduction must be kept on file.

REMEMBER: - Subtract the total amount of all deductions from TOTAL SALES (Item 1) and enter the result in TAXABLE SALES (Item 2).
- Report whole dollars only.
- If you have no TAXABLE SALES to report, enter "0."
- DO NOT ENTER DEDUCTIONS ON THIS RETURN.

Item 3 - Enter the total amount of taxable purchases that you made for your own use. This includes your cost of any taxable item you purchased, leased or rented for your own use tax free from out-of-state or in-state sellers. It also includes items you took out of your inventory for your own business or personal use. Do not enter any items that you hold in inventory exclusively for resale. Report whole dollars only. If none, enter "0." Examples of taxable purchases: - items given away for promotional purposes, - items purchased, leased or rented for an exempt use but actually used in a taxable manner, - machinery, equipment, capital assets and other taxable items purchased or rented for use from a Texas or out-of-state seller who failed to collect Texas sales and use tax, - items given away as gifts, - taxable labor or services purchased for business or personal use.

Items 5, 6 and 7 - Enter the amounts subject to applicable tax for each outlet: city (Item 5), MTA/CTD (Item 6) and/or county/SPD (Special Purpose District), (Item 7).

- If "USE LIST" IS PRINTED IN 9b, 9c or 9d, DO NOT ENTER ANY AMOUNT IN THE CORRESPONDING ITEMS 5, 6 OR 7. If there is an amount subject to the city, MTA/CTD and/or county/SPD tax for that outlet, enter the amount next to the appropriate local taxing unit on the enclosed "Texas Sales and Use Tax Return Supplement," form 01-116. *An entry is required for each local taxing unit marked with an asterisk (*) even if the amount is zero.* Return the supplement with your sales and use tax return.

- If "NOT APPLICABLE" is printed in Item 9b, 9c or 9d, DO NOT ENTER ANY AMOUNT IN ITEM 5, 6 OR 7.

Item 8 - Enter the five-digit outlet number shown on your Sales Tax Permit for each outlet you are reporting. If you do not have a permit, leave outlet number blank.
- Enter the trade name and actual location for each outlet. Use street address or meaningful directions. Do not use P.O. Box or Rural Route Number. Example: "3 miles south of FM 1960 on Jones Road."
- If any outlet is out of business, enter "Out of business" and date of closing next to the outlet.
- If a new outlet has been opened, enter the outlet trade name, actual location, opening date and a brief description of the business.

Item 11 - FOR PREPAYERS ONLY - The amount preprinted in Item 11 includes allowable prepayment discount for filing your return and paying the tax due on or before the due date. (If you prepaid timely and the amount is not printed here, calculate the credit by dividing the amount you paid by .9825 and enter the result in Item 11.)
- If you are filing your return and paying the tax late, mark out the printed amount and enter the actual amount you paid with your prepayment report.

DETERMINE THE ADDITIONAL TAX DUE OR THE OVERPAYMENT AMOUNT.

NOTE: If the difference between Item 10 and Item 11 is a credit in any of the tax columns and additional tax is due on this report, include the credit in Item 11 of the column(s) where additional tax is due.

- If Item 10 is GREATER THAN Item 11, multiply the difference by 1/2 of 1% (.005) and enter the result in Item 12. CONTINUE WITH Item 13.
- If Item 10 is LESS THAN Item 11 and the credit is to be refunded, multiply the difference by .9825 and enter the result in Item 13. SKIP Item 12.
- If Item 10 is LESS THAN Item 11 and the credit is to be taken on a future report, enter the credit in Item 13. SKIP Item 12.

DO NOT TAKE THE 1/2 of 1% DISCOUNT ON CREDIT BALANCES.

Item 12 - If you are filing your return and paying the tax due on or before the due date, enter 1/2 of 1% (.005) of the tax due (Item 10 minus Item 11). *(PREPAYERS: See instructions for Item 11.)*

Item 14 - If you are filing your return or paying the tax due AFTER the due date, enter penalty and interest. *Minimum penalty is $1 for each tax.*

PENALTY: If 1-30 days late, enter 5% of Item 13. If more than 30 days late, enter 10% of Item 13.

INTEREST: If any tax due is unpaid 61 days after the due date, enter 10% penalty PLUS interest calculated at the rate of 10% per annum on Item 13.

5a. Rule 3.335—Filing Reports

STATE OF TEXAS

COMPTROLLER OF PUBLIC ACCOUNTS

STATE SALES AND USE TAX

Rule 3.335. Filing Reports. (Texas Tax Code §§151.401, 151.402, 151.405, 151.406, 151.409).

(a) Monthly filing. The sales and use taxes are due and payable on or before the 20th day of the month following the end of each calendar month. Every taxpayer required to file city, county, and Metropolitan Transit Authority/City Transit Department (MTA/CTD) sales and use tax returns must file them at the same time the state sales and use tax returns are filed. Returns must be filed on a monthly basis unless a taxpayer qualifies as a quarterly filer or prepays tax on a quarterly basis. See subsections (b) and (e)(3) of this rule.

(b) Quarterly filing. A taxpayer who owes less than $1,500 in tax for any calendar quarter is required to file a return and pay the tax on or before the 20th day of the month following the end of the calendar quarter. Local (city, county, and MTA/CTD) liability is not included in determining the requirement for quarterly filing; however, every taxpayer required to file city, county, and MTA/CTD sales and use tax returns must file them at the same time the state sales and use tax returns are filed.

(c) Yearly filing.

(1) A taxpayer having less than $1,000 state sales and use tax to report during a calendar year may request authorization from the Comptroller's office to file returns on a yearly basis.

(2) Authorization to file returns on a yearly basis will be conditioned on the correct filing of prior returns.

(3) Authorization to file returns on a yearly basis will be denied if a taxpayer's liability exceeded $1,000 in the prior calendar year.

(4) A taxpayer filing on a yearly basis without authorization will be liable for applicable penalty and interest on any previously unreported quarter.

(5) Authority to file on a yearly basis is automatically revoked if a taxpayer's state sales and use tax liability is greater than $1,000 during a calendar year. The taxpayer must file a return for that month or quarter, depending on the amount, in which the liability is greater than $1,000. On that report, the taxpayer must report all accrued liability for the year and must file monthly or quarterly, as appropriate, as long as the yearly tax liability is greater than $1,000.

(6) Once each year all accounts will be reviewed to confirm yearly filing status and to authorize permit holders who meet the filing requirements to begin filing yearly returns.

(7) Yearly filers must report on a calendar year basis. The return and payment are due on or before January 20th of the next calendar year.

(d) State agencies. State agencies that deposit taxes directly into the State Treasury according to Accounting Policy Statement Number 12 are not required to file a separate tax return. A fully completed deposit request voucher is deemed to be the return filed by these agencies. Subsections (a), (b), and (c) of this rule do not apply to these state agencies. Taxes must be deposited into the State Treasury within the time period otherwise specified by law for deposit of state funds.

(e) Filing the return.

(1) The return for each reporting period must reflect the total sales, taxable sales, and taxable purchases for each outlet. The 0.5% discount for timely filing and payment may be claimed on the return for each reporting period and computed on the amount timely reported and paid with that return.

(2) The Comptroller will make forms available to all persons required to file returns. The failure of the taxpayer to obtain the forms will not relieve that taxpayer from the requirement to file and remit the tax timely.

(3) Prepayments may be made by taxpayers who file monthly or quarterly returns. The amount of the prepayment should be a reasonable estimate of the state and local tax liability for the entire reporting period. "Reasonable estimate" means at least 90% of the total amount due or an amount equal to the actual net tax liability due and paid for the same reporting period of the immediately preceding year.

(A) The monthly prepayment is due on or before the 15th day of the month for which the prepayment is made. Prepayments earn an additional 1.25% discount.

(B) The quarterly prepayment is due on or before the 15th day of the second month of the quarter for which the tax is due. See Rule 3.286 concerning Seller's and Purchaser's Responsibilities. Prepayments earn an additional 1.25% discount each quarter.

(4) Remittances which are less than a reasonable estimate as required by paragraph (3) of this subsection will not be regarded as a prepayment. The 1.25% discount will not be allowed. If the taxpayer owes more than $1,500 in a calendar quarter, the taxpayer will be regarded as a monthly filer. All monthly reports not filed because of the invalid prepayment will be subject to late filing penalty and interest.

(5) Filing late payments or filing late returns will cause all discounts to be disallowed and penalties for late filing or payment will be imposed. Reports filed late will result in disallowance of the prepayment discount.

(f) Direct payment. Yearly and quarterly filing requirements, prepayment procedures and discounts for timely filing do not apply to holders of direct payment permits. See Rule 3.288 concerning Direct Payment Procedures and Qualifications. Direct payment returns and remittances are due monthly on or before the 20th day of the month following the end of the calendar month for which payment is made.

Effective Date: November 6, 1990
Filed with Secretary of State: October 16, 1990

JOHN SHARP
Comptroller of Public Accounts

5b. Rule 3.286—Seller and Purchaser's Responsibilities

STATE OF TEXAS

COMPTROLLER OF PUBLIC ACCOUNTS

STATE SALES AND USE TAX

Rule 3.286. Seller's and Purchaser's Responsibilities. (Texas Tax Code §§111.0046, 151.008, 151.024, 151.051, 151.054, 151.103, 151.107, 151.202, 151.203).

(a) Definitions.

(1) Engaged in business. A retailer is engaged in business in Texas if the retailer is:

(A) maintaining, occupying, or using, permanently or temporarily, directly, or indirectly, or through an agent, by whatever name called, an office, place of distribution, sales or sample room, warehouse or storage place or other place of business;

(B) having any representative, agent, salesperson, canvasser, or solicitor operating in this state under the authority of the seller for the purpose of selling, delivering, or taking orders for any taxable items;

(C) promoting a flea market, trade day, or other event involving the sales of taxable items;

(D) utilizing independent salespersons in direct sales of taxable items by a company, corporation or other person;

(E) deriving receipts from a lease of tangible personal property located in this state;

(F) soliciting orders for taxable items by means of advertising that is broadcast from, printed at, or distributed from, a location in this state if the advertising is intended for consumers in this state and is only secondarily disseminated to bordering jurisdictions. Advertising will be considered to be intended for Texas consumers if 75% or more of the recipients are located in Texas;

(G) soliciting orders for taxable items by mail if:

(i) the solicitations are substantial and recurring; and

(ii) the retailer uses any banking, financing, debt collection, telecommunication, or marketing activities occurring in Texas, or benefits from a location in Texas of authorized installations, servicing, or repair facilities. A retailer located outside the state who is not otherwise engaged in business in this state will not be considered as engaging in business in this state by merely placing a request for financing, telecommunication, banking, marketing or debt collection services at an out-of-state location of a service provider even though the service is performed in whole or in part in Texas.

(H) allowing a franchisee or licensee to operate under its trade name if the franchisee or licensee is required to collect Texas sales or use tax; or

(I) soliciting orders for taxable items by mail or other media and federal law permits the state of Texas to require the retailer to collect Texas sales or use tax.

(2) Place of business of the seller - For tax permit requirement purposes means an established outlet, office or location operated by the seller, his agent or employee for the purpose of receiving orders for taxable items. A warehouse, storage yard, or manufacturing plant may not be considered a "place of business of the seller" for tax permit requirement purposes unless three or more orders are received by the seller in a calendar year at the warehouse, storage yard, or manufacturing plant.

(3) Seller - Every retailer, wholesaler, distributor, manufacturer or any other person who sells, leases, rents or transfers ownership of taxable items for a consideration. A promoter of a flea market, trade day or other event involving the sales of taxable items is a seller and is responsible for the collection and remittance of the sales tax collected by dealers, salespersons, or individuals at such events unless the participants hold active sales tax permits issued by the Comptroller. A direct sales organization engaged in business as defined in paragraph (1)(D) of this subsection is a seller and is responsible for the collection and remittance of the sales tax collected by the independent salespersons selling the organization's product.

(4) Special purpose district - A district funded by a sales tax that is governed by the County Sales and Use Tax Act, Chapter 323.

(b) Permits required.

(1) Every seller must apply to the Comptroller for a tax permit for each place of business.

(2) Every out-of-state seller engaged in business in this state must apply to the Comptroller for a tax permit.

(3) Independent salespersons of direct sales organizations will not be required to hold sales tax permits.

(c) Obtaining a permit.

(1) An application will be furnished by the Comptroller and must be filled out completely. After the application is filled out and returned to the Comptroller, together with whatever bond or other security is required by Rule 3.327 concerning Taxpayer's Bond or Other Security, a separate permit under the same account will be issued to the applicant for each place of business. The permit fee is $25.

(2) Each legal entity (corporation, partnership, sole proprietor, etc.) must apply for its own permit. The permit cannot be transferred from one owner to another. It is valid only for the person to whom it was issued and for the transaction of business only at the address shown on the permit. The permit must be renewed yearly on the date of issuance or renewal. The fee for renewal is $25 for each place of business. If a person operates two or more types of business under the same roof, only one permit is needed. It is the seller's responsibility to send an application for renewal and the permit fee to the Comptroller no later than the 30th day before the expiration date shown on the permit. Failure to renew causes automatic expiration on the renewal date and the seller is considered to be operating without a permit which is a misdemeanor punishable by a fine of not more than $500 per day.

(3) The permit must be conspicuously displayed at the place of business for which it is issued. However, a person who has traveling salesmen operating from one central office needs only one permit, which must be displayed at the central office.

(4) All permits of the seller will have the same taxpayer number; however, each business location will have a different outlet number. The outlet numbers assigned may not necessarily correspond to the number of business locations owned by a taxpayer.

(d) Collection and remittance of the tax.

(1) Each seller must collect the tax on each separate retail sale in accordance with the statutory bracket system. Copies of the bracket system should be displayed in each place of business so both the seller and the customers may easily use them. The tax is a debt of the purchaser to the seller until collected.

(2) The sales tax applies to each total sale, not to each item of each sale. For example, if two items are purchased, each costing $.07, the seller must collect the tax on the total selling price of $.14.

(3) The amount of the sales tax must be separately stated on the bill, contract or invoice to the customer or there must be a written statement to the customer that the stated price includes tax. Out-of-state sellers must identify the tax as Texas tax.

(4) It is unlawful for any seller to advertise or hold out to the public that the seller will assume, absorb, or refund any portion of the tax, or that the seller will not add the tax to the selling price of the taxable items being sold.

(5) The practice of rounding off the amount of tax due on the sale of a taxable item is prohibited. Tax must be added to the sales price according to the statutory bracket system.

(e) Payment of the tax.

(1) Each seller or purchaser owing tax not collected by a seller must remit tax on all receipts from the sales or purchases of taxable items less any applicable deductions. On or before the 20th day of the month following each reporting period, each person subject to the tax shall file a consolidated return together with the tax payment for all businesses operating under the same taxpayer number.

(2) The returns must be signed by the person required to file the report or by the person's duly authorized agent, but need not be verified by oath.

(3) The returns will be filed on forms prescribed by the Comptroller. The fact that the seller or purchaser does not receive the form or does not receive the correct forms from the Comptroller for the filing of the return does not relieve the seller or purchaser of the responsibility of filing a return and payment of the required tax.

(f) Reporting period.

(1) Sellers and purchasers owing tax not collected by sellers who have less than $1,500 in state tax per quarter to report may file returns quarterly. The quarterly reporting periods end on March 31st, June 30th, September 30th, and December 31st. The returns are to be filed on or before the 20th day of the month following the period ending date.

(2) Sellers and purchasers owing tax not collected by sellers having less than $1,000 state tax to report during a year may file yearly returns. The yearly reporting period ends on December 31st. See Rule 3.335 concerning Filing Reports. Yearly returns are to be filed on or before the 20th day of January.

(3) Sellers and purchasers owing tax not collected by sellers who have $1,500 or more in state tax per quarter to report must file monthly returns unless a seller prepays the tax. See Rule 3.335 concerning Filing Reports.

(g) Records required.

(1) Records must be kept for four years, unless the Comptroller authorizes in writing a shorter retention period. Exemption and resale certificates must be kept for four years following the completion of the last sale covered by the certificate. See Rule 3.281 concerning Records Required; Information Required and Rule 3.282 concerning Auditing Taxpayer Records.

(2) The Comptroller or an authorized representative has the right to examine any records or equipment of any person liable for the tax in order to verify the accuracy of any return made or to determine the tax liability in the event no return is filed.

(h) Prepaying the tax; discounts.

(1) Each seller may retain 0.5% of the amount of tax due as reimbursement for the expense of collecting the tax.

(2) A taxpayer who makes a prepayment based upon an estimate of tax liability may retain an additional 1.25% of the amount due. The prepayment must be made on or before the 15th day of the second month (February, May, August, and November) of the quarter for which the tax is due. Monthly prepayments are due on or before the 15th day of the month and are also entitled to the additional 1.25% deduction.

(A) On or before the 20th day of the month following the quarter for which a prepayment was made, the taxpayer must file a return showing the actual liability and remit any amount due in excess of the prepayment. If there is an additional amount due, the taxpayer may retain the 0.5% reimbursement provided that both the return and the additional amount due are timely filed. If the prepayment exceeded the actual liability, the taxpayer will be mailed an overpayment notice or refund warrant.

(B) If a taxpayer does not file a quarterly or monthly return together with payment on or before the due date, the taxpayer forfeits all discounts and incurs a mandatory 5.0% penalty. After the first 30 days delinquency, an additional mandatory penalty of 5.0% is assessed against the taxpayer, and after the first 60 days delinquency, interest begins to accrue at the rate of 10% per annum.

(i) Resale and exemption certificates.

(1) Any person selling taxable items in this state must collect a tax on the taxable items so sold unless a valid and properly completed resale, exemption or direct payment exemption certificate is received from the purchaser (Note: Simply having numbers on file without properly completed certificates does not relieve the seller from the responsibility for collecting tax.).

(2) A seller may accept a resale certificate only from a purchaser who is in the business of reselling the taxable items within the geographical limits of the United States of America, its territories and possessions. See Rule 3.285 concerning Resale Certificate; Sales for Resale. To be valid, the resale certificate must show the 11-digit number from the purchaser's Texas tax permit or the out-of-state registration number of the out-of-state purchaser.

(3) A seller may accept an exemption certificate in lieu of the tax on sales of items that will be used in an exempt manner or on sales to exempt entities. See Rule 3.287 concerning Exemption Certificates. There is no exemption number. An exemption certificate does not require a number to be valid.

(4) The purchaser claiming an exemption from the tax must issue to the seller a properly completed resale or exemption certificate. The seller must act in good faith when accepting the resale or exemption certificate. If a seller has actual knowledge that the exemption claimed is invalid, the seller must collect the tax.

(5) Direct payment permit holders are entitled to issue an exemption certificate when purchasing all taxable items, other than those purchased for resale. The direct payment exemption certificate must show the purchaser's direct payment permit number. See Rule 3.288 concerning Direct Payment Procedures and Qualifications.

(6) Maquiladora export permit holders are entitled to issue a maquiladora exemption certificate when purchasing all taxable items, other than those purchased for resale. Maquiladora export permit holders should refer to Rule 3.358 concerning Maquiladoras.

(7) The seller should obtain the properly executed resale or exemption certificates at the time the sale occurs. If the certificates are not obtained at the time of the sale, they are subject to verification before they will be honored. The seller has 60 days from the date written notice is given by the Comptroller to the seller in which to deliver certificates to the Comptroller. Any certificates delivered to the Comptroller during the 60-day period will be subject to verification before any deductions will be allowed. Certificates delivered to the Comptroller after the 60-day period will not be accepted and the deduction will not be granted. See Rule 3.285 concerning Resale Certificate; Sales for Resale, Rule 3.287 concerning Exemption Certificates, Rule 3.288 concerning Direct Payment Procedures and Qualifications and Rule 3.282 concerning Auditing Taxpayer Records.

(j) Suspension of permit.

(1) If a person fails to comply with any provision of the Tax Code, Title 2, or of the Bingo Enabling Act or with the rules issued by the Comptroller under those statutes, the Comptroller may suspend the person's permit or permits.

(2) Before a seller's permit is suspended, the seller is entitled to a hearing before the Comptroller to show cause why the permit or permits should not be suspended. The Comptroller shall give the seller at least 20 days notice, which shall be in accordance with the requirements of Rule 1.14 concerning Notice of Setting.

(3) After a permit has been suspended, a new permit will not be issued to the same seller until the seller has posted sufficient security and satisfied the Comptroller that the seller will comply with both the provisions of the law and the Comptroller's rules and regulations.

(k) Refusal to issue permit. The Comptroller is required by the Tax Code, §111.0046, to refuse to issue any permit to a person who:

(1) is not permitted or licensed for a different tax or activity administered by the Comptroller; or

(2) is currently delinquent in the payment of any tax collected by the Comptroller.

Effective Date: November 13, 1989
Filed with Secretary of State: October 23, 1989

JOHN SHARP
Comptroller of Public Accounts

5c. Rule 3.281—Records Required; Information Required

STATE OF TEXAS

COMPTROLLER OF PUBLIC ACCOUNTS

STATE SALES AND USE TAX

Rule 3.281. Records Required; Information Required. (Texas Tax Code §§151.010, 151.025, 151.202, 151,406, 151.709).

(a) Records required.

(1) Every person engaged in:

(A) making sales, leases, or rentals of tangible personal property;

(B) performing taxable labor, such as fabricating, processing, and producing tangible personal property; or

(C) performing taxable services, such as amusement services, cable television services, personal services, motor vehicle parking and storage services, and the repair, remodeling, maintenance, and restoration of certain tangible personal property; or

(D) purchasing taxable items must keep records in such form as may readily be examined by the Comptroller or his authorized agents or employees.

(2) The records must reflect the total gross receipts from sales, rentals, leases, taxable services, and taxable labor. Purchasers' records must reflect the total purchases of taxable items. Additional records must be kept to substantiate any claimed deductions or exclusions authorized by law. When records regarding the amount and applicability of any deductions or exclusions from the measure of the tax, or evidence of compliance with optional reporting methods, are insufficient, the Comptroller may estimate deductions or exclusions based on any records available or disallow all deductions and exclusions.

(b) Failure to keep accurate records. If any person fails to keep accurate records of gross receipts and gross purchases, the Comptroller will estimate the tax liability based on any information available, including, but not limited to, records of suppliers. In addition, the Comptroller may suspend the permit of the taxpayer, file misdemeanor charges, or take other action as authorized by statute to enforce compliance. Records may be written, kept on microfilm, or stored on data processing equipment.

(c) Information required.

(1) The Comptroller may require any person subject to the Limited Sales and Use Tax Act to furnish information necessary to:

(A) identify any person applying for a permit or any person required to file a return;

(B) determine the amount of bond required to commence or continue business;

(C) determine possible successor liability; and

(D) determine the amount of tax the person is required to remit.

(2) The information required may include, but is not limited to, the following:

(A) name of the actual owner of the business;

(B) name of each partner in a partnership;

(C) names of officers and directors of corporations and other organizations;

(D) all trade names under which the owner operates;

(E) mailing address and actual locations of all business outlets;

(F) license numbers, title numbers, and other identification of business vehicles;

(G) identification numbers assigned by other governmental agencies, including social security numbers, federal employers identification numbers, and drivers license numbers;

(H) names of suppliers, banks, and other persons with whom the taxpayer transacts business;

(I) names and last known addresses of former owners of the business.

Effective Date: October 30, 1984
Filed with Secretary of State: October 16, 1984

JOHN SHARP
Comptroller of Public Accounts

5d. Guidelines for Collecting Local Sales and Use Tax

Guidelines for Collecting Local Sales and Use Tax

If you sell taxable items, you must collect state sales or use tax plus the appropriate local sales or use taxes. Cities, counties, transit authorities and special purpose districts may impose a local tax. The local taxes apply to the same goods and services as does the state tax. We'll send you the forms you need to report both state and local taxes.

With all the various local taxing jurisdictions, we know it's a little overwhelming, so we've developed these guidelines to help you collect the correct local taxes.

Not More Than 2%

There is a difference between sales tax and use tax. For the most part you won't care which tax you are collecting. However, it does matter when it comes to deciding whether you need to collect tax for a local taxing jurisdiction because there is a rule of thumb in local taxes: "Don't collect more than 2%."

There is an order to follow. First, collect any local sales taxes. Then, collect local use taxes up to, but not more than, 2 percent. Collect the local use taxes in this order:

1. city
2. county
3. special purpose districts
4. transit tax

Don't collect a local use tax if the tax cannot be collected at its full rate without going over the 2-percent maximum.

Collecting Sales Tax for Cities, Counties and Special Purpose Districts

If the goods or taxable services you sell are delivered to Texas customers from an out-of-state location, skip this section and refer to the section on use tax.

With the exception of transit sales and use tax, local sales taxes are collected based on the location of your *place of business*. A place of business is a store, office or other location where you receive orders for taxable goods or services at least three times during a calendar year. A warehouse or other storage facility is not a place of business unless three or more sales are made or orders are taken there during a year.

One Place of Business

If your place of business is in a local taxing jurisdiction, collect city, county or special purpose district tax for that jurisdiction. For example, if your place of business is in Bastrop, collect Bastrop city tax and Bastrop county tax on all sales of taxable items delivered in Texas.

More Than One Place of Business

When you have more than one place of business, the local tax you collect is determined by the place of business from which your products are delivered. If you deliver your product from a place of business in a taxing jurisdiction, collect tax for that jurisdiction. For example, let's say you take an order from your place of business in Austin, but you ship the product from your store in Bastrop. In this situation, you collect the Bastrop city tax plus the Bastrop county tax.

Collecting Sales Tax for Transit Authorities

Transit tax is collected differently from other local taxes. The key element is *where* you deliver your service or product. Transit sales tax is due on all taxable items delivered from a place of business in a transit authority to a location in the same authority. Transit sales tax is not due on goods or services delivered to a location outside the transit authority. But you may need to collect transit use tax if that delivery is made to a location inside *another* transit authority (See the section on transit use tax).

Collecting Use Tax for Cities, Counties and Special Purpose Districts

Products Delivered From Out of State

If the goods or taxable services you sell are delivered to Texas customers from an out-of-state location, collect use tax for the city, county, special purpose district or transit authority where the product is delivered.

Products Delivered From Inside the State with One Place of Business

If your place of business is outside a local taxing jurisdiction, and you deliver your product inside a taxing jurisdiction, you must collect local use taxes if you are engaged in business in the jurisdiction.

Products Delivered From Inside the State with More Than One Place of Business

When you have more than one place of business, the local taxes you collect are determined by the place of business from which your products are delivered. If your goods or taxable services are delivered from a place of business outside a taxing jurisdiction to a location inside a taxing jurisdiction, collect taxes for that jurisdiction if you are engaged in business in that jurisdiction.

Collecting Transit Use Tax

If your products (taxable goods or services) are shipped into a transit authority, collect transit use tax if you are engaged in business in the transit authority. Don't forget the 2-percent limit on collecting local tax — transit tax is the last in line to be collected.

What is "Engaged in Business"?

If you have any of the following within a local jurisdiction, collect local use tax on taxable goods or services delivered into that jurisdiction.

A Location — This includes both permanent and temporary locations, whether operated by the retailer directly, a subsidiary or an agent. It may be an office, warehouse, distribution center, storage place, sales or sample room or any other place of business.

Delivery — When you use company vehicles (whether owned, leased or rented) to deliver to customers in the taxing jurisdiction.

Lease Equipment — Deriving income from the lease of equipment or other tangible personal property in the taxing jurisdiction.

Advertising — When the advertisement is for taxable goods or services, and is broadcast from, printed at or distributed from a location in a taxing jurisdiction, provided it is primarily distributed (75 percent or more) to people in the taxing jurisdiction.

Mail Order—If solicitations are frequent and recurring and if you benefit from any of the following services occurring within the taxing jurisdiction:

- banking
- financing
- debt collection
- telecommunications services
- marketing activities
- or if you have an authorized repairman or installer in the taxing jurisdiction.

Service Provider—This may include company employees or authorized service agents.

Independent Salespersons —This includes direct sales companies.

There Are Always Exceptions

The following services are the exception. If you sell these services, you don't have to worry about where your place of business is located; just follow the instructions for that service. The 2-percent cap on collecting local taxes still applies to these services.

Cable T.V. — Collect local taxes on cable television services based on where the customer receives the service.

Amusement Services — Collect local taxes on amusement services based on where the performance or event occurs.

Telecommunications Services — Collect local taxes on telecommunications ser- vices based on the location of the telephone or other device from which the call or other transmission originates. If you cannot determine where the communication originates, collect local tax based on the address to which the service is billed.

Waste Collection Services — Collect local taxes based on where the garbage is collected.

Natural Gas and Electricity — Collect local taxes based on where the customer receives the gas or electricity. Residential use of gas and electricity is exempt from county tax, special purpose district tax, transit tax and from tax in many cities.

Tax Assistance: 1-800-252-5555
Our local number is 512/463-4600
TDD ONLY: 1-800-248-4099

6. Sales and Use Tax Return—Metropolitan Transit Authority

01-116(2)
(Rev.1-91/4)

TEXAS SALES AND USE TAX RETURN

METROPOLITAN TRANSIT AUTHORITY/
CITY TRANSIT DEPARTMENT SUPPLEMENT

00

a. ■ 03350

•DO NOT STAPLE OR PAPER CLIP. Page of
•DO NOT WRITE IN SHADED AREAS.

c. Taxpayer number ■

d. Filing period

e. ■

f. Taxpayer name

g. Due date

• PRINT YOUR NUMERALS LIKE THIS
0 1 2 3 4 5 6 7 8 9

1. MTA/CTD NAME	2. MTA/CTD NUMBER ■	3. AMOUNT SUBJECT TO TAX ■ (Whole dollars only)	4. TAX RATE ■	5. MTA/CTD TAX DUE (Multiply Item 3 by Item 4)
				.
				.
				.
				.
				.
				.
				.
				.

			.
			.
			.
			.
			.
			.
			.
			.
			.
			.
			.
			.
			.

	MTA/CTD TAX
5. TOTAL MTA/CTD TAX DUE ON THIS PAGE	.

Combine the totals on all MTA/CTD supplement pages and enter the combined total in the MTA/CTD TAX column for Item 10 on the "Texas Sales and Use Tax Return," Form 01-114 or Form 01-123.

6a. Texas Mass Transit Tax Information

JOHN SHARP ▪ TEXAS COMPTROLLER OF PUBLIC ACCOUNTS

Texas Mass Transit Taxes

Texas has **eight transit authorities**, and all are financed with a transit tax.

More than half the Texas population lives in, or conducts business with retailers located inside, one of the state's transit authorities.

Transit authorities were created by citizens in major population areas to finance and improve mass transportation systems.

Guidelines presented here will help you to know how much transit tax to collect.

"I pledge to make sure you receive full value for each and every dollar you send to Austin. I guarantee that you will find the Comptroller's Office is a lean and efficient operation."

JOHN SHARP
Comptroller of Public Accounts

Businesses in the transit authorities collect a special transit sales and use tax of up to 1%, along with the state sales and use tax and any other applicable local sales and use taxes.

This brochure is designed to help taxpayers who collect the transit sales and use tax in one or more of the transit authority areas.

Transit Tax

Retailers collect the transit sales and use tax on the same items that are subject to state and other local sales and use taxes. All items exempt from state tax and taxable items delivered to an address outside any transit area are also exempt from the transit tax.

Sales of taxable items are subject to the combined rate of state and all applicable local sales and use taxes. Rate tables for combined tax rates can be obtained from the State Comptroller's Office.

Transit tax is paid to the State of Texas on a return the Comptroller furnishes each retailer. A retailer is responsible for paying any transit tax, as well as state and local taxes that are due, regardless of whether a return has been furnished.

Transit tax is due and must be paid to the Comptroller at the same time and for the same reporting period as state and local sales and use taxes.

Authority	Rate
Austin	¾%
Corpus Christi	½%
Dallas	1%
El Paso	½%
Fort Worth	½%
Houston	1%
Laredo	¼%
San Antonio	1%

When Is Transit Tax Due?

- Transit sales tax is due from the retailer or the purchaser on all taxable items delivered from a place of business in a transit area to an address **within** that transit area.
- Transit sales tax is **not** due if a taxable item is delivered by a retailer located inside a transit area to an address **outside** any transit area. (See MTA Rule 3.424 — Imposition of Sales Tax.)
- Transit **use** tax is due from the **retailer** or the **purchaser** on deliveries of taxable items to an address **within** a transit area, including taxable items shipped into a transit area from out of state or a foreign country. (See MTA Rule 3.425 — Administration of Use Tax.)
    - Transit **use** tax is due from the purchaser when taxable items are taken directly into a transit area from outside any transit area.

Follow these basic rules when collecting transit taxes in Texas.

Not More Than 2% Local Taxes Due

Retailers always must collect and report state sales tax and any local sales taxes due on a taxable transaction.

Retailers also must collect applicable **use** tax, **up to the maximum 2% rate** for all local taxes.

Local sales and use taxes should be collected in the following order:
1. Local (city, county, SPD, transit) sales taxes
2. City use tax
3. County use tax
4. Special purpose district (SPD) use tax
5. Transit use tax

If a local use tax cannot be collected at its full rate **without going over the 2% maximum**, the local tax for that jurisdiction **should not be collected**.

Texas' Eight Transit Authorities

El Paso City Transit Department

Known as Sun Metro
Code #3071889

This city is subject to the Sun Metro transit tax rate of ½%* —

The City of El Paso only.

* The Sun Metro transit tax rate of ½% became effective on April 1, 1988.

Laredo City Transit Department

Known as El Metro
Code #3240885

This city is subject to the El Metro transit tax rate of ¼%* —

The City of Laredo only.

* The El Metro transit tax rate of ¼% is effective July 1, 1991.

Dallas Area Rapid Transit

Known as DART
Code #3057994

These cities are subject to the DART transit tax rate of 1%* —

Addison	Glenn Heights
Buckingham	Highland Park
Carrollton	Irving
Cockrell Hill	Plano
Dallas	Richardson
Farmers Branch	Rowlett
Garland	University Park

* The DART transit tax rate of 1% became effective January 1, 1984.

Fort Worth Mass Transit Authority

Known as FWTA
Code #3220996

This city is subject to the FWTA transit tax rate of ½%* —

The City of Fort Worth only.

* The FWTA transit tax rate was ¼% from April 1, 1984, through December 31, 1988. Effective January 1, 1989, the rate increased to ½%.

Corpus Christi Mass Transit Authority

Known as the "B"
Code #3178998

These cities and areas are subject to the "B" transit tax rate of ½%* —

Agua Dulce
Corpus Christi
Driscoll
Gregory
Port Aransas
Robstown
San Patricio

The unincorporated areas of Nueces County.

* The "B" transit tax rate of ½% became effective January 1, 1986.

Austin Mass Transit Authority

Known as Capital Metro
Code #3227999

These cities and areas are subject to the Capital Metro transit tax rate of ¾%* —

Austin	Leander
Cedar Park	Manor
Jonestown	Pflugerville
Lago Vista	San Leanna

The unincorporated portion of southern Williamson County including Anderson Mill, Jollyville and Pond Springs; the unincorporated Travis County Commissioner's Precinct 2 (north and northwest Travis County).

* The Capital Metro transit tax rate was 1% from July 1, 1985, through March 31, 1989. Effective April 1, 1989, the rate decreased to ¾%.

San Antonio Mass Transit Authority

Known as VIA
Code #3015995

These cities and areas are subject to the VIA transit tax rate of 1%* —

Alamo Heights
Balcones Heights
Castle Hills
China Grove
Converse
Elmendorf
Grey Forest
Helotes
Hollywood Park
Kirby
Leon Valley
Olmos Park
Saint Hedwig**
San Antonio
Shavano Park
Terrell Hills
Windcrest

And the unincorporated areas of Bexar County.

* The VIA transit tax rate was ½% from January 1, 1978, through March 31, 1989. Effective April 1, 1989, the rate increased to 1%.

** Saint Hedwig became a part of the VIA effective October 1, 1988.

Houston Mass Transit Authority

Known as the Houston Metro
Code #3101990

These cities and areas are subject to the Houston Metro transit tax rate of 1%* —

Bellaire	Humble
El Lago	Katy
Houston	Missouri City

Bunker Hill Village
Hedwig Village
Hilshire Village
Hunters Creek Village
Piney Point Village
Spring Valley
Southside Place
Taylor Lake Village
West University Place

The unincorporated areas of southwest and northwest Harris County, including Bammel, Cypress, Hockley, Klein, Satsuma and Westfield; and the portions of Hufsmith, Kingwood and Spring that are within Harris County.

* The Houston Metro transit tax rate of 1% became effective October 1, 1978.

Comptroller Field Offices Located within Transit Authorities

Our experienced staff at each of our field offices can give you further help with transit taxes as well as other state taxes.

Austin

Taxpayer Assistance Office
111 West Sixth Street
Austin 78701
512/463-4865

3721 Executive Center Drive
Meredith Bldg., Suite 100
Austin 78731
512/345-0881

Corpus Christi

5155 Flynn Parkway
Suite 106
Corpus Christi 78411
512/854-2600

Dallas

1121 Rockingham Drive
Richardson 75080
214/690-9786

7222 S. Westmoreland Road
Suite 100
Dallas 75237
214/709-4357

1331 East Highway 80
Suite 2
Mesquite 75150
214/289-3400

El Paso

1421 N. Lee Trevino
Suite B-002
El Paso 79936
915/592-8827

Fort Worth

4040 Fossil Creek Boulevard
Suite 100, Fort Worth 76137
817/847-6201

4304-B Airport Freeway
Fort Worth 76117
817/834-5591

Houston

211 Highland Cross, Suite 110
Houston 77073
713/821-0162

1919 N. Loop West, Suite 100
Houston 77008
713/868-9112

650 FM 1959
Houston 77034
713/484-6533

11150 S. Wilcrest Drive, Suite 101
Houston 77099
713/879-8835

Laredo

602 E. Calton Road
Laredo 78041
512/722-2859

San Antonio

5825 Callaghan Road, Suite 100
San Antonio 78228
512/684-8652

103 SW Military Drive
San Antonio 78221
512/924-6434

We're here to help!

Call toll free 1-800-252-5555
(In Austin, call 463-4600.)

From a Telecommunication Device for the Deaf (TDD) only, call 1-800-248-4099 toll free. In Austin, the local TDD number is 463-4621.

Comptroller of Public Accounts, Tax Publications Division • Publication #96-285 – Revised May 1991.
For additional copies write Comptroller of Public Accounts, Account Maintenance, 111 E. 17th Street, Austin, Texas 78774-0100.

7. Texas Sales Tax Exemption Certificate

Comptroller of Public Accounts FORM 01-315 (Rev. 1-91/4)

TEXAS SALES AND USE TAX EXEMPTION CERTIFICATE

Name of purchaser, firm or agency

Address *(Street & number, P.O. Box or Route number)*

Phone *(Area code and number)*

City, State, ZIP code

I, the purchaser named above, claim an exemption from payment of sales and use taxes for the purchase of taxable items described below or on the attached order or invoice form:

Seller: ____________________

Street address: ____________________ City, State, ZIP code: ____________________

Description of items to be purchased or on the attached order or invoice:

____

____

____

Purchaser claims this exemption for the following reason:

____

____

____

I understand that I will be liable for payment of sales or use taxes which may become due for failure to comply with the provisions of the Tax Code: Limited Sales, Excise, and Use Tax Act, Municipal Sales and Use Tax Act, Sales and Use Taxes for Special Purpose Taxing Authorities, County Sales and Use Tax Act, County Health Services Sales and Use Tax and the Texas Health and Safety Code: Special Provisions Relating to Hospital Districts, Emergency Services Districts, and Emergency Services Districts in counties with a population of 125,000 or less.

I understand that it is a misdemeanor to give an exemption certificate to the seller for taxable items which I know, at the time of purchase, will be used in a manner other than that expressed in this certificate and that upon conviction may be fined not more than $500 per offense.

sign here ▶ Purchaser	Title	Date

Note: This certificate cannot be issued for the purchase, lease or rental of a motor vehicle.

THIS CERTIFICATE DOES NOT REQUIRE A NUMBER TO BE VALID

Sales and Use Tax "Exemption Numbers" or "Tax Exempt" Numbers do not exist.

This certificate should be furnished to the supplier. Do not send the completed certificate to the Comptroller of Public Accounts.

7a. Rule 3.287—Exemption Certificates

STATE OF TEXAS

COMPTROLLER OF PUBLIC ACCOUNTS

STATE SALES AND USE TAX

Rule 3.287. Exemption Certificates. (Texas Tax Code §§151.054, 151.155, 151.156, 151.418).

(a) Definition. Exemption certificate - A document which, when properly executed, allows the tax-free purchase of an item that would otherwise be subject to tax. A purchaser claiming an exemption because the item purchased is for resale must issue a resale certificate to the seller. See Rule 3.285 concerning Resale Certificate; Sales for Resale. There is no provision in the sales and use tax act for an exemption number or a tax exempt number to be issued or used in connection with an exemption certificate.

(b) Who may issue an exemption certificate. An exemption certificate of the type described in this rule may only be issued by one of the following:

(1) an organization that has qualified for exemption under the Tax Code, §151.309 and §151.310. See Rule 3.322 concerning Exempt Organizations;

(2) a person purchasing an item which is exempt under the Tax Code, Chapter 151, Subchapter H.

(c) Maquiladora exemption and direct payment permits.

(1) People who make purchases using direct pay permits should refer to Rule 3.288 concerning Direct Payment Procedures and Qualifications.

(2) People who make purchases using maquiladora exemption permits should refer to Rule 3.358 concerning Maquiladoras.

(d) Acceptance of exemption certificate.

(1) All gross receipts of a retailer are subject to sales or use tax unless a valid and properly completed exemption certificate is accepted by the seller.

(2) A sale is exempt if the exemption certificate is accepted in good faith at the time of the transaction and the seller lacks actual knowledge that the claimed exemption is invalid.

(3) A person who issues an exemption certificate when purchasing a taxable item who knows at the time of purchase the item will be used in a manner other than that expressed in the certificate is guilty of a misdemeanor and upon conviction shall be fined not more than $500 for each conviction.

(4) The seller should obtain the properly executed exemption certificate at the time the transaction occurs. Any certificates obtained after the transaction will be subject to verification by the Comptroller. If the certificates are not obtained at the transaction date, the seller has 60 days from the date written notice is given by the Comptroller to the seller in which to deliver them to the Comptroller. Any certificates delivered during the 60-day period will be subject to independent verification before any deductions will be allowed. Certificates delivered after the 60-day limit will not be allowed and the deduction will not be granted.

(5) The exemption certificate will be valid if the seller received it in good faith from a purchaser and if the certificate states valid qualifications for an exemption. A retailer must be familiar with the exemptions that are available for the items the retailer sells.

(6) An exemption certificate is not acceptable when an exemption is claimed because tangible personal property is exported outside the United States. For proper documentation required for proof of export, see Rule 3.323 concerning Imports and Exports.

(e) Improper use of items purchased under an exemption certificate.

(1) When an item purchased under a valid exemption certificate is used in a taxable manner, whether the use is in Texas or outside the state, the purchaser is liable for payment of sales tax based on the fair market rental value of the item for the period of time used. The fair market rental value is the amount the purchaser would pay on the open market to rent the item for use. If the item has no fair market rental value, sales tax is due on the original purchase price. If the exemption certificate was invalid at the time of its issuance, the purchaser owes tax on the original purchase price.

(2) At any time the person using the item purchased under a valid exemption certificate may stop paying tax on the fair market rental value and instead pay sales tax on the original purchase price. When the person elects to pay sales tax on the purchase price, credit will not be allowed for taxes previously paid on the fair market rental value.

(3) Sales tax is not due when an item purchased under a valid exemption certificate is donated to an organization exempt from tax under the Tax Code, §151.309 or §151.310(a)(1) or (a)(2).

(4) Contractors using equipment purchased under a valid exemption certificate on both taxable and exempt projects must account for tax based upon the provisions in Rule 3.291 concerning Contractors.

(f) Content of an exemption certificate. An exemption certificate must show:

(1) the name and address of the purchaser;

(2) a description of the item to be purchased;

(3) the reason the purchase is exempt from tax;

(4) the signature of the purchaser and the date; and

(5) the name and address of the seller.

(g) Form of an exemption certificate. An exemption certificate must be in substantially the form set out as follows.

Effective Date: February 19, 1990
Filed with Secretary of State: January 29, 1990

JOHN SHARP
Comptroller of Public Accounts

TEXAS CERTIFICATE OF EXEMPTION

____
Purchaser's name

____
Street Address

____
City, state, zip code

I claim an exemption from payment of sales and use taxes for the purchase of taxable items described below or on the attached order or invoice:

____
Description of items (or an attached order or invoice) to be purchased:

____

I claim this exemption for the following reason: ____________

____

I understand that I will be liable for payment of sales tax which may become due for failure to comply with the provisions of the state, city, county and/or metropolitan transit authority/city transit department sales and use tax laws and Comptroller rules regarding exempt purchases. Liability for the tax will be determined by the price paid for the taxable items purchased or the fair market rental value for the period of time used.

I understand that it is a misdemeanor to give an exemption certificate to the seller for taxable items which I know, at the time of purchase, will be used in a manner other than that expressed in this certificate and, upon conviction, may be fined up to $500 per offense.

Seller: ________________________________

Street address: ____________________________

City, state, zip code: ________________________

Purchaser's
signature: ____________ Date: _______ Phone: _______

Title: ________________________

This certificate does not require a number to be valid.

Sales and use tax exemption numbers or tax exempt numbers do not exist.

This certificate should be furnished to the supplier. Do <u>not</u> send the completed certificate to the Comptroller of Public Accounts.

8. Texas Sales Tax Resale Certificate

Comptroller of Public Accounts FORM 01-339 (11-87)

TEXAS SALES TAX RESALE CERTIFICATE

Name of purchaser, firm or agency	Phone *(Area code and number)*
Address (Street & number, P.O. Box or Route number)	
City, state, ZIP code	
Texas Limited Sales Tax Permit Number *(or out-of-state retailer's registration number or date applied for Texas permit)*	

I, the purchaser named above, claim the right to make a non-taxable purchase for resale of the taxable items described below or on the attached order or invoice from:

Seller

Street address

City, state, ZIP code

Description of the items to be purchased, or on the attached order or invoice:

Description of the type of business activity generally engaged in or type of items normally sold by the purchaser:

The taxable items described above, or on the attached order or invoice, will be resold, rented or leased by me within the geographical limits of the United States of America, its territories and possessions, in its present form or attached to other personal property to be sold.

I understand that if I make any use of the item other than retention, demonstration or display while holding it for sale, lease or rental, I must pay sales tax on the item at the time of use based upon either the purchase price or the fair market rental value for the period of time used.

I understand that it is a misdemeanor to give a resale certificate to the seller for taxable items which I know, at the time of purchase, are purchased for use rather than for the purpose of resale, lease, or rental, and that upon conviction I may be fined not more than $500 per offense.

sign here ▸ Purchaser	Title	Date

This certificate should be furnished to the supplier. Do not send the completed certificate to the Comptroller of Public Accounts

9. Texas Sales and Use Tax Bond—Security Information

01-707
(Rev. 4-87/6)

Do not write in the space above

TEXAS SALES AND USE TAX BOND-SECURITY INFORMATION

1. Taxpayer Name *(Legal name of owner)*			2. Social Security No. or F.E.I. No.	
3. Business Trade Name				Business phone *(Area code and number)*
Location *(Street and number)*	City	State	ZIP Code	

ESTIMATED AMOUNT SUBJECT TO SALES AND USE TAX PER MONTH				
4. 1st Qtr.	2nd Qtr.	3rd Qtr.	4th Qtr.	5. TOTAL ESTIMATED - 4 Qtrs.

5. Total Estimated $	÷ 6. Divided by 12	= 7. Average monthly amount subject to tax (Item 5 ÷ Item 6) $

Comments

____

____

I CERTIFY THAT THE ABOVE STATEMENTS ARE CORRECT TO THE BEST OF MY KNOWLEDGE AND BELIEF.

sign here Taxpayer	Title	Date
sign here E.O.	Field Office	Date

Instructions for Completing the Sales and Use Tax Bond-Security Information Worksheet

Purpose This is a worksheet for use by the taxpayers and Comptroller personnel to determine whether or not bond/security will be required for a new taxpayer. If bond is required, the taxpayer will be notified.

Taxpayers: send the completed worksheet along with the completed Sales and Use Tax Application, Form AP-100, to All Applications Unit, Revenue Management.

Items 1-3 Must exactly match the information on the Sales and Use Tax Application, Form AP-100.

Items 4-7 If purchasing a business, base estimates on prior owner's sales. For new businesses, base estimate on projected sales volume.

Signature Taxpayer: The owner, partner, corporate president, corporate secretary or someone with power of attorney must sign the form. Preferably, the same person who signed the application signs the form.

9a. Rule 3.327—Taxpayer's Bond or Other Security

STATE OF TEXAS

COMPTROLLER OF PUBLIC ACCOUNTS

STATE SALES AND USE TAX

Rule 3.327. Taxpayer's Bond or Other Security. (Tax Code §§151.251, 151.253, 151.254).

(a) Who must post bond or security. Every person who applies for a tax permit or who becomes delinquent in the payment of any taxes, penalties, or interest must furnish security in the amount determined by the Comptroller to be sufficient to protect the state against a failure to pay any amounts or costs which may become due under the state, city, and metropolitan transit authority sales and use tax laws.

(b) Conditional permit. An applicant may be issued a conditional permit to do business for a period of time not to exceed 14 days in order to furnish the security required.

(c) The amount of bond or security required of persons applying for a tax permit.

(1) Each applicant must post bond or security in an amount equal to two times the amount of the average monthly tax liability.

(2) If a bond amount for a person other than an itinerant vendor is calculated to be less than $3,000, an initial bond will not be required.

(3) If a bond amount for an itinerant vendor is calculated to be less than $100, an initial bond will not be required. For the purposes of this paragraph, an itinerant vendor is a person who does not operate any place of business as defined in Rule 3.286 concerning Seller's Responsibilities.

(d) The amount of bond or security required of a person who currently is or has been delinquent in payment of any amount due.

(1) Monthly filers. A retailer reporting on a monthly basis must post bond or security in an amount equal to two times the amount of the retailer's average monthly tax liability.

(2) Quarterly and yearly filers. A person reporting on a quarterly or yearly basis must post bond or security in an amount equal to three times the amount of the person's average monthly tax liability.

(3) Bond amounts calculated to be less than $100. If a bond amount is calculated to be less than $100, bond will not be required.

(e) Recalculation of amount of bond required under certain circumstances. If it is determined at any time that the amount of bond on file is inadequate or that a person is delinquent in the payment of any amount due, the Comptroller may recalculate the amount of security and require new or additional bond to be posted. Under no circumstances, however, will the amount required exceed $50,000 or be less than $100.

(f) Types of security.

(1) Acceptable types of security:

(A) irrevocable assignments of accounts in banks, savings and loan institutions, and credit unions, whose deposits are insured by an agency of the United States Government;

(B) cash (personal checks are acceptable);

(C) bank letters of credit which are deemed by the Comptroller to be sufficient in amount and secure;

(D) United States Treasury bonds, readily convertible to cash; and

(E) surety bonds.

(2) Unacceptable types of security.

(A) Corporate stocks and bonds.

(B) Personal guarantees.

(g) Assignments. An assignment of either a savings account or a certificate of deposit in an institution insured by an agency of the United States Government must be irrevocable and must be executed on an assignment form approved by the Comptroller.

(h) Surety bonds. A surety bond must be executed on a form approved by the Comptroller and can be issued only by a surety company chartered or authorized to do business in the State of Texas. The bond shall constitute a new and separate obligation in the penal sum named therein for each calendar year or a portion thereof while the bond is in force. The bond must be executed by an attorney-in-fact appointed by the surety. The appointing instrument must be properly notarized and physically attached to the bond.

(i) Forfeiture. In the event of forfeiture, the Comptroller will notify the person holding the security and demand payment. The Comptroller will also notify the retailer and demand that another or additional bond or security be furnished within 10 days of the date of such notice. The amount of bond or security specified in the notice shall be fixed by the Comptroller subject only to the limitations stated in subsection (e) of this rule. This notice shall become final at the expiration of 10 days. Failure to comply with the requirements of the notice within the 10-day period will result in the suspension of the retailer's tax permit.

(j) Retailer's bond or security when ownership is changed.

(1) The Tax Code, §151.201, requires a retailer holding a tax permit to apply for a new permit when the legal structure of the retailer's business changes; for example, a change from a sole ownership to a partnership, a partnership to a corporation, etc.

(2) When a retailer applies for a new permit because of a change in legal structure, the retailer must comply with the provisions of this rule. The Comptroller will review all records and such other information as the Comptroller may require regarding the prior taxpaying performance of the retailer.

(3) If, after the review, it appears that the interests of the state will not be endangered by the new ownership, the Comptroller may determine that no new or additional bond is required.

(4) If, however, it appears that there has been a substantial change in ownership or that security is required to guarantee payment of taxes by the new entity, the Comptroller may require security in accordance with the provisions of this rule.

Effective Date: September 18, 1990
Filed with Secretary of State: August 28, 1990

JOHN SHARP
Comptroller of Public Accounts

---

10. Publications Available from the Texas Comptroller

INDEX TO COMPTROLLER PUBLICATIONS
April 1991

Amusement Machine Regulation

Coin Operated Services Law - Booklet, 18 pages. August 1989. **#96-257.** Contains complete text of the Texas Coin-Operated Services Law including definitions, permits, collection of tax, rules and regulations. (Internal use only.) (Under revision.)

Texas Amusement Machine Regulation and Taxation - Brochure. September 1990. **#96-256.** Explains licensing and regulation of businesses that deal with coin-operated music, skill or pleasure machines. (Under revision.)

Business Tax

Franchise Tax Information - Brochure. January 1990. **#96-114.** Outlines reports, computation, penalties, deadlines, minimum prepayments, first year reports and annual reports. (Under revision.)

Franchise Tax Statutes - Booklet, 32 pages. February 1990. **#96-193.** Contains complete text of Franchise Tax law. (Internal use only.) (Under revision.)

Claims

State Employee Travel Allowance Guide - Booklet, 55 pages. September 1989. **#96-174.** Explains transportation allowances, per diem, voucher preparation. (Under revision.)

Texas State Agency Guide to State Accounting Operations - Booklet, 9 pages. July 1990. **#96-274.** A guide to the role and functions of various Comptroller divisions in the state's accounting operations. (Under revision.)

Communications/Research

Periodicals

1990-1991 Biennial Revenue Estimate: 71st Legislature -January 1989. The Comptroller's estimates of revenue for the remainder of fiscal year 1989 and for the 1990-1991 biennium and Legislature under Article III, Section 49a of the Texas Constitution. (Available in limited quantity from EAC.)

Fiscal Notes - Monthly publication. An in-depth look at timely topics in state economic, tax and financial matters. (Available only through EAC.)

Fiscal Notes Index - 1976-1989: 27 pages. February 1990. Indexes articles from the EAC's monthly newsletter Fiscal Notes by subject. (Available in limited quantity from EAC.)

Quarterly Survey of Business Expectations: 8 pages. Quarterly publication that reports the Comptroller's Index of Future Business Conditions, which measures overall business expectations for the next six-month period. (Available in limited quantity from EAC.)

General Information

A Special Financial Report - Crisis in the Classroom; An Immediate Solution - 6 pages. October 1989. State Comptroller Bob Bullock's plan to equalize funding for public schools. The solution would enable efficient and emergency distribution of monies to stop the Texas Supreme Court's May 1, 1990, cut-off of state funds.

A Special Financial Report - Decontrolling Natural Gas: The Impact on Texas Prices and Tax Revenue - 12 Pages. July 1983. Discusses the present federal natural gas regulation structure and two proposals before Congress to change the structure. Also reviewed are the influence of the current federal law on the Texas gas market, and the probable impact on the Texas gas industry and natural gas tax collections if the proposals are implemented. (Available in limited quantity from EAC.)

A Special Financial Report - Dollars We Deserve, Part I: How Texas is Short-Changed on Our Fair

Share of Federal Money - 9 pages. March 1990. First of five reports exploring the failure of Texas to receive all federal funds to which it is entitled — estimated at $2.4 billion a year.

A Special Financial Report - Dollars We Deserve, Part II: Fixing Federal Policies That Short-Change Texas - 34 pages. May 1990. Second of five reports exploring the failure of Texas to receive all federal funds to which it is entitled — estimated at $2.4 billion a year.

A Special Financial Report - Dollars We Deserve, Part III: Loss of Funds Brings Hard Times - 21 pages. August 1990. Third of five reports exploring the failure of Texas to receive all federal funds to which it is entitled — estimated at $2.4 billion a year.

A Special Financial Report - Dollars We Deserve, Part IV: Texas' Medicaid Suffers Federal Funds Shortfall - 24 pages. October 1990. Fourth of five reports exploring the failure of Texas to receive all federal funds to which it is entitled — estimated at $2.4 billion a year.

A Special Financial Report - Dollars We Deserve, Part V: Maximizing Federal Dollars for Texas - 31 pages. December 1990. Fifth and final report exploring the failure of Texas to receive all federal funds to which it is entitled — estimated at $2.4 billion a year.

A Special Financial Report - From the Capitol to the Schoolhouse - 10 pages. July 1990. An analysis of the 1990 Education Finance Act adopted by the Texas Legislature.

A Special Financial Report - Hazardous Waste in Texas - 8 pages. November 1983. Explores the production of hazardous waste in Texas and a proposed state tax that might be used to create incentives for safer disposal methods, pay for cleanup and provide research for long-term solutions. (Available in limited quantity from EAC.)

A Special Financial Report - Productivity Ideas and Cost-Cutting Alternatives to Control State Budget Growth - 35 pages. December 1984. An examination of ideas to increase productivity and reduce the costs of state government. (Available in limited quantity from EAC.)

A Special Financial Report - Public School Finance: A Realistic Alternative: 8 pages. May 1988. Discusses a plan that lays the foundation for a system of quality education. Looks at how Texas can finance a constitutional system of public education that overcomes the inequities discovered in the Edgewood v. Kirby lawsuit. (Available in English and Spanish editions in limited quantity from EAC.)

A Special Financial Report - Sales and Franchise Tax Exemptions - 10 pages. January 1991. An estimate of the value of each exemption, exclusion, special rate, deduction and discount available under Texas' sales and franchise tax laws. (Available in limited quantity from EAC.)

A Special Financial Report - Sales and Franchise Tax Exemptions: A Report to the Texas Legislature - January 1989. 12 pages. A report estimating the value of each exemption, exclusion, special rate, deduction and discount available under Texas' sales and franchise tax laws. (Available in limited quantity from EAC.)

A Special Financial Report - State Government's Use of Outside Services: Update for Fiscal Year 1985 -6 pages. April 1986. Discusses the use of consultants by state agencies. A look at the consulting services bought, the cost and the private firms that benefit. (Available in limited quantity from EAC.)

A Special Financial Report - The Geography of State Spending - 10 pages. May 1985. Report to the Legislature on state spending by geographic region. (Available in limited quantity from EAC.)

A Special Financial Report - The Geography of Texas Taxes - 8 pages. August 1984. Report to the Legislature on state spending by geographic region. (Available in limited quantity from EAC.)

A Special Financial Report - The High Finance of Higher Education - 8 pages. March 1985. An examination of non-appropriated local funds available to the state's public colleges and universities. (Available in limited quantity from EAC.)

A Special Financial Report - The Petroleum Industry and the Texas Sales Tax - 7 pages. April 1983. Discusses the slump in the state petroleum industry as a significant factor in the decline in sales tax revenue. Links both direct and indirect petroleum industry tax payments to the entire Texas economy. (Available in limited quantity from EAC.)

A Special Financial Report - The Texas-Mexico Border: 12 pages. March 1988. Discusses the economic situation and outlook for Texas' border area. Looks at job growth in the 1,000-mile long economic region, four

Border cities, specific industries, income and population and Winter Texans. (Available in limited quantity from EAC.)

A Special Financial Report - Time of Change, Time of Choice - 7 pages. August 1986. Proposes a restructure of the Texas tax system more in line with changes in the state economy. Proposes a broader sales tax base at lower rates. (Available in limited quantity from EAC.)

Texas and Taxes: A National Survey on Alternatives and Comparisons - 158 pages. January 1987. A report on alternative methods of raising state revenue along with comparisons nationwide. (Available in limited quantity from EAC.)

Texas Business Guide - A Handbook for Foreign Manufacturers and Service Industries - 40 pages. March 1989. **#96-270.** Provides information on the state's economic climate and federal and state laws and regulations of interest to foreign-owned businesses. (Available in limited quantity from EAC.)

Texas Fees—Putting a Price on State Services - 186 pages. May 1987. An overview of state fees, comparing Texas fees with those of other states and identifying some problems with the fee system in Texas. (Available in limited quantity from EAC.)

Field Operations - Audit

Notice of Routine Audit - Brochure. July 1988. **#96-146.** Notification to taxpayer of scheduled audit. Briefly describes audit procedures, documents needed. (For use only by Audit Offices.) (Under revision.)

Fuels Tax

Fuels Tax Review - Brochure. August 1989. **#96-248.** Briefly describes changes in state fuels tax law ordered by Texas Legislature.

Motor Fuels Tax Law - Booklet, 47 pages. February 1990. **#96-192.** Contains complete text of law describing motor fuels, gasoline, diesel fuel and liquefied gas taxes including explanations of tax rates, exceptions, permits, reports, penalties, offenses and allocation of taxes. (Internal use only.) (Under revision.)

Fund Accounting

Texas Comprehensive Annual Financial Report, 1990 – 262 pages. (Available in limited quantity.)

Annual Cash Report, 1990 Volume I - 46 pages. (Available in limited quantity.)

Annual Cash Report, 1990 Volume II - 842 pages. (Available in limited quantity.)

1989 Annual Financial Report, Unaudited GAAP Edition - 107 pages. (Available in limited quantity from Fund Accounting.)

1989 Annual Financial Report, Audited GAAP Edition -187 pages. (Available in limited quantity from Fund Accounting.)

Fiscal Facts - Bimonthly publication. 8 pages. Information link between the Comptroller's Office and other state agencies. (Available in limited quantity from Fund Accounting.)

General

Electronic Fund Transfer – Brochure. March 1991. **#96-275.** Information on electric funds transfer now required of taxpayers who paid a total of $500,000 or more in a payment category during the preceding state fiscal year.

Taxable Services - Brochure. July 1990. **#96-259.** A general discussion of services subject to sales tax. (Under revision.)

Services, Taxes Administered and Permits/Licenses Issued - Brochure. February 1990. **#96-268.** A complete listing of services provided by the Texas Comptroller of Public Accounts, including tax assistance, taxes administered, permits and licenses issued by the Comptroller. (Under revision.)

Tax Help - Brochure. January 1991. **#96-128.** Current listing of all field offices.

Taxpayer Bill of Rights - Brochure. February 1989. **#96-265.** A compilation of the rights of taxpayers in their dealings with the Comptroller of Public Accounts. A pledge that the tax laws are administered with fairness, uniformity, courtesy and common sense. (Under revision.)

Los Pagadores de Impuestos de Texas - Brochure. October 1988. **#96-265-s.** A Spanish translation of the Taxpayer Bill of Rights. (Under revision.)

Taxpayer Bill of Rights - Braille Brochure. April 1989. **#96-265B.** Braille version.

Taxpayer Bill of Rights- Large Print Brochure. March 1989. **#96-265L.** Large print version. (Under revision.)

Taxpayer Bill of Rights - Audio. **#96-265A.** Audio version.

Trade Show - Brochure. July 1990. **#96-276.** Defines responsibility of trade show exhibitors to collect Texas sales and use taxes. (Under revision.)

Human Resources

Career Opportunities for People with Disabilities - Brochure. April 1991. **#96-286.** Discusses career opportunities with the Comptroller's Office for people with disabilities.

Career Opportunities for People with Disabilities - Brochure. August 1990. **#96-286S.** Spanish version. (Under revision.)

Opportunities with the Comptroller - Brochure. February 1991. **#96-138.** Personnel Division's recruitment booklet.

Inheritance Tax

Inheritance Taxes In Texas - Booklet, 6 pages. January 1988. **#96-137.** Contains complete text of state inheritance tax law.(Internal use only.) (Under revision.)

Who? Me Need A Will - Brochure. December 1989. **#96-101.** Explains consequences of not having a will. (Under revision.)

Your Estate Under Texas Law - Brochure. August 1989. **#96-127.** Explains state inheritance tax law. (Under revision.)

Legal

The Rules of Practice and Procedure - Booklet, 29 pages. October 1990. **#96-145.** Explains administrative appeals system for taxpayers who disagree with audit assessments or tax law interpretations. (Under revision.)

The Rules of Practice and Procedure - Large Print Booklet. August 1990. **#96-145L.** Large print version. (Under revision.)

The Rules of Practice and Procedure - Audio. **#96-145A.** Audio version.

Administrative Remedies - Brochure. April 1989. **#96-129.** Explanation of taxpayer rights and how to exercise them in the event of a tax dispute with the Comptroller's Office. (Under revision.)

Administrative Remedies- Large Print Brochure. March 1989. **#96-129L.** Large print version. (Under revision.)

Administrative Remedies- Audio. **#96-129A.** Audio version.

Local Government

City and County Financial Management- Newsletter. Published quarterly as a service to Texas cities and counties by Comptroller's Local Government Assistance Section.

Minerals Tax

Oil and Gas Production Tax Laws - Booklet, 34 pages. January 1991. **#96-191.** Contains complete text of tax laws dealing with oil and gas production, cement and sulphur production and certain services connected with oil and gas wells. (Under revision.)

Miscellaneous Taxes

Hotel Occupancy Tax Law - Booklet, 4 pages. January 1990. **#96-100.** Contains complete text of law including definitions, tax exceptions, required reports and payments, enforcement procedures and disposition of revenue. (Under revision.)

Hotel Exemptions - Brochure. August 1989. **#96-224.** Discusses organizations and individuals qualified to claim exemption from the hotel occupancy tax. (Under revision.)

Miscellaneous Gross Receipts Tax Law - Booklet, 16 pages. December 1987. **#96-110.** Contains complete text of law for telegraph, utility, car and telephone companies with a section on tax collection and business permits, penalties and allocation of tax. (Internal use only.) (Under revision.)

Motor Vehicle Tax

Fair Market Value Deduction - Brochure. February 1990. **#96-141.** Describes deduction, who qualifies, when it is used, how to claim one, arriving at fair market value and how to compute the tax. (Under revision.)

Motor Vehicle, Interstate Motor Carrier & Manufactured Housing Tax Law - Booklet, 21 pages. May 1990. **#96-252.** Contains complete text of each of the three tax laws. (Internal use only.) (Under revision.)

Motor Vehicle Tax Guidebook - Booklet, 175 pages. January 1989. **#96-254.** A county tax assessor-collector's guide to the fair and equitable administration of the Motor Vehicle Tax Law. (Under revision.)

Sales Tax

Sales Tax Update- Quarterly. March 1991. **#96-237.** Contains information and tips on complying with the sales and use tax and rules.

Sales and Use Tax Rate Cards

6 1/4% Rate Card. $50. - #98-293.

6 3/4% Rate Card. $50. - #98-278.

7% Rate Card. $50. - #98-251.

7 1/4% Rate Card. $50. - #98-236.

7 3/4% Rate Card. $50. - #98-272.

8% Rate Card. $50. - #98-253.

8 1/4% Rate Card. $50.- #98-292.

A Guide to Local Sales & Use Taxes - Booklet, 21 pages. July 1990. **#96-108.** Guide to application of local and MTA sales and use taxes by persons doing business in Texas. (Under revision.)

Data Processing Services - Brochure. February 1990. **#96-279.** Information on taxable and non-taxable data services with examples of both. (Under revision.)

Exempt Entities - Brochure. November 1988. **#96-122.** Application of exempt status, types of exempt organizations, sales and purchases by exempt groups, and loss of exempt status. (Under revision.)

Local Sales & Use Tax Laws - Booklet. January 1991. **#96-281** Contains complete text of local sales and use tax law. (Under revision.)

Sales Tax Exemptions for Film Production Companies - Brochure. April 1990. **#96-283.** Provides information on tax-free purchases of material, equipment and supplies available to film production companies. (Under revision.)

Sales Tax for Flea Markets - Brochure. October 1990. **#96-211.** Describes the application of the Texas Sales Tax to flea markets. (Under revision.)

State Tax Exemptions for People With Disabilities - Brochure. January 1990. **#96-273.** Explains sales tax and motor vehicle tax exemptions available to people with disabilities. (Under revision.)

State Tax Exemptions for People With Disabilities - Braille Brochure. **#96-273B.** Braille version.

State Tax Exemptions for People With Disabilities - Large Print Brochure. October 1989. **#96-273L.** Large print version. (Under revision.)

State Tax Exemptions for People With Disabilities - Brochure. January 1990. **#96-273S.** Spanish version. (Under revision.)

State Tax Exemptions for People With Disabilities - Brochure. January 1990. **#96-273SL.** Large print and Spanish version. (Under revision.)

Taxable Items Sold in Grocery and Convenience Stores - Brochure. July 1990. **#96-280.** A guide to the sales and use tax as it should be applied to items sold in grocery and convenience stores. Lists items that are exempt from the tax. (Under revision.)

Taxpayer's Guide To The Texas Sales and Use Tax Tape Reporting System - Booklet, 19 pages. January 1991. **#96-209.** Explanation of procedure to follow in filing tax returns by magnetic tape.

Telecommunications Service Taxes - Brochure. November 1989. **#96-234.** Describes telecommunication services that are subject to sales tax. (Under revision.)

Texas Mass Transit Taxes – Brochure. January 1991. **#96-285.** Designed to assist taxpayers who collect the transit sales and use tax in one or more of the state's seven mass transit authority areas. (Under revision.)

Texas Sales Tax Rates - Booklet. January 1991. **#96-132.** Current listing of all cities that have adopted City Sales Tax or MTA Sales Tax.

Texas Sales & Use Taxes for Contractors - Booklet, 35 pages. January 1986. **#96-109.** Booklet provides information on sales tax as it applies to contractors. (Under revision.)

Texas State Sales & Use Tax Law - Booklet, 56 pages. January 1991. **#96-177.** Contains complete text of state sales and use tax law.

Your New Business and the Texas Sales Tax - Booklet, 44 pages. December 1989. **#96-144.** Outlines steps for starting business, sales and use tax provisions, franchise tax, exemptions, audits, rights and penalties, and list of other publications. (Under revision.)

Your New Business and the Texas Sales Tax - Large Print Book. December 1989. **#96-144L.** Large print version. (Under revision.)

Your New Business and the Texas Sales Tax - Audio. **#96-144A.** Audio version.

Your New Business and the Texas Sales Tax - Braille. **#96-144B.** Braille version.

Publications Index In Numerical Order
April 1991

Number	Date	Title
#96-100	January 1990	Hotel Occupancy Tax Law
#96-101	December 1989	Who? Me Need A Will
#96-108	July 1990	A Guide to Local Sales and Use Taxes
#96-109	January 1986	Texas Sales & Use Taxes for Contractors
#96-110	December 1987	Miscellaneous Gross Receipts Tax Law
#96-114	January 1990	Franchise Tax Information
#96-122	November 1988	Exempt Entities
#96-127	August 1989	Your Estate Under Texas Law
#96-128	January 1991	Tax Help
#96-129	April 1989	Administrative Remedies
#96-129L	March 1989	Administrative Remedies - Large print version
#96-129A		Administrative Remedies - Audio version
#96-132	January 1991	Texas Sales Tax Rates
#96-137	January 1988	Inheritance Taxes In Texas
#96-138	February 1991	Opportunities with the Comptroller
#96-141	February 1990	Fair Market Value Deduction
#96-144	December 1989	Your New Business and the Texas Sales Tax
#96-144A		Your New Business and the Texas Sales Tax - Audio version
#96-144B		Your New Business and the Texas Sales Tax - Braille version
#96-144L	December 1989	Your New Business and the Texas Sales Tax - Large print version
#96-145	October 1990	The Rules of Practice and Procedure
#96-145L	August 1990	The Rules of Practice and Procedure - Large print version

#96-145A		The Rules of Practice and Procedure - Audio version
#96-146	July 1988	Notice of Routine Audit
#96-174	September 1989	State Employee Travel Allowance Guide
#96-177	January 1991	Texas State Sales and Use Tax Law
#96-191	January 1991	Oil and Gas Production Tax Laws
#96-192	February 1990	Motor Fuels Tax Law
#96-193	February 1990	Franchise Tax Statutes
#96-209	January 1991	Taxpayer's Guide To The Texas Sales and Use Tax Tape Reporting System
#96-211	October 1990	Sales Tax for Flea Markets
#96-224	August 1989	Hotel Tax Exemptions
#96-234	November 1989	Telecommunications Service Taxes
#96-237	March 1991	Sales Tax Update
#96-248	August 1989	Fuels Tax Review
#96-252	May 1990	Motor Vehicle, Interstate Motor Carrier & Manufactured Housing Tax Law
#96-254	January 1989	Motor Vehicle Tax Guidebook
#96-256	September 1990	Texas Amusement Machine Regulation
#96-257	August 1989	Coin-Operated Services Law
#96-259	July 1990	Taxable Services
#96-265	February 1989	Taxpayer Bill of Rights
#96-265A		Taxpayer Bill of Rights - Audio version
#96-265-s	October 1988	Taxpayer Bill of Rights - Spanish version
#96-265L	March 1989	Taxpayer Bill of Rights - Large print version
#96-265B		Taxpayer Bill of Rights - Braille version
#96-268	February 1990	Services, Taxes Administered and Permits/Licenses Issued
#96-270	March 1989	Texas Business Guide
#96-273	January 1990	State Tax Exemptions for People With Disabilities
#96-273L	October 1989	State Tax Exemptions for People With Disabilities – Large print version

#96-273B		**State Tax Exemptions for People With Disabilities - Braille version**
#96-273S	January 1990	**State Tax Exemptions for People With Disabilities – Spanish version**
#96-273SL	January 1990	**State Tax Exemptions for People With Disabilities – Spanish and Large print version**

Bulletins In Numerical Order
April 1991

Number	Date	Title
#94-101	January 1991	**Agricultural Sales Tax Exemption**
#94-103	March 1991	**Surveying Services**
#94-104	February 1991	**Broadcasting Companies**
#94-105	January 1991	**Guidelines for Allocating/Collecting Local Sales & Use Taxes**
#94-106	February 1991	**Credit Reporting Services**
#94-107	March 1991	**Debt Collection Services**
#94-108	January 1991	**Engaged in Business**
#94-109	January 1991	**Information Services**
#94-110	January 1991	**Insurance Services**
#94-111	January 1991	**Janitorial Services**
#94-112	January 1991	**Landscaping Services**
#94-113	January 1991	**Motor Vehicle Repairs**
#94-114	January 1991	**Pest Control Services**
#94-115	January 1991	**Ready-To-Eat Food**
#94-116	January 1991	**Real Property Repair and Remodeling**
#94-117	January 1991	**Restaurant and Texas Sales Tax**
#94-118	January 1991	**Oil & Gas Well Servicing**
#94-119	March 1991	**Security Service Companies**
#94-120	January 1991	**Property Managers & Real Property Services**
#94-121	March 1991	**Tax on Fax**
#94-122	January 1991	**Local Tax/Industrial Development Corporations**

#94-123	January 1991	**Non-Profit Water Supply Corporations**
#94-124	January 1991	**Manufacturing Exemptions**
#94-125	January 1991	**Exemptions: Sales Tax Information for Non-Profit Organizations**
#94-126	January 1991	**Sales Tax Information for Schools and Associated Organizations**
#96-274	July 1990	**Texas State Agency Guide to State Accounting Operations**
#96-275	March 1991	**Electronic Fund Transfer**
#96-276	July 1990	**Trade Show Brochure**
#96-279	February 1990	**Data Processing Services**
#96-280	July 1990	**Taxable Items Sold in Grocery & Convenience Stores**
#96-281	January 1991	**Local Sales & Use Tax Laws**
#96-283	April 1990	**Sales Tax Exemptions for Film Production Companies**
#96-285	January 1991	**Texas Mass Transit Taxes**
#96-286	April 1991	**Career Opportunities for People With Disabilities**
#96-286S	August 1990	**Career Opportunities for People With Disabilities - Spanish Version**

Tax Rate Cards

Number	Title
#98-293	6 1/4% Rate Card. $50
#98-278	6 3/4% Rate Card. $50
#98-251	7% Rate Card. $50
#98-236	7 1/4% Rate Card. $50
#98-272	7 3/4% Rate Card. $50
#98-253	8% Rate Card. $50
#98-292	8 1/4% Rate Card. $50

11. Information Concerning the Texas Unemployment Tax

TEXAS UNEMPLOYMENT TAX

What is the Texas Employment Commission?

The Texas Employment Commission (TEC) is a State Agency, established in 1936 by the Texas Legislature, with two major objectives:

1. To find jobs for the unemployed, and
2. To pay unemployment insurance benefits to eligible workers unemployed through no fault of their own.

What is Unemployment Insurance (UI) Tax?

TEC collects UI Tax from Texas employers to finance the unemployment insurance benefits paid to eligible workers.

Who must pay the UI Tax?

Any sole proprietorship, partnership, corporation or other legal entity which qualifies as a subject employer as defined in Subsection 19 (f) of the Texas Unemployment Compensation Act, (TUCA).

Is UI Tax withheld from employee wages?

No. UI Tax is paid in full by subject employers.

Who is a subject employer?

An employing unit is a subject employer, and its workers are covered under the program, if:

1. In the current or preceding calendar year, it paid as much as $1,500 in wages in any calendar quarter or had in employment at least one individual for some portion of the day in each of 20 different days, each day being in a different calendar week.
2. It acquired the organization, trade, or business, or substantially all of the assets of a subject employer.
3. It is a nonprofit organization as described in Section 501 (c) (3) of the Federal Internal Revenue Code which is exempt from income tax under Section 501 (a) of such code and in the current or preceding calendar year had as many as four or more individuals in employment for some portion of 20 days, each day being in a different calendar week. (Churches and organizations operated primarily for religious purposes are excluded.)
4. It elected to become a subject employer.
5. It is subject to the Federal Unemployment Tax Act and had any employees in Texas.
6. It is a political subdivision of a State or an instrumentality of a political subdivision which is wholly owned by one or more political subdivisions.
7. It employed individuals in farm or ranch labor and paid cash wages of $6,250 or more in a calendar quarter or employed 3 or more workers for 20 weeks during the calendar year. Also, farm or ranch labor will be considered as covered employment if performed by a seasonal worker employed on a truck farm, orchard or vineyard. Migrant workers on a farm or ranch are covered immediately and seasonal workers will be covered immediately if work is performed at the same time and at the same location with migrant workers.
8. It paid wages in cash of $1,000 or more in a calendar quarter for domestic service.

What is employment?

Employment means any service, including service in interstate commerce, performed for wages or under any contract of hire, written or oral, expressed or implied. Any services performed by an individual for wages shall be deemed to be employment subject to the TUCA, **unless** it is shown to the satisfaction of TEC that such individual has been and will continue to be free from control or direction over the performance of such services both under the contract of service and in fact. Any employing unit which is in doubt as to employment being subject to the TUCA should contact TEC for a determination.

What constitutes wages?

Wages means all remuneration paid for personal services. Included in this definition are cash wages and the cash value of all remuneration paid in any medium other than cash and gratuities received by any employee in the course of employment.

What are the responsibilities of a subject employer?

A subject employer must:

1. Register with TEC;
2. On a quarterly basis report the name, social security number, and total earnings for each employee; and

3. On a quarterly basis pay the applicable UI Tax on each employee.

How much is the UI Tax?

Each subject employer must pay UI Tax on the first $9,000 of earnings, per employee at the employer's current tax rate.

How can employers obtain the necessary tax forms for filing and additional information concerning UI Tax?

Any employer wishing to obtain additional information or tax forms for filing, should contact their local TEC tax office, or write TEC, Tax Department, Austin, Texas 78778. TEC's experienced UI Tax representatives can provide special assistance on all UI Tax matters.

---

12. Memo to Texas Employers Concerning Texas Unemployment Compensation

M E M O

TO TEXAS EMPLOYERS

Texas Employment Commission
Congress Ave. & 15th St.
Austin, Texas 78778

From the office of:

Mary Scott Nabers
Commissioner
Representing
Employers

Introduction

The following information outlines step-by-step procedures that employers can follow in reducing state unemployment insurance tax costs. We have purposely avoided legalistic terms and exceptional situations that would only be confusing. For further details, refer to the law itself or call my office at **1—800—TEC-MARY.**

Background

The objectives of the unemployment compensation insurance law are:

- To encourage employers to stabilize their employment, and
- To provide for a limited degree of insurance to take care of the basic necessities of persons, temporarily unemployed, who have been separated from their last employment through no fault of their own.

> **NOTE:** A complete copy of the Texas Unemployment Compensation Act is available at your local TEC office or from this office. Not all aspects of the law are covered in this memo.

PLEASE REMEMBER

As the member of the Commission appointed to represent employers, I have a responsibility to each of you to see that you pay absolutely no more taxes than legally required. I would welcome the opportunity to discuss with you any problem which may arise from your participation in this program. I also welcome your correspondence and other comments.

Mary Nabers

Mary Scott Nabers

$ $ $

Texas Employers Pay The Costs

Even when employment is at a high level and the number of unemployed workers is at the lowest point, thousands of Texans file initial claims for unemployment benefits every year. The amount of these claims runs into millions of dollars. EMPLOYERS OF TEXAS PAY THE BILL.

An employer's tax rate is variable, depending in large part

upon the amount of chargebacks to its account based on benefits paid out to former employees. Employers can reduce rates by proper planning and operations. This brochure attempts to outline some definite steps all employers can follow to reduce costs.

Ways to Reduce Your Unemployment Costs

General and Ongoing

1. Select new employees carefully and stabilize your employment. If you have a vacancy, try to get the best qualified person. When you lay off a temporary employee, it may adversely affect your tax rate. Do not overemploy. Do try to utilize employees in various departments, rather than laying someone off in one department and hiring in another. If you must lay someone off, try to place them immediately with another company as it will mean a tax savings to you.

2. Establish responsibility for handling unemployment claims in your company. It is of primary importance that you keep adequate records. Responsibility for keeping such records should be assigned to a specific individual or department. A **written** record must be kept concerning the employment history of each employee, his job performance, and, specifically, the reasons for and conditions surrounding his separation from your employment. All warnings concerning job performance should be carefully documented and signed by the employee.

3. The individual handling the unemployment compensation function should be familiar with the provisions of the Texas Unemployment Compensation Act and the Texas Employment Commission Rules. They should also become acquainted with TEC representatives in the local office so they can work together to reduce unemployment costs.

Specific And Critical

Key points to remember in handling unemployment insurance matters:

1. When you receive any correspondence from the Texas Employment Commission **consider it PRIORITY MAIL!** It means your time is already running and a deadline is in effect for your response.

2. Read the letter carefully. Respond immediately, giving detailed facts concerning the claimant's work separation. Information provided by both you and the claimant will be considered by the local TEC office in making an initial determination on the claim.

   A. Even if you do not protest the payment of benefits, you should file a written response to any notice of claim. This will insure that you do not waive any rights connected with the claim during the benefit year.

   B. If you believe the claimant should be disqualified or held ineligible (See Section on Disqualifications and Eligibility Requirements) give all relevant facts on your protest. Your protest must be TIMELY POSTMARKED to protect your further appeal rights, so DO NOT DELAY!

3. If you discharged the claimant then YOU have the burden of proving work connected misconduct if benefits are to be denied and/or your account protected from charge. If the claimant quit, then the CLAIMANT has the burden of proving good work connected cause for quitting before he can receive benefits.

4. Misconduct is action adverse to the employer's interests that the claimant could have controlled. Misconduct is not simple inability to do a job or occasional errors in performance unaccompanied by carelessness or negligence.

5. A company policy is a must for any size business and will often be useful to you in proving misconduct. If you are going to a hearing, bring your company policy with you.

6. Be reasonable and consistent. Enforce company policy the same way for everyone and be reasonable in your actions when employees have adversity strike them.

7. Job descriptions should be broad enough to cover many areas of responsibility. Employers must be very careful about changing hiring agreements - a major change in responsibilities, schedule of work, or method of wage payment may constitute good work connected cause for quitting.

8. Failure to pass a polygraph exam does NOT constitute work connected misconduct.

You must have independent evidence of the misconduct. Considering the substantial changes in federal law concerning polygraph testing, employers are well advised to use extreme caution in this area.

9. Some of the most difficult work separations to judge involve the more serious allegations: Drugs, Alcohol, and Theft. Suspicions are not enough. Be ready to prove your allegations.

10. It is extremely hard to prove "bad attitude" and "insubordination" without witnesses who can relate specific instances of such behavior.

11. Above all ELSE — Understand that if a claim is contested and goes to a hearing, your success will most likely depend on the FIRSTHAND TESTIMONY that you provide. HEARSAY testimony and AFFIDAVITS are inferior forms of evidence and will NOT OUTWEIGH CONTRADICTORY FIRSTHAND TESTIMONY PROVIDED BY THE CLAIMANT.

Disqualifications and Eligibility Requirements

1. Disqualifying Circumstances that will prevent a charge to your account:

   If you have filed a protest with the Commission as set out in the preceding section of this publication, and you are a base period employer (not including reimbursing or special governmental tax account employers), the claimant will be disqualified, and the employer's account will not be charged if:

   a. The claimant **voluntarily left** employment with you without good cause connected with work, or

   b. The claimant was **discharged for misconduct** connected with work, or

2. There will be no chargeback to your account even when benefits are awarded if the work separation occurred under either of the following circumstances:

   a. A statute, either federal, state, or municipal, required that you separate the claimant.

   b. The claimant was separated due to medically verified illness.

3. Additional provisions of the law will not necessarily prevent a charge to your account but can prevent payment of benefits to a claimant and possibly reduce the chargeback.

   A claimant shall be disqualified from receipt of benefits for failure, without good cause, to accept suitable work. A claimant whose stoppage of work was due to a labor dispute is also subject to a disqualification, although the courts have held that even though a claimant initially went out on strike he is entitled to benefits if he has been locked out by the employer.

   Claimants are also subject to disqualification for weeks during which they receive wages in lieu of notice (not to be confused with severance pay) or workers' compensation. Social Security payments can reduce the amount of unemployment benefits received.

   A claimant is disqualified for the duration of any period of unemployment if the Commission finds he left his most recent full-time work for the purpose of attending an established educational institution. The law also denies benefits to professional athletes during the off-season of their particular sport, and to school employees during recesses and between academic terms if they have a reasonable assurance of return. Pensions or retirement pay from base period employers will be deducted from the benefit amount, and if it exceeds the benefit amount, no unemployment benefits shall be paid to the individual.

4. Benefit eligibility conditions: In addition to the disqualification provisions above, the law provides that a claimant shall not receive benefits unless the following eligibility conditions have been met. A claimant must:

   a. have registered for work at an employment office,

   b. have filed necessary claim papers in accordance with Commission Rules,

   c. be able to work,

   d. be available for work,

   e. have earned necessary qualifying wages from covered employers, and

   f. have been totally or partially unemployed for a waiting period of seven consecutive days prior to the first payment of benefits following an initial claim.

Rights and Appeals

Important Points to Bear in Mind

1. Rights of Claimants and Employers —

   a. The right of a claimant to receive unemployment insurance depends upon eligibility and the conditions surrounding the claimant's separation from his **last work.**

   b. The right of an individual employer to prevent a chargeback to his account depends upon a claimant's last separation from that particular employer's employment prior to the date of the initial claim.

2. Appeals —

   a. If you do not consider the determination of the Commission representative to be correct, you have the right to appeal to the Appeal Tribunal within 14 days from the date of a determination. IF YOU DO **NOT** FILE YOUR APPEAL WITHIN THIS 14 DAY PERIOD YOU WILL HAVE WAIVED YOUR RIGHT TO APPEAL AND A CHARGEBACK TO YOUR ACCOUNT IS AN **AUTOMATIC AND FINAL CONSEQUENCE.** You will be notified when and where the hearing is set, and you should have your witnesses present. Witnesses should have direct personal knowledge of the facts in dispute, as hearsay testimony has little value in administrative hearings. You should be prepared to introduce all pertinent evidence at the hearing.

   b. If you do not agree with the decision of the Appeal Tribunal, you may, within 14 days from the date of the decision, request a review by the Commission.

   c. If you do not agree with the Commission's decision, you have the further right of appeal to the courts.

   d. The claimant, of course, also has the right of appeal. Accordingly, when you think the original determination is correct and the claimant has appealed, you should appear at the appeal hearing when notified to do so and present your evidence.

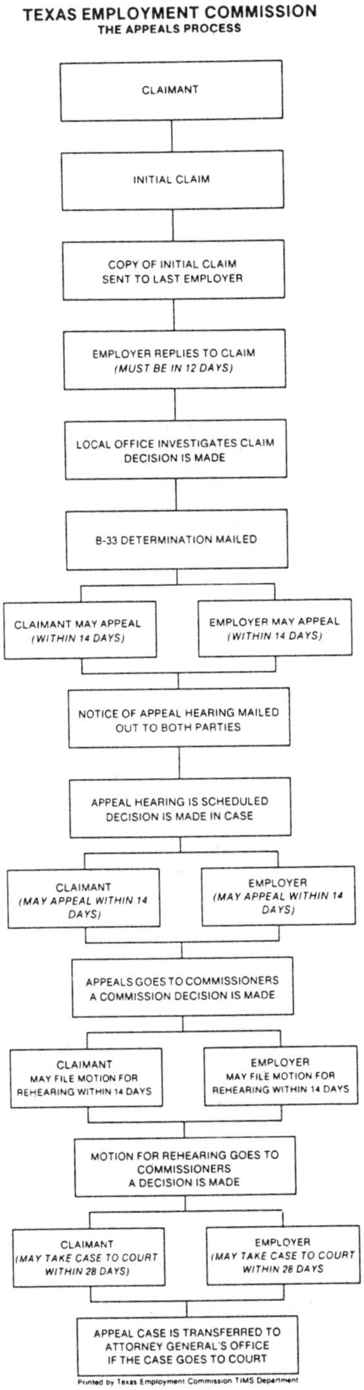

13. Unemployment Compensation and Tax Information

TEXAS EMPLOYMENT COMMISSION

Unemployment Compensation and Tax Information

UNEMPLOYMENT COMPENSATION AND TAXES

What is Unemployment Compensation?
Who Can Qualify for Benefits?
What Is a Base Period?
How Are Regular Benefits Determined?
What Is a Benefit Year?
What Must Claimants Do to Claim Unemployment Benefits?
What Are the Requirements for Receiving Payments?
Can Claimants Who Quit Work Draw Benefits?
Can Claimants Who Quit to Move With Their Spouse Draw Compensation?
What Is a "Voluntary" Separation?
What is "Good Cause Connected with the Work"?
Can Claimants Who are Discharged from Their Last Work Draw Benefits?
What Is "Misconduct"?
Can Claimants Refuse Suitable Work and Draw Compensation?
How Does a Claimant Requalify for Benefits?
Can Employees of Schools Draw Benefits During Summer Vacation or Holidays?
Can a Professional Athlete Draw Benefits Between Sport Seasons?
Can Aliens Draw Benefits?
Can Benefits Be Denied Solely Because of Pregnancy?
What Other Conditions Prevent Drawing Unemployment Benefits?
What Type of Earnings Must a Claimant Report on Weekly Claims for Benefits?
When is an Unemployment Compensation Overpayment Established?
What Are the Penalties Assessed When an Overpayment is Established?
Who Is Notified of Initial Claims Filed?
Can an Employer Protest Payment of a Claim?
What Notice Is Mailed in Response to a Protest?
Who Can Appeal from a Determination?
What Are Chargebacks?
How Is the Employer Notified of Maximum Potential Chargebacks?
Can Employers Protest Chargebacks to Their Account?
How Can an Employer Protest a Chargeback?
On What Basis Can an Employer Protest a Chargeback Notice?
Is the Employer Notified of the Action Taken on a Protested Chargeback?
What Happens When an Appeal Is Filed?
What Are Extended Benefits?
How Are Extended Benefits Financed?
Who Is a Subject Employer?
Are All Employees Covered by This Program?
What Tax Rates Are Applicable to Governmental Employers?
What Tax Rates Are Applicable to Employers Other Than Governmental Employers?
When Is an Employer Eligible for an Experience Tax Rate?
How Is an Experience Tax Rate Computed?
How Are Employees' Wages Reported?
How Much Tax Is to Be Paid?
What Are Wages?
What Is a Reimbursing Employer
Which Employers Pay Reimbursements Instead of Taxes?
What Are the Advantages and Disadvantages of Paying Reimbursements?
What Is a Group Account?
How May Disputed Issues involving Coverage, Taxes, or Penalties be Resolved?
What Is Shared Work Compensation?
How Does the Program Work?
How Long Is the Plan in Effect?

UNEMPLOYMENT COMPENSATION

AND TAXES

This pamphlet contains general information about claims, taxes, and reimbursements under the Texas Unemployment Compensation Act. It does not have the force or effect of statute or regulation.

WHAT IS UNEMPLOYMENT COMPENSATION? The Texas law provides that under certain conditions weekly payments of money may be made to unemployed individuals from an unemployment compensation fund contributed to by employers subject to payment of taxes or reimbursements under the Texas Unemployment Compensation Act.

WHO CAN QUALIFY FOR BENEFITS? An unemployed individual can qualify for benefits if during that claimant's Base Period (See "WHAT IS A BASE PERIOD?" explanation below) sufficient wage credits were earned by that claimant from employers covered by the Act on which the claim may be established in accordance with the Act (See "HOW ARE REGULAR BENEFITS DETERMINED?", below). Additionally, if you qualified for benefits on a prior claim, you must have since then earned 6 times your current computed Weekly Benefit Amount.

WHAT IS A BASE PERIOD? A base period is the first four of the last five completed calendar quarters immediately preceding the date of an initial claim for unemployment compensation. Base periods can be determined as follows:

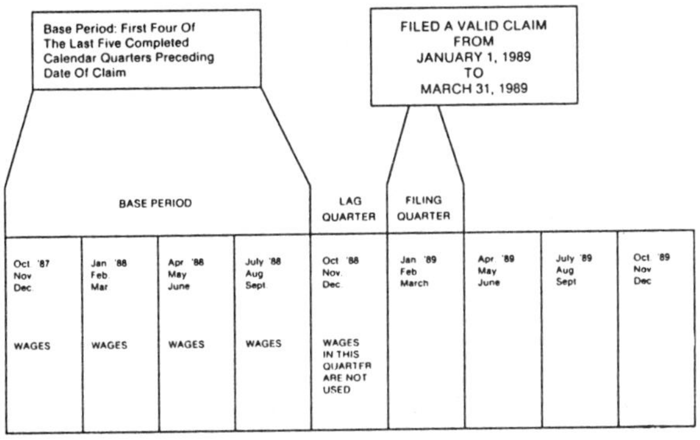

HOW ARE REGULAR BENEFITS DETERMINED? The amount of your benefits depends on the amount of qualifying wages you were paid during you base period. The weekly payment for a 7-consecutive day period of total unemployment is determined by taking the highest calendar quarter wage total in your base period and dividing that total by 25. This weekly payment is called the Weekly Benefit Amount (WBA). If the answer is not an exact dollar amount, it is raised to the next highest dollar amount not to exceed the maximum allowed under the law. The resulting answer (quotient) cannot be less or more than the current minimum or maximum amounts established in accordance with the Act. Current weekly benefit amount information can be obtained through your local claims representative. Your total earnings reported in your Base Period must exceed your WBA multiplied by 37 for your claim to be valid. If valid, your Maximum Benefit Amount, or the total benefits for a benefit year, will be the lesser of 27% of the total wages reported in your base period or 26 times your weekly benefit amount. A claimant may also qualify for extended benefits (See "WHAT ARE EXTENDED BENEFITS?").

WHAT IS A BENEFIT YEAR? A benefit year is a period of one year beginning with the effective date of a valid initial claim. The effective date is always the Sunday preceding the date of the claim.

WHAT MUST CLAIMANTS DO TO CLAIM UNEMPLOYMENT BENEFITS? To claim unemployment benefits, claimants must first register for work at a state employment office. After registering for work, they may then file an initial claim for unemployment compensation showing the name of the employer for whom they last worked and the reason for their unemployment.

The claimant's registration for work gives the Texas Employment Commission an opportunity to help the claimant find a job. A notice of the initial claim is mailed to the last employer named on the claim. Any issues arising as a result of statements made on the initial claim or as a result of information received from the employer will cause an investigation to determine a claimant's entitlement to benefits.

After filing an initial claim, claimants may file continued claims for periods of seven days following the initial claim. The initial claim is not a payable claim. The continued claims are the basis for making weekly payments of unemployment compensation.

WHAT ARE THE REQUIREMENTS FOR RECEIVING PAYMENTS? A claimant, during each seven-day period for which benefits are claimed must be less than full-time employed and must not have had earnings equal to or in excess of the weekly amount of unemployment insurance plus $5 or 25% of the weekly benefit amount, whichever is greater. In addition, the claimant must be able to work and must be available for work during the seven days for which the claims are filed. Furthermore, the claimant must make an active search for work. The claimant must also serve a waiting period of one week covered by a payable continued claim before qualifying for any payment of unemployment insurance. The claimant may be paid for this waiting period week claim if, during this benefit year, the claimant draws benefits totaling three times the weekly benefit amount for which the claimant qualified.

CAN CLAIMANTS WHO QUIT WORK DRAW BENEFITS? Claimants who quit their last work voluntarily without good cause connected with the work are disqualified for benefits. Also, claimants who quit voluntarily rather than provide servives to an individual with a communicable disease are disqualified. The disqualification remains in effect until the claimant returns to employment and either works for at least six weeks or earns wages equal to at least six times their weekly benefit amount. See HOW DOES A CLAIMANT REQUALIFY FOR BENEFITS? for requalification requirements. A claimant may not be disqualified for voluntarily leaving due to medically verified illness, injury, disability or pregnancy if the claimant is still available for work. Neither will an individual be disqualified if the claimant quit rather than provide services to an individual with a communicable disease if the employer failed to make available the facilities, equipment, training and supplies necessary to preclude infection of the claimant with the disease.

CAN CLAIMANTS WHO QUIT TO MOVE WITH THEIR SPOUSE DRAW COMPENSATION? If an individual quits work to move with a spouse from the area in which the individual worked, the claimant will be disqualified for not less than six nor more than twenty-five benefit periods. The claimant's maximum benefit amount will also be reduced by the number of weeks of disqualification.

WHAT IS A "VOLUNTARY" SEPARATION? A voluntary separation is a separation from work in which a claimant terminates work through personal choice and action. When claimants are forced to leave their last work for reasons beyond their control, they are considered to have left "involuntarily".

WHAT IS "GOOD CAUSE CONNECTED WITH THE WORK"? A claimant whose work-related reason for separation from employment was urgent, compelling, and of a necessitous nature so as to make separation involuntary has good cause connected with the work for quitting.

CAN CLAIMANTS WHO ARE DISCHARGED FROM THEIR LAST WORK DRAW BENEFITS? Claimants who are discharged from their last work for misconduct connected with the work are disqualified until they return to employment and either work for at least six weeks or earn wages at least equal to six times their weekly benefit amount. See HOW DOES A CLAIMANT REQUALIFY FOR BENEFITS? for requalification requirements.

WHAT IS MISCONDUCT? "Misconduct" means mismanagement of a position of employment by action or inaction, neglect that places in jeopardy the lives or property of others, intentional wrongdoing or malfeasance, intentional violation of a law, or violation of a policy or rule adopted to ensure orderly work and the safety of employees, but does not include an act of misconduct that is in response to an unconscionable act of an employer or superior.

CAN CLAIMANTS REFUSE SUITABLE WORK AND DRAW COMPENSATION? Claimants who fail, without good cause, to apply for available, suitable work when so directed by the Commission or to accept suitable work when offered will be disqualified until the claimant has returned to employment and either worked for six weeks or earned wages at least equal to six times the claimant's weekly benefit amount. See HOW DOES A CLAIMANT REQUALIFY FOR BENEFITS? for requalification requirements.

In determining whether or not any work is suitable for an individual, the Commission shall consider the degree of risk involved to health, safety, and morals at the place of performance of work, physical fitness and prior training, experience and prior earnings, length of unemployment and prospects for securing local work in the claimant's customary occupation, and the distance of the available work from the claimant's residence.

HOW DOES A CLAIMANT REQUALIFY FOR BENEFITS? In requalifying for benefits after a disqualification where the claimant must return to work for six weeks or earn wages at least equal to six times the weekly benefit amount, there are certain conditions that must be met. The claimant's employment must be in employment as defined in the Texas Unemployment Compensation Act or other States' unemployment compensation laws. The claimant must be separated from this new employment under nondisqualifying circumstances. For an individual to be considered to have worked for a week in satisfying the six weeks of work, it will be necessary for the individual to have worked a minimum of thirty hours during a seven consecutive day period not overlapping another seven day period.

It is the claimant's responsibility to present proof of the work and earnings necessary to requalify for benefits. The claimant must produce a document from the employer, or check stubs or other documentary evidence for the work and earnings.

CAN EMPLOYEES OF SCHOOLS DRAW BENEFITS DURING SUMMER VACATION OR HOLIDAYS? Individuals employed by any educational institution in any capacity cannot be paid benefits based on such services for any week of unemployment which begins during the period between two regular academic years or terms, if they performed such services in the first of such years or terms and have a contract to perform or there is a reasonable assurance that they will perform such services in the second of such years or terms. With respect to the foregoing services, individuals cannot be paid for any week of unemployment beginning during an established and customary vacation period or holiday recess if such individual performed services in the period immediately before and there is a reasonable assurance that they will perform services in the period immediately after such a vacation period or recess.

CAN A PROFESSIONAL ATHLETE DRAW BENEFITS BETWEEN SPORT SEASONS? Professional athletes are not entitled to payment of benefits on the basis of services, substantially all of which consist of participating in sports or are between two successive sport seasons (or similar periods) and they performed those services in the first of such seasons and there is reasonable assurance that they will perform those services in the latter of such seasons.

CAN ALIENS DRAW BENEFITS? Benefits are not payable on the basis of services performed by an alien unless the alien was lawfully admitted to the United States for permanent residence at the time such services were performed, was lawfully present for purposes of performing such services, or was permanently living in the United States under color of law at the time such services were performed.

CAN BENEFITS BE DENIED SOLELY BECAUSE OF PREGNANCY? No. While an individual must be both able to and available for work in order to be eligible for benefits, the law provides that benefits shall not be denied to an individual solely on the basis of pregnancy or termination of pregnancy.

WHAT OTHER CONDITIONS PREVENT DRAWING OF UNEMPLOYMENT BENEFITS? The law provides a disqualification preventing the claimant from receiving unemployment insurance if the stoppage of work is because of a labor dispute where the claimant was last employed or if the claimant quit the last job to go to school. Other disqualifications and penalties are applied as a result of misrepresentation or fraud.

Individuals shall be disqualified for benefits if they were involved in the sale of a corporation while an officer **and** a majority or controlling shareholder of that corporation. This also applies if the individual was a limited or general partner in a limited or general partnership and was involved in the sale of the business; or was a sole proprietor and sold the business.

Payments may also be denied or reduced by the claimant's receipt of wages in lieu of notice, Old Age Benefits (Social Security), Workmen's Compensation, wages from partial employment, and under certain conditions, receipt of vacation pay. Also, governmental or other pensions, retirement or retired pay, annuity, or any other similar periodic payment which is based on the previous work of the individual and which the individual receives after March 31, 1980, may cause a claimant's payments to be denied or reduced. Governmental payments include Social Security Old Age Benefits and Federal civilian and military pensions, and also disability payments based on retirement from work due to a disability. The phrase "based on the claimant's previous work" is intended to distinguish those payments received by the claimant as a result of work as an employee for an employer from those which the person financed in his capacity as an individual.

The law also provides for the deduction of unpaid child support obligations based on a signed agreement between the claimant and the Department of Human Resources. The deduction is to be paid to the appropriate state or local child support enforcement agency.

WHAT TYPE OF EARNINGS MUST A CLAIMANT REPORT ON WEEKLY CLAIMS FOR BENEFITS? Claimants must report gross earnings from any full-time, part-time, or temporary work; net profit from self-employment; vacation or holiday pay; and commissions. These earnings must be reported even though the claimant may not have yet received payment.

WHEN IS AN UNEMPLOYMENT COMPENSATION OVERPAYMENT ESTABLISHED? An overpayment is created when unemployment compensation benefits are received by an individual not legally entitled to such payment. An overpayment may be caused by a claimant error or may be intentional. There is no time limitation which prevents recording an overpayment that is detected or any set period of time when the overpayment can be removed from the record as uncollectible.

WHAT ARE THE PENALTIES ASSESSED WHEN AN OVERPAYMENT IS ESTABLISHED? Section 16 of the Texas Unemployment Compensation Act provides for administrative, civil action, and criminal penalties for fraudulent misrepresentation to obtain benefits as well as for recovery or recoupment of benefits improperly paid. It also provides penalties for fraudulent representation by an employing unit or any other person to prevent payment of benefits on legitimate claims or to reduce tax payments.

Penalties that may be assessed are fines of $20.00 to $500.00 and/or imprisonment or both; forfeiture of benefits received and the right to benefits which remain in the claimant's benefit year.

Subsection 16(d) of the TUC Act is the legal basis for initiating Civil Suit against a claimant for collection of past due benefits overpayments.

WHO IS NOTIFIED OF INITIAL CLAIMS FILED? The individual or organization for which the claimant last worked is mailed a notice of the filing of an initial claim.

CAN AN EMPLOYER PROTEST PAYMENT OF A CLAIM? Yes. An employer should protest a claim when knowledge of any facts is available that may adversely affect the claimant's right to receive unemployment benefits or that may affect a charge to the employer's account. The law provides that an employer has twelve (12) days from the date the notice is mailed in which to mail or deliver a protest. Such protest should be mailed or delivered to the office from which notice of the claim was mailed.

WHAT NOTICE IS MAILED IN RESPONSE TO A PROTEST? When a timely protest is received from an employer, the employer becomes an interested party to the claim and will be mailed a copy of the determination made in regard to the claim. This determination is furnished on Form B-33, Notice of Claim Determination, or occasionally by means of a letter. If the claimant received the wages from a taxed employer which is an interested party, and such wages were used to establish this claim, the Form B-33 will also indicate whether or not the benefits paid to the claimant during this benefit year will be charged to the account of such interested party. When a protest is not timely, employers will be mailed a letter providing this information.

If the claimant does not have sufficient wages to qualify for unemployment compensation, the interested party will be mailed a letter providing this information.

WHO CAN APPEAL FROM A DETERMINATION? Either the employer, if an interested party, or the claimant, can file an appeal. Each has fourteen (14) days from the date a determination is mailed in which to file an appeal.

WHAT ARE CHARGEBACKS? The sum of the regular unemployment benefits paid and 50% of the extended benefits paid to a claimant and charged to the tax account(s) of the base period employer(s) are called "Chargebacks." Chargebacks are used to compute an employer's tax rate and are not an amount owed by the employer. (For reimbursing employers, see "WHAT IS A REIMBURSING EMPLOYER?")

If claimants do not draw all of the benefits for which they qualify, the benefits not drawn will not become chargebacks. If at any time following the initial claim date an employer knows of circumstances which would prevent payment to the claimant, the employer should notify the Commission in writing of the circumstances and mail such notification to the Texas Employment Commission, Benefits Department, 101 East 15th Street, Austin, Texas 78778.

HOW IS THE EMPLOYER NOTIFIED OF MAXIMUM POTENTIAL CHARGEBACKS? After a claimant is paid the first benefit payment, a Form C-66, Notice of Maximum Potential Chargeback, is mailed to each of the base period taxed employers showing the maximum amount of unemployment benefits potentially chargeable to the employer's account for tax computation purposes.

CAN EMPLOYERS PROTEST CHARGEBACKS TO THEIR ACCOUNT? Yes. The taxed employer to which a Form C-66 is mailed has fourteen (14) days from the date the Form C-66 was mailed in which to protest the chargeback notice and present facts which will prevent the account from being charged with benefits paid to the claimant. If such an employer was the employer for whom the claimant last worked prior to the initial claim date, that employer will have been notified previously of the claim and will have no further right to protest the chargeback notice except for any clerical or machine error as to the amount of the maximum potential chargeback shown on Form Letter 62, To Employer - LEU Benefits Chargeable.

HOW CAN AN EMPLOYER PROTEST A CHARGEBACK? The lower part of the Form C-66, Notice of Maximum Potential Chargeback, should be used by the employer to protest the chargeback. It should be completed in detail and mailed to the Texas Employment Commission, Chargeback Determination Unit, 101 East 15th Street, Austin, Texas 78778, within fourteen (14) days after the date the Form C-66 is mailed.

ON WHAT BASIS CAN AN EMPLOYER PROTEST A CHARGEBACK NOTICE? An employer can file a protest to a Notice of Maximum Potential Chargeback when the claimant's last separation from work with the employer prior to the initial claim date shown on the Form C-66 was under one of the following circumstances:

- The claimant's separation was required by a Federal or Texas statute or a Texas municipal ordinance;
- The claimant left the work voluntarily without good cause connected with the work;

- The claimant left work voluntarily rather than provide services to an individual with a communicable disease;
- The claimant was discharged for misconduct connected with the work;
- The claimant was discharged for refusing to provide services to an individual with a communicable disease;
- Separation by medically verifiable illness.
- An involuntary separation resulting directly from a Presidentially declared natural disaster.

IS THE EMPLOYER NOTIFIED OF THE ACTION TAKEN ON A PROTESTED CHARGEBACK? Yes. When a determination is made with respect to a protest, the employer is mailed Form B-78, Notice of Decision of Potential Chargeback. Form B-78 will show whether the claimant's benefits are chargeable or not chargeable to the employer's account. If the employer desires to appeal the decision, he has fourteen (14) days after the date the Form B-78 is mailed in which to do so.

WHAT HAPPENS WHEN AN APPEAL IS FILED? When an appeal is received from either the employer or the claimant, the Appeal Tribunal schedules a hearing and notifies all interested parties of the time and place of the hearing. Testimony given in an appeal hearing is recorded and is under oath.

The employer and the claimant should present to the appeals referee evidence which they believe will support their contentions. This would include any documents, affidavits, or witnesses who have first hand information concerning the issue involved. Either party may be represented by legal counsel.

The appeals referee considers the record and testimony and renders a written decision. The decision includes the statement of the facts in issue, the applicable law, and the basis for the referee's decision. Copies of the decision are mailed to all interested parties. Further appeal may be made to the Commission within the fourteen (14) days after the mailing of the Appeal Tribunal decision.

When an appeal is received by the Commission, and the Commission has rendered a decision, a request for reconsider ation may be made to the Commission within fourteen (14) days after the date of the Commission's decision. If a request for reconsideration is not made to the Commission, appeal may be made to any court of competent jurisdiction in the county of the claimant's residence after the fourteenth day following the date of the Commission's decision and must be made before the end of the twenty-eighth (28) day.

WHAT ARE EXTENDED BENEFITS? Extended benefits are additional payments of unemployment benefits equal to 50% of regular benefits, which may be made to a claimant during a period of high unemployment after all of his regular unemployment benefits are exhausted. The period of time during which these additional payments may be made is called an "extended benefit period." Whether or not an extended benefit period exists is determined by the percentage rate of unemployment among insured workers statewide during a specific period of high unemployment.

HOW ARE EXTENDED BENEFITS FINANCED? Fifty percent of extended benefits paid is financed by the Federal government. The other fifty percent is financed in the same manner as regular benefits. Governmental employers must pay one hundred percent of any extended benefits paid to their former employees.

WHO IS A SUBJECT EMPLOYER? With respect to years after 1977, an employing unit is a subject employer, and its workers are covered under the program, if in the current or preceding calendar year:

(1) It paid as much as $1,500 in wages in any calendar quarter or had in employment at least one individual for some portion of the day in each of 20 different days, each day being in a different calendar week. (There are some exceptions. See (3) below and the list of excluded services under the next question.)

(2) It acquired the organization, trade, or business, or substantially all of the assets of a subject employer.

(3) It is a nonprofit organization as described in Section 501(c)(3) of the Federal Internal Revenue code which is exempt from income tax under Section 501(a) of such code and had as many as four or more individuals in employment for some portion of 20 days, each day being in a different calendar week. (Churches and organizations operated primarily for religious purposes are excluded.)

(4) It is subject to the Federal Unemployment Tax Act and had any employees in Texas.

(5) It elected to become a subject employer.

(6) It is a political subdivision of a State or an instrumentality of a political subdivision which is wholly owned by one or more political subdivisions.

(7) It employed individuals in agricultural labor and paid wages for such services in cash of $20,000 or more in any calendar quarter or employed 10 or more individuals in agricultural employment for some portion of the day in each of 20 different days, each day being in a different calendar week. Effective January 1, 1986 farm or ranch labor was considered as covered employment if performed by a seasonal worker employed on a truck farm, orchard or vineyard. Other farm or ranch employment is covered if the employing unit employs four (4) or more workers in 20 weeks or pays cash wages of $7,500 or more in a calendar quarter. (This changed to three (3) or more workers for 20 in a quarter effective January 1, 1987.) Migrant workers on a or $6,250 cash wages farm or ranch are covered immediately and seasonal workers will be covered immediately if work is performed at the same time and at the same location with migrant workers.

(8) It paid wages in cash of $1,000 or more in a calendar quarter for domestic service.

The State of Texas is a subject employer, and all services performed in the employ of the State of Texas or of any branch or department or instrumentality thereof are covered employment.

ARE ALL EMPLOYEES COVERED BY THIS PROGRAM? All employees who perform service for remuneration under the direction and control of a subject employer are covered unless such service is specifically excluded from the definition of employment. (An employer may elect to waive the exclusion.) Following are examples of serrvices which are excluded from covered employment:

(1) Services covered under the Railroad Retirement Act;

(2) Agricultural labor unless the employing unit is subject employer. (See preceding question regarding "WHO IS A SUBJECT EMPLOYER?"). The agricultural labor exemption is deleted effective January 1, 1986.

(3) Domestic service in a private home, local college club, or local chapter of a college fraternity or sorority unless the

employing unit is a subject employer. (See preceding question regarding "WHO IS A SUBJECT EMPLOYER?")

(4) Service of a minor child in the employ of his father or mother;

(6) Service performed in the employ of a church or organization operated primarily for religious purposes;

(7) Service performed for a political subdivision as an elected official, member of a legislative body, member of the judiciary, certain employees hired on a temporary basis due to fire and similar emergencies, and certain part-time policy-making or advisory employees;

(8) Service performed in the employ of a foreign government or instrumentality of a foreign government;

(9) Service performed as a student nurse or an intern in the employ of a hospital;

(10) Service performed as an insurance agent or solicitor if remuneration is solely by way of commission;

(11) Service of newsboys under the age of 18;

(12) Service performed in the employ of the United States Government;

(13) Service performed by an ordained minister in the exercise of his ministry or by a member of a religious order in the exercise of duties required by such order;

(14) Services performed by an individual receiving rehabilitation of the disabled;

(15) Service performed as part of an unemployment work relief or work training program assisted or financed by a Federal or State agency;

(16) Service performed by an inmate of a custodial or penal institution which is owned or operated by the State or a political subdivision thereof;

(17) Service performed by a student for a school, college, or university if he is enrolled and regularly attending classes;

(18) Certain services performed by a student who is enrolled at a nonprofit or public educational institution which combines academic instruction with work experience;

(19) Service performed by a patient of a hospital for the hospital; and

(20) Service performed on a fishing vessel normally having a crew of fewer than 10 if the crew member's reimbursement for services performed is a share of the catch and the services are determined not to be employment under the Federal Unemployment Tax Act.

(21) Service performed by a sales agent if seller is engaged in the direct sale of a product, and has a written contract whereby substantially all remuneration is to be by commission.

(22) Service performed by a full-time student employed by an organized camp which is operated seven months or less each year. The student must be enrolled full-time at an educational institution or be between terms with a reasonable assurance that he will be enrolled full-time the immediately succeeding academic term.

(23) Service performed by an individual as a real estate broker or salesman as defined in the Real Estate License Act (Vernon's Texas Civil Statutes, Article 657a); who holds a valid real estate license issued by the Texas Real Estate Commission, is being paid substantially by commission, and has a written cntract that provides that the individual is not treated as an employee for federal tax purposes with respect to those services.

(24) Service performed by an individual as an instructor of persons licensed or seeking licensure as real estate brokers or salesmen; who is instructing a program or course approved by the Texas Real Estate Commission, and who has a written contract that provides that the individual is not treated as an employee for federal tax purposes with respect to those services.

WHAT TAX RATES ARE APPLICABLE TO GOVERNMENTAL EMPLOYERS? Except for the answer to this question, the answers throughout this pamphlet with respect to tax rates pertain to nongovernmental employers.

There are no individual tax rates for governmental employers—all have the same rate. The tax rate for governmental employers was set by law at 1% for taxable wages paid in 1978 and 1979. Tax rates for governmental employers in 1980 and each year thereafter have been determined by how much this group of employers has cost the Fund in benefit payments to their ex-employees as compared to the amout of taxes which this group has paid.

WHAT TAX RATES ARE APPLICABLE TO EMPLOYERS OTHER THAN GOVERNMENTAL EMPLOYERS? Prior to January 1, 1986 each employer's tax rate is 2.7% until he becomes eligible for an experience tax rate after which his experience tax rate, or general rate, may range from 0% to 6.0%. Effective January 1, 1986 an employer shall pay contributions for the calendar year in which they become an employer at the rate established for that year for the major standard industrial classification group to which the employer is assigned, or at two and seven-tenths percent (2.7%) whichever rate is greater. Also January 1, 1986 an employer with an approved shared work unemployment compensation plan may be subject to a general tax rate up to 9.0%. Effective with tax rates for 1990, the general tax rate for employers using a shared work plan will cap at 6.00%.

Employers with Standard Industrial Classification (SIC) Code 0724 (cotton gins) may, for calendar years beginning 1988, elect to pay unemployment tax at a rate of 5.4%, instead of the rate assigned them by the Texas Employment Commission. This election must be made annually, on or before December 31, for the following year. Election forms will be provided by the Texas Employment Commission upon request.

WHEN IS AN EMPLOYER ELIGIBLE FOR AN EXPERIENCE TAX RATE? An employer is eligible for an experience tax rate as soon as his account has been chargeable with benefits throughout four calendar quarters. Since an employer's account is first chargeable when wages can be used in a claim for benefits, an employer will be liable for payment of the tax at his original tax rate for a period of six to eight quarters before he is eligible for an experience tax rate if the employer acquires all or a part of the business of a predecessor employer whose compensation experience is transferred to the successor employer as provided in Subsection 7(c)(7) of the Act. Effective June 10, 1985 the law was amended to require the mandatory transfer of compensation experince from the predecessor employer to the successor employer when a total acquisition occurs.

Total acquisitions effective September 1, 1989 or after will not have a mandatory transfer of compensation unless the previous owner(s) or any partner(s), officer(s), shareholder(s), or other owner(s) was related by blood or marriage, to any of the other owner(s) was related by blood or marriage, to any of the other owners, partners, officers, or shareholders of the successor or, if the previous owner holds an option to purchase an interest in the successor business. With the amendment effective September 1, 1989, there is no provision for voluntary total transfer of experience.

HOW IS AN EXPERIENCE TAX RATE COMPUTED? Annual experience tax rates are computed as of October 1 to be effective for the following calendar year, and notices of the rates are mailed to employers early in the year in which they are to be effective. An employer's general tax rate is determined by multiplying his benefit ratio by the statewide replenishment ratio for the preceding year.

An employer's benefit ratio is the result obtained by dividing the total benefits paid to his former employees and charged to his account during the preceding 36 months by the employer's total taxable payroll on which taxes have been paid for the same 36 months. If the employer has less than 36 months but at least four calendar quarters throughout which his account has been chargeable with benefits, his computation will be based on all calendar quarters immediately preceding the computation date.

The replenishment ratio is the result obtained by dividing the total effectively charged benefits paid during the 12 month period preceding the October 1 rate computation date plus one-half of the ineffectively charged benefits for the same period by the total amount of benefits paid for the same period that are effectively charged. Cancelled benefit warrants, repaid benefits which were overpaid, and benefits paid which are repayable from reimbursing employers, the Federal Government, or any other governmental entity are excluded from this computation.

Following is an example of the computation of an employer's experience tax rate or general rate:

Total amount of benefits paid to former employees of a taxed employer and charged to his account for the period from October 1, 1980, through September 30, 1983	=$ 400
Total taxable wages paid by an employer during above period on which the tax was paid	=$40,000
The employer's Benefit Ratio is, therefore, $400 — $40,000	= 1.00%
Assume that the statewide Replenishment Ratio for Texas for 1984 tax rates	= 1.40
Then, the employer's general tax rate will be 1.00% × 1.40	= 1.40%

The Texas Unemployment Compensation Act contains a table in Section 7 which provides an easy method to determine the computed experience tax rate or general rate. The table shows the various computed experience tax rates depending upon the replenishment ratios and the employer's benefit ratio. These rates vary from 0% to 6% for most employers through December 31, 1989. General rates for 1990 and beyond will cap at 6% for all employers.

The floor amount of the Unemployment Compensation Fund is the greater of four hundred million dollars ($400,000,000) or one percent (1%) of total taxable wages for the four calendar quarters ending June 30 preceding the rate computation date. Rate increases based on the floor amounts are computed according to a formula whereby a deficit ratio is obtained using the total amount of taxes due for the four calendar quarters preceding the computation date from experience rated employers under the general tax rate and the replenishment rate as the denominator and the numerator. Federal advances or other liabilities of the fund are not considered in computations made in 1984 and 1985. For years prior to 1988, the deficit ratio is multiplied by the employer's general tax rate for the prior year to obtain a deficit tax rate which is added to the employer's general tax rate. The deficit tax rate is limited to 2%.

Beginning with the rate computation for the calendar year 1988, the deficit ratio is multiplied by the sum of the employer's general tax rate, the replenishment rate as the denominator and the amount by which the fund balance is below the floor as the numerator. Federal advances or other liabilities of the fund are not considered in computations made in 1984 and 1985. For years prior to 1988, the deficit ratio is multiplied by the employer's general tax rate for the prior year to obtain a deficit tax rate which is added to the employer's general tax rate. The deficit tax rate is limited to 2%.

The ceiling amount of the Unemployment Compensation Fund is two percent (2%) of total taxable wages for the four calendar quarters ending June 30 preceding the rate computation date. Tax Credits based on the ceiling amounts are computed according to a formula whereby a surplus ratio is obtained using the total amount of taxes due from experience rated employers during the four calendar quarters preceding the computation date as the denominator and the amount by which the fund is above the ceiling as the numerator. The surplus ratio is multiplied by the employer's contributions due for the four calendar quarters ending September 30 preceding the computation date to obtain a credit amount which the employer may apply against his taxes in the ensuing year. The credit may not be applied against delinquent taxes or applied in any manner until the employer has paid any delinquent taxes he owes.

A Replenishment Tax is assessed against all experience rated employers. The tax rate is a percentage obtained by using one-half of the ineffectively charged benefits paid during the twelve months preceding the calculation date as the numerator and total taxable wages for the four quarters ending the preceding June 30 as the denominator.

The Commission has the authority to levy a separate interest tax on each experience rated employer. The rate may not exceed .2%. The proceeds of the interest tax can be used by the Governor solely to pay interest on advances from the Federal Unemployment Trust Fund.

HOW ARE EMPLOYEE'S WAGES REPORTED? During the month following each calendar quarter (April, July, October, and January), each employer submits an Employer's Quarterly Report. This report must show the total amount of wages paid during the quarter, the total amount of Benefit Wage Credits, and the total amount of Taxable Wages Paid.

The report contains a Wages List on which the employer reports each employee's Benefit Wage Credits for the quarter. Employees are listed by social security number and name, and the amount of Benefit Wage Credits applicable to each employee is shown.

Effective January 1, 1986 the Texas Unemployment Compensation Act was amended to define benefit wage credits as total wages.

The first $7,000 paid to an employee by an employer during a calendar year from January 1, 1983, through December 31, 1987, constituted taxable wages. January 1, 1988 that amount was increased to $8,000 and for calendar years 1989 and after, the taxable wage amount is $9,000. An employer cannot consider wages paid by another employer to the employee in the calendar year in arriving at this limit unless he is a successor to the prior employer, and a Joint Application for Transfer of Compensation Experience has been approved by the Commission. A total acquisition occurring on or after June 10, 1985, does not require the filing of a Joint Application for Transfer of Compensation Experience as the transfer of compensation experience has become mandatory.

This mandatory transfer of compensation experience will continue with acquisitions occurring on or after September 1, 1989, but will apply only to acquisitions where the predecessor is related by blood or marriage to the successor or where the predecessor holds an option to buy the business of the successor. There is no provision for voluntary total transfer of experience.

Following is an example of the amount of wages to be reported by an employer, assuming that he had only one employee in 1989 to whom he paid $4,000.00 per month.

Employer's Quarterly Report	1st Qtr.	2nd Qtr.	3rd Qtr.	4th Qtr.
Total Wages Paid	$12,000.00	$12,000.00	$12,000.00	$12,000.00
Wages over $9,000.00	3,000.00	12,000.00	12,000.00	12,000.00
Taxable Wages Paid	9,000.00	.00	.00	.00
Benefit Wage Credits	12,000.00	12,000.00	12,000.00	12,000.00
Effective Tax Rate	1.00%	1.00%	1.00%	1.00%
Amount of Tax	90.00	.00	.00	.00

The employer must file reports for the second, third and fourth quarters of 1989 even though he owes no tax.

Although reimbursing employers do not pay this tax, they must submit Employer's Quarterly Reports to report wages paid to their employees.

HOW MUCH TAX IS TO BE PAID? The amount of tax to be paid by an employer is computed by multiplying the amount of taxable wages paid during the quarter by the effective tax rate of the employer.

In the example under "HOW ARE EMPLOYEE'S WAGES REPORTED?,"the employer paid $9,000.00 in taxable wages in the first quarter of 1989 and his effective tax rate was 1.00%. Therefore, the amount of tax to be paid is 1.00% of $9,000.00 or $90.00. No tax is due for the second, third and fourth quarters.

WHAT ARE WAGES? "Wages" means all remuneration paid for personal services, including the cash value of all remuneration paid in any medium other than cash and gratuities received by any employee in the course of employment to the extent that the gratuities are considered as wages in the computation of taxes under the Federal Unemployment Tax Act, 26 U. S. C. Section 3301 et seq. (There are certain exceptions not included in this term which are listed in the Act.)

"Wages are wages (and reportable) when they are **paid** rather than when they are earned or accrued."

WHAT IS A REIMBURSING EMPLOYER? A reimbursing employer is an employer which pays to the Fund, in lieu of taxes, an amount equal to the amount of benefits which were paid to his former employees and were attributable to service in the employment of such employer. A reimbursing employer reports wages for his employees and is billed quarterly for the amount of regular benefits and 50% of the extended benefits paid to his former employees during the prior quarter. A reimbursing employer makes no tax payments but is subject to the same penalties as a taxed employer for failure to file reports and/or make payments on time. After December 31, 1978, a governmental employer must pay 100% of extended benefits based on wages earned from the governmental employer.

WHICH EMPLOYERS PAY REIMBURSEMENTS INSTEAD OF TAXES? The following employers pay reimbursements instead of taxes:

(1) A political subdivision of the State which elects to be a reimbursing employer;

(2) A nonprofit organization described in Section 501(c)(3) of the Internal Revenue Code of 1954 which is exempt from income tax under Section 501(a) of such code and which elects to be a reimbursing employer; and

(3) The State of Texas or any branch or department or instrumentality thereof.

WHAT ARE THE ADVANTAGES AND DISADVANTAGES OF PAYING REIMBURSEMENTS? Each political subdivision of the State and each nonprofit organization which is described in Section 501(c)(3) of the Internal Revenue Code of 1954 which is exempt from income tax under Section 501(a) of such code is entitled under the law to elect to pay reimbursements in lieu of paying taxes. Stated below are some matters to be considered when making the election.

To elect to become a reimbursing employer is comparable to making a decision to discontinue carrying casualty insurance. If no casualty occurs, the cost of the premium has been saved. Likewise, if no former employee is paid unemployment benefits, the organization has saved the cost of the tax but may have to pay the cost of a surety bond as a reimbursable employer which may be required to guarantee payment of reimbursements.

In the example under " HOW ARE EMPLOYEE'S WAGES REPORTED?," the employer's total tax for 1989 is $90.00. If his tax rate later increased to 8.44%, his tax will be $759.60 a year. If his tax rate should decrease to 0.63%, his tax will be $56.70 for a year. Of course, experience rates are subject to change from year to year.

In the same example, if the employer had one employee and elected to pay reimbursements in lieu of taxes, he could be charged in one year as much as $5,460.00 for regular benefits plus the cost of extended benefits. This employer could under certain unique circumstances get a large additional charge in a subsequent benefit year based on wage credits earned by this claimant which were not in the base period of the claimant's first benefit year.

A taxed employer normally knows in February of each year his tax rate for the calendar year. A reimbursing employer never knows his potential liability and may be required to pay reimbursements more than two years after the individual has been separated from his employment.

WHAT IS A GROUP ACCOUNT? The Act provides that two or more reimbursing employers may file a joint application with the Commission for the establishment of a group account for the purpose of sharing the costs of benefits paid to former employees of group members.

The members of a group must designate an individual to act as the group representative to make reports for the group, to pay reimbursements, to furnish any bond for the group that may be required, etc.

The advantage in forming such a group is that the risk to a member as to payment of reimbursements may be shared among all members. On the other hand, a member may be required to share in the reimbursements for other members of the group although none of his former employees have been paid benefits.

HOW MAY DISPUTED ISSUES INVOLVING COVERAGE, TAXES, OR PENALTIES BE RESOLVED? Commission Rule 13 provides in part that "In all situations not specifically provided for in the Act or in the rules of the Commission, a hearing may, at the discretion of the Commission, be afforded an employing unit, upon its written request, in any case involving tax liability or any question relating to contributions".

SHARED WORK UNEMPLOYMENT COMPENSATION PROGRAM

WHAT IS SHARED WORK COMPENSATION? Shared Work Compensation offers an alternative to employers facing a reduction in force. Instead of laying off employees, the employer reduces the hours of work among a specific group of employees. Wages lost to the worker as a result of reduced hours is supplemented by a partial unemployment benefit amount.

HOW DOES THE PROGRAM WORK? An interested employer submits to the Commission a plan for participating in the program. If the plan is approved, workers who qualify for unemployment benefits will receive both wages and Shared Work benefits. The workers will receive the percentage of their regular benefits that matches the percentage of reduction in the employer's plan.

HOW LONG IS THE PLAN IN EFFECT? An approved shared work plan is effective on the date approved by the Commission. It shall expire at the end of the 12th full calendar month after its effective date; provided, that the plan is not terminated previously by the Commission.

14. Information Concerning the Texas Employment Commission

Texas Employment Commission
101 E. 15th
Austin, Texas 78778

TEXAS EMPLOYMENT COMMISSION

SERVICES

For more details call 1-800-TEC-MARY

As a Texas Employer, you are entitled to use all the services offered by the Texas Employment Commission on a no-fee basis. Some of these services can be designed to meet your particular needs.

PLACEMENT SERVICES
Texas Employment Commission local offices have professional interviewers to assist you with your staffing needs, large or small, full-time, part-time or temporary. Additionally, employers who hire their permanent workers through Texas Employment Commission will receive an official certification of employment for each person hired. This certification serves in lieu of Form I-9 as required in the Immigration Reform and Control Act of 1986.

JOB SERVICE MATCHING SYSTEM
The Texas Employment Commission's computerized job matching system, the job service matching system, can assist you with your recruitment needs. When you request workers, the entire file of job seekers who are available in the area is searched to find the best qualified for the job. If we have difficulty in filling your job order in Texas, we can utilize the interstate job bank system, a national network of Employment Service Offices in 50 States.

ON-SITE RECRUITMENT AND MOBILE OFFICE
The Texas Employment Commission can assist you with job site recruitment designed to meet your particular needs. Our mobile offices can be used for staffing at construction sites, shopping centers or new factories.

JOB SERVICE TESTING
You often need to test a job seeker's skills or aptitudes in order to make a hiring decision. We offer aptitude and clerical proficiency tests that have been designed and validated by the Department of Labor to assist you with this need.

SAVE TAX $$$
The Targeted Job Tax Credit program allows employers to receive a tax credit for wages paid to certified workers enrolled in the program. The Emergency Veterans Job Training Act pays employers up to $10,000 to train and hire an eligible Vietnam-era or Korean conflict veteran.

ECONOMIC RESEARCH AND ANALYSIS DEPARTMENT
This department can provide you with labor market information on a State, local or regional basis, on past, present or future projections to assist you in planning and evaluation.

UNEMPLOYMENT COMPENSATION INSURANCE
This is an insurance program for people between jobs. It provides qualified individuals a weekly income while they are actively seeking work.

TAX DEPARTMENT SERVICES
Courteous field examiners are stationed State-wide to assist you in all Unemployment Insurance Tax matters.

These and other services are available through your local Texas Employment Commission office. The Texas Employment Commission is committed to serving the needs of employers by providing the means to bring workers and employers together. For more detailed information on these services, please telephone your local Texas Employment Commission office.

C-92 (987)

15. Information Concerning the Texas Business Council

A PARTNERSHIP IS THE QUICKEST ROUTE TO PROGRESS

By Mary Scott Nabers
Commissioner Representing Texas Employers

The goal of government is to accomplish on a grand scale what individuals, or small groups, lack the resources to achieve for themselves. It is a simple concept which should work better than it does.

In Texas the increasing difficulty experienced by the average taxpayer in accessing the system has created a real problem. A growing consensus of resentment and frustration toward government as a whole is obvious in every part of the state. Men and women complain bitterly about bureaucracy, red tape, regulation and escalating tax rates. Nothing good can come from a situation such as this. There can be no winners if taxpayers write off state government in exasperation.

Texas has always been a rich and powerful state, totally unaccustomed to difficult economic times and consequently unprepared for the recent downturn. Force people anywhere to face what Texans have encountered of late and the result would be the same: doubt, distrust, disagreement -- and endless searches for a place to lay the blame.

We simply cannot afford to think this way, not when we are in a race against time to turn the Texas economy around. Continued pessimism can only burden, delay, perhaps destroy the recovery we should nourish with every resource.

There are many areas of agreement. Laws and procedures are too complex; regulation is unnecessarily burdensome; our tax structure needs to be reexamined; there is incredible resistance to change; communication at best is hard to maintain. But understanding is essential, and an all-out effort is nothing less than an outright responsibility of every Texan -- whether in the private or the public sector.

State government is reaching out to taxpayers with a forum for communication called the Texas Business Council. It is open to everyone who will make a commitment to join in a united effort to (1) cut the cost of doing business in Texas; (2) put Texans back to work; and (3) stimulate the economy of a troubled state.

The council is a network linking business, government and labor. For the first time ever, various branches of state government have joined forces to travel into all regions of Texas to talk to and listen to the people they serve. Texas Business Council meetings have been scheduled throughout the state. Agencies that collect taxes and regulate will be on hand to explain their functions, answer questions, exchange ideas, and listen to complaints and suggestions. Information on the availability of state resources and expertise will be offered to the participants. The Council will encourage on-going relationships between public and private sector members, relationships which will foster increased understanding of the problems and needs which exist on both sides.

Participation in the Texas Business Council requires only a desire to become involved in this state government effort and a willingness to devote the time to attend one regional meeting this fall. For those who are most dissatisfied with how "the system" works, this is an opportunity to have valuable input. For those who want to see Texas returned to the economic position it once had and who believe that Texans no longer can afford the luxury of complacency, it is the place to begin.

Complete details on the program are available by writing to Mary Scott Nabers, Texas Employment Commission, 101 E. 15th, Austin, Texas 78778. There is no charge associated with the Council, but individuals are asked to pay the cost of food and refreshments at the meeting.

For more details call 1-800-TEC-MARY.

16. Texas Government and Licensing Offices

AGENCY ADDRESSES

1. **Texas State Board of Public Accountancy**
   1033 La Posada, Suite 340
   Austin, TX 78752-3892
   (512) 451-0241

2. **Board of Architetural Examiners**
   8213 Shoal Creek Blvd. #107
   Austin, TX 78758
   (512) 458-1363

3. **State Bar of Texas**
   P.O. Box 12487
   Capitol Station
   Austin, TX 78711
   (512) 463-1463

4. **Department of Licensing and Regulation**
   P.O. Box 12157
   Capitol Station
   Austin, TX 78711
   (512) 463-5522

5. **State Board of Barber Examiners**
   1300 E. Anderson Lane
   Building C, Suite 275
   Austin, TX 78752
   (512) 835-2040

6. **Texas Cosmetology Commission**
   1111 Rio Grande
   Austin, TX 78701
   (512) 463-5540

7. **Alcoholic Beverage Commission**
   1600 W. 38th Street
   Austin, TX 78731
   (512) 458-2500

8. **Texas Department of Health**
   1100 West 49th Street
   Austin, TX 78756
   (512) 458-7111

9. **Texas Funeral Commission**
   8100 Cameron Road
   Building B, Suite 550
   Austin, TX 78753
   (512) 834-9992

10. **Texas Education Agency**
    William B. Travis Building
    1701 N. Congress
    Austin, TX 78701
    (512) 463-9744

11. **Department of Public Safety**
    5805 North Lamar
    P.O. Box 4087
    Austin, TX 78773
    (512) 465-2000

12. **Department of Human Services**
    701 W. 51st Street
    P.O. Box 149030
    Austin, TX 78714-9030
    (512) 450-3011

13. **Chiropractic Examiners Board**
    8716 Mopac Expressway North, Suite 301
    Austin, TX 78759
    (512) 343-1895

14. **Texas Amusement Machine Commission**
    1005 E. 7th Street
    Austin, TX 78702
    (512) 473-2865

15. **Comptroller of Public Accounts**
LBJ State Office Building
111 East 17th Street
Austin, TX 78701
(800) 252-5555 (in Texas)
(512) 463-4070

16. **Department of Banking**
2601 North Lamar Blvd.
Austin, TX 78705
(512) 479-1200

17. **Texas State Board of Examiners of Psychologists**
1300 E. Anderson Lane
9101 Burnet Road, Suite 212
Austin, TX 78758
(512) 835-2036

18. **Credit Union Department**
914 E. Anderson Lane
Austin, TX 78752-1699
(512) 837-9236

19. **Board of Dental Examiners**
327 Congress, #500
Austin, TX 78701-4037
(512) 463-5536

20. **Texas Department of Agriculture**
P.O. Box 12847
Austin, TX 78711
(512) 463-7602

21. **Real Estate Commission**
1101 Camino La Costa
P.O. Box 12188
Capitol Station
Austin, TX 78711-2188
(512) 465-3940

22. **State Board of Registration for Professional Engineers**
1917 South I.H. 35
P.O. Drawer 18329
Austin, TX 78760
(512) 440-7723

23. **Railroad Commission of Texas**
P.O. Box 12967
Capitol Station
Austin, TX 78711
(512) 463-7288

24. **Savings and Loan Department**
2601 N. Lamar, #201
P.O. Box 1089
Austin, TX 78705
(512) 479-1250

25. **State Board of Veterinary Medical Examiners**
1946 South Inter-Regional Hwy, Suite 306
Austin, TX 78704
(512) 447-1183

26. **Texas Parks and Wildlife Department**
4200 Smith School Road
Austin, TX 78744
(512) 389-4800

27. **State Securities Board**
1800 San Jacinto
P.O. Box 13167
Capitol Station
Austin, TX 78711
(512) 474-2233

28. **Sate Board of Insurance**
State Insurance Building
1110 San Jacinto
Austin, TX 78701-1998
(512) 463-6169

29. **Texas Board of Land Surveyors**
7701 N. Lamar, #400
Austin, TX 78752
(512) 452-9427

30. **Texas Board of Examiners Fitting and Dispensing of Hearing Aids**
4800 N. Lamar Blvd. Suite 150
Austin, TX 78756
(512) 459-1488

31. **Texas Water Commission**
S.F. Austin Office Building
P.O. Box 13087
Capitol Station
Austin, TX 78711-3087
(512) 463-8028

32. **Board of Private Investigators and Private Security Agencies**
313 E. Anderson Lane, Suite 200
P.O. Box 13509
Austin TX 78711
(512) 463-5545

33. **Office of the Consumer Credit Commissioner**
2601 N. Lamar
Austin, TX 78705
(512) 479-1280

34. **Polygraph Examiners Board**
P.O. Box 4087
Austin, TX 78773
(512) 465-2058

35. **Texas Motor Vehicle Commission**
P.O. Box 2293
Austin, TX 78768
(512) 476-3587

36. **Board of Vocational Nurse Examiners**
9101 Burnet Road #105
Austin, TX 78758
(512) 835-2071

37. **Board of Nurse Examiners for the State of Texas**
9101 Burnet Road, Suite 104
Austin, TX 78756
(512) 835-4880

38. **Texas Board of Licensure for Nursing Home Administration**
4800 N. Lamar, Suite 310
Austin, TX 78756
(512) 458-1955

39. **Texas State Board of Medical Examiners**
1110 Camino La Costa, Suite 210
P.O. Box 13562
Capitol Station
Austin, TX 78711
(512) 452-1078

40. **Texas Optometry Board**
9101 Burnet Road, Suite 214
Austin, TX 78758
(512) 835-1938

41. **Structural Pest Control Board**
9101 Burnet Road, #201
Austin, TX 78758
(512) 835-4066

42. **State Board of Pharmacy**
8505 Cross Park Drive, #110
Austin, TX 78754-4533
(512) 832-0661

43. **Texas Board of Physical Therapy Examiners**
313 Rundberg lane, Suite 113
Austin, TX 78753
(512) 835-1846

44. **Texas State Board of Plumbing Examiners**
929 East 41st Street
P.O. Box 4200
Austin, TX 78751
(512) 458-2145

45. **State Board of Podiatry Examiners**
3420 Executive Center Drive, Suite 305
Austin, TX 78731
(512) 794-0145

46. **Department of Highways and Public Transportation**
125 E. 11th Street
Austin, TX 78701
(512) 463-8585

47. **Texas State Board of Examiners of Professional Counselors**
1100 West 49th Street
Austin, TX 78756-3183
(512) 459-2900

48. **Texas State Board of Examiners of Dietitians**
1100 West 49th Street
Austin, TX 78756-3183
(512) 458-7501

49. **State Committee of Examiners for Speech/Language Pathology and Audiology**
1100 West 49th Street
Austin, TX 78756
(512) 459-2935

17. Significant Aspects of Franchise Tax on Capital and Earned Surplus

- Problem areas of capital base would be amended to reduce the possibility of future litigation. The definition of employee benefits in the capital calculation would be more specifically defined to include pensions. A corporation could only use its federal income tax books to report its franchise tax on capital if the corporation had less than $1 million in taxable capital. Under current law, a corporation can report its tax using its federal tax books if it has less than $1 million in surplus. This provision has allowed many large companies to avoid using GAAP books in their tax calculation.
- The tax base would be broadened beyond capital to include earned surplus which is a measure of current business activity. Earned surplus would include net income plus compensation to directors and officers of corporations with more than 35 shareholders.
- Tax would be levied on capital at a rate of $2.50 per $1,000. The rate on earned surplus would be $4.50 per $100.
- The base tax would be on capital with a surtax on earned surplus for the amount that tax on earned surplus exceeds tax on capital. For example, if a corporation calculated a tax of $100 on capital and $150 on earned surplus, then the tax paid would be $150 composed of a $100 tax on capital plus a surtax of $50 on earned surplus.
- There would be no exemption from earned surplus or capital, but corporations with less than $100 in tax liability would not have to file a return.
- The tax base would be apportioned with the same single factor gross receipts formula used in the current franchise tax.
- Revenue gain would be $790.1 million for the 1992–93 biennium.
- The tax would combine the revenue potential of an income tax with the stability of a capital tax.
- The tax burden would be distributed by industry in a more equitable manner than either the current franchise tax, or a value added tax.
- The tax would be due in March for the privilege of doing business during the calendar year.
- There would be no loss from transferring to a quarterly prepayment system as under most income taxes.
- The effective date of the revised franchise tax is January 1, 1992.

THE FRANCHISE TAX AS AMENDED BY HOUSE BILL 11

House Bill 11 enacted several changes in the franchise tax. The tax has been levied on capital since its inception in 1907, but will now be assessed on capital and a measure of current business activity known as earned surplus. Virtually every aspect of the tax was amended by the bill.

Taxable Entities

The tax will continue to apply to corporations only. There were however some changes with regard to the entities who pay the tax.

The franchise tax paid by banks will be allocated to general revenue. Previously, bank franchise taxes were distributed to local entities to compensate them for the loss of the bank stock tax which was declared unconstitutional.

Savings and loans, which had historically been exempt from the tax, will now pay the franchise tax. Taxable savings and loans will also include state or federal savings banks.

Limited liability companies formed under the "Texas Limited Liability Company Act" will also be subject to the franchise tax. Total taxable capital of a limited liability company will consist of the members' contributions and surplus, which is defined as the excess of net assets over members' contributions.

Determination of Net Taxable Capital

The first step in determining a corporation's tax liability is to determine net taxable capital. The following procedure is followed:

1.) Determine the total taxable capital by adding the corporation's total stated capital and surplus. Stated capital is computed as the corporations par value of stock. Surplus is the value of the corporation's net assets over its stated capital. Net assets is defined as the corporation's total assets less its total debts.

2.) Determine the corporation's apportioned taxable capital by multiplying total taxable capital by the corporation's apportionment formula. The apportionment formula is the corporation's gross receipts derived in Texas divided by its total gross receipts.

The use of a single factor gross receipts formula for determining apportioned taxable capital is unchanged from the previous franchise tax. By continuing the use of a single factor formula based on receipts, the tax burden remains higher on out-of-state companies who have little or no plant, equipment or employees in the state.

3.) Compute net taxable capital by subtracting any allowable deductions from apportioned taxable capital. Allowable deductions include 50 percent of a corporation's capital investment in an enterprise zone project during the year, or the annual amortized cost of a solar energy device.

Miscellaneous Changes to Capital Tax Base

The capital tax base of the franchise tax has been the target of frequent litigation in the past decade. Previous attempts have been made to strengthen the base against future litigation. HB 11 enacted changes in the capital base in order to clarify certain areas of the base and prevent additional lawsuits.

1.) If a corporation's taxable capital is less than $1 million according to its federal income tax return, then the corporation may use the method to calculate its federal income tax return to compute its franchise tax. Under current law, companies with less than $1 million in surplus can use their federal income tax books to compute their franchise return. This provision created a loophole whereby certain large corporations were able to use their tax books in the franchise calculation.

2.) Deferred income taxes and investment tax credits will not be excluded from surplus. Historically, these accounts were not taxable, but it was determined that they did not meet the statutory definition of debt.

3.) The definition of taxable employee benefits was clarified to state that pensions would be part of the tax base. In the past there has been a great deal of uncertainty as to what constitutes taxable employee benefits.

4.) Corporations will be required to use double entry bookkeeping to account for all transactions that affect the computation of the tax. Certain taxpayers have attempted successfully to use items found in footnotes of a parent corporation to reduce taxable capital of a subsidiary.

Determination of Net Taxable Earned Surplus

The second portion of the new franchise tax base is net taxable earned surplus. It is calculated as follows:

1.) Determine the corporation's taxable earned surplus by adding compensation to directors and officers and reportable federal taxable income net of certain foreign source dividends. S corporations and other corporations with less than 35 shareholders are not required to add back compensation to officers and directors.

Reportable federal taxable income is federal taxable income after Schedule C special deductions and before net operating loss deductions. Schedule C special deductions are predominately dividend deductions. An S corporation's reportable federal taxable income is income reportable to the IRS as taxable to the corporation's shareholders.

If a parent corporation with 35 or more shareholders has a subsidiary with less than 35 shareholders, the subsidiary must add back officer compensation in determining taxable earned surplus.

Banks will only add compensation to executive officers and directors while other corporations add compensation of all officers and directors. This provision should adjust for the inordinately large number of officers at banks.

2.) **Apportion the corporation's taxable earned surplus to Texas to determine apportioned taxable earned surplus.** Multiply taxable earned surplus by an apportionment formula based on gross receipts.

The formula used to determine apportioned taxable earned surplus is substantially similar to the formula used to apportion taxable capital. The main difference is that neither the numerator nor denominator of the earned surplus apportionment formula includes foreign source dividends. The other difference is that this apportionment formula includes food and medicine receipts in the numerator.

3.) **Determine net taxable earned surplus by subtracting from apportioned taxable earned surplus any allowable deductions and business losses carried forward.**

Five percent of the capital investment in enterprise zone projects during the year will be allowed as a deduction against apportioned taxable earned surplus. Ten percent of the year's amortized cost of solar energy equipment may also be deducted from apportioned taxable earned surplus. If a deduction was taken against apportioned taxable capital for enterprise projects or solar energy devices then no deduction from earned surplus is allowed.

A business loss is any negative amount of apportioned taxable earned surplus. Any losses that occurring during a tax year that ended before January 1, 1991 cannot be used as an offset against the franchise tax. A business loss may be carried forward to the year following the loss year and for the next four years.

<u>Tax Rate and Calculation</u>

The tax rate on net taxable capital is .25 percent. This rate is less than half of the .525 percent rate levied on net taxable capital under the franchise tax prior to the passage of HB 11. The tax rate on net taxable earned surplus is 4.5 percent.

In principle, the tax liability is equal to the calculation on capital or earned surplus that yields the highest amount. In practice, the tax is levied on capital with a surtax on earned surplus for the amount that the tax on earned surplus exceeds the tax on capital. For example, if a corporation calculated a tax on capital of $100 and a tax on earned surplus of $150, then the tax paid would be $150, composed of a $100 tax on capital plus a $50 surtax on earned surplus. The effect is the same as if the calculation were a "higher of" measure.

The tax is calculated in this manner because only 14 states with a corporate income tax allow a deduction for income taxes paid to other states. By keeping part of the tax liability on capital for all corporations, multistate corporations doing business in Texas will most likely be able to keep a portion of the deduction they have historically enjoyed in other states for Texas franchise taxes paid.

<u>Tax Credit for Sales Tax on Manufacturing Machinery</u>

As part of the budget balancing package, the phase-out of the sales tax on manufacturing machinery and equipment will be removed from October 1, 1991 through September 30, 1993. Purchases made during this period will be subject to the full sales tax rate. The phase-out will continue as scheduled on October 1, 1993.

To compensate corporations for additional sales taxes paid because of this delay, a tax credit will be allowed on the 1994 franchise tax return equal to 25 percent of sales taxes paid on equipment purchased between October 1, 1991 and December 31, 1992, and 50 percent of the tax paid on equipment purchased between January 1, 1993 and September 30, 1993.

Corporations will be allowed to carry the credit forward to the next four privilege periods following the 1994 report. The credit may not exceed the amount of franchise tax due for any one privilege period.

<u>FAS 96 and the Temporary</u>
<u>Credit on Net Taxable Earned Surplus</u>

Under Federal Accounting Standards Board Statement 96 (FAS 96), a corporation must book as a deferred income tax expense the tax on the difference between the financial accounting basis and tax basis of its assets. The enactment of a new state tax based on income, or partially on income as is the revised Texas franchise tax, could produce an immediate loss in earnings as a result of a sudden increase in deferred income taxes for corporations who have adopted FAS 96.

To solve the problem, corporations could have been allowed to use the financial accounting basis of their assets in the earned surplus calculation. This would have resulted in a loss of revenue to the state from the tax on the difference between the financial accounting and tax basis of the assets.

A solution was reached that allows corporations the option of using the financial accounting basis of their assets to determine a credit against the tax on earned surplus. The credit consists of the tax rate times the difference between the financial accounting basis and tax basis of the assets in place at the close of the corporation's accounting year ending in 1991. The credit is limited to the tax on 1/20 of the difference in the basis of the assets.

Corporations opting for this credit will have to pay an additional tax on capital of 0.2 percent. With the option of this credit in place, FAS 96 corporations should be able to avoid a substantial loss in earnings.

<u>Additional Earned Surplus Tax</u>

There is an additional tax on earned surplus levied on corporations that are no longer subject to the taxing jurisdiction of the state. For example, if a corporation with an accounting year that coincides with the calendar year leaves the state on July 1, it would owe no tax on the earned surplus accumulated between January 1 and June 30. This is because the tax on this earned surplus would not be due until May 15 of the following year. The additional tax would be levied on that six months of earned surplus.

This corporation would owe the additional tax at the regular rate of 4.5 percent due within 60 days of ceasing business in the state. This additional tax is necessary because the regular tax is paid for a privilege period that exists the year following the year after the earned surplus is derived.

<u>Payment Dates and Privilege Period Covered</u>

The tax will be due on May 15 with an extension until November 15. On May 15, the corporation must pay either 90 percent of the tax due or 100 percent of the tax paid in the previous year to gain an extension. Because the tax liability will be drastically different for many corporations in 1992, corporations will be required to remit 90 percent of the tax due in order to be granted an extension during the initial year of the revised tax.

The extension runs until November since most corporations do not file their final income tax return with the IRS until October. If the tax due is less than $100, then the corporation does not owe tax and does not have to file a return.

The tax will still be levied as a privilege tax. This means that the tax is paid for the privilege of doing business in the state. For example, the tax on both earned surplus accumulated in 1991 and capital calculated at the close of the accounting year ending in 1991 will pay for the privilege of doing business in Texas during 1992.

In the past, the franchise tax was paid in March for the privilege of doing business during the following May 1 to April 30 period. Under the revised tax, the original payment will be in May for the privilege of doing business during the calendar year.

With the calendar year privilege period, corporations will pay the tax after the privilege period has begun. To make this adjustment, the privilege period for which the March 1991 franchise tax covers was shortened to May 1, 1991 through December 31, 1991.

The effective date of the revised tax is January 1, 1992 and the first report under the tax will be due on May 15, 1992.

A sample calculation of the franchise tax as amended by HB 11 follows on pages 9 and 10.

SAMPLE FRANCHISE TAX CALCULATION

RELEVANT FINANCIAL ITEMS

Total Assets	$8,000,000
Total Debt	6,500,000
Stated Capital	500,000
Net Assets (Total Assets-Total Debt)	1,500,000
Surplus (Net Assets-Stated Capital)	1,000,000
Net Income from Form 1120	360,000
Deductible Foreign Source Income	30,000
Director/Officer Compensation	150,000
Investment in Enterprise Zone	50,000
Amortized cost of Solar Energy Equip.	10,000

APPORTIONMENT PERCENTAGE

Texas Gross Receipts	$1,000,000
Total Gross Receipts	7,000,000
Apportionment Percentage	14.3%
(Texas Gross Receipts/Total Gross Receipts)	

CALCULATION OF TAX ON CAPITAL

Total Stated Capital	$500,000
+ <u>Surplus</u>	<u>$1,000,000</u>
Total Taxable Capital	$1,500,000

Total Taxable Capital	$1,500,000
x Apportionment Percentage	14.3%
Apportioned Taxable Capital	$214,286

Net Taxable Capital	$214,286
x Capital Tax Rate	0.25%
Tax owed on Capital	$536

CALCULATION OF TAX ON EARNED SURPLUS

Net Income from Form 1120	$360,000
- Deductible Foreign Source Income	$30,000
Net Income less Foreign Income	$330,000

Net Income less Foreign Income	$330,000
+ Director/Officer Compensation	$150,000
Taxable Earned Surplus	$480,000

Taxable Earned Surplus	$480,000
x Apportionment Percentage	14.3%
Apportioned Taxable Earned Surplus	$68,571

Apportioned Taxable Earned Surplus	$68,571
Cost of Solar Equip. x .1	$1,000
- Inv. in Ent. Zone x .05	$2,500
Net Taxable Earned Surplus	$65,071

Net Taxable Earned Surplus	$65,071
x Earned Surplus Tax Rate	4.50%
Tax owed on Earned Surplus	$2,928

TAX LIABILITY

Tax owed on Capital	$536
+ Tax owed on Earned Surplus net of tax owed on Capital	$2,392
Total Tax Owed the State	$2,928

CURRENT ISSUES RELATING TO THE FRANCHISE TAX ON CAPITAL AND EARNED SURPLUS

Even though a component of earned surplus is income, the tax is not a true income tax. The tax base is broader than income alone, and unlike most state corporate income taxes there is no quarterly prepayment provisions since it is a privilege tax.

In spite of these differences, the state will have to address many issues associated with corporate income taxation. The new franchise tax will require major adjustments by taxpayers and tax collectors alike.

Links to Federal Code

Because the franchise tax will now be levied in part on a measure of income, links to the Internal Revenue Code become important. The major question is whether to adopt federal changes to the code on a continuing basis or to tie-in to the code as of a certain date. In order to avoid deferring tax policy decisions to the federal level, the legislature decided to tie-in to the code as it existed on December 31, 1990.

Texas will join 16 other states who have adopted definitions in the code as of a certain date. Twenty four states who levy corporate income taxes adopt changes in the code on a continuing basis.

Reporting Methods

As a capital-based levy, the franchise tax has always been reported on a separate entity basis. This reporting requirement did not change with the passage of HB 11.

In addition to reporting the tax on a separate entity standard, states may allow or require either combined reporting and/or consolidated returns. The vast majority of states that levy corporate income taxes allow either combination or consolidation. Some require consolidated returns of unitary businesses. Texas will join six other states that allow neither combination nor consolidation.

As revenue from the tax is collected, the Comptroller will gain a better understanding of whether separate accounting will remain attractive from the state's standpoint. There is a possibility that some corporations may be able to shelter some income out of the state if reporting remains on a separate entity basis. On the other hand, some multistate corporations would achieve a tax reduction from either filing a combined report and/or a consolidated return.

At this time, the tax collection and audit mechanisms are in place for separate entity reports. During the early stages of the new tax, administrative ease may be preferred to the difficulties of adjusting to a new reporting method.

Foreign Source Dividends

The federal government allows a tax credit for foreign source income. Because federal relief is in the form of a tax credit, states who use federal income as a starting point must grant a deduction for foreign source dividends that are included in federal taxable income if taxation of these dividends is to be avoided.

There has been some question as to whether the bill as passed excludes all foreign source dividends or just the gross-up for foreign taxes and subpart F income. There appears to be some foreign source income that would still be taxable under the bill as passed.

Food and Medicine Deduction

Under the statute prior to HB 11, corporations could deduct sales of food and health care supplies from their gross receipts in Texas when calculating their apportionment formula. The food and medicine deduction referred to the existing apportionment formula for capital which was respecified in the bill to apply to capital only. A separate apportionment formula based on gross receipts was developed for earned surplus.

The result of this is that the statute as amended by the bill does not extend the food and medicine deduction to the new apportionment formula for the calculation of net taxable earned surplus. Certain corporations in the food and/or medical industries could be adversely affected by this treatment if it is not amended by either statute or rule.

Treatment of S Corporations

With the passage of the federal tax reform act of 1986, the number of S corporations increased dramatically. This was chiefly due to the fact that the highest personal income tax rate was now lower than the highest corporate income tax rate. Each state levying a corporate income tax must decide how it will treat S corporations. Since most states have a personal income tax, the vast majority recognize S corporations status and tax the distributions under the personal income tax.

Under the bill, Texas does not recognize S corporation status. S corporations must remit the tax like any other corporation. The major difference is that reportable federal taxable income to an S corporation for the purpose of defining earned surplus is 'the income reportable to the Internal Revenue Service as taxable to the corporation's shareholders.'

This definition has prompted some controversy in that it does not allow for an additional exemption for compensation to a shareholder for his or her services in the capacity of an officer when that shareholder does not draw an explicit salary for those services. In these instances the shareholder has chosen compensation in the form of dividends only.

Appendix D

Federal Publications

FEDERAL TAX MATERIAL

OSHA

Appendix D

Federal Publications

FEDERAL TAX MATERIAL

1. Guide to Free Tax Services

Free Tax Services

The Internal Revenue Service (IRS) provides free tax information and services to help you throughout the year. This publication lists the many free tax services the IRS offers. It gives helpful information about filing your return and briefly explains certain IRS procedures.

IRS free services include toll-free telephone service, tax information publications, tax assistance and educational programs, and audiovisual instructional materials that are available for loan to groups.

Most tax questions can be answered by reading the tax forms and instructions. If you need more information, you can turn to the free tax services described in this publication. You may call IRS toll-free or visit your local IRS office with questions about your tax account or tax law, or for general information about IRS procedures and services.

Telephone Service

Toll-free telephone assistance is available in all 50 states, the District of Columbia, Puerto Rico and the U.S. Virgin Islands. Using the toll-free telephone system, you can get answers to your tax questions and pay only local charges. There is no long distance charge for your call.

During periods of peak demand for telephone assistance, you may get a busy signal. Demand may be lower early in the morning or later in the week, so you may want to call at those times. Call the telephone number listed for your area on page 4 of this publication.

Tele-Tax

Tele-Tax is the IRS toll-free telephone service that provides both recorded tax information and automated refund information.

Recorded Tax Information. You can listen to tax information on about 140 topics such as filing requirements, dependents, itemized deductions, tax credits and free services available. Instructions on how to use Tele-Tax and a list of topics are on pages 5 and 6.

Automated Refund Information. If you filed your tax return and you have not received your refund, you can check on its status by using the Tele-Tax automated refund system. For information on how to use this service and what information you will need to provide, turn to page 5.

To Order Forms and Publications

Order tax forms and publications by using the order blank on page 31 of this publication, or by calling toll-free 1-800-TAX-FORM (1-800-829-3676).

Telephone Service for the Hearing-Impaired

Toll-free telephone tax assistance is available for deaf and hearing-impaired taxpayers with access to TDD (telecommunication device for the deaf) equipment. The hours of operation are:

January 1 through April 4	8:00 a.m. to 6:30 p.m. Eastern Standard Time
April 5 through April 15	9:00 a.m. to 7:30 p.m. Eastern Daylight Time

April 16 through October 24	9:00 a.m. to 5:30 p.m. Eastern Daylight Time
October 25 through December 31	8:00 a.m. to 4:30 p.m. Eastern Standard Time

Residents of all states, including Alaska, Hawaii, Puerto Rico, and the U.S. Virgin Islands, can call 1-800-829-4059.

Information for the Blind

Braille tax materials are available at Regional Libraries for the Visually Impaired in conjunction with National Library Services, the Library of Congress. Currently, these materials are limited to copies of Publication 17, *Your Federal Income Tax;* Publication 334, *Tax Guide for Small Business;* Forms 1040, 1040A, and 1040EZ, and related instructions; and the Tax Tables.

Walk-In Service

Assistors at most IRS offices throughout the country can help you prepare your own individual federal tax return.

If you want assistance with your tax return, you should bring the package of tax forms and instructions you received in the mail and all Forms W-2 and Forms 1099 showing interest or other income. Bring any other information (such as a copy of last year's return) that the assistors can use to help you.

Although the IRS will not prepare your tax return for you at these locations, assistors will provide line-by-line self-help tax return assistance with you and other taxpayers in a group setting. At most IRS offices you can also get tax forms, publications and help with questions about IRS notices or bills.

International Service

If you are a taxpayer who lives outside the United States, the IRS has full-time permanent staff at 13 U.S. Embassies and Consulates around the world. These offices maintain a supply of tax forms and publications. The staff can help you with account problems and answer your questions about notices and bills.

From January 1 through June 15 each year, taxpayer service representatives travel to many cities worldwide to assist taxpayers outside the U.S. In 1992 they will visit approximately 173 foreign cities. Note: The IRS office in Manila is now closed. If you were formerly serviced by this office, you may call the IRS office in Tokyo for information on available assistance in your area.

You may call your nearest U.S. Embassy, Consulate or IRS office listed below to find out when and where assistance will be available. These IRS telephone numbers are local numbers. Please check with your telephone company for any country or city codes required if you are outside the local dialing area. The Nassau and Ottawa numbers include the U.S. area codes.

Bonn, West Germany	339-2119
Caracas, Venezuela	285-3111, ext. 333
London, England	408-8076 or 408-8077
Mexico City, Mexico	211-0042, ext. 3559
Nassau, Bahamas	(809) 322-1181
Ottawa, Canada	(613) 238-5335
Paris, France	4296-1202, ext. 2214
Riyadh, Saudi Arabia	488-3800, ext. 206
Rome, Italy	4674-2560
Sao Paulo, Brazil	881-6511, ext. 206
Singapore	338-0251, ext. 247
Sydney, Australia	261-9275
Tokyo, Japan	224-5466

You can also write to the Assistant Commissioner (International), 950 L'Enfant Plaza SW, Washington, DC 20024, USA, for answers to your technical or tax account questions.

Volunteer and Education Programs

The IRS has programs designed to help you understand your rights and obligations under our nation's tax system. Volunteers trained by the IRS are an important part of all these programs. For times and locations of available services in your community, or to volunteer, call the IRS in your area and ask for the Taxpayer Education Coordinator.

Community Outreach Tax Education

Groups of taxpayers with common tax concerns, such as retirees, farmers, small business owners and employees, can get free tax help from IRS employees or trained volunteers at convenient community locations. The assistance may be provided during the day, in the evening, or on weekends.

Community Outreach Tax Education offers two kinds of assistance. One kind provides line-by-line self-help income tax return preparation for taxpayers who want to prepare their own returns. The other provides tax seminars discussing various tax topics. Outreach sessions may be co-sponsored by community organizations and other government agencies.

Volunteer Income Tax Assistance

Volunteer Income Tax Assistance (VITA) provides free help to people who cannot afford professional tax assistance. After completing IRS training, VITA volunteers help prepare basic tax returns for taxpayers with special needs, including persons with disabilities, the elderly, and non-English speaking taxpayers at libraries, community colleges, schools, shopping malls, and other convenient locations in the community.

Tax Counseling for the Elderly

Tax Counseling for the Elderly (TCE) provides free tax help to people aged 60 or older, especially those who are disabled or who have special needs. Volunteers who provide tax counseling are often retired individuals associated with non-profit organizations that receive grants from the IRS. The grants help pay out-of-pocket expenses for the volunteers to travel to homes, retirement homes, or special TCE sites. Sites are conveniently located in neighborhood centers, libraries, churches and other places in the community.

Small Business Tax Education Program

Small business owners and other self-employed individuals can learn about business taxes through a unique partnership between the IRS and community-based educational facilities. Seminars, workshops and in-depth tax courses, offered in a variety of settings, provide training on starting a business, recordkeeping, preparing business tax returns, self-employment tax issues and employment taxes. Resource materials provide instruction through practical examples and reinforcement exercises.

The costs for this program vary. Some courses are offered free as a community service. Some educational facilities may include costs for course materials in addition to tuition. Still others charge a nominal fee to offset the administrative costs of sponsoring organizations.

Bank, Post Office and Library Program

The IRS supplies free tax preparation materials to more than 16,000 banks and post offices and 14,000 libraries and reference areas in technical schools, military bases, prisons, community colleges and other locations. The materials at libraries may include reproducible tax forms, reference sets of IRS publications and audiovisual materials on preparing Forms 1040EZ, 1040A, 1040, and Schedules A and B. Banks, post offices and other sites have supplies of Forms 1040EZ, 1040A and 1040 available.

Student Tax Clinics

Student Tax Clinics are sponsored by law and graduate accounting schools. They are staffed by student volunteers who provide free tax assistance to taxpayers who would not normally obtain counsel when faced with a tax audit or examination. Students who have received special permission from the IRS may represent taxpayers before the IRS during examination and appeals proceedings.

Understanding Taxes

This is an introductory tax course taught in high schools, junior high schools, and basic adult education classes nationwide. Working students find immediate practical value in the section of the course that teaches them how to fill out their tax returns. Students also learn about the history, politics and economics of taxation and about taxpayer rights and responsibilities.

Teachers are provided with free instructional materials, including a videotape and computer software. In many areas, teachers may be able to enroll in workshops to help them prepare for course instruction.

Practitioner Education

Practitioner Education provides training to people who prepare tax returns for a fee. As part of this program, Practitioner Institutes are held in every state in cooperation with colleges, state bureaus of revenue, and professional associations. Tax professionals can learn about recent tax law changes at these Institutes, which will enhance the professional quality of the services they provide.

Taxes in U.S. History

This program contains instructional materials designed to complement eighth grade U.S. history courses. Teachers can use three video programs, a teacher's guide, and an instructional poster to portray three important events that played a key role in forging the U.S. tax system. These materials can reach a large number of students at an age when many soon will be required to file federal income tax returns for the first time.

Print and Audiovisual Information

The IRS provides a variety of print and audiovisual tax information materials to the news media for use in informing the public about current tax issues and assistance. Special audiovisual programming includes radio and TV shows where viewers can phone in their tax questions. For example, the IRS produces tax clinics for broadcast on public television stations. The clinics highlight the various tax forms and schedules, address changes in the tax law, give helpful filing hints and provide information on where to get free assistance.

Newspapers and other print media across the country receive tax information materials for their readers. IRS Public Affairs Officers send news releases, question and answer columns, and other items about taxes to their local media. Topics range from farming to electronic tax filing. One popular item the IRS produces is the Tax Supplement. It contains articles and graphics in a clipsheet format ready for paste up and printing. Newspapers can use it as a special tax section or publish articles from it as a regular series at tax time.

IRS-produced films and videotapes are available for loan to interested groups or organizations without charge. To order, call the Taxpayer Education Coordinator or Public Affairs Officer at your local IRS office.

"Why Us, the Lakens?"

This film, narrated by Lyle Waggoner, highlights taxpayers' rights during an IRS tax audit and their appeal rights. It follows Jeff and Kathy Laken, whose tax return has been selected for an IRS audit. Unhappy with the audit finding, the Lakens appeal and the viewer learns how the audit procedure and the appeals system work. (28 min.; 16mm film and 3/4" videocassettes; English-only.)

"¿Por Que Nosotros, Los Garcia?"

This Spanish-language film explains taxpayers' examination and appeal rights in a similar fashion to "Why Us, the Lakens?" (28 min.; l6mm film and 3/4" videocassettes.)

"¿Por Que Los Impuestos?"

Realizing that there is a lack of knowledge about the U.S. tax system in the Hispanic community, the editor of a Spanish weekly newspaper assigns an eager cub reporter to the story. The reporter uncovers the history of taxation, how taxes are used, the rights and responsibilities of taxpayers, and the different kinds of IRS assistance available. The film is especially suitable for social studies and history courses at adult education and community centers. (10 min.; 16mm film and 3/4" videocassettes, 1/2" VHS.)

"Line-by-Line Videotape"

This 90 minute videotape helps you select the most appropriate federal tax form for your circumstances. It takes you through Form 1040A, line by line, with explanations for each line in easy-to-understand everyday language. Also highlighted are areas on Form 1040 that many taxpayers find most difficult.

The line-by-line videotape is available for loan from most IRS offices. Many libraries also keep a copy.

It is also available in audiotape cassette (90 min.).

Call the IRS With Your Tax Question

If the instructions to the tax forms and our free tax publications have not answered your question, please call us TOLL-FREE. "Toll-Free" is a telephone call for which you pay only local charges.

Choosing The Right Number

Use only the number listed on this page for your area. Usè a local city number only if it is not a long distance call for you. **Please do not dial "1-800" when using a local city number.** However, when dialing from an area that does not have a local number, be sure to dial "1-800" before calling the toll-free number.

Before You Call

Remember that good communication is a two-way process. IRS representatives care about the quality of the service we provide to you, our customer. You can help us provide accurate, complete answers to your tax questions by having the following information available:

1. The tax form, schedule, or notice to which your question relates;

2. The facts about your particular situation (the answer to the same question often varies from one taxpayer to another because of differences in their age, income, whether they can be claimed as a dependent, etc.);

3. The name of any IRS publication or other source of information that you used to look for the answer.

Toll-free tax help telephone numbers

Alabama
1-800-829-1040

Alaska
Anchorage, 561-7484
Elsewhere, 1-800-829-1040

Arizona
Phoenix, 257-1233
Elsewhere, 1-800-829-1040

Arkansas
1-800-829-1040

California
Oakland, 839-1040
San Francisco, 839-1040
Elsewhere, 1-800-829-1040

Colorado
Denver, 825-7041
Elsewhere, 1-800-829-1040

Connecticut
1-800-829-1040

Delaware
1-800-829-1040

District of Columbia
1-800-829-1040

Florida
Jacksonville, 354-1760
Elsewhere, 1-800-829-1040

Georgia
Atlanta, 522-0050
Elsewhere, 1-800-829-1040

Hawaii
Oahu, 541-1040
Elsewhere, 1-800-829-1040

Idaho
1-800-829-1040

Illinois
Chicago, 435-1040
In area code 708,
1-312-435-1040
Elsewhere, 1-800-829-1040

Indiana
Indianapolis, 226-5477
Elsewhere, 1-800-829-1040

Iowa
Des Moines, 283-0523
Elsewhere, 1-800-829-1040

Kansas
1-800-829-1040

Kentucky
1-800-829-1040

Louisiana
1-800-829-1040

Maine
1-800-829-1040

Maryland
Baltimore, 962-2590
Elsewhere, 1-800-829-1040

Massachusetts
Boston, 523-1040
Elsewhere, 1-800-829-1040

Michigan
Detroit, 237-0800
Elsewhere, 1-800-829-1040

Minnesota
Minneapolis, 644-7515
St. Paul, 644-7515
Elsewhere, 1-800-829-1040

Mississippi
1-800-829-1040

Missouri
St. Louis, 342-1040
Elsewhere, 1-800-829-1040

Montana
1-800-829-1040

Nebraska
Omaha, 422-1500
Elsewhere, 1-800-829-1040

Nevada
1-800-829-1040

New Hampshire
1-800-829-1040

New Jersey
1-800-829-1040

New Mexico
1-800-829-1040

New York
Bronx, 732-0100
Brooklyn, 596-3770
Buffalo, 685-5432
Manhattan, 732-0100
Nassau, 222-1131
Queens, 596-3770
Staten Island, 596-3770
Suffolk, 724-5000
Elsewhere, 1-800-829-1040

North Carolina
1-800-829-1040

North Dakota
1-800-829-1040

Ohio
Cincinnati, 621-6281
Cleveland, 522-3000
Elsewhere, 1-800-829-1040

Before You Hang Up

If you do not fully understand the answer you receive, or you feel our representative may not fully understand your question, our representative needs to know this. The representative will be happy to take the additional time required to be sure he or she has answered your question fully and in the manner that is most helpful to you.

By law, you are responsible for paying your fair share of Federal income tax. If we should make an error in answering your question, you are still responsible for the payment of the correct tax. Should this occur, however, you will not be charged any penalty. To make sure that IRS representatives give accurate and courteous answers, a second IRS representative sometimes listens in on telephone calls. No record is kept of any taxpayer's identity.

Oklahoma
1-800-829-1040

Oregon
Portland, 221-3960
Elsewhere, 1-800-829-1040

Pennsylvania
Philadelphia, 574-9900
Pittsburgh, 281-0112
Elsewhere, 1-800-829-1040

Puerto Rico
San Juan Metro Area, 766-5040
Isla, 766-5549

Rhode Island
1-800-829-1040

South Carolina
1-800-829-1040

South Dakota
1-800-829-1040

Tennessee
Nashville, 259-4601
Elsewhere, 1-800-829-1040

Texas
Dallas, 742-2440
Houston, 541-0440
Elsewhere, 1-800-829-1040

Utah
1-800-829-1040

Vermont
1-800-829-1040

Virginia
Richmond, 649-2361
Elsewhere, 1-800-829-1040

Washington
Seattle, 442-1040
Elsewhere, 1-800-829-1040

West Virginia
1-800-829-1040

Wisconsin
Milwaukee, 271-3780
Elsewhere, 1-800-829-1040

Wyoming
1-800-829-1040

Phone Help for Hearing-Impaired People With TDD Equipment.

All areas in U.S., including Alaska, Hawaii, Virgin Islands, and Puerto Rico, 1-800-829-4059

Hours of Operation:

8:00 A.M. to 6:30 P.M. EST (Jan. 1–April 4)
9:00 A.M. to 7:30 P.M. EDT (April 5–April 15)
9:00 A.M. to 5:30 P.M. EDT (April 16–Oct. 24)
8:00 A.M. to 4:30 P.M. EST (Oct. 25–Dec. 31)

What Is Tele-Tax?

Recorded Tax Information *includes about 140 topics of tax information that answer many Federal tax questions. You can listen to up to three topics on each call you make.*

Automated Refund Information *is available so you can check the status of your refund.*

How Do I Use Tele-Tax?

Choosing The Right Number

Use only the number listed on this page for your area. Use a local city number only if it is not a long distance call for you. **Please do not dial "1-800" when using a local city number.** However, when dialing from an area that does not have a local number, be sure to dial "1-800" before calling the toll-free number.

Recorded Tax Information

Topic numbers are effective January 1, 1992. A complete list of these topics is on the next page.

Touch-tone service is available 24 hours a day, 7 days a week.

Rotary or pulse dial service is available Monday through Friday during regular office hours.

Select, by number, the topic you want to hear. **For the directory of topics, listen to topic no. 323.**

Have paper and pencil handy to take notes.

Call the appropriate phone number listed on this page.

- If you have a touch-tone phone, immediately follow the recorded instructions, or
- If you have a rotary or pulse dial phone, wait for further recorded instructions.

- Touch-tone service is available Monday through Friday from 7:00 A.M. to 11:30 P.M. (Hours may vary in your area.)
- Rotary or pulse dial service is available Monday through Friday during regular office hours.

Toll-free Tele-Tax telephone numbers

Alabama
1-800-829-4477

Alaska
1-800-829-4477

Arizona
Phoenix, 252-4909
Elsewhere, 1-800-829-4477

Arkansas
1-800-829-4477

California
Counties of: Alpine, Amador, Butte, Calaveras, Colusa, Contra Costa, Del Norte, El Dorado, Glenn, Humboldt, Lake, Lassen, Marin, Mendocino, Modoc, Napa, Nevada, Placer, Plumas, Sacramento, San Joaquin, Shasta, Sierra, Siskiyou, Solano, Sonoma, Sutter, Tehama, Trinity, Yolo, and Yuba, 1-800-829-4032
Los Angeles, 617-3177
Oakland, 839-4245
Elsewhere, 1-800-829-4477

Colorado
Denver, 592-1118
Elsewhere, 1-800-829-4477

Connecticut
1-800-829-4477

Delaware
1-800-829-4477

District of Columbia
882-1040

Florida
1-800-829-4477

Georgia
Atlanta, 331-6572
Elsewhere, 1-800-829-4477

Hawaii
1-800-829-4477

Idaho
1-800-829-4477

Illinois
Chicago, 886-9614
In area code 708, 1-312-886-9614
Springfield, 789-0489
Elsewhere, 1-800-829-4477

Indiana
Indianapolis, 631-1010
Elsewhere, 1-800-829-4477

Iowa
Des Moines, 284-7454
Elsewhere, 1-800-829-4477

Kansas
1-800-829-4477

Kentucky
1-800-829-4477

Louisiana
1-800-829-4477

Maine
1-800-829-4477

Maryland
Baltimore, 466-1040
Elsewhere, 1-800-829-4477

Massachusetts
Boston, 523-8602
Elsewhere, 1-800-829-4477

Michigan
Detroit, 961-4282
Elsewhere, 1-800-829-4477

Minnesota
St. Paul, 644-7748
Elsewhere, 1-800-829-4477

Mississippi
1-800-829-4477

Missouri
St. Louis, 241-4700
Elsewhere, 1-800-829-4477

Montana
1-800-829-4477

Nebraska
Omaha, 221-3324
Elsewhere, 1-800-829-4477

Nevada
1-800-829-4477

New Hampshire
1-800-829-4477

New Jersey
1-800-829-4477

New Mexico
1-800-829-4477

New York
Bronx, 406-4080
Brooklyn, 858-4461
Buffalo, 685-5533
Manhattan, 406-4080
Queens, 858-4461
Staten Island, 858-4461
Elsewhere, 1-800-829-4477

North Carolina
1-800-829-4477

Automated Refund Information

Be sure to have a copy of your tax return available since you will need to know the first social security number shown on your return, the filing status, and the **exact** amount of your refund.

Then, call the appropriate phone number listed on this page and follow the recorded instructions.

The IRS updates refund information every 7 days. If you call to find out about the status of your refund and do not receive a refund mailing date, please wait 7 days before calling back.

North Dakota
1-800-829-4477

Ohio
Cincinnati, 421-0329
Cleveland, 522-3037
Elsewhere, 1-800-829-4477

Oklahoma
1-800-829-4477

Oregon
Portland, 294-5363
Elsewhere, 1-800-829-4477

Pennsylvania
Philadelphia, 627-1040
Pittsburgh, 261-1040
Elsewhere, 1-800-829-4477

Puerto Rico
1-800-829-4477

Rhode Island
1-800-829-4477

South Carolina
1-800-829-4477

South Dakota
1-800-829-4477

Tennessee
Nashville, 242-1541
Elsewhere, 1-800-829-4477

Texas
Dallas, 767-1792
Houston, 850-8801
Elsewhere, 1-800-829-4477

Utah
1-800-829-4477

Vermont
1-800-829-4477

Virginia
Richmond, 783-1569
Elsewhere, 1-800-829-4477

Washington
Seattle, 343-7221
Elsewhere, 1-800-829-4477

West Virginia
1-800-829-4477

Wisconsin
Milwaukee, 273-8100
Elsewhere, 1-800-829-4477

Wyoming
1-800-829-4477

Tele-Tax Topic Numbers and Subjects

Topic No.	Subject
	IRS Procedures and Services
101	IRS help available—Volunteer tax assistance programs, toll-free telephone, walk-in assistance, and outreach program
102	Tax assistance for individuals with disabilities and the hearing impaired
103	Small Business Tax Education Program (STEP)—Tax help for small businesses
104	Problem Resolution Program—Help for problem situations
105	Public libraries—Tax information tapes and reproducible tax forms
106	Examination procedures and how to prepare for an audit
107	The collection process
108	Tax fraud—How to report
109	Types of organizations that qualify for tax-exempt status
110	Organizations—How to apply for exempt status
111	Examination appeal rights
112	Electronic filing
113	Special Enrollment Examination to practice before IRS
114	Power of attorney information
115	Change of address—How to notify IRS
911	Hardship assistance applications
999	Local information
	Filing Requirements, Filing Status, Exemptions
151	Who must file?
152	Which form—1040, 1040A, or 1040EZ?
153	When, where, and how to file
154	What is your filing status?
155	Dependents
156	Estimated tax
157	Amended returns
158	Decedents
	Types of Income
201	Wages and salaries
202	Tips
203	Interest received
204	Dividends
205	Refund of state and local taxes
206	Alimony received
207	Business income
208	Sole proprietorship
209	Capital gains and losses
210	Pensions and annuities
211	Pensions—The general rule and the simplified general rule
212	Lump-sum distributions
213	Rental income and expenses
214	Renting vacation property/Renting to relatives
215	Royalties
216	Farming and fishing income
217	Earnings for clergy
218	Unemployment compensation
219	Gambling income and expenses
220	Bartering income
221	Scholarship and fellowship grants
222	Nontaxable income
223	Social security and equivalent railroad retirement benefits
224	401(k) plans
225	Passive activities—Losses/credits
226	Tax statements from the Railroad Retirement Board
	Adjustments to Income
251	Individual retirement arrangements (IRAs)
252	Alimony paid
253	Bad debt deduction
254	Tax shelters
	Itemized Deductions
301	Should I itemize?
302	Medical and dental expenses
303	Taxes
304	Moving expenses
305	Interest expense
306	Contributions
307	Casualty losses
308	Miscellaneous expenses
309	Business use of home
310	Business use of car
311	Business travel expenses
312	Business entertainment expenses
313	Educational expenses
314	Employee business expenses
	Tax Computation
351	Tax and credits figured by IRS
352	Self-employment tax
353	Five-year averaging for lump-sum distributions
354	Alternative minimum tax
355	Gift tax
356	Estate tax
357	Standard deduction
358	Tax on a child's investment income
	Tax Credits
401	Child and dependent care credit
402	Earned income credit
403	Credit for the elderly or the disabled
	General Information
451	Substitute tax forms
452	Highlights of 1991 tax changes
453	Refunds—How long they should take
454	Copy of your tax return—How to get one
455	Forms/Publications—How to order
456	Tax shelter registration
457	Extension of time to file your tax return
458	Form W-2—What to do if not received
459	Penalty for underpayment of estimated tax
460	Recordkeeping
461	How to choose a tax preparer
462	Failure to pay child/spousal support and other Federal obligations
463	Withholding on interest and dividends
464	Highway use tax
465	Checklist/Common errors when preparing your tax return
466	Withholding on pensions and annuities
467	Foreign currency transactions
468	Desert Storm/Desert Shield
	IRS Notices and Letters
501	Notices—What to do
502	Notice of underreported income—CP 2000
503	IRS notices and bills/Penalty and interest charges
	Basis of Assets, Depreciation, Sale of Assets
551	Sale of your home—General
552	Sale of your home—How to report gain
553	Sale of your home—Exclusion of gain, age 55 and over
554	Basis of assets
555	Depreciation
556	Installment sales
	Employer Tax Information
601	Social security and Medicare withholding rates
602	Form W-2—Where, when, and how to file
603	Form W-4—Employee's Withholding Allowance Certificate
604	Federal tax deposits—General
605	Employer identification number—How to apply
606	Form 942—Employer's Quarterly Tax Return for Household Employees
607	Form 941—Deposit requirements
608	Form 941—Employer's Quarterly Federal Tax Return
609	Form 940—Deposit requirements
610	Form 940/940-EZ—Employer's Annual Federal Unemployment Tax Return

Topic No.	Subject
611	Targeted jobs credit
612	Tips—Withholding and reporting
	Form 1099 Series and Related Information Returns—Filing Magnetically or Electronically
651	Who must file—Originals and corrections
652	Acceptable media/Locating a third party to prepare your files
653	Applications, forms, and information
654	Waivers, extensions, and format deviations
655	Test files and combined Federal/state filing
656	Electronic filing of information returns
657	Information Returns Program Bulletin Board System
	Tax Information for Aliens and U.S. Citizens Living Abroad
701	Resident and nonresident aliens
702	Dual-status alien
703	Alien tax clearance
704	Foreign earned income exclusion—General
705	Foreign earned income exclusion—Who qualifies?
706	Foreign earned income exclusion—What qualifies?
707	Foreign tax credit
	The following topics are in Spanish:
751	Who must file?
752	Which form to use?
753	What is your filing status?
754	Earned income credit
755	Highlights of 1991 tax changes
756	Forms and publications—How to order
757	Alien tax clearance
758	Refunds—How long they should take
759	IRS help available—Volunteer tax assistance programs, toll-free telephone, walk-in assistance, and outreach program
760	Social security and equivalent railroad retirement benefits
761	Why do I have to turn in a Form W-4 to my employer?
	Tax Information for Puerto Rico Residents
851	Who must file a U.S. income tax return in Puerto Rico
852	Deductions and credits for Puerto Rico filers
853	Federal employment taxes in Puerto Rico
854	Tax assistance for residents of Puerto Rico

Topic numbers are effective January 1, 1992.

Free Tax Publications

The Internal Revenue Service publishes many free publications to help you "make your taxes less taxing." The publications listed on this page give general information about taxes for individuals, small businesses, farming, fishing, and recent tax law changes. (Forms and schedules related to the subject matter of each publication are indicated after each listing.) You may want to order one of these publications, and then, if you need more detailed information on any subject, order the specific publication about it.

Publications and forms listed in this booklet can be ordered by calling IRS toll-free at:

1-800-829-3676

or by using the order blank on page 29 of this publication.

1 Your Rights as a Taxpayer

To ensure that you always receive fair treatment in tax matters, you should know what your rights are. This publication clarifies your rights at each step in the tax process.

1S Derechos del Contribuyente (Your Rights as a Taxpayer) Spanish version of Publication 1.

3 Tax Information for Military Personnel

This publication gives information about the special tax situations of active members of the Armed Forces. It includes information on items that are includible in and excludable from gross income, alien status, dependency exemptions, sale of residence, itemized deductions, tax liability, and filing returns.

Forms 1040, 1040A, 1040EZ, 1040NR, 1040X, 1310, 2106, 2688, 2848, 3903, 3903F, 4868 and W-2.

4 Student's Guide to Federal Income Tax

This publication explains the federal tax laws that apply to high school and college students. It describes the student's responsibilities to file and pay taxes, how to file, and how to get help.

Examples illustrate typical situations. Filled-in forms and schedules show how to report income and deductions.

Forms 104EZ, W-2 and W-4.

17 Your Federal Income Tax

This publication can help you prepare your individual tax return. It takes you through the individual tax return and explains the tax laws that cover salaries and wages, interest and dividends, rental income, gains and losses, adjustments to income (such as alimony and IRA contributions), and itemized deductions. Also, it covers the new earned income credit rules.

Examples illustrate typical situations. Filled-in forms and schedules show how to report income and deductions.

The tax table, tax rate schedules, and earned income credit tables are included in this publication.

Forms 1040, 1040A, 1040EZ, Schedules A, B, D, E, R, SE, Forms W-2, 2106, 2119, 2441, 3903.

225 Farmer's Tax Guide

This publication explains the federal tax laws that apply to farming. It gives examples of typical farming situations and discusses the kind of farm income you must report and the different deductions you can take.

Schedules A, D, F, SE (Form 1040), and Forms 1040, 4136, 4562, 4684, 4797, 6251.

334 Tax Guide for Small Business

This book explains some federal tax laws that apply to businesses. It describes the four major forms of business organizations—sole proprietorship, partnership, corporation, and S corporation—and explains the tax responsibilities of each.

This publication is divided into eight parts. Part I contains general information on business organization and accounting practices. Part II discusses the tax aspects for the assets used in a business.

Parts III and IV explain how to figure your business income for tax purposes. They describe the kinds of income you must report and the different types of business deductions you can take.

Part V discusses the rules that apply when you sell or exchange business assets or investment property. It includes chapters on the treatment of capital gains and losses, and on involuntary conversions, such as theft and casualty losses. The chapters in Part VI bring together some specific tax considerations for each of the four major forms of business organizations.

Part VII explains some of the credits that can reduce your income tax and some of the other taxes you may have to pay in addition to income tax. It also discusses information returns that you may have to file. Part VIII shows how to fill out the main income tax forms businesses use.

Schedule C (Form 1040), Schedule K-1 (Forms 1065 and 1120S), Forms 1065, 1120, 1120-A, 1120S, 4562.

595 Tax Guide for Commercial Fishermen

This publication will familiarize you with the federal tax laws as they apply to the fishing industry. It is intended for sole proprietors who use Schedule C (Form 1040) to report profit or loss from fishing. It does not cover corporations or partnerships.

The last chapter includes a sample fisherman's recordkeeping system and illustrates filled-in tax forms.

Schedule C (Form 1040), Forms 1099-MISC, 4562, 4797.

More Free Tax Publications

Beginning on this page is a list of most often used free tax publications in numerical order.

15 Circular E, Employer's Tax Guide

Every employer automatically receives this publication on its revision and every person who applies for an employer identification number receives a copy.

Forms 940, 941, and 941E.

51 Circular A, Agricultural Employer's Tax Guide

Form 943

54 Tax Guide for U.S. Citizens and Resident Aliens Abroad

This publication discusses the tax situations of U.S. citizens and resident aliens who live and work abroad. In particular, it explains the rules for excluding income and excluding or deducting certain housing costs. Answers are provided to questions that taxpayers abroad most often ask.

Forms 2555, 1116, and 1040, Schedule SE (Form 1040).

80 Circular SS, Federal Tax Guide for Employers in the Virgin Islands, Guam, American Samoa, and the Commonwealth of the Northern Mariana Islands

Forms 940, 941SS and 943.

179 Circular PR, Guía Contributiva Federal Para Patronos Puertorriqueños (Federal Tax Guide for Employers in Puerto Rico)

Forms W-3PR, 940PR, 941PR, 942PR, and 943PR.

349 Federal Highway Use Tax on Heavy Vehicles

This publication explains which trucks, truck-tractors, and buses are subject to the federal highway use tax on heavy motor vehicles, which is one source of funds for the national highway construction program. You may be liable for this tax if a taxable highway motor vehicle is either registered or required to be registered in your name. The publication tells you how to figure and pay any tax due on your taxable vehicle.

Form 2290.

378 Fuel Tax Credits and Refunds

This publication explains the credit or refund allowable for the federal excise taxes paid on certain fuels, and the income tax credit available for alcohol used as a fuel.

Forms 843, 4136 and 6478.

448 Federal Estate and Gift Taxes

This publication explains federal estate and gift taxes.

Forms 706 and 709.

463 Travel, Entertainment, and Gift Expenses

This publication explains what expenses you may deduct for business-related travel, entertainment, local transportation, and gifts and it discusses the reporting and recordkeeping requirements for these expenses.

The publication also summarizes the reimbursement and accounting rules for employees and self-employed persons (including independent contractors).

Form 2106.

501 Exemptions, Standard Deduction, and Filing Information

This publication provides answers to some basic tax questions: who must file; who should file; what filing status to choose; how many exemptions to claim; and how to figure the amount of the standard deduction. It also covers the social security number requirement for dependents and rules for foster care providers.

Forms 2120 and 8332.

502 Medical and Dental Expenses

This publication tells you how to figure your deduction for medical and dental expenses. You may take this deduction only if you itemize your deductions on Schedule A (Form 1040).

It explains which specific expenses can be deducted and which cannot.

Schedule A (Form 1040).

503 Child and Dependent Care Expenses

This publication explains the credit you may be able to take if you pay someone to care for your dependent who is under age 13, your disabled dependent, or your disabled spouse. For purposes of the credit, "disabled" refers to a person physically or mentally not capable of self-care.

This publication also explains the tax rules covering benefits paid under an employer-provided dependent care assistance plan.

Publication 926 (listed below) explains the employment taxes you may have to pay if you are a household employer.

Schedule 2 (Form 1040A), and Form 2441.

504 Tax Information for Divorced or Separated Individuals

This publication explains tax rules of interest to divorced or separated individuals. It covers filing status, dependency exemptions, and the treatment of alimony and property settlements.

505 Tax Withholding and Estimated Tax

This publication explains the two methods of paying tax under our pay-as-you-go system.

They are:

1. Withholding. Your employer will withhold income tax from your pay. Tax is also withheld from certain other types of income. You can have more or less withheld, depending on your circumstances.

2. Estimated tax. If you do not pay your tax through withholding, or do not pay enough tax that way, you might have to pay estimated tax.

This publication also explains how to take credit on your 1991 return for your tax withholding and estimated tax payments, and how to figure the penalty for underpayment of estimated tax.

Forms W-4, W-4P, W-4S, 1040-ES, 2210, and 2210F.

508 Educational Expenses

This publication explains what work-related educational expenses qualify for deduction, how to report your expenses and any reimbursement you receive, and which forms and schedules to use.

Form 2106 and Schedule A (Form 1040).

509 Tax Calendars for 1992

510 Excise Taxes for 1992

This publication covers in detail the various federal excise taxes reported on Form 720. These include the following groupings: environmental taxes; facilities and service taxes on communications and air transportation; fuel taxes; manufacturers' taxes; vaccines; tax on heavy trucks, trailers, and tractors; luxury taxes; and tax on ship passengers. In addition, it briefly describes other excise taxes and tells which forms to use in reporting and paying the taxes.

Forms 637, 720, 6197, 6627, 8743, and 8807.

513 Tax Information for Visitors to the United States

This publication briefly reviews the general requirements of U.S. income tax laws for foreign visitors. You may have to file a U.S. income tax return during your visit. Most visitors who come to the United States are not allowed to work in this country. Please check with the Immigration and Naturalization Service before you take a job.

Forms 1040C, 1040NR, 2063, and 1040-ES (NR).

514 Foreign Tax Credit for Individuals

This publication may help you if you paid foreign income tax. You may be able to take a foreign tax credit or deduction to avoid the burden of double taxation. The publication explains which foreign taxes qualify and how to figure your credit or deduction.

Form 1116.

515 Withholding of Tax on Nonresident Aliens and Foreign Corporations

This publication provides information for withholding agents who are required to withhold and report tax on payments to nonresident aliens and foreign corporations. Included are three tables listing U.S. tax treaties and some of the treaty provisions that provide for reduction of or exemption from withholding for certain types of income.

Forms 1042 and 1042S, 1001, 4224, 8233, 1078, 8288, 8288-A, 8288-B, 8804, 8805, and W-8, 8813, and 8709.

516 Tax Information for U.S. Government Civilian Employees Stationed Abroad

This publication covers the tax treatment of allowances, reimbursements, and business expenses that U.S. government employees, including foreign service employees, are likely to receive or incur.

517 Social Security for Members of the Clergy and Religious Workers

This publication discusses social security coverage and the self-employment tax for the clergy.

It also tells you how, as a member of the clergy (minister, member of a religious order, or Christian Science practitioner), you may apply for an exemption from the self-employment tax that would otherwise be due for the services you perform in the exercise of your ministry. Net earnings from self-employment are explained and sample forms are shown.

Form 2106, Form 1040, Schedule SE (Form 1040), and Schedule C (Form 1040).

519 U.S. Tax Guide for Aliens

This comprehensive publication gives guidelines on how to determine your U.S. tax status and figure your U.S. tax.

Resident aliens, like U.S. citizens, generally are taxed by the United States on income from all sources. Nonresident aliens generally are taxed only on income from sources in the United States. The income may be from investments or from business activities such as performing personal services in the United States. An income tax treaty may reduce the standard 30% tax rate on nonresident aliens' investment income. Their business income is taxed at the same graduated rates that apply to U.S. citizens or residents.

Aliens admitted to the United States with permanent immigrant visas are resident aliens, while temporary visitors generally are nonresident aliens. Aliens with other types of visas may be resident aliens or nonresident aliens, depending on the length and nature of their stay.

Forms 1040, 1040C, 1040NR, 2063, and Schedule A (Form 1040).

520 Scholarships and Fellowships

This publication explains the tax laws that apply to U.S. citizens and resident aliens who study, teach, or conduct research in the United States or abroad under scholarships and fellowship grants.

Form 1040A, 1040EZ.

521 Moving Expenses

This publication explains how, if you changed job locations last year or started a new job, you may be able to deduct your moving expenses. You may qualify for a deduction whether you are self-employed or an employee. The expenses must be closely related to the start of work at your new job location. You must meet a distance test and a time test. You also may be able to deduct expenses of moving to the United States if you retire while living and working overseas or if you are a survivor or dependent of a person who died while living and working overseas.

To deduct your allowable moving expenses, you must itemize your deductions. You should use Form 3903, Moving Expenses, if your move is within or to the United States or its possessions. You should use Form 3903F, Foreign Moving Expenses, if your move is outside the United States or its possessions.

Forms 3903, 3903F, and 4782.

523 Tax Information on Selling Your Home

This publication explains how to treat any gain from selling your main home, how to postpone the tax on part or all of the gain on the sale of your home, and how to exclude part or all of the gain from your gross income if you are 55 or older.

Form 2119.

524 Credit for the Elderly or the Disabled

This publication explains how to figure the credit for the elderly or the disabled. You may be able to claim this credit if you are 65 or older, or if you are retired on disability and were permanently and totally disabled when you retired. Figure the credit on Schedule R (Form 1040), or Schedule 3 (Form 1040A), Credit for the Elderly or the Disabled. You cannot take the credit if you file a Form 1040EZ.

Schedule R (Form 1040).

525 Taxable and Nontaxable Income

This publication discusses wages, salaries, fringe benefits, and other compensation received for services as an employee. In addition, it discusses items of miscellaneous taxable income as well as items that are exempt from tax.

526 Charitable Contributions

If you make a charitable contribution or gift to, or for the use of, a qualified organization, you may be able to claim a deduction on your tax return. This publication explains what a charitable contribution is, how the deduction is claimed, and what limits apply.

Schedule A (Form 1040).

527 Residential Rental Property

This publication discusses rental income and expenses, including depreciation, and explains how to report them on your return. It covers casualty losses on rental property and limits on rental losses. It also provides information on reporting the sale of rental property.

Schedule E (Form 1040), and Forms 4562 and 4797.

529 Miscellaneous Deductions

This publication discusses expenses you generally may take as miscellaneous deductions on Schedule A (Form 1040), such as business employee expenses and expenses of producing income. It does not discuss other itemized deductions, such as the ones for charitable contributions, moving expenses, interest, taxes, or medical and dental expenses.

Schedule A (Form 1040), Form 2106.

530 Tax Information for Homeowners (Including Owners of Condominiums and Cooperative Apartments)

This publication gives information about home ownership and federal taxes. It explains how to determine basis, how to treat settlement and closing costs, and how to treat repairs and improvements you make. The publication discusses itemized deductions for mortgage interest, real estate taxes, and casualty and theft losses. It also explains the mortgage interest credit.

531 Reporting Income From Tips

This publication gives advice about keeping track of cash and charge tips and explains that all tips received are subject to federal income tax. The publication also explains the rules about the information that employers must report to the Internal Revenue Service about their employees' tip income.

Forms 4070 and 4070A.

533 Self-Employment Tax

This publication explains the self-employment tax, which is a social security and Medicare tax for people who work for themselves. It is similar to the social security and Medicare taxes withheld from the pay of wage earners.

Social security and Medicare benefits are available to people who are self-employed just as they are to wage earners. Your payments of self-employment tax contribute to your coverage under the social security system.

Schedule SE (Form 1040).

534 Depreciation

This publication discusses the various methods of depreciation, including the modified accelerated cost recovery system (MACRS). This publication covers:

- What can be depreciated
- Section 179 deduction
- MACRS-assets placed in service after 1986
- ACRS-assets placed in service after 1980 and before 1987
- The limitations for passenger automobiles and other "listed property" placed in service after June 18, 1984
- Methods used for assets placed in service before 1981 and for assets not qualifying for ACRS and MACRS
- Example with a filled-in Form 4562.

Form 4562.

535 Business Expenses

This publication discusses business expenses such as fringe benefits, rent, interest, taxes, insurance, and retirement plans. It also outlines the choice to capitalize certain business expenses, discusses amortization and depletion, covers some business expenses that may be deductible in some circumstances and not deductible in others, and points out some expenses that are not deductible.

536 Net Operating Losses

This publication explains how to figure a net operating loss (NOL) and when to use one. An NOL worksheet is included.

Form 1045, Schedule A.

537 Installment Sales

This publication discusses sales arrangements that provide for part or all of the selling price to be paid in a later year. These arrangements are "installment sales." If you finance the buyer's purchase of your property, instead of having the buyer get a loan or mortgage from a bank (or other lender), you probably have an installment sale.

Form 6252.

538 Accounting Periods and Methods

This publication explains which accounting periods and methods can be used for figuring federal taxes, and how to apply for approval to change from one period or method to another. Most individual taxpayers use the calendar year for their accounting period and the cash method of accounting.

Forms 1128 and 3115.

541 Tax Information on Partnerships

Form 1065, Schedules K and K-1 (Form 1065).

542 Tax Information on Corporations

Forms 1120 and 1120-A.

544 Sales and Other Dispositions of Assets

This publication explains how to figure gain and loss on various transactions, such as trading or selling an asset used in a trade or business, and it explains the tax results of different types of gains and losses. Not all transactions result in taxable gains or deductible losses, and not all gains are taxed the same way.

Schedule D (Form 1040) and Form 4797.

547 Nonbusiness Disasters, Casualties, and Thefts

This publication explains when you can deduct a disaster, casualty, or theft loss. Casualties are events such as hurricanes, earthquakes, tornadoes, fires, floods, vandalism, loss of deposits in a bankrupt or insolvent financial institution, and car accidents. The publication also explains how to treat the reimbursement you receive from insurance or other sources.

Form 4684.

550 Investment Income and Expenses

This publication explains which types of investment income are and are not taxable, when the income is taxed, and how to report it on your tax return. The publication discusses the treatment of tax shelters and investment-related expenses. The publication also explains how to figure your gain and loss when you sell or trade your investment property.

Forms 1099-INT, 1099-DIV, 6781, and 8815, Schedules B and D (Form 1040).

551 Basis of Assets

This publication explains how to determine the basis of property. The basis of property you buy is usually its cost. If you received property in some other way, such as by gift or inheritance, you normally must use a basis other than cost.

552 Recordkeeping for Individuals

This publication can help you decide what records to keep and how long to keep them for tax purposes. These records will help you prepare your income tax returns so that you will pay only your correct tax. If you keep a record of your expenses during the year, you may find that you can reduce your taxes by itemizing your deductions. Deductible expenses include medical and dental bills, interest, contributions, and taxes.

553 Highlights of 1991 Tax Changes

This publication discusses the more important changes in the tax rules brought about by recent legislation, rulings, and administrative decisions. It does not discuss all new tax rules or detail all changes. It highlights the important recent changes that taxpayers should know about when filing their 1991 tax forms and when planning for 1992.

554 Tax Information for Older Americans

This publication gives tax information of special interest to older Americans. An example takes you through completing a tax return and explains such items as the sale of a home, the credit for the elderly or the disabled, and pension and annuity income. The publication includes filled-in forms and schedules that show how these and other items are reported.

Schedules B, D, and R (Form 1040), and Forms 1040, 1040A, and 2119.

555 Federal Tax Information on Community Property

This publication may help married taxpayers who are domiciled in one of the following community property states: Arizona, California, Idaho, Louisiana, Nevada, New Mexico, Texas, Washington or Wisconsin. If you wish to file a separate tax return, you should understand how community property laws affect the way you figure your tax before completing your federal income tax return.

556 Examination of Returns, Appeal Rights, and Claims for Refund

This publication may be helpful if your return is examined by the Internal Revenue Service. It explains that returns are normally examined to verify the correctness of reported income, exemptions, or deductions, and it describes what appeal rights you have if you disagree with the results of the examination.

The publication also explains the procedures for the examination of items of partnership income, deduction, gain, loss, and credit. Information is given on how to file a claim for refund, the time for filing a claim for refund, and any limit on the amount of refund.

Forms 1040X and 1120X.

556S Revisión de las Declaraciones de Impuesto, Derecho de Apelación y Reclamaciones de Reemboisos (Examination of Returns, Appeal Rights, and Claims for Refund)

(Spanish version of Publication 556.)

Forms 1040X and 1120X.

557 Tax-Exempt Status for Your Organization

This publication discusses how organizations become recognized as exempt from federal income tax under section 501(a) of the Internal Revenue Code. (These include organizations described in Code section 501(c).) The publication explains how to get a ruling or determination letter recognizing the exemption, and it gives other information that applies generally to all exempt organizations.

Forms 990, 990EZ, 990PF, 1023, and 1024.

559 Tax Information for Survivors, Executors, and Administrators

This publication can help you report and pay the proper federal income tax if you are responsible for settling a decedent's estate. This publication also answers many questions that a spouse or other survivor faces when a person dies.

Questions answered include:

What was the decedent's tax liability for the year of death? When is the last return due? How is the income taxed from the date of the decendent's death to the distribution of the estate? Who is responsible for the decendent's tax? What are the tax problems of the heirs? How does the survivor (or beneficiary) treat bequests or inheritances received from the estate of a decendent?

Form 1040, Form 1041, and Form 4810.

560 Retirement Plans for the Self-Employed

This publication discusses retirement plans for self-employed persons and certain partners in partnerships. These retirement plans are sometimes called Keogh plans or HR-10 plans.

If you set up a retirement plan that meets certain legal requirements, you may be able to deduct your payments to the plan. In addition, income earned by the plan will be tax-free until it is distributed.

561 Determining the Value of Donated Property

This publication can help donors and appraisers determine the value of property (other than cash) that is given to qualified organizations. It explains what kind of information you need to support a charitable deduction you claim on your return.

Form 8283.

564 Mutual Fund Distributions

This publication discusses the federal income tax treatment of distributions paid or allocated to you as an individual shareholder of a mutual fund. A comprehensive example shows distributions made by a mutual fund and an illustration of Form 1040.

Form 1040, Schedules B and D (Form 1040), and Form 1099-DIV.

570 Tax Guide for Individuals With Income From U.S. Possessions

This publication is for individuals with income from American Samoa, Guam, the Commonwealth of the Northern Mariana Islands, Puerto Rico, and the U.S. Virgin Islands.

Forms 4563, 5074, and 8689.

571 Tax-Sheltered Annuity Programs for Employees of Public Schools and Certain Tax-Exempt Organizations

This publication explains the rules concerning employers qualified to buy tax-sheltered annuities, eligible employees who may participate in the program, and the amounts that may be excluded from income.

Form 5330.

575 Pension and Annuity Income (Including Simplified General Rule)

This publication explains how to report pension and annuity income on your federal income tax return. It also explains the special tax treatment for lump-sum distributions from pension, stock bonus, or profit-sharing plans.

Forms 1040, 1040A, 1099-R and 4972.

578 Tax Information for Private Foundations and Foundation Managers

This publication covers tax matters of interest to private foundations and their managers, including the tax classification of the foundations, filing requirements, the tax on net investment income, and various excise taxes on transactions that violate the foundation rules.

Form 990-F.

579S Cómo Preparar la Declaración de Impuesto Federal (How to Prepare the Federal Income Tax Return)

Forms 1040, 1040A, 1040EZ.

583 Taxpayers Starting a Business

This publication shows sample records that a small business can use if it operates as a sole proprietorship. Records like these will help you prepare complete and accurate tax returns and make sure you pay only the tax you owe. This publication also discusses the taxpayer identification number businesses must use, information returns businesses may have to file, and the kinds of business taxes businesses may have to pay.

Schedule C (Form 1040), and Form 4562.

584 Nonbusiness Disaster, Casualty, and Theft Loss Workbook

This workbook can help you to figure your loss from a disaster, casualty or theft. It will help you most if you list your possessions before any losses occur. The workbook has schedules to help you figure the loss on your home and its contents. There is also a schedule to help you figure the loss on your car, truck, or motorcycle.

586A The Collection Process (Income Tax Accounts)

This publication explains your rights and duties as a taxpayer who owes tax. It also explains the legal obligation of the Internal Revenue Service to collect overdue taxes, and the way we fulfill this obligation. It is not intended to be a precise and technical analysis of the law in this area.

586S Proceso de Cobro (Deudas Del Impuesto Sobre Ingreso)

(Spanish version of Publication 586A)

587 Business Use of Your Home

This publication can help you decide if you qualify to deduct certain expenses for using part of your home in your business. You must meet specific tests and your deduction is limited. Deductions for the business use of a home computer are also discussed.

Schedule C (Form 1040), Form 4562, and Form 8829.

589 Tax Information on S Corporations

This publication discusses the way corporations are taxed under subchapter S of the Internal Revenue Code. In general, an S corporation does not pay tax on its income. Instead, it passes through its income and expenses to its shareholders who then report them on their own tax returns.

Forms 1120S and Schedule K-1 (Form 1120S).

590 Individual Retirement Arrangements (IRAs)

This publication explains the rules for and the tax benefits of having an individual retirement arrangement (IRA). An IRA is a personal savings plan that offers you tax advantages to set aside money for your retirement. Your contributions to an IRA may be deductible in part or in full and the earnings and gains in your IRA are generally not taxed until they are distributed to you.

Topics covered in this publication include:

- Who can set up an IRA
- Kinds of IRAs
- Deductible and nondeductible contributions
- Rollovers and other transfers
- Distributions, including required minimum distributions
- Acts that result in penalties
- Simplified Employee Pensions (SEPs)

Forms 1040, 1040A, 5329 and 8606.

593 Tax Highlights for U.S. Citizens and Residents Going Abroad

This publication briefly reviews various U.S. tax provisions that apply to U.S. citizens or resident aliens who live or work abroad and expect to receive income from foreign sources.

594 The Collection Process (Employment Tax Accounts)

This booklet explains your rights and duties as a taxpayer who owes employer's quarterly federal taxes. It also explains how we fulfill the legal obligation of the Internal Revenue Service to collect these taxes. It is not intended as a precise and technical analysis of the law.

594S Proceso de Cobro (Deudas Del Impuesto Por Razón Del Empleo)

(Spanish version of Publication 594.)

596 Earned Income Credit

This publication discusses who may receive the earned income credit, and how to figure and claim the credit. There is a discussion on the three credits that are available under the earned income credit. There is also a worksheet for persons who are eligible for the self-employed health insurance deduction and want to take the health insurance credit. Included in this publication are the new earned income credit tax tables. Also discussed is how to receive advance payments of the earned income credit.

Forms W-5, 1040, 1040A, and Schedule EIC.

597 Information on the United States-Canada Income Tax Treaty

This publication reproduces the entire text of the U.S.-Canada income tax treaty, and also gives an explanation of provisions that often apply to U.S. citizens or residents who have Canadian source income. There is also a discussion that deals with certain tax problems that may be encountered by Canadian residents who temporarily work in the United States.

598 Tax on Unrelated Business Income of Exempt Organizations

This publication explains the unrelated business income tax provisions that apply to most tax-exempt organizations. An organization that regularly operates a trade or business that is not substantially related to its exempt purpose may be taxed on the income from this business. Generally, a tax-exempt organization with gross income of $1,000 or more from an unrelated trade or business must file a return.

Form 990-T

686 Certification for Reduced Tax Rates in Tax Treaty Countries

This publication explains how U.S. citizens, residents, and domestic corporations may certify to a foreign country that they are entitled to tax treaty benefits.

721 Tax Guide to U.S. Civil Service Retirement Benefits

This publication explains how the federal income tax rules apply to the benefits that retired federal employees or their survivors receive under the U.S. Civil Service Retirement System or Federal Employees' Retirement System. There is also information on estate taxes.

Forms 1040 and 1040A.

850 English-Spanish Glossary of Words and Phrases Used in Publications Issued by the Internal Revenue Service

901 U.S. Tax Treaties

This publication provides information about the reduced tax rates and exemptions from U.S. taxes provided under U.S. tax treaties with foreign countries. This publication is intended for residents of those countries who receive income from U.S. sources. Information for foreign workers and students is emphasized.

Form 1040NR.

904 Interrelated Computations for Estate and Gift Taxes

Forms 706 and 709.

907 Tax Information for Persons with Handicaps or Disabilities

This publication explains tax rules of interest to people who are handicapped or disabled and to those who have dependents who are disabled. For example, you may be able to take a tax credit for certain disability payments, you may be able to deduct medical expenses, and you may be able to take a credit for expenses of care of persons with disabilities.

Schedule A (Form 1040), Schedule R (1040), and Form 2441.

908 Bankruptcy and Other Debt Cancellation

This publication explains the income tax aspects of bankruptcy and discharge of debt for individuals and small businesses.

Forms 982, 1040, 1041, 1120.

909 Alternative Minimum Tax for Individuals

This publication discusses the alternative minimum tax which applies to individuals. It also discusses the credit for prior year minimum tax.

Forms 6251 and 8801.

911 Tax Information for Direct Sellers

This publication may help you if you are a "direct seller," a person who sells consumer products to others on a person-to-person basis. Many direct sellers sell door-to-door, at sales parties, or by appointment in someone's home. Information on figuring your income from direct sales as well as the kinds of expenses you may be entitled to deduct is also provided.

Schedules C and SE (Form 1040).

915 Social Security Benefits and Equivalent Railroad Retirement Benefits

This publication explains when you have to include part of your social security or equivalent railroad retirement benefits in income on Form 1040 or Form 1040A. It also explains how to figure the amount to include.

Forms SSA-1099 and RRB-1099, Social Security Benefits Worksheet. Notice 703, Forms SSA-1042S and RRB-1042S.

917 Business Use of a Car

This publication explains the expenses that you may deduct for the business use of your car. Car expenses that are deductible do not include the cost of commuting from your home to your regular workplace. The publication also discusses the taxability of the use of a car provided by an employer and rules on leasing a car for business.

Form 2106.

919 Is My Withholding Correct for 1992?

This publication helps employees check their withholding. This publication has worksheets that will help them estimate both their 1992 tax and their total 1992 withholding. The employees can then compare the two amounts. The publication tells employees what to do if too much or too little tax is being withheld.

Form W-4.

924 Reporting of Real Estate Transactions to IRS

This publication informs sellers of certain real estate about the information they must provide to the real estate reporting person in order that the reporting person can complete the Form 1099-S that must be filed with IRS.

925 Passive Activity and At-Risk Rules

This publication covers the rules that limit passive activity losses and the at-risk limits.

Form 8582.

926 Employment Taxes for Household Employers

This publication shows how a household employer reports federal income tax withholding, social security and Medicare taxes (FICA taxes), and unemployment taxes (FUTA). You may be a household employer if you have a babysitter, maid, or other employee who works in your house. The publication also shows what records you must keep.

Forms W-2, W-3, 940, 940-EZ and 942.

929 Tax Rules for Children and Dependents

This publication describes the tax laws affecting dependents and certain children. It explains their filing requirement and standard deduction amount for dependents. It also explains when and how a child's parents may include their child's interest and dividend income on their return, and when and how a child's parents are required to report part of their child's investment income on their return.

Forms 8615, 8814, and 8803.

936 Home Mortgage Interest Deduction

This publication covers the rules governing the deduction of home mortgage interest, including points. It also covers the limits to your deduction if your acquisition cost exceeds $1 million ($500,000 if you are married filing separately) or your home equity debt exceeds $100,000 ($50,000 if you are married filing separately). Worksheets are provided to determine what interest expenses qualify as home mortgage interest.

Form 1040 and Schedule A (Form 1040).

937 Business Reporting

This publication explains your responsibilities, if you have employees, to withhold federal income taxes and social security and Medicare taxes (FICA taxes) from their wages, and to pay social security and Medicare taxes and federal unemployment taxes (FUTA taxes). It discusses the rules for advance payment of the earned income credit, and for reporting and allocating tips.

It also provides information on reporting nonwage payments on Form 1099-MISC, discusses backup withholding, and contains a chart listing the reporting requirements for many information returns including the Form 1099 series.

Form W-2, W-4, 940, 941, and 1099-MISC.

938 Real Estate Mortgage Investment Conduits (REMICS) Reporting Information (And Other Collateralized Debt Obligations (CDOs))

This publication discusses reporting requirements for issuers of real estate mortgage investment conduits (REMICs) and collateralized debt obligations (CDOs). This publication also contains a directory of REMICS and CDOs to assist brokers and middlemen in fulfilling their reporting requirements.

939 Pension General Rule (Nonsimplified Method)

This publication covers the nonsimplified General Rule for the taxation of pensions or annuities, which must be used if the Simplified General Rule is not applicable or is not chosen. For example, the nonsimplified method must be used for payments under commercial annuities. The publication also contains the necessary actuarial tables for this method.

945 Tax Information for Those Affected by Operation Desert Storm

This publication describes the tax benefits available to those involved in Operation Desert Shield/Storm. It includes information on combat zone compensation exclusion and when to file returns. It also has answers to questions about persons who die in a combat zone or in a terroristic or military action.

946 How to Begin Depreciating Your Property

This new publication is intended for use by individuals who are depreciating property for the first time. It discusses:
- Section 179 deduction,
- MACRS, and
- Listed property.

The publication contains worksheets to help figure the deduction in all areas and contains a comprehensive example using these worksheets and Form 4562.

947 Power of Attorney and Practice Before the IRS

This publication explains who can represent a taxpayer before the IRS and what forms or documents are used to authorize a person to represent a taxpayer. The roles of practitioners and specially authorized nonpractitioners are discussed. Examples are included to help explain some of the different uses of power of attorney.

Form 2048 and 8821.

1004 Identification Numbers Under ERISA

1045 Information for Tax Practitioners

1212 List of Original Issue Discount Instruments

This publication explains the tax treatment of original issue discount (OID). It describes how:
- Brokers and other middlemen, including those who may hold the debt instruments as nominees for the owners, should report OID to IRS and to the owners on Forms 1099-OID or 1099-INT, and
- Owners of OID debt instruments should report OID on their income tax returns. The publication gives rules for figuring the discount amount to report each year, if required. It also gives tables showing OID amounts for certain publicly traded OID debt instruments, including short-term U.S. Government securities.

1244 Employee's Daily Record of Tips (Form 4070-A) and Employee's Report of Tips to Employer (Form 4070)

This publication explains how you must report tips if you are an employee who receives tips. Copies of the monthly tip report you must give your employer are included, as well as a daily list you can use for your own records.

Forms 4070 and 4070-A.

1544 Reporting Cash Payments of Over $10,000 (Received in a Trade or Business)

This publication explains when and how persons in a trade or business must file a Form 8300 when they receive cash payments of more than $10,000 from one buyer. It also discusses the substantial penalties for not filing the form.

Form 8300.

1581 Foreign Investment in U.S. Real Property

This publication explains the tax consequences of a sale of U.S. real property by a nonresident alien owner.

Form 1040NR, Schedule D (Form 1040), and Forms 4797, 6251, 8228, 8288A, 8288B.

Your Tax Package

The IRS will mail a tax package to you containing either Form 1040 and related schedules, or Form 1040A, or Form 1040EZ, depending on which form you filed previously. You should get this package in late December or early January. You also can pick up forms and schedules at many IRS offices, and some banks, post offices, and libraries.

Start early. By filing a complete and accurate return as soon as you can, you will help us to help you "make your taxes less taxing."

Preprinted label. Your tax package contains a preprinted name and address label. Attach it to your return for quicker processing and a quicker refund.

Your Mailing Label—What Does It Mean?

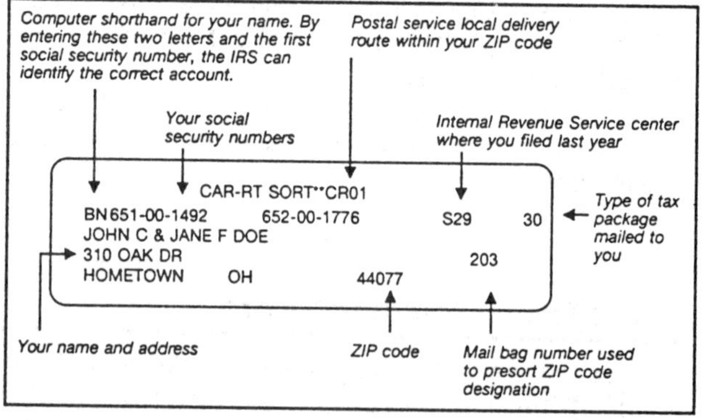

Make any necessary changes directly on the label. If you do not use the tax form in the package you received, attach the label to the return you do file. If someone prepares your return for you, ask that person to use the preprinted label.

Preaddressed envelope. Use the preaddressed envelope to mail your return. It will speed up the processing because it is coded for electronic sorting by type of tax return. If you do not have a preaddressed envelope or if you moved during the year, mail your return to the Internal Revenue Service Center for the area where you now live. Service Center addresses are on page 26 of this publication.

Social security number. Your social security number is your taxpayer identification number. It must appear on your tax returns, statements or documents when requested.

Write your social security number and the tax year on your check or money order when you pay any tax to the IRS.

Write your social security number in the appropriate space on your tax return if you do not use the IRS preprinted label.

If you are married, give the social security numbers for both you and your spouse, whether you file jointly or separately. If you file a joint return, list your social security numbers in the same order as you show your first names on the return. You must include the social security number of any dependent you claim on your return who is age 1 or older before the close of the taxable year.

If your name changes for reasons such as marriage or divorce, notify the Social Security Administration (SSA) so that the name on both IRS records and SSA records is the same. If you don't notify the SSA, then the IRS may have difficulty processing your return and issuing any refund due.

Tax deductions and credits. Deductions or credits reduce the tax a taxpayer owes. Allowable deductions include those for medical expenses, charitable contributions, and some state and local taxes. Many deductions are allowable only to taxpayers who itemize deductions on Schedule A (Form 1040). Certain types of deductions are subject to special rules and limitations.

Allowable credits include the earned income credit, the child and dependent care credit, and the credit for elderly or disabled individuals.

Deductions and credits are discussed in several free tax publications. For a list of these publications, please see page 8.

Avoid These Common Errors

The most common errors taxpayers make on their Forms 1040, 1040A and 1040EZ are explained below. Check your tax return carefully because these errors can delay any refund you may be expecting.

1. Checking the Age/Blindness box.
   — If you are age 65 or older or blind, or your spouse is age 65 or older or blind, make sure you check the appropriate box(es) on Form 1040 or Form 1040A.
2. Earned income credit is figured incorrectly.
   — You may be entitled to a credit of up to $2,020 if your adjusted gross income is less than $21,250 and you have a qualifying child. Schedule EIC is in the Form 1040 and 1040A instructions and is used to figure the credit. The amount of your credit is determined by your earned income and adjusted gross income. To figure the correct amount of your credit, follow the instructions on the Schedule EIC.
3. Earned income credit not claimed.
   — This is a special credit that can help some taxpayers who have a child and have incomes below a certain level. For more information on whether you qualify, refer to Publication 596, *Earned Income Credit.*
4. Social Security Tax, instead of Federal Income Tax Withheld, was entered on your tax return.
   — Form W-2 shows both the Federal Income Tax (Box 9) and FICA (Social Security Tax) (Box 11) withheld. Remember to use the amount in Box 9 on your return to calculate your total income tax withheld.
5. Omitting or making an incorrect entry for standard deduction amount.
   — If you do not itemize deductions, use the correct standard deduction chart to find the right amount.
6. Incorrect refund or balance due.
   — Verify your addition and subtraction. If your total payments are more than your total tax, you are due a refund. A "Balance Due" is figured when your taxes due are more than the amount you have already paid.
7. Incorrect tax entered from tax tables.
   — First, take the amount shown on the taxable income line of your Form 1040EZ, 1040, or 1040A and find the line in the tax table showing that amount. Next, find the column for your marital status (married filing jointly, single, etc.) and read down the column. The amount shown where the income line and filing status column meet is your tax.
8. Computation error when income amounts were totalled.
   — Verify the addition of all income amounts on your return.
9. Incorrect entries for social security number and zip code.
   — Check the preprinted address label that comes with your tax package. You can make any necessary changes on the label. Please make sure you have used the correct numbers.

Double Check Your Return Before Mailing

Take a moment to do the following:

- Put the preprinted address label on your return, and make any necessary corrections to your name, address, and social security number.
- Attach Copy B of all Forms W-2.
- Attach all required forms and related schedules.
- Check your return for math errors.
- Sign and date your return (on a joint return, both husband and wife must sign).
- If you owe additional tax, attach your check or money order payable to "Internal Revenue Service," not the "IRS." Remember to write your social security number, daytime telephone number, tax form number, and tax year on your check or money order.
- Make a copy of the return for your records.
- Use the envelope that came in the tax package to mail your return. If you do not have the preprinted envelope, address an envelope to the IRS Service Center for your state. Be sure to attach correct postage.

File Early — File Electronically

Electronic tax filing is a fast, accurate way to file your income tax return. Electronic filers (tax professionals or transmitters) send your return over telephone lines directly to the IRS. Computers automatically check for errors and missing information. Your electronic filer is notified by the IRS that your return has been received and accepted within two workdays after the original transmission. Minor errors can be corrected within days instead of weeks.

If you expect an income tax refund, you will get it within three weeks from the time IRS receives your return. By choosing to have your refund deposited directly into your savings or checking account, you could receive your money even faster. If you expect to have a balance due to the IRS, you can go ahead and file your return electronically just to get it behind you, and pay by April 15.

Electronic tax filing is simple. Just contact an electronic filer in your area. You can look in your local telephone directory for tax professionals who, for a fee, can transmit your return for you, whether they prepare the return or you do it yourself.

Where Do I File?

If an addressed envelope came with your return, please use it. If you do not have one, or if you moved during the year, mail your return to the **Internal Revenue Service Center** for the place where you live. **No street address is needed.**

Alabama—Memphis, TN 37501
Alaska—Ogden, UT 84201
Arizona—Ogden, UT 84201
Arkansas—Memphis, TN 37501
California—*Counties of Alpine, Amador, Butte, Calaveras, Colusa, Contra Costa, Del Norte, El Dorado, Glenn, Humboldt, Lake, Lassen, Marin, Mendocino, Modoc, Napa, Nevada, Placer, Plumas, Sacramento, San Joaquin, Shasta, Sierra, Siskiyou, Solano, Sonoma, Sutter, Tehama, Trinity, Yolo, and Yuba*—
Ogden, UT 84201
All other counties—
Fresno, CA 93888
Colorado—Ogden, UT 84201
Connecticut—Andover, MA 05501
Delaware—Philadelphia, PA 19255
District of Columbia—
Philadelphia, PA 19255
Florida—Atlanta, GA 39901
Georgia—Atlanta, GA 39901
Hawaii—Fresno, CA 93888
Idaho—Ogden, UT 84201
Illinois—Kansas City, MO 64999
Indiana—Cincinnati, OH 45999
Iowa—Kansas City, MO 64999
Kansas—Austin, TX 73301
Kentucky—Cincinnati, OH 45999
Louisiana—Memphis, TN 37501
Maine—Andover, MA 05501
Maryland—Philadelphia, PA 19255
Massachusetts—Andover, MA 05501
Michigan—Cincinnati, OH 45999
Minnesota—Kansas City, MO 64999
Mississippi—Memphis, TN 37501
Missouri—Kansas City, MO 64999
Montana—Ogden, UT 84201
Nebraska—Ogden, UT 84201
Nevada—Ogden, UT 84201
New Hampshire—Andover, MA 05501
New Jersey—Holtsville, NY 00501
New Mexico—Austin, TX 73301
New York—*New York City and counties of Nassau, Rockland, Suffolk, and Westchester*—
Holtsville, NY 00501
All other counties—
Andover, MA 05501
North Carolina—Memphis, TN 37501

North Dakota—Ogden, UT 84201
Ohio—Cincinnati, OH 45999
Oklahoma—Austin, TX 73301
Oregon—Ogden, UT 84201
Pennsylvania—Philadelphia, PA 19255
Rhode Island—Andover, MA 05501
South Carolina—Atlanta, GA 39901
South Dakota—Ogden, UT 84201
Tennessee—Memphis, TN 37501
Texas—Austin, TX 73301
Utah—Ogden, UT 84201
Vermont—Andover, MA 05501
Virginia—Philadelphia, PA 19255
Washington—Ogden, UT 84201
West Virginia—Cincinnati, OH 45999
Wisconsin—Kansas City, MO 64999
Wyoming—Ogden, UT 84201
American Samoa—Philadelphia, PA 19255
Guam—Commissioner of Revenue and Taxation
855 West Marine Dr.
Agana, GU 96910
Puerto Rico—Philadelphia, PA 19255
Virgin Islands: Nonpermanent residents—Philadelphia, PA 19255
Virgin Islands: Permanent residents—
V.I. Bureau of Internal Revenue
Lockharts Garden No. 1A
Charlotte Amalie
St. Thomas, VI 00802
Foreign country: *U.S. citizens and those filing Form 2555 or Form 4563*—
Philadelphia, PA 19255
All A.P.O. and F.P.O. addresses—
Philadelphia, PA 19255

After You File

Refunds

You can call a special IRS Tele-Tax telephone number to find out the status of your refund. For details on how to use this service, see "How Do I Use Tele-Tax" on page 5.

Amending Your Return

If you find that you made a mistake on your tax return, you can correct it by filing a Form 1040X, *Amended U.S. Individual Income Tax Return.* Generally, you must file this form within three years from the date you filed your original return or within two years from the date you paid your tax, whichever is later.

File Form 1040X with the IRS Service Center for your area. See the Service Center list on page 26.

Your state tax liability may be affected by a change made on your federal income tax return. For more information on this, contact your state tax authority.

Prior Year Returns

You can get a copy of your prior year tax returns by completing Form 4506, *Request for Copy of Tax Form,* and mailing it to the Service Center where you filed the return. Service Center addresses are listed on the back of Form 4506. The charge is $4.25 for each year's return. Send this fee to the Service Center along with your Form 4506.

Your authorized representative can request a copy of your prior year return. The representative must attach a signed copy of Form 2848, *Power of Attorney and Declaration of Representative,* or other document authorizing him or her to act for you with Form 4506.

If you do not have a Form 4506, you can send the Service Center a written request with your name and social security number, your spouse's name and social security number if you filed a joint return, the form number, the tax period, and your current address. You must sign this request. If you filed a joint return, only one of you need sign this request. Allow 45 days to receive your copy of the return.

Tax account information is free. You can get a printed copy of the information in your tax account by contacting most local IRS offices. The information will be mailed to you, generally within two weeks after your request. The tax account information you will receive includes your name and social security number, marital status, type of return filed, tax shown on return, adjusted gross income, taxable income, self-employment tax and the number of exemptions.

IRS Procedures

The Problem Resolution Program

If you have a tax problem with the IRS, and have been unable to resolve it after attempting to do so through normal IRS channels, you may use the Problem Resolution Program (PRP).

PRP personnel are taxpayer advocates. They have the authority to cut through red tape. Generally, you deal with one person from PRP, and that person keeps you informed of the case's progress.

You can contact PRP by calling the IRS assistance number listed on page 4 of this publication, by looking in your local telephone book under Internal Revenue Service, or by writing to your local IRS District Director and asking for Problem Resolution assistance. Deaf and hearing-impaired taxpayers who have access to TDD (telecommunication device for the deaf) equipment may call 1-800-829-4059 to ask for help from Problem Resolution.

While PRP staffs do everything they can to help you, there are some things they cannot do. Appeals of decisions made in tax examinations, Freedom of Information Act requests, Privacy Act inquiries, cases under criminal investigation and complaints about hiring practices are all outside of PRP's authority.

Examination of Returns

If the IRS selects your return for examination, you may be asked to show records such as canceled checks, receipts or other supporting documents to verify entries on your return.

You may act on your own behalf or you may have an attorney, a certified public accountant, or an individual enrolled to practice before the IRS represent or accompany you. Anyone can accompany you to an examination; however, the person that represents you must have a valid power of attorney.

Not all examinations result in changes in tax liability. If the examination of your return shows that you overpaid your tax, you will receive a refund. However, if the examination of your return shows that you owe additional tax, payment is expected. If you disagree with the examination results, you can appeal. Your appeal rights will be explained to you.

As mentioned earlier in this publication under "Volunteer and Education Programs," Student Tax Clinics are available in some IRS districts to help taxpayers during examinations and appeals proceedings.

Collection of Unpaid Taxes

The IRS checks tax returns for mathematical accuracy and to see if the correct payment has been made. If tax is owed, the IRS will send you a notice of tax due. Generally, you are then required by law to make payment within 10 days of the date of the bill.

If you believe a bill from the IRS is wrong, contact the IRS immediately. You need to provide information that supports your position. If the IRS agrees with you, then the IRS will make the necessary correction to your account.

However, if you owe the tax and it is not paid on time, then by law interest and penalties can be charged to you. If the liability, interest and penalties go unpaid, then a federal tax lien may also be filed on your property. There is also a penalty for failure to file a return by the due date.

If you cannot pay the entire amount due, contact your local IRS office. Depending on your financial condition, installment payments or deferred collection action may be arranged. Interest and penalties will continue to accrue until you pay the liability in full.

If you neglect the notice of tax due or refuse to pay, the IRS may enforce collection by levy on assets, including your income, or by the seizure and sale of property.

More information on the collection process and on your rights is in Publication 586A, *The Collection Process (Income Tax Accounts)*, and Publication 594, *The Collection Process (Employment Tax Accounts)*.

The Collection Process

To stop the process at any stage, you should pay the tax in full. If you cannot pay the tax in full, contact us right away to discuss possible ways to pay the tax.

Start here

First notice and demand for unpaid tax.

10 days later

Enforcement authority arises. Notice of Federal tax lien may be filed.

Up to 3 more notices sent over a period of time asking for payment.

Notice of intent to levy is sent by certified mail (final notice).

30 days later

Enforcement action to collect the tax begins (levy, seizure, etc.).

2. "Your Business Tax Kit" Order Form

Your Business Tax Kit

Department of the Treasury
Internal Revenue Service
Publication 454-A (Rev. 9-91)
Cat. No. 46525S

Here's Your Business Tax Kit (YBTK) to help make your taxes less taxing. You have the right to know all you can about your Federal tax benefits and responsibilities. The forms and publications apply solely to Federal taxes, therefore, you should consult with state or local taxing authorities for their requirements. In your kit you'll find Publication 334, Tax Guide for Small Business, an easy to read business tax reference which explains situations that apply to a small business.

To find out about educational programs for small businesses, complete the interest form on the enclosed Publication 1057, Small Business Tax Education Program (STEP) Brochure, and mail it to the nearest IRS office listed for your state. Through a unique partnership between IRS and many community and junior colleges, universities and business associations across the country, small business owners (sole-proprietors, partnerships and corporations) have an opportunity to learn what they need to know about taxes. Often educational programs are offered in conjunction with a variety of Federal and State agencies providing you with one-stop assistance. Contact your local Taxpayer Education Coordinator to find out about other IRS tax services available for small businesses, such as Community Outreach Tax Education. For more information, review the enclosed Publication 910, Guide to Free Tax Services.

WARNING!

IN ORDER TO AVOID ADDITIONAL TAXES AND SUBSTANTIAL PENALTIES THERE ARE IMPORTANT FACTS YOU SHOULD KNOW.

1. Formation of a corporation or a partnership does not release you from personal liability associated with employment taxes.

2. Classification of employees as "contract labor" and/or failure to properly withhold and report employment taxes could result in additional taxes and large penalities to the officers and owners of a business.

3. Employers are required to obtain valid social security numbers from all workers.

4. Corporate officers are employees, not contract labor, and are subject to withholding taxes.

YBTK ORDER BLANK

Form W-4	Form 1040 Sch SE	Form 1120	Inst 1120-S Sch D	Pub 15
Form 940	Form 1065	Form 1120 Sch D	Form 1120-W	Pub 393
Form 941	Inst 1065	Inst 1120/1120-A	Form 2553	Pub 505
Form 1040		Form 1120-A	Inst 2553	Pub 541
Inst 1040	Form 1065 Sch D	Form 1120-S	Form 4562	Pub 542
Form 1040 Sch C	Form 1065 Sch K-1	Inst 1120-S	Inst 4562	Pub 589
Form 1040 Sch E	Inst 1065 Sch K-1	Form 1120-S Sch D		

Internal Revenue Service **YBTK**

Name

Number and Street

City State Zip Code

THE FOLLOWING ITEMS ARE INCLUDED IN YBTK

Form SS-4, Application for Employer Identification Number
Form 1040ES, Estimated Tax for Individuals

Publication 334, Tax Guide to Small Business
Publication 454-A, YBTK Content Sheet
Publication 509, Tax Calendars for 1991
Publication 583, Taxpayers Starting a Busines

Publication 910, Guide to Free Tax Services
Publication 937, Business Reporting
Publication 1057, Small Business Tax Education Program Brochure

If a tax form, instruction or publication you want is not included in your kit, you may call the IRS toll-free number (1-800-829-3676) to order the item(s); or you may use the order blank provided below.

We will send you two (2) copies of each form and one (1) copy of each set of instructions or publication you circle. Please cut the order blank on the dotted line and be sure to print or type your name and address accurately on the bottom portion. Enclose this order blank in your own envelope and address your envelope to the IRS address shown on reverse for your state. Be sure to allow two (2) weeks for delivery.

THE FOLLOWING ITEMS MAY BE ORDERED ON THE ORDER BLANK PROVIDED

Sole Proprietorships

Form 1040 U.S. Individual Income Tax Return and Instructions
Schedule C (Form 1040) Profit or Loss From Business
Schedule SE (Form 1040) Social Security Self-Employment Tax
Form 4562 Depreciation and Amortization and Instructions

Publication 505 Tax Withholding and Estimated Tax
Publication 533 Self-Employment Tax

Corporations

Form 1120 U.S. Corporation Income Tax Return and Instructions
Schedule D (Form 1120) Capital Gains and Losses
Form 1120-A U.S. Income Tax Return and Instructions
Form 1120-S U.S. Income Tax for an S Corporation and Instructions
Schedule D (Form 1120S) Capital Gains and Losses and Built-In Gains and Instructions
Form 1120-W Corporation Estimated Tax
Form 2553 Election by a Small Business Corporation and Instructions
Form 4562 Depreciation and Amortization and Instructions

Publication 542 Tax Information on Corporations
Publication 589 Tax Information on S Corporations

Partnerships

Form 1065 U.S. Partnership Return of Income and Instructions
Schedule D (Form 1065) Capital Gains and Losses and Instructions
Schedule K-1 (Form 1065) Partner's Share of Income Credits Deductions, etc. and Instructions
Schedule E (Form 1040) Supplemental Income and Loss
Schedule SE (Form 1040) Social Security Self-Employment Tax
Form 4562 Depreciation and Amortization and Instructions

Publication 505 Tax Withholding and Estimated Tax
Publication 541 Tax Information on Partnerships

Employment Taxes

Form W-4 Employee's Withholding Allowance Certificate
Form 940 Employer's Annual Federal Unemployment (FUTA) Tax Return
Form 941 Employer's Quarterly Federal Tax Return

Publication 15 (Circular E) Employer's Tax Guide
Publication 393 Federal Employment Tax Forms

If you are located in:	Send to "Forms Distribution Center" for your state
Alabama, Arkansas, Illinois, Indiana, Iowa, Kansas, Kentucky, Louisiana, Michigan, Minnesota, Mississippi, Missouri, Nebraska, North Dakota, Ohio, Oklahoma, South Dakota, Tennessee, Texas, Wisconsin	P.O. Box 9903 Bloomington, IL 61799
Alaska, Arizona, California, Colorado, Hawaii, Idaho, Montana, Nevada, New Mexico, Oregon, Utah, Washington, Wyoming	Rancho Cordova CA 95743–0001
Connecticut, Delaware, District of Columbia, Florida, Georgia, Maine, Maryland, Massachusetts, New Hampshire, New Jersey, New York, North Carolina, Pennsylvania, Rhode Island, South Carolina, Vermont, Virginia, West Virginia	P.O. Box 25866 Richmond, VA 23289

Foreign Addresses — Taxpayers with mailing addresses in foreign countries should send their requests for forms and publications to: Forms Distribution Center, P.O. Box 25866, Richmond, VA 23289; Forms Distribution Center, Rancho Cordova, CA 95743–0001, whichever is closer.

Puerto Rico — Forms Distribution Center, P.O. Box 25866, Richmond, VA 23289

Virgin Islands — V.I. Bureau of Internal Revenue, Lockharts Garden, No. 1A, Charlotte Amalie, St. Thomas, VI 00802

*U.S. Government Printing Office: 1991 — 617-016/49135

3. Publication 937—Business Reporting

Department of the Treasury
Internal Revenue Service
Catalog Number 63126N

Publication 937

Business Reporting

- **Employment Taxes**
- **Information Returns**

For use in preparing
1991 Returns

Contents

Important Changes for 1991

Social security and Medicare taxes. Beginning in 1991, the computation of social security tax is separated into two parts. The old-age, survivors, and disability insurance part is referred to as social security. The hospital insurance part is referred to as Medicare. You must report each of these items separately on Forms 941 and W-2.

The tax rate for social security is 6.2% each for employers and employees (12.4% total) and the wage base for 1991 is $53,400. For 1992, the wage base is $55,500.

The tax rate for Medicare is 1.45% each for employers and employees (2.9% total) and the wage base for 1991 is $125,000. For 1992, the wage base is $130,200.

Form 1099–R replaces Form W-2P. Form W-2P, *Statement for Recipients of Annuities, Pensions, Retired Pay, or IRA Payments,* is obsolete after 1990. The information that was on the 1990 Form W-2P has been added to the 1991 Form 1099–R, *Distributions From Pensions, Annuities, Retirement or Profit-Sharing Plans, IRAs, Insurance Contracts, etc.* File the 1991 Form 1099–R with the Internal Revenue Service (IRS) by February 28, 1992, with ***Form 1096,*** *Annual Summary and Transmittal of U.S. Information Returns.*

Group legal service plans. Under the *Tax Extension Act of 1991,* the cost of group legal service plans is not subject to social security, Medicare, federal unemployment taxes, and income tax withholding if the cost is paid before July 1, 1992, for periods before that date. See *Withholding and Reporting Payments Other Than Wages* under *Income Tax Withholding.*

Educational assistance plans. Under the *Tax Extension Act of 1991,* the cost of educational assistance plans is not subject to social security, Medicare, federal unemployment taxes, and income tax withholding if the cost is paid before July 1,1992. See *Withholding and Reporting Payments Other Than Wages* under *Income Tax Withholding.*

Federal unemployment (FUTA) tax rate. The gross FUTA tax rate remains at 6.2% through 1992.

Introduction

This publication is mainly designed for small businesses. This includes self-employed persons such as sole-proprietors, independent contractors, and members of a partnership.

Free publications and forms. If you need information on a subject not covered in this publication, please check our other free publications. To order publications and forms, call our toll-free telephone number: 1–800–TAX–FORM (1–800–829–3676). You may also write to the IRS Forms Distribution Center for your area as shown in the income tax package.

Employment Taxes

If you have any employees, you will probably be required to withhold federal income tax from their wages. You may also have to withhold and pay social security and Medicare taxes. If you do not withhold these taxes, or withhold the taxes but do not deposit them, you may be subject to a penalty equal to the amount of the tax. See *Penalties* under *Deposits,* later.

This publication discusses an employer's responsibility for these taxes. It also discusses income tax withholding on payments other than wages, the federal unemployment (FUTA) tax, the rules for advance payment of the earned income credit, and the rules for tip reporting and allocation. Information useful for 1992 is also included.

If you need information on railroad taxes, see the instructions for Form CT–1, *Employer's Annual Railroad Retirement and Unemployment Repayment Tax Return,* and Form CT–2, *Employee Representative's Quarterly Railroad Tax Return.* Railroad retirement and railroad unemployment repayment taxes are explained in the *Instructions for Form CT–1.*

Note. After your employees file their 1991 income tax returns, you can help them correct any mistakes they may have made in figuring their income tax withholding for 1991 by making new 1992 Forms W–4 available. You should encourage them to check their income tax withholding situation if they owed a large amount of tax or received a large refund for 1991, and to give you a new Form W–4 for 1992 if necessary. An employee is most likely to have too little tax withheld if both the employee and his or her spouse work. See *Form W–4 Withholding Allowances,* under *Income Tax Withholding,* later.

After you receive completed Forms W–4 from your employees, you can help them determine whether they are having the right amount of income tax withheld in 1992 by giving them Publication 919, *Is My Withholding Correct for 1992?* This publication will help your employees compare the amount of tax they expect to show on their 1992 tax returns with the amount of tax to be withheld from their pay during 1992.

Employee's social security number. If one of your employees does not have a social security number and has not applied for one, you should tell the employee to submit an application on Form SS–5, *Application for a Social Security Card,* to the nearest Social Security office. Also, if an employee has changed his or her name, he or she should ask the Social Security Administration for a corrected social security card. Form SS–5 can be obtained from any Social Security office.

If any of your employees are under 18 years old, they must furnish evidence of age, identity, and U.S. citizenship along with the Form SS–5. Employees who are 18 years old or older must appear in person with this evidence at a Social Security office.

Employer identification number. If you do not have an employer identification number (EIN), you must get one. To get an EIN, file Form SS–4, *Application for Employer Identification Number*, with the IRS Service Center for your area listed in the *Instructions for Form SS–4*. If you prefer, you can ask for an EIN immediately by calling the tele-TIN phone number for your state's IRS Service Center listed in the *Instructions for Form SS–4*. You can get Form SS–4 and the *Instructions for Form SS–4* at IRS or Social Security Administration offices.

Who Are Employees?

Before you can know how to treat payments you make for services rendered to you, you must first know the business relationship that exists between you and the person performing those services. The person performing the services may be:

1) An independent contractor;
2) A common-law employee;
3) A statutory employee; or
4) A statutory nonemployee.

This discussion explains these four categories. A later discussion, *Employee or Independent Contractor?*, points out the differences between an independent contractor and an employee and gives examples from various types of occupations.

Independent Contractors

People such as lawyers, contractors, subcontractors, public stenographers, auctioneers, etc., who follow an independent trade, business, or profession in which they offer their services to the general public, are generally not employees. However, whether such people are employees or independent contractors depends on the facts in each case. The general rule is that an individual is an independent contractor if you, the employer, have the right to control or direct only the result of the work and not the means and methods of accomplishing the result.

You do not have to withhold or pay taxes on payments you make to independent contractors.

Common-law Employees

Under common-law rules, every individual who performs services subject to the will and control of an employer, as to both ***what*** must be done and ***how*** it must be done, is an employee. It does not matter that the employer allows the employee discretion and freedom of action, so long as the employer has the ***legal right*** to control both the method and the result of the services. For a discussion of the factors that indicate whether sufficient control is present to establish an employer-employee relationship, see *Employee or Independent Contractor?*, later.

Two usual characteristics of an employer-employee relationship are that the employer has the right to discharge the employee and the employer supplies the employee with tools and a place to work.

If you have an employer-employee relationship, it makes no difference how it is described. It does not matter if the employee is called an employee, partner, co-adventurer, agent, or independent contractor. It does not matter how the payments are measured, how they are made, or what they are called. Nor does it matter whether the individual is employed full time or part time.

No distinction is made between classes of employees. Superintendents, managers, and other supervisory personnel are all employees. An ***officer of a corporation*** is generally an employee, but a director is not. An officer who performs no services or only minor services, and neither receives nor is entitled to receive any pay, is not considered an employee.

You may have to withhold and pay taxes on wages you pay to common-law employees.

Statutory Employees

If an individual who works for you is not an employee under the common-law rules (see *Employee or Independent Contractor?*, later), you do not have to withhold federal income tax from that individual's pay. However, for social security and Medicare taxes, the term ***employee*** includes any individual who works for you for pay in one of the following four categories:

1) A driver who distributes meat products, vegetable products, fruit products, bakery products, or beverages (other than milk) or picks up and delivers laundry or dry cleaning, if the driver is your agent or is paid on commission.
2) A full-time life insurance sales agent whose principal business activity is selling life insurance or annuity contracts, or both, primarily for one life insurance company.
3) An individual who works at home on materials or goods which you supply and which must be returned to you or to a person you name, if you also furnish specifications for the work to be done.
4) A full-time traveling or city salesperson who works on your behalf and turns in orders to you from wholesalers, retailers, contractors, or operators of hotels, restaurants, or other similar establishments. The goods sold must be merchandise for resale or supplies for use in the buyer's business operation. The work performed for you must be the salesperson's principal business activity. See *Salespersons* under *Employee or Independent Contractor?*, later.

Social security and Medicare taxes. For social security and Medicare taxes, individuals within any of the above four categories are employees if:

- The service contract states or implies that almost all of the services are to be performed personally by them;
- The individual has little or no investment in the equipment and property used to perform the services (other than an investment in transportation facilities); and
- The services are performed on a continuing basis.

Federal unemployment tax. For federal unemployment tax, the term ***employee*** means the same as it does for social security and Medicare taxes, except that it does not include categories (2) and (3), above. Thus, any individual who is an employee under categories (1) or (4) is also an employee for federal unemployment tax purposes.

Reporting payments to statutory employees. Furnish a Form W-2 to a statutory employee, and check *Statutory employee* in box 6. Show your payments to the employee as other compensation in box 10. Also, show social security tax withheld in box 11, social security wages in box 12, Medicare wages in box 14, and Medicare tax withheld in box 15. The statutory employee can deduct his or her expenses from the payments shown on Form W–2. He or she reports earnings as a statutory employee on line 1 of Schedule C. (A statutory employee's business expenses are not subject to the reduction by 2% of his or her adjusted gross income that applies to common-law employees.)

Statutory Nonemployees

Two categories of statutory nonemployees have been established: ***direct sellers*** and ***licensed real estate agents***. They are treated as self-employed for federal income tax and employment tax purposes if:

1) Substantially all payments for their services as direct sellers or real estate agents are directly related to sales or other output, rather than to the number of hours worked; and
2) Their services are performed under a written contract providing that they will not be treated as employees for federal tax purposes.

Direct sellers. Direct sellers are persons:

1) Engaged in selling (or soliciting the sale of) consumer products in the home or at a place of business other than in a permanent retail establishment; or
2) Engaged in selling (or soliciting the sale of) consumer products to any buyer on a buy-sell basis, a deposit-commission basis, or any similar basis prescribed by regulations, for resale in the home or at a place of business other than in a permanent retail establishment.

Direct selling includes activities of individuals who attempt to increase direct sales activities of their direct sellers and who earn income based on the productivity of their direct sellers. Such activities include providing motivation and encouragement, imparting skills, knowledge, or experience, and recruiting.

For more information on direct sellers, get Publication 911, *Tax Information for Direct Sellers.*

Licensed real estate agents. This category includes individuals engaged in appraisal activities for real estate sales if they earn income based on sales or other output.

General Rules for Withholding

You may find it helpful to remember the following general rules for withholding:

1) ***Independent contractors.*** You do not have to withhold income tax or social security and Medicare taxes from amounts you pay an independent contractor. But, if you pay an independent contractor $600 or more during the year in the course of your trade or business, you must file a Form 1099–MISC, *Miscellaneous Income.*
2) ***Common-law employees.*** You may have to withhold income tax, social security tax, and Medicare tax from the wages you pay common-law employees. You may also have to pay federal unemployment tax and your share of social security and Medicare taxes on these wages.
3) ***Statutory employees.*** You do not withhold income tax from the wages of statutory employees. But you must withhold and pay social security and Medicare taxes. Unless they are full-time life insurance sales agents or work at home, you must also pay federal unemployment tax on their wages.
4) ***Statutory nonemployees.*** You do not withhold or pay taxes on payments to statutory nonemployees.

Penalty for treating an employee as an independent contractor. If you classify an employee as an independent contractor and you had no reasonable basis for doing so, you will have to pay employment taxes for that worker (the relief provisions, discussed below, will not apply). Further, if you do not withhold income, social security, and Medicare taxes from his or her wages, you may be held personally liable for a penalty of 100% of such taxes if you are the person responsible for the collection and payment of withholding taxes. See *Penalties* under *Deposits*, later.

Relief provisions. If you have a reasonable basis for not treating a worker as an employee, you may be relieved from having to pay employment taxes for that worker. To get this relief, you must file all required federal tax returns, including information returns, on a basis consistent with your treatment of the worker. You (or your predecessor) must not have treated any worker holding a substantially similar position as an employee for any periods beginning after 1977. For further information, see Revenue Procedure

85–18, in Internal Revenue Cumulative Bulletin 1985–1, page 518.

Technical service specialists. This relief provision does not apply to a worker who provides services for a client as a technical specialist under an arrangement between a taxpayer, such as a technical services firm, and the client. A technical service specialist is an engineer, designer, drafter, computer programmer, systems analyst, or other similarly skilled worker engaged in a similar line of work. (A taxpayer who directly contracts with a technical service specialist to provide services for itself rather than for a third party may still be entitled to the relief provision.) This rule does not automatically convert technical service specialists to employees for employment tax purposes. The common-law standards control whether the specialist is treated as an employee or an independent contractor. See *Employee or Independent Contractor?,* below.

Leased employees. Under certain circumstances, a corporation furnishing workers to various professional people and firms is the employer of those workers for employment tax purposes. For example, a professional service corporation may provide the services of secretaries, nurses, and other similarly trained workers to its subscribers. The service corporation enters into contracts with the subscribers under which the subscribers specify the services to be provided and the fee to be paid to the service corporation for each individual furnished. The contracts provide that the service corporation has the right to control and direct the worker's services for the subscriber including the right to discharge or reassign the worker. The service corporation hires the workers, pays their wages, provides them with unemployment insurance and other benefits, and is the employer for employment tax purposes. For information on employee leasing as it relates to pension plan qualification requirements, see *Employee leasing* in Publication 560, *Self-Employed Retirement Plans.*

Nonbusiness (personal) services by employees. Noncash payments by an employer for personal services by employees, not in the course of the employer's business, are not subject to employment taxes.

Cash payments by an employer, however, for personal services by employees not in the course of the employer's business, such as making repairs on the employer's home, are subject to the following rules:

1) Payments are subject to income tax withholding and federal unemployment taxes if the employee earns $50 or more in cash in a calendar quarter performing personal services for the employer, and works 24 or more days in that quarter or in the preceding quarter in the employer's business.
2) Payments are subject to social security and Medicare taxes if the employee receives $100 or more in cash in a calendar year from the employer for personal services.

These rules do not apply to corporate employees. They also do not apply to household and farm workers.

Additional information. For more information about the treatment of special types of employment, the treatment of special types of payments, and similar subjects, get a free copy of Publication 15 (Circular E), *Employer's Tax Guide,* or Publication 51 (Circular A), *Agricultural Employer's Tax Guide,* from the Internal Revenue Service.

Employee or Independent Contractor?

An employer must generally withhold income taxes, withhold and pay social security and Medicare taxes, and pay unemployment taxes on wages paid to an employee. An employer does not generally have to withhold or pay any taxes on payments to independent contractors.

Common law rules. To help you determine whether an individual is an employee under the common law rules, 20 factors have been identified that indicate whether sufficient control is present to establish an employer-employee relationship. The degree of importance of each factor varies depending on the occupation and the context in which the services are performed. It does not matter that the employer allows the employee freedom of action, so long as the employer has the right to control both the method and the result of the services. If an employer treats an employee as an independent contractor and the relief provisions discussed earlier do not apply, the person responsible for the collection and payment of withholding taxes may be held personally liable for an amount equal to the employee's income, social security, and Medicare taxes that should have been withheld.

The 20 factors indicating whether an individual is an employee or an independent contractor are:

1) ***Instructions.*** An employee must comply with instructions about when, where, and how to work. Even if no instructions are given, the control factor is present if the employer has the right to give instructions.
2) ***Training.*** An employee is trained to perform services in a particular manner. Independent contractors ordinarily use their own methods and receive no training from the purchasers of their services.
3) ***Integration.*** An employee's services are integrated into the business operations because the services are important to the success or continuation of the business. This shows that the employee is subject to direction and control.
4) ***Services rendered personally.*** An employee renders services personally. This shows that the employer is interested in the methods as well as the results.
5) ***Hiring assistants.*** An employee works for an employer who hires, supervises, and pays assistants. An independent contractor hires, supervises, and pays assistants under a contract that requires him or her to provide materials and labor and to be responsible only for the result.
6) ***Continuing relationship.*** An employee has a continuing relationship with an employer. A continuing relationship may exist where work is performed at frequently recurring although irregular intervals.
7) ***Set hours of work.*** An employee has set hours of work established by an employer. An independent contractor is the master of his or her own time.
8) ***Full-time work.*** An employee normally works full time for an employer. An independent contractor can work when and for whom he or she chooses.
9) ***Work done on premises.*** An employee works on the premises of an employer, or works on a route or at a location designated by an employer.
10) ***Order or sequence set.*** An employee must perform services in the order or sequence set by an employer. This shows that the employee is subject to direction and control.
11) ***Reports.*** An employee submits reports to an employer. This shows that the employee must account to the employer for his or her actions.
12) ***Payments.*** An employee is paid by the hour, week, or month. An independent contractor is paid by the job or on a straight commission.
13) ***Expenses.*** An employee's business and travel expenses are paid by an employer. This shows that the employee is subject to regulation and control.
14) ***Tools and materials.*** An employee is furnished significant tools, materials, and other equipment by an employer.
15) ***Investment.*** An independent contractor has a significant investment in the facilities he or she uses in performing services for someone else.
16) ***Profit or loss.*** An independent contractor can make a profit or suffer a loss.
17) ***Works for more than one person or firm.*** An independent contractor gives his or her services to two or more unrelated persons or firms at the same time.
18) ***Offers services to general public.*** An independent contractor makes his or her services available to the general public.
19) ***Right to fire.*** An employee can be fired by an employer. An independent contractor cannot be fired so long as he or she produces a result that meets the specifications of the contract.
20) ***Right to quit.*** An employee can quit his or her job at any time without incurring liability. An independent contractor usually agrees to complete a specific job and is responsible for its satisfactory completion, or is legally obligated to make good for failure to complete it.

Form SS–8. In doubtful cases, the facts will determine whether or not there is an actual employer-employee relationship. If you want the IRS to determine whether a worker is an employee, file Form SS–8, *Determination of Employee Work Status for Purposes of Federal Employment Taxes and Income Tax Withholding,* with the District Director.

The following examples may help you to properly classify your workers:

Building and Construction Industry

Example 1. John Brown has an oral agreement with Ace Building Co. to do carpentry work on any house designated by the Ace Building Co. He supplies his own hand tools. The Ace Building Co. supplies the material for each job. He has to do the work himself and he works on a full-time basis for the company. For some work he is paid on a piecework basis and for some on an hourly basis. He has no assistants, does not have an office, and does not advertise in newspapers or otherwise hold himself out to the public as being in the carpentry business. The Ace Building Co. can discharge him any time before he finishes a job without contractual liability. John is an employee of the Ace Building Co.

Example 2. Ron Smith, a mason, has an oral agreement with Jiffy, Inc., a contractor, to face a building with brick. Jiffy supplies all material for the job. He supplies only his hand tools. He has to do the work himself and is paid on an hourly basis. Jiffy employs two other masons on the job, who are supervised by Ron. Detailed supervision over him is neither necessary nor warranted because of his skill in the work. He can quit the job at any time, or Jiffy can discharge him at any time. He has no investment or proprietary interest in a business that offers the general public services similar to those he does for Jiffy. Ron is an employee of Jiffy, Inc.

Example 3. Tom Green is a painting subcontractor who has contracted to paint 264 houses. He hired 40 painters to do the work for him, although only about 15 are on the job at any one time. He supplies all the paint, brushes, and ladders. He designates the house to be painted and either pays the painters per house or by the hour. Detailed instructions about the work are not necessary because of the painters' skill in their trade. He inspects the work and requires them to repaint any unsatisfactory work. The painters cannot engage helpers without his consent. He can discharge them for any reason, and they are free to resign at any time. The painters are under no legal obligation to complete the painting of the houses. They assume no business risks and have no capital investment. None of them has an established business. The painters are employees of Tom Green.

Example 4. Jerry Jones has an agreement with Wilma White to supervise the remodeling of her house. She did not advance funds to help him carry on the work. She makes direct payments to the suppliers for all necessary materials. She carries liability and worker's compensation insurance covering Jerry and others he engaged to assist him. She pays them an hourly rate, and exercises almost constant supervision over the work. Jerry is not free to transfer his assistants to other jobs. He may not work on other jobs while working for Wilma. He assumes no responsibility to complete the work and will incur no contractual liability if he fails to do so. He and his assistants perform personal services for hourly wages. They are employees of Wilma White.

Example 5. Milton Manning, an experienced tilesetter, orally agreed with a corporation to perform full-time services at construction sites. He uses his own tools and performs services in the order designated by the corporation and according to its specifications. The corporation supplies all materials, makes frequent inspections of his work, pays him on a piecework basis, and carries worker's compensation insurance on him. He does not have a place of business or hold himself out to perform similar services for others. Either party can end the services at any time. Milton Manning is an employee of the corporation.

Example 6. Wallace Black agreed with the Sawdust Co. to supply the construction labor for a group of houses. The company agreed to pay all construction costs. However, he supplies all the tools and equipment. He performs personal services as a carpenter and mechanic for an hourly wage. He also acts as superintendent and foreman, and engages other individuals to assist him. The company has the right to select, approve, or discharge any helper. A company representative makes frequent inspections of the construction site. When a house is finished, Wallace is paid a certain percentage of its costs. He is not responsible for faults, defects of construction, or wasteful operation. At the end of each week, he presents the company with a statement of the amount he has spent, including the payroll. The company gives him a check for that amount from which he pays the assistants, although he is not personally liable for their wages. Wallace Black and his assistants are employees of the Sawdust Co.

Example 7. A local plumbers' union and a contractors' association agreed to set up an apprenticeship program. The program is financed by the contractors and is administered by a joint apprenticeship committee. Trainees are enrolled first in a preapprenticeship program, in which they attend vocational school full time 5 days a week for 6 to 8 weeks. During this period, they are paid an hourly rate and are furnished with all materials and supplies used in school.

After completion of the preapprenticeship program, the trainees are assigned to work for local contractors as apprentice plumbers. The apprentices must attend training classes related to the trade one day a week for 2 years. The apprenticeship program pays them for the time spent in attending classes at the same hourly rate they earn working for their contractor-employers.

While in the preapprenticeship program, the trainees are not employees. Their payments from the program are not subject to income tax withholding or social security, and Medicare taxes. The contractors and the administrators of the preapprenticeship program are not liable for federal unemployment tax. However, the apprentices assigned to contractors as apprentice plumbers are considered employees, even when attending classes under the apprenticeship program. Their payments from the program are subject to income tax withholding, social security and Medicare taxes, and federal unemployment tax.

Trucking Business

Example 1. Drivers for Rover Trucking Co. often engage laborers to unload their trucks with the express consent of the company. The drivers pay the unloaders from funds provided by the company. The unloaders are company employees. This also would be true if the drivers had only the implied consent of the company.

Example 2. A company engages Phil Blue to haul products to its customers. The company has legal ownership and control of the trucking equipment. Phil can be required, on an hour's notice, to make deliveries at times and places specified by the company. Refusal can jeopardize his relationship with the company. He has to operate and maintain the equipment and provide the necessary operators and helpers. He is not allowed to use the company's equipment to haul for others. He is paid on a tonnage basis and is not guaranteed a minimum amount of compensation. He has to pay the operators and helpers out of his tonnage receipts as well as pay for all insurance coverage required by the company. Phil and any operators or helpers engaged to assist him are employees of the company.

Fishing Industry

Example 1. Harry Rose is the captain of one of the Pan Fishing Company's schooners. He engages a crew of 15 to operate the schooner. He offers to pay each crew member on the ***lay*** (sharing of the profit) basis. He and the crew members (except the engineer, who is paid a straight fee) are jointly liable for any losses resulting from a voyage.

The schooner is an American vessel of more than 10 net tons. He and the Pan Fishing Company entered into a contract of service within the United States.

After the voyage, Captain Rose sells the catch through a fish exchange, which deducts its fees from the proceeds. After deducting certain specified expenses (such as fuel, oil, etc.), he turns one-fourth of the proceeds over to Pan Fishing Co., less 5%, which he keeps as his commission. From the remaining three-fourths, the expenses of food, bait, etc., are deducted. The remainder is then equally divided among the members of the crew, including himself.

The members of a crew engaged under these circumstances are employees of either the captain (if he is not an agent of the vessel owner) or of the vessel owner. Their lays are in the nature of wages, and the agreements under which the crews are engaged in these circumstances are contracts of hire.

In this example, Captain Rose is acting as an agent of Pan Fishing Co. Therefore, the company is the employer. As an employer of a crew working on an American vessel under a contract entered into in the U.S., the company must withhold income tax and social security and Medicare taxes from the entire crew's wages, including the wages of Captain Rose and the engineer. The company must also pay the employer's portion of social security and Medicare taxes.

Because the schooner is a vessel of more than 10 net tons with a crew of more than nine members, the company must also pay federal unemployment tax on these wages.

The value of ***meals and lodging furnished to the crew*** is not subject to income tax withholding, social security and Medicare taxes, and federal unemployment tax because the company must furnish meals and lodging on board the vessel so that the crew can do their work.

Federal unemployment tax. The work of catching fish is exempt from federal unemployment tax ***except*** for:

1) Work related to catching salmon or halibut for commercial purposes; or
2) Work performed on a vessel of more than 10 net tons.

However, work that is not exempt under this rule may qualify as exempt if the four conditions under *Certain crew members considered self-employed,* discussed next, are met.

Certain crew members considered self-employed. Wages paid to the members of a crew on a fishing boat are not subject to federal income tax withholding, social security and Medicare taxes, and the federal unemployment tax if all the following conditions are met:

1) The members neither get nor are entitled to any money for their work (other than as provided in condition (2), below);
2) The members get shares of the catch or of the proceeds from the sale of the catch;
3) Each member's share depends on the size of the catch; and
4) The operating crew of the boat (or each boat from which a member gets a share for a fishing operation involving more than one boat) normally numbers less than 10.

Each member of the crew who meets these conditions is considered self-employed. The earnings of these crew members are considered trade or business income and therefore subject to self-employment tax. See Publication 533, *Self-Employment Tax.*

Example 2. Mike Jones, an owner of a fishing boat of more than 10 net tons, employs a captain and eight others to work as crew members. The proceeds from the sale of the catch offset boat operating expenses, such as fuel, bait, and ice. The balance is divided 60% among the captain and the crew members and 40% between Mike and the captain. Between voyages the crew members do not receive any additional compensation, but they must do certain work, such as repairing nets, splicing cable, and transporting the catch. However, the mate, the engineer, and the cook receive an additional payment of $100 each. This payment does not depend on the boat's catch. Since the mate, the engineer, and the cook receive payment other than a share of the catch, they are not considered self-employed. The $100 payment and their share of the proceeds from the catch are subject to federal income tax withholding, social security and Medicare taxes, and the federal unemployment tax.

The other six crew members, including the captain, are considered self-employed because they do not receive any additional pay and are members of an operating crew of fewer than 10 members. Mike does not have to withhold federal income tax or social security and Medicare taxes from their pay. They must pay self-employment tax on their earnings. Also, because the boat has a crew of less than 10 members and meets the other conditions mentioned above under *Certain crew members considered self-employed,* Mike does not have to pay the federal unemployment tax for the other six crew members, even though the boat was more than 10 tons.

Example 3. Assume the same facts as in Example 2, except that, in addition to receiving a share of the catch, the captain and the other crew members are entitled to receive $10 per hour for repairing nets, constructing new nets, splicing cable, and other incidental work while in port. Since the crew members are entitled to receive payment other than a share of the catch, they are not considered self-employed. The $10 per hour payment and their share of the proceeds from the catch are subject to federal income tax withholding, social security and Medicare taxes, and the federal unemployment tax.

Reporting requirements. The operator of a boat must file with the IRS a completed Form 1099–MISC, *Miscellaneous Income,* if any of the crew members work as self-employed individuals. It must be filed with the IRS by February 28 of the year following the calendar year in which the crew member was paid. All amounts must be reported. The $600 or more rule does not apply.

Statement to crew member. Each operator who is required to file Form 1099–MISC must also furnish a statement to each crew member. You may use Copy B of Form 1099–MISC for this purpose. This statement must be furnished to all crew members by January 31 of the year following the calendar year in which the crew member was paid.

Shrimp Processing

Example. The Capital Shrimp Processing Co. hired Shirley Gray to devein shrimp. She works on a seasonal, part-time basis on the company's premises. The company pays her on a piecework basis. She or the company may end her services at any time. The percentage of her time spent in working for the Capital Shrimp Processing Co. varies. She also deveins shrimp under similar conditions for other processing firms. Shirley Gray is an employee of the Capital Shrimp Processing Co.

Dentistry

Example 1. Dr. Jean Red, a dentist, engaged James Jones, a dental hygienist, to clean the teeth of her patients at her office on designated days of each week. They have an agreement that he will receive 50% of the fee charged each patient, whether or not it is collected. The laws of the state where the services are performed state that a registered dental hygienist may operate only under the general direction or supervision of a licensed dentist in the dentist's office or in any public school or other institution giving dental services. Therefore, the dental hygienist is an employee of the dentist.

Example 2. Dr. James White, a dentist, entered into a verbal agreement with Dr. Henry Green under which Dr. Green agreed to perform dental services in Dr. White's office. Dr. Green agreed to work for a salary plus a percentage of all income over a stated amount resulting from his services. He has to observe designated office hours and obtain Dr. White's approval for any absences. Dr. White supplies all instruments, pays all office expenses, and realizes all losses from unpaid accounts. He also employs the nurse who assists Dr. Green. Either party can end this agreement at any time. Dr. Green is an employee of Dr. White.

Automobile Industry

Example 1. Donna Lee is a salesperson employed on a full-time basis by Bob Blue, an auto dealer. She works 6 days a week and is on duty in Bob's showroom on certain assigned days and times. She appraises trade-ins, but her appraisals are subject to the sales manager's approval. Lists of prospective customers belong to the dealer. She has to develop leads and report results to the sales manager. Because of her experience, she requires only minimal assistance in closing and financing sales and in other phases of her work. She is paid a commission and is eligible for prizes and bonuses offered by Bob. Donna is an employee of Bob Blue.

Example 2. Sam Sparks performs automobile repair services in the repair department of an automobile sales company. He works regular hours and is paid on a percentage basis. He has no investment in the repair department. The sales company supplies all facilities, repair parts, and supplies; issues instructions on the amounts to be charged, parts to be used, and the time for completion of each job; and checks all estimates and repair orders. Sam is an employee of the sales company.

Example 3. An auto sales agency furnishes space for Helen Smith to perform automobile repair services. She provides her own tools, equipment, and supplies. She seeks out business from insurance adjusters and other individuals and does all the body and paint work that comes to the agency. She hires and discharges her own helpers, determines her own and her helpers' working hours, quotes prices for repair work, makes all necessary adjustments, assumes all losses from uncollectible accounts, and receives, as compensation for her services, a large percentage of the gross collections from the auto repair shop. Helen is self-employed and the helpers are her employees.

Motel–Trailer Court

Example 1. The Hometown Corporation engaged Mr. and Mrs. James Smith to manage a motel it owns. They receive a specified amount per week for their services. They must furnish services 24 hours daily. The services include registering guests, collecting rent, maintaining rooms in good condition, making minor repairs, etc. The corporation provides all furnishings, equipment, and office supplies. No part of the operating cost is borne by the managing couple. Major maintenance and repair work has to be authorized by the corporation before it can be done. The corporation establishes guest service charges and operating policies and frequently gives instructions that it thinks will improve operating conditions. A corporation officer inspects the premises three or four times a week to assure its proper care and operation. The managers are employees of the Hometown Corporation.

Example 2. The Atlas Corporation operates a trailer court that is managed by George Brown, a real estate operator. Bill Grape was engaged to service the grounds. He reports to the trailer court each morning, observes regular working hours, follows a daily routine, and supplies whatever equipment is necessary to maintain the trailer court. He performs services on a full-time basis and is paid semimonthly. He does not perform services for others, has no business establishment, and does not advertise in newspapers or have a business telephone listing. His services can be ended at any time by either party. Bill is an employee of the Atlas Corporation because the corporation has the right to control him through George, the manager of the trailer court.

Barber Shops and Beauty Salons

Example 1. Paul Pick, a barber, signed a lease agreement with Larry Lord, the owner of a barber shop, to use a chair in Larry's shop. Larry bears all the shop expenses, including rent, utilities, advertising, linens, and other supplies.

The agreement provides that 70% of the receipts from Paul's chair go to him and 30% go to Larry. All receipts are put in Larry's cash register. At the end of the week, he pays Paul the agreed percentage of the receipts.

Shop hours are displayed on the shop door. Paul is expected to comply with them. He must take customers in turn, maintain clean premises, use clean towels and sterile equipment, and keep a clean personal appearance. Although Larry does not supervise Paul, Larry can dismiss him for acting in a manner that would cause the loss of patrons, or for any other reason.

Larry does not direct or control Paul in the actual performance of his services, but he has the right to do so and to discharge him. Larry's income depends on a percentage of Paul's receipts. Thus, Larry retains the right to direct and control Paul to protect his investment and to be assured a sufficient profit from the shop. Paul has no investment in the shop, assumes no liability for its operation, and furnishes nothing except his personal services. Paul is an employee of Larry.

Example 2. Beauty Salons, Inc., leases space for beauty shops in department stores. Each department store pays the wages of the shop manager and operators on the basis of payrolls prepared by the manager. The department stores receive a fixed percentage of shop receipts as rent. Although a department store can request removing an operator or manager from a particular store, Beauty Salons, Inc., controls the hiring, training, transfer, and dismissal of all beauty shop personnel. The managers and operators employed in the shop are employees of Beauty Salons, Inc.

Example 3. Charlie Green, the owner of a barber shop, and Sally Gold have an agreement under which Sally, a professional manicurist, furnishes manicuring services to shop patrons during business hours.

According to the agreement, Sally regulates her own hours, furnishes her own equipment and supplies, and keeps the proceeds from her work. She does not use the shop cash register nor does she report her earnings to Charlie. She does not have to perform her services personally but can hire a substitute. Charlie cannot direct the way she performs her services. Either party to the agreement can end the arrangement at any time.

Although Charlie has the right to dismiss her by ending the agreement, and although he furnishes her a place to work, he does not have the right to exercise over her work the degree of direction and control necessary to establish an employer-employee relationship. Therefore, Sally is self-employed.

Dry Cleaning

Example 1. Alfred East, under an agreement with Spotless Cleaners, collects garments regularly on a designated route and delivers them to Spotless for cleaning and pressing. He also solicits customers for Spotless and collects payments. Spotless specifies the prices charged to customers, supplies the truck, and bears all operating expenses. Alfred is paid a percentage of the money collected for garments he brings in and delivers. Either party can end the contract on 15 days written notice. However, Spotless can discharge him at any time for violating its rules, insubordination, being unavailable to customers, failure to account properly for money, or other unsatisfactory route work. Alfred is an employee of Spotless Cleaners.

Example 2. Roger Hemp owns a dry cleaning store. He has an agreement with John Brill and Fred Dant under which John and Fred will run the business for 3 years for half the net profit. John and Fred agreed to keep the store open during regular business hours, pay the bills from the gross receipts, use Roger's bookkeeping system, employ a bookkeeper approved by him, keep accurate books, keep the store equipment in good condition, and try to maintain and increase his business. Roger can end the agreement by giving 10 days' written notice. John and Fred have no investment in the store and furnish only their personal services. John, Fred, and the bookkeeper are employees of Roger Hemp.

Concessionaires and Caterers

Example 1. Snakko Corporation operates a food concession at a ball park. In addition to its regular staff, it hires school age boys and girls to work at its lunch counters and as vendors. They are engaged for each game, work on a commission basis, and are paid daily. They are employees of Snakko Corporation.

Example 2. Elmer, after working in Golda's restaurant for a salary, signed an agreement with her under which he will operate the business for half the net profits. The arrangement between the parties otherwise remains unchanged. He must keep the restaurant open during regular business hours. He purchases supplies in Golda's name and the parties consult frequently on management problems. Golda makes all final decisions concerning the business. Elmer made no capital investment and has no ownership interest in the business. All licenses are issued to Golda and she remains the owner of record of the real estate and the business. Elmer is an employee of Golda.

Example 3. A caterer contracted to render a customer complete service, including the furnishing of waiters. Services rendered by the waiters are necessary to the caterer's business. The caterer uses the control necessary to insure the satisfactory performance of the catering service. The waiters are employees of the caterer.

Salespersons

To determine whether salespersons are employees under the usual common-law rules, you must evaluate each individual case.

Not an employee Salespersons are generally not employees under common-law rules if they meet all four of the following tests:

1) They depend almost entirely on their own initiative, efforts, skill, and personality to retain old customers, develop new ones, and achieve a successful volume of sales.
2) They set their own working hours.
3) They pay their own expenses and are not reimbursed by the person or company they represent.
4) They are paid solely on a commission basis and their pay is derived from the results of their work. They are not guaranteed any minimum pay.

If a salesperson who works for you meets the above tests, you do not have to withhold federal income tax from his or her pay (see *Statutory Employees,* earlier). However, even if a salesperson is not an employee under the usual common-law rules, his or her pay may still be subject to social security and Medicare taxes and federal unemployment (FUTA) taxes. To determine whether a salesperson is an employee for social security, Medicare, and federal unemployment purposes, you must apply the statutory employee tests. A salesperson is an employee for social security, Medicare, and federal unemployment purposes if he or she:

1) Works full time for one person or company except, possibly, for sideline sales activities on behalf of some other person;
2) Sells on behalf of, and turns his or her orders over to, the person or company he or she works for;
3) Sells to wholesalers, retailers, contractors, or operators of hotels, restaurants, or similar establishments;
4) Sells merchandise for resale, or supplies for use in the customer's business;
5) Agrees to do most of this work personally;
6) Has no substantial investment in the facilities used to do the work, other than in facilities for transportation; and
7) Maintains a continuing relationship with the person or company he or she works for.

Household Employees

Household employees are persons you hire to perform services at your private home. If you file Form 941, *Employer's Quarterly Federal Tax Return,* for business employees, you can report wages you pay your household employees with wages you pay your other employees. Otherwise, report these wages on Form 942, *Employer's Quarterly Tax Return for Household Employees.* See the Form 942 instructions for further information, including reporting requirements. If your home is on a farm operated for a profit, also see the instructions for Form 943, *Employer's Annual Tax Return for Agricultural Employees.*

Companion Sitting Services

A person in the trade or business of referring sitters to individuals who need their services is not considered the employer of the sitters if:

1) He or she does not pay or receive the salary or wages of the sitters; and
2) He or she is paid a fee by the sitter or the persons who employ the sitter.

A sitter is any individual who furnishes personal attendance, companionship, or household care services to children or to individuals who are elderly or disabled.

Example. Mr. Jones operates a placement service for companion sitters. He put Sharon Silver in touch with Mrs. Smith, an elderly lady who needed a person to furnish personal attendance, companionship, and household care. Sharon receives her salary directly from Mrs. Smith. Mr. Jones charged Mrs. Smith a fee of $40 for locating a sitter. Sharon is not an employee of Mr. Jones.

Part-Time Workers

For income tax withholding, social security, Medicare, and federal unemployment purposes, there are no differences between full-time employees, part-time employees, and employees hired for short periods. It does not matter whether the worker has another job or has the maximum amount of social security and Medicare taxes withheld by another employer. Income tax withholding may be figured the same way as for full-time workers. Or it may be figured by the part-year employment method, explained in Circular E, *Employer's Tax Guide.*

Family Members

Children employed by parents. Payments for the services of a child under the age of 18 who works for his or her parent in a trade or business is not subject to social security and Medicare taxes. If these services are for work other than in a trade or business, such as domestic work in the parent's private home, they are not subject to social security and Medicare taxes until the child reaches 21.

Payments for the services of a child under the age of 21 who works for his or her parent whether or not in a trade or business are not subject to federal unemployment taxes.

The above rules apply even if the child is paid regular wages. The wages for these services are not subject to social security, Medicare, and federal unemployment taxes. But they may still be subject to income tax withholding.

One spouse employed by another. The wages for the services of an individual who works for his or her spouse in a trade or business are subject to income tax withholding and social security and Medicare taxes, but not to federal unemployment taxes. However, the services of one spouse employed by another in other than a trade or business, such as domestic service in a private home, are not subject to social security, Medicare, and federal unemployment taxes.

Covered services of a child or spouse. The wages for the services of a child or spouse are subject to income tax withholding as well as social security, Medicare, and federal unemployment taxes if he or she works for:

1) A corporation, even if it is controlled by the child's parent or the individual's spouse;
2) A partnership, even if the child's parent is a partner, unless each partner is a parent of the child;
3) A partnership, even if the individual's spouse is a partner; or
4) An estate, even if it is the estate of a deceased parent.

Parent employed by child. The wages for the services of a parent employed by a son or daughter in a trade or business are subject to income tax withholding and social security and Medicare taxes. Social security and Medicare taxes do not apply to wages paid to a parent for services not in a trade or business, but they do apply to domestic services if:

1) The parent cares for a child who lives with a son or daughter and is under 18, or requires adult supervision for at least 4 continuous weeks in a calendar quarter due to a mental or physical condition, and
2) The son or daughter is a widow or widower, divorced, or married to a person who, because of a physical or mental condition, cannot care for the child during such period.

Employees of Exempt Organizations

Many ***nonprofit organizations*** are exempt from income tax. Although they do not have to pay income tax themselves, they must still withhold income tax from the pay of their employees. However, there are special social security, Medicare, and federal unemployment tax rules that apply to the wages they pay their employees.

Section 501(c)(3) organizations. Nonprofit organizations described in section 501(c)(3) of the Internal Revenue Code include any community chest, fund, or foundation, organized and operated exclusively for religious, charitable, scientific, testing for public safety, literary, or educational purposes, or to foster national or international amateur sports competition, or for the prevention of cruelty to children or animals. These organizations are usually corporations and are exempt from income tax under section 501(a).

Social security and Medicare taxes. Wages paid to employees of section 501(c)(3) organizations are subject to social security and Medicare taxes unless one of the following situations applies:

1) A 501(c)(3) organization pays an employee wages of less than $100 in a calendar year.
2) A 501(c)(3) organization is wholly owned by a state or its political subdivision. Such an organization should contact the appropriate state official for information about reporting and getting social security and Medicare coverage for its employees. However, see *State and local government employees,* later.
3) A church or church-controlled organization that is opposed to the payment of social security and Medicare taxes for religious reasons can file Form 8274, *Certification by Churches and Qualified Church-Controlled Organizations Electing Exemption from Employer Social Security and Medicare Taxes,* to elect exemption from social security and Medicare taxes. The organization must file for exemption before the first date on which a quarterly employment tax return would otherwise be due. An employee of a church or church-controlled organization that is exempt from social security and Medicare taxes must pay the self-employment tax if the employee is paid $108.28 or more in a year. However, an employee who is a member of a qualified religious sect can apply for an exemption from the self-employment tax by filing Form 4029. See *Religious Exemptions,* below.

Federal unemployment tax. An organization described in section 501(c)(3) of the Internal Revenue Code that is exempt from income tax is also exempt from the federal unemployment tax. This exemption cannot be waived.

Other than section 501(c)(3) organizations. Nonprofit organizations that are not section 501(c)(3) organizations may also be exempt from paying income tax under section 501(a) or 521. These organizations are not exempt from income tax withholding, or social security, Medicare, or federal unemployment taxes. However, two special rules for social security, Medicare, and federal unemployment taxes apply to them:

1) If an employee is paid less than $100 during a calendar year, his or her wages are not subject to social security and Medicare taxes.
2) If an employee is paid less than $50 in a calendar quarter, his or her wages are not subject to federal unemployment tax for the quarter.

The above rules do not apply to employees who work for pension plans and other similar organizations described in section 401(a).

Religious Exemptions

Certain self-employed practitioners of religion or members of religious orders, and self-employed persons and their employees who are members of a recognized religious sect opposed to insurance can apply to exempt their earnings from social security and Medicare taxes (even if they are subject to income tax).

For more information on getting an exemption, or revoking an exemption, see Publication 517, *Social Security for Members of the Clergy and Religious Workers.*

Ministers, Christian Science practitioners, and members of religious orders who have not taken a vow of poverty. If you are in one of these categories, you can get an exemption from self-employment (social security and Medicare) tax on your earnings if you meet certain requirements. Members who have taken a vow of poverty are automatically exempt for amounts received while working for a church or an integral agency of the church. However, amounts received for performing services for an organization other than the church cannot be exempted from the tax.

To get the exemption, file Form 4361, *Application for Exemption From Self-employment Tax for Use by Ministers, Members of Religious Orders and Christian Science Practitioners.*

Members of recognized religious sects opposed to insurance. If you belong to a recognized religious sect or a division of such sect that is opposed to insurance, you may qualify for an exemption from the self-employment tax. To qualify, you must be conscientiously opposed to accepting the benefits of any public or private insurance that makes payments because of death, disability, old age, or retirement, or makes payments towards the cost of, or provides services for, medical care (including social security and Medicare benefits). If you buy a retirement annuity from an insurance company, you will not be eligible for this exemption. Religious opposition based upon the teachings of the sect is the only legal basis for the exemption. In addition, your religious sect (or division) must have existed since December 31, 1950.

Self-employed. If you are self-employed, you can get the exemption by filing an application, Form 4029, *Application for Exemption From Social Security and Medicare Taxes and Waiver of Benefits,* and waive all social security benefits.

Employees. The social security and Medicare tax exemption available to the self-employed who are members of a recognized religious sect opposed to insurance is also available to their employees who are members of such a sect. This applies to partnerships only if each partner is a member of the sect. This exemption for employees applies only if both the employee and the employer are members of such a sect, and the employer has an exemption. To get the exemption, the employee must file Form 4029.

An employee of a church or church-controlled organization that is exempt from social security and Medicare taxes can also apply for an exemption on Form 4029.

See Revenue Procedure 91–20 for guidelines used to determine whether an organization is a religious order or whether an individual is a member of a religious order.

Income Tax Withholding

You must generally withhold income tax from wages you pay employees if their wages for any payroll period exceed the amount of their withholding allowances for that period. The amount to be withheld is figured separately for each payroll period.

A ***payroll period*** is the period of time for which you usually make a payment of wages to an employee. ***Regular*** payroll periods can be daily, weekly, biweekly, semimonthly, monthly, quarterly, semiannually, or annually. A ***miscellaneous*** payroll period is any other period. Sundays and holidays are included in computing the number of days in a miscellaneous payroll period.

You should not withhold tax from the wages of employees who claim exemption from withholding on ***Form W–4,*** *Employee's Withholding Allowance Certificate.* Only employees who did not have to pay income tax last year and do not expect to pay any this year may claim exemption from withholding. Employees who claim exempt status on Form W–4 must renew their status by filing a new Form W–4 with you by February 15 of each year.

In addition to wages, other payments or benefits you give to your employees may or may not be subject to withholding, as discussed next.

Withholding and Reporting Payments Other Than Wages

Employee benefits. Certain employee benefits, including vacation leave, sick leave, compensatory time, severance pay, disability pay, and death benefit plans are not includible in income until paid to the employee. Nor are the benefits subject to social security and Medicare taxes, federal unemployment tax, and income tax withholding until paid to the employee.

Contributions to a simplified employee pension (SEP) plan. An employer's SEP contributions to an employee's individual retirement account (IRA) are excluded from the employee's gross income. These excluded amounts are not subject to social security, Medicare, and federal unemployment taxes, or income tax withholding. However, any employer SEP contributions paid under a salary reduction agreement are included in wages for purposes of social security and Medicare taxes and the federal unemployment tax.

Supplemental unemployment benefits. If you pay supplemental unemployment benefits to a former employee, all or part of the payments may be taxable. You should withhold income tax on the taxable part of the payments made, under a plan, to an employee who is involuntarily separated because of a reduction in force, discontinuance of a plant or operation, or other similar condition. It does not matter whether the separation is temporary or permanent.

Withholding on taxable supplemental unemployment benefits must be based on the withholding certificate the employee gave you.

Annuity or pension payments. Pension and annuity payments are generally subject to federal income tax withholding unless the recipient elects not to have tax withheld. The withholding rules apply to the ***taxable*** part of payments from an employer pension, annuity, profit-sharing, stock bonus, or other ***deferred compensation plan.*** The rules also apply to payments from an individual retirement arrangement, and an annuity, endowment, or life insurance contract issued by a life insurance company. There is no withholding on any part of a distribution that is not expected to be includible in the recipient's gross income.

Recipients of payments described above can choose not to have withholding apply to their pensions or annuities. The election remains in effect until the recipient revokes it. The payer must notify the recipient that this election is available.

For purposes of withholding income tax on periodic payments, a pension or annuity is treated as wages. The recipient of a pension or annuity should give the payer a completed withholding allowance certificate, ***Form W–4P,*** *Withholding Certificate for Pension or Annuity Payments,* or other form provided by the payer. If the recipient does not give the payer a certificate, the payer must withhold as if the recipient were married and claimed three withholding allowances.

You must withhold tax on qualified total distributions under a schedule designed to reflect the special tax treatment given to lump-sum payments. Qualified total distributions are generally made within one taxable year of the recipient. They include the balance to the credit of the recipient under the plan. The tables in Publication 493, *Alternative Tax Withholding Methods and Tables,* show the amount of income tax to withhold from qualified total distributions. You must withhold tax on other nonperiodic payments at a flat 10% rate.

You must furnish your employees and the IRS with Form 1099–R, *Distributions From Pensions, Annuities, Retirement or Profit-Sharing Plans, IRAs, Insurance Contracts, etc.*

Sick pay paid by third party. Employees can request that federal income tax be withheld from sick pay paid by third parties, such as insurance companies. An employee who wants income tax withheld from sick pay must file ***Form W–4S,*** *Request for Federal Income Tax Withholding from Sick Pay,* with the third-party payer.

For more information about sick pay paid by third parties, see *Circular E.*

Leave sharing plans. If you establish a leave sharing plan for your employees that allows them to donate leave to other employees for medical emergencies, the amounts paid to the recipients of the leave are considered wages. These amounts are includible in the gross income of the recipients and are subject to social security, Medicare, and federal unemployment taxes, and income tax withholding. Do not include these amounts in the income of the donors.

Bonuses and awards. If you pay bonuses, make taxable awards, or pay other supplemental wages to an employee, you must withhold income tax from the payment. If you add the payment to the employee's regular wages, you can figure the income tax to be withheld as if the total of the supplemental and regular wages were a single wage payment for the regular payroll period. However, if you withhold tax on the regular wage portion at the appropriate rate and specifically indicate on your payroll records the amount of each payment, you can withhold on the supplemental portion using a flat 20% rate without considering withholding allowances or the amount of regular wages.

If supplemental wages are paid separately, you can figure the tax to withhold by adding the supplemental wages to the regular wages for either the current payroll period or the last preceding payroll period within the same calendar year. If you have already withheld tax from the regular wages, you can figure the tax to withhold by using a 20% rate without considering withholding allowances and without referring to a regular wage payment.

You become liable for withholding income, social security, and Medicare taxes, and for paying federal unemployment tax, when you ***actually pay*** bonuses and vacation pay to your employees. This is true even though the employees earned the right to these payments at an earlier date and the vacation plan is unfunded.

Employee achievement awards. You can exclude the fair market value of an employee achievement award from your employee's gross income only if you can deduct the cost of the award. To be deductible, the award must be tangible personal property given to an employee for length of service or safety achievement, awarded as part of a meaningful presentation, and awarded under circumstances that do not indicate that the payment is disguised compensation. Amounts excluded for employee achievement awards are not subject to social security, Medicare, and federal unemployment taxes, or income tax withholding.

Limits. The most you can deduct for the cost of all employee achievement awards to the same employee for the year is $400. A higher limit of $1,600 applies to qualified plan awards. These awards are employee achievement awards under a written plan that does not discriminate in favor of highly compensated employees. An award cannot be treated as a qualified plan award if the average cost per recipient of all awards under all your qualified plans is more than $400.

If during the year an employee receives awards not made under a qualified plan and also receives awards under a qualified plan, your deduction for the total cost of all awards to that employee cannot be more than $1,600. The $400 and $1,600 limits cannot be added together to take a deduction of more than $1,600 for the cost of awards to any one employee during the year.

Wages not paid in money. If in the course of your trade or business you pay your employee in some medium that is neither cash nor a readily negotiable instrument, such as a check, you are said to pay them "in kind." Payments in kind may be in the form of goods, lodging, food, clothing, or services. The fair market value of such payments at the time they are provided is generally subject to income tax withholding.

Meals and lodging. The value of meals is not subject to income tax withholding if the meals are furnished for the employer's convenience and on the employer's premises. The value of lodging is not subject to withholding if the lodging is furnished for the employer's convenience, on the employer's premises, and as a condition of employment.

Dependent care assistance programs. The maximum amount you can exclude from your employee's gross income for dependent care assistance is $5,000 ($2,500 for married taxpayers filing separate returns). The excluded amount is not subject to social security, Medicare, and federal unemployment taxes, or income tax withholding. If the dependent is cared for in a facility at your place of business, the amount to exclude from the employee's income is based on his or her use of the facility and the value of the services provided.

Dependent care providers. If you were the provider of dependent care or pay the provider directly, your employee may ask you for help in obtaining a completed ***Form W–10,*** *Dependent Care Provider's Identification and Certification.* The dependent care credit and the exclusion for employer-provided dependent care assistance benefits cannot be claimed by your employee unless the dependent care provider is identified by name, address, and (if not an exempt organization) taxpayer identification number. The dependent care provider is required to furnish this information on Form W–10.

Health insurance plans. If you pay the cost of an accident or health insurance plan for your employees, your payments are not subject to social security and federal unemployment taxes, or income tax withholding.

Medical care reimbursements. Medical care reimbursements paid to or for an employee under an employer's self-insured medical reimbursement plan are not subject to income tax withholding.

Group legal service plans. For tax years beginning before July 1, 1992, you can exclude up to $70 of the cost you paid for a qualified group legal service plan for your employees from each employee's gross income. The excluded amount is not subject to social security, Medicare, and federal unemployment taxes, or income tax withholding. For 1992, the exclusion only applies to cost paid before July 1, 1992, for periods before that date.

Educational assistance programs. For tax years beginning before July 1, 1992, the amount you paid for the cost of tuition, fees, course supplies, and similar items for your employees under a qualified educational assistance program, up to $5,250 for each employee per year, is not includible in the gross income of your employees and is not subject to social security, Medicare, and federal unemployment taxes, or income tax withholding. For 1992, this only applies to amounts paid before July 1, 1992. Educational assistance includes any payments for graduate level courses that could lead to a law, business, medical, or other advanced academic or professional degree.

Scholarship and fellowship payments. Only amounts you pay as a qualified scholarship to a candidate for a degree may be excluded from the recipient's gross income. A qualified scholarship is any amount granted as a scholarship or fellowship that is used for tuition, fees, books, supplies, and equipment. Any amounts you pay for room and board, and any amounts you pay for teaching, research, or other services required as a condition of receiving the scholarship, are not excludable from the recipient's gross income. A qualified scholarship is not subject to social security, Medicare, and federal unemployment taxes, or income tax withholding.

Withholding for idle time. Payments made under a voluntary guarantee to employees for ***idle time*** (any time during which an employee performs no services) are wages for the purposes of social security, Medicare, and federal unemployment taxes, and the withholding of income tax.

Payments for ***lost time*** to an employee who was reinstated following a determination that he or she was dismissed without cause are also subject to income tax withholding.

Reimbursement and other expense allowance amounts. How you report a reimbursement or allowance arrangement depends on whether it was paid under an accountable plan or a nonaccountable plan. A reimbursement or allowance arrangement is a system or plan that you use to pay, substantiate, and recover the expenses, advances, reimbursements, and amounts charged to you for your employees' business expenses. If a single payment includes both wages and an expense reimbursement, you must specifically identify the amount of the reimbursement.

Accountable plan. To be an accountable plan, your reimbursement or allowance arrangement must require your employees to meet all three of the following rules:

1) They must have paid or incurred deductible expenses while performing services as your employees,
2) They must adequately account to you for these expenses, and
3) They must return any excess reimbursement or allowance.

Amounts paid under an accountable plan are not wages and are not subject to income tax withholding and payment of social security, Medicare, and federal unemployment taxes.

If the expenses covered by this arrangement are not substantiated or excess reimbursement is not returned within a reasonable period of time, the amount is treated as paid under a nonaccountable plan. This amount is subject to income tax withholding and payment of social security, Medicare, and federal unemployment taxes for the first payroll period following the end of the reasonable period.

A reasonable period of time depends on the facts and circumstances. Generally, it is considered reasonable if your employees adequately account for the expenses within 60 days after they were paid or incurred and return any excess reimbursement within 120 days after the expense was paid or incurred. Also, it is considered reasonable if you give your employees a periodic statement (at least quarterly) that asks them to either return or adequately account for outstanding amounts and they do so within 120 days.

Nonaccountable plan. A nonaccountable plan is an arrangement that does not meet the requirements for an accountable plan. All amounts paid under a nonaccountable plan are wages and are subject to income tax withholding and payment of social security, Medicare, and federal unemployment taxes when paid.

Per diem or other fixed allowance. If you give your employee a per diem or other fixed allowance for business expenses, your employee is considered to have adequately accounted to you for the amount of the expenses covered by this arrangement up to the amounts that have been specified by the federal government. The standard ***mileage*** rate is 27.5 cents a mile for auto expenses. However, see Revenue Procedure 90–34, 1990–1 C.B. 552, for information on using a fixed and variable rate (FAVR) allowance. The government per diem rate is listed in Publication 1542, *Per Diem Rates.* Other than the amount of these expenses, your employee's business expenses (for example, the business purpose of the travel or the number of business miles driven) must be substantiated.

If the per diem or allowance paid exceeds the amounts specified, you must report the amount in excess of the specified amount as wages. This excess amount is subject to income tax withholding and payment of social security, Medicare, and federal unemployment taxes. The amount equal to the specified amount is shown in box 17 of Form W–2, using code "L."

Penalties. If you made a substantial and good faith effort to comply with the withholding and reporting rules on employee business expense reimbursements, no penalties will be imposed for failure to pay or make timely deposits of employment taxes on (or for failure to report) payments made under reimbursement or other expense allowance arrangements before July 1, 1991.

Excessive termination payments (golden parachutes). A golden parachute is a contract entered into by a corporation and key personnel under which the corporation agrees to pay certain amounts to the key personnel in the event of a change in ownership or control of the corporation. Payments under golden parachute contracts, like any termination pay, are subject to social security, Medicare, and federal unemployment taxes, and income tax withholding.

Beginning with payments under contracts entered into, significantly amended, or renewed after June 14, 1984, no deduction is allowed to the corporation for *excess parachute payments.*

The employee is subject to a 20% nondeductible excise tax to be withheld by the corporation on all excess payments. The payment is generally considered an excess parachute payment if it equals or exceeds three times the average compensation of the recipient over the previous 5-year period. The amount over the average is the excess parachute payment.

Example. An officer of a corporation receives a golden parachute payment of $400,000. This is more than three times greater than his or her average compensation of $100,000 over the previous 5-year period. The excess parachute payment is $300,000 ($400,000 minus $100,000). The corporation cannot deduct the $300,000, and must withhold the excise tax of $60,000 (20% of $300,000). Get Circular E for information on reporting golden parachute payments.

Exempt payments. Payments from a small business corporation are exempt from the golden parachute rules. A small business corporation is generally a corporation that meets the requirements for electing S corporation status (discussed in Publication 589, *Tax Information on S Corporations.*) Also exempt are payments from a corporation that, immediately before a change in control, has no stock that is readily tradable on an established securities market or otherwise if: (1) the payments were approved by a vote of shareholders owning more than 75% of the voting power of the outstanding stock, and (2) there was adequate disclosure of all material facts concerning such payments.

For purposes of the shareholder approval requirements, the term "stock" does not include any stock:

1) That is not entitled to vote;
2) That has limited and preferred dividends and does not participate significantly in corporate growth;
3) That has redemption and liquidation rights not exceeding its issue price;
4) That cannot be converted into another class of stock; and
5) That has no rights adversely affected by the parachute payments.

Interest-free and below-market interest rate loans. If an employer loans an employee (or an independent contractor) more than $10,000 at less than the applicable federal interest rate, the employer is considered to have paid additional compensation to the employee equal to the difference between the applicable federal interest rate and the interest rate charged. This rule applies to any such loan, regardless of amount, if one of its principal purposes is the avoidance of federal tax.

This additional compensation to the employee is subject to social security, Medicare, and federal unemployment taxes, but not to income tax withholding. Include it in compensation on Form W-2 (or Form 1099-MISC for an independent contractor). For more information, see Chapter 6 in Publication 535, *Business Expenses.*

Cafeteria plans. Cafeteria plans must be written benefit plans under which all participants are employees who can choose from among cash and certain qualified benefits. If the employee elects qualified benefits, employer contributions are excluded from his or her wages if the benefits are excludable from gross income under a specific section of the Internal Revenue Code (other than scholarship and fellowship grants under section 117, educational assistance programs under section 127, and employee fringe benefits under section 132). The cost of group term life insurance that is includible in income only because the insurance exceeds $50,000 of coverage or is on the life of the employee's spouse or children is considered a qualified benefit under a special rule. Benefits under a cafeteria plan are not subject to social security, Medicare, and federal unemployment taxes, or income tax withholding. For more information, see Chapter 2 in Publication 535, *Business Expenses.*

Employee fringe benefits. The following fringe benefits that an employer provides to an employee are excluded from the employee's gross income. They are not subject to social security, Medicare, and federal unemployment taxes, or income tax withholding.

1) A no-additional cost service, which is a service offered for sale to customers in the course of the employer's line of business in which the employee works. It is provided at no substantial additional cost, including lost revenue, to the employer. Examples: airline, bus, and train tickets and telephone services provided free or at reduced rates by an employer in the line of business in which the employee works.
2) A qualified employee discount that, if offered for property, is not more than the employer's gross profit percentage. If offered for services, the discount is not more than 20% of the price for services offered to customers.
3) A working condition benefit, which is property or a service the employee could deduct as a business expense if he or she had paid for it. Examples: company car for business use, subscriptions to business magazines, and parking facilities provided to the employee on or near the employer's business premises. Under special rules, all of the use of a demonstrator car by an auto salesperson is excluded if there are substantial restrictions on personal use.
4) A de minimis benefit, which is a service or an item of such small value as to make accounting for the benefit unreasonable or administratively impracticable. Examples: typing of a personal letter by a company secretary; occasional personal use of a company copying machine; monthly transit passes provided at a discount not in excess of $15; occasional parties or picnics for employees; occasional supper money and taxi fare for employees working overtime; holiday gifts with a low fair market value; occasional tickets for entertainment events; and coffee and doughnuts furnished to employees. Also, meals at an eating facility operated by the employer for the employees' benefit on or near the employer's business premises if the income from the facility equals or exceeds the direct operating costs of the facility.
5) An on-premises gym or other athletic facility provided and operated by the employer if substantially all the use is by employees, their spouses, and their dependent children.
6) A qualified tuition reduction, which an educational organization provides its employees for education, generally below the graduate level. For more information on a qualified tuition reduction, get Publication 520, *Scholarships and Fellowships.*

Special fringe benefit rules for airlines and their affiliates. Employees of a qualified affiliate of an airline (a member of a group in which another member operates the airline) who are directly engaged in providing airline-related services may exclude from their income as a no-additional-cost service the fair market value of air transportation provided by the other member. Airline-related services means providing any of the following services in connection with air transportation: catering; baggage handling; ticketing and reservations; flight planning and weather analysis; service at restaurants and gift shops located at an airport; and similar services.

Any use of air transportation provided by an airline to parents of the airline's employees is also treated as use by the employees. The employees are entitled to exclude the fair market value of such transportation from their income as a no-additional-cost service.

Note. In order to be excluded from the income of highly compensated employees, all of the above items except a working condition benefit or a de minimis benefit (other than eating facilities) must be offered to employees on a nondiscriminatory basis.

More information. For more detailed information on fringe benefits, get Publication 535, *Business Expenses.*

Withholding and Reporting Taxable Noncash Fringe Benefits

Use the following guidelines for reporting and withholding tax on taxable noncash fringe benefits.

Choice of period for withholding, depositing, and reporting. For employment tax and withholding purposes, you can treat fringe benefits (including personal use of employer-provided highway motor vehicles) as paid on a pay period, quarter period, semi-annual period, annual period, or other basis. But the benefits must be treated as paid no less frequently than annually. You do not have to choose the same period for all employees. You can withhold more frequently for some employees than for others.

You can change the period as often as you like as long as you treat all the benefits provided in a calendar year as paid no later than December 31 of the calendar year.

You can also treat the value of a single fringe benefit as paid on one or more dates in the same calendar year, even if the employee receives the entire benefit at one time. For example, if your employee receives a fringe benefit valued at $1,000 in one pay period during 1991, you can treat it as made in four payments of $250, each in a different pay period of 1991. You do not have to notify the IRS of the use of the periods discussed above.

Transfer of property. The above choice for reporting and withholding does not apply to a fringe benefit that is a transfer of tangible or intangible personal property of a kind normally held for investment, or a transfer of real property. For this kind of fringe benefit, you must use the actual date provided.

Withholding and depositing taxes. You can add the value of fringe benefits to regular wages for a payroll period and figure income tax withholding on the total. Or you can withhold federal income tax on the value of fringe benefits at the flat 20% rate presently applicable to supplemental wages.

You must withhold the applicable income, social security, and Medicare taxes on the date or dates you chose to treat the benefits as paid. Deposit the amounts withheld as discussed under *Deposits*, later.

Amount of deposit. To estimate the amount of income and employment taxes and to deposit them on time, make a reasonable estimate of the value of the fringe benefits provided on the date or dates you chose to treat the benefits as paid. Determine the estimated deposit by figuring the amount you would have had to deposit had you paid cash wages equal to the estimated value of the fringe benefits and withheld taxes from those cash wages. Even if you do not know which employee is the recipient of the fringe benefit on the date the deposit is due, you should follow this procedure.

If you underestimate the value of the fringe benefits and deposit less than the amount you would have had to deposit if the applicable taxes had been withheld, you may be subject to a penalty.

If you overestimate the value of the fringe benefit and overdeposit, you can either claim a refund or have the overpayment applied to the next employment tax return.

If you paid the required amount of taxes to IRS but withheld a lessor amount from the employee, you can recover from the employee the social security, Medicare, or income taxes you paid on the employee's behalf, and included on the employee's Form W-2. However, you must recover the income taxes before April 1 of the following year.

Election not to withhold—special rule for highway motor vehicles. You can choose not to withhold income tax on the value of an employee's personal use of a highway motor vehicle you provided. You do not have to make this choice for all employees. You can withhold income tax from the wages of some employees but not others. You must, however, withhold the applicable social security and Medicare taxes on such benefits.

You can choose not to withhold income tax by:

1) Notifying the employee as described below that you choose not to withhold; and
2) Including the value of the benefits in boxes 10, 12, and 14 on a Form W-2 furnished on time.

The notice must be in writing and must be provided to the employee by January 31 of the election year or within 30 days after a vehicle is first provided to the employee, whichever is later. This notice must be provided in a manner reasonably expected to come to the attention of the affected employee. For example, the notice may be mailed to the employee, included with a paycheck, or posted where the employee could reasonably be expected to see it. You can also change your election not to withhold at any time by notifying the employee in the same manner.

Special accounting rule for valuation. Under the general income tax and reporting rule, you must determine the value of fringe benefits provided in a calendar year by January 31 of the following calendar year. If the benefit is the personal use of a highway motor vehicle, you can either determine the value for the calendar year, or determine the value as if the entire use of the vehicle for the year by the employee is personal and include 100% in the employee's income.

Instead of using the general rule, you can use the special accounting rule explained in the following paragraphs. The special accounting rule cannot be used, however, for a fringe benefit that is a transfer of tangible or intangible personal property of a kind normally held for investment, or a transfer of real property.

Special accounting period. You can treat the value of benefits provided during the last 2 months of the calendar year or any shorter period as paid in the next year. Thus, the value of benefits actually provided in the last 2 months of 1991 would be treated as provided in 1992 together with the value of benefits provided in the first 10 months of 1992. This does not mean that all benefits treated as paid during the last 2 months of a calendar year can be deferred until the next year. Only the value of benefits actually provided during the last 2 months of the calendar year can be treated as paid in the next calendar year.

Conformity rules. Use of the special accounting rule is optional. You can use the rule for some fringe benefits but not others. The period of use need not be the same for each fringe benefit. However, if you use the rule for a particular fringe benefit, you must use it for all employees who receive that benefit.

If you use the special accounting rule, your employee must use it and for the same period as you use it. But your employee cannot use the special accounting rule unless you do.

You do not have to notify the IRS if you use the special accounting rule. You can also, for appropriate reasons, change the period for which you use the rule without notifying the IRS. But you must report the income and deposit the withheld taxes as required, for the changed period.

Amount to report on Forms 941 and W-2. The actual value of fringe benefits provided during a calendar year (or other period as explained under *Special accounting rule for valuation,* earlier) must be determined by January 31 of the following year. You must report the actual value on Form W-2 and also on Form 941 for the 4th quarter of the prior year and pay any tax due. If you choose, you can use a separate Form W-2 for fringe benefits and any other benefit information.

Include the value in box 10 of Form W-2. Also include it in boxes 12 and 14 if applicable. Show the total value of the fringe benefits provided in the calendar year or other period in box 23 of Form W-2. If you provided your employee with the use of a highway motor vehicle and included 100% of the value of the vehicle in the employee's income, you must also report it separately in box 23. If there is not enough space on the Form W-2, you must report it to the employee on a separate schedule so that the employee can compute the value of any business use of the vehicle.

If you use the special accounting rule, you must notify the affected employees of the period in which you used it. You must give the notice at or near the date you give the Form W-2 but not earlier than with the employee's last paycheck of the calendar year.

For more information on fringe benefits, see Chapter 3 in Publication 535.

Form W-4 Withholding Allowances

In general, an employee can claim withholding allowances equal to the number of allowances the employee will be entitled to in figuring income tax on his or her annual return. An employee may also be able to claim a special withholding allowance and allowances for estimated deductions and credits. See *Special withholding allowance* and *Additional withholding allowances,* later.

You should ask each new employee to give you a ***Form W-4*** on or before his or her first day of work. This certificate is effective for the first payment of wages and will last until the employee files another one unless the employee claims exemption from withholding. The certificate must include the employee's social security number.

If an employee does not give you a Form W-4, you must withhold tax as if the employee were a single person who has claimed no withholding allowances. Married employees (and widows and widowers qualified to file their income tax returns as married persons) who have not indicated on Form W-4 that they are married will be treated as single persons for withholding purposes.

Changes in allowances or marital status. An employee who wants to change the number of allowances claimed or show a change in marital status should file a new Form W-4. Near the end of each year, you should ask each of your employees to file a new Form W-4 for the following year if there has been a change in allowances or marital status since the last Form W-4 was filed. If the employee has a change in name because of a changed marital status, advise the employee to report this to the Social Security Administration. This will ensure that wage reports showing the new name will be correctly credited to the employee's social security records.

Effective date of Form W-4. You must put a new Form W-4 into effect no later than the start of the first payroll period ending on or after the 30th day from the date you receive it. If you pay wages without regard to a payroll period, you must put the new Form W-4 into effect no later than the first payment of wages on or after the 30th day from the date you receive it.

Repayment or reimbursement. If an employee gives you a new Form W-4 claiming additional withholding allowances, you cannot reimburse the employee for income taxes collected during the year before the effective date of the new W-4. But you can reimburse the employee for income taxes you overcollected on or after the effective date if you did not take the new certificate into account.

Note. A Form W-4 that makes a change for the next calender year will not take effect in the current calendar year.

Two jobs. An employee who holds two jobs at the same time and claims all withholding allowances on the Form W-4 filed with one employer, must claim zero allowances on the Form W-4 filed with the second employer.

Married employees. You should inform your married employees that, if a husband and wife both work, they can divide their allowances any way they like. But one spouse may not claim an allowance claimed by the other.

Exempt employees. An employee can claim an exemption from income tax withholding on Form W-4 if he or she had a right to a refund of all federal income tax withheld last year because of no income tax liability, and expects the same situation to exist this year. An employee who can be claimed as a dependent by someone else usually cannot claim this exemption if he or she has nonwage income, and that income plus wages is expected to be more than $550. Student status does not automatically exempt the employee from income tax withholding. An employee who has claimed exemption from withholding and later discovers he or she will incur tax liability must give you a new Form W-4 within 10 days.

An employee who wants to continue claiming exemption from withholding must file a new Form W-4 by February 15 each year. If the employee does not do so, withhold tax as if the employee is single with zero withholding allowances.

Special withholding allowance. An employee can claim a special withholding allowance if the employee is single and works for only one employer, or is married and works for only one employer and the employee's spouse is not employed. The employee can also claim this allowance if the total wages earned on other jobs by the employee or the employee's spouse (or both) are $1,000 or less.

Additional withholding allowances. An employee can claim additional withholding allowances on Form W-4 for estimated deductions, adjustments to income, or tax credits. For more information, see the instructions for Form W-4. If an employee has estimated tax credits that are not covered in the Form W-4 instructions, he or she can also use an alternative method to figure withholding allowances. For more information, see Publication 505, *Tax Withholding and Estimated Tax.*

An employee should complete the *Deductions and Adjustments Worksheet* on page 2 of Form W-4 to figure the number of additional allowances. The additional allowances remain in effect until the employee files a new Form W-4 with you. Each employee must file a new form within 10 days if the number of allowances he or she is entitled to claim decreases to less than the number the employee is now claiming.

Additional withholding. If an employee determines that his or her income tax liability for the year will be more than the total amount to be withheld, the employee can have an additional amount withheld by showing the amount on line 5 of Form W-4.

A married employee may also have tax withheld at the higher "single" rate by checking the appropriate box on Form W-4.

Invalid withholding certificate. Any alteration of, or unauthorized addition to, a withholding certificate makes it invalid. If an employee indicates to you, either orally or in writing, that the information on the withholding certificate is false, the certificate will be invalid even if it is not yet in effect. If you realize the certificate is invalid, then you must ask your employee to furnish a new one. If the employee does not comply, you must withhold from the employee the same amount you would withhold from a single person claiming no exemptions. However, if a prior certificate is still in effect, you should withhold according to that certificate.

If you have reason to believe that a withholding certificate has incorrect information, you should advise the District Director.

Filing Form W–4 with the Internal Revenue Service. You must send the IRS a copy of any Form W–4 received from an employee who is still employed by you at the end of the quarter if:

1) The employee filing it claims 11 or more withholding allowances; or
2) The employee filing it claims exemption from income tax withholding, but the employee's wages are more than $200 a week.

Copies of the Forms W–4 that must be submitted because of either of the above conditions should be sent along with your quarterly employment tax returns, Forms 941 and 941E. You can send them more often if you like. But if you do, please include a statement giving your name, address, employer identification number, and the number of forms you are sending. If you would like to report this material on magnetic tape, you should get a copy of Revenue Procedure 90–9. It is published in Internal Revenue Cumulative Bulletin 1990–1 on page 460.

Figuring Withholding

You should figure withholding on gross wages before any deductions for social security and Medicare taxes, pension, union dues, insurance, etc., are made. You can figure the withholding by any of several methods, the most common of which are the ***percentage method*** and the ***wage bracket method.***

Circular E contains the applicable tables and more detailed instructions for using both of these withholding methods.

Percentage method. Under the percentage method, figure the income tax to withhold as follows:

1) Multiply the dollar amount of one withholding allowance for a payroll period (see *Circular E*) by the number of allowances claimed on Form W–4 by the employee;
2) Subtract that amount from the employee's wages; and
3) Figure the amount to be withheld according to the employee's wage level and marital status as listed in the *Tables for Percentage Method of Withholding* in *Circular E*.

The amount of one withholding allowance for payroll periods of varying lengths and the rates to apply to the taxable wages are given in *Circular E.*

You can also figure withholding using your employee's yearly wages. To do so, find in the percentage tables the income tax to be withheld from the employee's wages (less withholding allowances) for the year. Then divide this amount by the number of payroll periods in the year. The result is the withholding for each payroll period.

Wage bracket method. Under the wage bracket method, use tables based on wage ranges to figure the income tax to be withheld. These tables are reproduced in *Circular E.* Tables are for weekly, biweekly, semimonthly, monthly, and daily or miscellaneous payroll periods, for both married and unmarried employees.

To figure the income tax to withhold under this method, determine the employee's correct payroll period, marital status, total wage payment, and the number of withholding allowances claimed on Form W–4. Then use the table for the correct payroll period and marital status, and find the amount of tax you must withhold.

Other methods. Three alternative methods that usually produce the same result are the ***average estimated wages, annualized wages,*** and ***cumulative wages methods.*** Any alternative method must provide acceptable results over the full range of salary and exemption situations. You cannot use a method that consistently deducts amounts less than those required under the percentage method.

Any method can be used if it produces the same result as the percentage method or the wage bracket method or a result that falls between these two methods. A result roughly within $10 of the amount that would be withheld annually under either the percentage or wage bracket method is considered the same result.

For more information on alternative methods of figuring income tax withholding, get Circular E, *Employer's Tax Guide,* and Publication 493, *Alternative Tax Withholding Methods and Tables.*

Social Security and Medicare Taxes

The ***Federal Insurance Contributions Act (FICA)*** provides for a federal system of old age, survivors, disability, and hospital insurance. The old age, survivors, and disability insurance part is financed by the social security tax. The hospital insurance part is financed by the Medicare tax. Beginning in 1991, each of these taxes is reported separately.

Social security and Medicare taxes are levied on both you and your employees (unless you or your employees are not subject to these taxes; see *Family Members, Employees of Exempt Organizations* and *Religious Exemptions,* earlier). You, as an employer, must collect and pay the employee's part of the taxes and you must pay a matching amount.

Tax rates and wage bases. These taxes have different tax rates and wage bases. The wage base is the maximum wage that is subject to the tax for the year. You can multiply each payment by the tax rate or you can use the tables provided in Circular E. There are no withholding allowances for social security and Medicare taxes.

The tax rate for social security is 6.2% each for employers and employees (12.4% total) and the wage base for 1991 is $53.400. For 1992, the wage base is $55,500.

The tax rate for Medicare is 1.45% each for employers and employees (2.9% total) and the wage base for 1991 is $125,000. For 1992, the wage base is $130,200.

Meals and lodging. Meals, lodging, clothing, services, and other payments in kind are generally subject to the same social security and Medicare taxes as wages paid in cash. However, the value of meals that are nontaxable because they are furnished for the employer's convenience and on the employer's premises are not subject to these taxes. Nor is nontaxable lodging that is furnished for the employer's convenience, on the employer's premises, and as a condition of employment.

Successor employer. If you acquire all or substantially all of the property used in the business of another employer, or a unit of that employer's business, you may, in determining the wage bases for each of your new employees who worked for the other employer, include the wages the other employer paid to the employee.

Example. Early in 1991, you bought all the assets of a plumbing business from Mr. Martin. Mr. Brown, who had been employed by Mr. Martin and received $2,000 in wages before the date of purchase, continued to work for you. You and Mr. Brown are subject to social security taxes on the first $51,400 ($53,400 less $2,000) and Medicare taxes on the first $123,000 ($125,000 less $2,000) of wages you pay him during the rest of the calendar year.

Employee's portion of taxes paid by employer. If you are not a household or agricultural employer and you pay your employee's liability for social security and Medicare taxes without deducting them from the employee's pay, you must include the amount of the payments in the employee's wages for social security, Medicare, and federal unemployment taxes, and income tax withholding. This increase in the employee's wage payment for your payment of the employee's social security and Medicare taxes is also subject to employee social security and Medicare taxes. This again increases the amount of the additional taxes you must pay. For the formula you must use to figure the employee's income, social security and Medicare, and federal unemployment taxes in this situation, see Revenue Ruling 86–14 in Cumulative Bulletin 1986–1, page 304. Change the rate of the employee social security and Medicare (FICA) tax in the formula to 7.65% for 1991 wages of up to $53,400. For wages over $53,400, repeat the formula using 1.45% for wages over $53,400, but not over $125,000.

However, if you are a household employer in a private home or an agricultural employer, any employee social security and Medicare tax you pay for an employee is additional income to the employee for income tax purposes. But it is not considered wages for social security, Medicare, and federal unemployment taxes.

Supplemental unemployment payments. Employer provided supplemental unemployment payments are not subject to social security and Medicare taxes if the payments are linked to state unemployment payments. A lump sum payment is not considered linked to state unemployment payments because the amount is not linked to the period of unemployment.

Federal employees. Federal employees are subject to Medicare taxes. Covered federal employment can be used in determining eligibility for Medicare benefits. Federal employees hired after 1983 are subject to social security and Medicare taxes just as other employees. This coverage counts for figuring social security benefits on the same basis as other covered employment. Certain services performed by penal inmates, medical interns, student nurses, and temporary emergency employment are not covered under either of these provisions.

Uniformed services. The pay for services of a member of a uniformed service on active duty or on inactive duty training (generally weekend training and drills) is subject to social security and Medicare taxes.

State and local government employees. State and local government employees can be covered by social security and Medicare under a section 218 agreement (voluntary agreement) entered into by the state and the Secretary of Health and Human Services. The state decides which employees are covered by the voluntary agreement. The wages of an employee covered by the agreement are subject to social security and Medicare taxes.

The wages of ***an employee hired after March 31, 1986,*** who is not covered under a voluntary agreement are subject to Medicare tax. This does not apply to:

1) Individuals hired to relieve unemployment;
2) Patients or inmates working in hospitals, homes, or other institutions;
3) Temporary workers hired for snow, flood, or similar emergencies;
4) Certain student employees of hospitals of the District of Columbia;
5) Election officials or workers receiving less than $100 in a calendar year for such service; and

6) Individuals paid on a fee basis who are subject to self-employment tax.

Wages ***for services performed after July 1, 1991,*** by an employee who is not covered under a voluntary agreement and who is not a member of the retirement system of the state or local government are subject to social security and Medicare taxes. The same exceptions discussed in the previous paragraph apply to these wages.

An employee is considered a member of the retirement system only if that employee actually participates in the program. Therefore, if participation in a retirement system is elective and an employee elects not to participate, that employee's wages are subject to social security and Medicare taxes.

Group-term life insurance. The cost of group-term life insurance you provided to an employee for coverage over $50,000, or for coverage that discriminated in favor of the employee, is taxable and subject to social security and Medicare taxes. This taxable insurance cost can be treated as paid by the pay period, by the quarter, or on any basis so long as the cost is treated as paid at least once a year.

For coverage after 1990 of taxable group-term life insurance you provided to former employees (including retirees), the former employees must pay the employee's share of social security and Medicare taxes with their income tax returns. The employer must separately include on the Form W-2 the portion of wages that consists of payments for group-term life insurance and the amount of social security and Medicare taxes owed by the former employee for coverage provided after separation from service.

Sick pay. Employers and third-party payers, such as insurance companies, must withhold employee social security and Medicare taxes and pay employer social security and Medicare taxes on most sick pay payments. In general, sick pay is any amount paid by an employer to an employee because of the employee's sickness or injury. Third-party sick pay is any amount paid by a third party to an employee in place of wages for any period the employee is absent due to sickness or injury. Liability for paying the employer portion of social security and Medicare taxes, however, shifts from the third party to the employer for whom the employee normally works if the third party notifies the employer, within the time required for a tax deposit, of the amount of the sick pay payment. For more information, see Notice 91-26 in Internal Revenue Bulletin 1991-31.

The following kinds of payments are not subject to social security and Medicare taxes:

1) Payments made more than 6 months after the last calendar month the employee worked.
2) Payments received under worker's compensation law.
3) Payments, or portions of payments, attributable to the employee's contribution to a sick pay plan.
4) Payments made for medical care.
5) Payments (generally for injury) not related to absence from work.
6) Most payments made to a state or local government employee. The third-party payer should contact the state or local government employer for instructions.

Deferred compensation arrangements. Employer contributions to a cash or deferred compensation arrangement that is part of a qualified profit-sharing or stock bonus plan are included in social security and Medicare wages even though they may not be included in the gross incomes of the employees.

An amount deferred under a nonqualified deferred compensation plan is treated as social security and Medicare wages when the services are performed or when the employee no longer has any substantial risk of forfeiting the right to the deferred compensation, whichever is later.

Tax sheltered annuities. Employer payments made by an educational institution or a tax-exempt organization to purchase a tax-sheltered annuity for an employee are included in the employee's social security and Medicare wages if the payments are made because of a salary reduction agreement.

Concurrent employment by related corporations. If two or more related corporations employ the same individual at the same time and pay this individual through a common paymaster, which is one of the corporations, the corporations are considered a single employer. They have to pay, in total, no more in social security and Medicare taxes than a single employer would.

Each corporation must pay its own part of the employment taxes and may deduct only its own part of the wages. The deductions will not be allowed unless the corporation reimburses the common paymaster for the wage and tax payments.

International social security agreements. The United States has social security agreements with many countries to eliminate dual taxes under two social security systems. Under these agreements, you must generally pay social security taxes only to the country you live in. Employees and employers who are subject only to foreign social security taxes under these agreements are exempt from U.S. social security taxes including the Medicare portion.

The United States now has social security agreements with the following countries: Austria, Belgium, Canada, France, Germany, Italy, the Netherlands, Norway, Portugal, Spain, Sweden, Switzerland, and the United Kingdom. Additional agreements are expected in the future. For more information, contact:

Social security Administration
Office of International Policy
P.O. Box 17741
Baltimore, MD 21235

Paying Social Security, Medicare, and Withheld Income Taxes

Social security and Medicare taxes and withheld income tax are reported and paid together. The following sections discuss some rules that apply equally to both types of taxes.

Employee Tips

Your employees must report to you each month cash tips of $20 or more that they receive while on the job. This includes both tips received directly from customers and those that charge customers add to the bill and you pay over to the employee. However, no report needs to be made for any month in which the tips were less than $20. Otherwise, they should be reported every month regardless of the total wages and tips the employee receives for the year. The written report must be made by the 10th day of the month after the month the tips are received. It should show:

1) The name, address, and social security number of the employee;
2) The name and address of the employer;
3) The calendar month or period covered by the statement; and
4) The total amount of the tips the employee received during the period covered by the statement.

Tips received by your employees in December 1990 and reported to you in January 1991 are considered income in 1991.

Form 4070, *Employee's Report of Tips to Employer,* available from the IRS, may be used for reporting tips.

Gratuities. So-called gratuities collected by a club or other establishment through mandatory charges added to its members' bills are considered wages. These amounts are subject to both employer and employee taxes under social security and Medicare, the employer tax under federal unemployment, and income tax withholding.

Both income tax and employee and employer social security and Medicare taxes apply. You must collect employee social security tax, Medicare tax, and income tax on tips reported by an employee. You can withhold these taxes either from wages due the employee or from other funds the employee makes available. You must also pay the employer portion of the social security and Medicare taxes on tips reported by an employee. Stop collecting ***employee social security tax*** and paying ***employer social security tax*** when the employee's combined wages and reported tips total $53,400 for 1991. Stop collecting ***employee Medicare tax*** and paying ***employer Medicare tax*** when the employee's combined wages and reported tips total $125,000 for 1991.

You are not required to withhold or pay on tips not reported to you.

Income tax withholding applies to the entire year, even if the social security and Medicare limits have been reached.

How to figure withholding on tips. If your employees get both regular wages and tips, you can, in figuring the income tax to withhold, either:

1) Treat the tips as part of the employee's current or preceding wage payment and use the regular graduated withholding rates; or
2) Determine the tax to withhold from tips by using a flat 20% rate if income tax has already been withheld from the regular wage payment.

Form W-2. Employers must report on Form W-2 an employee's compensation, including the tips reported by the employee to the employer.

Pooling or splitting of tips. Employees who participate in a tip-splitting or tip-pooling arrangement must report to their employer only the tips they actually receive and keep. They may use Form 4070 or any other form provided by their employer.

Example. A restaurant pays its waiter $400 in charged tips. The waiter then splits the tips with the busboy, giving the busboy one-fourth. The waiter reports to the employer only the $300 he kept. The busboy reports the $100 he received from the waiter. Both the waiter and the busboy may use Form 4070 to make their reports.

Reporting by large food and beverage establishments. Most large food and beverage establishments must report to the IRS more information about their employees' tip income. See *Tip Reporting and Allocation Rules,* near the end of this publication.

Liability for Tax Withheld

You are required by law to deduct and withhold income, social security, and Medicare taxes from the salaries and wages of your employees. You are liable for the payment of these taxes to the federal government whether or not you collect them from your employees. If, for example, you deduct less than the correct tax from your employees' wages, you are still liable for the full amount.

Liability of third parties. Any lender, surety, or other third party who pays wages directly to the employees of an employer, or to the employee's agent, is responsible for any required withholding on those wages. This includes the withholding of income, social security, Medicare, and railroad retirement taxes. The third party is also liable for any interest and penalties accruing on these accounts.

If a third party supplies funds to an employer so that the employer can pay the employees' wages, and if the third party knows that the employer will not pay or deposit the taxes that are required to be withheld when due, then the third party must pay the taxes withheld from the employee's wages but not paid by the employer. However, the third party does not have to pay more than 25% of the amount that is specifically supplied for paying wages. The third party supplier must also pay interest on the taxes if they are paid after the due date of the employer's return.

Third parties are liable only for payment of the employees' part of payroll taxes. They are not liable for the employer's part. The employer must file an employment tax return for wages that he or she or a third party pays and must furnish statements to employees of wages paid and taxes withheld. The employer also remains liable for any withholding taxes not paid by the third party.

Liability of trustee in bankruptcy. A trustee in bankruptcy must withhold, report, and pay income, social security, and Medicare taxes from the payment of priority claims for employee's wages earned prior to, but unpaid at the time of, an employer's bankruptcy.

How to pay withheld tax. Third parties who pay employment taxes must file two copies of Form 4219, *Statement of Liability of Lender, Surety, or Other Person For Withholding Taxes under Sec. 3505 of the IRC.* A separate set of forms must be filed for each employer and calendar quarter.

Form 4219 must be filed with the IRS Service Center where the employer for whom wages were paid, or funds were supplied, files federal employment tax returns.

Each Form 4219 should be accompanied by a check or money order made out to the Internal Revenue Service. To avoid interest, full payment should be made on or before the due date of the employer's federal employment tax return.

Tax Returns

Generally, social security and Medicare taxes and withheld income tax are reported together on ***Form 941,*** *Employer's Quarterly Federal Tax Return.* However, there are three exceptions:

1) If your employees are agricultural workers, use ***Form 943,*** *Employer's Annual Tax Return for Agricultural Employees*.
2) If your employees work in your home rather than in your business—for example, to do child care, housekeeping, or gardening work —use ***Form 942,*** *Employer's Quarterly Tax Return for Household Employees.*
3) If your employees are not covered by social security taxes, use ***Form 941E,*** *Quarterly Return of Withheld Federal Income Tax and Medicare Tax.*

When to file returns. Form 943 is an annual return due one month after the calendar year ends. The other forms are quarterly returns due one month after the end of each calendar quarter. The periods covered by these forms are the same whether you use a fiscal year or the calendar year as your tax year. The due dates are given below:

Return and Period	Due Date
Form 943: Calendar year	January 31
Forms 941, 941E, and 942:	
1st quarter:	
January–February–March	April 30
2nd quarter:	
April–May–June	July 31
3rd quarter:	
July–August–September	October 31
4th quarter:	
October–November–December	January 31

However, if you must deposit the tax (see following discussion) and you deposit it on time and in full, you have an extra 10 days to file the return:

Return and Period	Due Dates
Form 943: Calendar year	February 10
Forms 941 and 941E:	
1st quarter:	
January–February–March	May 10
2nd quarter:	
April–May–June	August 10
3rd quarter:	
July–August–September	November 10
4th quarter:	
October–November–December	February 10

If a due date falls on a Saturday, Sunday, or legal holiday, it is postponed until the next day that is not a Saturday, Sunday, or legal holiday. A statewide legal holiday delays a due date only if the IRS office where you are required to file is located in that state.

Seasonal or intermittent employers. If you are a seasonal or intermittent employer, you do not have to file Form 941 or Form 941E when you have paid no wages during a quarter. However, you must check the seasonal filer box on Form 941, or the intermittent filer box on Form 941E, on each return you file so IRS will not expect a return each quarter.

Paying the tax. When you pay social security, Medicare, and withheld income taxes—whether through deposits or with your return—you should write the following information on your check or money order:

1) Your employer identification number;
2) The type of tax you are paying; and
3) The period covered by the payment.

Deposits

You will generally have to make deposits of social security and Medicare taxes and withheld income taxes before the return is due. You must deposit both your part and your employees' part of social security and Medicare taxes. Deposits are not required for taxes reported on Form 942, *Employer's Quarterly Tax Return for Household Employees.* For Form 942, you should pay the tax when you file the return.

Figuring deposits. Each return period is divided into a number of shorter deposit periods. Whether or not you must make a deposit depends on your tax liability at the end of the deposit period. If your tax liability has reached a certain amount, a deposit is required. Voluntary deposits during a deposit period do not affect the determination of the tax liability for that period.

If by the end of a deposit period your tax liability has not reached the amount requiring a deposit, the undeposited tax is carried over and added to the tax for the next period. If the total tax at the end of that period still has not reached the amount requiring a deposit, it will all be carried over again to the next period —and so on until either a deposit is required or the return period ends. Once a tax amount requiring a deposit is reached, that amount is not considered when figuring whether any future deposits are required.

To determine if a deposit is required and the amount of the deposit, reduce your tax liability by the amount of any advanced earned income credit payments (discussed later) you made to your employees.

Deposit rules. Each month of the return period is divided into eight deposit periods. These periods end on the 3rd, 7th, 11th, 15th, 19th, 22nd. 25th, and last day of every month. When you must deposit social security, Medicare, and withheld income taxes depends on the following rules:

1) ***$100,000 rule.*** If your total tax liability plus any undeposited taxes reach $100,000 or more in any eighth-monthly deposit period, you must deposit at least 95% of such taxes on the next banking day after the day the taxes reach $100,000. If, by the end of that same eighth-monthly period, your additional tax liability is at least $3,000 but less than $100,000, you must deposit at least 95% of these additional taxes within 3 banking days after the end of that period. See Schedule B (Form 941), *Supplemental Record of Federal Tax Liability,* for more information if your tax liability is $100,000 or more. File Schedule B with your quarterly return.
2) ***$3,000 rule.*** If at the end of any eighth-monthly period your tax liability plus undeposited taxes is $3,000 or more but less than $100,000, you must deposit at least 95% of what you owe within three banking days after the end of that period.
3) ***$500 rule.*** If your tax liability plus undeposited taxes is $500 or more but less than $3,000 at the end of the month, you must deposit all of it by the 15th of the next month. If your tax is less than $500, you may carry it over to the next month. This rule does not apply if the $3,000 rule applies during the same month.
4) ***End-of-return-period rule.*** If, at the end of the return period, your total tax liability for the quarter is less than $500, you may deposit the taxes by the end of the next month, or pay them when you file your quarterly return.

Example. In 1992, Jim Black's first deposit is for the period ending January 31. On that date, he has a tax liability of $2,900 for social security, Medicare, and withheld income taxes. Because he is not required to make a deposit for any other period in January, this amount triggers a deposit under the $500 rule. Jim plans to mail in his deposit around February 12, in time to arrive before the February 18 due date. (February 15 is on a Saturday and the following Monday is a holiday.)

For the next deposit period ending February 3, Jim's social security, Medicare, and withheld income tax liability stands at $3,250. But $2,900 of this amount has already triggered a deposit requirement. He therefore excludes it when figuring whether a deposit is required. Because the remaining $350 is not enough to trigger a deposit, he carries it over to the next period.

If Jim had been required to make a deposit for an earlier period in January, the $2,900 he owes at the end of the month would not trigger a deposit. The $3,250 owed on February 3 would then trigger a 3-day deposit under the $3,000 rule.

Exception to $3,000 rule. When the tax you owe triggers the $3,000 rule, you can make the deposit by the 15th day of the next month, instead of within 3 banking days, if:

1) It is the first time you were required to make a deposit under the $3,000 rule within the previous 4 calendar quarters and earlier months of the current calendar quarter, and
2) The deposit is less than $10,000.

95% rule. If under the $100,000 or $3,000 rule you deposited at least 95% of the tax liability, you must then make up the difference in another deposit later. If the deposit is triggered during the last month of the return period, make up the difference no later than the end of the next month, as required by the end-of-return-period rule. If the deposit is triggered during any other month of the return period, make up the difference no later than the first deposit that is required after the 15th of the next month.

Tax calendar. If you would like a calendar that lists the various due dates on which employers must file returns and make deposits, get Publication 509, *Tax Calendars for 1992.*

How to make deposits. Make your deposit by mailing or delivering a single check or money order covering social security, Medicare, and withheld income taxes to an authorized financial institution or a Federal Reserve bank. The Federal Unemployment Tax, explained later, must be paid separately. To help ensure proper crediting to your account when depositing taxes, write your employer identification number, the tax return number, and the tax period the deposit applies to on your check or money order. You can get the names of authorized institutions from a Federal Reserve bank. To be on time, mailed deposits must arrive at the depository by the due date. Each deposit must be accompanied by a federal tax deposit (FTD) coupon. It is very important to clearly mark the correct type of tax and tax period on each deposit coupon. This information is used by the IRS to credit your account.

A Federal Tax Deposit Coupon Book containing a supply of ***Form 8109**, Federal Tax Deposit Coupon*, and instructions will automatically be sent to you after you apply for an employer identification number. If you do not receive a book of coupons, contact your local IRS office. If you need more coupons, order them using Form 8109A, *FTD Reorder Form*, in the coupon book. Be sure to show your name, employer identification number, and address on the reorder form. If you need to change your address, mark an "x" in the box for an address change and show the address where you want the coupon book sent on the reorder form. This will not change your address for the mailing of returns, refunds, or notices.

It takes about 5 or 6 weeks for delivery of the coupons. Allow ample time to reorder before using up your current supply. If you have a deposit due and there is not enough time to obtain a coupon book, blank forms (Form 8109–B, *Federal Tax Deposit Coupon*), are available at IRS offices.

If you have not received your employer identification number and must make a deposit, mail your payment with an explanation to the IRS Service Center where you file your return. Make your check payable to the Internal Revenue Service and show on it your name, address, kind of tax, period covered, and the date you applied for your employer identification number.

Note. Do not use a Federal Tax Deposit Coupon to deposit delinquent taxes you have been assessed by the IRS. These payments should be mailed to the IRS Service Center that assessed the taxes together with copies of any related notices. Also, do not mail estimated tax payments for your own income tax return with social security, Medicare, and withheld income taxes.

Timeliness of deposits. The timeliness of a deposit depends on the date the authorized financial institution or Federal Reserve bank receives it. A deposit received after the due date will be considered timely if you can establish that it was mailed at least two days before the due date. However, deposits of $20,000 or more by an employer required to deposit tax more than once a month must be received by the due date to be timely.

Penalties. If you do not deposit social security, Medicare, and withheld income taxes on time with an authorized financial institution or a Federal Reserve bank, you may have to pay a penalty. In addition, the IRS can require you to file monthly returns for these taxes on Form 941–M, *Employer's Monthly Federal Tax Return.*

If you do not withhold income, social security, and Medicare taxes from employees, or withhold the taxes but do not pay them to IRS or deposit them, you may be subject to a penalty of 100% of the tax. If you are the person responsible for the collection and payment of withholding taxes, you can be subject to this penalty even if you are an officer or employee of a corporation or a member or employee of a partnership.

Federal tax deposit penalties. The penalty for a late tax deposit is based on the length of time the deposit is late. The following penalties apply for late deposits:

1) If the deposit is not more than 5 days late, the penalty is 2% of the underpayment.
2) If the deposit is more than 5 days late but not more than 15 days late, the penalty is 5% of the underpayment.
3) If the deposit is more than 15 days late, the penalty is 10% of the underpayment.
4) If the deposit is not made within 10 days after IRS issues the first notice demanding payment or by the day that notice and demand for immediate payment is given, the penalty is 15% of the underpayment.

Be sure to follow all the tax laws that apply to you. In addition to civil penalties, criminal penalties may be imposed for intentionally not paying taxes, not filing returns, or filing a false return.

Other Forms

Form W–2. You must furnish copies of Form W–2, *Wage and Tax Statement,* to each employee from whom income, social security, or Medicare taxes have been withheld. (Sole proprietors do not report their own income on Forms 941 and W–2.) You must also furnish it to employees from whom income tax would have been withheld if the employee had claimed no more than one withholding allowance or had not claimed exemption from withholding on Form W–4. The Form W–2 must show the total wages and other compensation paid (whether or not subject to withholding), total wages subject to social security taxes, total wages subject to Medicare taxes, the amounts deducted for income, social security, and Medicare taxes, and any other information required on the statement. For information on preparing Form W–2, see the *Instructions for Forms W–2.*

Form W–2 is a six-part combined federal-state form designed for use by employers in states where both federal and state taxes must be withheld. This form may also be used where city or other subdivision taxes are withheld. It is printed in sets of six copies so that copies are available for filing and for the employee's records.

Furnish Form W–2 to employees as soon after December 31 as possible, so they may file their income tax returns early. In any event, you ***must*** furnish the employee Form W–2 or its equivalent no later than January 31 of the following year. However, when an employee who leaves your employment gives you a written request for the form earlier, you must give it to him or her within 30 days after you receive the request or, if later, the final wage payment, if the 30–day period ends before January 31. You should keep any undeliverable employee copies (copies B and C) of Form W–2 as a part of your records for a period of 4 years.

Form W–3. Employers must file Form W–3, *Transmittal of Income and Tax Statements,* annually by the last day of February to transmit Copy A of Forms W–2 to the Social Security Administration. Form W–2 will be processed by the Social Security Administration, which will then furnish the IRS with the income tax data that it needs from these forms. You must file 1991 Forms W–2 on magnetic media if you file 250 or more forms. The 250 requirement applies separately to each type of form.

Additional forms. Forms W–2 and W–3 are available on request from the IRS.

Extensions. If you are unable to file Forms W–2 with IRS on either paper forms or magnetic media by the due date, get ***Form 8809**, Request for Extension of Time To File Information Returns.* You must, however, furnish the required statements to recipients by the due date.

Reconciliation of Forms 941 and W–3. Amounts reported for the current calendar year on the 4 quarterly Forms 941 must agree with the totals reported on Form W–3. The amounts that must agree are: social security wages, social security tips, Medicare wages and tips, and the advance earned income credit.

Correcting Forms 941 and W–2. Use ***Form 941c**, Statement To Correct Information,* to correct income, social security, and Medicare tax information reported on Form 941 (or Forms 941E, 942, or 943). Attach Form 941c to the tax return making the adjustment. Social security and Medicare tax information can be corrected for prior years, but income tax information can be corrected only for earlier periods of the current calendar year.

Since Form W–2 is used by the Social Security Administration (SSA) to post the employee's social security and Medicare wages and tips to his or her earnings record, you must file a ***Form W–2c**, Statement of Corrected Income and Tax Amounts,* with SSA and give copies to the employee for any social security or Medicare correction made after you have filed Form W–2 with SSA. Send Form W–2c to SSA with ***Form W–3c**, Transmittal of Corrected Income and Tax Statements.* If you are correcting only the employees' names and social security numbers, Form W–3c is not needed.

Form 1099–R. Use Form 1099–R, *Distributions From Pensions, Annuities, Retirement or Profit-Sharing Plans, IRAs, Insurance Contracts, etc.,* to report any designated distribution from profit-sharing or retirement plans, IRAs, annuities, pensions, etc., whether or not you withheld income tax. Form W–2P, *Statement for Recipients of Annuities, Pensions, Retired Pay, or IRA Payments,* is now obsolete. The information that was on the 1990 Form W–2P has been added to the 1991 1099–R. File the 1991 Form 1099–R with IRS by February 28, 1992, along with Form 1096, *Annual Summary and Transmittal of U.S. Information Returns.* Provide the recipient of a distribution with a statement by January 31, 1992.

Change of Address. If you move or change your mailing address, be sure to notify the IRS by using ***Form 8822**, Change of Address.* Mail it to the Internal Revenue Service Center for your old address. If you are changing both your home and business addresses, you should complete two separate forms.

Federal Unemployment Tax

The ***Federal Unemployment Tax Act (FUTA),*** along with the state systems, provides unemployment payments to workers who have lost their jobs. Most employers pay both a state and federal unemployment tax. However, even if you are exempt from state tax, you may still have to pay the federal tax.

Use the following three tests to determine whether you must pay federal unemployment (FUTA) tax. Each test applies to a different category of employee, and each is independent of the others. It is possible to be liable for the tax in one category, but not in another. If a test describes your situation either during the current calendar year or during the preceding calendar year, you are subject to federal unemployment tax on the wages you pay to employees in that category during the current calendar year.

1) **In general.** You are subject to federal unemployment tax on the wages you pay employees who are not farm workers or household workers if:
   a) In any calendar quarter, the wages you paid to employees in this category totaled $1,500 or more, or

b) In each of 20 different calendar weeks, there was at least a part of a day in which you had an employee in this category. The 20 weeks do not have to be consecutive. Nor does it have to be the same employee each week. Individuals on sick leave or vacations are counted as employees.

2) **Household workers.** You are subject to federal unemployment tax on the cash wages you pay to household workers if the wages you paid to employees in this category totaled $1,000 or more in any calendar quarter. A household worker is an employee who performs domestic services in a private home, local college club, or local fraternity or sorority chapter.

3) **Farm workers.** You are subject to federal unemployment tax on the wages you pay to farm workers if:

   a) In any calendar quarter, the cash wages you paid for the farm labor totaled $20,000 or more, or

   b) In each of 20 different calendar weeks, there was at least one day in which you had 10 or more farm worker employees. The 20 weeks do not have to be consecutive. Nor does it have to be the same 10 employees each week. Nor do all 10 employees have to work a full day or the same part of the day. Individuals on sick leave or vacation are counted as employees.

Tips. All tip income (including credit card tips) reported by the employee to the employer for social security and Medicare tax purposes is considered wages for federal unemployment tax purposes.

Wages not paid in money. If in the course of your trade or business you pay your employees in some medium that is neither cash nor a readily negotiable instrument (such as a check), you are said to pay them "in kind." Payments in kind may be in the form of goods, lodging, food, clothing, or services. Generally, wages paid in kind are treated as wages paid in money. The value of a wage payment in kind is the fair market value it would have on the day it is made. For the treatment of ***meals and lodging,*** see the discussion under *Social Security and Medicare Taxes,* earlier.

Payments in kind for farm labor are not considered wages. Do not count them either to figure whether you are subject to federal unemployment tax under test (3) above or to figure how much tax you owe. Nor count payments in kind to household workers when figuring whether you are subject to federal unemployment tax under test (2) above.

Employee liability for taxes paid by employer. Generally, if you pay an employee's liability for any state unemployment taxes or social security or Medicare taxes (without deduction from the employee's pay), include the payments in the employee's wages for purposes of the federal unemployment tax. This rule does not apply to payments for domestic service in your home or for agricultural labor.

Supplemental unemployment payments. The federal unemployment tax does not apply to employer provided supplemental unemployment payments if the payments are linked to state unemployment payments and are not made in a lump sum.

Wages of foreign workers. The federal unemployment tax does not apply to the wages of a worker admitted to the United States under contract to perform farm labor for you before 1993 and who returns to his or her own country when the contract is completed. However, count the wages you pay to an alien worker in figuring whether you are subject to federal unemployment tax for your other farm workers under rule (3) above.

Wages paid by crew leaders. To obtain farm labor, some farmers use the services of, or employ, individuals called "crew leaders." A crew leader is defined as anyone who:

1) Furnishes workers to perform farm labor;
2) Pays the workers (either on his or her own behalf or on behalf of the farmer) for the work they do; and
3) Has not entered into a written agreement with the farmer under which he or she is designated as an employee of the farmer.

Depending on the circumstances, workers furnished by a crew leader may be considered employees of the crew leader or employees of the farmer for federal unemployment tax.

The crew leader is considered the employer of the workers if:

1) He or she is registered under the Migrant and Seasonal Agricultural Worker Protection Act, or
2) Substantially all crew members operate or maintain mechanized equipment provided by the crew leader as part of the service to the farmer.

The farmer is considered the employer of the workers in all other situations. The farmer is also considered the employer of workers furnished by a registered crew leader if the workers are employees of the farmer under the common-law test. For example, some farmers employ crew leaders to recruit farm workers exclusively for them. Although these crew leaders may be required to register under the Migrant and Seasonal Agricultural Worker Protection Act, the workers are hired directly by the farmer. The farmer is considered to be the employer in these cases.

Payments to survivor or estate. Payments made by an employer to a survivor or the estate of a former employee after the calendar year in which the employee died are not subject to federal unemployment tax.

Camp counselor. An exemption from federal unemployment tax applies to wages paid by certain camps to employees who are full-time students. The students must have worked for the camp less than 13 weeks in the calendar year.

To qualify, the camp must have operated 7 months or less in the current year and 7 months or less in the preceding year, or had gross receipts for any 6 months in the preceding year which were 1/3 or less of its average gross receipts for the other 6 months.

Other exceptions. Not all payments you make to your employees are considered wages for federal unemployment tax. For example, payments made under the worker's compensation law are not counted as wages.

Nor does the tax apply to certain types of employment. For example, if you hire cooperative education students, you are not subject to the federal unemployment tax on their wages.

Additional information. Get *Circular E* (*Circular A* for farm labor) for a chart indicating whether payments are exempt from federal unemployment tax.

Figuring the Tax

The federal unemployment tax is figured on the first $7,000 in wages paid to each employee during 1991. This $7,000 maximum is scheduled to remain the same for 1992. The tax is imposed on you as the employer. You must not collect it or deduct it from the wages of your employees.

Example. In November 1990, you hire Alice Green and pay her $3,500 in wages before the year ends. All $3,500 is subject to the federal unemployment tax. The first $7,000 you pay her in 1991 is also subject to the tax. Her total wages for 1991 reach the $7,000 mark in mid-March. The wages you pay her after that in 1991 are not subject to the tax. Then, in July, she quits her job, and you hire someone to replace her. The first $7,000 you pay her replacement in 1991 is also subject to the tax.

Tax rate and credit. The federal unemployment tax rate for 1991 is 6.2%. The rate is scheduled to remain the same for 1992. However, you are given a credit of up to 5.4% for the state unemployment tax you pay. The tax rate, therefore, can be as low as 0.8% (6.2% minus 5.4%) if your state is not subject to a credit reduction. If your state tax rate (experience rate) happens to be less than 5.4%, you are still allowed the full 5.4% credit. But you cannot take the credit for any state taxes you do not pay. If for any reason you are exempt from state unemployment tax, the full 6.2% rate applies.

Credit reduction. The 5.4% credit may be reduced for employers in some states. A credit reduction is required if a state's unemployment fund borrows from the federal government and keeps an outstanding balance for two or more years. For 1991, Michigan is the only state subject to a credit reduction.

Successor employer. If you take over the business of an employer who was subject to the federal unemployment tax, you may, in figuring the $7,000 limit, count wages paid by that employer to employees who continue to work for you.

Concurrent employment by related corporations. If two or more related corporations employ the same individual at the same time and they pay this individual through only one of the corporations (the "common paymaster"), the corporations are considered a single employer. They have to pay, in total, no more in federal unemployment taxes than a single employer would pay.

Each corporation must pay its own share of employment taxes and may deduct only its own share of the wages paid.

To take the deduction, the corporation must reimburse the common paymaster for its share of wages and tax payments. The common paymaster cannot deduct wage and tax payments for employee services performed for another corporation in the related group.

Reporting and Paying the Tax

The federal unemployment tax is reported on ***Form 940.*** This form covers one calendar year and is generally due one month after the year ends. However, you may have to make deposits of the tax before filing the return.

Form 940–EZ. Form 940–EZ, a simplified version of Form 940, can be used by employers: (1) who paid state unemployment taxes to only one state; (2) who paid all the state unemployment taxes by the due date of Form 940–EZ; (3) whose wages taxable for FUTA tax were also taxable for state unemployment tax; and (4) who paid no wages in 1991 subject to the unemployment compensation laws of the State of Michigan.

Deposit due dates. If at the end of any calendar quarter, you owe, but have not yet deposited, more than $100 in federal unemployment (FUTA) tax for the year, you must make a deposit by the end of the next month. The due dates are shown in the following chart:

If your undeposited FUTA tax is more than $100 on:	Deposit the full amount by:
March 31	April 30
June 30	July 31
September 30	October 31
December 31	January 31

If the tax is $100 or less at the end of a quarter, you do not have to deposit it. But you must add it to the tax for the next quarter. Then, in the next quarter, if the total undeposited tax is more than $100, a deposit will be required.

If a due date falls on a Saturday, Sunday, or legal holiday, it is postponed until the next date that is not a Saturday, Sunday, or legal holiday. A statewide legal holiday delays a due date only if the IRS office where you are required to file is located in that state.

Figuring deposits for 1992. To figure whether you must make a deposit for 1992, assume that you will be able to take the full credit of 5.4%, that is, use an effective tax rate of 0.8% (6.2% minus 5.4%). Next, figure what part of the wages you paid during the quarter is subject to the tax. Multiply that amount by 0.8% (.008). The result is the amount of federal unemployment tax you owe for the quarter.

Additional liability because of credit reduction. If your state is subject to a credit reduction for 1992, the state's name and the amount of the credit reduction will be shown on the 1992 Form 940. If the 5.4% credit for 1992 is reduced for employers in your state, it creates an additional 4th quarter liability. Before the 4th quarter, you are not liable for depositing any tax owed because of a credit reduction. The credit reduction becomes final on November 10 each year. To figure the amount of federal unemployment tax you owe for the 4th quarter of 1992 if you are subject to a credit reduction, follow these steps:

1) First, using an effective tax rate of 0.8% for 1992, figure the tax you owe on wages paid during the 4th quarter.
2) Next, multiply the total wages subject to federal unemployment tax in all 4 quarters by your state's credit reduction rate shown on the 1992 Form 940.
3) Then, add together the amounts from these two steps. The result is the federal unemployment tax you owe for the 4th quarter.

Making deposits. Make deposits of FUTA tax as discussed earlier for depositing social security, Medicare, and withheld income taxes. See *How to make deposits* under *Deposits,* earlier.

Filing the return. If you deposit the tax on time and in full, you have an extra 10 days beyond the usual January 31 due date, or until February 10, to file Form 940 or 940–EZ.

Additional information. More information about the federal unemployment tax can be found in the instructions to Form 940.

Example of How To Figure Employment Taxes

Peter Cone owns a small furniture business which he runs with three full-time employees. In 1991, he paid one employee $600 a week, one employee $500 a week, and one employee $400 a week. He did not hire anyone else during the year, and the employees stayed with him the entire year.

It is Peter's practice to pay his employees on Monday. If Monday is a holiday, payday is Tuesday.

The sections that follow discuss how Peter figured his employment taxes for the year. They show how he figured his deposits and how he filled out Forms 940 and 941. Only the 4th quarter Form 941 is illustrated.

Peter files Form 941 quarterly. On it, he reports:

1) Income tax he withholds from his employees' wages; and
2) Social security and Medicare taxes, both the part he withholds from his employees' wages and the part he pays as an employer.

Before filing Form 941 for the 4th quarter, Peter must deposit the taxes at various times during the quarter because the tax owed at the end of each month in that quarter was enough to trigger a deposit requirement.

Each of Peter's employees has already filled out a Form W–4. Form W–4 tells him:

1) How many withholding allowances the employee claims; and
2) Whether to withhold at the "married" or at the "single" rate.

Using this information, Peter finds the correct amount to withhold in Publication 15 (Circular E), *Employer's Tax Guide.* He uses the wage bracket tables in the January 1991 Circular E to find the correct amount to withhold during the 4th quarter. The tables are for wages paid after December 1990.

In the 4th quarter of 1991, the first payday for Peter's employees is Monday, October 7. His income tax withholding for this payday is shown in the chart below:

Employee	Wages for the week	Withholding rate and allowances	Amount to be withheld
R. Apple	$ 600	married–3	$ 62.00
J. Jones	500	married–2	53.00
F. Plum	400	single–1	51.00
Total	$1,500		$166.00

Peter's liability for withheld income tax on this payday totals $166.00. If any of his employees had asked him (on Form W–4) to withhold an extra amount, he would have included it with the total.

Peter also withholds 6.2% of each employee's wages as social security tax and pays a 6.2% share himself, for a total of 12.4% in 1991. In addition, he withholds 1.45% of each employee's wages as Medicare tax and pays a 1.45% share himself, for a total of 2.9%. The total social security tax for this payday is $186.00 ($1,500 total wages times 12.4%), and the total Medicare tax is $43.50 ($1,500 total wages times 2.9%).

Social security tax applies to only the first $53,400 paid to each employee in 1991. The Medicare tax applies to the first $125,000. If any of Peter's employees had already earned $53,400, or reached this limit on the October 7 payday, he would have included only the Medicare tax (up to $125,000) when figuring the tax. However, none of his employees will earn more than $53,400 in 1991.

None of the employees is eligible for advanced earned income credit payments (discussed later).

On this payday, Peter's total liability for social security tax, Medicare tax, and withheld income tax is $395.50 ($186.00 plus $43.50 plus $166.00). The following chart shows his tax liability for the paydays in the 4th quarter:

Payday	Total wages paid	Income tax withheld	Social Security (12.4%)	Medicare (2.9%)
Oct. 7	$ 1,500	$ 166.00	$ 186.00	$43.50
Oct. 15	1,500	166.00	186.00	43.50
Oct. 21	1,500	166.00	186.00	43.50
Oct. 28	1,500	166.00	186.00	43.50
Nov. 4	1,500	166.00	186.00	43.50
Nov. 12	1,500	166.00	186.00	43.50
Nov. 18	1,500	166.00	186.00	43.50
Nov. 25	1,500	166.00	186.00	43.50
Dec. 2	1,500	166.00	186.00	43.50
Dec. 9	1,500	166.00	186.00	43.50
Dec. 16	1,500	166.00	186.00	43.50
Dec. 23	1,500	166.00	186.00	43.50
Dec. 30	1,500	166.00	186.00	43.50
Total	$19,500	$2,158.00	$2,418.00	$65.50

Making Deposits

Peter's schedule for making deposits depends on the total amount of social security tax, Medicare tax, and withheld income tax he owes at the end of each of eight deposit periods within the month. The eight periods end on the 3rd, 7th, 11th, 15th, 19th, 22nd, 25th, and last day of every month.

On the first payday of the 4th quarter, Peter's liability for social security tax, Medicare tax, and withheld income tax totals $395.50. Because this payday falls on October 7, he owes this amount for the October 4–7 deposit period. Since the amount he owes is less than $3,000, no deposit is required.

The second payday for Peter's employees during the 4th quarter falls within the October 12–15 deposit period. His payroll and liability for social security tax, Medicare tax, and withheld income tax are the same as for the first payday. Therefore, his liability for this deposit period totals $791.00 ($395.50 times 2 paydays). This total is still under $3,000. So again no deposit is required.

By the end of October, Peter's liability for social security tax, Medicare tax, and withheld income tax grows to $1,582.00 ($395.50 times 4 paydays). Peter meets the requirements to make a deposit under the $500 rule. (If at the end of the month, an employer owes $500 or more (but less than $3,000), a deposit is required by the 15th of the next month.)

During November, Peter's payroll remains the same. The following chart shows how the social security tax, Medicare tax, and withheld income tax he owes add up during November:

Payday	Total wages paid on the payday	Taxes owed for the payday	Taxes owed since last deposit requirement
November 4	$1,500	$395.50	$ 395.50
November 12	1,500	395.50	791.00
November 18	1,500	395.50	1,186.50
November 25	1,500	395.50	1,582.00

At the end of the month, Peter meets the $500 rule and must make a deposit by December 16 (December 15 is on a Sunday).

Note that when figuring his deposit requirements, Peter does not add any of the taxes owed for October to those he owes in November, even though he did not have to deposit the October taxes until November 15. If his October taxes had not triggered a deposit requirement, he would have carried them over and added them to the taxes he owes for November. But because the October taxes were already subject to a deposit requirement, they do not have to be considered when figuring later deposits.

During December, Peter's payroll remains the same. The following chart shows how the social security tax, Medicare tax, and withheld income tax he owes add up during December.

Payday	Total wages paid on the payday	Taxes owed for the payday	Taxes owed since last deposit requirement
December 2	$1,500	$395.50	$ 395.50
December 9	1,500	395.50	791.00
December 16	1,500	395.50	1,186.50
December 23	1,500	395.50	1,582.00
December 30	1,500	395.50	1,977.50

A deposit by January 15, 1992, is required.

Filling Out Form 941

Peter begins filling out Form 941 by using the preaddressed form with his name, address, and employer identification number. The form identifies the quarter the return is for as ending on December 31, 1991. Since it is a 4th quarter return, he does not have to fill in lines 1a and 1b. If he had gone out of business in 1991, he would fill in the entries above line 1a on the Form 941.

Line 2. Peter enters the total wages he paid in the quarter, $19,500.

Line 3. Peter enters the total income tax he withheld from his employees' wages during the quarter, $2,158.

Line 5. Peter does not have to make any adjustments for errors in the withholding he reported for the first 3 quarters of the year (line 4). He enters the amount from line 3 on line 5.

Line 6a. None of Peter's employees earned more than the $53,400 limit for 1991. The amount they were paid during the quarter, $19,500, is counted as "taxable social security wages." He enters 12.4% of this amount, or $2,418, as his social security tax on this line. This includes both his share and the amount he withheld from his employees' wages.

Line 6b. Peter's employees did not earn any taxable tips.

Line 7. Peter again enters the wages he paid. He enters 2.9% of this amount, or $565.50, as his Medicare tax on this line. This includes both his share and the amount he withheld from his employees' wages.

Lines 8 and 10. Peter does not have to make any adjustments for errors in social security or Medicare taxes he reported previously (line 9). He enters the total amount of social security and Medicare taxes on lines 8 and 10.

Line 14. Peter adds the withheld income, social security, and Medicare taxes. He enters the total, $5,141.50.

Line 16. None of Peter's employees received advance payments of the earned income credit (line 15). He enters the amount from line 14 on line 16.

Lines 16 and 17. Peter shows that the amount of tax he owed for the quarter and the amount he deposited are the same. He does not have to make a payment with his return (line 18). Nor is he owed a refund (line 19).

Record of liability. Peter completes the *Record of Federal Tax Liability* section of Form 941 by filling in lines I, II, III, and IV.

Signature and date. Peter signs the return, prints his name and title, and enters the date. Because Peter deposited the tax on time and in full, he has an extra 10 days to file his return.

Form 940 or Form 940–EZ

Peter must pay state as well as federal unemployment tax. His state gave him an experience rating of 3.0% for 1991. Since his state bases its tax on the first $7,000 of wages paid to each employee, and since he paid each of his employees more than that amount in 1991, he must pay the state tax on $21,000 ($7,000 times 3 employees). He paid $630 (3.0% of $21,000) in state unemployment tax during 1991.

For federal unemployment tax, Peter must fill out a Form 940, or Form 940–EZ if he qualifies, for the year and make any deposits required. A deposit is required if an employer has more than $100 of tax outstanding at the end of a calendar quarter.

Making Deposits

The federal unemployment tax rate is 6.2% of the first $7,000 in wages paid to each employee in 1991. Peter figures his deposits under the assumption that he will receive full credit for the state unemployment tax he paid. The maximum credit allowed is 5.4%. He figures his deposits using an effective tax rate of 0.8% (6.2% minus 5.4%). Although he has a state experience rate of less than 5.4%, he is still able to take the 5.4% credit.

Peter will not know until the end of the year whether the 5.4% credit will be reduced for employers in his state. If it is reduced, he must take the reduction into account when figuring the deposit for the 4th quarter.

First quarter. There were 12 paydays for Peter's employees in the 1st quarter of 1991. Each employee's wages remained the same on all 12 paydays. The following table shows how much of each employee's total wages for the 1st quarter is subject to federal unemployment (FUTA) tax:

Employee	Wages paid in 1st quarter	Wages subject to FUTA in 1st quarter
R. Apple	$ 7,200	$ 7,000
J. Jones	6,000	6,000
F. Plum	4,800	4,800
Total	$18,000	$17,800
Tax rate		×.008
Tax liability for 1st quarter		$142.40

Peter figures his tax for the quarter as 0.8% of $17,800, or $142.40. Because this is more than $100, he must deposit it by the end of April.

Second quarter. There were 13 paydays for Peter's employees in the 2nd quarter of 1991. Each employee's weekly wages remained the same. The following table shows how much of each employee's total wages for the 2nd quarter is subject to federal unemployment (FUTA) tax:

Employee	Wages paid in 2nd quarter	Wages already subject to FUTA	Wages subject to FUTA in 2nd quarter
R. Apple	$ 7,800	$ 7,000	$ -0-
J. Jones	6,500	6,000	1000
F. Plum	5,200	4,800	2,200
Total	$19,500	$17,800	$ 3,200
Tax rate			×.008
Tax liability for 2nd quarter			$ 25.60

The wages he paid to all his employees reached the yearly $7,000 limit during the quarter. For example, all the wages paid to J. Jones in the 1st quarter, $6,000, were subject to the tax. Therefore, only $1,000.00 ($7,000 minus $6,000) of Jones's 2nd quarter wages are subject to the tax.

Peter's federal unemployment tax liability for the 2nd quarter is $25.60. This is figured by multiplying the total wages subject to the tax in the quarter ($3,200) by the tax rate (0.8%). He does not have to make a deposit for the 2nd quarter because the amount he owes is not more than $100.

Third quarter. Peter carried over his 2nd quarter tax liability of $25.60 to the 3rd quarter. However, since he already reached the $7,000 limit for all his employees in the 2nd quarter, none of the wages paid in the 3rd quarter are subject to FUTA tax.

Fourth Quarter. Peter carried his tax liability of $25.60 to the 4th quarter. Since Peter did not pay wages that are subject to the unemployment compensation laws of the State of Michigan, he does not have to figure a credit reduction for the 4th quarter. He can either deposit the $25.60 or pay it with his Form 940 by January 31, 1992.

Peter can file Form 940–EZ, a simplified version of Form 940, because: (1) he paid state unemployment taxes to only one state; (2) he paid all the state unemployment taxes by the due date of Form 940–EZ; (3) all his wages taxable for FUTA tax were also taxable for state unemployment tax; and (4) he paid no wages in 1991 subject to the unemployment compensation laws of the State of Michigan. If Peter did not meet these 4 conditions, he would have to file Form 940, a 4-part form. Form 940–EZ is a 2-part form.

Filling Out Form 940–EZ

Peter begins filling in Form 940–EZ by using the preaddressed form with his name, address, and employer identification number. If he uses a trade name, he also adds it if it is not already on the form.

Items A and B. Peter enters the amount he paid to the state unemployment fund, $630.00. He then enters the name of his state and his state reporting number.

Peter is now ready to fill out the rest of the form.

Part I

Line 1. Peter enters the total amount he paid to his employees during 1991. His payroll was $78,000 for 1991.

Line 2. None of the wages he paid in 1991 was exempt from federal unemployment tax. Peter does not enter anything on this line. (Wages paid to a family member are an example of exempt wages.)

Line 3. Peter enters $57,000, the amount of wages he paid that was over the $7,000 limit for each employee. Any amount included on line 2 should not be included on this line.

Line 4. Peter enters $57,000, the sum of lines 2 and 3.

Line 5. Peter subtracts his total exempt payments on line 4 from his total payments on line 1. He enters the difference, $21,000, on line 5. This is the amount of his 1991 wage payments subject to federal unemployment tax.

Line 6. Peter enters $168, 0.8% of the $21,000 in taxable wages listed on line 5.

Line 7. Peter enters $142.40, the amount of his federal unemployment tax deposit for the 1st quarter. He made no other deposits during the year.

Line 8. Because his deposits do not equal his tax liability for the year, Peter writes a check for the additional amount.

Line 9. Because he did not overpay the tax, Peter leaves this line blank.

Part II (Tax Liability Record)

Peter enters his tax for the 1st quarter, $142.40, in the first column.

Peter enters his tax for the 2nd quarter, $25.60, in the second column. He makes no entries in the 3rd and 4th quarter columns because he has no tax liability for those quarters.

Peter enters his total tax liability, $168, in the last column.

Signature and date. Peter signs the return, enters his title as "owner," and enters the date.

Form **941** (Rev. January 1991) Department of the Treasury Internal Revenue Service | 4141

Employer's Quarterly Federal Tax Return

▶ See Circular E for more information concerning employment tax returns.

Please type or print.

Your name, address, employer identification number, and calendar quarter of return. (If not correct, please change.) ▶

DD 10-1234567 9112 S28 C
Peter Cone
362 Main Street
Anytown VA 23000

OMB No. 1545-0029
Expires: 5-31-93

T
FF
FD
FP
I
T

If address is different from prior return, check here ▶ ☐ IRS Use

If you do not have to file returns in the future, check here . . . ▶ ☐ Date final wages paid . . . ▶

If you are a seasonal employer, see **Seasonal employers** on page 2 and check here . ▶ ☐

Line	Description		Amount
1a	Number of employees (except household) employed in the pay period that includes March 12th . ▶	1a	
b	If you are a subsidiary corporation AND your parent corporation files a consolidated Form 1120, enter parent corporation employer identification number (EIN) . . ▶ 1b –		
2	Total wages and tips subject to withholding, plus other compensation ▶	2	19,500 00
3	Total income tax withheld from wages, tips, pensions, annuities, sick pay, gambling, etc. ▶	3	2,158 00
4	Adjustment of withheld income tax for preceding quarters of calendar year (see instructions) ▶	4	
5	Adjusted total of income tax withheld (line 3 as adjusted by line 4—see instructions)	5	2,158 00
6a	Taxable social security wages (Complete line 7) $ 19,500 00 × 12.4% (.124) =	6a	2,418 00
b	Taxable social security tips $ × 12.4% (.124) =	6b	
7	Taxable Medicare wages and tips $ 19,500 00 × 2.9% (.029) =	7	565 50
8	Total social security and Medicare taxes (add lines 6a, 6b, and 7)	8	2,983 50
9	Adjustment of social security and Medicare taxes (see instructions for required explanation)	9	
10	Adjusted total of social security and Medicare taxes (line 8 as adjusted by line 9—see instructions) ▶	10	2,983 50
11	Backup withholding (see instructions)	11	
12	Adjustment of backup withholding tax for preceding quarters of calendar year ▶	12	
13	Adjusted total of backup withholding (line 11 as adjusted by line 12)	13	
14	**Total taxes** (add lines 5, 10, and 13)	14	5,141 50
15	Advance earned income credit (EIC) payments made to employees, if any ▶	15	
16	Net taxes (subtract line 15 from line 14). **This should equal line IV below** (plus line IV of Schedule A (Form 941) if you have treated backup withholding as a separate liability)	16	5,141 50
17	**Total deposits for quarter,** including overpayment applied from a prior quarter, from your records. ▶	17	5,141 50
18	**Balance due** (subtract line 17 from line 16). This should be less than $500. Pay to IRS. ▶	18	
19	**Overpayment,** if line 17 is more than line 16, enter here ▶ $ ________ and check if to be: ☐ Applied to next return **OR** ☐ Refunded.		

Record of Federal Tax Liability (You must complete if line 16 is $500 or more and Schedule B is not attached.) See instructions before checking these boxes.

Check only if you made deposits using the 95% rule ▶ ☐ Check only if you are a first time 3-banking-day depositor. ▶ ☐

Show tax liability here, **not deposits.** IRS gets deposit data from FTD coupons.

Date wages paid		First month of quarter		Second month of quarter		Third month of quarter
1st through 3rd	A		I		Q	
4th through 7th	B		J		R	
8th through 11th	C		K		S	
12th through 15th	D		L		T	
16th through 19th	E		M		U	
20th through 22nd	F		N		V	
23rd through 25th	G		O		W	
26th through the last	H		P		X	
Total liability for month	I	1,582.00	II	1,582.00	III	1,977.50

Do NOT Show Federal Tax Deposits Here

IV Total for quarter (add lines *I, II,* and *III*). **This should equal line 16 above** ▶ 5,141.50

Sign Here Under penalties of perjury, I declare that I have examined this return, including accompanying schedules and statements, and to the best of my knowledge and belief, it is true, correct, and complete.

Signature ▶ Peter Cone Print Your Name and Title ▶ Peter Cone Owner Date ▶ 2-6-92

For Paperwork Reduction Act Notice, see page 2.

Form **940-EZ**

Department of the Treasury
Internal Revenue Service

Employer's Annual Federal Unemployment (FUTA) Tax Return

OMB No. 1545-1110

1991

If incorrect, make any necessary changes.

DD 10-1234567 9112 S28 B
Peter Cone
362 Main Street
Anytown VA 23000

Calendar year

IRS

Employer identification number

T	
FF	
FD	
FP	
I	
T	

Follow the chart under "Who Can Use Form 940-EZ" on page 2. If you cannot use Form 940-EZ, you must use Form 940 instead.

A Enter the amount of contributions paid to your state unemployment fund. (See instructions for line A on page 4.) ▶ $ 630.00

B (1) Enter the name of the state where you have to pay contributions ▶ Virginia

(2) Enter your state reporting number(s) as shown on state unemployment tax return. ▶ 98765432

If you will not have to file returns in the future, check here (see *Who Must File a Return* on page 2) **complete, and sign the return** ▶ ☐

If this is an Amended Return check here ▶ ☐

Part I Taxable Wages and FUTA Tax

			Amount paid		
1	Total payments (including payments shown on lines 2 and 3) during the calendar year for services of employees			1	78,000.00
2	Exempt payments. (Explain all exempt payments, attaching additional sheets if necessary.) ▶	2			
3	Payments for services of more than $7,000. Enter only amounts over the first $7,000 paid to each employee. Do not include any exempt payments from line 2	3	57,000.00		
4	Total exempt payments (add lines 2 and 3)			4	57,000.00
5	**Total taxable wages** (subtract line 4 from line 1) ▶			5	21,000.00
6	**FUTA tax.** Multiply the wages on line 5 by .008 and enter here. (If the result is over $100, also complete Part II.)			6	168.00
7	Total FUTA tax deposited for the year, including any overpayment applied from a prior year (from your records)			7	142.40
8	**Amount you owe** (subtract line 7 from line 6). This should be $100 or less. Pay to "Internal Revenue Service". ▶			8	25.60
9	**Overpayment** (subtract line 6 from line 7). Check if it is to be: ☐ **Applied to next return, or** ☐ **Refunded** ▶			9	

Part II Record of Quarterly Federal Unemployment Tax Liability (Do not include state liability.) Complete only if line 6 is over $100.

Quarter	First (Jan. 1 – Mar. 31)	Second (Apr. 1 – June 30)	Third (July 1 – Sept. 30)	Fourth (Oct. 1 – Dec. 31)	Total for Year
Liability for quarter	142.40	25.60			168.00

Under penalties of perjury, I declare that I have examined this return, including accompanying schedules and statements, and, to the best of my knowledge and belief, it is true, correct, and complete, and that no part of any payment made to a state unemployment fund claimed as a credit was, or is to be, deducted from the payments to employees.

Signature ▶ Peter Cone Title (Owner, etc.) ▶ Owner Date ▶ 1-24-92

Advance Payment of Earned Income Credit

You must pay part of the earned income credit (EIC) in advance to eligible employees who have filed a Form W-5, *Earned Income Credit Advance Payment Certificate,* for 1992 with you. If an employee does not file a Form W-5, he or she cannot receive any advance payment. Any eligible employee who chooses not to get advance payment of the EIC will still get full benefit of the EIC on his or her tax return.

Earned income credit notification. You must notify each employee who worked for you at any time during the year and from whom you did not withhold any income tax about the EIC. However, you do not have to notify employees who claim exemption from withholding on Form W-4, *Employee's Withholding Allowance Certificate.*

You can meet the notification requirement by giving each employee the official IRS Form W-2, *Wage and Tax Statement,* which contains the notification on the back of Copy C, or you can give each employee Notice 797, *Notice of Possible Federal Tax Refund Due to the Earned Income Credit (EIC).* You can also use your own written statement as long as it has the exact wording of Notice 797, or you can furnish substitute Forms W-2, containing the exact wording shown on the back of Copy C of the official Form W-2. You must so notify each employee, either in person or by first class mail, with his or her 1991 Form W-2, or within one week before or after that time, unless you use a substitute Form W-2 as the notice. If you do not furnish Form W-2 on time, you must notify the employee about the EIC by the date Form W-2 was required to be furnished. If Form W-2 is not required, you must notify the employee about the EIC by February 7, 1992.

You can request supplies of Notice 797 by calling the IRS toll-free telephone number 1-800-TAX-FORM (1-800-829-3676).

Eligible employee. To receive advance payment of part of the EIC for 1992, your employee must first expect to be eligible for the EIC. An employee is eligible if he or she expects to meet all the following requirements.

1) The employee's earned income and adjusted gross income must both be less than $22,370 in 1992. Do not continue advance payments to an employee once the employee's wages are $22,370 or more in 1992.
2) The employee must not claim the foreign earned income or housing expense exclusion, or the foreign housing expense deduction.
3) The employee, if married, must not file as married filing separately. He or she must file a joint return or qualify to file as a head of household.
4) The employee must have a qualifying child living with him or her for more than half the tax year, except when the child is away at school or on vacation. This time is counted as time at home. The requirement for a foster child is a full year.
5) The employee must claim a married child as a dependent unless the employee does not claim the child because the child's other parent claims the exemption since the employee released his or her claim in writing, or because the exemption is granted to the child's other parent by a pre-1985 separation agreement or divorce decree. This rule also applies if the employee files a joint return with his or her present spouse.

Qualifying child. A qualifying child is the employee's son, daughter, adopted child, or their descendants. It also includes a stepchild or foster child. The child must be under age 19, a full-time student under age 24, or permanently and totally disabled. The child must have a social security number if the child is age 1 or older.

Form W-5. The employee must file Form W-5 with you before any advance EIC payment can be made. On Form W-5, the employee certifies that he or she expects to be eligible for the EIC and has no other certificate in effect with any other current employer. Once filed, it will stay in effect for one calendar year, unless it is revoked by the employee or another Form W-5 is filed to replace it. Employees must file a new Form W-5 each year.

On the Form W-5, the employee must show if his or her spouse has a Form W-5 in effect for the year with the spouse's employer. If your employee's spouse has one in effect, the maximum amount of the advance payments you can make to your employee will be reduced.

If after giving you a signed Form W-5, the employee later becomes ineligible for the EIC or the employee's spouse files a Form W-5, the employee must either revoke the previously filed form or file a new one within 10 days. If your employee gives you a Form W-5 certifying that his or her spouse has a Form W-5 in effect, and later the spouse revokes his or her form, your employee may file a new one showing the change. But he or she is not required to do so.

Effective date. The first Form W-5 filed by an employee each year becomes effective for the first payroll period ending on or after the day the form is received. If wage payments are made without regard to a payroll period, it becomes effective for the first payment on or after the day the form is filed. If a revised Form W-5 is filed, it takes effect on:

1) The day the first payment of wages is made on or after the first status determination date (January 1, May 1, July 1, or October 1) that occurs at least 30 days after the form is received; or
2) The day any wages are paid that is on or after the day the form is received, if you so choose.

Figuring the payment. To figure the amount of advance payment, take into account the wages paid, including reported tips, as well as whether your married employee's spouse has a Form W-5 in effect.

Wages for the advance EIC payment are generally the same as wages subject to income tax withholding. For employees who claim exemption from income tax withholding on Form W-4, the wages for advance EIC payments are those that would have been subject to income tax withholding. For domestic employees, the wages for advance EIC payments are the same as wages subject to social security and Medicare taxes.

After considering these factors, you can figure the amount to include in the eligible employee's wage payments by using the tables contained in Circular E. The advance EIC payment does not change the amount of income or social security and Medicare taxes that you withhold from your employee's wages. The advance EIC payment you make is treated as if you paid the IRS on the day you paid that amount to your employee. The payment would normally be paid to the IRS through federal tax deposits or with your employment tax return. The advance EIC payment you make to your employee is not considered compensation for services and is not subject to payroll taxes.

You generally will make the advance EIC payment from withheld income, social security, and Medicare taxes (both the employee's and your share). If for any payroll period the advance EIC payments are more than the total withheld income, social security, and Medicare taxes (both the employee's and your share), you can:

1) Lower each advance EIC payment proportionately. Each payment is reduced by an amount with the same ratio to the excess as the payment has to total advance EIC payments for the payroll period; or
2) Elect to make full payment of the advance EIC amount and have the full amounts treated as an advance payment of your tax liability. See *Election to treat excess amounts as advance tax payment,* next.

Election to treat excess amounts as advance tax payment. If the advance EIC payments you will make are more than the total income tax withholding and social security taxes due for the period, you can elect not to lower the advance payment but to pay in full all advance EIC amounts for the payroll period. If you elect to make full payment, you must state on your employment tax return (Form 941, 941E, 942, or 943) the amount of excess advance amounts paid and the payroll period to which the excess relates. If this is not done, you must proportionately lower each advance EIC payment.

You can make this election for each separate payroll period. When this election is made, the excess advance amounts you paid are treated as an advance payment of your employment taxes (income tax withholding, social security and Medicare taxes) that are due for the period reported on the Form 941, 941E, 942, or 943 which includes the payroll period during which the excess was paid. If your remaining employment tax liability for that period is less than the excess payment, you can claim a credit or refund of the difference.

Employment tax returns. The advance EIC payment that you make is added to each employee's pay. It does not change the amount you must withhold from that employee's pay for income, social security, and Medicare taxes. Instead, the advance EIC payments you make are treated as made from the total of all amounts you withheld as income and employee social security and Medicare taxes and that you must pay as employer social security and Medicare taxes. Furthermore, the advance EIC payments you made are treated as if you had paid over that amount to the IRS on the day you paid the wages. You will then take these payments into account when you file your employment tax return (Form 941, 941E, 942, or 943).

Forms 941, 941E, and 943. If you must file any of these employment tax forms, include the amount of advance EIC payments you made in completing the form. When you figure your total employment tax liability, use these amounts together with any actual federal tax deposits you made to lower any payment that may be due when you file the form.

The same rules that require you to show your employment tax liability for a specific period also apply for showing advance payments you made. If you have to show your employment tax liability on the form for each eighth monthly period, you show your tax liability (income tax withheld plus both the employee and employer social security and Medicare taxes minus any advance EIC payments) for the period.

Form 942. This form does not have a part for the Record of Federal Tax Liability. If you must file this form, show the total amount of payments made on the line for advance EIC payments.

Guam and U.S. Virgin Islands. Employers in Guam and the U.S. Virgin Islands should consult their local tax office for information on the earned income credit. These employers cannot take advance EIC payments into account on Form 941SS.

Form W-2. Show the total advance EIC payments made during the year on the employee's Form W-2. On the 1991 Form W-2, this amount is shown in box 8.

The amounts shown on Form W-2 for income, social security, and Medicare taxes withheld are not affected by any advance EIC payments the employee received. No other entries on Form W-2 are changed because of these payments.

Tip Reporting and Allocation Rules

Most large food or beverage establishments must make annual reports to the IRS concerning receipts from food or beverage operations and their employees' tip income. If you are subject to these reporting rules, you must provide the required information annually by filing ***Form 8027,*** *Employer's Annual Information Return of Tip Income and Allocated Tips,* with the IRS. File this form with the Internal Revenue Service Center, Andover, MA 05501 by the end of February for the preceding calendar year.

You must file a separate Form 8027 for each establishment. If you need to file more than one Form 8027, use Form 8027-T, *Transmittal of Employer's Annual Information Return of Tip Income and Allocated Tips.* If you file 250 or more Forms 8027, you must file on magnetic media. For information on magnetic media, get Publication 1239, *Requirements and Conditions for Submitting Form 8027 on Magnetic Tape.*

These rules only impose additional reporting requirements. Therefore, all the other rules for reporting employee tips and for withholding income tax and social security and Medicare taxes, discussed earlier in this publication under *Employee Tips,* continue to apply.

Reporting rules. You must file Form 8027 if you provide food or beverages for consumption on your premises, tipping is customary, and you normally employ more than 10 people on a typical business day during the preceding calendar year. If you did not operate at least one month during the preceding year, see *New businesses,* later.

Exceptions. Food or beverage operations where tipping is not customary do not file Form 8027. For example, a cafeteria or "fast food" operation would generally not be covered by the tip reporting rules because tipping is not customary at such places. Your operation is likewise not covered by the rules if you add a service charge of 10% or more to 95% or more of your food or beverage sales. Nor do these rules apply to food or beverage operations outside the United States.

If your business operates as a cafeteria for part of the day and as a full-service restaurant with tipping customary for the rest of the day, it is treated as a single operation covered by the rules if it employed more than 10 people. However, if you record gross receipts for the two operations separately, the receipts from your cafeteria-style service are not covered by the rules.

Most restaurants that provide table or counter service for seated customers and cocktail lounges with similar service are covered by the rules if they employ more than 10 people. An establishment may be part of a larger operation such as a hotel.

More than 10 employees. You are considered to have normally employed more than 10 people on a typical business day if the average number of hours worked by all employees in all your food or beverage operations on a typical business day is more than 80 hours. An individual who owns 50% or more in value of the stock of a corporation that operates a business is not considered an employee for this purpose. To figure this average:

1) Consider the month of your greatest and the month of your least gross receipts during the preceding calendar year. The month of your least gross receipts must be a month your establishment was open for business. If your establishment was not open for business during the preceding year, see *New businesses,* later.
2) Include the hours worked by all your employees at all your food or beverage operations, not just tipped employees.
3) Treat all members of a group of businesses under common control as one employer.
4) Estimate the number of hours an employee worked for a given food or beverage operation in a month if he or she worked for more than one of your food or beverage operations during the month, or worked for both your food or beverage operation and your non-food or beverage operation.

Example. You had three food or beverage operations open for business in January (the month of your greatest total gross receipts) and September (the month of your least total gross receipts). In January, operation A was open 31 days with 2,500 hours worked. Operation B was open 20 days with 1,000 hours worked. Operation C was open 24 days with 1,500 hours worked. This made a total of 75 days and 5,000 hours. The average number of days your operations were open for business in January is 25 days (75 days divided by 3 operations). The average number of employee hours worked per business day during January is 200 (5,000 hours divided by 25 days). During September, the average number of employee hours worked per business day is 60. You are considered to have normally employed more than 10 employees on a typical business day because the 2-month average is greater than 80 hours (200 + 60 = 260; 260 divided by 2 = 130 hours).

Note that if the average number of employee hours worked per business day during any month is more than 160 hours, you meet the more-than-10-employees test and your food or beverage operations are covered by the rules, regardless of what the average is during any other month.

New businesses. If your food or beverage operation is a new business, you must use a special method to figure whether you normally employ more than 10 people on a typical business day and are thus subject to the tip allocation rules.

Your food or beverage operation is a new business if you did not have any food or beverage operations during the preceding calendar year. You are not considered to have had a food or beverage operation during a calendar year if each of your food or beverage operations was operated for less than one calendar month during the year.

If your food or beverage operation is a new business, you must figure the average number of employee hours worked per business day over each of any 2 consecutive calendar months of the current calendar year. If there are any 2 consecutive calendar months in which the average number of hours worked per business day by all of your employees is more than 80 hours, your new business is considered to have more than 10 employees on a typical business day. To figure this average, follow the rules discussed for all other businesses under *More than 10 employees,* earlier.

Your new business must comply with the tip reporting rules from the first payroll period that begins after the first 2-month period in which the average employee hours worked per business day exceeds 80 hours.

What you must report. If the reporting rules apply to your food or beverage operation, you must report the following information to the IRS each calendar year for each of your separate food or beverage operations:

1) Your name, address, and employer identification number.
2) Your establishment's name, address, and number.
3) Your total gross receipts from providing food and beverages.
4) Your total charge receipts on which customers showed tips.
5) The total tips on your charge receipts.
6) The total tips your employees reported to you.
7) The total service charges of less than 10% you collected from customers and paid to employees as wages.
8) The name and social security number of each employee you allocated tips to under these reporting rules and the amount of tips you allocated to each one. This requirement will be satisfied by including an employee's tip allocation in box 7 of the employee's Form W-2.

Do not include carryout sales, state or local taxes, or sales with a service charge of 10% or more in figuring items (3) and (4), above.

The allocated amount in item (8) above is for information purposes only. ***Do not withhold any taxes from the allocated amount.*** However, you report allocated tips on Form W-2 separately from wages and reported tips.

If an employee leaves your employment before the end of the calendar year and requests an early Form W-2, you do not have to include a tip allocation on the Form W-2. However, you may show either the actual allocated amount if you know how much it is, or an estimated allocation. If you show an estimate, put the word "estimate" next to the allocated amount. In January of the next year, you must provide an amended Form W-2 to the employee if the earlier Form W-2 showed no allocation or the estimated allocation was wrong by more than 5%.

Allocation rules. You must allocate tips among your employees only if the total amount of tips they reported to you during any allocation period is less than 8% (or a lower percentage approved by the District Director) of your establishment's total food and beverage sales during that period. These sales do not include carryout sales, state or local taxes, and sales with a service charge of 10% or more. But they do include the retail value of certain complimentary food and beverages. An allocation period can be your regular payroll period, the calendar year, or some reasonable division of a year, such as a calendar month or calendar quarter.

If your employees report tips totaling less than 8% of your total sales, you must allocate the excess of 8% of total sales over reported tips either among your employees who receive tips directly from customers or among all tipped employees if your agreement with your employees provides for allocating them this way. However, do not allocate any tips to an employee who reports tips at least equal to his or her share of 8% of your total sales.

If your customers tip less than 8% on average, you or a majority of your employees may apply to have the allocation percentage reduced from 8%. However, it cannot be reduced below 2%. The application should be made in writing to the District Director for the Internal Revenue District in which your establishment is located. See Revenue Procedure 86–21 in Cumulative Bulletin 1986–1, page 560, for guidelines in applying for the allocation reduction.

Allocation methods. You can allocate tips under a formula agreed to by both you and your employees. If you cannot agree on a formula, you must allocate them according to IRS regulations. If you allocate tips according to a good-faith agreement between you and your employees or according to the regulations, you will not be liable to any employee for any amount allocated improperly.

According to the formula in the regulations, you make tip allocations only to your directly tipped employees. A directly tipped employee receives tips directly from customers, even if the tips are turned over to a tip pool. For example, waiters, waitresses, and bartenders are usually considered directly tipped employees. An employee who does not normally receive tips directly from customers is an indirectly tipped employee. Busboys, service bartenders, and cooks are examples of indirectly tipped employees. If an employee receives tips both directly and indirectly, such as through a tip-splitting or tip-pooling arrangement, the employee is treated as a directly tipped employee.

You may allocate tips under the regulations on the basis of each directly tipped employee's share of either gross receipts or total hours worked.

However, the method of allocation based on the number of hours worked may be used only if you employ less than the equivalent of 25 full-time employees at an establishment during a payroll period. For this purpose, less than the equivalent of 25 full-time employees means that the average number of employee hours worked each business day during a payroll period is less than 200 hours.

The following example illustrates the allocation method provided in the regulations using gross receipts as the basis for allocations.

Example. Smith's is a large restaurant with gross receipts of $100,000 for the allocation period ending April 30. Employees reported tips totaling $6,200 for this period. Directly tipped employees reported $5,700. Indirectly tipped employees reported $500.

Directly tipped employees	Gross receipts for payroll period	Tips reported
A	$ 18,000	$1,080
B	16,000	880
C	23,000	1,810
D	17,000	800
E	12,000	450
F	14,000	680
	$100,000	$5,700

Smith's figured its allocation as follows:

1) $100,000 (gross receipts) × 0.08 = $8,000
2) Tips reported by indirectly tipped employees = $500
3) $8,000 − $500 (indirect tips) = $7,500

4)

Directly tipped employees	Directly tipped share of 8% gross		Gross receipts ratio		Employee share of 8% gross
A	$7,500	x	18,000/100,000	=	$1,350
B	7,500	x	16,000/100,000	=	1,200
C	7,500	x	23,000/100,000	=	1,725
D	7,500	x	17,000/100,000	=	1,275
E	7,500	x	12,000/100,000	=	900
F	7,500	x	14,000/100,000	=	1,050
					$7,500

5)

Directly tipped employees	Employee share of 8% gross		Tips reported		Employee shortfall
A	$1,350	—	$1,080	=	$ 270
B	1,200	—	880	=	320
C	1,725	—	1,810	=	-0-
D	1,275	—	800	=	475
E	900	—	450	=	450
F	1,050	—	680	=	370
			Total shortfall		$1,885

Since employee C has no reporting shortfall, there is no allocation to C.

6) $8,000 — $6,200 (total tips reported) = $1,800 (amount allocable among employees with shortfall)

7)

Shortfall employees	Allocable amount		Shortfall ratio		Amount of allocation
A	$1,800	x	270/1885	=	$258
B	1,800	x	320/1885	=	306
D	1,800	x	475/1885	=	454
E	1,800	x	450/1885	=	430
F	1,800	x	370/1885	=	353

If Smith's wanted to allocate tips in the above example on the basis of hours worked, the computation would be the same except an "hours worked ratio" would be used in step (4) instead of the gross receipts ratio. The hours worked ratio for each directly tipped employee is the number of hours the employee worked in the allocation period divided by the total number of hours worked by all directly tipped employees during the allocation period.

Note: The tip allocation amount may be added to a tipped employee's gross income unless he or she is able to prove a lesser amount with adequate records. The IRS may determine that a tipped employee received more tip income than reflected in the tip allocation.

Information Returns

In your trade or business activities, you may make payments that are not wages that you must report to the IRS. ***Form 1099–MISC,*** *Miscellaneous Income,* is the information return used most often by a small business to report these payments.

File Form 1099–MISC with ***Form 1096,*** *Annual Summary and Transmittal of U.S. Information Returns,* by February 28, 1992, with IRS if you:

1) Made payments of $600 or more for ***fees, commissions,*** or other forms of payments to persons not treated as your employees for services rendered in your trade or business;
2) Gave ***prizes, awards,*** or made other payments, of $600 or more that are not for services rendered, or made direct sales of $5,000 or more of ***consumer products for resale;***
3) Made payments of $10 or more for ***royalties,*** or $600 or more for ***rents*** other than rent payments to real estate agents;
4) Withheld federal income tax on miscellaneous income under the ***backup withholding*** rules;
5) Made payments of $600 or more to physicians or other suppliers or providers of health care services in connection with ***medical assistance programs,*** or ***health, accident, and sickness insurance programs;***
6) Made payments in connection with the sale of a ***fishing*** catch, or made a distribution in-kind reported at the fair market value of the catch, to each crew member of fishing boats with normally fewer than 10 members;
7) Received payments of $10 or more as a ***broker*** on behalf of a customer, in lieu of a dividend or tax-exempt interest, as a result of the transfer of a customer's securities for use in a short sale.

Report only payments made in the course of your trade or business (including government agencies and nonprofit activities), or from which you withheld federal income tax or foreign tax. Payments include the fair market value of exchanges of property or services between individuals in the course of a trade or business.

You must furnish a statement to each recipient by January 31, 1992. A copy of Form 1099–MISC can be used for this purpose. However, if you file Form 1099–MISC to report substitute payments in lieu of dividends or tax-exempt interest, you must furnish a copy of Form 1099–MISC to the recipient.

Royalty payments. Examples of royalty payments to be reported on Form 1099–MISC include payments for the right to exploit natural resources, such as oil, gas, coal, timber, sand, gravel, and other mineral interests. Also included are payments for the right to exploit intangible property, such as copyrights, trade names, trademarks, franchises, books and other literary compositions, musical compositions, artistic works, secret processes and formulas, and patents.

Nonemployee compensation. The kinds of nonemployee compensation to be reported on Form 1099–MISC include fees, commissions, prizes, awards, or other forms of compensation for services rendered for your trade or business by an individual who is not your employee. Also include expenses incurred for the use of an entertainment facility that you treat as compensation to a nonemployee.

Examples of payments to be reported as nonemployee compensation are:

1) Fees paid to attorneys and accountants for professional services.
2) Fees paid by one professional to another, such as fee-splitting or referral fees.
3) Payments by attorneys to witnesses or experts in legal adjudication.
4) Payments by insurance companies for labor and parts to an auto repair shop under a repair contract indicating an amount for labor and another amount for parts, as long as the repair shop does not hold itself out as a parts dealer. See *Example 2,* later.
5) Commissions paid to nonemployee salespersons, subject to repayment but not repaid during the calendar year.
6) Fees paid to a nonemployee and travel reimbursement for which the nonemployee did not account to the payer, if the fees and reimbursements aggregate at least $600.
7) Payments to nonemployee entertainers for services.
8) Exchanges of services between individuals in the course of their trades or businesses.
9) Taxable fringe benefits for nonemployees. See Publication 535, *Business Expenses,* for information on the valuation of fringe benefits.
10) Oil or gas payments for a working interest.

Guidelines for reporting nonemployee compensation. If you answer "yes" to the four questions below, you must generally report a payment as nonemployee compensation on Form 1099–MISC:

1) Did you make the payment to a nonemployee?
2) Did you make the payment for services rendered in your trade or business, including government agencies and nonprofit organizations?
3) Did you make the payment to a payee who is not a corporation? If the payment was made to a corporation, see *Payments to corporations,* below.
4) Did the payments total $600 or more during the year? Total payments include payments for parts or materials used by the payee in rendering the services.

Payments to corporations. Payments to corporations are not reported on Form 1099–MISC except for medical payments and substitute payments in lieu of dividends and tax exempt interest.

Treat a payee as a corporation if the payee's name ends with the corporate status, such as *Incorporated, Inc., Corporation,* or *Corp.* Do not treat a payee as a corporation if the payee's name ends with *Company* or *Co.* or without any business status.

Payments exempt from these requirements. Payments that do not require a Form 1099–MISC include the following:

1) Payments for merchandise and inventory, including freight, storage, and similar charges;
2) Payments for utilities, such as electricity, gas, oil, and water;
3) Payments for telephone, telegraph, and similar services;
4) Payments of rent to real estate agents;

5) Payments to employees (including federal, state, and local government employees) for traveling and other business expenses;
6) Payments to corporations except for those payments listed above; and
7) Payments to informers for information about criminal activities, but only if these payments are made by federal, state, or local agencies, or by nonprofit organizations described in section 501(c)(3) of the Internal Revenue Code.

Examples. The following examples illustrate the filing of information returns for miscellaneous payments:

Example 1. Mrs. Taylor, an attorney, obtains the assistance of Mr. Johnson, another attorney, in serving a client. In return for the assistance, Mrs. Taylor agrees to split the fee received from the client with Mr. Johnson. Mrs. Taylor pays a $900 fee to Mr. Johnson. Mrs. Taylor must report $900 to IRS on Form 1099–MISC and furnish a statement to Mr. Johnson (a copy of Form 1099–MISC may be used for this purpose).

Example 2. An insurance company pays $1,000 to an unincorporated auto repair shop for a repair. The repair contract states that $300 is for labor and $700 is for parts. The insurance company must report the entire $1,000 on Form 1099–MISC. In this situation, the obligation to furnish parts is incidental to the obligation to repair the car.

Example 3. Mrs. Green, a contestant on a television quiz show, wins a fur coat. The producer of the show must report the fair market value of the coat. Since the fair market value is not easy to determine, the producer can report the manufacturer's suggested retail selling price of $5,000 on Form 1099–MISC.

Example 4. Mr. Black, a real estate agent, collected $1,000 in rental payments from the tenants of a building. He deducted his commission of $100 and paid $900 to the building owner. He must report the gross amount of $1,000 on Form 1099–MISC even though he deducted his commission of $100 from the $1,000 and paid the owner $900.

Example 5. Mr. Jones, owner of an unincorporated home repair business, is paid $1,000 for repair work on a church. Even though the church is exempt from federal income tax, the church must report the $1,000 on Form 1099–MISC.

Example 6. An attorney and a painter agree to an ***exchange of services*** whereby the attorney represents the painter for non-payment of business debts in return for painting the attorney's law offices. The fair market value of the services performed by each is $1,000. The attorney and the painter are not incorporated, and the agreement is not made through a barter exchange. The attorney must report $1,000 on Form 1099–MISC, and the painter must also report $1,000 on Form 1099–MISC. In this situation, the attorney's payment in services to the painter (representing the painter for non-payment of business debts) is for a business expense of the attorney (painting law offices). The painter's payment in services to the attorney (painting the law offices) is for a business expense of the painter (representation for non-payment of business debts). Each is making a payment for expenses incurred in the course of a trade or business.

Note. In the above example, if the attorney represented the painter in a divorce proceeding, the painter would not have to report $1,000 because the painter's services for the attorney would be payment for a personal rather than business expense of the painter. This is true even though the painter's services are of the kind normally performed in the course of his business. However, the attorney would still report $1,000 on Form 1099–MISC, because the attorney's services to the painter are a payment for an expense incurred in the course of the attorney's business.

Example 7. Mr. Jones is in the business of renting houses. He pays Mr. Smith, who operates a painting business as a sole proprietor, $1,750 to paint one of his rental houses. Mr. Jones must report the $1,750 on Form 1099–MISC.

Other information returns. Other information returns that you may be required to file are listed below:

Form 1098 for mortgage interest (including certain points) of $600 or more that you received in the course of your trade or business from individuals.

Form 1099–A for lenders to report acquisitions or abandonment of property that secures a loan.

Form 1099–B for: (a) brokers to report the gross proceeds from the sale of stocks, bonds, commodities, regulated futures or forward contracts, debt instruments, etc.; or (b) barter exchanges to report the exchange of property or services.

Form 1099–DIV for: (a) payments of $10 or more in gross dividends and other distributions on stock; (b) withheld foreign tax eligible for the recipient's foreign tax credit on dividends and other distributions on stock; or (c) distributions of $600 or more in liquidation.

Form 1099–G for certain payments made by a unit of a Federal, State, or local government, such as unemployment compensation and state and local income tax refunds.

Form 1099–INT for: (a) interest of $10 or more paid or credited on earnings from savings and loan associations, credit unions, bank deposits, corporate bonds, etc.; (b) interest of $600 or more from sources other than those listed in (a) if paid in the course of your trade or business; (c) forfeited interest due to premature withdrawals of time deposits; (d) withheld foreign tax eligible for the recipient's foreign tax credit on interest; or (e) payments of any interest on bearer certificates of deposit.

Form 1099–OID for original issue discount of $10 or more on obligations including bonds or other evidences of indebtedness, time and savings deposits, and certificates of deposit made, purchased, or renewed after 1970 if the term of the obligation or deposit arrangement is more than one year.

Form 1099–PATR for patronage dividends or other distributions of $10 or more by cooperatives.

Form 1099–R for distributions from retirement or profit-sharing plans, IRAs, SEPs, or insurance contracts. (Form W–2P was merged into Form 1099–R.)

Form 1099–S for most real estate transactions.

Form W–2G for certain gambling winnings.

Form 4789 for cash payments or transfers by, through, or to a financial institution of $10,000 or more.

Form 5498 for contributions to an individual retirement arrangement (IRA) and the value of an IRA or simplified employee pension (SEP).

Form 8300 for cash payments of over $10,000 received in the course of your trade or business.

Form 8308 for the sale or exchange of a partnership interest involving unrealized receivables or substantially appreciated inventory items.

See the *Guide to Information Returns for 1991* at the back of this publication. For more information, get a booklet titled: *1991 Instructions for Forms 1099, 1098, 5498, and W-2G.*

For more information on the requirements for withholding taxes on payments made to nonresident aliens, and the requirements for exemption from tax withholding, see Publication 515, *Withholding of Tax on Nonresident Aliens and Foreign Corporations.*

For more information on the requirements for reporting cash payments received in a trade or business, see Publication 1544, *Reporting Cash Payments of Over $10,000.*

Backup Withholding

In certain cases, you may be required to withhold income tax at 20% (backup withholding) on payments of interest, dividends, patronage dividends, rents, royalties, commissions, nonemployee compensation, and certain other payments you make in the course of your trade or business. In addition, transactions by brokers and barter exchanges and certain payments made by fishing boat operators are subject to backup withholding. Real estate transactions, however, are not subject to backup withholding.

You must withhold 20% of the payment if the payment is a reportable interest, dividend, or other payment and:

1) The payee does not furnish a taxpayer identification number (TIN) to you;
2) IRS notifies you to impose backup withholding because the payee furnished an incorrect TIN;
3) You are notified by IRS that the payee is subject to backup withholding on interest or dividends;
4) For interest and dividend accounts opened (or instruments acquired) after 1983, the payee does not certify to you, under penalties of perjury, that he or she is not subject to backup withholding under item (3) above; or
5) For interest, dividend, broker, or barter exchange accounts opened (or instruments acquired) after 1983, or broker accounts considered inactive in 1983, the payee does not certify to you, under penalties of perjury, that the TIN furnished is correct.

Form W–9. You can use Form W–9, *Request for Taxpayer Identification Number and Certification,* to request payees to furnish a taxpayer identification number and to certify that the number furnished is correct.

You can also use Form W–9 to obtain certifications from payees that they are not subject to backup withholding or that they are exempt from backup withholding. Form W–9 includes a list of payees who are exempt from backup withholding.

Form W–8. Form W–8, *Certificate of Foreign Status,* is used by nonresident aliens and foreign entities to certify that they are not subject to United States information return reporting or backup withholding rules on payments of interest broker transactions, or barter exchange transactions. Payers of interest, brokers, and barter exchanges should send Form W–8 to nonresident alien individuals and foreign corporations, partnerships, estates, and trusts to get this certification.

Length of backup withholding period. Generally, the period for which the 20% backup withholding should be withheld is as follows:

1) Taxpayer identification number (TIN) not furnished. Withhold on payments made until the TIN is furnished unless the payee is waiting for a TIN. The payee may certify on Form W-9 that he or she is waiting for a TIN by writing "Applied for" in the space for a TIN and signing the form. If the TIN is not received within 60 days, begin withholding and continue until a TIN is furnished.

During this 60-day period, you must backup withhold either on:

- Any withdrawals of reportable interest and dividends made after the 7th business day after you receive the awaiting-TIN certificate, or
- Any payments of reportable interest and dividends made during the 60-day period (whether or not a withdrawal is made). Under this method, you must (1) begin backup withholding no later than the 7th business day after you receive the awaiting-TIN certificate, and (2) refund the amounts withheld if the TIN is received during the 60-day period.

2) No certification by payee that the TIN is correct. Withhold on reportable interest and dividends until you receive the certification. If the payee does not have a TIN, see (1) above.

3) No certification by payee that he or she is not subject to backup withholding. Withhold on reportable interest and dividends until the certification is provided.

4) Notice from IRS that payee is subject to backup withholding. Start withholding on payments made after the 30th day from the date you receive notification from IRS. Stop withholding when you receive a written IRS notice to stop from IRS or from the payee. You must notify the payee when withholding under this procedure starts. In most cases, withholding will stop on January 1 of the year following the year of the notice.

5) Notice from IRS that payee furnished an incorrect TIN. Start withholding on payments made more than 30 business days after the date you receive notification from IRS. (You may elect to withhold on payments made at any time after receiving the notification from IRS.) Stop withholding within 30 calendar days after a certified TIN is furnished.

Incorrect TIN. A TIN will be considered incorrect if:

- The TIN does not match any number on IRS or Social Security Administration (SSA) records, or
- The TIN matches a number on an IRS or SSA record, but the name associated with the TIN does not match the name on the information return.

If you receive an IRS notice of an incorrect TIN for a prior year's return, you must send a copy of the notice and a Form W–9 to the payee and notify the payee of the following:

- The IRS has determined that the TIN furnished by the payee is incorrect, and
- The payee is subject to income tax withholding at 20% on each reportable payment.

Start withholding on payments you make after the 30th day from the date you receive notification from IRS. Stop withholding when you receive a certified TIN or certified TIN and name combination. If the payee gives you another certified TIN, use that TIN on information returns you are required to file.

Reporting. Report amounts withheld under backup withholding on Form 941, *Employer's Quarterly Federal Tax Return* (or Form 941E, *Quarterly Return of Withheld Federal Income Tax and Medicare Tax*). If you file Form 943, *Employer's Annual Tax Return for Agricultural Employees,* you must also report backup withholding on Form 941 (or Form 941E). You can combine these amounts with your employment taxes for deposit purposes. If you choose to treat them separately, you can show the backup withholding amounts on Schedule A (Form 941), *Record of Federal Backup Withholding Tax Liability.* At the end of the year, report these amounts on forms in the 1099 series.

Recordkeeping

As an employer, you must keep all your records on employment taxes (income tax withholding, social security taxes, Medicare taxes, federal unemployment tax, and advance earned income credit (EIC) payments) for a minimum of 4 years after the due date of the tax for the return period to which the records relate or the date the tax is paid, whichever is later. In addition to the following items required for each specific type of employment tax, your records should also contain your employer identification number, copies of the returns you have filed, and the dates and amounts of deposits you have made.

Income tax withholding. The specific records you must keep for income tax withholding are:

1) Each employee's name, address, and social security number;
2) The total amount and date of each wage payment and the period of time the payment covers;
3) The amount subject to withholding for each wage payment;
4) The amount of withholding tax collected on each payment and the date it was collected;
5) The reason why the taxable amount is less than the total payment if they differ;
6) Copies of any statements furnished by employees relating to nonresident alien status, residence in Puerto Rico or the Virgin Islands, or residence or physical presence in a foreign country;
7) The fair market value and date of each payment of noncash compensation made to a retail commission salesperson, if no income tax was withheld;
8) Information about the amount of each payment for wage continuation plans;
9) The withholding allowance certificates (Form W–4) filed by each employee;
10) Any agreement between you and the employee on Form W–4 for the voluntary withholding of additional amounts of tax;
11) The dates in each calendar quarter on which the employee worked for you, but ***not*** in the course of your trade or business, and the amount paid for that nonbusiness work;
12) Copies of statements furnished by employees reporting tips received in their work, unless the information shown on the statements appears in another item on this list; and
13) Requests by employees to have the tax withheld figured on the basis of their individual cumulative wages.

An employee's earnings ledger, which you can buy at most office supply stores, normally has space for the information required in items (1) through (4).

Social security and Medicare taxes. You must also maintain the following information in your records on the social security and Medicare taxes of your employees:

1) The amount of each wage payment subject to social security tax;
2) The amount of each wage payment subject to Medicare tax;
3) The amount of social security and Medicare taxes collected for each payment and the date collected; and
4) The reason why the total wage payment is more than the taxable amount if they differ.

Federal unemployment tax. For federal unemployment tax purposes, your records must include:

1) The total amount paid to your employees during the calendar year;
2) The amount of compensation subject to the unemployment tax, and why it differs from the total compensation if they differ;
3) The amount you paid into the state unemployment fund; and
4) Any other information required to be shown on the unemployment tax return, and the amount of the tax.

Earned income credit (EIC). The following records must be kept for advance EIC payments:

1) Copies of employees' Forms W–5;
2) Amounts and dates of all wage payments and advance EIC payments; and
3) Dates of each employee's employment.

Magnetic media reports. Copy A of Form W–2 may be filed on magnetic media with the Social Security Administration. Employers and other payers who are required to file 250 or more Forms W–2 for 1991 must use magnetic media. The 250 requirement applies separately to each type of form. All filers must obtain approval of their magnetic medium before filing Forms W–2 on magnetic media by submitting an SSA authorization request. The request forms are in Technical Information Bulletin 4 (TIB-4), discussed below. If you are unable to comply with the magnetic media requirements, you may request a waiver for up to one year on ***Form 8508,*** *Request for Waiver From Filing Information Returns on Magnetic Media.*

The reporting specifications and procedures for magnetic media filing of Copy A of Forms W–2 are in TIB-4, *Magnetic Media Reporting, Submitting Annual W–2 Copy A Information to the Social Security Administration.* Specifications for tape and diskette reporting for Forms W–2 are included in TIB-4. You can obtain a copy of this bulletin by writing to the Social Security Administration, P.O. Box 2317, Baltimore, Maryland 21203, Attn: Reports Preparation Section.

Guide to Information Returns for 1991

FORM NUMBER	TITLE	WHAT TO REPORT	AMOUNTS TO REPORT	DUE DATE IN 1992	
				TO IRS	TO RECIPIENT (unless indicated otherwise)
1042S	Foreign Person's U.S. Source Income Subject to Withholding	Payments subject to withholding under Chapter 3 of the Côde, including interest, dividends, royalties, pensions and annuities, gambling winnings, and compensation for personal services.	All amounts	March 15	March 15
1098	Mortgage Interest Statement	Mortgage interest (including certain points) you received in the course of your trade or business from individuals.	$600 or more	February 28	(To Payer/Borrower) January 31

Guide to Information Returns for 1991 *(Continued)*

FORM NUMBER	TITLE	WHAT TO REPORT	AMOUNTS TO REPORT	DUE DATE IN 1992: TO IRS	DUE DATE IN 1992: TO RECIPIENT (unless indicated otherwise)
1099-A	Acquisition or Abandonment of Secured Property	Information about the acquisition or abandonment of property that is security for a debt for which you are the lender.	All amounts	February 28	(To Borrower) January 31
1099-B	Proceeds From Broker and Barter Exchange Transactions	Sales or redemptions of securities, futures transactions, commodities, and barter exchange transactions.	All amounts	February 28	January 31
1099-DIV	Dividends and Distributions	Distributions, such as dividends, capital gains, or nontaxable distributions, that were paid on stock, and distributions in liquidation.	$10 or more, except $600 or more for liquidations	February 28	January 31
1099-G	Certain Government Payments	Unemployment compensation, state and local income tax refunds, agricultural payments, taxable grants, and discharge of indebtedness.	$10 or more for unemployment and tax refunds; $600 or more for all others	February 28	January 31
1099-INT	Interest Income	Interest payments not including interest on an IRA.	$10 or more ($600 or more in some cases)	February 28	January 31
1099-MISC	Miscellaneous Income	Rent or royalty payments; prizes and awards that are not for services, such as winnings on TV or radio shows.	$600 or more, except $10 or more for royalties	February 28	January 31
	(Also, use this form to report the occurrence of direct sales of $5,000 or more of consumer goods for resale.)	Payments to crew members by owners or operators of fishing boats. Report payments of proceeds from sale of catch.	All payments		
		Payments to a physician, physicians' corporation, or other supplier of health and medical services. Issued mainly by medical assistance programs or health and accident insurance plans.	$600 or more		
		Payments for services performed for a trade or business by people not treated as its employees. Examples: fees to subcontractors or directors, expenses incurred for use of an entertainment facility treated as compensation to a nonemployee, and golden parachute payments.	$600 or more		
		Substitute dividend and tax-exempt interest payments reportable by brokers.	$10 or more		
		Crop insurance proceeds.	$600 or more		
1099-OID	Original Issue Discount	Original issue discount.	$10 or more	February 28	January 31
1099-PATR	Taxable Distributions Received From Cooperatives	Distributions from cooperatives to their patrons.	$10 or more	February 28	January 31
1099-R	Distributions From Pensions, Annuities, Retirement or Profit-Sharing Plans, IRAs, Insurance Contracts, etc.	Distributions from retirement or profit-sharing plans, IRAs, SEPs, or insurance contracts.	All amounts	February 28	January 31
1099-S	Proceeds From Real Estate Transactions	Gross proceeds from the sale or exchange of real estate.	All amounts	February 28	January 31
4789	Currency Transaction Report	Each deposit, withdrawal, exchange of currency, or other payment or transfer, by, through, or to a financial institution (other than casinos) that involves a transaction in cash.	Over $10,000	Within 15 days after the date of the transaction	Not required
5498	Individual Retirement Arrangement Information	Contributions (including rollover contributions) to an individual retirement arrangement (IRA), and the value of an IRA or simplified employee pension (SEP) account.	All amounts	June 1	(To Participant) January 31 (for value of account) June 1 (for contributions)
8027	Employer's Annual Information Return of Tip Income and Allocated Tips	Receipts from food or beverage operations, tips reported by employees, and allocated tips	See separate instructions	March 2	Allocated tips are shown on Form W–2, due January 31
8300	Report of Cash Payments Over $10,000 Received in a Trade or Business	Payments in cash or foreign currency received in one transaction, or two or more related transactions, in the course of a trade or business. (This does not apply to financial institutions filing **Form 4789,** above, casinos that are required to report such transactions on **Form 8362,** or, generally, to transactions outside the United States.	Over $10,000	Within 15 days after the date of the transaction	(To Payer) January 31
8308	Report of a Sale or Exchange of Certain Partnership Interests	Sales or exchanges of a partnership interest involving unrealized receivables or substantially appreciated inventory items.	(Transaction only)	(Attach to Form 1065)	(To Transferor and Transferee) January 31
W-2G	Certain Gambling Winnings	Gambling winnings from horse racing, dog racing, jai alai, lotteries, raffles, drawings, bingo, slot machines, and keno.	Generally, $600 or more ($1,200 or more from bingo or slot machines; $1,500 or more from keno)	February 28	January 31
				TO SSA	TO RECIPIENT
W-2	Wage and Tax Statement	Wages, tips, other compensation, withheld income and social security and Medicare taxes, and advance earned income credit (EIC) payments. Include bonuses, vacation allowances, severance pay, moving expense payments, some kinds of travel allowances, and third-party payments of sick pay.	See separate Instructions	March 2	January 31

Note. If a due date falls on a Saturday, Sunday, or legal holiday, this chart shows the next day that is not a Saturday, Sunday, or legal holiday. A statewide legal holiday delays a due date only if the IRS office where you are required to file is located in that state.

4. Publication 583—Taxpayers Starting a Business

Department of the Treasury
Internal Revenue Service
Catalog Number 15150B

Publication 583
(Rev. Dec. 1990)

Taxpayers Starting a Business

Note: This publication has not been updated, but you can still use it to answer your questions. If there are any significant changes affecting the contents, they are explained in an addendum included with the publication. If you do not find all of your answers in this publication, please call the toll-free number for tax help shown in your phone directory under U.S. Government, Internal Revenue Service. If there is no number listed, call 1-800-829-1040.

The toll-free phone number for requesting free IRS forms and publications has changed. The new number is 1-800-TAX-FORM (1-800-829-3676).

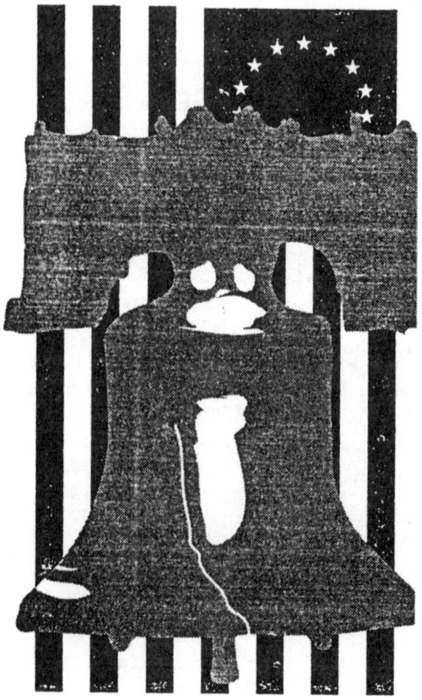

Contents

Introduction

This publication discusses some topics of interest to an individual starting a small business. It covers the following topics:

- The identification numbers used by businesses.
- The kinds of federal taxes businesses may have to pay.
- The kinds of information returns businesses may have to prepare.
- The kinds of records a small business may find helpful to keep.

The publication looks at some of the decisions you must make when setting up a recordkeeping system, and the types of books and records included in a typical system for a small business. Sample records and filled-in forms are illustrated at the end of the publication.

Penalties. To ensure that all taxpayers pay their fair share of taxes, the law provides penalties for failure to file returns or pay taxes as required. Some other penalties that may be charged include those pointed out later under *Business Taxes* and *Information Returns.* Some penalties may not be charged if noncompliance was due to reasonable cause.

Criminal penalties may be imposed for willful failure to file, tax evasion, or making a false statement.

Free publications and forms. If you need information on a subject not covered in this publication, you may check our other free publications. For a subject matter index to IRS publications and information about other free tax services, get Publication 910, *Guide to Free Tax Services.*

To order publications and forms, call our toll-free telephone number 1-800-829-FORM (3676) or write the IRS Forms Distribution Center for your area as shown in the income tax package.

Identification Numbers

You must have a taxpayer identification number so that the Internal Revenue Service can process your return. There are two kinds of taxpayer identification numbers—a social security number and an employer identification number.

Employer Number

If you are a sole proprietor, you don't need an employer identification number (EIN) unless you have a Keogh plan or are required to file an employment, excise, fiduciary, or alcohol, tobacco, and firearms tax return. Otherwise, use your social security number. You are a sole proprietor if you are self-employed (work for yourself) and are the only owner of your unincorporated business.

How To Get an EIN

To get an EIN, file Form SS–4, *Application for Employer Identification Number,* with the Internal Revenue Service Center for your area listed in the instructions to Form SS–4. You can get Form SS–4 at Internal Revenue Service or Social Security Administration offices.

When to apply. You should file Form SS–4 early enough so that you will have a number by the time you need to file a return or statement or to make a tax deposit. It takes about four weeks for Form SS–4 to be processed.

If you do not receive your EIN by the time a return is due, file your return anyway and write "Applied for" and the date you applied in the space for the EIN. If a tax deposit (discussed under *Business Taxes)* is due before you receive your number, send your payment to the Internal Revenue Service Center where you file your returns. Make your check or money order payable to the Internal Revenue Service and write in your name (as it appears on the Form SS–4 you completed), your address, the kind of tax you are paying, the period covered, and the date you filed Form SS–4.

How To Use an EIN

You must include your taxpayer identification number (SSN or EIN) on all your returns or other documents sent to the Internal Revenue Service. You are also required to furnish your number to other persons who must use your identification number on any returns or documents they send to the Internal Revenue Service. This includes returns or documents they file to report:

1) Interest, dividends, royalties, etc., paid to you,
2) Amounts paid to you (in the course of your business) that total $600 or more for the year,
3) Any amount paid to you as a dependent care provider, and
4) Any amount paid to you as alimony.

If you fail to furnish your identification number as required, you will be subject to penalties.

More than one EIN. If you have more than one EIN and are not sure which to use, please contact the Internal Revenue Service Center where you file your return. Tell them the numbers you have, the name and address you used on each application, and the address of your main place of business. They will tell you which number to use.

When To Get a New EIN

You may need to get a new EIN if either the organization or the ownership of your business changes.

Change in organization. A new EIN is required when any of the following changes occur:

1) A sole proprietorship incorporates,
2) A sole proprietorship takes in partners and operates as a partnership,
3) A partnership incorporates,
4) A partnership is taken over by one of the partners and is operated as a sole proprietorship, or

5) A corporation changes to a partnership or to a sole proprietorship.

If a corporation chooses to be taxed as an S corporation, it does not need a new EIN.

Change in ownership. A new EIN is required when any of the following changes occur:

1) You purchase or inherit an existing business that you will operate as a sole proprietorship (You cannot use the EIN of the former owner, even if he or she is your spouse.),
2) You represent an estate that operates a business after the owner's death, or
3) You terminate an old partnership and begin a new one.

Employee and Other Payee Numbers

In the operation of a business, you normally will make certain payments that you have to report on information returns, discussed later. Also, you must give the recipient of these payments (the payee) a statement showing the total amount paid during the year. The forms used to report these payments must include the payee's identification number as well as your own identification number.

Employee. If you are an employer, you must get a social security number (SSN) from each of your employees. When you hire an employee, you should give him or her a Form W-4, *Employee's Withholding Allowance Certificate.* The employee must complete the form and return it to you so that you will have his or her SSN and the information you need to figure the amount of income tax to withhold from the employee's salary. You will use the SSN of each employee when you make the required report of his or her wages and the amount of withheld social security and income taxes. Using the SSN will ensure that each employee's account is properly credited.

If your employee does not have an SSN, he or she should file Form SS-5, *Application for a Social Security Card,* with the Social Security Administration. Forms are available at Social Security Administration offices.

Other payee. If you make payments to a nonemployee that must be reported on an information return, get a social security number (SSN) from each individual (including sole proprietors) to whom you make payments. If you make payments to an organization such as a corporation or partnership, you must get the employer identification number (EIN) of the organization.

To get the payee's SSN or EIN, use Form W-9, *Request for Taxpayer Identification Number and Certification.* This form is available from Internal Revenue Service offices. A payee who does not provide you with an identification number may be subject to a 20% backup withholding. For information on backup withholding, see Form W-9 and the 1990 *Instructions for Forms 1099, 1098, 5498, 1096, and W-2G.*

Business Taxes

The type of business you operate determines what taxes you must pay and how you pay them. There are four general kinds of business taxes:

1) Income tax,
2) Self-employment tax,
3) Employment taxes, and
4) Excise taxes.

Publication 509, *Tax Calendars for 1990,* contains a general tax calendar, an employer's tax calendar, and an excise tax calendar which explain when to file returns and make tax payments.

Income Tax

Every business must file an annual income tax return. Which form you use depends on how your business is organized.

Organization:	File:
Sole proprietorship	Schedule C (Form 1040)
Farming	Schedule F (Form 1040)
Partnership	Form 1065
Corporation	Form 1120 or 1120–A
S corporation	Form 1120S

If you are a sole proprietor or farmer and have more than one business, file a separate Schedule C or Schedule F for each business.

How to pay. Federal income and self-employment taxes are pay-as-you-go taxes.

Individuals. Income from your business is not subject to withholding. Generally, you will pay the tax during the year as you earn your income. Sole proprietors, partners, or shareholders of an S corporation pay as they go by making regular payments of estimated tax during the year. If your estimated income tax and self-employment tax are $500 or more for 1989, you generally have to make estimated tax payments. For information on estimated tax, see Publication 505, *Tax Withholding and Estimated Tax.*

Corporations. Corporations pay as they go by making periodic deposits of their estimated income tax. See *Depositing Taxes,* later, for information on how to make tax deposits.

Self-Employment Tax

Self-employment tax is the social security tax for individuals who work for themselves, such as sole proprietors, self-employed farmers, and members of a partnership. This tax is figured and reported on Schedule SE (Form 1040), which is attached to and filed with Form 1040.

For more information, get Publication 533, *Self-Employment Tax.*

Employment Taxes

If you have employees, you will probably be required to pay employment taxes. These taxes include:

1) Federal income tax withholding,
2) Social security tax, and
3) Federal unemployment (FUTA) tax.

Federal Income and Social Security Taxes

You withhold federal income tax from your employee's wages. For social security tax, you withhold part from your employee's wages and you pay a matching amount yourself.

Tax returns. Social security taxes and withheld income tax are reported and paid together. Farm employers report these taxes on Form 943, *Employer's Annual Tax Return for Agricultural Employees.* Other employers use Form 941, *Employer's Quarterly Federal Tax Return.*

Federal Unemployment (FUTA) Tax

Federal unemployment tax is reported and paid separately from social security taxes and withheld income tax. You pay FUTA tax only from your own funds. Employees do not pay this tax or have it withheld from their pay.

Tax return. Form 940, *Employer's Annual Federal Unemployment (FUTA) Tax Return,* is used to report federal unemployment tax.

Simplified form. Form 940EZ is a simplified version of Form 940. You can use Form 940EZ if:

1) You pay employment taxes to only one state,
2) You pay all state employment tax by the due date for filing Form 940EZ, and
3) The wages you pay that are taxable for FUTA are also taxable for state unemployment tax.

How to Pay

You generally have to pay employment taxes before you file an employment tax return. This is done through a system of tax deposits. See *Depositing Taxes,* later, for information on how deposits are made.

For more information on employment taxes and reporting and deposit requirements, get Publication 15, *Circular E, Employer's Tax Guide,* and Publication 937, *Business Reporting.* Publication 15 also contains the withholding tax tables to use to figure the amount of social security taxes and federal income tax to withhold.

Excise Taxes

If you are in the business of manufacturing or selling certain products, you may have to pay excise taxes. There are also excise taxes on certain kinds of businesses, on certain transactions, and on the use of various kinds of equipment, facilities, and products.

Form 720. The federal excise taxes reported on Form 720, *Quarterly Federal Excise Tax Return,* consist of several broad categories, such as:

1) Environmental taxes imposed on crude oil received at a United States refinery, on imported petroleum products, and on certain chemicals sold by producers, manufacturers, or importers.
2) Facilities and services taxes, including taxes on amounts paid for telephone communications and air transportation.
3) Fuel taxes, including taxes on the sale or use of gasoline, gasohol, diesel fuel, and special motor fuels.
4) Manufacturers taxes on the sale or use of a variety of different products.
5) Retail taxes on the first retail sale of heavy trucks and trailers.
6) Other excise taxes, including taxes on policies issued by foreign insurers and obligations not in registered form.

Form 720 generally must be filed within one month after the end of a calendar quarter.

You may have to make deposits of the excise taxes reported on Form 720 before the return is due. See *Depositing Taxes,* later, for information on making deposits. For more information on the excise taxes you report on Form 720, get Publication 510, *Excise Taxes for 1990.*

Form 2290. There is a federal tax for the use of highways on certain trucks, truck tractors, and buses. This tax is reported on Form 2290, *Heavy Vehicle Use Tax Return.* For more information, get Publication 349, *Federal Highway Use Tax on Heavy Vehicles.* The tax applies to trucks and buses operated on U.S. highways, whether registered in the United States, Canada, or Mexico.

ATF Form 5630.5. If you produce, sell, or import guns or tobacco or alcohol products, or if you manufacture equipment for their production, you may be liable for one or more excise taxes. Many of these taxes are reported on ATF Form 5630.5, *Special Tax Registration and Return.* This form is filed with the Bureau of Alcohol, Tobacco and Firearms, and may be ordered by calling the ATF Distribution Center at (703) 455-7801 or writing the ATF Distribution Center, 7943 Angus Court, Springfield, VA 22153.

Form 730. If you are in the business of accepting bets or running a betting pool or lottery, you may be liable for federal excise taxes on wagering. Form 730, *Tax on Wagering,* is used to report a tax on the bets you receive. For more information, see the Form 730 instructions.

Form 11–C. Form 11–C, *Special Tax Return and Application for Registry—Wagering,* is used to pay an annual tax and to register your place of business. For more information, get the Form 11–C instructions.

Depositing Taxes

In some cases, you may have to deposit the tax you owe before you file your return. A return can cover more than one deposit period.

Mail or deliver deposits with completed *deposit coupons* to an authorized financial institution or a Federal Reserve bank or branch for your area. To help ensure proper crediting of your account, include your EIN, the type of tax, and the tax period to which the payment applies on your check or money order.

To be on time, deposits that are mailed generally must arrive at the depository by the due date. You may be charged a penalty for not making deposits when due, unless you have reasonable cause.

The following types of tax, reported on the forms listed below, are paid by deposit.

Type of Tax	Reported on
Corporate income tax	Form 1120
Social security taxes and withheld income tax (non-agricultural)	Form 941
Social security taxes and withheld income tax (agricultural)	Form 943
Federal unemployment (FUTA) tax	Form 940
Excise tax	Form 720

Deposit coupons. Form 8109, *Federal Tax Deposit Coupon Book,* contains coupons for depositing all types of taxes. On each coupon you must show the deposit amount, the type of tax, the period for which you are making a deposit, and your telephone number. Use a separate coupon for each tax and period. A coupon must be included with each deposit you make.

When you apply for an employer identification number (EIN), as discussed earlier, the tax deposit coupon book will be sent to you. If you need more coupons, you can order them from your Internal Revenue Service Center, using Form 8109A, *FTD Reorder Form,* which is included in the coupon book. On the reorder form, enter the number of coupon books you will need for a one-year period and mail it in the return envelope provided with the coupon book. In the event you have a deposit due and there is not enough time to obtain a coupon book, blank coupons (Form 8109–B) are available at most Internal Revenue Service offices. You cannot use photocopies of the coupons to make your deposits.

If you have not received your EIN and must make a deposit, mail your payment with an explanation to the Internal Revenue Service Center where you file your return. Make your check or money order payable to Internal Revenue Service. On the check show your name (as shown on Form SS–4), address, kind of tax, period covered, and date you applied for an EIN.

For more information. Get Publication 509, Publication 937, and Publication 15 for more information on when deposits and business tax returns are due.

Information Returns

In the course of your business activities, you may make or receive payments that you must report to the Internal Revenue Service.

You must report on information returns various kinds of payments made to, or certain payments received from, persons who are not your employees. The principal purpose of information returns is to match the payments with each person's income tax returns to see whether the payments were included in income. You must give each of these persons a statement showing the total amount paid to, or received from, that person during the year.

Form 1099–MISC. Form 1099–MISC, *Statement for Recipients of Miscellaneous Income,* must be filed to report certain payments you make in the course of your trade or business. These include payments of $10 or more for royalties, and payments of $600 or more for rents, prizes and awards that were not for services rendered, and payments to persons who were not your employees (such as an independent contractor).

Form 8300. Form 8300, *Report of Cash Payments Over $10,000 Received in a Trade or Business,* which you must file if, in the course of your trade or business, you receive more than $10,000 in cash or foreign currency in one or more related transactions.

Other returns. In addition to the above Forms 1099–MISC and 8300, other returns are used to report certain kinds of payments or transactions. For information on other returns, and on the general requirements for filing information returns get Publication 937, *Business Reporting.*

Penalties

Caution: As this publication was being prepared for print, Congress was considering legislation that would change many of the penalty provisions mentioned below. For additional information on any late legislative changes, get Publication 553, *Highlights of 1989 Tax Changes.*

If you do not follow the requirements for filing, completing, and furnishing information returns, the following penalties may be charged for each failure.

1) $50 penalty if you do not file an information return with the Internal Revenue Service on time.
2) $50 penalty if you do not furnish a copy of an information return to a payee or payer on time.
3) $50 penalty if you do not include a payee's or a payer's taxpayer identification number on an information return.
4) $5 penalty if you do not include your own taxpayer identification number on an information return filed with the Internal Revenue Service.
5) $5 penalty if you do not include all of the information required to be shown, or include incorrect information, on a return filed with the Internal Revenue Service or a statement furnished to a payee or payer.

The maximum penalty for (1), (2), (3), and (4) is $100,000 a year for each of these penalties except for returns reporting interest or dividend income. The maximum penalty for (5) is $20,000 a year except for returns reporting interest or dividend income. For more information on penalties, see Publication 937.

Waiver of penalty. Except in the case of interest and dividend payments, to which special rules apply, the penalties discussed here will not be imposed if you can show that the failures were due to reasonable cause and not willful neglect.

Recordkeeping

Everyone in business must keep records. Your records should help you prepare accurate tax returns so that you pay only the amount of tax you owe.

Good records are needed for good management. The following list shows what good records can do for you.

1) **Identify source of receipts.** The money or property you receive can come from many sources. Your records can identify the source of your receipts. You need this information to separate business receipts from nonbusiness receipts and taxable income from nontaxable income.
2) **Keep track of deductible expenses.** Expenses may be forgotten when you prepare your tax return unless you record them when they occur.
3) **Figure depreciation allowance.** You should record the assets you can depreciate in a permanent record. Without a record of the cost and other information on your assets, you cannot figure your depreciation deductions. If the assets are sold or become fully depreciated, or if capital improvements are made to them, only a permanent record will show how much of their cost you have not recovered.
4) **Record details of assets.** If your records are good and complete, they will show the date an asset was acquired, the percentage of its business use, and any changes in the basis of each asset. This information is required to figure (and to know how to report) the amount of your gain or loss from the disposition of the asset if you later sell, trade, or otherwise dispose of it or it is destroyed.
5) **Determine your earnings for self-employment tax purposes.** The self-employment tax is part of the system for providing social security coverage for people who work for themselves. Your social security benefits when you retire, or are disabled, or that your family can get when you die, depend on how much you earn. Your records should show how much self-employment tax you pay on your earnings.
6) **Support items reported on your tax returns.** If any of your tax returns are examined by the Internal Revenue Service, you may be asked to explain the items reported. A complete set of records will speed up the examination. Adequate and complete records are always supported by sales slips, invoices, receipts, deposit slips, canceled checks, and other documents.

Records Required

The law does not require any special kind of records. You may choose any system that is suited to your business and that will clearly show your income.

Your permanent books (including inventory records) must show not only your gross income, but also your deductions and credits. In addition, you must keep any other records and data necessary to support the entries in your books and on your tax and information returns. Paid bills, canceled checks, etc., that support entries in your books should be filed in an orderly fashion and kept in a safe place. For most small businesses, the business checkbook is the main source for entries in the business records.

The type of business you are in affects the kinds of business records that you will need to keep for federal tax purposes. You should set up your books using an accounting method that clearly shows your income for your tax year. If you are in more than one business, you should keep a complete and separate set of books for each business.

The sample records in this publication show the kinds of records that can be used by a small business operating as a sole proprietorship.

Car expense records. If you use your car for business, get Publication 917, *Business Use of a Car,* for information on the records you must keep to figure your deduction for the business use of your car.

Tax Year

You must be able to figure your taxable income and file an income tax return based on an annual accounting period called a tax year. A tax year is usually 12 consecutive months.

There are 2 kinds of tax years:

1) Calendar, and
2) Fiscal.

If you operate a business as a sole proprietor, the tax year for your business must be the same as your individual tax year.

Calendar year. A calendar year is 12 consecutive months beginning January 1, and ending on December 31. If you are a calendar year taxpayer, and you operate your business as a sole proprietorship, the business must also be on the calendar year basis.

Fiscal year. A fiscal year is 12 consecutive months ending on the last day of any month other than December, or a 52–53 week year. To report on a fiscal year, your books must be kept on that basis.

If you are considering the use of a fiscal year, get Publication 538, *Accounting Periods and Methods.*

Short tax year. A short tax year is a tax year of less than 12 months. You will have a short tax year if your business is not in existence for an entire tax year or if you change your tax year. Each situation results in a different way of figuring tax for the short tax year and is explained in Publication 538.

S corporations. Generally, for tax years beginning after 1986, all S corporations, regardless of when they became S corporations, are required to use a calendar tax year (however, see *Special election* below). Also, an S corporation can use any other accounting period for which the corporation establishes a business purpose to the satisfaction of the Internal Revenue Service.

Partnerships. For tax years beginning after 1986, all partnerships, including existing partnerships, are required to use a tax year that conforms to their partners' tax year (however, see *Special election,* next). Also, a partnership can use any other accounting period for which it establishes a business purpose to the satisfaction of the Internal Revenue Service. For information, get Publication 538.

Special election. S corporations, partnerships, and personal service corporations may be able to make a special election on Form 8716 to use a tax year other than their required year. For more information, get Publication 538.

First-time filer. If you have never filed an income tax return, you may choose either a calendar or a fiscal tax year. You must choose a tax year by the time set by law (not including extensions) for filing your first return.

If your records are not adequate or you have no accounting period or your annual accounting period does not qualify as a fiscal year, your tax year must be the calendar year.

Accounting Method

An accounting method is a set of rules used to determine when and how to report income and expenses in your books and income tax returns.

You may choose any of the following accounting methods if you use it regularly and it clearly shows your income:

1) The cash method,
2) The accrual method,
3) Special methods, such as the installment or long-term contract method, or
4) Any other method or combination of methods as long as income is clearly shown. A combination of methods is known as a hybrid method.

If inventories are needed to show income correctly, you generally must use the accrual method of accounting for purchases and sales.

You must use the same accounting method from year to year to figure your taxable income and keep your books if that method clearly shows your income. In general, any accounting method that consistently uses accounting principles suitable for your trade or business clearly shows income. An accounting method clearly shows income only if all items of gross income and all expenses are treated the same from year to year.

Cash method—reporting income. Under this method you report income when actually or constructively received, and you report expenses when actually paid.

Constructive receipt occurs when an amount is credited to your account or made available to you without restriction as to the time or manner of payment. You do not need to have possession of it.

Holding checks or similar property from one tax year to another does not put off payment of tax on the income. Such income is properly included in the year when the checks or other property are set aside for you and are subject to your demand.

Example 1. Interest credited to your bank account near the end of a tax year is included in your gross income for that year and not for the following year when it is withdrawn or is entered in your passbook.

General Journal

DATE		DESCRIPTION OF ENTRY	POST REF	DEBIT	CREDIT
Oct	5	Rent Expense		780 00	
		Cash			780 00

Example 2. A check or payment received on December 31, 1989, but not cashed or deposited until January 2, 1990, is included in your gross receipts for 1989, the year in which you actually received the amount.

Example 3. On January 2, 1990, you received and deposited a check dated December 28, 1989, for payment of goods. This amount must be included in gross receipts for 1990, the year the check is received.

Cash method—deducting expenses. Usually, you must deduct expenses in the tax year in which you actually pay them. However, expenses you pay in advance can be deducted only in the year to which they apply.

Example. If you are a calendar year taxpayer and you pay $3,000 for an insurance policy that is effective on July 1, 1989, for a 3-year period, you may deduct $500 in 1989, $1,000 in 1990, $1,000 in 1991, and $500 in 1992.

Limits on use of cash method. Corporations (other than S corporations) and certain partnerships with average yearly gross receipts of more than $5,000,000, and all tax shelters, cannot use the cash method of accounting. Get Publication 538 for more information.

Accrual method—reporting income. Income under the accrual method is generally reported in gross income when you earn it, even though you may receive the payment in a later year. It is not the actual receipt of payment but the right to receive it that is important. All events that fix your right to receive the income must have happened, and you must be able to figure the amount with reasonable accuracy.

Example. You are a calendar year taxpayer. You sold a radio in November 1989. You billed the customer 2 days later, but you did not receive payment until February 1990. You must include the amount of the sale in your income for 1989 because you earned the income in that year.

Accrual method—deducting expenses. Under this method, expenses are deducted when you incur them, whether or not you pay them in the same year. All events that set the amount of the liability must have happened, and you must also be able to figure the amount of expense with reasonable accuracy.

Economic performance rule. Business expenses are generally not deductible until economic performance occurs. If your expense is for property or services provided to you, or for use of property by you, economic performance occurs as the property or services are provided, or as the property is used. If your expense is for property or services that you provide to others, economic performance occurs as you provide the property or service. An exception allows certain recurring expenses to be treated as incurred during a tax year even though economic performance has not occurred. See Publication 538 for a discussion of the economic performance rule.

Example. You are a calendar year taxpayer, and, in December 1989, you buy office supplies. You received the supplies and are billed for them in December, but you pay for the supplies in January 1990. The expense is deductible in 1989 because all events that set the amount of the liability and economic performance occurred in that year. Your office supplies may qualify as a recurring expense enabling you to deduct that expense in 1989, even if delivery of the supplies (economic performance) does not occur until 1990.

Cash or accrual. If you use the accrual method of accounting for purchases and sales, you may use the cash method for figuring all other income and expenses. However, if you use the cash method for figuring gross income from your business, you must use the cash method for figuring business expenses. If you use an accrual method for figuring business expenses, you must use an accrual method for figuring all items that affect your gross income from your business.

Business and personal items may be accounted for under different accounting methods. Thus, you may figure the income from your business under an accrual method even though you use the cash method to figure personal items.

More than one business. If you own more than one business, you can use a different accounting method for each separate business if the method you use for each clearly shows your income. If you use different accounting methods, you must keep a complete and separate set of books and records for each business.

Example. You run a personal service business and a manufacturing business. You may use the cash method for the personal service business, but you must use the accrual method for the manufacturing business because inventories are required in accounting for your income.

Changing your method of accounting. Once you have set up your accounting method, you must get the consent of the Internal Revenue Service before you can change to another method of accounting. A change in the method of accounting includes a change not only in your overall system of accounting, but also in the treatment of any material item. For examples of changes that require consent and the information on how you get consent, get Publication 538.

Bookkeeping System

You must decide whether to use a single- or a double-entry bookkeeping system. The single-entry system of bookkeeping is the simplest to maintain, but it may not be good for everyone. You may find that the double-entry system is better because it has built-in checks and balances to assure accuracy and control.

Single-entry. A single-entry system is based on the income statement (profit or loss statement). It can be a simple and practical system if you are starting out in a small business. For tax purposes, the system records the flow of income and expenses through the use of a daily summary of cash receipts, a monthly summary of cash receipts, and a monthly summary of disbursements.

Double-entry. A double-entry bookkeeping system uses journals and ledgers. Transactions are first entered in a journal and then are posted to ledger accounts to show income, expenses, assets (property that a business owns), liabilities (debts of a business), and net worth (excess of assets over liabilities). Income and expense accounts are closed at the end of each accounting period. Asset, liability, and net worth accounts are kept open on a permanent basis.

In the double-entry system, each account has a left side for debits and a right side for credits. It is self-balancing because every transaction is recorded as a debit entry in one account and as a credit entry in another. An example of a journal showing a payment of rent in October is shown at the bottom left of this page.

Under this system, after the journal entries are posted to the ledger accounts, the total of the amounts entered as debits must equal the total of the amounts entered as credits. If the amounts do not balance, an error has been made and steps must be taken to find and correct the error.

At the end of each accounting period, financial statements may be prepared. These statements are generally the income statement and the balance sheet. The income statement reflects current operations for the year. The balance sheet shows the financial position of the business in terms of assets, liabilities, and net worth on any given date.

Automatic data processing (ADP) system. You may use a computer accounting system if the system can maintain adequate permanent records and can produce a legible print-out.

Additional information. You can get more information on accounting systems and on basic accounting terms and procedures from various Small Business Administration (SBA) publications. Write for the free *Directory of Business Development Publications,* at the following address:

SBA Publications
P.O. Box 1000
Fort Worth, TX 76119

Recordkeeping System

You are not required to keep your records in bound books. Records are adequate if they show current income on the basis of an annual accounting period.

A recordkeeping system for a small business might include the following:

- Business Checkbook
- Daily Summary of Cash Receipts
- Monthly Summary of Cash Receipts
- Check Disbursements Journal
- Depreciation Record
- Employee Compensation Record

You must have the books and records of your business available for inspection by the Internal Revenue Service.

How long to keep records. Your records must be kept as long as they may be needed for the administration of any provision of the Internal Revenue Code. Keep records that support an item of income or deduction on a return until the statute of limitations runs out. Usually, the statute of limitations for an income tax return is 3 years after the return is due or filed, or 2 years from the date the tax was paid, whichever occurs later.

If you are an employer, you must keep all your employment tax records for at least 4 years after the date the tax becomes due or is paid, whichever is later.

Keep records that verify your basis in property for as long as they are needed to figure the basis of the original or replacement property. Occasionally, Congress passes laws giving relief to taxpayers in certain situations. You will be able to take advantage of these laws only if your records show that you are eligible. Your records can prove that you had the needed transactions in earlier years.

Copies of tax returns. You should keep copies of your filed tax returns. They help in preparing your future tax returns and in making computations if you later file a claim for refund. They may also be helpful to the executor or administrator of your estate, or to the Internal Revenue Service if your original return is not available.

The Business Checkbook

The business checkbook is your basic source for keeping a record of your business expenses. You should deposit all daily receipts in your business checking account. You should check your account for errors by reconciling your checking account. See *Reconciling Your Checking Account* under the *Sample Record System,* later.

Consider using a checkbook that allows you enough space to enter information to determine later what money represents income and what money represents personal funds or loans deposited. You should note on the deposit slips the source of the deposit and keep copies of all the slips.

You may need to set up a petty cash fund for small expenses. See *Petty cash fund* under the *Sample Record System,* later. All business expenses paid by cash should be clearly supported by documents that show they are for business purposes.

You should make all payments by check so that business expenses are well documented. Write checks payable to yourself only when making withdrawals of income from your business for personal use. Avoid writing checks payable to cash. If you must write a check payable to cash or to yourself to pay for a business expense by cash, you should include the receipt for the cash payment in your records. If you cannot get a receipt for a cash payment, you should make an adequate explanation in your records at the time of payment.

Sample Record System

The bookkeeping system illustrated on the following pages uses the principles described earlier. This is a single-entry system used by Henry M. Brown, the sole proprietor of a small automobile body shop. Henry, who uses part-time help and has no inventory of items held for sale, uses the cash method of accounting.

These sample records ***should not*** be viewed as a recommendation that your records be kept this way. They are used only to show one form in which business records can be kept and how these records are used to complete a Schedule C (Form 1040), *Profit or Loss From Business.*

The design of Schedule C may change from year to year. You should make sure that all items are entered on the correct line of the current form.

Amounts on Schedule C have been rounded to the nearest dollar.

The following explanations are keyed to the numbers and letters on the sample records and the Schedule C. Use the bracketed numbers to help you relate the text to the illustrations. The bracketed letters and the related discussions identify and explain the progression of certain transactions throughout the sample system.

[1] Daily Summary of Cash Receipts. This summary records cash sales for the day and accounts for the cash over and above the amount in your Change and Petty Cash at the beginning of the day.

You may take the Cash Sales entry from your cash register tape, or if you have no cash register, you may simply total your cash sale slips and any other cash received for the day.

[A] The total of cash receipts ($267.80) including cash sales ($263.60) and sales tax ($4.20) for January 2, 1989, is taken from the *Daily Summary of Cash Receipts* [1] and is entered in the *Monthly Summary of Cash Receipts* [2]. This gives you the total monthly receipts from which total monthly taxable income is figured.

Petty cash fund. You can use a petty cash fund to make small payments without having to write checks for small amounts. Each time you make a payment from this fund, you should make out a petty cash slip and attach it to your receipt as proof of payment. You should set up a fixed amount in your petty cash fund ($50 is the amount shown for this example). The total of the unspent petty cash and the amounts on the petty cash slips should equal the fixed amount of the fund. When the total amounts on the petty cash slips approach the fixed amount, you should bring the cash in the fund back to the fixed amount by writing a check to "Petty Cash" for the amounts on the outstanding slips (see the *Check Disbursements Journal* [4] entry for check number 90). This will restore the fund to its fixed amount of $50. The slips are then summarized and entered in the proper columns in the monthly check disbursements journal.

[2] Monthly Summary of Cash Receipts. This provides the income activity for the month showing such items as net sales, sales tax, daily receipts, and deposits in separate columns. A single figure can be arrived at for each account in its separate column. The net sales for the year is the principal income item (Gross receipts or sales) on Schedule C.

[B] The total monthly net sales ($4,865.05) is carried to the *Annual Summary for Schedule C Entries* [5] to figure gross receipts for the year.

To figure total monthly net sales, reduce the total monthly receipts by the actual amount of sales tax to be turned over to the state. You may not take a deduction for the sales tax turned over to the state because you have only collected the tax. You have not included the amount in your income.

Another way to handle sales tax is to include the total sales tax collected in your gross receipts and take a deduction for sales taxes paid over to the state on the taxes line of your Schedule C. Because the various states and local jurisdictions have different requirements for the collection of sales taxes, you should contact the taxing authorities in your area for sales tax regulations.

[3] An Employee Compensation Record. This record is kept for each employee. It records the number of hours worked by each employee in a pay period and the individual's total pay for the period. Deductions withheld are recorded to show the computation of the employee's net pay. It also records monthly gross payroll [C], which is carried to your *Annual Summary of Schedule C Entries* [5].

[4] Check Disbursements Journal. You should enter checks drawn on your business checking account in your *Check Disbursements Journal* each day. All checks should be prenumbered, and every check number should be listed and accounted for in the column provided for check numbers in the journal.

The more frequent expenses are set up with their own headings across the sheet. You should enter in a separate account column expenses that normally require comparatively numerous or large payments each month, such as materials, gross payroll, and rent. You may enter under the general account column small expenses that normally have only one or two monthly payments, such as payments for licenses and postage.

Personal or nonbusiness expenses should not be paid by checks drawn on the business account. If they are drawn on the business account, you should record them in the journal, even though they are not deductible as business expenses.

[D] The monthly total of materials ($1,083.50) is carried to the *Annual Summary for Schedule C Entries* [5]. Similarly, monthly expenses for telephone, truck, auto, etc., are entered in the appropriate columns of this summary.

[5] Annual Summary for Schedule C Entries. This annual summary of monthly cash receipts and expense totals provides final annual amounts you enter on your tax return. The annual summary is taken from the total of monthly cash receipts items such as [B], which is taken from the *Monthly Summary of Cash Receipts* [2], and from monthly expenditures like [D], which is taken from the *Check Disbursements Journal* [4]. As in the case of this journal, each major expense is kept in a separate column.

[E] The cash receipts total ($47,440.95) arrived at on the annual summary is entered on line 1, Part I of Schedule C.

[F] The annual expense total for materials ($9,872.11) is carried from the annual summary and entered on the materials and supplies line of Part III to determine the cost of operations. This total is then entered on line 4, Part I of Schedule C.

There are no inventories of materials and supplies in this example since the buying of parts and supplies is on a per-job basis and the parts and supplies are used only in connection with body work services. A business carrying materials and supplies on hand, unless they are incidental and records of use are not kept, must complete the appropriate lines dealing with inventory in Part III of Schedule C.

Annual totals for interest, rent, taxes, and wages are entered on the appropriate lines of Schedule C. The total for taxes includes the employer's share of social security taxes, the federal unemployment (FUTA) tax, and business license fee. Other annual business expense totals are entered as miscellaneous items on line 28 of Schedule C.

[6] Depreciation Record. Another major item entered on Schedule C is the depreciation allowed on the depreciable assets used in your trade or business. The sample depreciation record shows examples of items depreciated on the modified accelerated cost recovery system (MACRS) and the declining balance methods of depreciation. Depreciation is discussed in Publication 534, *Depreciation.*

You must take depreciation in the year in which it is sustained. You cannot deduct in any one year the allowable depreciation that you failed to take in a prior year.

You may elect to deduct up to $10,000 of the cost of certain depreciable property purchased and placed in service in your trade or business during 1989. This is referred to as the "section 179 deduction." For each dollar of investment in section 179 property in excess of $200,000 in a tax year, the $10,000 maximum is reduced (but not below zero) by one dollar. The section 179 deduction is discussed in Publication 534.

[G] The amount of depreciation that you can claim for the tax year is shown in your depreciation record. It should agree with the depreciation shown on line 18, Section C of Form 4562, *Depreciation and Amortization.* The amount of the depreciation for the tax year ($11,120) is carried from line 19, Section D of Form 4562 to line 13, Part II of Schedule C (Form 1040).

Reconciling Your Checking Account

When you get your checking account statement, you should make sure that your checkbook, the statement, and your books agree. The statement balance may not agree with the balance in your checkbook and books because the statement:

- May include bank charges that you will need to enter in your books and subtract from your checkbook balance, or
- Does not include deposits made after the statement date or checks that did not clear your account before the statement date.

By reconciling your checking account you will:

1) Verify how much money you have in it,
2) Ensure that your checkbook and books reflect all bank charges and the correct balance in the checking account, and
3) Correct any errors in the bank statement, your checkbook, and books.

You should reconcile your checking account each month.

Before you start to reconcile your monthly bank statement, check your own figures. Begin with the balance as shown in your checkbook at the end of the prior month. To this balance add the total cash deposited during the month and subtract total cash disbursements.

You can figure the amount of your bank deposits from the monthly total in the *Monthly Summary of Cash Receipts* [2]. The amount of cash disbursements is the total in the "Amount of Check" column of your *Check Disbursements Journal* [4]. The result should agree with your checkbook balance at the end of the month.

If, after adding total cash deposits and subtracting total cash disbursements from last month's checkbook balance, the result does not agree with your checkbook's balance at the end of the month, you may have made an error in recording check or deposit amounts. You can find such errors by taking the following steps:

1) Add the amounts on your check stubs, and compare that total with the total in the "Amount of Check" column of your *Check Disbursements Journal* [4]. If the totals do not agree, check the individual amounts to see if an error was made in your check stub record or in the related entry in the "Amount of Check" column of your *Check Disbursements Journal.*
2) Add the deposit amounts in your checkbook. Compare that total with the monthly total of "Daily Receipts" in the *Monthly Summary of Cash Receipts* [2]. If the totals do not agree, check the individual amounts to find any errors.

If your checkbook and journal entries still disagree, then recompute the running balance in your checkbook to make sure additions and subtractions are correct.

Steps to reconciling your checking account. When your checkbook balance agrees with the balance figured from the journal entries, you may begin reconciling your checkbook record with the bank statement. Many banks print reconciliation forms on the back of the statement.

To reconcile your account:

1) Compare the amounts on all canceled checks and other debit slips (such as service charges) with the amounts listed on the statement. Make sure that you issued all the checks correctly and that you charged the correct amounts against your account.
2) Compare the deposits listed on the bank statement with the deposit amounts shown in your checkbook. Account for all differences. List in the first section of the reconciliation any deposits entered in your checkbook that do not appear on the bank statement. In the sample reconciliation, the bank prepares the statement near the end of the month and the deposits of $701.33 and $380.65 do not appear on the bank statement.
3) Put all the canceled checks in numerical order.
4) Compare each canceled check, including both check numbers and dollar amount, with the entry on your checkbook stubs. If correct, mark that number on the checkbook as having cleared the bank. After accounting for all checks returned by the bank, those not marked on your checkbook are your outstanding checks. List in the next section of the reconciliation these outstanding checks. In the sample reconciliation, checks numbered 88, 89, 92, and 93 were still outstanding.
5) Enter the errors you find while carrying out any of the preceding steps in the last section of the reconciliation under "Add" or "Subtract."
6) Enter service charges and other bank debits, determined in step (1) in the last section of the reconciliation under "Add" or "Subtract."
7) Update your checkbook by entering items on the reconciliation but not recorded (such as service charges). At this point, the adjusted bank statement should equal your adjusted checkbook balance. If you still have differences, check to find out whether errors in the prior steps have been made.

In the illustrated sample reconciliation, the checkbook balance must be decreased to reflect the net adjustment of $4 ($10 minus $6). The only book adjustment needed is to the *Check Disbursements Journal* [4] for the $10 bank service charge. No adjustment is needed on the *Monthly Summary of Cash Receipts* [2] because the January 8 deposit of $600.40 was correctly entered in that record.

[1]— **Daily Summary of Cash Receipts**

January 2, 1989

Cash Sales		263 60
Sales Tax		4 20
Total Receipts		267 80 —[A]
Cash on Hand		
Cash in Register (Including unspent petty cash)		
Coins	23 75	
Bills	143 00	
Checks	134 05	
Total Cash in Register		300 80
Petty Cash Slips		17 00
Total Cash		317 80
Less: Change and Petty Cash		
Petty Cash Slips	17 00	
Coins and Bills (unspent petty cash)	33 00	
Total Change and Petty Cash Fund		50 00
Total Cash Receipts		267 80

[2]— **Monthly Summary of Cash Receipts**

Date 1989	Net Sales	Sales Tax	Daily Receipts	Deposit
Jan. 2	263 60	4 20	267 80	—[A]
3	212 00	3 39	215 39	
4	194 40	3 10	197 50	680 69
5	222 40	3 54	225 94	
6	231 15	3 68	234 83	
7	137 50	2 13	139 63	600 40
9	187 90	2 99	190 89	
10	207 56	3 31	210 87	401 76
11	128 95	2 05	131 00	
12	231 40	3 77	235 17	
13	201 28	3 21	204 49	
14	88 01	1 40	89 41	660 07
17	210 95	3 36	214 31	
18	221 80	3 53	225 33	439 64
19	225 15	3 59	228 74	
20	221 93	3 52	225 45	
21	266 83	4 26	271 09	725 28
23	130 84	2 08	132 92	
24	216 37	3 45	219 82	352 74
25	220 05	3 50	223 55	
26	197 80	3 15	200 95	
27	272 49	4 34	276 83	701 33
30	150 64	2 40	153 04	
31	224 05	3 56	227 61	380 65
[B]—	4865 05	77 51	4942 56	4942 56

[3]— **Employee Compensation Record**

NAME John E. Marks
ADDRESS 1 Elm St., Newark, NJ
PHONE 768-6075

FULL TIME
PART TIME X

SOC. SEC. NO. 567-00-8901
DATE OF BIRTH 12-21-65
NO. OF EXEMPTIONS Single-1

Pay Period Ending	Hours Worked														Total Reg. Hours	Over-time	Earnings			Deductions				Net Pay
	S	M	T	W	T	F	S	S	M	T	W	T	F	S			Regular Rate	Overtime Rate	Total	Social Security	Fed. Income Tax	State Income Tax	Other	
1/7/89		5	5	5	5				5	5	4	6			40		6.50		$260.00	$ 19.53	$ 22.00	$ 6.00		$212.47
1/21/89		4	4	4	4	4	2		4	3	4	4	3		40		6.50		$260.00	$ 19.53	$22.00	$ 6.00		$ 212.47
															80				$520.00	$ 39.06	$44.00	$12.00		$ 424.94
QUARTERLY TOTALS																								

[C]

[4]—— **Check Disbursements Journal**

1989		Paid To	Ck. No.	Amount of Check	Materials	Gross Payroll	Federal Withheld Income Tax	FICA Reserve	State Withheld Income Tax
Jan	2	Dale Advertising	74	85 00					
	4	City Treasurer	75	35 00					
	5	Auto Parks, Inc.	76	203 00	203 00				
	6	Henry Brown	77	250 00					
	6	Bill's Delicatessen	78	36 00					
	6	Joe's Service Station	79	74 50	29 50				
	6	ABC Auto Paint	80	137 50	137 50				
	7	Henry Brown	81	225 00					
	7	John E. Marks	82	212 47		260 00	(22 00)	(19 53)	(6 00)
	14	Telephone Co.	83	27 00					
	19	National Bank	84	90 74					
	19	Auto Parks, Inc.	85	472 00	472 00				
	19	Henry Brown	86	275 00					
	21	Electric Co.	87	175 30					
	21	A. J. Ignition	88	66 70	66 70				
	21	Baker's Fender Co.	89	9 80	9 80				
	21	Petty Cash	90	17 00	15 00				
	21	Henry Brown	91	225 00					
	21	John E. Marks	92	212 47		260 00	(22 00)	(19 53)	(6 00)
	26	Baker's Fender Co.	93	150 00	150 00				
	26	Enterprise Properties	94	300 00					
	26	National Bank (Tax Deposit)	95	122 12			44 00	39 06	
	26	State Treasurer	96	12 00					12 00
	26	State Treasurer	97	73 90					
				3,487 50	1,083 50	520 00	-0-	-0-	-0-
		Bank Service Charge		10 00					
				3,497 50	1,083 50	520 00	-0-	-0-	-0-

[D] [C]

[4]—— Check Disbursements Journal (Cont'd)

Employer's FICA Tax	Electric	Interest	Rent	Telephone	Truck/ Auto	Drawing	General Accounts	
							Advertising	85 00
							License	35 00
						250 00		
							Shop Holiday Party	36 00
					45 00			
						225 00		
				27 00				
		18 09					Loan	72 65
						275 00		
	175 30							
							Postage	2 00
						225 00		
			300 00					
39 06								
							Sales Tax	73 90
39 06	175 30	18 09	300 00	27 00	45 00	975 00		304 55
								10 00
39 06	175 30	18 09	300 00	27 00	45 00	975 00		314 55

[5]—Annual Summary for Schedule C Entries

	Cash Receipts [B]	Materials [D]	Gross Payroll [C]	FICA Taxes	Bank Charges	Electric	Interest	Insurance	Rent	Telephone	Truck/Auto	Miscellaneous
January	4865 05	1083 50	520 00	39 06	10 00	175 30	18 09		300 00	27 00	45 00	36 00
February	3478 32	874 93	235 40	17 68	7 50	153 10	18 09	210 00	300 00	21 50	28 50	15 90
March	3942 00	724 90	507 00	38 08	11 25	145 81	18 09		300 00	32 10	51 30	32 15
April	4077 02											
May	4066 32											
June	4151 62											
July	3812 12											
August	3741 82											
September	4126 52											
October	3877 72											
November	3645 92											
December	3656 52											
Totals	[E]—47440 95	[F]—9872 11	5434 00	408 09	92 50	1642 37	217 08	420 00	3600 00	324 09	571 46	314 25
Enter on Schedule C	Line 1a	Line 4, Part III	Line 28a	Line 25	Line 6	Line 27	Line 17b	Line 16	Line 22	Line 27	Line 9	Line 6 65 Line 20 40 Line 24 129 Line 25 218: Line 29 314

[6]—Depreciation Record

Property	Date Placed in Service	Cost	Section 179 Deduction	Investment Credit	Balance for Depreciation	Recovery Period	Method	ACRS %	Depreciation Prior Years	Depreciation for 1989
Equipment – Transmission Jack	7/1/84	1,366	1,366	—	—	5	—	–	—	—
Pickup Truck (used)	4/2/85	3,500	2,000	60*	1,500	3	ACRS	37	1,500	—
Heavy Duty Tow Truck	2/1/89	14,000	8,400	—	5,600	5	DDB (HY)	40	—	1,120
Equipment – Engine Hoist	4/1/89	1,600	1,600	—	—	5	—	—	—	—

* Investment credit--Reduced credit taken instead of reducing basis. Investment credit repealed for most property placed in service after 1985.

Depreciation for 1989	1,120
Section 179 Deduction	10,000
Total Depreciation for 1989	11,120 [G]

SCHEDULE C (Form 1040)
Department of the Treasury Internal Revenue Service

Profit or Loss From Business
(Sole Proprietorship)
Partnerships, Joint Ventures, Etc., Must File Form 1065.
▶ Attach to Form 1040 or Form 1041. ▶ See Instructions for Schedule C (Form 1040).

OMB No 1545 0074
1989
Attachment Sequence No 09

Name of proprietor: Henry M. Brown
Social security number (SSN): 123 00 6789

A Principal business or profession, including product or service (see Instructions): Auto Repair Services
B Principal business code (from page 2) ▶ 8854

C Business name and address ▶ Brown's Auto Body Shop, 5 Amherst Ave., Newark, NJ 07103
D Employer ID number (Not SSN): 10-9999999

E Method(s) used to value closing inventory: (1) ☐ Cost (2) ☐ Lower of cost or market (3) ☐ Other (attach explanation) (4) ☐ Does not apply (if checked, skip line G)

F Accounting method: (1) ☒ Cash (2) ☐ Accrual (3) ☐ Other (specify) ▶

	Yes	No
G Was there any change in determining quantities, costs, or valuations between opening and closing inventory? (If "Yes," attach explanation.)	NA	
H Are you deducting expenses for business use of your home? (If "Yes," see Instructions for limitations.)		X
I Did you "materially participate" in the operation of this business during 1989? (If "No," see Instructions for limitations on losses.)	X	

J If this schedule includes a loss, credit, deduction, income, or other tax benefit relating to a tax shelter required to be registered, check here. ▶ ☐
If you checked this box, you MUST attach Form 8271.

Part I Income

[E]

Line	Description		Amount
1	Gross receipts or sales	47,441	
2	Returns and allowances		
3	Subtract line 2 from line 1. Enter the result here		47,441
4	Cost of goods sold and/or operations (from line 39 on page 2)		9,872 [F]
5	Subtract line 4 from line 3 and enter the **gross profit** here		37,569
6	Other income, including Federal and state gasoline or fuel tax credit or refund (see Instructions)		
7	Add lines 5 and 6. This is your **gross income** ▶		37,569

Part II Expenses

[G]

Line	Expense	Amount	Line	Expense	Amount
8	Advertising	85	22	Repairs	
9	Bad debts from sales or services (see Instructions)		23	Supplies (not included in Part III)	129
10	Car and truck expenses	571	24	Taxes	626
11	Commissions		25	Travel, meals, and entertainment:	
12	Depletion		25a	Travel	
13	Depreciation and section 179 deduction from **Form 4562** (not included in Part III)	11,120	25b	Meals and entertainment	
14	Employee benefit programs (other than on line 20)		25c	Enter 20% of line 25b subject to limitations (see Instructions)	
15	Freight (not included in Part III)		25d	Subtract line 25c from line 25b	
16	Insurance (other than health)	420	26	Utilities (see Instructions)	1,966
17	Interest:		27	Wages (less jobs credit)	5,434
17a	Mortgage (paid to banks, etc.)		28	Other expenses (list type and amount):	
17b	Other	217		Bank service charge 93	
18	Legal and professional services			Miscellaneous 314	
19	Office expense	40			
20	Pension and profit-sharing plans				
21	Rent or lease:				
21a	Machinery and equipment				
21b	Other business property	3,600	28		*407

Line	Description	Amount
29	Add amounts in columns for lines 8 through 28. These are your **total expenses** ▶	24,615
30	**Net profit or (loss).** Subtract line 29 from line 7. If a profit, enter here and on Form 1040, line 12, and on Schedule SE, line 2. If a loss, you MUST go on to line 31. (Fiduciaries, see Instructions.)	12,954

31 If you have a loss, you MUST check the box that describes your investment in this activity (see Instructions). 31a ☐ All investment is at risk. 31b ☐ Some investment is not at risk.
If you checked 31a, enter the loss on Form 1040, line 12, and Schedule SE, line 2.
If you checked 31b, you MUST attach **Form 6198**.

For Paperwork Reduction Act Notice, see Form 1040 Instructions. Schedule C (Form 1040) 1989

* Part III is not shown.

Form **4562** Department of the Treasury Internal Revenue Service

Depreciation and Amortization

▶ See separate instructions.
▶ Attach this form to your return.

OMB No 1545-0172
1989
Attachment Sequence No 67

Name(s) as shown on return: Henry M. Brown
Identifying number: 123-00-6789

Business or activity to which this form relates: Auto Repair Service

Part I **Depreciation** *(Use Part III for automobiles, certain other vehicles, computers, and property used for entertainment, recreation, or amusement.)*

Section A.—Election To Expense Depreciable Assets (Section 179)

1 Maximum dollar limitation	1	$10,000
2 Total cost of section 179 property placed in service during the tax year (see instructions)	2	15,600
3 Threshold cost of section 179 property before reduction in limitation	3	$200,000
4 Reduction in limitation (Subtract line 3 from line 2, but do not enter less than -0-.)	4	-0-
5 Dollar limitation for tax year (Subtract line 4 from line 1, but do not enter less than -0-.)	5	10,000

	(a) Description of property	(b) Date placed in service	(c) Cost	(d) Elected cost
6	Heavy duty tow truck	2/1/89	14,000	8,400
	Engine hoist	4/3/89	1,600	1,600

* 7 Listed property—Enter amount from line 28	7	-0-
8 Tentative deduction (Enter the lesser of: (a) line 6 plus line 7; or (b) line 5.)	8	10,000
9 Taxable income limitation (Enter the lesser of :(a) Taxable income; or (b) line 5) (see instructions)	9	10,000
10 Carryover of disallowed deduction from 1988 (see instructions)	10	-0-
11 Section 179 expense deduction (Enter the lesser of: (a) line 8 plus line 10; or (b) line 9.)	11	10,000
12 Carryover of disallowed deduction to 1990 (Add lines 8 and 10, less line 11.) ▶ 12 -0-		

Section B.—MACRS Depreciation

(a) Classification of property	(b) Date placed in service	(c) Basis for depreciation (Business use only—see instructions)	(d) Recovery period	(e) Convention	(f) Method	(g) Depreciation deduction
13 General Depreciation System (GDS) (see instructions): *For assets placed in service ONLY during tax year beginning in 1989*						
a 3-year property						
b 5-year property		5,600	5	HY	DDB	1,120
c 7-year property						
d 10-year property						
e 15-year property						
f 20-year property						
g Residential rental property			27.5 yrs.	MM	S/L	
			27.5 yrs.	MM	S/L	
h Nonresidential real property			31.5 yrs.	MM	S/L	
			31.5 yrs.	MM	S/L	
14 Alternative Depreciation System (ADS) (see instructions): *For assets placed in service ONLY during tax year beginning in 1989*						
a Class life					S/L	
b 12-year			12 yrs.		S/L	
c 40-year			40 yrs.	MM	S/L	

15 Listed property—Enter amount from line 27	15	
16 GDS and ADS deductions for assets placed in service before 1989 (see instructions)	16	

Section C.—ACRS and/or Other Depreciation

17 Property subject to section 168(f)(1) election (see instructions)	17	
18 ACRS and/or other depreciation (see instructions)	18	

Section D.—Summary

19 Total (Add deductions on line 11 and lines 13 through 18.) Enter here and on the appropriate line of your return (Partnerships and S corporations—see instructions.)	19	11,120 [G]
20 For assets shown above and placed in service during the current year, enter the portion of the basis attributable to section 263A costs (see instructions)	20	-0-

For Paperwork Reduction Act Notice, see page 1 of the separate instructions. Form **4562** (1989)

* Part III is not shown

Check Reconciliation as of January 31, 1989

Balance shown on bank statement		1593 55
Add deposits not credited:		
1/27	701 33	
1/30	380 65	
		1081 98
		2675 53
Subtract outstanding checks:		
No. 88	66 70	
89	9 80	
92	212 47	
93	150 00	
		438 97
		2236 56
Adjusted balance per bank statement		
Balance shown in checkbook		2240 56
Add: Deposit of $600.40 for 1/8		
entered as $594.40 (difference)		6 00
		2246 56
Subtract		
Bank service charge		10 00
Adjusted checkbook balance		2236 56

*U.S. Government Printing Office: 1990 — 282-015/20025

5. Circular E—Employer's Tax Guide

Department of the Treasury

Internal Revenue Service

Circular E
Employer's Tax Guide

What's Inside

Separate Reporting of Withholding Required for Social Security and for Medicare

The wage base for social security is $55,500 for 1992. The wage base for Medicare is $130,200 for 1992. For social security, the tax rate is 6.2% each for employers and employees. For Medicare, the rate is 1.45% each for employers and employees.

Two separate tables are provided to help you figure these taxes. The social security table begins on page 48 and the Medicare table is on page 50. Be sure to use **BOTH** tables.

1992 Federal Unemployment (FUTA) Tax Rate is 6.2%.

1991 Form W-2

The 1991 Form W-2 has been revised extensively. Please see the separate instructions for more details.

Advance Earned Income Credit

The amount of the advance earned income credit is limited to the amount allowed for only one qualifying child, even though for 1992 employees may be eligible to claim an additional amount on their returns for more than one qualifying child. This package contains the tables needed to figure the advance earned income credit.

Form 1099-R Changes—Form W-2P Eliminated

Form W-2P, Statement for Recipients of Annuities, Pensions, Retired Pay, or IRA Payments, has been eliminated effective for tax year 1991. The information previously reported on Form W-2P must be included on **Form 1099-R**, Distributions From Pensions, Annuities, Retirement or Profit-Sharing Plans, IRAs, Insurance Contracts, etc.

Notice

Keep this booklet for reference. It has information that you will need during the year. The booklet may be needed by more than one department in your company; to order more copies, call 1-800-829-3676.

Deposit Rules

Effective for deposit periods beginning after March 31, 1991, an employer's deposit obligation is determined by reference to the total amount of **tax liability** accumulated for the period. The obligation is no longer determined by the total amount of **undeposited taxes** on hand at the close of the period. See Treasury Decision 8341, 1991-16 I.R.B. 4. The rules for depositing taxes can be found in Section 13 of this booklet.

Calendar

The following is a list of important dates during the year that you should take note of.

Note: *If any date shown falls on a Saturday, Sunday, or legal holiday, use the next regular workday.*

By January 31

Give each employee a completed **Form W-2,** Wage and Tax Statement. Give each annuitant a completed **Form 1099-R,** Distributions from Pensions, Annuities, Retirement or Profit-Sharing Plans, IRAs, Insurance Contracts, etc., by January 31. For pension payments made prior to 1991, use **Form W-2P,** Statement for Recipients of Annuities, Pensions, Retired Pay, or IRA Payments. (See section 17.)

Federal Unemployment (FUTA) Tax.—File **Form 940** or **Form 940-EZ,** Employer's Annual Federal Unemployment (FUTA) Tax Return. If you deposited all the tax when due, you have 10 additional days to file the return.

By February 15

Ask for a new **Form W-4,** Employee's Withholding Allowance Certificate, from each employee who claimed total exemption from withholding during the prior year.

On February 16

Begin withholding for each employee who previously claimed exemption from withholding but has not given you a new Form W-4 for the current year. If the employee does not give you a new completed Form W-4, withhold tax as if he or she is single, with zero withholding allowances. The Form W-4 previously given you claiming exemption is now expired. (See section 10(h).)

February 28

Send Copy A of all Forms 1099-R with **Form 1096,** Annual Summary and Transmittal of U.S. Information Returns, to the Internal Revenue Service Center for your locality. (See section 16.)

By The Last Day of February

Income Tax Withholding.—File **Form W-3,** Transmittal of Income and Tax Statements, with the Social Security Administration (SSA) and include Copy A of all Forms W-2 for employees for the year before. (See section 16.)

Allocated Tip Reporting.—File **Form 8027,** Employer's Annual Information Return of Tip Income and Allocated Tips, with the Internal Revenue Service. (See section 7.)

By April 30, July 31, October 31, and January 31

Deposit Federal unemployment tax due if it is more than $100. File **Form 941,** Employer's Quarterly Federal Tax Return, or **Form 941E,** Quarterly Return of Withheld Federal Income Tax and Medicare Tax, and pay any undeposited income, social security, and Medicare taxes. If you deposited all the taxes when due, you have 10 additional days to file the return.

File **Form 942,** Employer's Quarterly Tax Return for Household Employees, if you have such employees, and pay the tax due. (See section 14.)

Before December 1

Income Tax Withholding.—Ask for a new Form W-4 from each employee whose withholding allowances will change for the next year.

On December 31

Form W-5, Earned Income Credit Advance Payment Certificate, expires. Employees who want to continue receiving advance payments of the earned income credit for the next year must file a new Form W-5.

Reminders

When Hiring New Employees

Eligibility for Employment.—You will have to verify that each new employee is legally eligible to work in the U.S. This will include completing the Immigration and Naturalization Service (INS) **Form I-9,** Employment Eligibility Verification Form. The form can be obtained from INS offices. Contact the INS for further information concerning your responsibilities.

Income Tax Withholding.—Ask each new employee to complete Form W-4. Use the 1992 Form W-4.

Social Security and Medicare Taxes.—Record each new employee's name and number from his or her social security card. Any employee without a social security card should apply for one. (See section 5.)

When Paying Wages or Annuities

Income Tax Withholding.—Withhold tax from each wage payment or supplemental unemployment compensation plan benefit payment according to the employee's Form W-4 and the correct withholding rate. (Employers who have nonresident alien employees, see section 10.) Withhold from periodic pension and annuity payments as if the recipient is married claiming three withholding allowances, unless he or she has filed Form W-4P either electing no withholding or giving a different number of allowances, marital status, or additional amount to be withheld. (See sections 6, 10, 11, and 12.)

Social Security and Medicare Taxes.—Withhold 6.2% from each wage payment in 1992 for social security. Stop when you reach $55,500 in taxable wages. Withhold 1.45% from each wage payment in 1992 for Medicare. Stop when you reach $130,200 in taxable wages. (If the employee reported tips, see section 7.)

Backup Withholding

Payers must generally withhold 20% of taxable interest, dividend, and certain other payments if payees fail to furnish payers with their correct taxpayer identification numbers. There are other circumstances when the payer is also required to withhold. This withholding is referred to as backup withholding. Please see **Form W-9,** Request for Taxpayer Identification Number and Certification, and the **Instructions for Forms 1099, 1098, 5498, and W-2G** for more details.

Report backup withholding amounts on the same Form 941 you use to report social security, Medicare, and income tax withholding (or Form 941E if only reporting income tax withholding and the Medicare tax). See section 13 for information on depositing backup withholding.

Information Returns

You may have to file information returns to report certain types of payments made during the year. For example, you must file **Form 1099-MISC,** Miscellaneous Income, to report payments of $600 or more to persons not treated as employees (e.g., independent contractors) for services performed for your trade or business. You can use the chart on pages 58 and 59 as a quick reference guide to 1991 information returns. For details about forms of the 1099 series and for information about required magnetic media filing, please see the **Instructions for Forms 1099, 1098, 5498, and W-2G.** Do not use the Form 1099 series to report wages and other compensation you paid to employees; report these on Form W-2. See the separate Instructions for Form W-2 for details. "Other compensation" to be reported on Form W-2 is described in sections 6 and 17.

Information Return Penalties

A penalty may be imposed if a person either fails to file (on paper or on magnetic media) an information return or files with incorrect information.

The amount of the penalty is based on when the correct information returns are filed. The penalty is as follows:

- $15 for each information return if the correct information is filed within 30 days after the due date (by March 30 if the due date is February 28) with a maximum penalty of $75,000 per year ($25,000 for small businesses, defined later).
- $30 for each information return if the correct information is filed more than 30 days after the due date but by August 1, with a maximum penalty of $150,000 per year ($50,000 for small businesses, defined later).
- $50 for each information return that is not filed at all or is not filed correctly by August 1, with a maximum penalty of $250,000 per year ($100,000 for small businesses, defined later).
- $100 for each information return that is not filed or is not filed correctly due to intentional disregard of the filing requirements with a maximum penalty of 10% of the amounts of items required to be reported correctly.

Exceptions to the Penalty.—In general, the penalty will not apply to any failure that was due to reasonable cause.

In addition, the penalty will not apply to a de minimis number of failures. These failures are information returns that were filed timely but with incomplete or incorrect information and were corrected by August 1. The penalty will not apply to the greater of 10 information returns or ½ of 1% of the total number of information returns that are required to be filed for the year.

Definition of Small Business.—A small business is a firm with average annual gross receipts of $5 million or less for the 3 most recent taxable years.

Failure to Provide Payee Statement or Providing Incorrect Payee Statement.—A penalty may be imposed if a person either fails to furnish a payee statement by the due date or fails to include correct information on a payee statement. The penalty is $50 for each failure. The maximum penalty for such failures is $100,000.

Business Reporting

If you are a small business, self-employed, sole proprietor, independent contractor, or a member of a partnership, you may want to get **Pub. 937,** Business Reporting, for useful information on business reporting. You can order Pub. 937 by calling 1-800-829-3676.

Unresolved Problems

If you have a tax problem you have been unable to resolve with the IRS, write to your local IRS district director or call your local IRS office and ask for Problem Resolution assistance. This office will take responsibility for your problem and ensure that it receives proper attention. Although this office cannot change the tax law or technical decisions, it can frequently clear up misunderstandings that resulted from previous contacts.

Hearing-impaired taxpayers who have access to TDD equipment, may call 1-800-829-4059 to ask for Problem Resolution assistance.

General Information

1. Purpose

This guide explains your tax responsibilities as an employer. It explains the requirements for withholding, depositing, reporting, and paying taxes. It explains the forms you must give your employees, those your employees must give you, and those you must send to IRS and SSA. (Detailed filing requirements and instructions for completing the forms, including instructions for correcting previously filed forms, are usually on the forms themselves. However, some forms do have separate instructions.) This guide also has tax tables you need to figure the taxes to withhold for each employee after December 1991.

Most employers must withhold, deposit, report, and pay—

- Income tax,
- Social security and Medicare taxes.

They must also deposit, report, and pay—

- Federal unemployment tax (FUTA).

There are exceptions to these requirements. See pages 18 through 23. Railroad retirement and railroad unemployment repayment taxes are explained in the Instructions for Form CT-1.

2. Are You an Employer?

Generally, an employer is a person or organization for whom a worker performs a service as an employee. The employer usually gives the worker the tools and place to work and has the right to fire the worker. A person or organization paying wages to a former employee after the work ends is also considered an employer.

Specific definitions of employers apply for income and FUTA tax purposes.

Income Tax Withholding.—For income tax withholding purposes, the term employer includes organizations that are exempt from income, social security, Medicare, and FUTA taxes.

FUTA Tax.—For FUTA tax purposes, an employer is:

(1) Any person or organization that during this year or last year either:

(a) Paid wages of $1,500 or more in any calendar quarter, or

(b) Had one or more employees at any time in each of any 20 different calendar weeks.

(2) Any agricultural employer who during this year or last year either:

(a) Paid cash wages of $20,000 or more for farm labor in any calendar quarter, or

(b) Employed 10 or more farmworkers during some part of a day for at least 1 day during any 20 different weeks.

(3) Any household employer who during this year or last year paid cash wages of $1,000 or more during any calendar quarter for household service in a private home, local college club, or local chapter of a college fraternity or sorority.

Federal Government Employers.—If you are a Federal agency, the information in this guide applies, except:

(a) Deposit Federal taxes only at Federal Reserve banks, and

(b) The due date for Federal tax deposits is the payroll date. Refer to the **Treasury Fiscal Requirements Manual (I TFRM 3-4000)** for procedures to use in accounting for withheld Federal income tax, social security, and Medicare taxes.

State and Local Government Employers.— Wages of your employees are generally subject to Federal income tax withholding. In addition, wages of your employees hired after March 31, 1986, are subject to the Medicare tax (1.45% of the first $130,200 paid to each employee for the year), unless they are otherwise covered by a section 218 agreement between the State and the Social Security Administration. Wages of any employees covered by a section 218 agreement are subject to the social security and Medicare taxes. Wages for services performed after July 1, 1991, by employees who are not members of retirement systems of state and local government employers, with certain exceptions, are subject to the social security and Medicare taxes. For rules for determining whether an employee is a "member of a retirement system," see T.D. 8354 1991-30 I.R.B. 4.

You can get information on reporting and social security coverage from your local IRS office. If you have any questions about coverage under a section 218 agreement, contact the appropriate state official.

See **Deposit Instructions for State and Local Government Employers** on page 11 for information on tax deposits for state and local government employers.

3. Employer Identification Number

If you are required to report employment taxes or give tax statements to employees or annuitants, you need an employer identification number.

The employer identification number (EIN) is a 9-digit number the IRS issues. The digits are arranged as follows: 00-0000000. It is used to identify the tax accounts of employers and certain others that have no employees.

If you have not asked for a number, request one on **Form SS-4,** Application for Employer Identification Number. You can get this form at IRS or Social Security Administration (SSA) offices.

You should have only one number. If you have more than one and are not sure which one to use, please check with the Internal Revenue Service Center where you file your return. Give the numbers you have, the name and address to which each was assigned, and the address of your main place of business. IRS will tell you which number to use. **Use your employer identification number on all the items you send to IRS and SSA.**

If you took over another employer's business, do not use that employer's number. If you don't have your own number by the time a return is due, write "Applied for" and the date you applied in the space shown for the number.

Please see **Pub. 583,** Taxpayers Starting a Business, for more information on how to make deposits, file returns, etc., if due before you have received your number.

4. Who Are Employees?

Generally, employees can be defined either under common law or under special statutes for special purposes.

Employment Status Under Common Law.— Anyone who performs services is an employee if you, as an employer, can control what will be done and how it will be done. This is so even when you give the employee freedom of action. What matters is that you have the legal right to control the method and result of the services. Also see **Statutory Employees,** on page 4.

Generally, people in business for themselves are not employees. For example, doctors, lawyers, veterinarians, construction contractors, and others in an independent trade in which they offer their services to the public are usually not employees. Also see **Statutory Nonemployees** on page 4.

If an employer-employee relationship exists, it does not matter what it is called. The employee may be called a partner, agent, or independent contractor. It also does not matter how payments are measured or paid, what they are called, or whether the employee works full- or part-time.

There is no employee class difference. An employee can be a superintendent, manager, or supervisor. Generally, an officer of a corporation is an employee, but a director is not. An officer who performs no services or only minor ones, and who neither receives nor is entitled to receive pay of any kind, is not considered an employee.

Whether an employer-employee relationship exists under the usual common law rules will be determined, when there is any doubt, by the facts in each case.

If you have good reason for treating a worker other than as an employee, you will not be liable for employment taxes on the payments to that worker.

To get this relief, you must file all required Federal tax returns, including information returns, on a basis consistent with your treatment of the worker. You (or your predecessor) must not have treated any worker holding a substantially similar position as an employee for any period after 1977. See Rev. Proc. 85-18, 1985-1 C.B. 518, for further details.

This relief is not available, however, to a business that furnishes technical service specialists (e.g., engineers, computer programmers, and systems analysts) to clients. In these cases, the employment relationship between the business and the technical service specialist will be determined under the common law rules. **Note:** *If you, as the business that furnishes technical service specialists to clients, correctly treat a technical service specialist as an independent contractor under the common law rules, you will not be liable for employment taxes on that individual.* See Rev. Rul. 87-41, 1987-1 C.B. 296, for guidelines for determining the employment status of a technical service specialist.

Statutory Employees.—If someone who works for you is not an employee under the common law rules explained above, do not withhold Federal income tax from his or her pay. Although the following persons may not be common law employees, they are considered employees for social security and Medicare purposes if tests (1) through (3) below are met. Persons in (a) and (d) are employees for FUTA tax purposes if tests (1) through (3) are met.

(a) An agent (or commission) driver who delivers food or beverages (other than milk) or laundry or dry cleaning for someone else.

(b) A full-time life insurance salesperson.

(c) A homeworker who works by the guidelines of the person for whom the work is done, with materials furnished by and returned to that person or to someone that person designates.

(d) A traveling or city salesperson (other than an agent-driver or commission-driver) who works full time (except for sideline sales activities) for one firm or person getting orders from customers. The order must be for items for resale or use as supplies in the customer's business. The customers must be retailers, wholesalers, contractors, or operators of hotels, restaurants, or other businesses dealing with food or lodging.

Tests.—

(1) It is understood from a service contract that the services will be performed by the person.

(2) The person does not have a substantial investment in facilities (other than transportation) used to perform the services.

(3) The services involve a continuing relationship with the person for whom they are performed.

Pub. 937, Business Reporting, gives examples of the employer-employee relationship.

If you want a decision about whether a worker is an employee, file **Form SS-8,** Determination of Employee Work Status for Purposes of Federal Employment Taxes and Income Tax Withholding. You can get the form at IRS offices. The Form SS-8 should be sent to your district director.

Statutory Nonemployees.—Direct sellers and qualified real estate agents are by law considered nonemployees. They are instead treated as self-employed for income tax and employment tax purposes. See Pub. 937 for details on these two groups.

Treating Employees as Nonemployees.—You will be liable for income tax and employee social security and Medicare taxes if you don't deduct and withhold these taxes because you consider an employee as a nonemployee. See Internal Revenue Code section 3509 for details.

5. Employee's Social Security Number

Record the name and number of each employee exactly as they are shown on the employee's social security card. Any employee without a social security card can get one from any SSA office by completing **Form SS-5,** Application for a Social Security Card. You can get this form at SSA offices or by calling 1-800-772-1213.

If the employee's name is not correct as shown on the card, including if the employee's name has changed due to marriage or divorce, the employee should request a new card from SSA.

If your employee has been given a new social security card because of an adjustment to his or her alien residence status, which shows a different name or social security number, correct your records for 1992 and show the new information on the 1992 Form W-2. If you filed Form W-2 for the same employee in prior years under the old name and social security number, file **Form W-2c,** Statement of Corrected Income and Tax Amounts, to correct the name and number. Advise the employee to contact their local SSA office later in the year to ensure that their records have been updated.

6. Taxable Wages

Wages subject to Federal employment taxes include all pay you give an employee for services performed. The pay may be in cash or in other forms. It includes salaries, vacation allowances, bonuses, and commissions. It does not matter how you measure or pay the payments.

Any employee social security tax, Medicare tax, and employee state unemployment compensation tax you pay for your employees (rather than deducting it) is includible in social security, Medicare, and FUTA wages. (This does not apply to household workers or farmworkers.)

(See pages 18 through 23 for exceptions to wages. See section 7 for a discussion of tips. See section 17 for reporting "other compensation" not subject to withholding.)

Measure pay that is not in money (such as goods, lodging, and meals) by its fair market value. This kind of pay may be subject to tax and withholding. See pages 20 and 21.

Payments to your employee for travel and other necessary expenses of your business generally are taxable if: (1) your employee is not required to **or** does not substantiate those expenses to you with receipts or other documentation, or (2) you advance an amount to your employee for business expenses and your employee is not required to **or** does not return any amount he or she does not use for business expenses. See **What To Include on the 1991 Form W-2** on page 13 for more information.

Partially Exempt Employment.—If an employee spends half or more of his or her time in a pay period performing services subject to employment taxes, all the employee's pay in that pay period is taxable. If the employee spends less than half the time performing services subject to taxes, none of the pay in that pay period is subject to employment taxes.

Supplemental Unemployment Compensation Benefits.—Treat supplemental unemployment compensation benefits as wages for income tax withholding to the extent they are includible in your employee's gross income. This applies if you pay benefits to your employee because of his or her involuntary separation from the job under a plan to which you are a party. Involuntary separation includes a reduction in force or closing a plant or operation. It does not include separation because of disciplinary problems or because of age. Also see Rev. Rul. 90-72, 1990-2 C.B. 211.

Moving Expenses.—Reimbursements to employees for moving expenses are not subject to withholding if you believe the employee is entitled to a deduction for them. They are subject to withholding if you believe the employee is not entitled to a deduction. For more information, see **Pub. 521,** Moving Expenses.

Golden Parachutes.—If you make parachute payments to certain "disqualified" individuals (personal services corporations, or similar entities, are treated as individuals for purposes of this provision), you are subject to reporting and withholding requirements. Parachute payments (also called "golden parachutes") are certain payments in the nature of compensation which corporations make to key individuals, often in excess of their usual compensation, in the event that ownership or control of the corporation changes. The golden parachute provision does not apply to payments made to or for a disqualified individual by a corporation that immediately before the change in ownership or control was: (1) an S corporation; or (2) a corporation that had no readily tradable securities. If (2) applies, shareholders must have consented to the payments. Excess parachute payments are not deductible by the payer, and the recipient of the excess payments is subject to a 20% excise tax. If you make the payments to an employee, see section 17 for instructions for reporting to the employee. If you make parachute payments to a nonemployee, use Form 1099-MISC for reporting. See the Instructions for Forms 1099, 1098, 5498, and W-2G. The parachute payments provision applies to payments made under agreements entered into or renewed after June 14, 1984, in tax years ending after that date. For further information, see Internal Revenue Code sections 280G and 4999.

Payments to Nonresident Aliens.—In general, if you pay wages to nonresident aliens, you must withhold income tax (unless excepted by regulations), social security, and Medicare taxes as you would for a U.S. citizen. You must also give a Form W-2 to the nonresident alien. The wages are subject to FUTA tax as well. However, see the chart on page 18 for exceptions to these general rules.

In some cases, a Code section or a U.S. treaty provision will exempt payments to a nonresident alien from "wages." These payments are not subject to income tax withholding. Do not give Form W-2 in these cases. These payments, unless exempt from tax because of a Code or U.S. tax treaty provision, are subject to withholding at a flat 30%, or lower treaty rate. You must report the payments and any withheld tax on **Form 1042S,** Foreign Person's U.S. Source Income Subject to Withholding. Form 1042S is sent to IRS with **Form 1042,** Annual Withholding Tax Return for U.S. Source Income of Foreign Persons. You may have to make deposits of the withheld income tax, using **Form 8109,** Federal Tax Deposit Coupon. See **Pub. 515,** Withholding of Tax on Nonresident Aliens and Foreign Corporations, for more information.

Social Security Totalization Agreements.— The U.S. has entered into totalization agreements with several countries. Under the terms of these agreements, employees and employers who would otherwise have to pay social security taxes to both countries will only have to pay to one country. Thus, items shown as taxable for social security and Medicare in this publication may be exempt if covered by a totalization agreement. Employees and employers who are exempt under one of the agreements are exempt from both the social security (6.2%) portion and the Medicare (1.45%) portion. At this time, we have agreements in effect with Austria, Belgium, Canada, France, Italy, the Netherlands, Norway, Portugal, Spain, Sweden, Switzerland, the United Kingdom, and Germany. For more information about social security totalization agreements, contact the Social Security Administration, Office of International Policy, P.O. Box 17,741, Baltimore, MD 21235. (See Rev. Proc. 80-56, 1980-2 C.B. 851, and Rev. Proc. 84-54, 1984-2 C.B. 489 for information on how to prove the exemption.)

Fringe Benefits

Unless the law says otherwise, you must include fringe benefits in an employee's gross income. The benefits are subject to income and employment taxes. Fringe benefits include cars you provide, flights on aircraft you provide, free or discounted commercial flights, vacations, discounts on property or services, memberships in country clubs or other social clubs, and tickets to entertainment or sporting events. In general, the amount you must include is the amount by which the fair market value of the benefits is more than the sum of what the employee paid for it plus any amount the law excludes. There are other rules you and your employees may use to value certain fringe benefits. See **Pub. 535,** Business Expenses, and the regulations under Code section 61 for more information. This includes special valuation rules for certain fringe benefits, provided that you have timely notified your employees of your election to use one of the special rules.

Nontaxable Fringe Benefits.—Some fringe benefits are not taxable if certain conditions are met. Examples are services provided to your employees at no additional cost to you, qualified employee discounts, working condition fringes (including parking and the use of on-premises athletic facilities), minimal value fringes (including meals you provide at eating places you run for your employees provided the meals are not furnished at below cost), and reduced tuition for education. However, services you provide at no additional cost to you, qualified employee discounts, meals at eating places you run for your employees, and reduced tuition provided to officers, owners, or highly paid employees are only excluded from income and the wage base if the benefits are given to employees on a nondiscriminatory basis. For further information, including who is considered an officer, owner, or highly paid employee, see Pub. 535 and the regulations under Code section 132.

When Fringe Benefits Are Treated as Paid.— You may choose to treat certain noncash fringe benefits as paid by the pay period, or by the quarter, or on any other basis you choose as long as you treat the benefits as paid at least as often as once a year. You do not have to make a formal choice of payment dates or notify IRS of the dates you choose. You do not have to make this choice for all employees. You may change methods as often as you like, as long as you treat all benefits provided in a calendar year as paid by December 31 of the calendar year. (However, see **Special Accounting Rule for Fringe Benefits Provided During November and December** on this page.) You may treat a single fringe benefit as paid on one or more dates in the same calendar year, even if the employee gets the entire benefit at one time. However, once you choose the payment dates, you must report the taxes on your return in the same tax period in which you treated them as paid. This election does not apply to a fringe benefit where real property or investment personal property is transferred.

Withholding on Fringe Benefits.—You may add the value of fringe benefits to regular wages for a payroll period and figure withholding taxes on the total, or you may withhold Federal income tax on the value of the fringe benefits at the flat 20% supplemental wage rate.

If you withhold less than the required amount of taxes from an employee in a calendar year but report the proper amount, you should ask the employee for the social security, Medicare, or railroad retirement and income taxes you paid on his or her behalf. You must recover income taxes before April 1 of the next year.

Election Not To Withhold Income Tax on Personal Use of a Highway Motor Vehicle.— You may choose not to withhold income tax on the value of an employee's personal use of a vehicle you provide. You must, however, withhold social security, Medicare, or railroad retirement taxes on the use of the vehicle. You do not have to make the choice for all employees. If you make the choice, you must do it in such a way that all of your affected employees will be aware of it. For example, you can do this by including the notice with the employee's paycheck, or by displaying the notice. You may change methods at any time by notifying affected employees in a similar way. You must give notice by the later of January 31 of the year to which you want a different method to apply, or within 30 days after you first give a vehicle to the employee.

Depositing Taxes on Fringe Benefits.— Once you choose payment dates for fringe benefits, you must deposit taxes in the same tax period you have determined to treat the fringe benefit as paid. To avoid a penalty, deposit the taxes following the general deposit rules for that tax period. You may reasonably estimate the value of the fringe benefits provided on the date(s) you choose, for purposes of making your deposits on time.

You may claim a refund for overpayments or have them applied to your next employment tax return. If you deposit too little, you may be subject to the failure to deposit penalty. See section 13 for details.

When To Report Fringe Benefits.—In general, you must figure the value of fringe benefits no later than January 31 of the next year. If you provide a vehicle, you may either figure the actual value of the benefit for the whole calendar year or consider the employee's use of the vehicle during the year to be entirely personal and include 100% in the employee's income. See **Fringe Benefits** on page 14 for additional information on this option.

Special Accounting Rule for Fringe Benefits Provided During November and December.— You may choose to treat the value of certain noncash fringe benefits provided during November and December, or any shorter period, as paid in the next year. However, this applies only to those benefits you actually provided during November and December, not to those you merely treated as paid during those months.

If you use this rule, you must notify each affected employee between the time of the employee's last paycheck of the calendar year and at or near the time you give Form W-2. If you use the special accounting rule, your employee must also use it for all purposes (e.g., for deductions related to the fringe benefit) and for the same period. You cannot use this rule for a fringe benefit where you transfer real property or investment personal property to your employee.

Employer "Line of Business" Requirement and Election.—In general, you can only exclude qualified employee discounts and services you provide to employees at no additional cost to you from the income of employees who perform substantial services in the line of business in which the benefits are offered for sale to your customers.

If you have more than one line of business, employees in your other lines of business are not entitled to nontaxable treatment of qualified employee discounts and services you provide at no additional cost to you. However, you can choose to consider all your employees to be in one line of business, and to receive fringe benefits from that line of business. If you make this choice, you will be charged a 30% excise tax on the excess fringe benefits. This is the excess of the total value of these two types of fringe benefits provided during the calendar year over 1% of the total taxable compensation paid to all employees during the calendar year. You must report the tax on **Form 5330,** Return of Excise Taxes Related to Employee Benefit Plans, and it is not deductible. In general, this provision applies only to employment within the United States. For further information, see Code section 4977 and related regulations.

Note: *If you include the value of a noncash fringe benefit in an employee's gross income, you cannot deduct this amount as compensation for services. You can only deduct what it cost you to provide the benefit to the employee.*

Sick Pay

In general, sick pay is any amount you pay, under a plan you take part in, to an employee because of sickness or injury. These amounts are sometimes paid by a third party, such as an insurance company or employees' trust. In either case, these payments are subject to social security, Medicare, or railroad retirement (RRTA) taxes, and Federal unemployment (FUTA) taxes. The payments are also subject to income tax. If you make the payments, withhold on the basis of the employee's Form W-4. If a third party makes the payments, the employee may request income tax withholding by giving the third-party payer a **Form W-4S,** Request for Federal Income Tax Withholding From Sick Pay. Even though the third party makes the payments, you may be responsible for paying social security and Medicare taxes and reporting on Form W-2. See section 19 for details.

The following kinds of payments are not subject to social security, Medicare, RRTA, RURT, or FUTA taxes:

(1) Payments received under a workmen's compensation law.

(2) Payments, or portions of payments, attributable to the employee's contributions to a sick pay plan.

(3) Payments received under the Railroad Retirement Act.

(4) Payments of benefits under the Railroad Unemployment Insurance Act for an on-the-job injury.

(5) Payments made more than 6 months after the last calendar month in which the employee worked.

See section 19 for details on reporting sick pay and for details on withholding and reporting the income, social security, Medicare, or RRTA taxes on sick pay, and for paying the FUTA tax.

7. Taxable Tips

Tips your employee receives are generally subject to withholding. Your employee must report cash tips to you by the 10th of the month after the month the tips are received. The report should include tips you paid over to the employee for charge customers, and tips the employee received directly from customers. No report is required for months when tips are less than $20. Your employee reports the tips on **Form 4070,** Employee's Report of Tips to Employer, or on a similar statement.

The statement must be signed by the employee and must show the following:

- The employee's name, address, and social security number
- Your name and address
- The month or period the report covers
- The total tips

You must collect:

- Income tax, employee social security tax, and employee Medicare tax on the employee's tips.

You can collect these taxes from the employee's wages or from other funds he or she makes available. (See **Tips Treated as Supplemental Wages** in section 8 for further information.) Stop collecting the employee social security tax when his or her wages and tips for the year reach the social security limit.

Stop collecting the employee Medicare tax when his or her wages and tips for the year reach the Medicare limit.

You are responsible for the employer social security and Medicare taxes on wages and tips until the wages (including tips) reach the limits. You must withhold income tax for the whole year on wages and tips, even when the limits are reached.

Use Form 941 to show all tips your employees report during the quarter. See the discussion of Form 941 in section 14 for more information.

On line 6b of Form 941, show all tips your employees report during the quarter until tips and wages paid for each employee reach the social security limit for the year. On line 7 of Form 941, include all tips your employees report during the quarter until tips and wages reach the Medicare limit for the year. Do this even if employee funds were not available for collection of the tax.

If, by the 10th of the month after the month you received an employee's report on tips, you don't have enough employee funds available to deduct the employee tax, you no longer have to collect it. Show any uncollected social security and Medicare taxes on Form W-2. (See the Instructions for Form W-2.)

The chart on page 23 shows how tips are treated for Federal unemployment tax purposes.

Allocated Tips.—If you are a large food or beverage establishment, you must report allocated tips under certain circumstances. A large food or beverage establishment is one that provides food or beverages for consumption on the premises, where tipping is customary, and where there are normally more than 10 employees on a typical business day in all food or beverage operations.

If employees report tips totalling 8% or more of your gross receipts, less carryout sales and sales with at least a 10% service charge added, you do not need to allocate tips. However, you must still file **Form 8027,** Employer's Annual Information Return of Tip Income and Allocated Tips.

If the 8% reporting threshold is not met, you must allocate to tipped employees an amount equal to the difference between 8% of gross receipts (less carryout sales and sales with at least a 10% service charge added) and the total tips reported by the employees. This 8% threshold percentage may be reduced, but not below 2%, by your petition or that of a majority of your employees. See Rev. Proc. 86-21, 1986-1 C.B. 560, for details. The allocation may be made according to an agreement between you and your employees or according to the methods in the regulations. However, all establishments cannot use the method of allocation described in the regulations that is based on the number of hours worked. Only establishments employing fewer than the equivalent of 25 full-time employees during the payroll period can use this method. Do not withhold income, social security, or Medicare taxes on allocated tips. For further information, including required magnetic media filing if 250 or more Forms 8027 are filed, see the separate Instructions for Form 8027.

8. Supplemental Wage Payments

If you pay supplemental wages along with regular wages but do not specify the amount of each, withhold income tax as if the total were a single payment for a regular payroll period. Supplemental wages include but are not limited to bonuses, commissions, overtime pay, accumulated sick leave, severance pay, or payments to an employee for moving expenses he or she cannot deduct.

If you pay supplemental wages separately (or combine them in a single payment and specify the amount of each), the income tax withholding method depends partly on whether you withhold income tax from your employee's regular wages:

- If you withhold income tax from an employee's regular wages, you can use one of the following methods for the supplemental wages:

(a) Withhold a flat 20%.

(b) Add the supplemental and regular wages for the most recent payroll period this year. Then figure the income tax as if the total were a single payment. Subtract the tax already withheld from the regular wages. Withhold the remaining tax from the supplemental wages.

- If you did not withhold income tax from the employee's regular wages, use method (b). (This would occur, for example, when the value of the employee's withholding allowances claimed on Form W-4 is more than the wages.)

Tips Treated as Supplemental Wages.—Withhold the income tax on tips from wages or from other funds the employee makes available. If an employee receives regular wages and reports tips, figure income tax as if the tips were supplemental wages. If you have not withheld income tax from the regular wages, add the tips to the regular wages. Then withhold income tax on the total. If you withheld income tax from the regular wages, you can withhold on the tips by method (a) or (b) on page 6.

Vacation Pay.—Vacation pay is subject to withholding as if it were a regular wage payment. When vacation pay is in addition to regular wages for the vacation period, treat it as a supplemental wage payment. If the vacation pay is for a time longer than your usual payroll period, spread it over the pay periods for which you pay it.

9. Payroll Period

The payroll period is that period of service for which you usually pay wages.

When you have a regular payroll period, withhold income tax for that time period even if your employee does not work the full period.

When you don't have a payroll period, withhold the tax as if you paid wages on a daily or miscellaneous payroll period. Figure the number of days (including Sundays and holidays) in the period covered by the wage payment. If the wages are unrelated to a specific length of time (e.g., commissions paid on completion of a sale), count back the number of days from the payment period to the latest of:

(a) The last wage payment made during the same calendar year,

(b) The date employment began, if during the same calendar year, or

(c) January 1 of the same year.

When you pay an employee for a period of less than 1 week, and the employee signs a statement under penalties of perjury that he or she is not working for any other employer during the same calendar week for wages subject to withholding, figure withholding based on a weekly payroll period. If the employee later begins to work for another employer for wages subject to withholding, the employee is required to notify you within 10 days. You should then figure withholding based on the daily or miscellaneous period.

10. Withholding From Employees

Form W-4.—To know how much income tax to withhold from employees' wages, you should have a Form W-4 on file for each employee. Ask all new employees to give you a signed Form W-4 when they start work. Make the form effective with the first wage payment. If a new employee does not give you a completed Form W-4, withhold tax as if he or she is single, with no withholding allowances. A Form W-4 remains in effect until the employee gives you a new one. If an employee gives you a Form W-4 that replaces an existing Form W-4, begin withholding no later than the start of the 1st payroll period ending on or after the 30th day from the date you received the replacement Form W-4. For exceptions, see the discussion on page 8 on invalid Forms W-4, Forms W-4 that must be sent to IRS, and exemption from income tax withholding.

Note: *A Form W-4 that makes a change for the next calendar year will not take effect in the current calendar year.*

If you need to order Forms W-4 or **Pub. 505,** Tax Withholding and Estimated Tax, or **Pub. 919,** Is My Withholding Correct for 1992?, call the IRS toll-free number 1-800-829-3676.

Withholding.—To determine income tax withholding, take the following into account:

(a) Wages paid, including tips reported.

(b) Marital status.— The withholding tables are different for single and for married employees. A nonresident alien, or a person married to one, is considered single for withholding tax purposes.

There are special rules for an employee whose spouse has recently died. An employee whose spouse has died during the year can show status as Married for the year on Form W-4.

An employee whose spouse died in either of the two preceding tax years can claim Married status if:

(1) The employee's home is maintained as the main household of a child or stepchild for whom the employee can claim an exemption; and

(2) The employee could file a joint return with the decedent in the year of the spouse's death.

An employee who qualifies as a "head of household" is considered single for withholding purposes.

(c) Withholding allowances.— Exemptions are allowable on the Federal income tax return for the employee, spouse, and dependents. Elderly and blind persons receive an increased standard deduction on their tax return if they do not itemize their deductions.

You are not responsible for verifying the withholding allowances your employees claim. However, the following tests may help your employees decide whether they can claim a withholding allowance for a dependent.

Each dependent your employee claims must meet all of the following tests:

(1) Income.—Receives income less than $2,300. (If your employee's child (see Chart A below) was under 19 or a full-time student under 24, ignore this test.)

(2) Support.—Gets more than half of his or her support from your employee.

(3) Married dependents.—Does not file a joint return with his or her spouse.

(4) Citizenship or residence.—Is a citizen or resident of the United States; a resident of Canada or Mexico; or an alien child adopted by and living with a U.S. citizen in a foreign country.

(5) Relationship.—Is either:

Chart A—Relationship

1. Related to the employee (if your employee files jointly, the dependent can be related to either spouse) as one of the following:

Child*	Half-brother	Sister-in-law
Mother	Half-sister	Son-in-law
Father	Stepbrother	Daughter-in-law
Grandparent	Stepsister	Or if related
Great grand-parent, etc.	Stepmother	by blood:
Brother	Stepfather	Uncle
Sister	Mother-in-law	Aunt
Grandchild	Father-in-law	Nephew
Great grand-child, etc.	Brother-in-law	Niece

*Child includes:

Your employee's son, daughter, stepson, or stepdaughter.

A child who lived in your employee's home as a member of the family, if placed with your employee by an authorized placement agency for legal adoption.

A foster child (any child who lived in your employee's home as a member of the family for the whole year).

2. Or a person who lived in your employee's home as a member of the family for the whole year.

(d) Special withholding allowance.—For withholding purposes only, each single person with only one job and each married person with only one job whose spouse is not working can claim one additional withholding allowance. Any person with two jobs can also claim the allowance if one job paid $1,000 or less. A married person with two jobs or a working spouse can claim the allowance if one job paid $1,000 or less.

(e) Additional withholding allowance for heads of households.—For withholding purposes only, each person entitled to head of household filing status can claim one additional withholding allowance on Form W-4.

(f) Additional withholding allowances based on deductions and tax credits.—These allowances are only for withholding purposes; they are not claimed on a tax return. To take these allowances into account, the employee must figure and claim them on Form W-4. See Form W-4 for details. For information for figuring withholding allowances for tax credits, see **Pub. 505,** Tax Withholding and Estimated Tax.

(g) Fewer withholding allowances because of a working spouse, more than one job, or nonwage income.—If any of the above apply, the number of withholding allowances an employee claims may be reduced.

(h) Exemption from income tax withholding for eligible persons.—An employee may claim to be exempt from income tax withholding because he or she had no income tax liability last year and expects none this year. However, the wages may still be subject to social security and Medicare taxes.

An employee must file a Form W-4 each year by February 15 to claim exemption from withholding. Employers should begin withholding for each employee who previously claimed exemption from withholding but has not submitted a new Form W-4 for the current year. Withhold tax as if the employee is single with zero withholding allowances.

An employee who can be claimed as a dependent on someone else's tax return may not be exempt. If that employee has any nonwage income (such as interest on savings), and wages plus the nonwage income are expected to be more than $600 for 1992, he or she usually **cannot** claim exemption from withholding.

Note: *Student status does not automatically exempt the employee from income tax withholding.*

Withholding on Nonresident Aliens.— Employers should remind nonresident aliens when completing Form W-4 that to avoid under withholding of income taxes they should (1) not claim exemption from income tax withholding; (2) request withholding as if they are single, regardless of their actual marital status; and (3) claim only one allowance. However, if the nonresident alien is a resident of Canada, Mexico, Japan, or Korea he or she may claim one allowance for each dependent. In addition, nonresident aliens should request that their employer withhold an extra $3 per week to avoid being underwithheld. For more information, get **Pub. 515,** Withholding of Tax on Nonresident Aliens and Foreign Corporations.

Sending Certain Forms W-4 to IRS.—You must send to IRS copies of certain Forms W-4 received during the quarter from employees still employed by you at the end of the quarter. Send copies when the employee: (1) claims more than 10 withholding allowances, or (2) claims exemption from withholding and his or her wages would normally exceed $200 per week. You are not required to send any others unless IRS notifies you in writing to do so.

Send in each quarter with Form 941 or 941E copies of any Forms W-4 that meet either of the above conditions. Complete boxes 9 and 11 on any Forms W-4 you send in. Box 10 is for the employer's use only, and may be used by the employer to identify the office responsible for processing the employee's payroll information. Also send copies of any written statements from employees in support of the claims made on Forms W-4. Do this even if the Forms W-4 are not in effect at the end of the quarter. You can send them to your Internal Revenue Service Center more often if you like. If you do so, include a cover letter giving your name, address, employer identification number, and the number of forms included. In certain cases, IRS may notify you in writing that you must submit specified Forms W-4 more frequently to your district director separate from your Form 941 or 941E.

Base withholding on the Forms W-4 that you send in unless IRS notifies you in writing that a Form W-4 is defective and that you should do otherwise.

If the IRS notifies you about a particular employee, base withholding on the number of withholding allowances shown in the IRS notice. You will get a copy of the notice to give to the employee. Also, the employee will get a similar notice directly from the IRS. If the employee later gives you a new Form W-4, follow it only if: (1) exempt status is not claimed, or (2) the number of withholding allowances is equal to or fewer than the number in the IRS notice. Otherwise, disregard it and do not submit it to the IRS. Continue to follow the IRS notice. If the employee prepares a new Form W-4 explaining any difference with the IRS notice, he or she may either submit it to IRS or to you. If submitted to you, send the Form W-4 and explanation to the IRS office shown in the notice. Continue to withhold based on the notice unless and until IRS tells you to follow the new Form W-4.

Form W-4 information may be filed with IRS on magnetic tape instead of sending copies of Forms W-4. If you wish to file on magnetic tape, you must submit **Form 4419,** Application for Filing Information Returns Magnetically/ Electronically, to request authorization. See Rev. Proc. 90-9, 1990-1 C.B. 460, also published as Pub. 1245, which contain information concerning magnetic media filing. To obtain these documents or additional information, call the IRS Martinsburg Computing Center at (304) 263-8700.

Invalid Forms W-4.—Any unauthorized change or addition to Form W-4 makes it invalid. This includes taking out any language by which the employee certifies that the form is correct. A Form W-4 is also invalid if, by the date an employee gives it to you, he or she indicates in any way that it is false.

When you get an invalid Form W-4, do not use it to figure withholding. Tell the employee it is invalid and ask for another one. If the employee does not give you a valid one, withhold taxes as if the employee were single and claiming no withholding allowances.

However, if you have an earlier Form W-4 for this worker that is valid, withhold as you did before.

Amounts Exempt From Levy on Wages, Salary, and Other Income.—If you receive a Notice of Levy on Wages, Salary, and Other Income (Forms 668W or 668W(c)), you must withhold amounts as described in the instructions for these forms. **Pub. 1494,** Table for Figuring Amount Exempt from Levy on Wages, Salary, and Other Income (Forms 668W and 668W(c)), shows the exempt amount. If you need the exemption rates for 1992, they are included in Notice 91-36, 1991-44, I.R.B. 13. You may also get these rates by calling 1-800-829-3676 and ordering a copy of the 1992 revision of Pub. 1494.

11. Figuring Withholding

There are several ways to figure income tax withholding. You can use any of the following:

- Percentage method (see pages 26 and 27).
- Wage bracket tables (see pages 28 through 47).

Also see page 24 for directions on how to use the tables for employees claiming more than 10 allowances.

- Alternative formula tables for percentage withholding (see **Pub. 493,** Alternative Tax Withholding Methods and Tables).
- Wage bracket percentage method withholding tables (see Pub. 493).

Employers with automated payroll systems will find the two alternative formula tables and the two alternative wage bracket percentage method tables useful.

- Combined income, employee social security, and employee Medicare tax table (see Pub. 493).
- Annualized wages method (see page 24).
- Average estimated wages method (see page 24).
- Cumulative wages and part-year employment methods (see page 24). These may be used if your employee requests that you use them, and you agree to this.
- Other alternative methods (see page 24).

If an employee wants additional tax withheld, have the employee show the extra amount on Form W-4.

Social Security and Medicare Taxes, Employer's and Employee's Share.—For wages paid in 1992, the social security tax rate is 6.2% and the Medicare tax rate is 1.45% for both the employer and the employee. You can multiply each wage payment by these percentages or use the tables on pages 48 through 50. You can use the amounts in the boxes in the lower right corners of the tables on pages 49 and 50 if the wage payment is $100 or more. For example, the social security tax on a wage payment of $355 would be $22.01 ($18.60 + $3.41) each. The Medicare tax would be $5.15 ($4.35 + $.80) each.

12. Income Tax Withholding From Pensions and Annuities

Generally, payers or plan administrators must withhold Federal income tax at specified rates on certain periodic pension, annuity, deferred income payments, and on nonperiodic distributions, including qualified total distributions. Recipients may also choose to have additional amounts withheld from periodic payments and nonperiodic distributions, or may choose exemption from withholding (however, see **Periodic Payments and Nonperiodic Distributions Delivered Outside the U.S.** on page 9). They do this by filing with the payer or administrator a Form W-4P, and completing the appropriate lines. Payers and administrators may substitute their own forms for this purpose.

Note: *Since military retirement pay is generally considered as wages, and not as a pension or annuity, military retirees should give you a Form W-4 to request income tax withholding, not Form W-4P.*

Also, see section 14 for information on reporting withheld income tax on Form 941.

Withholding on Periodic Payments.—Generally, periodic payments are those payable over a period of more than a year. Because these payments are treated as if they are wages, you can figure withholding by using the income tax withholding tables and methods in this publication or in Pub. 493.

Recipients of periodic payments can file a Form W-4P with you to claim an exemption from withholding, to revoke a previously filed exemption, or to specify the number of withholding allowances and any additional amount they want withheld. If they do not file a Form W-4P, you must figure withholding by treating a recipient as married with three withholding allowances. If a recipient already has a previously filed Form W-4P in effect with you under the prior law and does not file a new one, you may continue to withhold the flat dollar amount shown on the form. However, you must have notified the recipient that his or her previously filed Form W-4P will remain in effect unless he or she elects exemption from withholding or files a new Form W-4P.

After the end of the year, give each recipient a Form 1099-R showing the required information. (See section 16.)

Withholding on Nonperiodic Payments.—For information on withholding from nonperiodic payments and the tables for withholding on qualified total distributions, see Pub. 493.

Periodic Payments and Nonperiodic Distributions Delivered Outside the U.S.—A recipient of any such payment or distribution that is delivered outside the U.S. or its possessions cannot choose exemption from withholding unless the recipient certifies to the payer that the recipient is not: (1) a U.S. citizen who is a bona fide resident of a foreign country; or (2) an individual to whom Internal Revenue Code section 877 applies (concerning expatriation to avoid tax). The certification can be made in a statement to the payer under the penalties of perjury.

Nonresident aliens who choose such exemption will be subject to withholding under section 1441 of the Code. See Pub. 515.

Note: *There is an automatic withholding rule for foreign-delivered pension benefits and similar payments made to individuals subject to U.S. income taxation on their worldwide income. Recipients of pension benefits or payments delivered in any U.S. possession may elect an exemption from withholding. However, recipients choosing exemption from withholding must certify that they were not U.S. citizens or resident aliens.*

13. Depositing Taxes

In general, you must deposit backup withholding, income tax withheld, and both the employer and employee social security and Medicare taxes that total $500 or more.

Use **Form 8109,** Federal Tax Deposit Coupon, to deposit employment taxes and all other types of taxes that are deposited. Do **not** use the deposit coupons to pay delinquent taxes that have been assessed by the IRS. These payments should be sent directly to your Internal Revenue Service Center along with a copy of any related notice the IRS sent you.

The IRS will send you a coupon book after you apply for an employer identification number. The coupons will be preprinted with your name, address, and employer identification number. They have entry boxes for indicating the type of tax and the tax period against which the deposit is to be applied.

Note: *It is very important to clearly mark the correct type of tax and tax period on each deposit coupon. This information is used by the IRS to credit your account.*

When you need more coupons, order them from your Internal Revenue Service Center, using **Form 8109A,** FTD Reorder Form, that is included in the coupon book. Your coupons will be sent to the address preprinted on the reorder form, which may not be your IRS account address (the address the IRS uses to send you your tax returns, refunds, and notices). If you want them sent to a different address, show the new information on the reorder form and deposit coupons will be sent to the new address. Your IRS account address will not change even if you have your coupons sent to a different address.

Note: *You should receive your reorder in approximately 5-6 weeks. Be sure to allow ample reorder time before you use up your current supply.*

If you have branch offices depositing taxes, give them coupons and complete instructions so they can deposit the taxes when due.

Please use only your coupons. If you use anyone else's coupon, you may be subject to the failure to deposit penalty. This is because your account will be underpaid by the amount of the deposit credited to the other person's account. See **Penalties** below for details.

Mail or deliver each deposit coupon and a single payment covering the taxes to be deposited to a financial institution qualified as a depositary for Federal taxes or to the Federal Reserve bank or branch (FRB) serving your geographical area. Follow the instructions in the front of the coupon book. Make the check or money order payable to the depositary or FRB where you make your deposit. To help ensure proper crediting of your account, include your employer identification number, the type of tax (e.g., Form 940), and tax period to which the payment applies on your check or money order.

Reporting Agents.—Reporting agents who submit Federal employment tax deposits for their clients should see Rev. Proc. 89-48, 1989-2 C.B. 599 for details.

Deposits at Authorized Financial Institutions.—Authorized depositaries must accept cash, a postal money order drawn to the order of the depositary, or a check or draft drawn on and made payable to the depositary. You can deposit taxes with a check drawn on another financial institution only if the depositary is willing to accept that form of payment.

Deposits at FRBs.—If you use a check to deposit taxes at an FRB, please deposit with the FRB that serves your area. The check must be considered by that FRB as an immediate credit item. Deposits may be subject to the failure to deposit penalty if the check is not considered an immediate credit item by that FRB. You can learn which FRB serves your area, and what checks are immediate credit items, from any commercial bank or FRB.

Note: *Please be sure that the financial institution where you make deposits is an authorized depositary. Deposits made at an unauthorized institution may be subject to the failure to deposit penalty.*

Depositing on Time.—FRBs accept deposits in accordance with their check collection schedule and only process immediate credit items. Generally, immediate credit items include checks drawn on commercial banks located in the same city as the FRB on the date that the commercial bank processes the check. If you use a check to deposit taxes at an FRB, please deposit with the FRB that serves your area by the cut-off time necessary for the check to be considered an immediate credit item. Deposits may be subject to the failure to deposit penalty if the check is not considered an immediate credit item on the day it is received by that FRB.

Note: *Deposits of $20,000 or more, which are made by taxpayers required to deposit any taxes more than once a month, must be received by the due date of the deposit to be timely.*

If a deposit that does not comply with the deposit payment requirements is made at an FRB, that deposit will be dated on collection of the funds by the FRB, regardless of when mailed.

If you hand-deliver your deposit to the depositary on the due date, be sure to deliver it before the depositary closes its business day.

Depositing Without a Coupon or EIN.—If you have applied for an employer identification number but have not received it, and you must make a deposit, make the deposit with your Internal Revenue Service Center rather than with a depositary or FRB. Make it payable to IRS and show on it your name (as shown on Form SS-4), address, kind of tax, period covered, and date you applied for an EIN. Attach an explanation to the deposit.

If you have reordered coupons and have not received them in time to make a deposit, or if you are a new employer and have already received your employer identification number but have not yet received your initial supply of deposit coupons, use **Form 8109-B.** You can get this over-the-counter deposit coupon at most IRS offices. When you use Form 8109-B, be sure your EIN, name and address, type of tax (i.e., 940, 941, etc.), tax period for which you are depositing, and the month your tax year ends are on the form. Use Form 8109-B to make deposits with an authorized depositary or FRB only.

Deposit Record.—For your records, a stub is provided with each coupon in the coupon book. The coupon itself will not be returned. It is used to credit your account. Your check or money order is your receipt.

How To Claim Credit for Overpayments.—If you deposited more than the right amount of taxes for a quarter, you can ask on the tax return you file to have the overpayment refunded or applied as a credit to your next return.

Penalties.—The penalties for failure to make deposits of taxes are based on applicable percentages of the amount of underpayment determined by the number of days the deposit is late. If the failure is:

(1) not more than 5 days late, the applicable percentage is 2% of the underdeposited taxes;

(2) more than 5 days but not more than 15 days late, the applicable percentage is 5% of the underdeposited taxes; or

(3) if the failure is more than 15 days late, the penalty is 10%.

Also, a penalty of 15% may be imposed if the underdeposited taxes are not paid on or before the earlier of:

(1) 10 days after the first delinquency notice; or

(2) the day on which notice and demand for immediate payment is given.

Separate Accounting When Deposits Are Not Made or Withheld Taxes Are Not Paid.— Separate accounting may be required if you do not pay over withheld employee social security tax, Medicare tax, or income tax, deposit required taxes, make required payments, or file tax returns. In this case, you would receive written notice from the district director requiring you to deposit taxes in a special trust account for the U.S. Government. You would also have to file monthly tax returns on **Form 941-M,** Employer's Monthly Federal Tax Return. Penalties are provided for not depositing taxes and not making payments.

When To Deposit.—The amount of taxes determines the frequency of deposits. You owe these taxes when you pay the wages, not when your payroll period ends. The rules and examples below explain how often to deposit taxes. **Pub. 509,** Tax Calendars for 1992, shows the due dates for deposits required under rules 2 through 4.

Note: *If any date shown falls on a Saturday, Sunday, or legal holiday, use the next regular workday for depositing taxes.*

Depositing Social Security, Medicare, and Withheld Income Taxes

Note: *Effective for deposit periods beginning after March 31, 1991, an employer's deposit obligation is determined by reference to the total amount of liability accumulated for the period and no longer by the total amount of undeposited taxes on hand at the close of the period.*

Rule 1—Less than $500 at end of quarter.— If at the end of the calendar quarter your total tax liability for the quarter is less than $500, you do not have to deposit the taxes. You may pay the taxes to IRS with Form 941 (or 941E), or you may deposit them by the end of the next month.

Rule 2—Less than $500 at the end of any month.—If at the end of any month your total tax liability is less than $500, you do not have to make a deposit. You may carry the taxes over to the following month within the quarter. (See Example A.)

Rule 3—$500 or more but less than $3,000 at the end of any month.—If at the end of any month your total tax liability is $500 or more but less than $3,000, you must deposit the taxes within 15 days after the end of the month, unless the exception to rule 3 below applies.

Exception to rule 3: If you are required to make a deposit of $3,000 or more during the month under rule 4 below, carry over any balance of less than $3,000 at the end of the first or second month of the quarter to the next month. Follow rules 3 and 4 to determine when the next deposit is due (see Example D).

If you are required to make a deposit of $3,000 or more during the third month of the quarter, deposit any balance of $500 or more but less than $3,000 by the end of the next month. A balance due of less than $500 can be paid with the return following rule 1 (see Example E).

Rule 4—$3,000 or more but less than $100,000 at the end of any eighth-monthly period.—Each month is divided into eight deposit periods called eighth-monthly periods, that end on the 3rd, 7th, 11th, 15th, 19th, 22nd, 25th, and last day of the month. If at the end of any eighth-monthly period your total tax liability is $3,000 or more, deposit the taxes within 3 banking days after the end of that eighth-monthly period. (See Examples B, C, D, and E, below.) Do not count as banking days local holidays observed by authorized financial institutions, Saturdays, Sundays, and legal holidays. If your tax liability is $100,000 or more at the end or at any time during the eighth-monthly period, deposit the taxes on the next banking day as described in rule 5.

Exception to rule 4: If this is the first time you are required to make a deposit within 3 banking days after the end of an eighth-monthly period, you may deposit the taxes by the 15th of the next month (instead of within 3 banking days after the eighth-monthly period) if you meet **all** of the following conditions:

- You were not required to deposit taxes under rule 4 during the 4 quarters preceding the current quarter.
- You were not required to deposit taxes under rule 4 during earlier months of this quarter.
- Your total tax liability for any eighth-monthly period during this month is less than $10,000.

Rule 5—$100,000 or more during any eighth-monthly period.—If your total tax liability is $100,000 or more on any day in any eighth-monthly period, you are required to deposit the payroll taxes by the close of the next banking day. You must also complete **Schedule B (Form 941),** Supplemental Record of Federal Tax Liability, and attach it to your Form 941 or Form 941E.

You will be considered to meet rules 4 and 5 if:

- When your tax liability is $3,000 or more for any eighth-monthly period, you deposit at least 95% of the tax liability for that eighth-monthly period within 3 banking days after the end of that period. However, if you accumulate a tax liability of $100,000 or more on any day in an eighth-monthly period, you deposit at least 95% of that amount on the next banking day.
- You deposit any underpayment as follows:

(a) If the eighth-monthly period is in the first or second month of the quarter, you deposit the underpayment with the first deposit that is otherwise required to be made after the 15th of the following month.

(b) If the eighth-monthly period is in the last month of the quarter, you deposit any underpayment of $500 or more by the due date of the return. (Any underpayment less than $500 can be paid with Form 941 (or 941E) as explained in rule 1.)

The following examples explain the five deposit rules and tell where the tax liability should be shown on the Record of Federal Tax Liability on Form 941 and Form 941E.

Example A: The taxes on wages paid in October are $450, and the taxes on wages paid in November are $550. No deposit is required for October (because of rule 2), but add the $450 to the $550 for November and deposit the total ($1,000) by December 15 (as required by rule 3). Show $1,000 on line *II.*

Example B: The taxes on wages paid from the 1st through the 3rd of the month are $3,500. Deposit these taxes within 3 banking days after the 3rd of the month (as required by rule 4). Show $3,500 on line A.

Example C: The taxes on wages paid from the 4th through the 7th of January are $2,500 and the taxes on wages paid from the 8th through the 11th are $2,000. A separate deposit is not required for the $2,500, but add it to the $2,000 and deposit the total ($4,500) within 3 banking days after the 11th of the month (as required by rule 4). Show $2,500 on line B and $2,000 on line C.

Example D: The taxes on wages paid from the 23rd through the 25th of January are $3,500. Deposit these taxes within 3 banking days after the 25th of the month (as required by rule 4). Show $3,500 on line C. The taxes on wages paid from the 26th through the end of January are $2,500. Since a deposit was already required to be made for an eighth-monthly period during the month, a separate deposit is not required for the $2,500 (because of the exception to rule 3). Show $2,500 on line H. Carry the $2,500 over and add it to the taxes on wages paid in February. Then follow rules 3 and 4 to determine when the next deposit is required. (However, if this occurs in the last month of a quarter, deposit any balance due of $500 or more but less than $3,000 by the end of the next month.)

Example E: Wages are paid on Friday for the prior week. In the first quarter of 1992, paydays are on January 3, 10, 17, 24, and 31; February 7, 14, 21, and 28; and March 6, 13, 20, and 27. Taxes are $1,050 for each payday.

Enter $1,050 on lines A, C, E, G, H, J, L, N, P, R, T, V and X of Form 941. Enter $5,250 on Total line I; $4,200 on Total lines II and III; and $13,650 on line IV.

You must make a deposit within 3 banking days of January 19, February 7, February 29, and March 22 because the liability for taxes reached at least $3,000 for the eighth-monthly periods ending on those dates.

The liability for taxes at the end of January of $2,100 (for paydays on the 24th and 31st) may be carried over to February because of the exception to rule 3 as explained in Example D. A deposit will be required within 3 banking days of February 29th when the liability for taxes reached at least $3,000. A deposit is required within 3 banking days of March 22 for the paydays of March 6, 13, and 20. At the end of March, the liability for taxes of $1,050 (for the payday on the 27th) must be deposited by April 30 (because of the exception to rule 3 for the last month of a quarter as explained in Example D).

Chart B—Summary of Deposit Rules for Social Security and Medicare Taxes and Withheld Income Tax

Deposit Rule	Deposit Due
(1) If at the end of the quarter your total tax liability for the quarter is less than $500:	(1) No deposit is required. You may pay the taxes to IRS with Form 941 (or 941E), or you may deposit them by the due date of the return.
(2) If at the end of any month your total tax liability is less than $500:	(2) No deposit is required. You may carry the tax liability over to the following month within the quarter.
(3) If at the end of any month your total tax liability is $500 or more but less than $3,000:	(3) Within 15 days after the end of the month. (No deposit is required if you were required to make a deposit for an eighth-monthly period during the month under rule 4. However, if you were required to make a deposit under rule 4 in the last month of the quarter, deposit any balance due of less than $3,000 by the due date of the return.)
(4) If at the end of any eighth-monthly period (the 3rd, 7th, 11th, 15th, 19th, 22nd, 25th, and last day of each month) your total tax liability is $3,000 or more but less than $100,000:	(4) Within 3 banking days after the end of that eighth-monthly period.
(5) If at the end of any day during an eighth-monthly period your total tax liability is $100,000 or more:	(5) By the end of the next banking day.

Example F: Wages are paid every two weeks. Paydays for December of 1992 are:

Payroll Date	Payroll Tax Liability	Eighth-Monthly Period
December 3, 1992	$105,000	Q
December 17, 1992	90,000	U
December 31, 1992	130,000	X

The December 3rd liability of $105,000 is due by December 4, 1992. (Rule 5 applies.)

The December 17th liability of $90,000 is due by December 23, 1992. (Rule 4 applies.)

The December 31st liability of $130,000 is due by January 2, 1993 (January 1st is a banking holiday). (Rule 5 applies.)

Depositing Backup Withholding.—For tax deposit purposes, you can either combine backup withholding with other taxes reported on Form 941 or 941E and deposit the combined total, or you can treat backup withholding as a separate tax and deposit it separately following the same deposit rules used for social security, Medicare, and withheld income taxes.

If you treat backup withholding as a separate tax, show the amounts for deposit purposes on **Schedule A (Form 941),** Record of Federal Backup Withholding Tax Liability, and when depositing this tax, darken the "Sch. A" entry box on the deposit coupon. Schedule A (Form 941) must be attached to Form 941 or 941E.

Deposit Instructions for State and Local Government Employers.—If you are not covered by a section 218 agreement, deposit withheld income tax and (for employees hired after March 31, 1986) the Medicare tax. If you are covered by a section 218 agreement (or (for services performed after July 1, 1991) have employees that are not members of a state or local government retirement system), deposit income tax and social security and Medicare taxes following rules 1 through 5 on page 10.

Deposit with authorized depositaries and FRBs only; do not send the social security taxes to the state.

Depositing Federal Unemployment (FUTA) Taxes.—For deposit purposes, figure FUTA tax quarterly. Deposit any amount due by the last day of the first month after the quarter ends.

Determine whether you must deposit tax for any of the first 3 quarters in a year. Figure the total tax by multiplying by .008 that part of the first $7,000 of each employee's annual wages that you paid during the quarter. If this amount (plus any amount not yet deposited for any earlier quarter of the year) is more than $100, deposit it during the first month after the quarter. But if it is $100 or less, you do not have to deposit it. Just add it to the amount for deposit for the next quarter.

If the tax reportable on Form 940-EZ or Form 940 (including any credit reductions under Code section 3302(c)), minus amounts deposited for the year, is more than $100, deposit all of the tax by January 31. If your tax for the year (minus deposits) is $100 or less, you may either deposit it or pay it with Form 940 or Form 940-EZ by January 31.

14. Filing the Quarterly Return of Withheld Income Tax, Social Security, and Medicare Taxes

Form 941.—Generally, all employers who are subject to income tax withholding (including withholding on pensions, annuities, sick pay, gambling winnings, and supplemental unemployment benefits) or social security and Medicare taxes must file Form 941 quarterly. However, there are the following exceptions:

(a) Seasonal employers no longer file for quarters when they regularly have no tax liability because they have paid no wages. To alert IRS that you will not have to file a return for one or more quarters during the year, check the "Seasonal employer" box above line 1 on Form 941. The IRS will mail two Forms 941 to the seasonal filer once a year after March 1. The preprinted label will not include the date the quarter ended. You must enter the date the quarter ended when you file the return. IRS will generally not inquire about unfiled returns if at least one taxable return is filed each year. However, you must check the "Seasonal employer" box on every quarterly return you file. Otherwise, IRS will expect a return to be filed for each quarter.

(b) Employers who report only withheld income tax or who withheld only the Medicare tax. These include some payers of supplemental unemployment compensation benefits, churches and church-controlled organizations that have filed **Form 8274**, Certification by Churches and Qualified Church-Controlled Organizations Electing Exemption From Employer Social Security Taxes and certain payers of pensions, annuities, and sick pay. These employers should use Form 941E.

(c) Household employers reporting social security and Medicare taxes and/or withheld income tax. Report these on Form 942.

(d) Employers reporting wages for employees in American Samoa, Guam, the Commonwealth of the Northern Mariana Islands, or the Virgin Islands. If the employees are not subject to U.S. income tax withholding, use Form 941SS. Employers in Puerto Rico use Form 941PR.

(e) Agricultural employers reporting social security and Medicare taxes and withheld income tax. Report these on Form 943.

Penalties.—For each whole or part month a return is not filed when required (disregarding any extensions of the filing deadline), there is a penalty of 5% of the amount that should have been shown on that return. The maximum penalty is 25%. Also, for each whole or part month the tax is paid late (disregarding any extensions of the payment deadline), a penalty of 0.5% of the amount of tax generally applies. The maximum for this penalty is also 25%. The penalties will not be charged if there is an acceptable reason for failing to file or pay.

In cases where income, social security, and Medicare taxes that should be withheld are not withheld or are not paid to the IRS, the **100% penalty** may be applied. Under this penalty, certain officers or employees of a corporation, or certain members or employees of a partnership become personally liable for the payment of the taxes and penalized an equal amount.

When To File.—Due dates for returns and tax payments are:

Chart C—Due Dates

Quarter	Ending	Due Date
Jan.-Feb.-Mar.	Mar. 31	Apr. 30
Apr.-May-June	June 30	July 31
July-Aug.-Sept.	Sept.30	Oct. 31
Oct.-Nov.-Dec.	Dec. 31	Jan. 31

If you deposited all taxes when due for the quarter, you may file the return by the 10th

Chart D—Social Security and Medicare Tax Rate Table (for 3 prior years)

Calendar Year	Wage Base (each employee)	Tax Rate on Taxable Wages	Tax Rate on Taxable Tips
1991-Social Security	$53,400	12.40%	12.40%
1991- Medicare	125,000	2.90	2.90
1990	51,300	15.30	15.30
1989	48,000	15.02	15.02

Note: *Prior to 1991, the social security and Medicare tax rates were combined and the wage bases were the same.*

day of the second month following the quarter.

Where To File.—File Form 941 (or Form 941E) with the Internal Revenue Service Center for the region serving your legal residence, main place of business, or office or agency. The addresses are listed in the Form 941 and 941E instructions.

Hints on Filing.—Do not report more than one calendar quarter on one return.

Use the preaddressed form mailed to you. If you don't have the form, get one from any IRS office in time to file the return when due. If you use a form that is not preaddressed, please show your name and employer identification number on it. Be sure they are exactly as they appeared on earlier returns.

If you go out of business or stop paying wages, file a final return.

Successor Employer.—If you received all or most of the property used in the trade or business of another employer, or a unit of that employer's trade or business, you may, when you figure the annual wage limit, include the wages the other employer paid to your employees. See Regulations section 31.3121(a)(1)-1, for more information. Also see Rev. Proc. 84-77, 1984-2 C.B. 753, for the procedures used in filing returns in a predecessor-successor situation.

Common Paymaster.—For information on concurrent employment by related corporations with a common paymaster, see Regulations section 31.3121(s).

Adjustments.—For every return on which you report an adjustment, attach a statement. It should explain why you are making the adjustment, the period covered, and any other information required by the instructions on the return. You cannot adjust income tax withholding after the end of the calendar year.

If you withhold no social security and Medicare taxes or less than the right amount from an employee's wages, you can make it up from later pay to that employee. But you are the one who owes the underpayment. Reimbursement is up to you and the employee. (This does not apply to tax on tips.)

If you withhold more than the right amount of social security and Medicare taxes from wages paid, give the employee the excess. Be sure to keep in your records the employee's written receipt showing the date and amount of the repayment. If you don't have a receipt, you must report and pay each excess amount when you file the return for the quarter in which you withheld too much tax.

Form 941 tells how to correct mistakes in reporting withheld income, social security, and Medicare taxes, including the use of **Form 941c,** Statement to Correct Information. Generally, you can adjust social security and Medicare taxes reported on previous Forms 941 on your current Form 941. However, if you use Form 941c to correct social security and Medicare taxes because of a change in the wage totals reported for a previous year, you may also need to file **Forms W-2c,** Statement of Corrected Income and Tax Amounts, and **Form W-3c,** Transmittal of Corrected Income and Tax Statements. Also, if you cannot adjust social security and Medicare taxes you overwithheld, you may be able to claim a refund of these taxes by filing **Form 843,** Claim for Refund and Request for Abatement.

Household Employees.—If you are a sole proprietor and file Form 941 for business employees, you can include household employees on it. Otherwise, report them on Form 942. Use Form 943 to report household employees in a private home on a farm operated for profit. They are considered farmworkers. You can withhold income tax from wages you pay your household employees if you and your employees agree to this arrangement.

Generally, household work includes services performed in or about your private home by cooks, butlers, housekeepers, governesses, maids, cleaning people, babysitters, janitors, caretakers, handy persons, gardeners, and drivers of cars for family use.

You are liable for social security and Medicare taxes if you pay a household employee cash wages of $50 or more in a calendar quarter. It doesn't matter when the wages were earned.

The $50 test applies to each household employee. Checks, money orders, etc., are the same as cash. The value of food, lodging, clothing, bus or subway tokens, and other noncash items you give to the employee is not subject to social security and Medicare taxes.

You do not have to pay social security and Medicare taxes on cash wages for any household service done in your home by your mother or father unless both (a) and (b) below apply.

(a) You have in your home a son or daughter, or stepson or stepdaughter, who is under 18, or who has a physical or mental condition requiring the personal care of an adult for at least 4 weeks in the quarter. (The weeks must be continuous.)

(b) You are a widow or widower, or are divorced, or have a spouse in your home who, because of a physical or mental condition, is unable to care for your son or daughter, or stepson or stepdaughter, for at least 4 weeks in the quarter. (The weeks must be continuous.)

Send Copy A of Forms W-2 for household employees with a Form W-3 to the **Social Security Administration, Albuquerque Data Operations Center, Albuquerque, NM 87180** by the last day of February of the following year. (If you are sending only one Form W-2, Form W-3 is not needed.)

For social security and Medicare taxes on household employees only, you may round each wage payment to the nearest whole dollar to figure taxes and report wages on your returns. If you do this, you must round off every wage payment made to every household employee during the same quarter. Get **Pub. 926,** Employment Taxes for Household Employers, for more information.

Modifying Forms 941 and 942 for Prior Years.—You will have to modify Forms 941 and 942 if you are using a current year's form to report taxes from a prior year. **Caution:** *The instructions on the form may be inappropriate for the year for which you are reporting taxes, because of changes in the law, regulations, or procedures. Contact the IRS if you have any questions. The revision date (found under the form number at the top of the form) will tell you the year for which the form was developed.*

Note: *A form for a particular year can generally be used without modification for any quarter within that year. For example, a form with any 1991 revision date (for example, January or October 1991) can generally be used without modification for any quarter of 1991.*

In all cases, however, be sure to correctly fill out the "Date quarter ended" section at the top of the form. If you are modifying a form with a label, change the date on the label (the date is shown with the month and year the quarter ends; for example, JUN91 would be for the quarter ending June 30, 1991). Cross out any inapplicable tax rate(s) shown on the form and write in the rate from the table above. You can get tax rates and wage bases for years not shown in the table from the IRS.

15. Filing the Federal Unemployment (FUTA) Tax Return (Form 940 or 940-EZ)

The Federal Unemployment Tax Act (FUTA), together with state unemployment systems, provides for payments of unemployment compensation to workers who have lost their jobs. Most employers pay both a Federal and state unemployment tax. Only the employer pays this tax. Use Form 940 or 940-EZ, Employer's Annual Federal Unemployment (FUTA) Tax Return, to report Federal unemployment tax.

For 1991, IRS will mail preaddressed Forms 940 or 940-EZ to employers who filed returns the year before. If you do not receive Form 940 or 940-EZ in the mail, you can get them from the IRS.

By January 31, file Form 940 or 940-EZ and deposit or pay the balance of tax. If you deposit all FUTA tax when due, you have 10 additional days to file Form 940 or Form 940-EZ.

You may be able to use Form 940-EZ if: (1) you paid unemployment taxes ("contributions") to only one state; (2) you paid these taxes by the due date of Form 940 or 940-EZ; and (3) all wages that were taxable for FUTA tax purposes were also taxable for your state's unemployment tax. Otherwise, use Form 940. For example, if you paid wages to corporate officers (these wages are subject to FUTA tax) in a state that exempts these wages from its unemployment taxes, you cannot use Form 940-EZ.

For 1992, the FUTA tax is 6.2% of wages paid during the year. The tax applies to the first $7,000 you pay each employee as wages during the calendar year. Generally, you can take a credit against your FUTA tax for amounts you paid into state unemployment funds. This credit cannot be more than 5.4% of taxable wages. You are responsible for paying FUTA tax. You cannot deduct it from employees' wages.

If you have acquired a business from someone else who was an employer liable for FUTA tax, you may count the wages that employer paid to the employees who continue to work for you when you figure the wage limit. If the prior owner was not subject to FUTA tax, you may be eligible for a credit based on the state unemployment contributions paid by that owner, under Code section 3302(e) and Regulations section 31.3302(e)-(1).

16. Reporting Withheld Taxes

Forms W-2 and 1099-R.—By the last day of February, send to SSA Copy A of all Forms W-2 issued for the previous year. File Form W-3 with the copies you send. The SSA addresses are listed in the Form W-3 instructions.

By February 28, send Copy A of all Forms 1099-R with Form 1096 to the Internal Revenue Service Center for your locality.

If you file a final return on Form 941 or 941E before the end of the year, send SSA all Copies A of the Forms W-2 issued for the year along with Form W-3. Do this when you send IRS your final return. However, you may file these forms as late as the last day of February of the following year.

If your payroll includes several separate establishments, you may group the copies for each establishment and send each group with a separate Form W-3, or you may use a single Form W-3.

If you have a very large number of forms, you may use several packages. Be sure to put your name on each package. Number the packages in order. Write the number of packages below the title on Form W-3 and put it in the first package.

Use first class postage to mail the forms to SSA.

Keep any payee copies of Forms W-2 and 1099-R that you have tried to deliver without success for 4 years. You must make a reasonable effort to deliver these statements. An example would be mailing the statement to the recipient's last known address.

Filing on Magnetic Media.—In general, if you file 250 or more information returns (Forms W-2, 1099, 1098, 5498, or W-2G) you must use magnetic media to file. If you file on magnetic media, do not file the same returns on paper. The due dates for filing on magnetic media are the same as for paper documents.

If filing on magnetic media would be an undue hardship, you may be able to get a waiver from this requirement, for a period of time not to exceed one tax year, by filing **Form 8508,** Request for Waiver From Filing Information Returns on Magnetic Media. You must apply for this waiver at least 90 days before the due date of the return. For more information on obtaining a waiver, get Form 8508. If you are filing Forms W-2 using magnetic media, you may also need **Form 6559,** Transmitter and Summary Report of Magnetic Media Filing, and **Form 6559-A**, Continuation Sheet for Form 6559.

If you are filing Form W-2 data for the first time, you must obtain SSA approval of the data formats you plan to use.

For additional information on filing information returns on magnetic media, including approval procedures for use of your particular magnetic medium, you may write to the addresses below.

Chart E—Magnetic Media Addresses

1. *For Form W-2—*
Social Security Administration
P.O. Box 2317
Baltimore, MD 21235
Attn: Magnetic Media Group

Note: *You may also get this information from your local SSA office.*

2. *For Forms 1099, 1098, 5498, or W-2G—*
Internal Revenue Service
Martinsburg Computing Center
P.O. Box 1359
Martinsburg, WV 25401-1359

17. Reporting to Employees

Form W-2.—Give a Form W-2 to each employee from whom you withheld income tax and to each employee from whom you would have withheld income tax if the employee had claimed no more than one withholding allowance, or had not claimed exemption from withholding on Form W-4.

If you have a trade or business, give a Form W-2 to each employee you pay for services. Pay includes cash and the cash value of anything else used to pay an employee for services.

Give a Form W-2 to each recipient of supplemental unemployment compensation benefits or third-party sick pay.

You must give a Form W-2 to any employee if the wages were also subject to social security and Medicare taxes. The Form W-2 must show the following social security and Medicare information: wages paid, tips reported, and taxes withheld (or paid on behalf of the employee).

Example.—You hired a part-time maid in 1991. You paid $48.50 in the first quarter, $60 in both the second and third quarters, and $49.25 in the fourth quarter. On your quarterly Form 942 (or Form 941 for certain sole proprietors), report the wages and pay the social security and Medicare tax for the second and third quarters. On Form W-2, show $217.75 as wages, tips, and other compensation in box 10. In box 12 show $120 as wages subject to social security. The employee social security tax is $7.44 ($120 × 6.2%), reported in box 11. In box 14 show $120 as wages subject to Medicare. The employee Medicare tax is $1.74 ($120 × 1.45%), reported in box 15.

What To Include on the 1991 Form W-2 (also see the 1991 Instructions for Form W-2).—Use Form W-2 to report all wages, tips, and other compensation you pay an employee. "Other compensation" means amounts includible in gross income but not subject to income tax withholding. It applies to both cash and noncash payments. Add the cash value of other compensation to the wages paid and tips reported. Show the total (excluding elective deferrals) in box 10 on Form W-2. If you have a payroll system that makes it difficult to combine other compensation with wages and tips, you may file two Forms W-2. One can show wages and tips; the other can show the other compensation. Also include items such as:

(a)(1) Reimbursements you made to an employee for moving expenses that he or she cannot deduct and from which you withheld income tax. Report these reimbursements as wages. Report any other reimbursements for moving expenses as other compensation.

When you reimburse or pay your employee's moving expenses (whether to your employee, to a third party for your employee, or by providing services in-kind to the employee), give the employee a completed **Form 4782,** Employee Moving Expense Information. Do this for each such move. (**Note:** *There are different rules for services in-kind given to military personnel. See* ***Pub. 521,*** *Moving Expenses.*)

(a)(2) Certain reimbursements for employee business expenses. Generally, payments made under an accountable plan are excluded from the employee's gross income and are not reported on Form W-2. However, if your employees receive per diem or mileage allowance payments in excess of the standard mileage rate, or the per diem or high-low substantiation methods (i.e., government specified rates), you must include as income any amount in excess of the government specified rates. The excess amounts are subject to income tax withholding, social security tax, Medicare tax, and Federal unemployment tax. Use code "L" in Box 17 to report the amount that is equal to the government specified rates.

Payments made under a nonaccountable plan are reportable as wages on Form W-2, and are subject to income tax withholding, social security tax, Medicare tax, and Federal unemployment tax.

For more information on accountable plans, nonaccountable plans, the standard mileage rate, the per diem substantiation method, and the high-low substantiation method, see Regulations section 1.62-2, Rev. Proc. 90-59, 1990-2 C.B. 644, Rev. Proc. 90-60, 1990-2 C.B. 651, **Pub. 463,** Travel, Entertainment, and Gift Expenses, and **Pub. 1542**, Per Diem Rates.

(b) The cost of group-term life insurance in excess of $50,000 that you buy for an employee. Show only the amount that is includible in the employee's gross income. The amount of group-term life insurance costs includible as income is also subject to social security and Medicare taxes. (See **Pub. 525,** Taxable and Nontaxable Income, for details.)

Note: *The social security and Medicare taxes will be paid by the employee for coverage during which an employment relationship no longer exists. See the Instructions for the 1991 Form W-2.*

(c) The value of noncash prizes or awards to retail commission salespersons. Show the value of noncash prizes or awards from which you do not withhold income tax. This applies only to employees whom you ordinarily pay on a cash commission basis.

(d) Employer contributions to a section 403(b) annuity contract that are more than the limitation for the tax year. See **Pub. 571,** Tax-Sheltered Annuity Programs for Employees of Public Schools and Certain Tax-Exempt Organizations.

(e) Amounts paid to or on behalf of an employee for educational assistance that are not job related. Generally, amounts paid for educational assistance that are job related are not included as income. However, see **Pub. 508,** Educational Expenses, for more information.

Deceased Worker's Wages.—Employers must report wages or other compensation for services performed by a deceased former employee and paid to the estate or the person entitled to receive the payment of the deceased employee. For information on how to report, see Rev. Rul. 86-109, 1986-2 C.B. 196.

Dependent Care Benefits.—Include the total amount paid (or incurred) to your employee (or a third party for your employee) for dependent care benefits under section 129 of the Internal Revenue Code in box 22 on Form W-2. Employers who provide dependent care services on their premises or who pay a dependent care provider directly for their services should assist employees in obtaining a completed **Form W-10,** Dependent Care Provider's Identification and Certification. For more information on the amount to report, see Notice 89-111, 1989-2 C.B. 449.

Employees Covered by a Pension Plan.—If an employee was an active participant (for any part of the year) in a retirement plan you maintained (including a simplified employee pension (SEP) plan) or if your employee participates in a collectively bargained plan (i.e., union pension plan), check the "Pension plan" box in box 6 of Form W-2. If you made contributions to a section 401(k), 403(b), 408(k)(6) salary reduction SEP, or 501(c)(18)(D) plan, check the "Deferred compensation" box in box 6 (in addition to checking the "Pension plan" box), and enter these elective deferrals in box 17.

Repayments.—Where employees or recipients of pensions and annuities make repayments to you for amounts received in error, do not offset the repayments against current year payments unless the repayments are for amounts received in error in the current year. Repayments made in the current year, but related to a prior year or years, require special tax treatment by employees or recipients in some cases. You may want to advise these individuals of the total repayments made during the current year and the amount (if any) related to prior years. This information will help them account for such repayments on their Federal income tax returns.

Uncollected Tax on Tips.—If enough funds were not available during the year to collect the employee social security and Medicare tax on tips, enter the uncollected amounts in box 17 of Form W-2.

Allocated Tips.—Large food or beverage employers with employees who receive tips and who report less than 8% of adjusted gross receipts as tips must show the allocated tips in box 7 on Form W-2. See the separate instructions for Form 8027 for details.

Advance Payment of the EIC.—If during the year you made advance earned income credit (EIC) payments to an employee, enter the amount in box 8 on Form W-2. See section 18 for details.

Fringe Benefits.—Include all taxable fringe benefits in box 10 of the employee's Form W-2, as wages, tips, and other compensation and, if applicable, in boxes 12 and 14 as social security and Medicare wages. You must show the total value of the fringe benefits in box 23 on Form W-2 (or you may issue a separate Form W-2 showing just the value of the fringe benefits in boxes 10, 12, and 14 and a note in box 23). The amounts reported in boxes 17 and/or 22 of the Form W-2 should not be included in the amount reported in box 23. If you gave the employee a vehicle and included 100% of the value of the use in the employee's income, you must separately report this value to the employee in box 23 or on a separate statement. The employee can then figure the value of any business use of the vehicle and report it on **Form 2106,** Employee Business Expenses.

Note: *If you used the commuting rule or the vehicle cents-per-mile rule to value the personal use of the vehicle, you cannot include 100% of the value of the use of the vehicle in the employee's income. See Pub. 535 for details.*

Scholarships and Fellowship Grants.—Only give a Form W-2 to each recipient of a scholarship or fellowship grant if you are reporting amounts includible in income under section 117(c) of the Internal Revenue Code (relating to payments for teaching, research, or other services required as a condition for receiving the qualified scholarship). (See **Pub. 937,** Business Reporting, for further information.) Such amounts are subject to income tax withholding. However, their taxability for social security, Medicare, and FUTA taxes depends on the nature of the employment and the status of the organization (see **Students** on page 22).

Golden Parachute Payments.—Include the amount of the payments in boxes 10, 12, and 14 of Form W-2. Withhold income, social security, and Medicare taxes as usual and report them in boxes 9, 11, and 15, respectively, of Form W-2. Excess payments are also subject to a 20% excise tax. If the excess payments are considered wages, the tax is treated as income tax withholding. Include this tax amount in box 9 and report it separately in box 17 of Form W-2.

Third-Party Payments of Sick Pay.—Third-party payments of sick pay must be reported to the recipients on Form W-2. Whether you or the third-party payer must report the amounts depends on certain conditions. See section 19 for the conditions and details on reporting.

When To Give Form W-2 to Employees.—Give employees Forms W-2 for the calendar year, and any corrected statements made in the year, by January 31 of the following year. If an employee stops working for you before the end of the year, you may give him or her Forms W-2 any time after employment ends but not later than January 31 of the following year. However, if the employee asks you for Form W-2, give him or her the completed form within 30 days after the request or the final wage payment, whichever is later. Keep Copy A of Form W-2 to file with Form W-3.

Correcting Form W-2.—Use **Form W-2c,** Statement of Corrected Income and Tax Amounts, to correct errors on previously filed Forms W-2 and W-2P. Send Forms W-2c with **Form W-3c,** Transmittal of Corrected Income and Tax Statements, to the SSA Data Operations Center where you file your Forms W-2 and W-3.

If an employee loses or destroys his or her copies, give your employee copies of Form W-2 marked "Reissued Statement." Do not send Copy A of the reissued form to SSA.

If a form is corrected before you file Copy A with SSA, give the employee the corrected copies. Mark the original Copy A "Void" in the proper box and send the new Copy A to SSA. Do Not write "corrected" on the new Copy A.

How To Get Forms.—You can get Form W-2 from the IRS (see page 63). Private printers also produce this form. You can use these substitute forms for filing returns with SSA and for giving statements to employees. Unless you are filing on magnetic media, the paper forms you file with SSA must be in scannable format.

A revenue procedure reprinted as Pub. 1141 explains the format that must be used on substitute paper Forms W-2 and W-3. You can get a copy by calling the IRS Forms Distribution Center at 1-800-829-3676.

Penalties.—For penalty provisions for Form W-2, see **Information Return Penalties** on page 2.

18. Advance Payment of the Earned Income Credit

Employees eligible for the earned income credit (EIC) may either receive it on their tax returns or in advance payments during the year. Those who want it in advance must file Form W-5 with you. Eligible employees who do not file Form W-5 will not receive advance payments, but they will still get the full benefit of the EIC on their annual tax returns. For 1992 the advance EIC can be as much as $1,324.

You are required to notify employees not having income tax withheld that they may be eligible for a tax refund because of the EIC.

This is because the amount of EIC that exceeds tax liability is refunded. However, you do not have to notify employees claiming exemption from withholding on Form W-4. You can notify your employees by using Form W-2 which contains a statement on the back of Copy C concerning the earned income credit (EIC). If you use a substitute Form W-2 which does not have the statement on the back of Copy C, you may have to give Notice 797 to your employees. If Form W-2 is required to be furnished and is furnished on time, you must give the notice within one week before or after you give the employee his or her Form W-2 or at the same time you give the employee Form W-2. If Form W-2 is not furnished on time, you must give the notice on or before the date the Form W-2 was required to be furnished. If Form W-2 is not required to be furnished, you must give the notice on or before February 7, 1992. You can use your own written statement as long as it has the exact wording of Notice 797 or if you furnish a substitute Form W-2, you may, on Copy C, use the language contained in Notice 89-95, 1989-2 C.B. 417 in place of Notice 797. You can order this notice, and **Pub. 1325,** that contains notification information for employers, through the IRS toll-free telephone number 1-800-829-3676.

Eligible Employees.—Employees who want to receive advance EIC payments must first expect to be eligible for the EIC. Eligibility requirements are shown on Form W-5 and are summarized below:

(a) The employee's expected earned income and adjusted gross income must each be less than $22,370. (An employer who has paid total wages of at least $22,370 during the year to an employee must stop making advance payments to that employee.)

(b) If married, the employee must file a joint return or (if eligible) as head of household.

(c) The employee must not be able to exclude any income earned abroad, housing expense exclusion, or foreign housing expense deduction.

(d) The employee cannot be a qualifying child of another person who is claiming the EIC.

(e) The employee generally must have a child living with him or her more than half the year, including time when the child is away at school or on vacation (the entire year for a foster child).

(f) A married child generally must be claimed as a dependent by the employee. However, there are special rules that may apply if the child is the child of divorced or separated parents, or if the employee qualifies as an unmarried head of household. See Form W-5 for details.

(g) The child must be under age 19 at the end of the year, a full-time student under age 24, or permanently and totally disabled.

Form W-5.—On Form W-5 an employee must show if he or she is married and if his or her spouse has a Form W-5 in effect for the year with an employer.

If the employee shows that his or her spouse has filed a Form W-5 with an employer, use the advance EIC tables in this publication (either the wage bracket or percentage method table) titled "Married with both spouses filing certificate."

Form W-5 remains in effect until the end of the calendar year. Eligible employees must file a new certificate each year.

Make the signed form effective with the first payroll period ending (or the first wage payment made without regard to a payroll period) on or after the date the certificate is given to you.

If an employee has given you a signed Form W-5 and later becomes ineligible for the credit, the employee must revoke the previously filed form within 10 days. If the employee's situation changes because his or her spouse files a Form W-5, your employee must file a new Form W-5 showing that his or her spouse has a Form W-5 in effect with an employer.

If an employee has a Form W-5 certifying that his or her spouse has a Form W-5 in effect and the spouse's form is no longer in effect, the employee may file a new Form W-5 with you. This form will certify that the spouse does not have a Form W-5 in effect.

Figuring the Advance EIC Payment.—You must include the advance EIC payment with wages paid to eligible employees who have filed Form W-5.

For purposes of the advance EIC payment, "wages" means amounts subject to income tax withholding. For employees who have claimed the exemption from income tax withholding on Form W-4, "wages" means amounts that would have been subject to income tax withholding.

For household employees, "wages" means amounts subject to social security and Medicare taxes.

To determine the amount of the advance payment, take into account:

(a) Wages paid—including tips reported, and

(b) Whether a married employee's spouse has a Form W-5 in effect with an employer. There are separate tables for married employees whose spouses have a certificate in effect.

Figure the amount of the payment to include in eligible employees' wage payments by using the tables beginning on page 52. Be sure to use the right table for married employees.

Paying the Advance EIC to Employees.—The advance EIC payment does not change the amount of income tax, social security, or Medicare taxes that you withhold from employees' wages. The advance EIC payment is not compensation for services rendered and is not subject to payroll taxes.

Generally, employers will pay the amount of the advance EIC payment from withheld income, social security, and Medicare taxes. These taxes are normally required to be paid over to IRS either through Federal tax deposits or with employment tax returns.

If for any payroll period the advance EIC payments are more than the withheld income, social security, and Medicare taxes (including the employer's share of social security and Medicare taxes), you may:

(a) Reduce each advance EIC payment proportionately. (Each payment must be reduced by an amount that has the same ratio to the excess as the payment has to the total of all advance payments for the payroll period); or

(b) Elect to make full payment of the advance EIC amount and have these full amounts treated as an advance payment of the employer's tax liability. If excess EIC payments are applied against any other taxes, attach an explanation to that tax return on which the credit for overpayment is taken.

Employer's Returns.—As stated above, the amount of the advance EIC payment does not change the amount you must deduct and withhold from employees' pay for income, social security, and Medicare taxes. Advance EIC payments you make to employees must be treated on your tax return as made from amounts withheld as income tax, employee social security tax, employee Medicare tax, and owed as employer social security and employer Medicare taxes. For deposit due date purposes, the day you make an advance EIC payment to your employee is treated as the day you deposited that amount with the IRS.

Take the amount of advance EIC payments into account on your employment tax returns, Forms 941, 941E, 942, and 943. Enter the total payments on the advance EIC payments line of your return.

Penalty.—You must make advance EIC payments to employees who correctly fill out Form W-5. If you do not, you are subject to a penalty equal to the amount of the advance EIC payments not made.

If you are in American Samoa, the Commonwealth of the Northern Mariana Islands, Guam, or the Virgin Islands, consult your local tax office for information on the EIC. You cannot take advance EIC payments into account on Form 941SS.

Reporting Advance EIC Payments on Form W-2.—You must show the total amount of advance EIC payments made during the year on the employee's Form W-2.

The amounts shown on Form W-2 for income tax withheld (if any), social security, and Medicare taxes withheld are not affected by any advance EIC payments. Likewise, no other entries on Form W-2 are changed because of these payments.

19. Social Security, Medicare, and Income Tax Withholding, and FUTA Tax Payments, on Sick Pay

Employer Payments of Sick Pay.—If you make your own sick pay payments, treat the payments as you treat other social security or Medicare wages or RRTA compensation. Withhold income tax from the payments on the basis of the employee's Form W-4. Include payments subject to social security taxes on line 6a of Form 941. Also include payments subject to Medicare taxes on line 7 of Form 941. Report payments subject to RRTA taxes on **Form CT-1,** Employer's Annual Railroad Retirement and Unemployment Repayment Tax Return. Pay FUTA tax as you normally would for any other type of taxable wages. Include the amount of sick pay payments on line 1, Part I of Form 940 or 940-EZ.

Note: *If a third party makes the sick pay payments, the third party may be liable for withholding the employee's share of social security and Medicare taxes. See Third Party Payments of Sick Pay below and Notice 91-26, 1991-31 I. R. B. 14.*

Third-Party Payments of Sick Pay.—If you are a third-party payer of sick pay (such as an insurance company), employees may request that Federal income tax be withheld from the payments by giving the third party a Form W-4S. This request remains in effect until the employee gives the third party written notice to change or cancel the request.

The third party should start the withholding of income tax (or change or cancel it) with all payments made 8 or more days after receiving the request. If you prefer, you can use an earlier date. The minimum amount of income tax that can be withheld is $20 a week. The request must be in whole dollars. The sick pay remaining after withholding must be at least $10. For a payment other than a full payment, the amount withheld must be in the same proportion that regular withholding is to the full payment.

If third-party sick pay payments were made to employees covered under social security and Medicare, the third party must withhold and deposit the employee portions of the social security and Medicare taxes and pay the employer portions of the taxes. If third-party sick pay payments were made to employees covered under RRTA, the third party must withhold and deposit the employee portion of Tier I RRTA tax and Tier I Medicare tax and pay the employer portion of Tier I RRTA tax and Tier I Medicare tax. Liability for paying the employer portion of the social security and Medicare or Tier 1 RRTA and Tier I Medicare taxes, may be transferred to the employer for whom the employee normally works. The third party should do this by notifying the employer, within the time required for the deposit of tax, of the amounts of the sick pay payments made.

If the payments are subject to social security and Medicare taxes, include them with any other social security wages and figure the tax on line 6a of Form 941. Also include them with any other Medicare wages and figure the tax on line 7 of Form 941. If you have notified the employer of the payments and the employer is, therefore, liable for the employer portions of the social security and Medicare taxes, deduct the employer's portions of both taxes on line 9 of Form 941. The employer deducts the employee's portions on line 9 of the employer's Form 941.

If the payments are subject to Tier I RRTA tax and Tier I Medicare tax, report them on Form CT-1. Although the annual return is not due until the end of February of next year, you must withhold and deposit the employee RRTA tax. For 1992, the employee Tier I RRTA tax rate is 6.2% on the first $55,500 paid to each employee for the year and the Tier I Medicare tax is 1.45% on the first $130,200 paid to each employee for the year. See the instructions for Form CT-1 for information on deposit rules.

If the payments are subject to FUTA tax, the third party will be liable for payment of the tax unless the employer for whom the employee normally works is notified of the amount of the sick pay payments. The third party must give notice within the time required for the deposit of the FUTA tax for that sick pay payment. If the third party has already notified the employer that he or she is liable for the employer share of social security and Medicare taxes on sick pay, that notice can serve for FUTA purposes as well.

If the third party does not notify the employer, the third party will be considered the employer and will have to pay the FUTA tax on the sick pay payments, and file Form 940 or 940-EZ.

Note: *If you make sick pay payments solely as an agent of the employer, you will not be considered the employer.*

Special Rule for Third-Party Payers Under an Insurance Contract With Certain Multiemployer Plans.—If you are a third-party payer providing sick pay payments under an insurance contract with a collectively bargained multiemployer plan, special rules apply: If the third party provides timely notice to the plan, the plan, rather than the third party, is liable for social security, Medicare, RRTA, and FUTA taxes. However, if the plan notifies the employer for whom the employee normally works within 6 business days of receiving your notice, then the employer, and not the plan, is liable for these taxes.

Note: *The sick pay is considered paid when the employer or plan receives the notice.*

Reporting Third-Party Sick Pay to Employees.—If the third party made third-party payments of sick pay and did not notify the employer, the third party must give each employee a Form W-2 by January 31 that shows the **third party's** name, address, and employer identification number, the employee's name, address, and social security number, and the following information:

(a) The Federal income tax withheld, if any;

(b) The amount of the sick pay the employee must include in income. (Show this in the box titled *Wages, tips, other compensation.*);

(c) The amount not includible, if any, because the employee contributed to the sick pay plan. (Show this in the box for the employer's use, box 18.);

(d) The amount of sick pay subject to employee social security tax. (Show it in the box titled *Social security wages.*);

(e) The employee social security tax you withheld. (Show it in the box titled *Social security tax withheld.*);

(f) The amount of sick pay subject to employee Medicare tax. (Show it in the box titled *Medicare wages and tips*.); and

(g) The employee Medicare tax you withheld. (Show it in the box titled *Medicare tax withheld.*)

If third-party payments of sick pay were made and the employer was notified, the third party must give the employer a statement by January 15 showing for each person to whom sick pay was paid during the preceding year:

(a) The employee's name;

(b) The social security number of each employee who had any income, social security, Medicare, or RRTA taxes withheld;

(c) The amount of sick pay for each employee; and

(d) The amount of Federal income tax withheld, if any, and the amount of social security, Medicare, or RRTA taxes withheld from each employee's sick pay.

Where the employer is given the above information, the employer, by January 31, must give to each employee who received sick pay from a third-party payer a Form W-2 that shows the employer's name, address, and employer identification number, the employee's name, address, and social security number, and the following information:

(a) The Federal income tax withheld, if any;

(b) The amount of the sick pay the employee must include in income. (Show this in the box titled *Wages, tips, other compensation.*);

(c) The amount not includible, if any, because the employee contributed to the sick pay plan. (Show this in the box for the employer's use, box 18.);

(d) The amount of sick pay subject to employee social security tax. (Show it in the box titled *Social security wages.*);

(e) The employee social security tax withheld by the third-party payer. (Show it in the box titled *Social security tax withheld.*);

(f) The amount of sick pay subject to employee Medicare tax. (Show it in the box titled *Medicare wages and tips*.); and

(g) The employee Medicare tax you withheld. (Show it in the box titled *Medicare tax withheld.*)

You may include these amounts in the Form W-2 that shows the employee's wages, or you may give the employee a separate Form W-2 that shows these amounts. If you give a separate Form W-2, please state in the box for the employer's use that the amounts are third-party sick pay.

Note: *See Form W-3 instructions for more information on reporting third-party sick pay.*

Reducing Discrepancies Between Reports Filed with IRS and SSA

When there are discrepancies between reports filed with IRS and those filed with SSA, we must contact you to resolve the discrepancies. This costs time and money, both for the government and for you the employer. To help reduce the number of these discrepancies, please:

(a) Reconcile the social security wages, social security tips, Medicare wages, total compensation, advance earned income credit, income tax withheld, social security taxes, and Medicare taxes, on the four quarterly Forms 941 to your Form W-3. The amounts may not match for various reasons. If they do not match, you should determine that the reason is a valid one (such as some income tax withheld was reported on Form 1099, or adjustments were made on Form 941c). Please retain your reconciliation. This way, if there are inquiries in the future, you will know why the amounts did not match.

(b) Use Form W-2 for the current year.

(c) File all Forms W-2 with SSA not with IRS.

(d) Report bonuses as social security and Medicare wages.

(e) Report **both** social security and Medicare wages and taxes separately for each employee.

(f) Show social security taxes in the box for social security taxes withheld, not as social security wages.

(g) Show Medicare taxes in the box for Medicare taxes withheld, not as Medicare wages.

(h) Make sure social security and Medicare wage amounts for each employee do not exceed the annual social security and Medicare wage bases.

Department of the Treasury
Internal Revenue Service

Notice 967

(November 1991)

Corrections to Circular E—Employer's Tax Guide (Publication 15)

The following changes should be made on pages 10 and 11 of Circular E (Rev. January 1992) which you recently received or will receive shortly.

- On page 10, third column, the last sentence of **Example A** should be changed to read, "Show $450 on line ***I*** and $550 on line ***II***."

- On page 10, third column, the third sentence of **Example D** should be changed to read, "Show $3,500 on line G."

- On page 11, first column, the second to last sentence of **Example F** should be changed to read "The December 31st liability of $130,000 is due by January 4, 1993. (January 1st is a banking holiday and the 2nd and 3rd are Saturday and Sunday.)"

Please keep this notice with your copy of Circular E.

Cat. No. 14079D

6. Small Business Tax Information

Addresses and Telephone Numbers for IRS Taxpayer Education Coordinators

Unless otherwise noted telephone numbers are not toll free and will involve long distance charges to callers outside of the local calling area. Contacts by mail should be made to the attention of the *"Taxpayer Education Coordinator."*

ALABAMA
500 22nd St., S., Stop 117
Birmingham, AL 35233
(205) 731-0403
Toll Free 1 (800) 829-1040

ALASKA
P.O. Box 101500
Anchorage, AK 99510
(907) 561-7484
Toll Free 1 (800) 829-1040

ARIZONA
2120 N Central
Stop 6610-PX
Phoenix, AZ 85004
(602) 379-6076
Toll Free 1 (800) 829-1040

ARKANSAS
P.O. Box 3778, Stop 25
Little Rock, AR 72203
(501) 378-5685
Toll Free 1 (800) 829-1040

CALIFORNIA
Los Angeles
300 N. Los Angeles St.
Room 5202
Los Angeles, CA 90012
Los Angeles City Area
(213) 894-4574
Toll Free 1 (800) 829-1040
San Francisco
1221 Broadway, 6th Fl.
Oakland, CA 94612
(415) 273-4233
Toll Free 1 (800) 829-1040
Laguna Niguel
Chet Holifield Fed. Bldg.
P.O. Box C-10
Laguna Niguel
CA 92677-1000
(714) 643-4060
Toll Free 1 (800) 829-1040
Sacramento
P.O. Box 2900, Stop SA5650
Sacramento, CA 95812
(916) 978-4083
Toll Free 1 (800) 829-1040
San Jose
P.O. Box 100
Stop 77-01-6400
San Jose, CA 95113
(408) 291-7114
Toll Free 1 (800) 829-1040

COLORADO
600 17th Street
Stop 6610-DEN
Denver, CO 80202-2490
(303) 844-3349
Toll Free 1 (800) 829-1040

CONNECTICUT
135 High Street, Stop 115
Hartford, CT 06103
(203) 240-4154
Toll Free 1 (800) 829-1040

DELAWARE
P.O. Box 28
Wilmington, DE 19899
(302) 573-6270
Toll Free 1 (800) 829-1040

DISTRICT OF COLUMBIA
P.O. Box 538
Baltimore, MD 21203
(202) 488-3100, Ext. 2222

FLORIDA
Jacksonville
400 W. Bay St., Stop 6250
Jacksonville, FL 32202
(904) 791-2514
Toll Free 1 (800) 829-1040
Ft. Lauderdale
P.O. Box 292590, Stop 6030
Building A, Room 270
Ft. Lauderdale
FL 33329-2590
(305) 424-5124
Toll Free 1 (800) 829-1040

GEORGIA
P.O. Box 1037, Rm. 526
Summit Building
Atlanta, GA 30370
(404) 331-3808
Toll Free 1 (800) 829-1040

HAWAII
PJKK Federal Building
P.O. Box 50089
Honolulu, HI 96850
(808) 541-3329
Toll Free 1 (800) 829-1040

IDAHO
550 W. Fort St., Box 041
Boise, ID 83724
(208) 334-1307
Toll Free 1 (800) 829-1040

ILLINOIS
Chicago
P.O. Box 1132, DPN 7-5
Chicago, IL 60604
(312) 886-4609
Toll Free 1 (800) 829-1040
Springfield
P.O. Box 19201, Stop 8
Springfield, IL 62794-9201
(217) 492-4386
Toll Free 1 (800) 829-1040

INDIANA
P.O. Box 44211, Stop 60
Indianapolis, IN 46244
(317) 226-6543
Toll Free 1 (800) 829-1040

IOWA
P.O. Box 1337, Stop 30-2
Des Moines, IA 50305
(515) 284-4870
Toll Free 1 (800) 829-1040
Ext. 4870

KANSAS
412 S. Main Street
Stop 6610-WIC
Wichita, KS 67202
(316) 291-6610
Toll Free 1 (800) 829-1040

KENTUCKY
P.O. Box 1216, Stop 531
Louisville, KY 40201
(502) 582-6259
Toll Free 1 (800) 829-1040

LOUISIANA
501 Magazine Street
New Orleans, LA 70130
(504) 589-2801
Toll Free 1 (800) 829-1040

MAINE
P.O. Box 1020
Augusta, ME 04332
(207) 622-8328
Toll Free 1 (800) 829-1040

MARYLAND
31 Hopkins Plaza
Room 615A
Baltimore, MD 21201
(301) 962-2222
Toll Free 1 (800) 829-1040
Ext. 2222

MASSACHUSETTS
JFK Federal Building
P.O. Box 9088
Boston, MA 02203
(617) 565-1645
Toll Free 1 (800) 829-1040

MICHIGAN
P.O. Box 330500, Rm. 1196
Detroit, MI 48232-6500
(313) 226-3674
Toll Free 1 (800) 829-1040

MINNESOTA
316 Robert Street, Stop 6500
St. Paul, MN 55101
(612) 290-3320
Toll Free 1 (800) 829-1040

MISSISSIPPI
100 W. Capitol Street
Suite 504, Stop 30
Jackson, MS 39269
(601) 965-4142
Toll Free 1 (800) 829-1040

MISSOURI
P.O. Box 1147, Stop 612
St. Louis, MO 63188
(314) 539-3660
Toll Free 1 (800) 829-1040

MONTANA
Federal Building, 301 S. Park
Drawer 10016
Helena, MT 59626-0016
(406) 449-5375
Toll Free 1 (800) 829-1040

NEBRASKA
106 South 15th, Stop 27
Omaha, NE 68102
(402) 221-3501
Toll Free 1 (800) 829-1040

NEVADA
4750 W. Oakey Blvd.
Las Vegas, NV 89102
(702) 455-1039
Toll Free 1 (800) 829-1040

NEW HAMPSHIRE
80 Daniel Street
Portsmouth, NH 03801
(603) 433-0519
Toll Free 1 (800) 829-1040

NEW JERSEY
425 Raritan Ctr. Pkwy.
Edison, NJ 08818
(201) 417-4075
Toll Free 1 (800) 829-1040

NEW MEXICO
517 Gold Ave., S.W.
Stop 6610-ALB
P.O. Box 1967
Albuquerque, NM 87101
(505) 766-2537
Toll Free 1 (800) 829-1040

NEW YORK
Manhattan
P.O. Box 3036
Church Street Station
New York, NY 10008
(212) 264-3310
Brooklyn
P.O. Box 606, RM G-14
Brooklyn, NY 11202
(718) 780-6020
Albany
Leo O'Brien Federal Bldg.
Clinton & N. Pearl Sts.
Room 616
Albany, NY 12207
(518) 472-3636
Buffalo
P.O. Box 1040
Niagara Square Station
Buffalo, NY 14201
(716) 846-4007
Toll Free 1 (800) 829-1040

NORTH CAROLINA
320 Federal Place, Rm. 128
Greensboro, NC 27401
(919) 333-5620
Toll Free 1 (800) 829-1040

NORTH DAKOTA
P.O. Box 2461
Fargo, ND 58108
(701) 239-5105
Toll Free 1 (800) 829-1040

OHIO
Cincinnati
P.O. Box 3459
Cincinnati, OH 45201
(513) 684-2828
Toll Free 1 (800) 829-1040
Cleveland
P.O. Box 99184
Cleveland, OH 44199
(216) 522-3414
Toll Free 1 (800) 829-1040

OKLAHOMA
200 Northwest 4th Street
Stop 6610-OKC
Oklahoma City, OK 73102
(405) 231-4989
Toll Free 1 (800) 829-1040

OREGON
P.O. Box 2709
Portland, OR 97208
(503) 326-6565
Toll Free 1 (800) 829-1040

PENNSYLVANIA
Philadelphia
600 Arch St., Rm. 6424
Philadelphia, PA 19106
(215) 597-0512
Toll Free 1 (800) 829-1040
Pittsburgh
P.O. Box 2488, Rm. 1117
Pittsburgh, PA 15230
(412) 644-6504
Toll Free 1 (800) 829-1040

RHODE ISLAND
P.O. Box 6627
Providence, RI 02940
(401) 528-4276

SOUTH CAROLINA
Strom Thurmond Fed. Bldg.
1835 Assembly St., Rm. 408
Columbia, SC 29201
(803) 253-3031
Toll Free 1 (800) 829-1040

SOUTH DAKOTA
P.O. Box 370
Aberdeen, SD 57402-0370
(605) 226-7230
Toll Free 1 (800) 829-1040

TENNESSEE
P.O. Box 1107, MDP 46
Nashville, TN 37202
(615) 736-2280
Toll Free 1 (800) 829-1040

TEXAS
Austin
300 E. 8th Street
Stop 6610-AUS
Austin, TX 78701
(512) 499-5314
Toll Free 1 (800) 829-1040
Houston
4100 Westheimer
Stop 6610H-SW, Suite 280
Houston, TX 77027
(713) 541-7610
Toll Free 1 (800) 829-1040
Dallas
1100 Commerce Street
Stop 6610-DAL
Dallas, TX 75242
(214) 767-1428
Toll Free 1 (800) 829-1040

UTAH
465 South 400 East St.
Stop 6610-SLC
Salt Lake City, UT 84111
(801) 524-6095
Toll Free 1 (800) 829-1040

VERMONT
Courthouse Plaza
199 Main Street
Burlington, VT 05401
(802) 860-2089

VIRGINIA
P.O. Box 10049, Rm. 5223
Richmond, VA 23240
(804) 771-2289
Toll Free 1 (800) 829-1040

WASHINGTON
915 Second Ave., MS-425
Seattle, WA 98174
(206) 442-4230
Toll Free 1 (800) 829-1040

WEST VIRGINIA
P.O. Box 1138, Stop 2019
Parkersburg, WV 26102
(304) 420-6612
Toll Free 1 (800) 829-1040
Ext. 6612

WISCONSIN
P.O. Box 493
Milwaukee, WI 53201
(414) 297-3302
Toll Free 1 (800) 829-1040

WYOMING
308 W. 21st Street
Stop 6610-CHE
Cheyenne, WY 82001
(307) 772-2325
Toll Free 1 (800) 829-1040

Outside 50 States:

PUERTO RICO
Mercantil Plaza Bldg., GF
Ave. Ponce de Leon, Stop 271/2
Hato Rey, PR 00918
(809) 498-5946

Other:

OFFICE OF ASSISTANT COMMISSIONER (INTERNATIONAL)
950 L'Enfant Plaza
IN:C:TPS
Washington, DC 20024
(202) 287-4507

7. List of IRS Publications

Instructions

Tax Practitioner Program

The purpose of this program is to provide: **two** informational copies of most tax forms and schedules; **one** copy of instructions and publications and Practitioner **newsletters** relating to recent law changes. We accept only one request per firm/company, per address, **for ordering forms and bulk shipments of Package X, and Publications 17 and 334.** Orders from different practitioners within the same firm will be removed at the discretion of IRS without further notification. However, we **will** accept multiple names per firm to receive **Practitioner Newsletters.** A Form 3975 must be completed for each person wishing to receive a newsletter.

Package X bulk distribution from the contractor is being expanded in order to process your order more efficiently. If you are requesting more than 40 copies, please order in increments of 5.

Federal agencies are required by law (Joint Committee on Printing (JCP) Regulation, Title III) to update their mailing list periodically. You **must** submit **Form 3975** to remain on the mailing list, even if you only want to receive the newsletter. Failure to annually submit Form 3975 will result in the removal of your name from the Tax Practitioner Mailing List.

Responsibilities of Return Preparers— The importance of the roles of income tax preparers is recognized in the Internal Revenue Code which contains provisions that regulate their conduct. For more information, see Notice 90-20, 1990-1 C.B. 328, IRC Sections 6060, 6109, 6694, 6695, 7216.

Paperwork Reduction Notice—We ask for the information on this form to furnish you information and to send you the items you ordered. Your compliance is voluntary.

The time needed to complete and file this form will vary depending on individual circumstances. The estimated average time is 3 minutes.

If you have comments concerning the accuracy of this time estimate or suggestions for making this form more simple, we would be happy to hear from you. You can write to both the **Internal Revenue Service,** Washington, DC 20224, Attn: IRS Reports Clearance Officer T:FP; and **Office of Management and Budget,** Paperwork Reduction Project (1545-0351), Washington, DC 20503. **DO NOT** send the form to either of these offices. Instead, see the instructions for information on where to mail your Form 3975.

Other Items

After December 15, 1991, written requests on company letterhead may be submitted for items **not listed on pages 2–7.** We cannot honor requests before this date. Send requests to the distribution center for your state (see page 12), or call 1-800-829-3676 and ask for the practitioner gate. You will receive the maximum quantity of two copies of tax forms and one copy of publications. You can also use this toll free number if you have a problem with your order.

The forms **listed** on pages 2–7 will be available only in **Package X** and the **Reproducible Kits.**

Bulk Quantities Of Forms

Multiple copies of tax forms which exceed our quantity limits, may be obtained by: (1) ordering from Superintendent of Documents using GPO Form 3565 on page 13, (2) ordering from a commercial forms broker or private printer, or (3) photocopy using the reproducible masters provided in the kits (page 10).

Superintendent of Documents (Sup Docs)

The Superintendent of Documents is part of the Government Printing Office and **is not affiliated with the Internal Revenue Service.** Sup. Docs. is the only government agency authorized to sell printed materials. Use GPO Form 3565 (page 13) for bulk forms requests and send directly to Sup. Docs., **not to the IRS.** All orders received at IRS will be returned to the requestor, thus delaying the processing time of your order. Checks must be included with your order and made payable to the Superintendent of Documents. If there is a problem with your GPO Form 3565 order, you should contact Sup. Docs. at (301) 953-2298. Partial shipments will begin as soon as forms become available.

Titles For Items Listed On Form 3975 (Refer to "Other Items" when requesting items not listed)

Tax Practitioner Kits
Reproducible Copies of Various Tax Forms (refer to pages 3-7 for items listed).

Package X
Informational Copies of Federal Tax Forms (refer to pages 3-7 for items listed).

Publication 1 *
Your Rights as a Taxpayer

Publication 15
Circular E—Employer's Tax Guide

Publication 17
Your Federal Income Tax

Publication 51 †
Circular A—Agricultural Employer's Tax Guide

Publication 54
Tax Guide for U.S. Citizens and Resident Aliens Abroad

Publication 225
Farmer's Tax Guide

Publication 334
Tax Guide for Small Business

Publication 393 †
Federal Employment Tax Forms

Publication 463 *
Travel, Entertainment, and Gift Expenses

Publication 501 *
Exemptions, Standard Deductions, Filing Information

Publication 502 *
Medical and Dental Expenses

Publication 503 *
Child and Dependent Care Expenses

Publication 504 *
Tax Information for Divorced or Separated Individuals

Publication 505 *
Tax Withholding and Estimated Tax

Publication 508 *
Educational Expenses

Publication 509 *
Tax Calendar for 1992

Publication 520 *
Scholarships and Fellowships

Publication 521 *
Moving Expenses

Publication 523 *
Tax Information on Selling Your Home

Publication 524 *
Credit for the Elderly or the Disabled

Publication 525 *
Taxable and Nontaxable Income

Publication 526 *
Charitable Contributions

Publication 527 *
Residential Rental Property

* Item also available in Pub. 1194.

† New item added this year.

Publication 529 *
Miscellaneous Deductions

Publication 530 *
Tax Information for Homeowners

Publication 531 *
Reporting Income From Tips

Publication 533 *
Self-Employment Tax

Publication 534 *
Depreciation

Publication 535 *
Business Expenses

Publication 537
Installment Sales

Publication 538
Accounting Periods and Methods

Publication 541 *
Tax Information on Partnerships

Publication 542 *
Tax Information on Corporations

Publication 544 *
Sales and Other Dispositions of Assets

Publication 545 * †
Interest Expense

Publication 547 *
Nonbusiness Disasters, Casualties, and Thefts

Publication 550 *
Investment Income and Expenses

Publication 551 *
Basis of Assets

Publication 552 *
Recordkeeping for Individuals

Publication 553 *
Highlights of 1991 Tax Changes

Publication 554 *
Tax Information for Older Americans

Publication 556 *
Examination of Returns, Appeal Rights, and Claims for Refund

Publication 559 *
Tax Information for Survivors, Executors, and Administrators

Publication 560 *
Retirement Plans For The Self-Employed

Publication 561
Determining the Value of Donated Property

Publication 564 *
Mutual Fund Distributions

Publication 570
Tax Guide for Individuals in U.S. Possessions

Publication 575 *
Pension and Annuity Income

Publication 583
Taxpayers Starting a Business

Publication 584
Nonbusiness, Disaster, Casualty and Theft Loss Workbook

Publication 587 *
Business Use of Your Home

Publication 589 *
Tax Information on S Corporations

Publication 590 *
Individual Retirement Arrangements (IRAs)

Publication 596 *
Earned Income Credit

Publication 776 † (Foreign Accounts Only)
Overseas Filers of Form 1040

Publication 907 *
Tax Information for Handicapped and Disabled Individuals

Publication 908
Bankruptcy and Other Debt Cancellation

Publication 909 *
Alternative Minimum Tax for Individuals

Publication 910 *
Guide to Free Tax Services

Publication 915 *
Social Security Benefits and Equivalent Railroad Retirement Benefits

Publication 917 *
Business Use of a Car

Publication 925 *
Passive Activity and At-Risk Rules

Publication 929 *
Tax Rules for Children and Dependents

Publication 936 *
Limits on Home Mortgage Interest Deduction

Publication 937 *
Business Reporting (Employment Taxes, Information Returns)

Publication 1167
Substitute Printed Computer-Prepared and Computer-Generated Tax Forms and Schedules

Publication 1220
Requirements for Filing Forms 1098,1099, 5498 & W-2G on Magnetic Tape 5¼ & 3½ Inch Diskettes

Publication 1345
Revenue Procedure for Electronic Filing of Individual Income Tax Returns (Tax Year 1991)

List of Various Tax Forms, Schedules and Instructions

The following list of tax forms, schedules and related instructions are **anticipated to be included in Package X and the Tax Practitioner Kits. Do not order items individually.** This list of items may vary due to the availability and approval to print.

SS-4
Application for Employer Identification Number

SS-4 Instructions

W-2 (1991)
Wage and Tax Statement
See W-2 Instructions (1991)

W-2 Instructions (1991)

W-2c
Statement of Corrected Income and Tax Amounts

W-3 (1991)
Transmittal of Income and Tax Statements

W-3c
Transmittal of Corrected Income and Tax Statements

W-4
Employee's Withholding Allowance Certificate

W-4P
Withholding Certificate for Pension or Annuity Payments

W-4S
Request for Federal Income Tax Withholding from Sick Pay

W-5
Earned Income Credit Advance Payment Certificate

W-9
Request for Taxpayer Identification Number and Certification

W-10
Dependent Car Provider's Identification and Certification

706
United States Estate (and Generation-Skipping Transfer) Tax Return

706 Instructions

709
United States Gift (and Generation-Skipping Transfer) Tax Return

* Item also available in Pub. 1194.
† New item added this year.

709 Instructions

720 (4th Qtr. 1991)
Quarterly Federal Excise Tax Return

843
Claim

843 Instructions

851
Affiliations Schedule

911
Application for Taxpayer Assistance Order To Relieve Hardship

940
Employer's Annual Federal Unemployment (FUTA) Tax Return

940 Instructions

940EZ
Employer's Annual Federal Unemployment (FUTA) Tax Return

Sch. A (Form 941)
Record of Federal Backup Withholding Tax Liability

942 (4th Qtr. 1991)
Employer's Quarterly Tax Return for Household Employees

943
Employer's Annual Tax Return for Agricultural Employees

943A
Agricultural Employer's Record of Federal Tax Liability

990
Return of Organization Exempt From Income Tax (Except Black Lung Benefit Trust or Private Foundation)

990 Instructions

990EZ
Short Form Return of Organization Exempt From Income Tax

990EZ Instructions

Sch. A (Form 990)
Organization Exempt Under Section 501(c)(3) (Supplementary Information)

Sch. A (Form 990) Instructions

990W
Estimated Tax on Unrelated Business Taxable Income for Tax-Exempt Organizations

1040
U.S. Individual Income Tax Return

1040 Instructions

Schs. A&B (Form 1040)
Itemized Deductions, Interest and Dividend Income
See 1040 Instructions

Sch. C (Form 1040)
Profit or Loss from Business
See 1040 Instructions

Sch. D (Form 1040)
Capital Gains and Losses
See 1040 Instructions

Sch. D-1 (Form 1040)
Continuation Sheet for Sch. D (Form 1040)
See 1040 Instructions

Sch. E (Form 1040)
Supplemental Income and Loss
See 1040 Instructions

Sch. EIC (Form 1040)
Earned Income Credit

Sch. F (Form 1040)
Farm Income and Expenses
See 1040 Instructions

Sch. R (Form 1040)
Credit for the Elderly or the Disabled

Sch. R (Form 1040) Instructions

Sch. SE (Form 1040)
Social Security Self-Employment Tax
See 1040 Instructions

1040A
U.S. Individual Income Tax Return

1040A Instructions

Sch. 1 (Form 1040A)
Interest and Dividend Income for Form 1040A Filers
See 1040A Instructions

Sch. 2 (Form 1040A)
Child and Dependent Care Expenses for Form 1040A Filers
See 1040A Instructions

Sch. 3 (Form 1040A)
Credit for the Elderly or the Disabled for Form 1040A Filers
See Sch. 3 (Form 1040A) Instructions

Sch. 3 (Form 1040A) Instructions

Sch. 4 (Form 1040A)
Earned Income Credit

1040-ES (1991)
Estimated Tax for Individuals

1040EZ
Income Tax Return for Single Filers With No Dependents
See 1040EZ Instructions

1040EZ Instructions

1040NR
U.S. Nonresident Alien Income Tax Return

1040NR Instructions

1040X
Amended U.S. Individual Income Tax Return

1040X Instructions

1041
U.S. Fiduciary Income Tax Return

1041 Instructions

Sch. D (Form 1041)
Capital Gains and Losses
See 1041 Instructions

Sch. J (Form 1041)
Information Return—Trust Allocation of an Accumulation Distribution (IRC Section 665)
See 1041 Instructions

Sch. K-1 (Form 1041)
Beneficiary's Share of Income, Deductions, Credits, etc.
See 1041 Instructions

1041-ES (1991)
Estimated Tax for Fiduciaries

1045
Application for Tentative Refund

1065
U.S. Partnership Return of Income

1065 Instructions

Sch. D (Form 1065)
Capital Gains and Losses

Sch. K-1 (Form 1065)
Partner's Share of Income, Credits, Deductions, etc.

Sch. K-1 (Form 1065) Instructions

1096 (1991)
Annual Summary and Transmittal of U.S. Information Returns
See 1099 Instructions (1991)

1098 (1991)
Mortgage Interest Statement
See 1099 Instructions (1991)

1099 Instructions (1991)
For Forms 1099, 1098, 5498, 5754, 1096, and W-2G

1099-A (1991)
Information Return for Acquisition or Abandonment of Secured Property
See 1099 Instructions (1991)

1099-B (1991)
Statement for Recipients of Proceeds From Broker and Barter Exchange Transactions
See 1099 Instructions (1991)

1099-DIV (1991)
Statement for Recipients of Dividends and Distributions
See 1099 Instructions (1991)

1099-G (1991)
Statement for Recipients of Certain Government Payments
See 1099 Instructions (1991)

1099-INT (1991)
Statement for Recipients of Interest Income
See 1099 Instructions (1991)

1099-MISC (1991)
Statement for Recipients of Miscellaneous Income
See 1099 Instructions (1991)

1099-OID (1991)
Statement for Recipients of Original Issue Discount
See 1099 Instructions (1991)

1099-PATR (1991)
Statement for Recipients (Patrons) of Taxable Distributions Received From Cooperatives
See 1099 Instructions (1991)

1099-R (1991)
Statement for Recipients of Total Distributions From Profit-Sharing, Retirement Plans, Individual Retirement Arrangements, Insurance Contracts, etc.
See 1099 Instructions (1991)

1099-S (1991)
Statement for Recipients of Proceeds From Real Estate Transactions
See 1099 Instructions (1991)

1116
Computation of Foreign Tax Credit (Individual, Fiduciary, or Nonresident Alien Individual)

1116 Instructions

1118
Computation of Foreign Tax Credit—Corporation

1118 Instructions

1120
U.S. Corporation Income Tax Return

1120 and 1120-A Instructions

Sch. D (Form 1120)
Capital Gains and Losses

Sch. PH (Form 1120)
U.S. Personal Holding Company Tax

Sch. PH (Form 1120) Instructions

1120-A
U.S. Corporation Short-Form Income Tax Return

1120S
U.S. Income Tax Return for an S Corporation

1120S Instructions

Sch. D (Form 1120S)
Capital Gains and Losses and Built-in Gains

Sch. D (Form 1120S) Instructions

Sch. K-1 (Form 1120S)
Shareholder's Share of Income, Credits, Deductions, etc.

Sch. K-1 (Form 1120S) Instructions

1120-W
Corporation Estimated Tax

1120X
Amended U.S. Corporation Income Tax Return

1127
Application for Extension of Time for Payment of Tax

1310
Statement of Person Claiming Refund Due a Deceased Taxpayer

2106
Employee Business Expenses

2106 Instructions

2119
Sale of Your Home

2119 Instructions

2120
Multiple Support Declaration

2210
Underpayment of Estimated Tax by Individuals

2210 Instructions

2220
Underpayment of Estimated Tax by Corporations

2220 Instructions

2290
Heavy Vehicle Use Tax Return

2350
Application for Extension of Time To File U.S. Income Tax Return

2441
Credit for Child and Dependent Care Expenses

2441 Instructions

2553
Election by a Small Business Corporation

2553 Instructions

2688
Application for Additional Extension of Time To File U.S. Individual Income Tax Return

2758
Application for Extension of Time To File Certain Excise, Income, Information and Other Returns

2848
Power of Attorney and Declaration of Representative

3115
Application for Change in Accounting Method

3115 Instructions

3468
Investment Credit

3468 Instructions

3800
General Business Credit

3800 Instructions

3903
Moving Expenses

3903 Instructions

3911
Taxpayer Statement Regarding Refund

4136
Computation of Credit for Federal Tax on Fuels

4137
Computation of Social Security Tax on Unreported Tip Income

4255
Recapture of Investment Credit

4506
Request for Copy of Tax Form

4562
Depreciation and Amortization

4562 Instructions

4626
Alternative Minimum Tax—Corporations

4626 Instructions

4684
Casualties and Thefts

4684 Instructions

4782
Employee Moving Expense Information

4797
Sale of Business Property

4797 Instructions

4804
Transmittal of Information Returns Reported on Magnetic Media

4835
Farm Rental Income and Expenses

4852
Substitute for Form W-2, Wage and Tax Statement for Recipients of Annuities, Pensions, Retired Pay, or IRS Payments

4868
Application for Automatic Extension of Time To File U.S. Individual Income Tax Return

4952
Investment Interest Expense Deduction

4952 Instructions

4970
Tax on Accumulation of Distribution of Trusts

4972
Tax on Lump-Sum Distribution

4972 Instructions

5329
Return for Additional Taxes Attributable to Qualified Retirement Plan (Including IRA's), Annuities and Modified Endowment Contracts

5329 Instructions

5498 (1991)
Individual Retirement Arrangement Information
See 1099 Instructions (1991)

5500
Annual Return/Report of Employee Benefit Plan (with 100 or more participants)

5500 Instructions

Sch. A (Form 5500)
Insurance Information

Sch. B (Form 5500)
Actuarial Information

Sch. B (Form 5500) Instructions

Sch. C (Form 5500)
Service Provider Information

Sch. P (Form 5500)
Annual Return of Fiduciary of Employee Benefit Trust

Sch. SSA (Form 5500)
Annual Registration Statement Identifying Separated Participants with Deferred Vested Benefits

5500-C/R
Return/Report of Employee Benefit Plan (with fewer than 100 participants)

5500-C/R Instructions

5500EZ
Annual Return of One-Participant (owners and their spouses) Pension Benefit Plan

5500EZ Instructions

5558
Application for Extension of Time to File Certain Employee Plan Returns

5754
Statement By Person(s) Receiving Gambling Winnings
See 1099 Instructions (1991)

5884
Jobs Credit

6198
At-Risk Limitations

6198 Instructions

6251
Alternative Minimum Tax Individuals

6251 Instructions

6252
Installment Sale Income

6252 Instructions

6781
Gains and Losses from Section 1256 Contracts and Straddles

7004
Application for Automatic Extension of Time To File Corporation Income Tax Return

8027
Employer's Annual Information Return of Tip Income and Allocated Tips

8027 Instructions

8082
Notice of Inconsistent Treatment or Amended Return (Administrative Adjustment Request (AAR))

8082 Instructions

8264
Application for Registration of Tax Shelter

8264 Instructions

8271
Investor Reporting of Tax Shelter Registration Number

8275
Disclosure Statement Under Section 6661

8275 Instructions

8283
Non-cash Charitable Contributions

8283 Instructions

8300
Report of Cash Payments Over $10,000 Received in a Trade or Business

8308
Report of a Sale or Exchange of Certain Partnership Interests

8332
Release of Claim to Exemption for Child of Divorced or Separated Parents

8379
Injured Spouse Allocation

8453
U.S. Individual Income Tax Declaration for Electronic Filing

8582
Passive Activity Loss Limitations

8582 Instructions

8582-CR
Passive Activity Credit Limitations

8582-CR Instructions

8586
Low-Income Housing Credit

8594
Asset Acquisition Statement

8606
Nondeductible IRA Contributions, IRA Basis, and Nontaxable IRA Distributions

8609
Low-Income Housing Credit Allocation Certification

Sch. A (Form 8609)
Annual Statement

8615
Computation of Tax for Children Under Age 14 Who Have Investment Income of More Than $1,000

8633
Electronic Filer Application to File 1991 Individual Income Tax Return Electronically

8656
Alternative Minimum Tax—Fiduciaries

8656 Instructions

8716
Election To Have a Tax Year Other Than a Required Tax Year

8717
User Fee for Employee Plan Determination Letter Request

8736
Application for Automatic Extension of Time To File Return/U.S. Partnerships or for Certain Trusts

8800
Application for Additional Extension of Time To File Return for U.S. Partnerships or Certain Trusts

8801
Credit for Prior Year Minimum Tax

8803
Limit on Alternative Minimum Tax for Children Under Age 14

8809
Requests for Extension of Time To File Information Returns

8810
Corporate Passive Activity Loss and Credit Limitations

8810 Instructions

8814
Parent's Election To Report Child's Interest and Dividends

8815
Exclusion of Interest From Series EE U.S. Savings Bonds Issued After 1989

8817
Allocation of Patronage and Nonpatronage Income and Deductions

8818
Redemption of College Savings Bonds, Optional Form To Record

8821
Taxed Information Authorization

8822
Change of Address

8824
Like-Kind Exchanges

8824 Instructions

8825
Rental Real Estate Income & Expenses of a Partnership S Corporation

9041
Application for Electronic/Magnetic Tape Filing of Tax Year 1991 Forms 1041, 1065, and 5500 C/R

TD F 90-22.1
Report of Foreign Bank and Financial Accounts

7a. Form 3975-A—Tax Practitioner Annual Mailing List Application and Order Blank

Form **3975**

Department of the Treasury
Internal Revenue Service

Tax Practitioner Annual Mailing List Application and Order Blank

▶ For Paperwork Reduction Notice, see instructions in Publication 1045.

OMB No. 1545–0351
Expires: 6-30-94

1991

Section A

Attach peel off label from front cover here.

Section B—Nature of Request (must be completed).

1 ☐ New application 2 ☐ Reapplication no change 3 ☐ Reapplication with change 4 ☐ Delete record

Section C—List daytime office phone number.

Office Telephone Number ☐☐☐ ☐☐☐ - ☐☐☐☐

Section D—Number of professional tax return preparers in your firm.

Section E—Mailing adddress information for the months of **October through April.**

First name

Last name

Firm/Company

Firm/Company street address

City or Town

State or Province

ZIP code (left justified)

(Foreign Countries)

Section F—Job Code

What is your principal occupation or business? (Check ONLY ONE.)

1 ☐ Association
4 ☐ CPA
7 ☐ Enrolled agent
2 ☐ Attorney
5 ☐ Accountant
8 ☐ Other
3 ☐ Banker
6 ☐ Preparer of tax returns

Section G—Purpose for being on the Tax Practitioner Mailing List? (Check ONLY ONE.)
Complete order blank (page 10) if you checked Box 1 or 3.

1 ☐ To order information copies of tax forms only 2 ☐ To receive the practitioner newsletter only 3 ☐ Both

Section H—Check if you **do not** want your firm/company name and address released to the public as part of a practitioner mailing list . . . . ☐ No

Section I—Check if you share office space at the same address with another practitioner firm? ☐ Yes

Cat. No. 41235N

Form 3975 (1991) Page **2**

Section J—Tax Practitioner Order Blank (See pages 2-7 for Titles).

(Items are listed in numerical order, reading from left to right.)

ID No.	Pub.	X	ID No.	Pub.	X	ID No.	Pub.	X	ID No.	Pub.	X
001	1		002	15		003	51		004	54	
005	225		006	393		007	463		008	501	
009	502		010	503		011	504		012	505	
013	508		014	509		015	520		016	521	
017	523		018	524		019	525		020	526	
021	527		022	529		023	530		024	531	
025	533		026	534		027	535		028	537	
029	538		030	541		031	542		032	544	
033	545		034	547		035	550		036	551	
037	552		038	553		039	554		040	556	
041	559		042	560		043	561		044	564	
045	570		046	575		047	583		048	584	
049	587		050	589		051	590		052	596	
053	776		054	907		055	908		056	909	
057	910		058	915		059	917		060	925	
061	929		062	936		063	937		064	1167	
065	1220		066	1345		067	KITS				

Section K—Request For Miscellaneous Products

ID No.	ITEM	Quantity	ID No.	ITEM	Quantity	ID No.	ITEM	Quantity
071	Pub. 17		072	Pub. 334		073	Pkg. X	

Section L—1991 Informational Return Forms

ID No.	Form	Quantity	ID No.	Form	Quantity	ID No.	Form	Quantity	ID No.	Form	Quantity
075	W-2		076	W-3		077	1096		078	1098	
079	1099-A		080	1099-B		081	1099-DIV		082	1099-G	
083	1099-INT		084	1099-MISC		085	1099-OID		086	1099-PATR	
087	1099-R		088	1099-S		089	5498				

8. Publication 1—Your Rights as a Taxpayer

Your Rights AS A TAXPAYER

As a taxpayer, you have the right to be treated fairly, professionally, promptly, and courteously by Internal Revenue Service employees. Our goal at the IRS is to protect your rights so that you will have the highest confidence in the integrity, efficiency, and fairness of our tax system. To ensure that you always receive such treatment, you should know about the many rights you have at each step of the tax process.

Department of the Treasury
Internal Revenue Service
Publication 1 (Rev. 10-90)

Cat. No. 64731W

Free Information and Help in Preparing Returns

You have the right to information and help in complying with the tax laws. In addition to the basic instructions we provide with the tax forms, we make available a great deal of other information.

Taxpayer publications. We publish over 100 free taxpayer information publications on various subjects. One of these, Publication 910, *Guide to Free Tax Services*, is a catalog of the free services and publications we offer. You can order all publications and any tax forms or instructions you need by calling us toll-free at 1-800-TAX-FORM (829-3676).

Other assistance. We provide walk-in tax help at many IRS offices and recorded telephone information on many topics through our *Tele-Tax* system. The telephone numbers for *Tele-Tax*, and the topics covered, are in certain tax forms' instructions and publications. Many of our materials are available in Braille (at regional libraries for the handicapped) and in Spanish. We provide help for the hearing-impaired via special telephone equipment.

We have informational videotapes that you can borrow. In addition, you may want to attend our education programs for specific groups of taxpayers, such as farmers and those with small businesses.

In cooperation with local volunteers, we offer free help in preparing tax returns for low-income and elderly taxpayers through the Volunteer Income Tax Assistance (VITA) and Tax Counseling for the Elderly (TCE) Programs. You can get information on these programs by calling the toll-free telephone number for your area.

Copies of tax returns. If you need a copy of your tax return for an earlier year, you can get one by filling out Form 4506, *Request for Copy of Tax Form*, and paying a small fee. However, you often only need certain information, such as the amount of your reported income, the number of your exemptions, and the tax shown on the return. You can get this information free if you write or visit an IRS office or call the toll-free number for your area.

Privacy and Confidentiality

You have the right to have your personal and financial information kept confidential. People who prepare your return or represent you *must* keep your information confidential.

You also have the right to know why we are asking you for information, exactly how we will use any information you give, and what might happen if you do not give the information.

Information sharing. Under the law, we can share your tax information with State tax agencies and, under strict legal guidelines, the Department of Justice and other federal agencies. We can also share it with certain foreign governments under tax treaty provisions.

Courtesy and Consideration

You are always entitled to courteous and considerate treatment from IRS employees. If you ever feel that you are not being treated with fairness, courtesy, and consideration by an IRS employee, you should tell the employee's supervisor.

Protection of Your Rights

The employees of the Internal Revenue Service will explain and protect your rights as a taxpayer at all times. If you feel that this is not the case, you should discuss the problem with the employee's supervisor.

Complaints

If for any reason you have a complaint about the IRS, you may write to the District Director or Service Center Director for your area. We will give you the name and address if you call our toll-free phone number listed later.

Representation and Recordings

Throughout your dealings with us, you can represent yourself, or, generally with proper written authorization, have someone represent you in your absence. During an interview, you can have someone accompany you.

If you want to consult an attorney, a certified public accountant, an enrolled agent, or any other person permitted to represent a taxpayer during an interview for examining a tax return or collecting tax, we will stop and reschedule the interview. We cannot suspend the interview if you are there because of an administrative summons.

You can generally make an audio recording of an interview with an IRS Collection or Examination officer. Your request to record the interview should be made in writing, and must be received 10 days before the interview. You must bring your own recording equipment. We also can record an interview. If we do so, we will notify you 10 days before the meeting and you can get a copy of the recording at your expense.

Payment of Only the Required Tax

You have the right to plan your business and personal finances so that you will pay the least tax that is due under the law. You are liable only for the correct amount of tax. Our purpose is to apply the law consistently and fairly to all taxpayers.

If Your Return is Questioned

We accept most taxpayers' returns as filed. If we inquire about your return or select it for examination, it does not suggest that you are dishonest. The inquiry or examination may or may not result in more tax. We may close your case without change. Or, you may receive a refund.

Examination and inquiries by mail. We handle many examinations and inquiries entirely by mail. We will send you a letter with either a request for more information or a reason why we believe a change needs to be made to your return. If you give us the requested information or provide an explanation, we may or may not agree with you and we will explain the reasons for any changes. You should not hesitate to write to us about anything you do not understand. If you cannot resolve any questions through the mail, you can request a personal interview. You can appeal through the IRS and the courts. You will find instructions with each inquiry or in Publication 1383, *Correspondence Process.*

Examination by interview. If we notify you that we will conduct your examination through a personal interview, or you request such an interview, you have the right to ask that the examination take place at a reasonable time and place that is convenient for both you and the IRS. If the time or place we suggest is not convenient, the examiner will try to work out something more suitable. However, the IRS makes the final determination of how, when, and where the examination will take place. You will receive an explanation of your rights and of the examination process either before or at the interview.

If you do not agree with the examiner's report, you may meet with the examiner's supervisor to discuss your case further.

Repeat examinations. We try to avoid repeat examinations of the same items, but this sometimes happens. If we examined your tax return for the same items in either of the 2 previous years and proposed no change to your tax liability, please contact us as soon as possible so we can see if we should discontinue the repeat examination.

Explanation of changes. If we propose any changes to your return, we will explain the reasons for the changes. It is important that you understand these reasons. You should not hesitate to ask about anything that is unclear to you.

Interest. You must pay interest on additional tax that you owe. The interest is generally figured from the due date of the return. But if our error caused a delay in your case, and this was grossly unfair, we may reduce the interest. Only delays caused by procedural or mechanical acts not involving the exercise of judgment or discretion qualify. If you think we caused such a delay, please discuss it with the examiner and file a claim for refund.

Business taxpayers. If you are in an individual business, the rights covered in this publication generally apply to you. If you are a member of a partnership or a shareholder in a small business corporation, special rules may apply to the examination of your partnership or corporation items. The examination of partnership items is discussed in Publication 556, *Examination of Returns, Appeal Rights, and Claims for Refund.* The rights covered in this publication generally apply to exempt organizations and sponsors of employee plans.

An Appeal of the Examination Findings

If you don't agree with the examiner's findings, you have the right to appeal them. During the examination process, you will be given information about your appeal rights. Publication 5, *Appeal Rights and Preparation of Protests for Unagreed Cases*, explains your appeal rights in detail and tells you exactly what to do if you want to appeal.

Appeals Office. You can appeal the findings of an examination within the IRS through our Appeals Office. Most differences can be settled through this appeals system without expensive and time-consuming court trials. If the matter cannot be settled to your satisfaction in Appeals, you can take your case to court.

Appeals to the courts. Depending on whether you first pay the disputed tax, you can take your case to the U.S. Tax Court, the U.S. Claims Court, or your U.S. District Court. These courts are entirely independent of the IRS. As always, you can represent yourself or have someone admitted to practice before the court represent you.

If you disagree about whether you owe additional tax, you generally have the right to take your case to the U.S. Tax

Income Tax Appeal Procedure

At any stage
- ☐ You can agree and arrange to pay.
- ☐ You can ask for a notice of deficiency so you can file a petition with the Tax Court.
- ☐ You can pay the tax and file a claim for refund.

*Further appeals to the courts may be possible, except there is no appeal under the Tax Court's small tax case procedure.

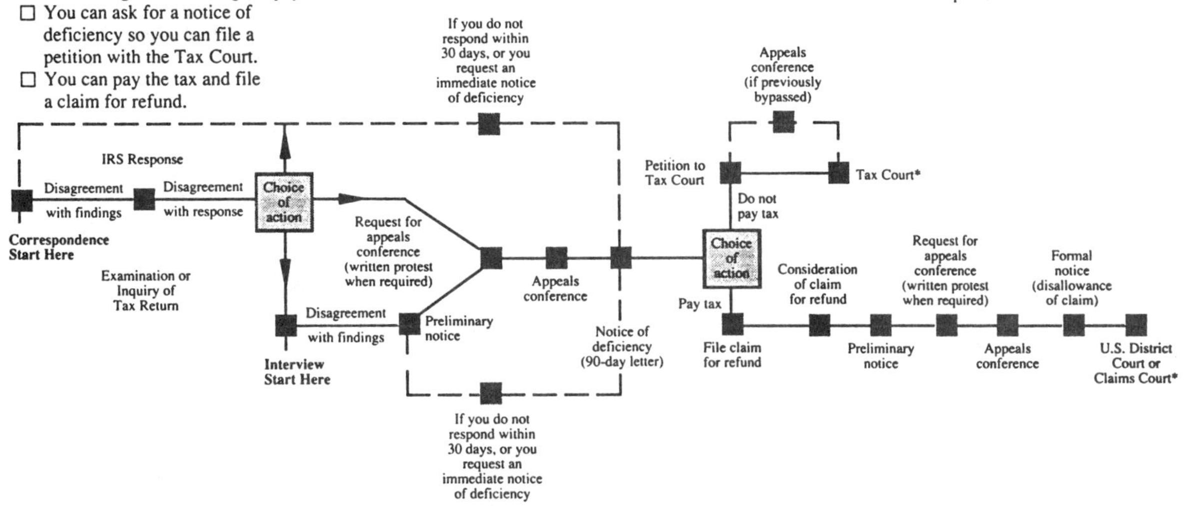

Court if you have not yet paid the tax. Ordinarily, you have 90 days from the time we mail you a formal notice (called a "notice of deficiency") telling you that you owe additional tax, to file a petition with the U.S. Tax Court. You can request simplified small tax case procedures if your case is $10,000 or less for any period or year. A case settled under these procedures cannot be appealed.

If you have already paid the disputed tax in full, you may file a claim for refund. If we disallow the claim, you can appeal the findings through our Appeals Office. If you do not accept their decision or we have not acted on your claim within 6 months, then you may take your case to the U.S. Claims Court or your U.S. District Court.

Recovering litigation expenses. If the court agrees with you on most issues in your case, and finds that our position was largely unjustified, you may be able to recover some of your administrative and litigation costs. To do this, you must have used all the administrative remedies available to you within the IRS. This includes going through our Appeals system and giving us all the information necessary to resolve the case.

Publication 556, *Examination of Returns, Appeal Rights, and Claims for Refund*, will help you more fully understand your appeal rights.

Fair Collection of Tax

Whenever you owe tax, we will send you a bill describing the tax and stating the amounts you owe in tax, interest, and penalties. Be sure to check any bill you receive to make sure it is correct. You have the right to have your bill adjusted if it is incorrect, so you should let us know about an incorrect bill right away.

If we tell you that you owe tax because of a math or clerical error on your return, you have the right to ask us to send you a formal notice (a "notice of deficiency") so that you can dispute the tax, as discussed earlier. You do not have to pay the additional tax at the same time that you ask us for the formal notice, if you ask for it within 60 days of the time we tell you of the error.

If the tax is correct, we will give you a specific period of time to pay the bill in full. If you pay the bill within the time allowed, we will not have to take any further action.

We may request that you attend an interview for the collection of tax. You will receive an explanation of your rights and of the collection process either before or at the interview.

Your rights are further protected because we are not allowed to use tax enforcement results to evaluate our employees.

Payment arrangements. You should make every effort to pay your bill in full. If you can't, you should pay as much as you can and contact us right away. We may ask you for a complete financial statement to determine how you can pay the amount due. Based on your financial condition, you may qualify for an installment agreement. We can arrange for these payments to be made through payroll deduction. We will give you copies of all agreements you make with us.

If we approve a payment agreement, the agreement will stay in effect only if:

You give correct and complete financial information,

You pay each installment on time,

You satisfy other tax liabilities on time,

You provide current financial information when asked, and

We determine that collecting the tax is not at risk.

Following a review of your current finances, we may change your payment agreement. We will notify you 30 days before any change to your payment agreement and tell you why we are making the change.

We will not take any enforcement action (such as recording a tax lien or levying on or seizing property), until after we have tried to contact you and given you the chance to voluntarily pay any tax due. Therefore, it is very important for you to respond right away to our attempts to contact you (by mail, telephone, or personal visit). If you do not respond, we may have no choice but to begin enforcement action.

Release of liens. If we have to place a lien on your property (to secure the amount of tax due), we must release the lien no later than 30 days after finding that you have paid the entire tax and certain charges, the assessment has become legally unenforceable, or we have accepted a bond to cover the tax and certain charges.

Recovery of damages. If we knowingly or negligently fail to release a lien under the circumstances described above, and you suffer economic damages because of our failure, you can recover your actual economic damages and certain costs.

If we recklessly or intentionally fail to follow the laws and regulations for the collection of tax, you can recover actual economic damages and certain costs.

In each of the two situations above, damages and costs will be allowed within the following limits. You must exhaust all administrative remedies available to you. The damages will be reduced by the amount which you could have reasonably prevented. You must bring suit within 2 years of the action.

Incorrect lien. You have the right to appeal our filing of a Notice of Federal Tax Lien if you believe we filed the lien in error. If we agree, we will issue a certificate of release, including a statement that we filed the lien in error.

A lien is incorrect if:

You paid the entire amount due before we filed the lien,

The time to collect the tax expired before we filed the lien,

We made a procedural error in a deficiency assessment, or

We assessed a tax in violation of the automatic stay provisions in a bankruptcy case.

Levy. We will generally give you 30 days notice before we levy on any property. The notice may be given to you in person, mailed to you, or left at your home or workplace. On the day you attend a collection interview because of a summons, we cannot levy your property unless the collection of tax is in jeopardy.

Property that is exempt from levy. If we must seize your property, you have the legal right to keep:

Necessary clothing and schoolbooks,

A limited amount of personal belongings, furniture, and business or professional books and tools,

Unemployment and job training benefits, workers' compensation, welfare, certain disability payments, and certain pension benefits,

The income you need to pay court-ordered child support,

Mail,

An amount of weekly income equal to your standard deduction and allowable personal exemptions, divided by 52, and

Your main home, unless collection of tax is in jeopardy or the district director (or assistant) approves the levy in writing.

If your bank account is levied after June 30, 1989, the bank will hold your account up to the amount of the levy for 21 days. This gives you time to settle any disputes concerning ownership of the funds in the account.

We generally must release a levy issued after June 30, 1989, if:

You pay the tax, penalty, and interest for which the levy was made,

The IRS determines the release will help collect the tax,

You have an approved installment agreement for the tax on the levy,

Thc IRS determines the levy is creating an economic hardship, or

The fair market value of the property exceeds the amount of the levy and release would not hinder the collection of tax.

If at any time during the collection process you do not agree with the collection officer, you can discuss your case with his or her supervisor.

If we seize your property, you have the right to request that it be sold within 60 days after your request. You can request a time period greater than 60 days. We will comply with your request unless it is not in the best interest of the government.

Access to your private premises. A court order is not generally needed for a collection officer to seize your property. However, you don't have to allow the employee access to your private premises, such as your home or the non-public areas of your business, if the employee does not have court authorization to be there.

Withheld taxes. If we believe that you were responsible for seeing that a corporation paid us income and social security taxes withheld from its employees, and the taxes were not paid, we may look to you to pay an amount based on the unpaid taxes. If you feel that you don't owe this, you have the right to discuss the case with the collection officer's supervisor. You may also request an appeals hearing within 30 days of our proposed assessment of employment taxes. You generally have the same IRS appeal rights as other taxpayers. Because the U.S. Tax Court has no jurisdiction in this situation, you must pay at least part of the withheld taxes and file a claim for refund in order to take the matter to the U.S. District Court or U.S. Claims Court.

The amount of tax withheld from your wages is determined by the W-4, *Employees Withholding Allowance Certficate*, you give your employer. If your certificate is incorrect, the IRS may instruct your employer to increase the amount. We may also assess a penalty. You have the right to appeal the decision. Or, you can file a claim for refund and go to the U.S. Claims Court or U.S. District Court.

Publications 586A, *The Collection Process (Income Tax Accounts)*, and 594, *The Collection Process (Employment Tax Accounts)*, will help you understand your rights during the collection process.

The Collection Process

To stop the process at any stage, you should pay the tax in full. If you cannot pay the tax in full, contact us right away to discuss possible ways to pay the tax.

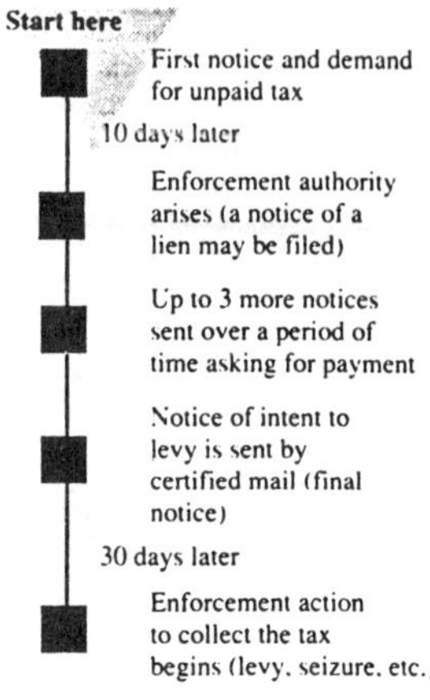

Refund of Overpaid Tax

Once you have paid all your tax, you have the right to file a claim for a refund if you think the tax is incorrect. Generally, you have 3 years from the date you filed the return or 2 years from the date you paid the tax (whichever is later) to file a claim. If we examine your claim for any reason, you have the same rights that you would have during an examination of your return.

Interest on refunds. You will receive interest on any income tax refund delayed more than 45 days after the **later** of either the date you filed your return or the date your return was due.

Checking on your refund. Normally, you will receive your refund about 6 weeks after you file your return. If you have not received your refund within 8 weeks after mailing your return, you may check on it by calling the toll-free Tele-Tax number in the tax forms' instructions.

If we reduce your refund because you owe a debt to another Federal agency or because you owe child support, we must notify you of this action. However, if you have a question about the debt that caused the reduction, you should contact the other agency.

Cancellation of Penalties

You have the right to ask that certain penalties (but not interest) be cancelled (abated) if you can show reasonable cause for the failure that led to the penalty (or can show that you exercised due diligence, if that is the applicable standard for that penalty).

If you relied on wrong advice you received from IRS employees on the toll-free telephone system, we will cancel certain penalties that may result. But you have to show that your reliance on the advice was reasonable.

If you relied on incorrect written advice from the IRS in response to a written request you made after January 1,

1989, we will cancel any penalties that may result. You must show that you gave sufficient and correct information and filed your return after you received the advice.

Special Help to Resolve Your Problems

We have a Problem Resolution Program for taxpayers who have been unable to resolve their problems with the IRS. If you have a tax problem that you cannot clear up through normal channels, write to the Problem Resolution Office in the district or Service Center with which you have the problem. You may also reach the Problem Resolution Office by calling the IRS taxpayer assistance number for your area. If you are hearing-impaired with TV/Telephone (TTY) access, you may call 1-800-829-4059.

If your tax problem causes (or will cause) you to suffer a significant hardship, additional assistance is available. A significant hardship may occur if you cannot maintain necessities such as food, clothing, shelter, transportation, and medical treatment.

There are two ways you can apply for relief. You can submit Form 911, *Application for Taxpayer Assistance Order to Relieve Hardship*, which you can order by calling 1-800-TAX-FORM (829-3676). You can choose instead to call 1-800-829-1040, to request relief from your hardship. The Taxpayer Ombudsman, Problem Resolution Officer, or other official will then review your case and may issue a Taxpayer Assistance Order (TAO), to suspend IRS action.

Taxpayer Assistance Numbers

You should use the telephone number shown in the white pages of your local telephone directory under U.S. Government, Internal Revenue Service, Federal Tax Assistance. If there is not a specific number listed, call toll-free 1-800-829-1040.

You can also find these phone numbers in the instructions for Form 1040. You may also use these numbers to reach the Problem Resolution Office. Ask for the Problem Resolution Office when you call.

U.S. taxpayers abroad may write for information to:

Internal Revenue Service
Attn: IN:C:TPS
950 L'Enfant Plaza South, S.W.
Washington, D.C. 20024

You can also contact your nearest U.S. Embassy for information about what services and forms are available in your location.

☆U.S. GOVERNMENT PRINTING OFFICE: 1991-286-335

9. Form 941—Employer's Quarterly Federal Tax Return

Form **941**
(Rev. January 1991)
Department of the Treasury
Internal Revenue Service

4141

Employer's Quarterly Federal Tax Return

► See Circular E for more information concerning employment tax returns.

Please type or print.

Your name, address, employer identification number, and calendar quarter of return. (If not correct, please change.)

Name (as distinguished from trade name)	Date quarter ended	OMB No. 1545-0029 Expires: 5-31-93
Trade name, if any	Employer identification number	T
Address and ZIP code		FF
		FD
		FP
		I
		T

IRS Use: 1 1 1 1 1 1 1 1 1 1 2 3 3 3 3 3 3 4 4 4
5 5 5 6 7 8 8 8 8 8 8 9 9 9 10 10 10 10 10 10 10 10 10 10

If address is different from prior return, check here ► ☐

If you do not have to file returns in the future, check here . . . ► ☐ Date final wages paid . . . ►

If you are a seasonal employer, see **Seasonal employers** on page 2 and check here . ► ☐

1a	Number of employees (except household) employed in the pay period that includes March 12th . ►		1a	
b	If you are a subsidiary corporation AND your parent corporation files a consolidated Form 1120, enter parent corporation employer identification number (EIN) . . ► 1b –			
2	Total wages and tips subject to withholding, plus other compensation . . . . ►		2	
3	Total income tax withheld from wages, tips, pensions, annuities, sick pay, gambling, etc. . . ►		3	
4	Adjustment of withheld income tax for preceding quarters of calendar year (see instructions) . . ►		4	
5	Adjusted total of income tax withheld (line 3 as adjusted by line 4—see instructions)		5	
6a	Taxable social security wages (Complete line 7)	$ × 12.4% (.124) =	6a	
b	Taxable social security tips	$ × 12.4% (.124) =	6b	
7	Taxable Medicare wages and tips	$ × 2.9% (.029) =	7	
8	Total social security and Medicare taxes (add lines 6a, 6b, and 7)		8	
9	Adjustment of social security and Medicare taxes (see instructions for required explanation) . . .		9	
10	Adjusted total of social security and Medicare taxes (line 8 as adjusted by line 9—see instructions) ►		10	
11	Backup withholding (see instructions)		11	

12	Adjustment of backup withholding tax for preceding quarters of calendar year. . . . . ▶	12	
13	Adjusted total of backup withholding (line 11 as adjusted by line 12)	13	
14	**Total taxes** (add lines 5, 10, and 13)	14	
15	Advance earned income credit (EIC) payments made to employees, if any . . . . ▶	15	
16	Net taxes (subtract line 15 from line 14). **This should equal line IV below** (plus line IV of Schedule A (Form 941) if you have treated backup withholding as a separate liability)	16	
17	**Total deposits for quarter,** including overpayment applied from a prior quarter, from your records. ▶	17	
18	**Balance due** (subtract line 17 from line 16). This should be less than $500. Pay to IRS . . . . ▶	18	

19 **Overpayment,** if line 17 is more than line 16, enter here ▶ $ ______________ and check if to be:

☐ Applied to next return **OR** ☐ Refunded.

Record of Federal Tax Liability (You must complete if line 16 is $500 or more and Schedule B is not attached.) See instructions before checking these boxes.

Check only if you made deposits using the 95% rule ▶ ☐ Check only if you are a first time 3-banking-day depositor. . . ▶ ☐

Date wages paid (Do NOT Show Federal Tax Deposits Here)	Show tax liability here, **not deposits.** IRS gets deposit data from FTD coupons. First month of quarter		Second month of quarter		Third month of quarter	
1st through 3rd	A		I		Q	
4th through 7th	B		J		R	
8th through 11th	C		K		S	
12th through 15th	D		L		T	
16th through 19th	E		M		U	
20th through 22nd	F		N		V	
23rd through 25th	G		O		W	
26th through the last	H		P		X	
Total liability for month	*I*		*II*		*III*	

▶ *IV* Total for quarter (add lines *I*, *II*, and *III*). **This should equal line 16 above** . . . . ▶

Sign Here Under penalties of perjury, I declare that I have examined this return, including accompanying schedules and statements, and to the best of my knowledge and belief, it is true, correct, and complete.

Signature ▶ Print Your Name and Title ▶ Date

For Paperwork Reduction Act Notice, see page 2.

Form 941 (Rev. 1-91) Page **2**

Paperwork Reduction Act Notice.—We ask for the information on this form to carry out the Internal Revenue laws of the United States. You are required to give us this information. We need it to ensure that taxpayers are complying with these laws and to allow us to figure and collect the right amount of tax.

The time needed to complete and file this form will vary depending on individual circumstances. The estimated average time is: **Recordkeeping** 12 hrs., 40 min.; **Learning about the law or the form** 34 min.; **Preparing the form** 1 hr., 44 min.; **Copying, assembling, and sending the form to IRS** 16 min. If you have comments concerning the accuracy of these time estimates or suggestions for making this form more simple, we would be happy to hear from you. You can write to both the **Internal Revenue Service,** Washington, DC 20224, Attention: IRS Reports Clearance Officer, T:FP; and the **Office of Management and Budget,** Paperwork Reduction Project (1545-0029), Washington, DC 20503. DO NOT send the tax form to either of these offices. Instead, see the instructions below for information on where to file.

Important Tax Law Changes for 1991.—The wage bases for the two parts of the social security tax (social security and Medicare) now are different. Employers can no longer combine and report the withholding as a single amount. Social security wages must be reported on line 6a, social security tips must be reported on line 6b, and Medicare wages and tips must be reported on line 7. The wage bases are $53,400 for social security and $125,000 for Medicare.

The cost of group-term life insurance in excess of $50,000 provided former employees is subject to both the employer and employee portion of social security and Medicare taxes. Include the cost of the excess coverage on lines 6a and 7. Any uncollected social security and Medicare taxes must be reported as an adjustment on line 9.

Forms W-4.—Each quarter, send in with Form 941 copies of any Forms W-4 received during the quarter from employees: (1) claiming more than 10 withholding allowances, or (2) claiming exemption from income tax withholding if their wages will normally be more than $200 a week. For details, see section 10 of Circular E.

Circular E, Employer's Tax Guide, explains the rules for withholding, paying, depositing, and reporting Federal income tax, social security and Medicare taxes, and Federal unemployment (FUTA) tax on wages, fringe benefits, and sick pay paid by third-party payers. **Circular A,** Agricultural Employer's Tax Guide, explains different rules for employers who have farmworkers. These circulars are available free at IRS offices.

General Instructions

Purpose of Form.—To report:

- Income tax you withheld from wages, tips, annuities, supplemental unemployment compensation benefits, certain gambling winnings, and third-party payments of sick pay.
- Income tax withheld as backup withholding.
- Social security and Medicare taxes.

Who Must File.—Employers who withhold income tax, and both social security and Medicare taxes, must file Form 941 quarterly. Exceptions are:

- **Seasonal employers** are relieved from filing Form 941 for quarters when they regularly have no tax liability because they have paid no wages. To alert IRS that you will not have to file a return for one or more quarters during the year, check the Seasonal employers box above line 1. IRS will generally not inquire about unfiled returns if at least one taxable return is filed each year. However, you must check the Seasonal employers box on every quarterly return you file. Otherwise, IRS will expect a return to be filed for each quarter.
- Employers who report payments not subject to social security, see **Form 941E,** Quarterly Return of Withheld Federal Income Tax and Medicare Tax, and Circular E.
- Employers who report wages on household employees, see **Form 942,** Employer's Quarterly Tax Return for Household Employees, and Circular E.
- Employers who report wages on farmworkers, see **Form 943,** Employer's Annual Tax Return for Agricultural Employees, and Circular A.
- Business Reorganization or Termination. If you sell or transfer your business, both you and the new owner must file a return for the quarter in which the change took place. Neither should report wages paid by the other. (An example of a transfer is when a sole proprietor forms a partnership or corporation.) If a change occurs, please attach to your return a statement that shows: new owner's name (or new name of the business); whether the business is now a sole proprietorship, partnership, or corporation; kind of change that took place (sale, transfer, etc.); and date of the change.

When a business is merged or consolidated with another, the continuing firm must file the return for the quarter in which the change took place. The return should show all wages paid for that quarter. The other firm should file a final return.

But if you go out of business or stop paying wages, file a final return. Be sure to fill in the entries above line 1. You may also file Form W-2 with the Social Security Administration now but not later than March 2, 1992.

When To File.—File starting with the first quarter in which you are required to withhold income tax or pay wages subject to social security and Medicare taxes.

Quarter	Ending	Due Date
Jan.-Feb.-Mar.	March 31	April 30
Apr.-May-June	June 30	July 31
July-Aug.-Sept.	Sept. 30	Oct. 31
Oct.-Nov.-Dec.	Dec. 31	Jan. 31

If you deposited all taxes when due for a quarter, you have 10 more days after the above due date to file. If the due date for filing a return falls on a Saturday, Sunday, or legal holiday, you may file the return on the first day afterward that is not a Saturday, Sunday, or legal holiday.

After you file your first return, we will send you a form every 3 months. Please use this form. If you don't have a form, get one from an IRS office in time to file the return when due.

Where To File.—

If your legal residence, principal place of business, office, or agency is located in:	Use the following Internal Revenue Service Center address:
Florida, Georgia, South Carolina	Atlanta, GA 39901
New Jersey, New York (New York City and counties of Nassau, Rockland, Suffolk, and Westchester)	Holtsville, NY 00501
New York (all other counties), Connecticut, Maine, Massachusetts, New Hampshire, Rhode Island, Vermont	Andover, MA 05501
Illinois, Iowa, Minnesota, Missouri, Wisconsin	Kansas City, MO 64999
Delaware, District of Columbia, Maryland, Pennsylvania, Virginia	Philadelphia, PA 19255
Indiana, Kentucky, Michigan, Ohio, West Virginia	Cincinnati, OH 45999
Kansas, New Mexico, Oklahoma, Texas	Austin, TX 73301
Alaska, Arizona, California (counties of Alpine, Amador, Butte, Calaveras, Colusa, Contra Costa, Del Norte, El Dorado, Glenn, Humboldt, Lake, Lassen, Marin, Mendocino, Modoc, Napa, Nevada, Placer, Plumas, Sacramento, San Joaquin, Shasta, Sierra, Siskiyou, Solano, Sonoma, Sutter, Tehama, Trinity, Yolo, and Yuba), Colorado, Idaho, Montana, Nebraska, Nevada, North Dakota, Oregon, South Dakota, Utah, Washington, Wyoming	Ogden, UT 84201
California (all other counties), Hawaii	Fresno, CA 93888
Alabama, Arkansas, Louisiana, Mississippi, North Carolina, Tennessee	Memphis, TN 37501
If you have no legal residence or principal place of business in any state	Philadelphia, PA 19255

Employer Identification Number (EIN).—If you have not asked for a number, apply for one on **Form SS-4,** Application for Employer Identification Number. Get this form from IRS or the Social Security Administration (SSA). If you do not have a number by the time a return is due, write "Applied for" and the date you applied in the space shown for the number.

Penalties and Interest.—There are penalties for filing a return late and paying or depositing taxes late, unless there is reasonable cause. If you are late, please attach an explanation to your return. There are also penalties for willful failure to file returns and pay taxes when due, furnish Forms W-2 to employees and file copies with SSA, keep records, deposit taxes when required, and for filing false returns or submitting bad checks. See Circular E for additional information.

Interest is charged on taxes paid late at the rate set by law.

Depositing Taxes.—Use **Form 8109,** Federal Tax Deposit Coupon, to deposit your taxes. See Circular E, section 13, for information and rules concerning Federal tax deposits.

Do not use the deposit coupons to pay delinquent taxes for which you have received a notice from the IRS. These payments should be sent directly to your Internal Revenue Service Center along with a copy of any related notice the IRS sent you.

Specific Instructions

Reconciliation of Forms 941 and W-3.—Certain amounts reported on the four quarterly Forms 941 for 1991 should agree with the **Forms W-2,** Wage and Tax Statement, totals reported on **Form W-3,** Transmittal of Income and Tax Statements, or with information filed on equivalent magnetic media reports filed with the SSA. The amounts that should agree are: social security wages, social security tips, Medicare wages and tips, and the advance earned income credit. If the totals do not agree, IRS will require you to explain any differences and correct any errors. You can avoid this by making sure that correct amounts (including adjustments) are reported on Forms 941 and W-3.

Line 1—Number of employees.—Complete for the January-March calendar quarter only. Do not include household employees, persons

(continued on page 4)

Form **941**
(Rev. January 1991)
Department of the Treasury
Internal Revenue Service

4141

Employer's Quarterly Federal Tax Return

▶ **See Circular E for more information concerning employment tax returns.**

Please type or print.

Type or print your name, address, employer identification number, and calendar quarter of return as shown on original. ▶

Name (as distinguished from trade name) | Date quarter ended | OMB No. 1545-0029 Expires: 5-31-93

Trade name, if any | Employer identification number

Address and ZIP code

YOUR COPY

If you do not have to file returns in the future, check here . . . ▶ ☐ Date final wages paid . . . ▶

If you are a seasonal employer, see **Seasonal employers** on page 2 and check here . ▶ ☐

1a Number of employees (except household) employed in the pay period that includes March 12th . ▶ **1a**

b If you are a subsidiary corporation AND your parent corporation files a consolidated Form 1120, enter parent corporation employer identification number (EIN) . . ▶ **1b** –

2	Total wages and tips subject to withholding, plus other compensation . . . . ▶	2		
3	Total income tax withheld from wages, tips, pensions, annuities, sick pay, gambling, etc. . . ▶	3		
4	Adjustment of withheld income tax for preceding quarters of calendar year (see instructions) . . ▶	4		
5	Adjusted total of income tax withheld (line 3 as adjusted by line 4—see instructions)	5		
6a	Taxable social security wages (Complete line 7) $ × 12.4% (.124) =	6a		
b	Taxable social security tips $ × 12.4% (.124) =	6b		
7	Taxable Medicare wages and tips . . . . . . $ × 2.9% (.029) =	7		
8	Total social security and Medicare taxes (add lines 6a, 6b, and 7)	8		
9	Adjustment of social security and Medicare taxes (see instructions for required explanation) . . .	9		
10	Adjusted total of social security and Medicare taxes (line 8 as adjusted by line 9—see instructions) ▶	10		
11	Backup withholding (see instructions)	11		
12	Adjustment of backup withholding tax for preceding quarters of calendar year. . . . . ▶	12		
13	Adjusted total of backup withholding (line 11 as adjusted by line 12)	13		
14	**Total taxes** (add lines 5, 10, and 13)	14		
15	Advance earned income credit (EIC) payments made to employees, if any . . . . ▶	15		
16	Net taxes (subtract line 15 from line 14). **This should equal line IV below** (plus line IV of Schedule A (Form 941) if you have treated backup withholding as a separate liability)	16		
17	**Total deposits for quarter,** including overpayment applied from a prior quarter, from your records. ▶	17		
18	**Balance due** (subtract line 17 from line 16). This should be less than $500. Pay to IRS. . . . ▶	18		
19	**Overpayment,** if line 17 is more than line 16, enter here ▶ $ ______________ and check if to be: ☐ Applied to next return **OR** ☐ Refunded.			

Record of Federal Tax Liability (You must complete if line 16 is $500 or more and Schedule B is not attached.) See instructions before checking these boxes.

Check only if you made deposits using the 95% rule ▶ ☐ Check only if you are a first time 3-banking-day depositor. . . ▶ ☐

Do NOT Show Federal Tax Deposits Here

Date wages paid	Show tax liability here, **not deposits.** IRS gets deposit data from FTD coupons.					
	First month of quarter		Second month of quarter		Third month of quarter	
1st through 3rd	A		I		Q	
4th through 7th	B		J		R	
8th through 11th	C		K		S	
12th through 15th	D		L		T	
16th through 19th	E		M		U	
20th through 22nd	F		N		V	
23rd through 25th	G		O		W	
26th through the last	H		P		X	
Total liability for month	*I*		*II*		*III*	
IV Total for quarter (add lines *I, II,* and *III*). **This should equal line 16 above** . . . . . . ▶						

Sign Here Under penalties of perjury, I declare that I have examined this return, including accompanying schedules and statements, and to the best of my knowledge and belief, it is true, correct, and complete.

Signature ▶ **Print Your Name and Title ▶** **Date ▶**

Form 941 (Rev. 1-91) Page **4**

who received no pay during the pay period, pensioners, or members of the Armed Forces. If you have only household employees in the pay period, enter -0-. An entry of 250 or more on line 1a indicates a need to file wage reports on magnetic media. You should immediately request Publication TIB-4 from SSA if not already a magnetic media filer.

Line 2.—Enter the total of all wages paid, tips reported, taxable fringe benefits provided, and other compensation paid to your employees, even if you do not have to withhold income or social security and Medicare taxes on it. Do not include pensions, annuities, supplemental unemployment compensation benefits, or gambling winnings, even if you withheld income tax on them.

When an employer receives timely notice from its insurance carrier concerning the amount of third-party sick pay paid, the employer should include the third-party sick pay on this line. In these cases, an insurance company should not include third-party sick pay that it paid to the employees of policy holders. See section 19 of Circular E for more details.

Line 3.—Enter the income tax you withheld on wages, tips, taxable fringe benefits, annuities, supplemental unemployment compensation benefits, and gambling winnings. An insurance company should enter the income tax it withheld on third-party sick pay here.

Line 4—Adjustment of withheld income tax.—Use line 4 to correct errors in income tax withheld from wages paid in earlier quarters of the same calendar year. Explain any amount on **Form 941c,** Statement to Correct Information, or attach a statement that shows: (a) what the error was, (b) quarter in which the error was made, (c) the amount of the error for each quarter, (d) quarter in which you found the error, and (e) how you and your payees have settled any overcollection or undercollection. Do not use this line to adjust income tax withholding for earlier years.

Line 5—Adjusted total of income tax withheld.—Add line 4 to line 3 if you are reporting additional income tax withheld for an earlier quarter in this calendar year. Subtract line 4 from line 3 if you are reducing the amount of income tax withheld. If there is no entry on line 4, the entry will be the same as line 3.

Line 6a—Taxable social security wages.—Enter the total wages subject to social security taxes that you paid your employees during the quarter. Include the employee social security tax and the employee state unemployment compensation tax you paid for your employees rather than deducting it from their wages. Also include any sick pay and taxable fringe benefits subject to social security taxes. Enter the amount before deductions. Do not include tips on this line. Stop reporting when an employee's wages (including tips) reach $53,400 for 1991. However, continue to withhold income tax for the whole year on wages and tips even when the social security wage base of $53,400 is reached. See line 7 below for Medicare tax. If none of the payments are subject to social security tax, enter -0- and attach a statement explaining why the wages are not subject to social security tax.

Line 6b—Taxable tips.—Enter all tips your employees reported during the quarter, until tips and wages for each employee reach $53,400 in 1991. Do this even if you were not able to withhold the employee tax (6.2%). However, see line 9 instructions below.

An employee must report to you cash tips, including tips you paid the employee for charge customers, totaling $20 or more in a month by the 10th of the next month. The employee may use **Form 4070,** Employee's Report of Tips to Employer, or a written statement.

Do not include allocated tips on this line. Instead, report them on **Form 8027,** Employer's Annual Information Return of Tip Income and Allocated Tips. Allocated tips are not reportable on Form 941 and are not subject to withholding of income, social security, or Medicare taxes.

Line 7—Taxable Medicare wages and tips.—Use this line to report all wages and tips subject to the Medicare portion of social security. Stop reporting when an employee's wages and tips reach $125,000 for 1991. If none of the payments are subject to Medicare tax, enter -0- and attach a statement explaining why the wages are not subject to the Medicare tax.

Include all tips your employees reported during the quarter, even if you were not able to withhold the employee tax (1.45%). However, see line 9 instructions below.

Line 9—Adjustment of social security and Medicare taxes.—Use line 9 to correct errors in social security and Medicare taxes reported on an earlier return or to correct errors in credits for overpayments of penalty or interest paid on tax for an earlier quarter. If you report both an underpayment and an overpayment, show only the difference. Except for fractions of cents or third-party sick pay, explain any amount on line 9 on Form 941c, or attach a statement that shows: (a) what the error was, (b) ending date of each quarter in which the error was made and the amount of the error, (c) quarter in which you found the error, (d) that you repaid the employee tax or got each affected employee's written consent to this refund or credit, if the entry corrects an overcollection, and (e) if the entry corrects social security and Medicare taxes overcollected in an earlier year, that you got from the employee a written statement that he or she has not claimed and will not claim a refund or credit for the amount. If you are adjusting an employee's social security wages, tips, Medicare wages, Medicare tips, or tax withheld for a prior year, you must also file **Form W-2c,** Statement of Corrected Income and Tax Amounts, and **Form W-3c,** Transmittal of Corrected Income and Tax Statements, with the Social Security office where you filed Forms W-2. You can get these from IRS.

Enter on Form 941c or include in the statement the total wages or tips for all your employees as previously reported and as corrected. You can get Form 941c from IRS.

Adjustments of tax on tips and group-term life insurance premiums paid for former employees.—Include on line 9 the total uncollected employee social security and Medicare taxes. Attach a statement explaining each adjustment. (See Circular E for details.)

Adjustment of tax on third-party sick pay.—Deduct on line 9 the social security and Medicare taxes on third-party sick pay for which you are not responsible, and write "Sick pay" in the margin.

Fraction of cents.—If there is a difference between the total tax on line 8 and the total deducted from your employees' wages or tips because of fractions of cents added or dropped in collecting the tax, report the difference on line 9. If this difference is the only entry, write "Fractions only" in the margin.

Line 10—Adjusted total of social security and Medicare taxes.—Add line 9 to line 8 if you are reporting additional taxes for an earlier quarter. Subtract line 9 from line 8 if you are reducing the amount of taxes reported for an earlier quarter or claiming credit for overpayments of penalty or interest paid on tax for an earlier quarter.

Line 11—Backup withholding.—Enter the income tax withheld as backup withholding.

Line 12.—Use line 12 to correct errors in backup withholding tax for earlier quarters of this year.

Line 17—Total deposits for quarter.—Enter the total deposits for the quarter including backup withholding reported on Schedule A (Form 941) and any overpayment applied from the previous quarter from your records.

Line 18—Balance due.—If you deposited all taxes when due, any balance will be less than $500. Enter your EIN, "Form 941," and the tax period to which the payment applies on your check or money order.

Line 19—Overpayment.—If you deposited more than the correct amount for a quarter, you can have the overpayment refunded or applied to your next return. Also, the IRS may apply your overpayment to any past due tax account that we have under your EIN.

Completing the Record of Federal Tax Liability (ROFT).—Note: *This is a record of when you were liable for taxes, NOT a record of when you made a deposit.*

(a) Line 16 is less than $500.—You do not have to complete the ROFT.

(b) Your tax liability is $500 or more but less than $3,000 for each month of the quarter.—Only enter your total liability for each month on the "Total liability for month" lines (I, II, and III). No entries are required in A through X.

(c) Your tax liability is $3,000 or more for at least one month during the quarter but less than $100,000 during each eighth-monthly period.—Each month is divided into eight deposit periods (called eighth-monthly periods) that end on the 3rd, 7th, 11th, 15th, 19th, 22nd, 25th, and last day of the month as shown in the record. Find the eighth-monthly period(s) during the quarter in which you had a payday. Make entries only on the lines next to these periods. (For example, if you pay wages on the 1st and 15th of each month, complete lines A, D, I, L, Q, T, and the monthly Total lines.) Enter your tax liability (income tax withheld plus both the employee and employer social security and Medicare taxes minus any advance earned income credit payments) for each eighth-monthly period during which you had a payday.

(d) Your tax liability is $100,000 or more during any eighth-monthly period.—You do not have to complete the ROFT. Instead, you must complete and attach **Schedule B (Form 941),** Supplemental Record of Federal Tax Liability. You must enter the total of Column 2 from Schedule B (Form 941) on line IV of the ROFT.

Do NOT show Federal tax deposits here. This information is obtained from the deposit coupon.

The total of the tax liability column, line IV (plus line IV on Schedule A (Form 941) if you treat backup withholding as a separate liability) should equal "Net taxes" (line 16). Otherwise, you may be charged a penalty, based on your average tax liability, for not making deposits of taxes.

Check the first box at the top of the ROFT only if you are making deposits using the 95% rule. This is explained in Circular E.

Check the second box at the top of the ROFT only if you qualify for the exception under Rule 4 explained on page 9 of Circular E and attach a statement showing your net taxes for each of the preceding 4 calendar quarters.

☆ U.S.G.P.O. 1991 289-181

OSHA

10. OSHA Information

Digests and Standards

The Occupational Safety and Health Administration (OSHA) has prepared a series of pocket digests covering the following areas:

- Construction Industry
- General Industry
- Longshoring Industry
- Shipyard Industry

These digests have been compiled to aid employers, supervisors, and safety and health personnel in their efforts to comply with OSHA standards in the workplace.

Unless otherwise noted, a single free copy of each these digests are available from OSHA regional and area offices or from the OSHA publications office, 200 Constitution Avenue NW, Room N-3101, Washington, D.C. 20120.

The information contained in these digests should in no way be considered as a complete substitute for any provisions of the Occupational Safety and Health Act of 1970 or for any standards promulgated under the Act. The actual source standards are noted in the indexes to these booklets and should be consulted for complete reference to OSHA standards in their entirety.

Explanation of Contents

The *Construction Industry Digest* (OSHA 2202) and the *General Industry Digest* (OSHA 2201) contain those standards most frequently overlooked by employers, and those that are particularly hazardous. These two booklets only summarize the basic applicable standards; they do not list OSHA standards verbatim. The actual standards, in their entirety, are sold by the Superintendent of Documents, U.S. Government Printing Office, Washington, D.C. 20402-0325 (fax number 202-275-0019).

The *Shipyard Industry Digest* (OSHA 2268) contains all the safety and health standards in Title 29 Code of Regulations (CFR) Part 1915, as of January 31, 1989. Hazards not covered by the shipyard industry standards may be covered by general industry standards in 29 CFR Part 1910.

The *Longshoring Industry Digest* (OSHA 2232) contains all the safety and health standards to marine terminals (29 CFR 1917) and longshoring (29 CFR 1918) operations, as of September 1985. Consequently, the current digest does not include single-piece rim wheels or hazard communication. Other booklets on these topics are available from the OSHA Publications Office. Ask for "Chemical Hazard Communications (OSHA 3084)" or "Safe Operating Procedures: Single-Piece Rim Wheels (OSHA 3086)."

---

11. Texas OSHA Offices

A number of booklets concerning OSHA requirements and information are available from any OSHA office. The location of Texas OSHA offices is listed below. The publications available include:

Fort Worth, TX 76115
Fort Worth Federal Center
4900 Hemphill Bldg. 24—Rm. 145
P.O. Box 6477
Telephone: 817-334-5274

Harlingen, TX 78550
Riverview Professional Bldg.
1324 S. 77 Sunshine Strip—Suite 9
Telephone: 512-425-6811

Houston, TX 77004
2320 LaBranch Street—Rm. 2118
Telephone: 713-226-5431

Houston, TX 77058
1100 NASA Road 1—Suite 505
Telephone: 713-226-4357

Irving, TX 75061
1425 W. Pioneer Drive
Telephone: 214-749-7555

Lubbock, TX 79401
Federal Bldg.—Rm. 421
1205 Texas Avenue
Telephone: 806-762-7681

Tyler, TX 75702
FOB-USPO & Courthouse
Room 208
211 W. Ferguson St.
Telephone: 214-595-1404

---

12. Required Posters in the Workplace

There are several posters that employers are mandated by law to display on their work premises. These are listed below, with the appropriate telephone number for contact purposes.

1. State law requires all employers to post the notice by the Texas Employment Commission (TEC) that advises employees of their rights under the Texas Unemployment Compensation Act. Employers are also required by the Texas Payday Law to post notice of their paydays.

   CONTACT: TEC, Payday Law Unit, 800-342-3836.

2. Under the Texas Workers' Compensation Act, employers are required to post notice as to whether or not the employer has workers' compensation insurance coverage, and how employees can report workplace safety violations.

   CONTACT: Texas Workers' Compensation Commission, 512-448-7900.

3. A poster entitled "Equal Employment Opportunity is the Law" meets the requirements of the Age Discrimination in Employment Act of 1967 and Title VII of the Civil Rights Act of 1964.

   CONTACT: Equal Employment Opportunity Commission, Dallas, 214-767-7015; Houston, 713-653-3377; San Antonio, 512-229-4810.

4. Posters detailing provisions of the Fair Labor Standards Act and the Polygraph Protection Act are required for display.

   CONTACT: U.S. Department of Labor, 713-750-1683 or 512-229-6126.

5. The "OSHA Poster" explains the Occupational Safety and Health Act of 1970.

   CONTACT: Occupational Safety & Health Administration, 214-767-4731.

Houston One Stop Business Center
P.O. Box 1562
Houston, Texas 77251
Phone: 713-663-7867

Appendix E

Immigration Law Supplement

Appendix E

Immigration Law Supplement

1. Employment Eligibility Verification Form

EMPLOYMENT ELIGIBILITY VERIFICATION (Form I-9)

1 EMPLOYEE INFORMATION AND VERIFICATION: (To be completed and signed by employee.)

Name: (Print or Type) Last	First	Middle	Birth Name
Address: Street Name and Number	City	State	ZIP Code
Date of Birth (Month/Day/Year)		Social Security Number	

I attest, under penalty of perjury, that I am (check a box):

☐ 1. A citizen or national of the United States.
☐ 2. An alien lawfully admitted for permanent residence (Alien Number A ____________________).
☐ 3. An alien authorized by the Immigration and Naturalization Service to work in the United States (Alien Number A ____________________, or Admission Number ____________________, expiration of employment authorization, if any ____________________).

I attest, under penalty of perjury, the documents that I have presented as evidence of identity and employment eligibility are genuine and relate to me. I am aware that federal law provides for imprisonment and/or fine for any false statements or use of false documents in connection with this certificate.

Signature	Date (Month/Day/Year)

PREPARER/TRANSLATOR CERTIFICATION (To be completed if prepared by person other than the employee). I attest, under penalty of perjury, that the above was prepared by me at the request of the named individual and is based on all information of which I have any knowledge.

Signature	Name (Print or Type)		
Address (Street Name and Number)	City	State	Zip Code

2 EMPLOYER REVIEW AND VERIFICATION: (To be completed and signed by employer.)

Instructions:
Examine one document from List A and check the appropriate box, ***OR*** examine one document from List B ***and*** one from List C and check the appropriate boxes. Provide the ***Document Identification Number*** and ***Expiration Date*** for the document checked.

List A Documents that Establish Identity and Employment Eligibility	List B Documents that Establish Identity	and	List C Documents that Establish Employment Eligibility
☐ 1. United States Passport ☐ 2. Certificate of United States Citizenship ☐ 3. Certificate of Naturalization ☐ 4. Unexpired foreign passport with attached Employment Authorization ☐ 5. Alien Registration Card with photograph	☐ 1. A State-issued driver's license or a State-issued I.D. card with a photograph, or information, including name, sex, date of birth, height, weight, and color of eyes. (Specify State)________) ☐ 2. U.S. Military Card ☐ 3. Other (Specify document and issuing authority) ________		☐ 1. Original Social Security Number Card (other than a card stating it is not valid for employment) ☐ 2. A birth certificate issued by State, county, or municipal authority bearing a seal or other certification ☐ 3. Unexpired INS Employment Authorization Specify form # ________
Document Identification # ________ *Expiration Date (if any)* ________	*Document Identification* # ________ *Expiration Date (if any)* ________		*Document Identification* # ________ *Expiration Date (if any)* ________

CERTIFICATION: I attest, under penalty of perjury, that I have examined the documents presented by the above individual, that they appear to be genuine and to relate to the individual named, and that the individual, to the best of my knowledge, is eligible to work in the United States.

Signature	Name (Print or Type)	Title
Employer Name	Address	Date

Employment Eligibility Verification

> **NOTICE:** Authority for collecting the information on this form is in Title 8, United States Code, Section 1324A, which requires employers to verify employment eligibility of individuals on a form approved by the Attorney General. This form will be used to verify the individual's eligibility for employment in the United States. Failure to present this form for inspection to officers of the Immigration and Naturalization Service or Department of Labor within the time period specified by regulation, or improper completion or retention of this form, may be a violation of the above law and may result in a civil money penalty.

Section 1. Instructions to Employee/Preparer for completing this form

Instructions for the employee.

All employees, upon being hired, must complete Section 1 of this form. Any person hired after November 6, 1986 must complete this form. (For the purpose of completion of this form the term "hired" applies to those employed, recruited or referred for a fee.)

All employees must print or type their complete name, address, date of birth, and Social Security Number. The block which correctly indicates the employee's immigration status must be checked. If the second block is checked, the employee's Alien Registration Number must be provided. If the third block is checked, the employee's Alien Registration Number ***or*** Admission Number must be provided, as well as the date of expiration of that status, if it expires.

All employees whose present names differ from birth names, because of marriage or other reasons, must print or type their birth names in the appropriate space of Section 1. Also, employees whose names change after employment verification should report these changes to their employer.

All employees must sign and date the form.

Instructions for the preparer of the form, if not the employee.

If a person assists the employee with completing this form, the preparer must certify the form by signing it and printing or typing his or her complete name and address.

Section 2. Instructions to Employer for completing this form

(For the purpose of completion of this form, the term "employer" applies to employers and those who recruit or refer for a fee.)

Employers must complete this section by examining evidence of identity and employment eligibility, and:

- checking the appropriate box in List A ***or*** boxes in both Lists B and C;
- recording the document identification number and expiration date (if any);
- recording the type of form if not specifically identified in the list;
- signing the certification section.

NOTE: Employers are responsible for reverifying employment eligibility of employees whose employment eligibility documents carry an expiration date.

Copies of documentation presented by an individual for the purpose of establishing identity and employment eligibility may be copied and retained for the purpose of complying with the requirements of this form and no other purpose. Any copies of documentation made for this purpose should be maintained with this form.

Name changes of employees which occur after preparation of this form should be recorded on the form by lining through the old name, printing the new name and the reason (such as marriage), and dating and initialing the changes. Employers should not attempt to delete or erase the old name in any fashion.

RETENTION OF RECORDS.

The completed form must be retained by the employer for:

- three years after the date of hiring; or
- one year after the date the employment is terminated, whichever is later.

Employers may photocopy or reprint this form as necessary.

U.S. Department of Justice
Immigration and Naturalization Service

OMB #1115-0136
Form I-9 (05/07/87)
☆ U.S.G.P.O.: 1987- 183-918/69085

For sale by the Superintendent of Documents, U.S. Government Printing Office
Washington, D.C. 20402

2. Employer Instructions for Completing Employment Eligibility Verification Form

M-274 (5-87)

Handbook for Employers

Instructions for Completing Form I-9

(Employment Eligibility Verification Form)

To American Employers:

When the Congress passed and the President signed into law the Immigration Reform and Control Act of 1986, the result was the first major revision of America's immigration laws in decades. The new law seeks to preserve jobs for those who are legally entitled to them: American citizens and aliens who are authorized to work in our country.

The Immigration and Naturalization Service is responsible for implementing this new law. Public cooperation is crucial to the success of this national effort.

Put briefly, the law says that you should hire only American citizens and aliens who are authorized to work in the United States. You will need to verify employment eligibility of anyone hired after November 6, 1986, and complete and retain a one-page form (I-9) contained in this handbook.

We have worked to make the process as simple as possible. This handbook provides a step-by-step explanation of what you must do. We hope you will find it helpful.

All Americans stand to benefit from the successful implementation of the Immigration Reform and Control Act. We seek your cooperation.

Alan C. Nelson

Alan C. Nelson
Commissioner
U.S. Immigration and Naturalization Service

Contents

This Handbook is divided into nine parts:

This Handbook includes two copies of the Form I-9. At the back, you will also find a list of INS offices for you to contact if you need more information.

Part One

Why Employers Must Verify Employment Eligibility of New Employees

The Immigration Reform and Control Act of 1986 is the most comprehensive reform of our immigration laws since 1952. In recent years, our nation has been increasingly affected by illegal immigration. This law, passed by Congress through a bipartisan effort, preserves our tradition of legal immigration while closing the back door to illegal entry. By combining prohibitions against employing illegal entrants (or those aliens, such as tourists, who legally enter the United States but are not authorized to work while they are here) with increased border enforcement, the law represents a step forward in the effort to secure our nation's borders.

Employment is often the magnet that attracts persons to come to or stay in the United States illegally. The purpose of the new law is to remove the magnet by requiring employers to hire only citizens and aliens who are authorized to work here.

This new law was strongly supported by the American public. Employers will want to join the effort to protect our heritage of legal immigration and to preserve jobs for those who are legally entitled to them. This cooperation will make jobs available to American citizens and to aliens who are authorized to work in our country. It also can be a means to help people get off welfare and into jobs. Further, it is a good business practice for you to verify the identity of your workers. The law deserves your support.

The Form I-9 has been developed for verifying that persons are eligible to work in the United States. The following instructions will help you assess your responsibilities for completing the Form and understanding the law.

The law requires you as an employer to do five things:

1. Have your employees fill out their part of the Form I-9 when they start to work;
2. Check documents establishing employees' identity and eligibility to work;
3. Properly complete the Form I-9;
4. Retain the Form for at least three years (if you employ the person for more than three years, you must retain the Form until one year after the person leaves your employment); and
5. Present the Form for inspection to an INS or Department of Labor (DOL) officer upon request. You will be given at least three days advance notice.

Part Two

When You Must Complete Form I-9

IF YOU EMPLOY PERSONS TO PERFORM LABOR OR SERVICES IN RETURN FOR WAGES OR OTHER PAY, **YOU MUST COMPLETE FORM I-9 FOR:**

Persons hired after May 31, 1987. For these employees, you must complete a Form I-9 within three business days of the date of the hire. (If you employ the person for less than three days, you must complete the Form I-9 before the end of the employee's first working day.)

Persons hired between November 7, 1986 and May 31, 1987. For these employees, you must complete Form I-9 before September 1, 1987.

NOTE: If you employ people for domestic work in your private home on a regular (such as weekly) basis, these requirements also apply to you.

YOU **DO NOT** NEED TO COMPLETE FORM I-9 FOR:

—Persons hired before November 7, 1986.

—Persons hired after November 6, 1986, who left your employment before June 1, 1987.

—Persons you employ for domestic work in a private home on an intermittent or sporadic basis.

—Persons who provide labor to you who are employed by a contractor providing contract services (e.g., employee leasing).

—Persons who are independent contractors.

Persons who are self-employed do not need to complete Form I-9.

Part Three

How to Complete Form I-9

Form I-9 contains two sections. The **employee** completes the first section (Steps 1, 2, and 3). If a preparer or translator assists the individual, he or she completes Step 4. The second section (Steps 5 and 6) should be completed by the **employer**.

When completing the Form I-9, the employee will need to provide a document or documents that establish identity and employment eligibility. Some documents establish *both* identity and employment eligibility. These documents appear in *List A* on the bottom half of the Form. Other documents establish identity alone (*List B*) or employment eligibility alone (*List C*). If the person does not provide a document from List A, he or she must produce one from List B *and* one from List C. A complete list of acceptable documents appears in Part Nine.

The employer should review the document or documents provided by the person. Documents should appear to be genuine and to relate to the individual.

If employees cannot complete Section 1 by themselves or need the Form translated, someone may assist them. The preparer or translator should read the Form to the employee, help with Step 1 and Step 2 as needed, have the employee sign or mark the Form, and follow Step 4.

Until September 1, 1987, if an employee indicates that he or she intends to or has applied for legalization, Special Agricultural Worker (SAW), or Cuban/Haitian entrant status, the employee is covered by a "special rule" and the employer should follow the instructions on page 4.

If a minor (under age 16) cannot produce a List A document or one of the identity documents listed in Part Nine (List B), he or she is exempt from producing one if: (1) a parent or legal guardian completes Section 1 and writes in the space for the minor's signature the words, "minor under age 16;" (2) the parent or legal guardian completes the "Preparer/Translator Certification," and (3) the employer writes in Section 2 the words, "minor under age 16" under List B in the space after the words "Document Identification #." If this procedure is followed, the minor must still produce a List C document showing employment eligibility.

SECTION 1: TO BE COMPLETED BY THE **EMPLOYEE**

STEP 1
Fill in the personal information.

STEP 2
Check the box for work eligibility. Give other information where needed.

STEP 3
Read, sign, and date.

STEP 4
(Preparer/Translator only)
Read, fill in information, and sign.

EMPLOYMENT ELIGIBILITY VERIFICATION (Form I-9)

1 **EMPLOYEE INFORMATION AND VERIFICATION:** (To be completed and signed by employee.)

Name: (Print or Type) Last: Smith — First: Mary — Middle: Ellen — Birth Name: Adams

Address: Street Name and Number: 4502 Birch Ln — City: Danville, TN — State — ZIP Code: 37832

Date of Birth (Month/Day/Year): 6/26/53 — Social Security Number: 408-08-4503

I attest, under penalty of perjury, that I am (check a box):

☒ 1. A citizen or national of the United States.
☐ 2. An alien lawfully admitted for permanent residence (Alien Number A ________).
☐ 3. An alien authorized by the Immigration and Naturalization Service to work in the United States (Alien Number A ________, or Admission Number ________, expiration of employment authorization, if any ________).

I attest, under penalty of perjury, the documents that I have presented as evidence of identity and employment eligibility are genuine and relate to me. I am aware that federal law provides for imprisonment and/or fine for any false statements or use of false documents in connection with this certificate.

Signature: Mary Ellen Smith — Date (Month/Day/Year): 6/15/87

PREPARER/TRANSLATOR CERTIFICATION (To be completed if prepared by person other than the employee). I attest, under penalty of perjury, that the above was prepared by me at the request of the named individual and is based on all information of which I have any knowledge.

Signature — Name (Print or Type)

Address (Street Name and Number) — City — State — Zip Code

SECTION 2: TO BE COMPLETED BY THE **EMPLOYER**

STEP 5
Examine the document and check the box that corresponds to the document. Fill in document number and expiration date.

STEP 6
Read, fill in information, and sign.

2 **EMPLOYER REVIEW AND VERIFICATION:** (To be completed and signed by employer.)

Instructions:
Examine one document from List A and check the appropriate box, *OR* examine one document from List B *and* one from List C and check the appropriate boxes.
Provide the ***Document Identification Number*** and ***Expiration Date*** for the document checked.

List A — Documents that Establish Identity and Employment Eligibility

☒ 1. United States Passport
☐ 2. Certificate of United States Citizenship
☐ 3. Certificate of Naturalization
☐ 4. Unexpired foreign passport with attached Employment Authorization
☐ 5. Alien Registration Card with photograph

Document Identification # Y016534
Expiration Date (if any) Oct 21, 1991

List B — Documents that Establish Identity

and

☐ 1. A State-issued driver's license or a State-issued I.D. card with a photograph, or information, including name, sex, date of birth, height, weight, and color of eyes. (Specify State) ________)
☐ 2. U.S. Military Card
☐ 3. Other (Specify document and issuing authority) ________

Document Identification # ________
Expiration Date (if any) ________

List C — Documents that Establish Employment Eligibility

☐ 1. Original Social Security Number Card (other than a card stating it is not valid for employment)
☐ 2. A birth certificate issued by State, county, or municipal authority bearing a seal or other certification
☐ 3. Unexpired INS Employment Authorization Specify form # ________

Document Identification # ________
Expiration Date (if any) ________

CERTIFICATION: I attest, under penalty of perjury, that I have examined the documents presented by the above individual, that they appear to be genuine and to relate to the individual named, and that the individual, to the best of my knowledge, is eligible to work in the United States.

Signature: J. W. Walsh — Name (Print or Type): JOSEPH W. WALSH — Title: PRESIDENT

Employer Name: JOSEPH WALSH, INC. — Address: 807 N. MAIN ST., DANVILLE, TN — Date: 6/25/87

Form I-9 (05/07/87)
OMB No. 1115-0136

U.S. Department of Justice
Immigration and Naturalization Service

Under the new immigration law, charges of national origin discrimination against employers with four through fourteen employees and charges of citizenship discrimination against employers with four or more employees should be filed with the Office of Special Counsel in the Department of Justice. Discrimination charges may be filed either by persons who believe they were discriminated against in employment on the basis of national origin or citizenship status (or by a person on their behalf) or by INS officers who have reason to believe that discrimination has occurred. Discrimination charges must be filed within 180 days of the discriminatory act. The Office of the Special Counsel will notify the employer by certified mail within ten days upon receipt of a charge of discrimination. After investigating the charge, the Special Counsel may file a complaint with an administrative law judge. If the Special Counsel does not file a complaint within 120 days of receiving the charge, the person making the charge (other than an INS officer) may initiate filing a complaint with an administrative law judge. The administrative law judge will conduct a hearing and issue a decision.

Employers found to have engaged in discriminatory practices under the new immigration law will be ordered to stop the prohibited practice. They may also be ordered to hire, with or without back pay, individuals directly injured by the discrimination; pay a fine of up to $1,000 for each individual discriminated against (up to $2,000 for each such individual in cases of employers previously fined); and keep certain records regarding the hiring of applicants and employees. If a court decides that the losing party's claim has no reasonable basis in fact or law, the court may award attorneys' fees to prevailing parties other than the United States.

For more information concerning the antidiscrimination section of the new immigration law, write the Office of the Special Counsel for Immigration-Related Unfair Employment Practices, P.O. Box 65490, Washington, D.C. 20035-5490 or call (202) 653-8121.

For more information on Title VII and policies and procedures of the Equal Employment Opportunity Commission, call 1-800-USA-EEOC.

Part Five

Penalties for Prohibited Practices

1. Civil Penalties

If an investigation reveals that an employer has violated the new immigration law with respect to employees hired after November 6, 1986, INS may take action. During the first year of implementation (June 1, 1987–May 31, 1988) INS will continue to assist employers in complying with the law. In addition, INS will only issue a citation for first violations. Further violations during this period may result in the penalties described below. When INS intends to impose those penalties, the Service first issues a Notice of Intent to Fine. Employers who receive a Notice may request a hearing before an administrative law judge. If a hearing is not requested within 30 days, the penalty will be imposed. After May 31, 1988, INS will no longer issue warning citations, and first violations may result in penalties.

- *Hiring or continuing to employ unauthorized employees.* Employers determined to have knowingly hired unauthorized employees (or to be continuing to employ persons knowing that they are or have become unauthorized) may be fined as follows:

  —*First Violation.* Not less than $250 and not more than $2,000 for each unauthorized employee.

  —*Second Violation.* Not less than $2,000 and not more than $5,000 for each unauthorized employee.

  —*Subsequent Violations.* Not less than $3,000 and not more than $10,000 for each unauthorized employee.

- *Failing to comply with record-keeping requirements.* Employers who fail to properly complete, retain, and present for inspection the Form I-9 as required by law may face civil fines of not less than $100 and not more than $1000 for each employee for whom the Form was not completed, retained, or presented. In determining penalties, consideration shall be given to the size of the business, good faith efforts to comply, the seriousness of the violation, and whether the violation involved unauthorized employees.

- *Requiring indemnification.* Employers found to have required a bond or indemnity from an individual against liability under the new law may be fined $1000 and ordered to make restitution, either to the person who was required to pay the indemnity, or, if that person cannot be located, to the United States Treasury.

- *Recruiting unauthorized seasonal agricultural workers outside the United States.* Employers who knowingly recruit unauthorized workers outside the United States to perform seasonal agricultural labor may face the same penalties as for hiring unauthorized workers, unless the workers recruited have been granted Special Agricultural Worker (SAW) status.

2. Criminal Penalties.

- *Engaging in a pattern or practice of knowingly hiring or continuing to employ unauthorized employees.* Employers convicted for having engaged in a pattern or practice of knowingly hiring unauthorized aliens after November 6, 1986, may face fines of up to $3000 per employee and/or six months imprisonment. The same penalties apply to engaging in a pattern or practice of recruiting unauthorized seasonal agricultural workers outside the United States. Criminal sanctions will be reserved for serious or repeated violations.

- *Engaging in fraud or false statements, or otherwise misusing visas, immigration permits, and identity documents.* Persons who use fraudulent identification or employment eligibility documents or documents that were lawfully issued to another, or who make a false statement or attestation, for purposes of satisfying the employment eligibility requirements may be imprisoned for up to five years or fined or both.

Part Six

Timetable for Employer Verification Requirements

December 1, 1986 through May 31, 1987

Public Education Period. This is an initial period established by law for the publication of regulations and dissemination of forms and information. During this period, citations are not issued and fines are not levied.

June 1, 1987 through May 31, 1988

Citation Period. This is a one-year period for public education, voluntary compliance and initial enforcement. INS will work with employer associations, labor unions, and others to provide assistance, develop voluntary cooperation, and encourage efforts to hire legal employees. Penalties are not imposed for first-offense violations during this time. Instead, a warning citation is issued which explains the nature of the violation. For subsequent or repeated violations, civil or in some cases criminal penalties can be imposed.

June 1, 1987 through September 1, 1987

Special Rule Period. Employers may hire or continue to employ employees who attest on the Form I-9 that they have applied or intend to apply for legalization, Special Agricul-

HOW TO FILL OUT FORM I-9 IF THE **SPECIAL RULE** APPLIES

The new immigration law also provides that certain qualified aliens who have resided illegally in the United States can legalize their status. In order to legalize their status, aliens must apply under the legalization, Special Agricultural Worker (SAW), or Cuban/Haitian entrant programs.

Employers may hire applicants or prospective applicants for legalization, SAW, or Cuban/Haitian entrant status. *Until September 1, 1987*, these applicants are covered by a "special rule" that authorizes them to work without providing employment eligibility documents. "Special rule" employees will need to fill out the I-9 as shown below and provide one of the specified documents that establish identity (see List B in Part Nine). The employer should review the identity document. It should appear to be genuine and to relate to the individual.

After September 1, 1987, the "special rule" expires, and these applicants will need to show a work authorization document to be hired or to continue to work. Employers must update the Form I-9 by recording the work authorization document information on the Form.

STEP 1
Fill in the personal information.

STEP 2
Check box #3. Write "special rule" in the space for alien number and "September 1, 1987" for the expiration date.

STEP 3
Read, sign, and date.

STEP 4
(Preparer/Translator only)
Read, fill in information, and sign.

STEP 5
Under List B, check the box that corresponds to the identity document and fill in document number and expiration date. Under List C, write "special rule" in the space for document number, and "September 1, 1987" for the expiration date.

STEP 6
Read, fill in information, and sign.

EMPLOYMENT ELIGIBILITY VERIFICATION (Form I-9)

(1) **EMPLOYEE INFORMATION AND VERIFICATION:** (To be completed and signed by employee.)

Name: (Print or Type) Last	First	Middle	Birth Name
JONES	DAVID	ALAN	
Address: Street Name and Number	**City**	**State**	**ZIP Code**
407 ELM ST.	HARRISON	RHODE ISLAND	02912
Date of Birth (Month/Day/Year)		**Social Security Number**	
NOVEMBER 19, 1955			

I attest, under penalty of perjury, that I am (check a box):

- ☐ 1. A citizen or national of the United States.
- ☐ 2. An alien lawfully admitted for permanent residence (Alien Number A ________).
- ☒ 3. An alien authorized by the Immigration and Naturalization Service to work in the United States (Alien Number A SPECIAL RULE or Admission Number ________, expiration of employment authorization, if any SEPT 1, 1987).

I attest, under penalty of perjury, the documents that I have presented as evidence of identity and employment eligibility are genuine and relate to me. I am aware that federal law provides for imprisonment and/or fine for any false statements or use of false documents in connection with this certificate.

Signature	Date (Month/Day/Year)
David A. Jones	7/14/87

PREPARER/TRANSLATOR CERTIFICATION (To be completed if prepared by person other than the employee). I attest, under penalty of perjury, that the above was prepared by me at the request of the named individual and is based on all information of which I have any knowledge.

Signature		Name (Print or Type)	
Address (Street Name and Number)	City	State	Zip Code

(2) **EMPLOYER REVIEW AND VERIFICATION:** (To be completed and signed by employer.)

Instructions:
Examine one document from List A and check the appropriate box, ***OR*** examine one document from List B ***and*** one from List C and check the appropriate boxes. Provide the ***Document Identification Number*** and ***Expiration Date*** for the document checked.

List A Documents that Establish Identity and Employment Eligibility	List B Documents that Establish Identity	and	List C Documents that Establish Employment Eligibility
☐ 1. United States Passport ☐ 2. Certificate of United States Citizenship ☐ 3. Certificate of Naturalization ☐ 4. Unexpired foreign passport with attached Employment Authorization ☐ 5. Alien Registration Card with photograph	☒ 1. A State-issued driver's license or a State-issued I.D. card with a photograph, or information, including name, sex, date of birth, height, weight, and color of eyes. (Specify State) Rhode Island ☐ 2. U.S. Military Card ☐ 3. Other (Specify document and issuing authority) ________		☐ 1. Original Social Security Number Card (other than a card stating it is not valid for employment) ☐ 2. A birth certificate issued by State, county, or municipal authority bearing a seal or other certification ☐ 3. Unexpired INS Employment Authorization Specify form # ________
Document Identification # ________	***Document Identification*** # 323-750-1031		***Document Identification*** # Special Rule
Expiration Date (if any) ________	***Expiration Date (if any)*** February 26, 1989		***Expiration Date (if any)*** September 1, 1987

CERTIFICATION: I attest, under penalty of perjury, that I have examined the documents presented by the above individual, that they appear to be genuine and to relate to the individual named, and that the individual, to the best of my knowledge, is eligible to work in the United States.

Signature	Name (Print or Type)	Title
Barbara Evans	Barbara Evans	Personnel Officer
Employer Name	**Address**	**Date**
Apex Corporation	8204 Oak St; Harrison, RI 02912	7/14/87

Form I-9 (05/07/87)
OMB No 1115-0136

U.S. Department of Justice
Immigration and Naturalization Service

Part Four

Unlawful Discrimination

The new immigration law also prohibits discrimination. Under this law, if you have four or more employees, you may not discriminate against any individual (other than an unauthorized alien) in hiring, discharging, or recruiting or referring for a fee because of that individual's national origin or, in the case of a citizen or intending citizen, because of his or her citizenship status.

Title VII of the Civil Rights Act of 1964 and the remedies against discrimination it provides also remain in effect. Title VII prohibits discrimination against any individual on the basis of national origin in hiring, discharge, recruitment, assignment, compensation, and other terms and conditions of employment with respect to employers subject to its coverage. Claims of national origin discrimination against employers with fifteen or more employees should be filed with the Equal Employment Opportunity Commission.

tural Worker, or Cuban/Haitian status even if the workers have not yet received work authorization documents from the INS.

June 1, 1988

Effective Date for Full Enforcement. As of this date, citations will no longer be issued for first violations. Employers who violate the law may face civil or criminal penalties.

June 1, 1987 through November 30, 1988

Deferral Period for Employers of Seasonal Agricultural Workers. Penalties will not apply to employers of seasonal agricultural workers during this period. This deferral does not apply to the prohibition against recruitment of unauthorized employees who are outside the United States. As of December 1, 1988, INS will begin full enforcement of the law with respect to these agricultural employers.

Part Seven

Instructions for Recruiters and Referrers for a Fee

The provisions of the new law that apply to employers also apply to those who **recruit** persons and refer them to potential employers in return for a fee and those who **refer** or provide documents or information about persons to employers in return for a fee. The provisions do not apply to persons who recruit for their own company or business. In addition, union hiring halls that refer union members or nonunion individuals who pay membership dues are not considered to be recruiters or referrers for a fee.

Recruiters and referrers for a fee are **not** required to verify the status of persons referred between November 6, 1986, and May 31, 1987. **Starting June 1, 1987, they should complete Form I-9 when a person they refer to an employer is hired by that employer.** The Form should be completed within three business days of the hire.

Recruiters and referrers for a fee may also refer individuals covered by the "special rule" and should follow the procedures for completing the Form I-9 on page 4.

Recruiters and referrers may designate agents to complete the verification procedures on their behalf, such as national associations, or employers. If the employer who hires the referred individual is designated as the agent, the employer needs only to provide the recruiter or referrer with a photocopy of the Form I-9. Recruiters or referrers who designate someone to complete the verification procedures on their behalf are still responsible for compliance with the law and may be found liable for violations of the law.

Recruiters and referrers must **retain** the Form I-9 for three years after the date the referred individual was hired by the employer. They must also present Forms for inspection to an INS or DOL officer after three days advance notice.

The penalties described in Part Five apply to recruiting and referring unauthorized employees for a fee which occurs on or after June 1, 1987.

Part Eight

Some Questions You May Have About the Form I-9

Q. Do United States citizens need to prove they are eligible to work?

A. Yes. While United States citizens are automatically eligible for employment, they too must provide the required documents and complete the Form I-9.

Q. Do I need to complete an I-9 for everyone who applies for a job with my company?

A. No. You need to complete I-9's only for people you actually hire. For purposes of the new law, a person is "hired" when he or she begins to work for you.

Q. If someone accepts a job with my company but will not start work for a month, can I complete the I-9 when the employee accepts the job?

A. Yes. While the law requires you to complete the I-9 when the person actually begins working, you may complete the Form when he or she accepts the job.

Q. Do I need to fill out an I-9 for independent contractors or their employees?

A. No. For example, if you contract with another company to provide temporary secretarial services, you do not have to complete I-9's for that company's employees. The other company is responsible for completing the I-9's for its own employees. However, you must not knowingly use contract labor to circumvent the law against hiring unauthorized workers.

Q. Do I need to complete an I-9 for people I hired after November 6, 1986, if they left the job before June 1, 1987?

A. No.

Q. Does the new law apply to my current employees if I hired them before it was passed?

A. No. You are not required to verify status or complete I-9's for current employees hired before November 7, 1986. However, if you choose to complete I-9's for these employees, you should do so for all your current employees hired before November 7, 1986.

Q. What if a current employee was hired before November 7, 1986, but has recently taken an approved leave of absence?

A. You do not need to complete an I-9 for that employee if he or she was temporarily absent from work for approved paid or unpaid leave, strike, or temporary layoff, or was transferred to another location of your business. However, if you rehire an employee who quit or was terminated, you should complete the employment verification process as you would for others hired after November 6, 1986. You must also verify employment eligibility and complete an I-9 if an employee leaves or is removed from the United States because of an order by a judge or INS.

Those conditions also apply to employees hired after November 6, 1986. Once you have completed an I-9 for those employees, you will not need to fill out a new Form if they have a temporary absence for approved leave, strike, layoff, or transfer.

Q. Will I be subject to employer sanctions penalties if a current employee I hired before November 7, 1986, is an illegal alien?

A. No. You will not be subject to employer sanctions penalties for merely retaining in your workforce an illegal alien hired before November 7, 1986. The fact that an illegal alien was on your payroll before November 7, 1986, does *not* give him or her any right to remain in the United States. Unless the alien is legalized or otherwise obtains permission from INS to remain in the United States, he or she is subject to apprehension and removal.

Q. What should I do if illegal alien employees ask me to help them in legalizing their status?

A. You can assist past and present employees who may qualify by providing documentation of employment history. Employment documentation furnished by employers and presented by legalization applicants will be used only to determine the applicant's eligibility for legal status. The government will not use the documents against the employer except in cases of fraud by the employer.

If aliens do not know how to apply for legal status, they may be able to get help from various organizations, such as churches, community groups, or business associations, which have been designated by INS to advise aliens and help them prepare applications.

You can also advise them that the Internal Revenue Service (IRS) may be able to provide them with documentation to verify residence. To obtain this documentation, employees should contact IRS in person or by correspondence to the service center where they filed their tax return(s). A letter to IRS should include name, address of filing, social security number (both spouses' numbers if a joint return was filed), tax year or years required and copies of any correspondence received from IRS relating to the requested years. IRS will then issue them a Form 6166 (Certification of Filing a Tax Return) if the tax information is verifiable.

Q. May I specify which documents I will accept for verification?

A. No. You must accept any document or combination of documents listed on the I-9 or in Part Nine of this Handbook that appear to be genuine.

Q. What should I do if the person I hire is unable to provide the required documents within three days?

A. If an employee is unable to provide the required document or documents within three days he or she must at least produce a receipt showing that he or she has applied for the document. The employee must produce the document itself within 21 days of the hire.

Q. What is my responsibility concerning the authenticity of documents?

A. You should examine the documents and if they appear to be genuine on their face and to relate to the person, you should accept them. If on their face the documents do not appear to be genuine or to relate to the person, you should not accept them. In addition, if the work authorization documents carry restrictions, you should abide by them.

You should also be aware that any social security number starting with a "9" is an invalid number. Employees who are using such numbers should be instructed to get a proper social security number using Form SS-5, available from the Social Security Administration.

Q. What identity documents are acceptable for minors?

A. If the minor does not have any of the identity documents listed in Part Nine, he or she does not have to produce an identity document if a parent or legal guardian completes the appropriate sections of the Form for the minor.

Q. When do I fill out the I-9 if I hire someone for less than three days?

A. You do need to complete an I-9 before the end of the employee's first working day. However, if the person is providing intermittent domestic service in your home, you do not need to complete an I-9.

Q. What if the person I hire after November 6, 1986, is an illegal alien who has applied or intends to apply for legalization?

A. There is a "special rule" for these applicants. Up until September 1, 1987, you should fill out the I-9 as illustrated on page 4.

After September 1, 1987 even these aliens must provide work authorization documents and you should update the I-9 to reflect the authorization.

Q. What if I rehire someone who previously filled out an I-9?

A. You do not need to complete a new I-9 if you rehire the person within three years of the initial hire, and the information on the Form indicates that the person is still authorized to work.

Q. Do I need to complete a new I-9 when one of my employees is promoted within my company or transfers from one of my company's offices to another at a different location?

A. No. You do not not need to complete a new I-9 if the employee is promoted or transferred within your company.

Q. What do I do when an employee's work authorization expires?

A. You will need to update the I-9 if you want to continue employing the person. At that time, the employee must present a document that either shows an extension of employment eligibility or that is a new grant of work authorization. If the employee cannot produce such a document, that person is no longer eligible to work. Continuing to employ that person is a violation of the law, even if the employee was previously authorized to work.

Q. As an employer, do I have to fill out all the I-9's myself?

A. No, you may designate someone to fill out the Form for you such as a personnel officer, foreman, agent, or anyone else acting in your interest. However, you are still responsible for compliance with the new law.

Q. Can I contract with someone to complete I-9's for my business?

A. Yes. You can contract with another person or business to verify employees' work eligibility and complete the I-9's for you. If you do so, of course, you are still responsible for the contractor's actions and could be liable for any violations of the new law.

Q. As an employer, can I negotiate my responsibility to complete the I-9's in a collective bargaining agreement with a union?

A. Yes. However, you are still responsible for compliance with the new law.

Q. When I review the identity and work authorization documents, should I make photocopies of them?

A. The law does not require you to photocopy documents. However, if you wish to make photocopies, you must retain them with the I-9. Photocopies must not be used for any other purpose.

Q. What are the requirements for retaining the I-9?

A. You must retain the Form for at least three years. If you employ the person for more than three years, you must retain the Form for one year after the person leaves your employment.

Q. Will I get any advance notice if an INS or DOL officer wishes to inspect my I-9's?

A. Yes. The officer will give you at least three days advance notice before the inspection. He or she will not need to show you a subpoena or warrant at that time. Failure to provide the I-9's for inspection could result in civil money penalties.

Q. What happens if I do everything the new law requires and INS discovers that one of my employees is not actually authorized to work?

A. Unless the government can show that you had actual knowledge of the illegal status of the employee, you will have an affirmative defense against the imposition of employer sanctions penalties if you have done the following things:

—Had employees fill out their part of the I-9 when they started to work;

—Checked the required documents (they should appear to be genuine and to relate to the individual);

—Properly completed the I-9;

—Retained the Form for the specified time; and

—Presented the Form upon request to an INS or Department of Labor officer. You will receive at least three days advance notice.

Q. How can I avoid discrimination while complying with the new immigration law?

A. Employers can avoid discrimination by applying the verification procedures of the Act to *all* newly hired employees and by hiring without respect to the national origin or citizenship status of those authorized to work in the United States. Seeking identity and employment eligibility documents only from individuals of a particular national origin or from those who appear or sound foreign violates the new immigration law and may also be a violation of Title VII of the Civil Rights Act of 1964. Employers should not discharge present employees, refuse to hire new employees, or otherwise discriminate on the basis of foreign appearance, language, or name. It is also a violation of Title VII to discriminate against employees or applicants for employment on the basis of national origin.

Q. I have heard that state employment agencies can certify that people they refer are eligible to work. Is that true?

A. Yes. State employment agencies may elect to provide individuals they refer to employers with a certification of employment eligibility. If one of these agencies refers potential employees to you and an employee presents you with one of these certifications, you do not have to check documents or complete an I-9 if you hire that person. However, you must retain the certification as you would an I-9 and present it for inspection if requested. Employers who hire people referred by state employment agencies should become familiar with what an authorized state employment agency certification looks like.

Q. Where can I get the Form I-9?

A. There are two copies of the Form I-9 in this Handbook. If you need more, you can photocopy or print the Forms. You may obtain a limited number of copies from INS. Or you may order them in bulk from the Superintendent of Documents at the following address:

Superintendent of Documents
U.S. Government Printing Office
Washington, D.C. 20402
Tel. (202) 783-3238

Q. What if one of my employees tells me that his or her Social Security Number is invalid?

A. You should tell the employee to get a proper Social Security Number by completing a Form SS-5. This Form is available from the Social Security Administration. You do not need to amend your employment tax returns. However, when the employee gives you the new number, you should file Form W-2C with the Social Security Administration for the years in which you reported income and withholding under the incorrect number.

Q. What advice should I give to my employees applying to legalize their status concerning their Federal Tax obligations?

A. You can advise employees that when they apply to INS for permanent resident status, they will be given an IRS publication explaining requirements for filing Form W-4 or W-4A to insure correct withholding of tax on wages, procedures for correcting prior year tax records (if an invalid social security number was used) and other guidelines relating to tax benefits.

Q. What advice should I give to newly-hired employees who ask about their Federal income tax obligations?

A. First, you can tell them it is important to have a valid social security number and to properly complete a W-4 or W-4A so that the employer can withhold the proper amount for income tax. Second, you can encourage employees to apply for social security numbers for their dependent children who will be five years old or older by the end of the year. Beginning in 1987, such numbers are required to be provided for dependents claimed on tax returns.

Part Nine

Acceptable Documents for Verifying Employment Eligibility

The following documents have been designated for determining employment eligibility by the Immigration Reform and Control Act of 1986 and the implementing regulations. As stated in Part Two, the employee will need to provide a document or documents that establish identity and employment eligibility. A complete list of acceptable documents is given on the next page. Samples of many of the acceptable documents appear on the following pages.

Some documents establish **both** identity and employment eligibility. These are listed on the Form I-9 under *List A*, "Documents that Establish Identity and Employment Eligibility."

If a person does not provide a document from *List A* he or she must provide one document that establishes identity **and** one document that establishes employment eligibility.

In order to establish **identity**, the person must provide a state-issued driver's license, a state-issued identification card, or one of the other documents in *List B*.

In order to establish **employment eligibility**, the person must provide a Social Security card, a United States birth certificate, or one of the immigration documents in *List C*.

If an employee is unable to provide the required document or documents within three days, he or she must at least produce (within three days) a receipt showing that he or she has applied for the document. The employee must produce the document itself within 21 days of the hire.

LIST A
Documents That Establish Identity and Employment Eligibility

- United States Passport
- Certificate of United States Citizenship. (INS Form N-560 or N-561)
- Certificate of Naturalization. (INS Form N-550 or N-570)
- Unexpired foreign passport which:
  - —Contains an unexpired stamp which reads "Processed for I-551. Temporary Evidence of Lawful Admission for permanent residence. Valid until ____. Employment authorized;" or
  - —Has attached thereto a Form I-94 bearing the same name as the passport and contains an employment authorization stamp, so long as the period of endorsement has not yet expired and the proposed employment is not in conflict with any restrictions or limitations identified on the Form I-94.
- Alien Registration Receipt Card (INS Form I-151) or Resident Alien Card (INS Form I-551), provided that it contains a photograph of the bearer.
- Temporary Resident Card. (INS Form I-688)
- Employment Authorization Card. (INS Form I-688A)

LIST B
Documents That Establish Identity

For individuals 16 years of age or older:

- State-issued driver's license or state-issued identification card containing a photograph. If the driver's license or identification card does not contain a photograph, identifying information should be included, such as name, date of birth, sex, height, color of eyes, and address.
- School identification card with a photograph
- Voter's registration card
- United States Military card or draft record
- Identification card issued by federal, state or local government agencies
- Military dependent's identification card
- Native American tribal documents
- United States Coast Guard Merchant Mariner Card
- Driver's license issued by a Canadian government authority

For individuals under age 16 who are unable to produce one of the documents listed above:

- School record or report card
- Clinic doctor or hospital record
- Daycare or nursery school record

LIST C
Documents That Establish Employment Eligibility

- Social Security number card, other than one which has printed on its face "not valid for employment purposes."
  Note: This must be a card issued by the Social Security Administration; a facsimile (such as a metal or plastic reproduction that people can buy) is not acceptable.
- An original or certified copy of a birth certificate issued by a state, county, or municipal authority bearing an official seal
- Unexpired INS employment authorization
- Unexpired re-entry permit. (INS Form I-327)
- Unexpired Refugee Travel Document. (INS Form I-571)
- Certification of Birth issued by the Department of State. (Form FS-545)
- Certification of Birth Abroad issued by the Department of State. (Form DS-1350)
- United States Citizen Identification Card. (INS Form I-197)
- Native American tribal document
- Identification Card for use of Resident Citizen in the United States. (INS Form I-179)

DOCUMENT LIST A.

United States Passport

Issued by the Department of State to United States citizens and nationals.

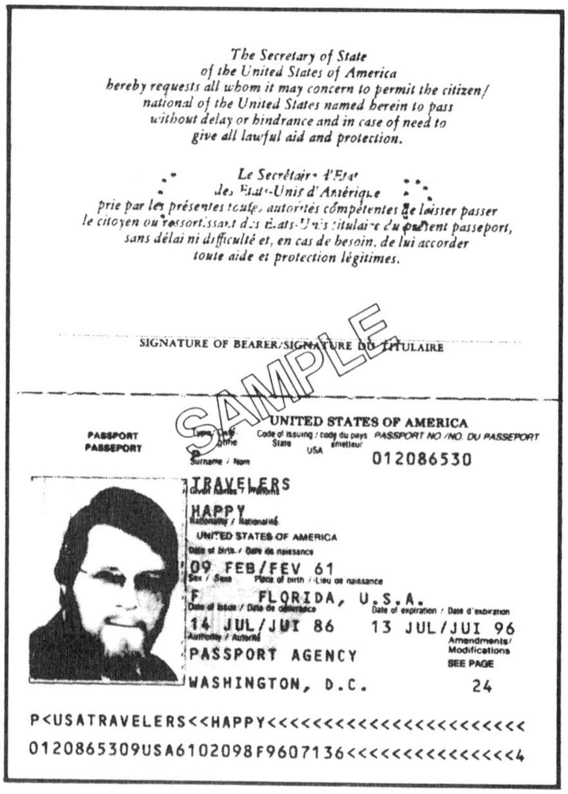

Certificate of United States Citizenship N-560

Issued by INS to individuals who derived citizenship through parental naturalization; acquired citizenship at birth abroad through a United States parent or parents; acquired citizenship through application by United States citizen adoptive parents; and who, pursuant to section 341 of the Act, have applied for a certificate of citizenship.

Certificate of Naturalization N-550 or N-570

Issued by INS to naturalized United States citizens.

I-94 Arrival-Departure Record

Arrival-departure record issued by INS to nonimmigrant aliens and attached to an unexpired foreign passport. An individual in possession of this document may only be employed if the document bears an employment authorization stamp. The expiration date is noted on the face of the document.

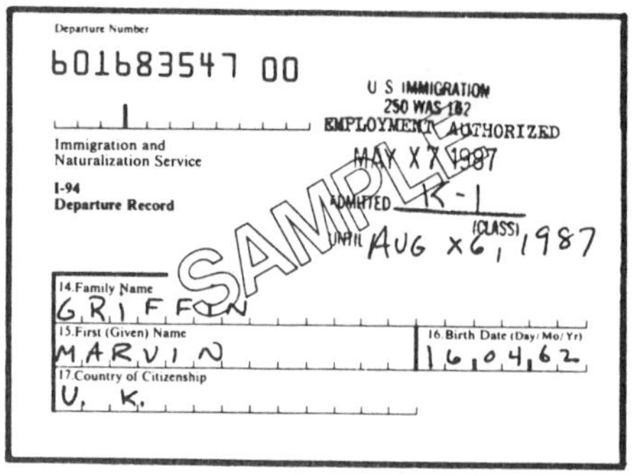

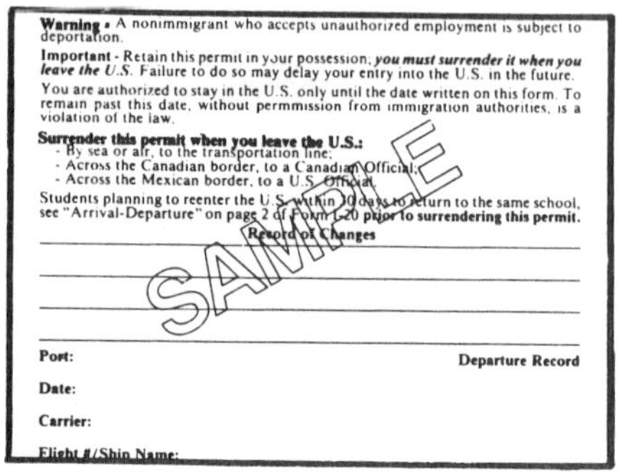

Alien Registration Receipt Card I-151

Issued by INS, prior to June 1978, to lawful permanent resident (lawful immigrant) aliens. There are numerous versions of this card because it was periodically revised. Although this card is no longer issued, it is valid indefinitely. This card is also commonly referred to as a "green card."

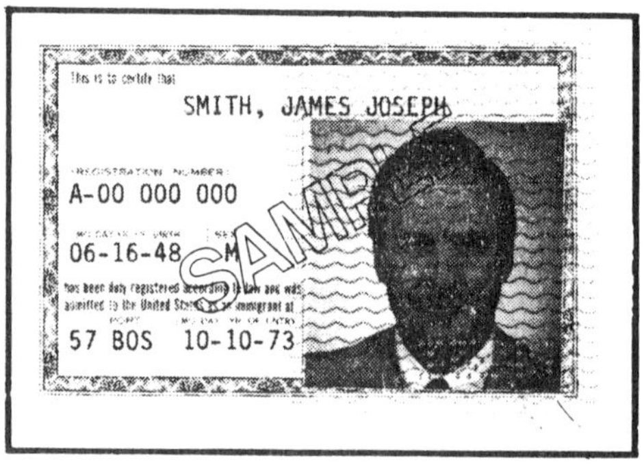

Alien Registration Receipt Card (Resident Alien Card) I-551

Issued by INS to lawful permanent resident (lawful immigrant) aliens. Valid indefinitely, this card is commonly referred to as a "green card" and is a revised edition of Form I-151.

Alien Registration Receipt Card (Conditional Resident Alien Card) I-551

Issued by INS to conditional permanent residents such as alien spouses of United States citizens or lawful permanent residents. Although it is the same card as the I-551 issued to permanent resident aliens, this card is valid for a limited period of time. The expiration date is stated on the back of the card.

Temporary Resident Card I-688

Issued by INS to aliens granted temporary resident status under the legalization or SAW programs. It is valid until the expiration date stated on the face of the document.

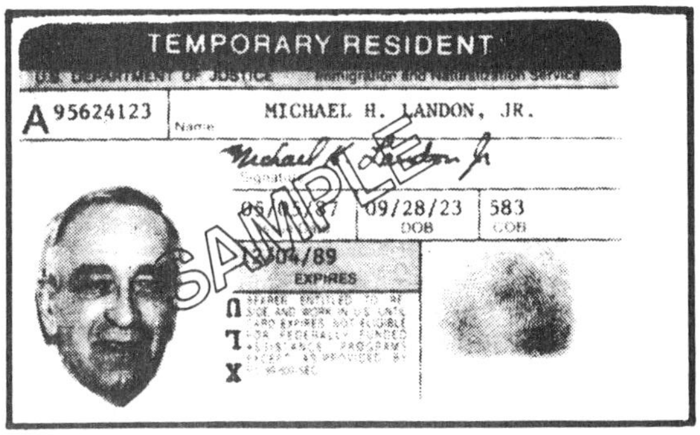

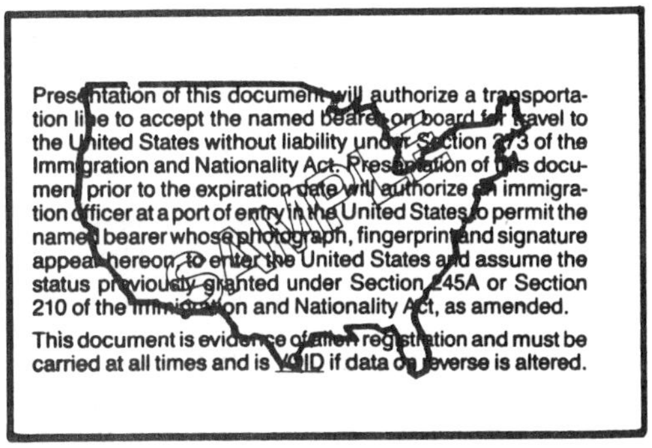

Employment Authorization Card I-688A

Issued by INS to applicants for temporary resident status after their interview for legalization or SAW status. It is valid for a period of six months from issuance and has the expiration date stated on the face of the card.

DOCUMENT LIST B.

Sample Driver's License

A driver's license issued by any state (including the District of Columbia, Puerto Rico, the Virgin Islands and Guam) or by a Canadian government authority is acceptable if it contains a photograph or other indentifying information such as name, date of birth, sex, height, color of eyes and address.

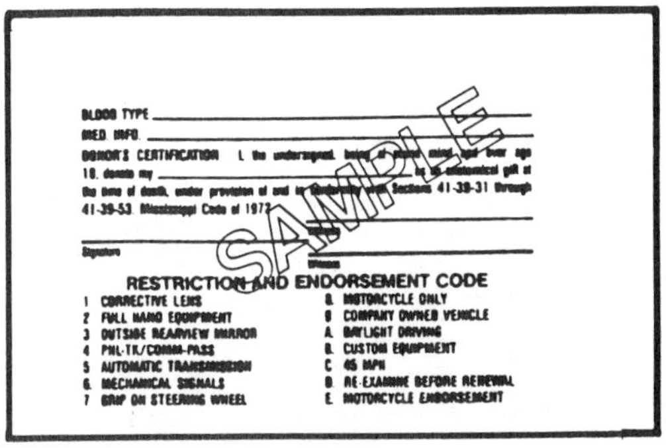

Sample State Identification Card

An identification card issued by any state (including the District of Columbia, Puerto Rico, the Virgin Islands and Guam) is acceptable if it contains a photograph or other identifying information such as name, date of birth, sex, height, color of eyes and address.

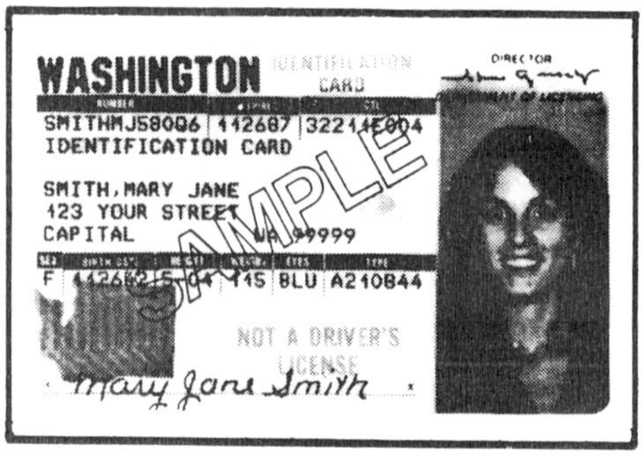

DOCUMENT LIST C.

Social Security Card

This card is invalid if laminated.

This card is invalid if not signed by the number holder unless health or age prevents signature.

Improper use of this card and/or number by the number holder or any other person is punishable by fine, imprisonment or both.

This card is the property of the Social Security Administration and must be returned upon request. If found, return to:
SSA—PO Box 17087
Baltimore, MD 21203
ATTN: FOUND SSN CARD (Return postage guaranteed)

Department of Health and Human Services
Social Security Administration
Form OA-702 (10-83) B05193176

SAMPLE

Sample Birth Certificates

BIRTH CARD CERTIFICATION
KENTUCKY DEPARTMENT FOR HEALTH SERVICES
REGISTRAR OF VITAL STATISTICS

BIRTH NUMBER 116 60 29839-26
NAME OMAR L GREEMAN
BIRTHDATE 6-11-1926 SEX MALE
BIRTHPLACE McCRACKEN COUNTY KENTUCKY
RECORD FILED 6-17-1926 DATE ISSUED 10-11-83
CARD NUMBER 0000

SAMPLE
OMAR L. GREEMAN, STATE REGISTRAR

THIS CERTIFICATION IS A TRUE ABSTRACT OF THE ORIGINAL BIRTH RECORD OF THE PERSON NAMED ON THE REVERSE SIDE, WHICH RECORD IS ON FILE WITH AND IN OFFICIAL CUSTODY OF THE STATE REGISTRAR OF VITAL STATISTICS AT FRANKFORT, KENTUCKY.

ISSUED UNDER AUTHORITY OF CHAPTER 213 KENTUCKY REVISED STATUTES.

SAMPLE

STATE OF MICHIGAN
DEPARTMENT OF PUBLIC HEALTH
CERTIFICATE OF LIVE BIRTH

LF 000001
CF
STATE FILE NUMBER
0455013B

CHILD	1. CHILD - NAME (FIRST) JOHN	(MIDDLE) LEE	(LAST) DOW
	2. SEX MALE	3a. THIS BIRTH - SINGLE, TWIN, TRIPLET, ETC. (SPECIFY) SINGLE	3b. IF NOT SINGLE - BORN 1ST, 2ND, 3RD, ETC. (SPECIFY)
	4a. DATE OF BIRTH 4 (MO) 1 (DAY) 01 (YEAR)	4b. HOUR 12:00PM	
PLACE	5a. HOSPITAL NAME - (IF NOT HOSPITAL GIVE STREET AND NUMBER) OUTER DRIVE HOSPITAL	5b. CITY, VILLAGE, OR TOWNSHIP OF BIRTH LINCOLN PARK	5c. COUNTY OF BIRTH WAYNE
CERTIFICATION	I CERTIFY THAT THE ABOVE NAMED CHILD WAS BORN ALIVE AT THE PLACE AND TIME AND ON THE DATE STATED ABOVE. 6a. SIGNATURE: DR. WALTER SMITH DATE: 4-2-1901	6b. NAME AND TITLE OF ATTENDANT AT BIRTH IF OTHER THAN CERTIFIER	
	6c. CERTIFIER NAME AND TITLE (PRINT OR TYPE) DR. WALTER SMITH	6d. MAILING ADDRESS (ST. NO., CITY OR VILLAGE, STATE, ZIP) 100000 SOUTHFIELD RD, LINCOLN PARK, MICH. 48146	
	7a. REGISTRAR'S SIGNATURE Irene B. Bristol	7b. DATE RECEIVED BY LOCAL REGISTRAR - (MO. DAY. YEAR) April 6, 1901	
MOTHER	8a. MOTHER - MAIDEN NAME (FIRST) MARY (MIDDLE) LOU (LAST) JONES	8b. SOCIAL SECURITY NUMBER 111-111-3647	8c. AGE (AT TIME OF THIS BIRTH) 22 · 8d. STATE OF BIRTH - NAME COUNTRY IF NOT USA MICH.
	8e. RESIDENCE (Check one box and specify) [X] INSIDE CITY LIMITS OF [ ] INSIDE VILLAGE LIMITS OF [ ] TWP. OF LINCOLN PARK	8f. COUNTY WAYNE	8g. STATE MICH.
FATHER	9a. FATHER - NAME (FIRST) HENRY (MIDDLE) JOHN (LAST) DOW	9b. SOCIAL SECURITY NUMBER 222-333-4786	9c. AGE (AT TIME OF THIS BIRTH) 23 · 9d. STATE OF BIRTH - NAME COUNTRY IF NOT USA MICH.
	I CERTIFY THAT THE PERSONAL INFORMATION PROVIDED ON THIS CERTIFICATE IS CORRECT TO THE BEST OF MY KNOWLEDGE AND BELIEF. 10a. SIGNATURE (PARENT OR OTHER INFORMANT) MARY DOW DATE: 4-3-1901	10b. RELATION TO CHILD MOTHER	

B213b (1/80)
MDPH

SAMPLE

Unexpired Re-Entry Permit I-327

Issued by INS to lawful permanent resident (lawful immigrant) aliens before they leave the United States for a one to two year period.

UNITED STATES
DEPARTMENT OF JUSTICE
★
Immigration and Naturalization Service
PERMIT TO REENTER THE UNITED STATES
★

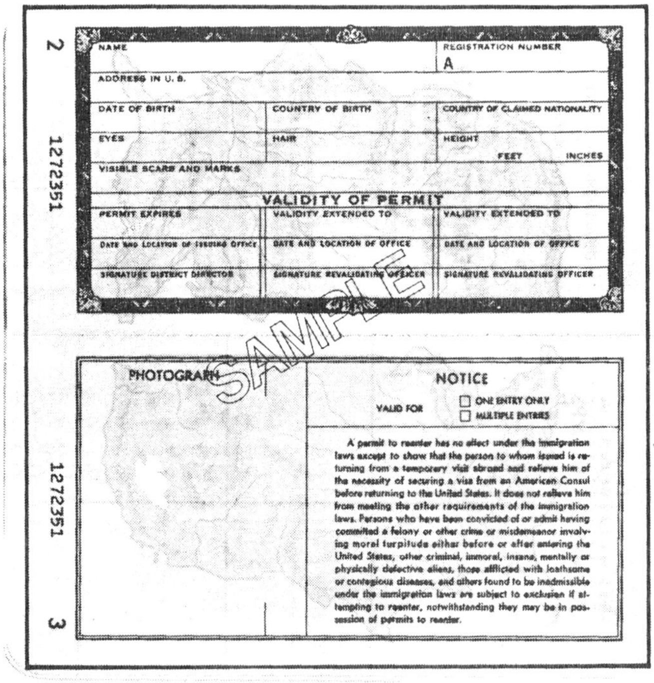
2
1272351
NAME | REGISTRATION NUMBER A
ADDRESS IN U. S.
DATE OF BIRTH | COUNTRY OF BIRTH | COUNTRY OF CLAIMED NATIONALITY
EYES | HAIR | HEIGHT FEET INCHES
VISIBLE SCARS AND MARKS
VALIDITY OF PERMIT
PERMIT EXPIRES | VALIDITY EXTENDED TO | VALIDITY EXTENDED TO
DATE AND LOCATION OF ISSUING OFFICE | DATE AND LOCATION OF OFFICE | DATE AND LOCATION OF OFFICE
SIGNATURE DISTRICT DIRECTOR | SIGNATURE REVALIDATING OFFICER | SIGNATURE REVALIDATING OFFICER
SAMPLE
PHOTOGRAPH
NOTICE
VALID FOR ☐ ONE ENTRY ONLY ☐ MULTIPLE ENTRIES
A permit to reenter has no effect under the immigration laws except to show that the person to whom issued is returning from a temporary visit abroad and relieve him of the necessity of securing a visa from an American Consul before returning to the United States. It does not relieve him from meeting the other requirements of the immigration laws. Persons who have been convicted of or admit having committed a felony or other crime or misdemeanor involving moral turpitude either before or after entering the United States, other criminal, immoral, insane, mentally or physically defective aliens, those afflicted with loathsome or contagious diseases, and others found to be inadmissible under the immigration laws are subject to exclusion if attempting to reenter, notwithstanding they may be in possession of permits to reenter.
1272351
3

Unexpired Refugee Travel Document I-571

Issued by INS to aliens who have been granted refugee status. The expiration date is stated on page four.

UNITED STATES OF AMERICA
ESTADOS UNIDOS DE AMÉRICA
REFUGEE TRAVEL DOCUMENT
DOCUMENTO DE VIAJE PARA REFUGIADOS

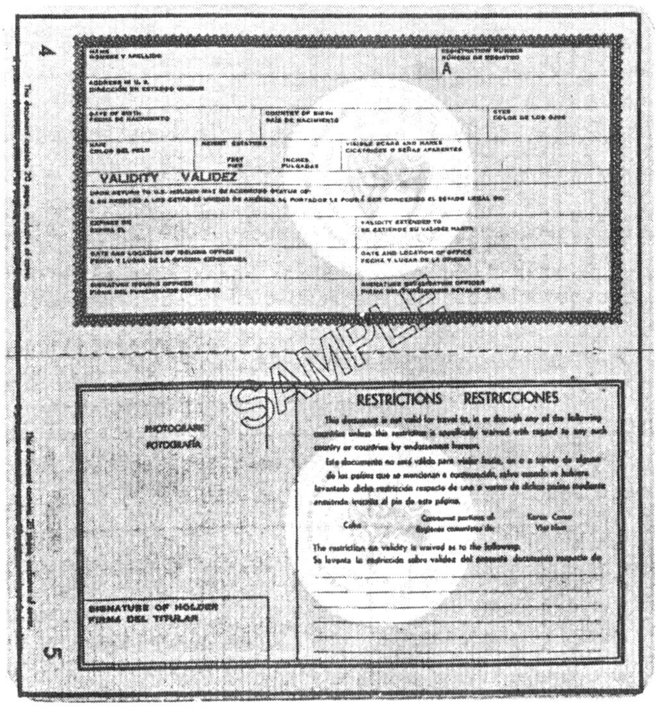
4
A
VALIDITY VALIDEZ
SAMPLE
PHOTOGRAPH
FOTOGRAFÍA
RESTRICTIONS RESTRICCIONES
SIGNATURE OF HOLDER
FIRMA DEL TITULAR
5

Certification of Birth issued by the Department of State FS-545

Issued by U.S. embassies and consulates overseas to United States citizens born abroad.

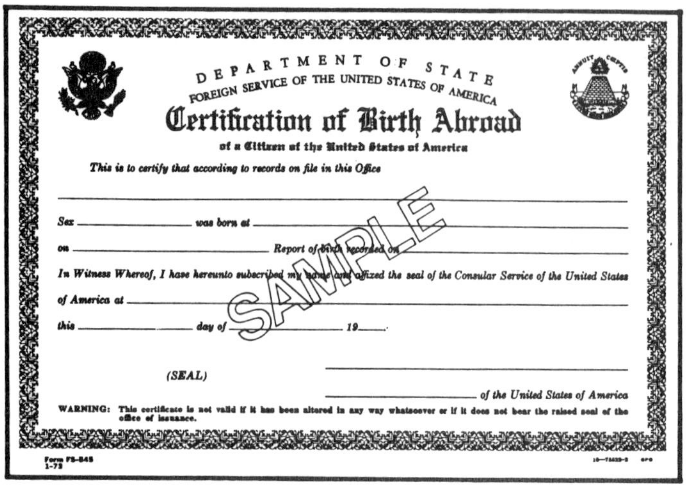

DEPARTMENT OF STATE
FOREIGN SERVICE OF THE UNITED STATES OF AMERICA
Certification of Birth Abroad
of a Citizen of the United States of America
This is to certify that according to records on file in this Office
Sex ________ was born at ________
on ________ Report of birth recorded on ________
In Witness Whereof, I have hereunto subscribed my name and affixed the seal of the Consular Service of the United States of America at ________
this ________ day of ________ 19__.
(SEAL)
________ of the United States of America
WARNING: This certificate is not valid if it has been altered in any way whatsoever or if it does not bear the raised seal of the office of issuance.
Form FS-545
1-73
SAMPLE

Certification of Birth issued by the Department of State DS-1350

Issued by the U.S. Department of State to United States citizens born abroad.

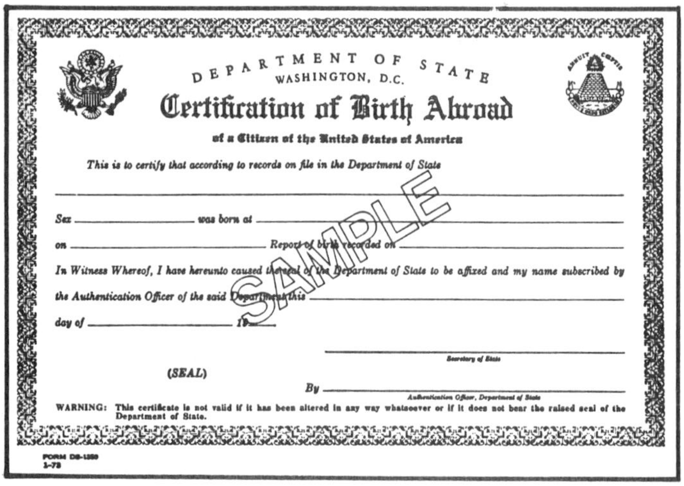

DEPARTMENT OF STATE
WASHINGTON, D.C.
Certification of Birth Abroad
of a Citizen of the United States of America
This is to certify that according to records on file in the Department of State
Sex ________ was born at ________
on ________ Report of birth recorded on ________
In Witness Whereof, I have hereunto caused the seal of the Department of State to be affixed and my name subscribed by the Authentication Officer of the said Department this ________
day of ________ 19__.
Secretary of State
(SEAL)
By ________
Authentication Officer, Department of State
WARNING: This certificate is not valid if it has been altered in any way whatsoever or if it does not bear the raised seal of the Department of State.
FORM DS-1350
1-73
SAMPLE

United States Citizen Identification Card I-197

Issued by INS to United States citizens. INS no longer issues this card.

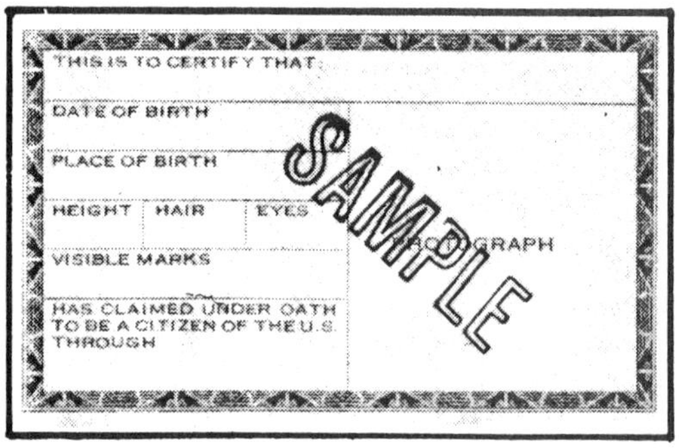

THIS IS TO CERTIFY THAT:
DATE OF BIRTH
PLACE OF BIRTH
HEIGHT | HAIR | EYES
VISIBLE MARKS
HAS CLAIMED UNDER OATH TO BE A CITIZEN OF THE U.S. THROUGH
PHOTOGRAPH
SAMPLE

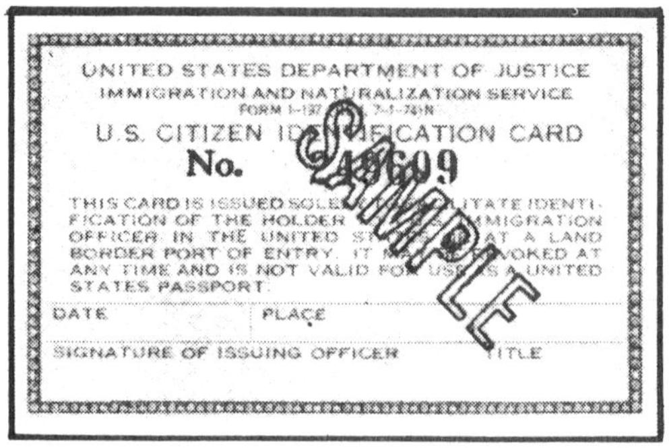

UNITED STATES DEPARTMENT OF JUSTICE
IMMIGRATION AND NATURALIZATION SERVICE
U.S. CITIZEN IDENTIFICATION CARD
No. 249609
THIS CARD IS ISSUED SOLELY TO FACILITATE IDENTIFICATION OF THE HOLDER TO AN IMMIGRATION OFFICER IN THE UNITED STATES AT A LAND BORDER PORT OF ENTRY. IT MAY BE REVOKED AT ANY TIME AND IS NOT VALID FOR USE AS A UNITED STATES PASSPORT.
DATE | PLACE
SIGNATURE OF ISSUING OFFICER | TITLE
SAMPLE

Identification Card for use of Resident Citizen in the United States I-179

Issued by INS to United States citizens who are residents of the United States. INS no longer issues this card.

PHOTOGRAPH
IDENTIFICATION CARD
FOR THE USE OF RESIDENT CITIZEN IN THE UNITED STATES
ISSUED BY THE IMMIGRATION AND NATURALIZATION SERVICE
UNITED STATES
DEPARTMENT OF JUSTICE
No. 231024
Form I-179
(Rev. 1-1-73) N
(Signature of holder)
SAMPLE

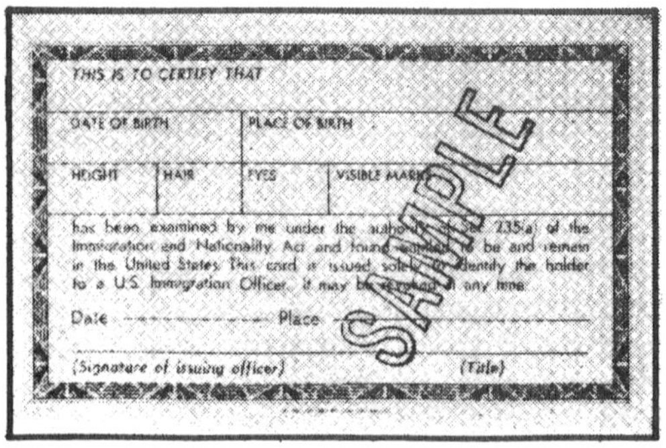

THIS IS TO CERTIFY THAT
DATE OF BIRTH | PLACE OF BIRTH
HEIGHT | HAIR | EYES | VISIBLE MARKS
has been examined by me under the authority of 235(a) of the Immigration and Nationality Act and found entitled to be and remain in the United States. This card is issued solely to identify the holder to a U.S. Immigration Officer. It may be revoked at any time.
Date ________ Place ________
(Signature of issuing officer) (Title)
SAMPLE

How to Obtain More Information

If you have questions after reviewing this Handbook, you may obtain information from one of the following local INS offices. Direct your letter to the attention of the *Employer Relations Officer*.

ALABAMA
75 Spring Street S.W.
Atlanta, GA 30303

ALASKA
701 "C" Street, Room D-251
Lock Box 16
Anchorage, AK 99513

ARIZONA
230 North First Avenue
Phoenix, AZ 85025

ARKANSAS
701 Loyola Avenue, Room T-8005
New Orleans, LA 70113

CALIFORNIA
300 North Los Angeles Street
Los Angeles, CA 90012

880 Front Street
San Diego, CA 92188

630 Sansome Street
San Francisco, CA 94111

COLORADO
1787 Federal Building
1961 Stout Street
Denver, CO 80202

CONNECTICUT
JFK Federal Building
Government Center
Boston, MA 02203

DELAWARE
601 Market Street
Room 1321, U.S. Courthouse
Philadelphia, PA 19106

DISTRICT OF COLUMBIA
4420 North Fairfax Drive
Arlington, VA 22203

FLORIDA
7880 Biscayne Boulevard
Miami, FL 33138

GEORGIA
75 Spring Street S.W.
Atlanta, GA 30303

GUAM
595 Ala Moana Boulevard
Honolulu, HI 96813

HAWAII
595 Ala Moana Boulevard
Honolulu, HI 96813

IDAHO
Federal Building, Room 512
310 South Park, Drawer 10036
Helena, MT 59626-0036

ILLINOIS
219 South Dearborn Street
Chicago, IL 60604

INDIANA
219 South Dearborn Street
Chicago, IL 60604

IOWA
Federal Building, Room 1008
106 South 15th Street
Omaha, NE 68102

KANSAS
9747 North Conant Avenue
Kansas City, MO 64153

KENTUCKY
701 Loyola Avenue, Room T-8005
New Orleans, LA 70113

LOUISIANA
701 Loyola Avenue, Room T-8005
New Orleans, LA 70113

MAINE
P.O. Box 578, Downtown Station
Portland, ME 04112

MARYLAND
101 West Lombard Street
Baltimore, MD 21201

MASSACHUSETTS
JFK Federal Building
Government Center
Boston, MA 02203

MICHIGAN
333 Mount Elliott Street
Detroit, MI 48207

MINNESOTA
927 Main Post Office Building
St. Paul, MN 55101

MISSISSIPPI
701 Loyola Avenue, Room T-8005
New Orleans, LA 70113

MISSOURI
9747 North Conant Avenue
Kansas City, MO 64153

MONTANA
Federal Building, Room 512
310 South Park, Drawer 10036
Helena, MT 59626-0036

NEBRASKA
Federal Building, Room 1008
106 South 15th Street
Omaha, NE 68102

NEVADA
230 North First Avenue
Phoenix, AZ 85025

NEW HAMPSHIRE
JFK Federal Building
Government Center
Boston, MA 02203

NEW JERSEY
970 Broad Street
Newark, NJ 07102

NEW MEXICO
343 U.S. Courthouse
P.O. Box 9398
El Paso, TX 79984

NEW YORK
68 Court Street
Buffalo, NY 14202

26 Federal Plaza
New York, NY 10278

NORTH CAROLINA
75 Spring Street S.W.
Atlanta, GA 30303

NORTH DAKOTA
927 Main Post Office Building
St. Paul, MN 55101

OHIO
1240 East 9th Street, Room 1917
Cleveland, OH 44199

OKLAHOMA
Federal Building, Room 6A 21
1100 Commerce Street
Dallas, TX 75242

OREGON
511 N.W. Broadway
Portland, OR 97209

PENNSYLVANIA
601 Market Street
Room 1321, U.S. Courthouse
Philadelphia, PA 19106

PUERTO RICO
GPO Box 5068
San Juan, Puerto Rico 00936

RHODE ISLAND
JFK Federal Building
Government Center
Boston, MA 02203

SOUTH CAROLINA
75 Spring Room S.W.
Atlanta, GA 30303

SOUTH DAKOTA
927 Main Post Office Building
St. Paul, MN 55101

TENNESSEE
701 Loyola Avenue, Room T-8005
New Orleans, LA 70113

TEXAS
Federal Building, Room 6A 21
1100 Commerce Street
Dallas, TX 75242

P.O. Box 9398
El Paso, TX 79984

2102 Teege Road
Harlingen, TX 78550

2627 Caroline Street
Houston, TX 77004

727 East Durango, Suite A301
San Antonio, TX 78206

UTAH
1787 Federal Building
1961 Stout Street
Denver, CO 80202

VERMONT
P.O. Box 578, Downtown Station
Portland, ME 04112

VIRGINIA
4420 North Fairfax Drive
Arlington, VA 22203

VIRGIN ISLANDS
GPO Box 5068
San Juan, Puerto Rico 00936

WASHINGTON
815 Airport Way South
Seattle, WA 98134

WEST VIRGINIA
601 Market Street
Room 1321, U.S. Courthouse
Philadelphia, PA 19106

WISCONSIN
219 South Dearborn Street
Chicago, IL 60604

WYOMING
1787 Federal Building
1961 Stout Street
Denver, CO 80202

BORDER PATROL HEADQUARTERS

1590 H Street
P.O. Drawer V
Blaine, WA 98230

P.O. Box 2020
Del Rio, TX 78841-2020

P.O. Box 32639
Detroit, MI 48232

1111 North Imperial Avenue
P.O. Box 60
El Centro, CA 92243

P.O. Box 9578
El Paso, TX 79986

P.O. Box 1657
Grand Forks, ND 58206-1657

P.O. Box 112
Havre, MT 59501

P.O. Box 706
Houlton, ME 04730

207 West Del Mar Boulevard
Laredo, TX 78041

P.O. Box 1
Marfa, TX 79843

2301 South Main Street
McAllen, TX 78501

161 N.E. 183rd Street
P.O. Box 3663 Norland Branch
Miami, FL 33169

P.O. Box 6218
New Orleans, LA 70174

P.O. Box 880
Pleasanton, CA 94566

3752 Beyer Boulevard
San Ysidro, CA 92073-9022

P.O. Box 18930
Spokane, WA 99208

Grand Avenue
P.O. Box 705
Swanton, VT 05488

1970 West Ajo Way
Tucson, AZ 85713

231 Grand Island Boulevard
Tonawanda, NY 14150

P.O. Box 2708
Yuma, AZ 85364

For Employer Information
Call this toll-free number:

1-800-777-7700

2a. Summary of Immigration Reform & Control Act, Prepared by the Texas Employment Commission

EMPLOYMENT ELIGIBILITY

The Immigration Reform & Control Act

URGENT for JUNE 1st 1987

- What it means
- Who it affects
- Acceptable documents

Texas Employment Commission

ACCEPTABLE DOCUMENTS

In many cases, a single document will provide evidence of both identity and employment eligibility. For this purpose the following documents establish both identity and employment eligibility:

A. United States passport

B. Certificate of Citizenship issued by the United States Immigration and Naturalization Service

C. United States Citizen Identification Card issued by the United States Immigration and Naturalization Service

D. Certificate of Naturalization

E. Unexpired foreign passport which:

   1. contains an unexpired stamp therein which reads, "processed for I-551...", or

   2. has attached thereto a Form I-94 in the same name (with identical biographic information) which contains an employment authorization stamp so long as the period of endorsement has not yet expired and the proposed employment is not in conflict with any restrictions or limitations identified on the Form I-94

F. Alien Registration Card provided that it contains a photograph of the bearer.

G. Unexpired Work Permit issued by the United States Immigration and Naturalization Service

When such papers as these are not available, applicants must provide one document to establish identity and another for employment eligibility.

Acceptable documents for identity include the following:

A. An original driver's license issued by any state which

   1. bears a photograph of the individual, or

   2. contains personal identifying information which, at a minimum, includes his/her full name, date of birth, height, weight, color of eyes, and residence address.

B. An original identifying document issued by any State for the purpose of identification which either:

   1. bears a photograph of the individual, or

   2. contains personal identifying information which, at a minimum, includes his/

her full name, date of birth, height, weight, color of eyes, and residence address.

C. In the case of individuals residing in a State which does not provide for issuance of an identification document (other than a driver's license), the following:

   1. Document evidencing active duty or reserve status in the United States Armed Forces.

Some of the items deemed satisfactory for establishing employment eligibility include the following:

A. Social Security account number card issued by the Department of Health and Human Services or previously issued by the Health, Education, and Welfare (other than such a card which specifies on the face that the issuance of the card does not authorize employment in the United States).

B. A certificate of birth in any State. The certificate must contain the given surname, name, date of birth, place of birth, date the birth record was filed, and an official seal or other certification by the official custodian of such record. Official custodian refers to the governmental agency with which the birth is registered.

C. Report of United States Citizen Birth Abroad issued by the United States Department of State.

D. Form I-94 with employment authorization stamp.

This is **not** an all-inclusive list as the Immigration and Naturalization Service may add others.

WHO IT AFFECTS

All persons entering employment must provide the necessary documents to employers for examination. In addition, all persons entering employment must also complete a new form developed by the Immigration and Naturalization Service called the Form I-9. The form provides biographic information and attests to the applicant's United States citizenship or status as a legally authorized alien worker. The Form I-9 must be completed and supporting documents provided within 3 business days after the commencement of employment.

THE LAW . . .
THE IMMIGRATION REFORM AND CONTROL ACT OF 1986

The President of the United States signed into law on November 6 the Immigration Reform and Control Act of 1986. The Act popularly referred to as the Simpson/Rodino Bill establishes procedures by which employers may legally hire applicants.

The Act requires an employer when hiring must reasonably satisfy himself or herself that the new employee is either a United States citizen or an alien who is legally eligible to work in this country. To be eligible for hiring, an employee must provide evidence of **both identity** and **employment eligibility.** Every individual will be required to provide documents to the employer, recruiter or referrer for the purpose of establishing his/her identity and employment eligibility.

Index